W9-CES-292

HANDBOOK OF FINANCIAL MATHEMATICS, FORMULAS AND TABLES

HANDBOOK OF FINANCIAL MATHEMATICS, FORMULAS AND TABLES

Robert P. Vichas

PRENTICE-HALL, INC.
Englewood Cliffs, N.J.

Prentice-Hall International, Inc., *London*
Prentice-Hall of Australia, Pty. Ltd., *Sydney*
Prentice-Hall of Canada, Ltd., *Toronto*
Prentice-Hall of India Private Ltd., *New Delhi*
Prentice-Hall of Japan, Inc., *Tokyo*
Prentice-Hall of Southeast Asia Pte. Ltd., *Singapore*
Whitehall Books, Ltd., *Wellington, New Zealand*

Sixth Printing . . . . August, 1981

Library of Congress Cataloging in Publication Data

Vichas, Robert P
Handbook of financial mathematics, formulas, and tables.

Includes bibliographical references and index.
1. Business and mathematics. I. Title.
HF5691.V42 513'.93 78-15748
ISBN 0-13-378000-7

Printed in the United States of America

TO

MY

WIFE

DOLORES

About the Author

Dr. Robert P. Vichas, having owned and operated several of his own businesses, has acquainted himself with multifarious financial problems common to a broad spectrum of industries. The author, as credit and financial analyst and assistant mercantile claims manager for several years with Dun & Bradstreet, Inc., observed that most managers of medium and small businesses simply lack time to become proficient in major business functions. In subsequent years he and a team of experts formed a consulting firm to assist enterprises in these areas, in addition to compliance with government regulations. Also the writer was research director of American Commodities Exchange, Inc.

Dr. Vichas has earned university degrees here and abroad (most recently at the Swiss Institute of International Graduate Studies in Geneva) studying diverse domestic and international economic and financial problems—ranging from developing financial incentives to attract investors, to financing a country's economic growth. Additionally, he is presently or has been a member of the American Finance Association, Financial Management Association, Academy of International Business, and others.

Besides writing articles for magazines and journals, his two most recent books are: *Getting Rich in Commodities, Currencies, or Coins* (Arlington House Publishers) and *Coeval Economics* (McCutchan Publishing Co.).

A Word from the Author

Crammed into a single volume are selected formulas, tested mathematical short cuts, and frequently used tables—essential to daily operations of any profit-maximizing business, large or small; financial institutions and investment funds; nonprofit organizations; educational entities and hospitals; governmental bodies and even cost-conscious households—pinpointing practical principles of sound financial management. This valuable *reference book:*

*signals where to minimize costs, conserve cash.
*illustrates how to predict potential bankruptcies up to three years in advance.
*employs continuous compounding and continuous discounting.
*interprets application of latest inflation accounting techniques.
*demonstrates how to reduce losses under unfavorable conditions.
*breaks the seal on liquidity improvement.
*shows how to acquire property cheaper by paying more for it.
*cuts through the mystery of foreign exchange transactions.
*lays bare short-cut methods for nonmathematicians.

Dividend-yielding formulas—quickly grasped and instantly applied by any businessman, executive, manager or investor—are equal time-savers for analysts, accountants, advisors, portfolio managers, lawyers, financial officers, securities and insurance salesmen, and other profit-motivated individuals. Because this book is filled with proven financial and investment survival techniques, it will feed fruitful ideas to its readers and users for many years.

Who should use this handbook? Whoever needs to solve financial, investment, insurance, credit, real estate, foreign exchange, inflation, risk, loan, interest, or a general personal or related business problem, for example, will find formulas, tables, intelligible examples, and simple solutions that require no more than elementary arithmetic for fast, profitable decision-making. Topics range from computing daily interest on a $100 savings account to acquisition analysis of a multimillion dollar transnational enterprise. Techniques range from the uncomplicated to the complex; and since complexity does not necessarily insure better results, a simple rule-of-thumb or short-cut approach may be quickly located in the Table of Contents, chapter contents, or comprehensive Index.

Each precept has been concisely explained in words, and with numerical examples extracted from mini-case studies to demonstrate its operability. That is, vague and incomplete theories, no matter how interesting, do not find a place in the practical approach of this prescriptive guide. Further, remedies limited to those most cogent and germane to financial decision-making are restricted to those problem areas addressed. Criteria for topic selection, the linking threads in this money-saving formulary, are profits, practicality, and applicability.

Why should this reference occupy a conspicuous spot on your bookshelf?

For example, in CHAPTER ONE alone there are: Twenty-eight valuable formulas. Ten short-cut examples. An interpretation of how different techniques produce divergent answers; a simple, but pragmatic, step-by-step explanation of continuous compounding; inexpensive, noncomputerized solutions to burdensome compounding issues; three methods to determine a firm's compound growth rate; profitable use of effective versus nominal rates; three disclosures of fast solutions to complex problems; plus several actual case studies.

The other side of compounding, discounting, in CHAPTER TWO, focuses on the significance of present value mathematics in borrowing decisions, in maximizing rates of return, in achieving some specific target growth rate, in differentiating between the size and shape of income streams. Seventeen techniques are elucidated by such examples as evaluating a training program, discounting a promissory note, establishing a retirement fund, funding debt, solving for a deferred annuity, finding an unknown interest rate, arranging beneficial terms in a real estate purchase, calculating annual and monthly installments under conditions of uncertainty, purchasing a de-nationalized business (should such a happy event occur), accounting for steadily rising maintenance costs and comparing discrete and continuous results. Although continuous discounting is less known than continuous compounding, Chapter Two not only unveils how to quickly master this concept but also how to profitably apply tables in the Appendix which engage continuous compounding noumenon.

Rate of return calculations, CHAPTER THREE, are not only troublesome to compute but no two popular methods yield invariable results. Although rules-of-thumb, clearly explicated in Chapter Three, may suffice for certain decisions, among the 16 methods cast, the superior present value techniques provide preferred, consistent outcomes. Four basic approaches for better decision-making can be quickly penetrated by the reader. The benefits, of course, are lower costs of debt servicing, adequate accounting for risks, profitable discrimination among investment alternatives, and assessment of sensitivity of profit changes to variations in key variables; i.e., this chapter reports on the communication link between users and suppliers of capital.

Figuring the cost of various sources of funds in CHAPTER FOUR begins with specific costs of long term funds and ends by combining all sources into an average weighted cost of capital. Too, the chapter deals explicitly with taxes and risks. Because borrowing is an important source of capital, the question arises: How much leverage? Although CHAPTER FIVE does not moralize on the virtues of solvency and sound financial management, especially important in recessionary times, it does zero in on leveraging for profits rather than for bankruptcy. Leverage arises not only from borrowing (financial leverage) but from the particular technique of production chosen, the combination of labor and capital selected (operating leverage). Operating leverage is especially significant in regional analysis and plant relocation, domestically or internationally.

Applying marginal, opportunity, and sunk cost analysis to the profit concept in CHAPTER SIX relates the marginal principle to such cost problems as incremental outlays for electricity, money-losing options which actually translate into more profits, increasing efficiency in production schedules, and, for investors in scotch whisky, tables depict the best time to sell. An interesting cost minimization problem supports a decision to either remodel an old building or invest in a new one. The historical insignificance of sunk costs is aptly recounted and a capital recovery factor clarified by formula and table.

Although sunk costs are not relevant to new investment decisions, depreciation of previously purchased assets are important in tax decisions. CHAPTER SEVEN not only interprets straight time, accelerated time, compound interest, and service life methods of depreciation but also furnishes the reader with a profitable, time-saving short-cut improvement. Related to depreciation accounting, leasing, buying, and borrowing options significantly affect the timing and magnitude of cash flows. Check lists in CHAPTER EIGHT on the advantages of owning and leasing quickly substantiate which of these alternatives will best benefit the decision-maker. Twelve formulas, along with clear-cut examples, point to whether a firm should lease or buy or lease or borrow, and to elements of risk shifting in leasing. Such methods as discounted cash flow, basic interest rate, and the Penney method steer toward the best decisions under varying conditions of risk. Further, the chapter affirms how a lessor should price his equipment. And a high interest factor alone does *not* imply that a lessee can necessarily take over the profits of a lessor. This chapter asserts both why and how.

The next three chapters pinpoint profit factors in inventory, receivables, and cash management. A former vice president of Dun and Bradstreet cautions that inventories are the graveyards of American businesses. CHAPTER NINE tells how to keep out of the graveyard. Dun and Bradstreet also frequently admonishes that "a sale is never complete until the money is collected." Many methods of controlling receivables for liquidity and profits have enjoyed wide-spread application. CHAPTER TEN clearly limns why most control techniques trigger inconstant responses under variant conditions and then introduces the reader to a high-powered approach that certainly will improve both performance and evaluation of those involved in credit decisions. Converting receivables into cash does not end the chain of events, for unemployed cash (liquidity) is just as disastrous to long term profitability as illiquidity is to short run operations and solvency. CHAPTER ELEVEN clearly guides the user of this reference manual to scientifically seek out this delicate liquidity-solvency balance under conditions of certainty and uncertainty of cash flows.

If bankruptcy can be predicted well enough in advance, corrective action taken in time can restore an unbalanced firm; if creditors foresee a potential bankruptcy in the making, a stitch in time makes a hero out of the financial decision-maker. CHAPTER TWELVE is a hero builder with its set of bankruptcy-predicting formulas. In fact, 60 basic ratios in all will encourage any enterpriser to plan for profit and growth.

And growth, not always achieved internally, may originate in a properly executed merger and acquisition plan. CHAPTER THIRTEEN, in developing a comprehensive valuation model, instructs how to value a going business, avoid pitfalls of dilution to stockholders' equity, and strike a bargain acceptable to both buyer and seller.

CHAPTER FOURTEEN deals with a subject that might well have been omitted had this handbook appeared several years earlier. Fortunately, the decision-maker can now refer to this chapter on international investment, foreign exchanges, and hedging against devaluations and revaluations. No firm is totally isolated from fluctuating foreign exchange rates in a politically uncertain world. This chapter communicates, with a condensed case study, how a firm which has never exported or imported, has no foreign subsidiaries, and owns no foreign investments (either direct or portfolio) had substantial foreign exchange exposure and how the company treasurer built a success aura by taking positive, low-cost action. The chapter also portrays how speculators, investors, exporters, importers, and multinational corporations can shift risks and hedge foreign exchange transactions to minimize losses and save even millions of dollars.

CHAPTER FIFTEEN tackles a controversial subject, price-level, or inflation, accounting. The illustrated procedure, akin to foreign exchange hedging, highlights debt in inflationary times, when a profit is hardly a profit (all the way to bankruptcy proceedings), and a new use of ratio analysis. Recognition of monetary items in adjusted income may enable a firm to show adjusted profits although its cash position is deteriorating. Step-by-step Chapter Fifteen demonstrates how to translate financial statements into current nominal terms. Finally, CHAPTER SIXTEEN introduces the reader to computer logic in profitable decision-making. The quality of the decision, of course, depends upon the individual(s) making it; the computer helps to explore decision alternatives faster.

The remainder of the handbook, as a convenience to you, its user, comprises valuable tables used to facilitate calculations in profitable analysis. Many factors are carried out to eight decimal places, some even ten, to furnish better, more accurate, answers. Another unusual feature of these tables in the Appendix is the series based on continuous compounding formulations. Most of the tables based on end-of-period computations are redeciphered on beginning-of-period assumptions of contiuous compounding (or discounting). Another uncommon set of tables relates nominal to effective rates and effective to nominal rates under different assumptions of compounding ranging from annual to continuous. Supplementing these data are tables of exponential functions, e^x and e^{-x}, vital in converting nominal rates to continuously compounded ones. Two other features also merit mention. To convert accelerated depreciation to straight line for price-level accounting, two tables of age-reducing factors greatly simplify these otherwise complex calculations. The other set of tables, although available from government sources, refer to implicit price deflators for GNP going back to 1947. Two tables employ 1972 as the base year, one uses 1958; however, a note in the text defines the statistical technique for shifting base years. Other convenience tables include six- and seven-place mantissas and tables of roots and powers.

Some of these techniques have averted hundreds of thousands of dollars in losses. Some of these techniques have saved money managers from embarrassing mistakes. Some of these techniques may be too complex to implement for a given situation. Some of these techniques must be combined with others, or modified, to fit a specific instance. In all events, this Handbook is a valuable aid in asset management and the author hopes that frequent referral to it will profit your enterprise.

> "If the iron be blunt and he do not whet the edge, then must he put to more strength: but wisdom is profitable to direct." (*Ecclesiastes 10:10*)

Robert P. Vichas

ACKNOWLEDGMENTS

The author acknowledges an intellectual debt to those who have reviewed, tested, and further refined many of these concepts. A partial list of creditors includes:

Stephen H. Archer
Frank Ayres, Jr.
Harold Bierman, Jr.
Eugen von Böhn-Bäwerk
Kenneth E. Boulding
John H. Cooper
Arthur B. Curtis
Charles A. D'Ambrosio
Sidney Davidson
George N. Engler
Irving Fisher
Milton Friedman
Eugene L. Grant
Erich A. Helfer
Pearson Hunt
W. Grant Ireson
Robert W. Johnson
Louis M. Killeen
James D. Kimes
Dennis A. Kraebel
Wilbur G. Lewellen
J. Robert Lindsay
James C. T. Mao
John J. Marszalek
Harry Markowitz
Ludwig von Mises
Garnet D. Olive
David E. Peterson
George C. Philipatos
C. David Quirin
James L. Riggs
Arnold W. Sametz
Seymour Smidt
Robert M. Soldofsky
Ezra Solomon
Milford S. Tysseland
James C. van Horne
David W. Wycoff

The author is also indebted to:

The Federal Reserve Bank of St. Louis for providing data on Implicit Price Deflators for Gross National Product;

The McGraw-Hill Book Company for permission to reproduce the tables on age-reducing factors for depreciable assets from Sidney Davidson, Clyde P. Stickney, and Roman L. Weil, *Inflation Accounting; a Guide for the Accountant and Financial Analyst* (1976);

Prentice-Hall, Inc. for permission to reproduce tables of six- and seven-place mantissas from Simpson, Pirenian, Crenshaw, Riner, *Mathematics of Finance,* 4th edition (1969); and

Dolores M. Vichas, without whom this volume would not have materialized and to whom this book is dedicated.

The author also expresses his appreciation for the valuable suggestions made by:

Mr. R. A. Hohner of Westvaco Corporation, New York City;

Mr. Edward M. Rollins, Manager of Financial Communications, R. J. Reynolds, Inc., Winston Salem, North Carolina;

Mr. J. J. Kelly, Secretary-Treasurer, Lewis Business Forms, Inc., Jacksonville, Florida;

Mr. Carl R. Pite, Vice President-Finance, Bowne & Co. Inc., New York City.

R.P.V.

For God shall bring every work into judgment, with every secret thing, whether it be good, or whether it be evil. (*Ecclesiastes 12:14*)

Table of Contents

List of Tables in Appendix

HANDBOOK OF FINANCIAL MATHEMATICS, FORMULAS AND TABLES

List of Symbols

A = any amount or sum or stream of payments.

a = any constant quantity or sum.

B = book value.

b = a constant, or rate.

C = total costs.

c = cost per unit.

D = dividends.

d = dividend rate.

E = (total) value of firm or asset.

e = 2.71828182845. . . .

F = future amount or flow.

f = factor or rate.

G = growth or production, absolute amount of change.

g = rate of growth or change or production.

H = dollar amount of taxes.

h = tax rate.

I = dollar amount of interest.

i $= \frac{j}{m}$ = rate per conversion period; or annual rate of interest if interest is converted once a year.

J = inventory lot size (in units).

j = im = nominal rate converted m times per year; a continuous interest rate.

K = dollar amount of costs (flotation costs, e.g.), or expenses.

k = a constant; or cost of capital (%).

L = salvage value.

ln = natural logarithm (base e).

M = market price (or value).

m = number of conversion periods per year.

N = number.

n = number of interest periods, or number of years.

P = principal or investment.

p = periodic payment; or price per unit.

Q = balance due, or net proceeds, at beginning of period; or cash balance.

q = interim balance.

R = coupon (rate) on bonds; annual rent from annuity.

r = effective rate of return.

S = any sum; or, e.g., a payment to reduce principal and interest.

s = any sum or partial or interim payment.

T = time, like number of days, months, etc.

t = time periods.

V = present value of a future sum.

v = credit (such as investment tax credit), credit line, or discount.

W = price level index; or deflator.

w = rate of price change.

X = any unknown, or quantity.

x = any unknown, or quantity.

Y = any unknown, or value.

y = any unknown, or value.

Z = total debt, obligations, or liabilities.

β = business risk.

Δ = change.

θ = financial risk.

π = profit(s).

ρ = probability.

Σ = sum of.

σ = standard deviation.

$(A/F_{i,n})$ = sinking fund factor of a uniform series.

$(A/G_{i,n})$ = uniform gradient series factor.

$(A/P_{i,n})$ = capital recovery factor of a uniform series.

$(F/A_{i,n})$ = compound amount of a uniform series.

$(F/P_{i,n})$ = compound amount factor of a single payment.

$(P/A_{i,n})$ = present value factor of a uniform series.

$(P/F_{i,n})$ = present value factor of a single payment.

$(P/G_{i,n})$ = present value factor of a gradient series.

CONTENTS

Chapter One: Twenty-Eight Money-Building Formulas

ONE

Twenty-Eight Money-Building Formulas

Miracles and wonders of compounding, rediscovered anew each generation and probably several times over as each generation matures and contemplates wealth accumulation, embody an interesting array of formulas and techniques for savers, borrowers, and financial decision-makers. For *savers* compounding means savings grow faster without expending more energy. For *borrowers* compounding means the cost of borrowing time, a piece of tomorrow—both an obligation and opportunity. For the *decision-maker* compounding means an analytical tool.

For example, grammar school history tells us that a fellow named Peter Minuit of the Dutch West India Company spun a fantastic bargain when he bought, swindled, or boondoggled (depending on which historian wrote it) Manhattan Island from the natives for $24 worth of costume jewelry. Did Peter really drive that unprincipled, ignominious, picaresque, oblique bargain we are led to believe? Or did the Indians put one over on the Dutch West India Company? We will never know with complete certainty, but compounding that $24 at 6 per cent may provide some insight into the original deal consummated over 350 years ago (apparently by Indians who did not even live on or own Manhattan but happened to be over for a few days of hunting).

Here is what $24 will amount to at various intervals if it earns 6 per cent compounded only once a year. (Figure 1-1.)

Figure 1-1

Year	*Value of Investment ($)*
1626	24.00
1726	8,143.00
1826	2,763,022.00
1926	937,499,017.00
1976	17,268,876,531.00
1991	74,115,785,544.00
2026	318,095,369,846.00

Looking at it from Peter Minuit's point of view back in 1626, if he could have accurately predicted Manhattan's value 350 years later at, say, $10 billion instead of more than $17 billion, he would have offered considerably less than $24, and the Indians would have accepted less than $24 if they had agreed with his lower estimates and if 6 per cent were an acceptable rate.

Whether we look forward into the future, *compounding,* or state the future in terms of the present, *discounting,* the same factors operate to determine future or present values. Let's examine how time, interest rates, frequency of compounding all influence future values of sums invested today.

SIMPLE INTEREST

Interest rates reflect more than the time value of money. Generally, when we speak of interest rates, or a banker quotes an interest rate, there are three underlying elements which enter into every transaction. While the lender of funds thinks of interest as income, the borrower treats interest as a cost of obtaining funds, and the interest rate for both parties consists of:

(a) the time value of money,
(b) risks,
(c) inflation (or deflation, a negative inflation rate).

For every borrower there must a lender be. And what does a lender, or saver, give up when he allows others to draw on his funds? The lender postpones spending. He professes greater preference for the future. He surrenders time, the present; therefore, he expects to be paid for his sacrifice, lost time. Hence, the time value of money.

Risks infer that the lender may never see his funds again. The borrower may default. Since the borrower has shifted certain risks to the lender, he must compensate the lender for extra burden the lender has assumed because "there's no such thing as a free lunch."

Inflation erodes purchasing power of money. A lender, repaid in constant dollars, for example, is worse off if the purchasing power of those dollars has declined; ergo, the lender expects protection against inflation losses and adds something to the interest rate to cover at least part of this anticipated cost. To focus on formulas and methods, this handbook will continue to compound the error of lumping together these various costs, tagging them "interest."

Ordinary Simple Interest

Passing from the simple to the complex, simple interest is based on a 360-day year equally spaced among 12 months. A simple interest rate is directly proportional to the sum b͏orrowed.

To calculate interest due (or earned) at the end of a period, multiply principal times interest rate per period times number of interest periods.

Formula:

$$I = Pin$$

I = dollar amount of interest due (earned).

P = principal or present amount of original loan or investment.

i = interest rate (expressed as a decimal) per time period.

n = number of interest periods.*

However, the lender expects repayment of principal as well as interest; therefore, the future sum of money (F) comprises principal plus interest. Interest costs (I) depend on *amount* borrowed, interest *rate,* and length of *time* funds are employed.

$$F = P + I$$

---

*As frequently as necessary formulas will be expressed in words and symbols. Symbols will have uniform designation throughout this handbook and are listed in the front for quick reference.

Substituting the previous formula for I, we have,

$$F = P + Pin$$

which gives us the following:

Formula: $F = P(1 + in)$

Now let's apply this formula to a case study to calculate *ordinary simple interest* and *exact simple interest.*

Case Study: What did Lorrie Hargis do?

Mrs. Lorrie Hargis, a housewife, decided to initiate her own business venture representing Mary Kay Cosmetics of Dallas. To qualify for a dealership discount of 50 per cent, Mrs. Hargis must purchase a minimum inventory of \$300. However, the Mary Kay representative urged her to order \$1,200 initially. Carrying a larger inventory lessens the possibility of a *stock-out* and sales lost during a facial show. Additionally, \$1,200 monthly purchases entitle Mrs. Hargis to a 14-karat gold-plated goblet each time. The Mary Kay representative accompanied Lorrie to her bank to obtain an inventory loan. Mrs. Hargis, although confident of her sales ability, preferred loan repayment to coincide with receipt of extra funds expected 14 months later.

The bank loaned Mrs. Hargis \$1,200, on July 1, due on August 31, the following year, at simple interest rate of 9.5%. What is the sum Mrs. Hargis must repay at the end of the 14-month loan period?

A 360-day year, used in simple interest calculations, implies 12 months of equal length, 30 days each. Fourteen months, then, is 12 months plus 2, or $1\frac{1}{6}$ years. Using the *ordinary simple interest formula* in this manner, after 14 months, Mrs. Hargis will repay:

$$\begin{aligned} F &= P(1 + in) \\ &= \$1{,}200\left[1 + 0.095\left(1 + \frac{1}{6}\right)\right] \\ &= \$1{,}200 + \$114(1\tfrac{1}{6}) \\ &= \$1{,}200 + \$133 = \$1{,}333.00 \text{ (principal \& interest)} \end{aligned}$$

By rearranging the basic formula, we can also determine the interest rate. Since $I = Pin$, then:

Formula:

$$i = \frac{I}{Pn}$$

Example: At what rate will \$7,350 generate \$793.80 in simple interest in 9 months?

$$i = ?;\ I = \$793.80;\ P = \$7{,}350;\ n = 9/12 = 3/4$$

$$i = \frac{I}{Pn} = \frac{793.80}{7{,}350(3/4)} = \frac{4 \times 793.80}{7{,}350 \times 3} = 0.144 = 14.4\%$$

To check your answer, solve, $I = Pin = 7{,}350 \times 0.144 \times 3/4 = \$793.80$

However, the objective of a 360-day year is to increase interest income for the lender, which leads to the Banker's Rule.

Banker's Rule

Ordinary interest, based on a 360-day year, simplifies calculations but increases total interest collected by lenders when ordinary interest accrues for an exact number of days. For example, this loan runs for 1 year and 62 days. With a 360-day year, the loan's duration exceeds 1 1/6 years, Mrs. Hargis will repay \$1,333.63.

$$F = \$1200 + \$1200\left[0.095\left(1 + \frac{62}{360}\right)\right] = \$1{,}333.63$$

Having once been a common practice of commercial banks, it is known as the *Banker's Rule.*

Accountant's Method, a Short-Cut

Ensuing short-cut rules, widely practiced by budding practitioners of the trade and accountants, underscore how to locate correctly a decimal point when interest is 6 per cent, based on a 360-day year.

$$I = \frac{Pit}{360}, \text{ where } t = \text{number of days and } \frac{t}{360} = n.$$

RULE I: To find ordinary interest on P, when i = 6%, for 60 days, shift the decimal point *two* places to the left.

Example: Interest on \$825.43 for 60 days @ 6% is \$8.25.

RULE II: To find ordinary interest on P, when i = 6%, for 6 days, shift the decimal point *three* places to the left.

Example: Interest on \$825.43 for 6 days @ 6% is \$0.83.

RULE III: To find ordinary interest on P, when i = 6%, for any multiple of 60, divide by that multiple and add or subtract the result from interest on 60 days.

Example: (a) 15 days is ¼ of 60; therefore, \$8.25 ÷ 4 = \$2.06 interest cost for 15 days @ 6%.
(b) 75 days = 60 + 15; therefore, \$8.25 + \$2.06 = \$10.31, interest cost for 75 days @ 6%.

RULE IV: To find multiples of multiples, extend and apply Rule III.

Example: Interest for 30 days is ½ of \$8.25, or \$4.13; to find interest for 3 days, shift the decimal point *one* place to the left (equals \$0.41).

Example: To find interest on \$825.43 for 82 days @ 6%, the steps are:

(i) interest @ 6% for 60 days =	\$8.25	
(ii) interest @ 6% for 20 days =	2.75	(1/3 of (i))
(iii) interest @ 6% for 2 days =	0.28	(move decimal one place to left
Interest @ 6% for 82 days =	\$11.28	and round.)

RULE V: To find interest for rates other than 6%,
(i) shift decimal 3 places to the left;
(ii) multiply by *number* of per cents in interest rate;
(iii) divide by 6;
(iv) multiply by number of days;
(v) divide by 6.

Example: Find ordinary interest on \$825.43 @ 4% for 72 days:
(i) \$0.825
(ii) \$0.825 X 4 = \$3.30
(iii) 3.30 ÷ 6 = \$0.55
(iv) 0.55 X 72 = \$39.60
(v) 39.60 ÷ 6 = \$6.60

or, $$\frac{[(0.825 \times 4) \div 6] \times 72}{6} = \$6.60$$

At some point a hand calculator will replace these short-cut operations, but certainly mental exercises stimulate cerebral impulses.

Merchant's Rule

With the Merchant's Rule, total payment of an obligation amounts to initial loan principal (P), length of loan (n), and simple interest rate (i). Periodic payments plus interest reduce the obligation. Interest is computed on the original debt and on each interim payment (s) to the due date of the debt. The final payment comprehends balance due on principal plus interest minus partial payments already made. In the following formula three payments are assumed: s_1 and s_2 symbolize interim payments, plus s_3, the unknown final payment.

$$s_3 + s_2 + s_1 = P(1 + in)$$

where

$$s = p\left(1 + \frac{i}{n}\right)$$

and p stands for reduction of principal plus interest based on time remaining until the loan's due date.

Formula:

$$s_3 + p_2\left(1 + i\frac{1}{n}\right) + p_1\left(1 + i\frac{1}{n}\right) = P(1 + in)$$

Applying this formula to our case study, we may assume that Mrs. Hargis arranges to repay the loan principal on the following schedule: \$400 in 7 months (p_1), \$300 in 10 months (p_2), and the balance, s_3, on the loan's due date, August 31.

$$s_3 + \$300\left[1 + 0.095\left(\frac{2}{7}\right)\right] + \$400\left(1 + \frac{0.095}{2}\right) = 1{,}200\ [1 + 0.095\ (1\tfrac{1}{6})]$$

$$s_3 + \$308.14 + \$419.00 = \$1{,}333.00$$

$$s_3 = \$1{,}333.00 - \$727.14 = \$605.86$$

Observe carefully. Total debt, \$1,200 plus interest at 9.5% for 14 months, is the same sum calculated with the ordinary simple interest formula; but Mrs. Hargis will not have use of the full \$1,200 for the entire 14-month period. Therefore, the actual interest rate must necessarily exceed 9.5%, the same as in the *Banker's Rule.** Notice, too, in the formula, that s_2 consists

---

*See the "Residuary Formula" in this chapter to determine the approximate interest rate she would have paid.

of \$300 contributed to principal reduction plus \$8.14 on interest according to time remaining on the loan; viz., 14 months minus 10 months equals 4 months, or $^{4}/_{14}$, or $^{2}/_{7}$ ths of the remaining loan period. All other interim payments are figured in the same manner.

In order to pay a true rate of 9.5 per cent, interest ought to be calculated on the unpaid balance, where q_1, q_2, and q_3 represent balance due on principal at the end of each interest period, and F is the total sum paid (principal plus interest).

Formula:

$$F = (p_1 + q_1 \text{ in}) + (p_2 + q_2 \text{ in}) + (p_3 + q_3 \text{ in})$$

For example,

$$F = \left[\$400 + \$1{,}200\ [0.095(^{7}/_{12})]\right] + \left[\$300 + \$800\left(\frac{0.095}{4}\right)\right]$$

$$+ \left[\$500 + \$500\left(\frac{0.095}{3}\right)\right]$$

$$= \$466.50 + \$319.00 + \$515.83 = \$1{,}301.33$$

Because the loan balance was not a constant \$1,200 outstanding over the 14-month period, interest payments totaled \$101.33. Under the *Merchant's Rule,* interest payments were higher for funds borrowed over an identical period.

Equal Payments Rule

In situations where principal is steadily reduced by equal sums so that interest payments decrease by uniform amounts at the end of each interest period, calculated on the unpaid balance, total interest (I) paid for the entire loan term is:

Formula:

$$I = \frac{n}{2}\ [2I_i + (n - 1)\ G]$$

n = number of payments.

I_i = interest paid at end of the first interest period.

G = constant dollar decrease in interest at end of each period.

For example, Mr. Kevin owes \$6,000 on a leasehold improvement which he will repay in semi-annual installments of \$500 on principal plus 5% interest on outstanding principal every 6 months. To how much will total interest payments aggregate?

Mr. Kevin will make 12 payments $\left(\frac{6{,}000}{500}\right)$. The first interest payment equals \$300 (\$6,000 X 0.05); the second one will be \$275 (\$5,500 X 0.05); and consecutive interest payments will decrease by \$25. Solving the equation, Mr. Kevin will pay:

$$I = \frac{12}{2}[2(\$300) + (12 - 1)(-\$25)]$$

$$= 6(600 - 275) = \$1{,}950.$$

Note—Because interest costs diminish periodically by a uniform \$25, the decrement is registered as a negative figure (–\$25).

Exact Simple Interest

However, if *exact simple interest* applies, the ordinary simple interest formula must be modified to include a 365-day year (366 days for leap years). Ordinary simple interest computations assume each day is $\frac{1}{365}$th of a year. Denoting the letter t for days, we can modify the basic formula by substituting $\frac{t}{360}$ for n in ordinary simple interest problems so that for exact simple interest we have $n = \frac{t}{365}$.

Formula: $$I = \frac{Pit}{365}$$

Formula: $$F = P\left[1 + i\left(\frac{t}{365}\right)\right]$$

With exact simple interest Lorrie Hargis would have repaid:

Formula: $$F = P\left[1 + i\left(1 + \frac{t}{365}\right)\right]$$

Note: In this example (1 + t) is used because her loan extends for more than one year. It could have been left t = 427 days divided by 365, instead of being expressed as one plus a fraction of a year.

$$F = \$1{,}200\left[1 + 0.095\left(1 + \frac{62}{365}\right)\right]$$

$$F = \$1{,}200\ (P) + \$133.36\ (I) = \$1{,}333.36$$

But real multiplication begins when interest is compounded more frequently.

COMPOUND INTEREST

Simple interest, earned on the original value of the investment (bond, for example) or loan, is due at the end of the period. With compound interest the life of investment, savings account, for example, or loan, is divided into several interest periods. Interest for the first period is calculated on the original sum. Interest for the second period is calculated on the original sum plus interest earned during the preceding period, so that interest earned in a preceding period becomes principal for the next period.

Example: A \$1,000 bond paying a *stated interest* of 6½%, at the end of 3 years, will pay out:

$$I = Pin$$

$$I = \$1{,}000\ (.065)3 = \$195.$$

But a \$1,000 (P) savings account paying 6½% (i) *compounded annually* over 3 (n) years will produce:

First year: $I = \$1{,}000(.065) = \$65.00$

Second year: $I = (\$1{,}000 + \$65)\ 0.065 = \$69.23$

Third year: $I = (\$1{,}000 + \$65 + \$69.23)\ 0.065 = \$73.72$

Total interest earned: $I = I_1 + I_2 + I_3 = \$207.95$

Frequency of Conversion

Interest may be compounded any number of times during the year; the number of times interest is converted annually is designated *frequency of conversion;* the period of time between conversions is called the *conversion* (or interest) *period.* Which three important variables manifest in compounding?

(1) original principal,
(2) rate of interest per period, and
(3) the number of interest periods during the life of the transaction.

Formula: $F = P(1 + i)^n$

Example: The above $1,000 (P) compounded annually at 6.5% (i) for 3 years (n) can be quickly toted up:

$$F = \$1{,}000\,(1 + 0.065)^3$$
$$= \$1{,}000\,(1.20795) = \$1{,}207.95$$

(A "Table of Powers," Table XXVII, is also available in the Appendix.)

Quick Method

Complicated problems, to reckon compound amounts by actual computations, require much time, but Table I in the Appendix provides a practical short-cut. Briefly examine Table I. *Numbers* under the n column denote *conversion periods; per cent* corresponds to various *interest rates; figures* in each per cent column result from application of the *compounding formula,* $F = P(1 + i)^n$, and each corresponds to the *future value* of $1 at different interest rates and for different time periods. Operate as many decimal places as required for the problem, rounding off accordingly. If principal is $10,000.00, read 7 decimal places; if principal is $10.00, read 4 decimal places.

Suppose that a $1,000 time deposit yields 7% compounded annually for 3 years; find the 7% column and n = 3 row. The factor in Table I reads 1.225043. Multiply by $1,000.

$$\$1{,}000\,(1.225043) = \$1{,}225.04$$

The product marks the future value of $1,000 today compounded annually at 7% for 3 years. Any amount, lesser than or greater than $1, multiplied by the factor found in the table will yield the future value of an original principal.

Suppose, however, that $1,000 is invested for a fraction of a year more, such as 3 years and 3 months ($3\frac{1}{4}$ years), at 5% interest. In this case, P = 1,000, i = 0.05, n = $^{13}\!/_{4}$.

Theoretical Method

Although seldom used, the theoretical method meets with a slightly smaller value than the practical method below.

$$F = 1{,}000(1.05)^{13/4} = 1{,}000(1.05)^3\,(1.05)^{1/4}$$
$$= 1{,}000(1.157625)\,(1.012272) = \$1{,}171.83$$

The compounded future sum is computed in two parts. First, determine the compound amount by $F = P(1 + i)^n$ at the end of the last whole period contained within the given duration of investment, second, interest for the remaining fraction of a conversion period.

Practical Method

The practical method is easier to compute.

$$F = P\left(1 + \frac{i}{m}\right)^{mn}\left(1 + \frac{i}{m}\right)$$

Where n equals number of years and m the number of conversions per year.

$$F = 1{,}000\,(1.05)^3\left(1 + \frac{0.05}{4}\right)$$
$$= 1{,}000\,(1.157625)\,(1.012500) = \$1{,}172.10$$

With the practical method annual interest rate is divided by the number of periods; in this case m = 1 for the first 3 years and for the fraction of the 4th year, 3 months equals ¼ of a year.

Now let's examine differences between nominal interest and effective interest.

Nominal Interest Rate

For a year divided into several interest periods, interest is compounded during each period. For example, when a year is divided into four periods with interest at 1½ per cent compounded every 3 months, the nominal annual interest rate may also be stated as 6 per cent compounded quarterly.

Interest for the first quarter is calculated on the original principal; interest for the second quarter is calculated on the original principal plus interest earned during the first quarter; interest for the third quarter is calculated on the original principal plus interest accrued during the first two quarters, and so on.

Effective Interest Rate

The effective annual interest rate is the ratio of annual return to the original principal. The actual rate of interest cited above exceeds 6 per cent per annum because interest earned on interest compounds the effect.

Formula:

$$r = \frac{F - P}{P}$$

Example: Invested at 6% compounded *annually* \$1,000 will produce an effective interest rate (r):

$$r = \frac{\$1{,}060 - \$1{,}000}{\$1{,}000} = 0.06 = 6\%$$

But if the same sum is compounded *quarterly,* the future sum (F) will now amount to \$1,061.36. Therefore, the original investment (P) \$1,000, at 6% compounded quarterly, will sire an effective interest rate:

$$r = \frac{\$1{,}061.36 - \$1{,}000}{\$1{,}000} = 0.0614 = 6.14\%$$

In other words, we can state that the foregoing interest rates are equivalent if they yield the same results, so that 6% compounded *quarterly* matches 6.14% compounded *annually.* Both evolve an interest income of \$61.36 on \$1,000 for the first year. These are called *equivalent rates,* or *corresponding rates.*

Two Tables of interest appear in the Appendix: Table XIV, "Nominal Rates of Interest from Effective Rates," and Table XV, "Effective Interest Rates from Nominal Rates."

What if the future amount is unknown, can the effective interest rate be obtained directly from the nominal interest rate?

Example: What *effective rate* (r) compares with the *nominal rate* (i) of 12% compounded quarterly on an original investment of \$1,000?

In one year, \$1,000, at effective rate, r, will amount to (1 + r) and at

12% compounded quarterly will multiply to $\left(1 + \frac{0.12}{4}\right)^4$ times original investment. Since they equal each other we can state that:

Formula:

$$r = \left(1 + \frac{j}{m}\right)^m - 1$$

where m denotes number of times interest is converted within a year and j the nominal rate converted m times per year $\left(i = \frac{j}{m}\right)$. In this case we find that:

$$r = \left(1 + \frac{0.12}{4}\right)^4 - 1$$

$$= 1.1255088 - 1 = 0.12551 = 12.551\%$$

Of course, the procedure is reversible and the effective rate corresponding to a nominal rate can also be known.

Example: Let's call the unknown nominal rate, j, compounded quarterly, and now assume an effective rate, r, of 12%.

Formula:

$$j = m\ [(1 + r)^{1/m} - 1]$$

In this case we find that

$$\left(1 + \frac{j}{4}\right)^4 = (1 + 0.12)$$

$$\text{or, } 1 + \frac{j}{4} = (1 + 0.12)^{1/4}$$

$$j = 4\ [(1.12)^{1/4} - 1] = 4(0.0287374) = 0.11495 = 11.495\%$$

The *nominal rate,* then, is the expressed *annual* rate when interest is compounded more than once a year; while the rate of interest actually earned with more frequent conversions is the *effective rate.* Referring again to the two above examples, in the first one the *nominal rate* is 12.000%, the *effective rate,* 12.551%; while in the second one the *nominal rate* is 11.495%, the *effective rate,* 12.000%. Banks, saving and loan associations, and other thrift institutions will quote both nominal and effective rates. The case study on Austin Federal Savings toward the end of the chapter illustrates the point.

Short-Cut Method to Find Time

In solving for various elements in the compounding formula, $F = P(1 + i)^n$, we have known the time element. Suppose, however, you want to know how long it will take \$50,000 to multiply to \$250,000 at 8% compounded quarterly.

Example:

$$\$250{,}000 = \$50{,}000\left(1 + \frac{.08}{4}\right)^n$$

$$\text{and, } (1.02)^n = \frac{250}{5} = 5.00000$$

What we need to discover here is the value of $(1.02)^n$ that equals 5.00000. In Table I, $F = P(1 + i)^n$, run down the 2% column until you find an entry close to 5.00000. Where n = 81 the factor is 4.9729479, and where n = 82 the factor is 5.0724069. Multiplying the first factor 4.9729479, times \$50,000 (P) renders \$248,647, and \$50,000 × 5.0724069 = \$253,620. That is, in order to attain the objective, investment must be carried through the 82nd period which yields \$3,620 more than targeted. The answer, then, is n = 82, or 20 years and 6 months.

Short-Cut Method for n Values Beyond Table Limit

Assume that a problem requires a time span that extends beyond available compound interest tables. You may still define the compound amount by application of a *Law of Exponents* which, in general form, states that $a^x \cdot a^y = a^{x+y}$.

Example: How much will \$50,000 at 8% compounded quarterly amount to in 40 years? Since the table stops at n = 100, and we need n = 160, by the mentioned Law of Exponents we know that $(1 + i)^{100} \times (1 + i)^{60} = (1 + i)^{160}$. From Table I,

$$(1.02)^{100} = 7.2446461$$

$$(1.02)^{60} = 3.2810308$$

$$\text{and, } (1.02)^{160} = 7.2446461 \times 3.2810308 = 23.7699070$$

$$\text{so that } F = \$50{,}000\,(23.7699070) = \$1{,}188{,}495.35$$

Compounding with Changing Rates

Most problems and examples in this chapter assume a constant interest rate throughout the investment period, but interest rates may change periodically. By modifying known formulas we can handle changing interest rates.

Formula: $$F = P\left(1+\frac{j}{m}\right)^{mn}\left(1+\frac{j}{m}\right)^{mn}\left(1+\frac{j}{m}\right)^{mn}$$

Where m substitutes for the number of conversions within a given year, n for numbers of years, and j for (im) the nominal rate, expand or contract the formula to compensate for each applicable interest rate.

Example: H. G. Zavalakas, controller of an American firm, deposited $10,000, personal funds, in a 12-month time deposit at Barclay's Bank in London. The account is designated in Swiss francs. His contract states that unless he notifies the bank to the contrary by the end of the eleventh month the bank will automatically renew the deposit contract at the prevailing interest rate. During the 7 years he has maintained funds on deposit, for the first 3 years, the bank paid 3% compounded quarterly, then for 2 years paid 4% compounded semi-annually, and for the last 2 years paid 2.50% compounded annually.

Applying the above formula we can determine by how much H. G. Zavalakas' deposit has grown in 7 years. (Assume a constant exchange ratio.)

$$\begin{aligned} F &= \$10{,}000\left(1+\frac{.03}{4}\right)^{4\cdot 3}\left(1+\frac{.04}{2}\right)^{2\cdot 2}\left(1+\frac{.025}{1}\right)^{1\cdot 2} \\ &= 10{,}000\,(1.0075)^{12}\,(1.02)^{4}\,(1.025)^{2} \\ &= 10{,}000\;(1.0938)\,(1.0824)\,(1.0506) \\ &= 10{,}000\,(1.2438) = \$12,438.36 \end{aligned}$$

(This formula, of course, does not consider exchange rate appreciation or depreciation when foreign funds are converted into equivalent dollar amounts. See Chapter Fourteen on foreign exchange hedging and Chapter Fifteen on price-level accounting.)

Residuary Formula

To approximate true interest rate when partial payments are applied against the principal, the *residuary formula* rules that partial payments, s, first contribute to the unpaid loan balance, P, and then to the interest cost, I.

In the following formula, the letter m designates number of payments made in one year, while n still refers to the total number of interest periods, that is, the total number of payments.

Formula:

$$r = \frac{2mI}{P(n+1) + I(n-1)}$$

r = effective interest rate.

m = number of payments during one year.

I = total dollar amount of interest paid.

P = unpaid principal.

n = number of interest periods.

Turning once again to the case of Mrs. Hargis, where we modified her original payment schedule in order to illustrate the Merchant's Rule, we observe that she paid more than the simple interest rate of 9.5% because loan payment prior to the end of the 14-month period means that the entire sum of $1,200 is not available at all times. What, then, is the *effective interest rate* under modified assumptions when m = 2, I = $133, P = $1,200, and n = 3?

$$r = \frac{2(2)(133)}{1{,}200\,(3+1) + 133\,(3-1)} = \frac{532}{4{,}800 + 266} = 0.1050 = 10.50\%$$

If Mrs. Hargis had chosen an early repayment schedule without negotiating a reduction in total interest paid, she would have been paying an effective interest rate of 10.50 per cent on her loan.

Direct Ratio Formula

However, H. E. Stelson offers a reputedly more accurate formula, one which may produce significantly different results from the Residuary Formula. Symbols are identical but weighting of each expression differs.

Formula:

$$r = \frac{6mI}{3P(n+1) + I(n-1)}$$

Once again Mrs. Hargis supplies the data.

$$r = \frac{6(2)(133)}{3(1{,}200)(3+1) + 133(3-1)} = \frac{1{,}596}{14{,}400 + 266} = 0.1088 = 10.88\%$$

While both formulas indicate significantly higher interest rates, differences may be slight on a small loan, substantial on a larger one. Similarly, the interest rate actually paid may substantially differ from the stated rate.

Monthly and Annual Rates

For example, a certain firm charges its accounts a monthly carrying charge of 1½ per cent. Is the annual rate equal to 12 times the monthly rate, or 18 per cent? No, because the annual rate should reflect monthly compounding. The effective annual rate is:

Formula: $r = (1 + i)^m - 1$ (where i = the monthly rate)

For example:

$$r = (1 + 0.015)^{12} - 1 = (1.015)^{12} - 1$$
$$= 1.1956 - 1 = 0.1956 = 19.56\%$$

Case Study: How much did the First National Bank really charge its clients?

Several years ago the First National Bank in Mansfield pioneered an eye-catching advertisement well-placed throughout its marketing area in which they offered new car loans at 4 per cent interest. This rate was about one-half the advertised rate of most other leading institutions and substantially lower than rates offered by Universal CIT and General Motors Acceptance Corporation (GMAC). Their approach appealed to enough people in this high-income area so that other area and regional banks quickly imitated this ploy.

Wayne Purcell, a draftsman at Westinghouse, decided to buy a new car at the beginning of the model year to take advantage of these "low rates" rather than wait until vacation time the following June as he had planned. After trade-in allowance he still needed to finance $3,000. The bank loaned him this sum at 4 per cent interest repayable in 24 equal monthly installments. How much will he pay monthly, and, using the *Direct Ratio Formula,* what will be the effective interest rate?

Formula: $s = \frac{P + I}{n}$

To summarize the facts, we have

$n = 24 \qquad P = \$3{,}000$

$m = 12 \qquad I = \$3{,}000\ (0.04)\ (2) = \$240$

The monthly installments will be:

$$s = \frac{3{,}000 + 240}{24} = \$135$$

Employing the *Direct Ratio Formula,* the effective interest rate is:

$$r = \frac{6\ (12)\ 240}{3(3{,}000)\ (24 + 1) + 240\ (24 - 1)}$$

$$= \frac{17{,}280}{225{,}000 + 5{,}520} = 0.07496 = 7.50\%$$

By today's standards, of course, such low-cost loans are scarce. Nevertheless, versions of this approach spring up as important marketing tools. For a store engaging in substantial credit business, heavy carrying charges facilitate greater pricing flexibility and greater profits.

Constant Ratio Formula

An appliance store in Managua promoted refrigerators at a price noticeably lower than most of its smaller competitors and at prices certainly competitive with large dealers such as Sears and Casa Mantica. In equivalent dollars they advertised General Electric refrigerators at \$790 cash or, on terms, \$100 down and the balance in 12 monthly installments of \$71. Assuming that each monthly payment (\$71) includes repayment of principal plus interest in the same ratio as the original unpaid balance to interest, we can resort to the *Constant Ratio Formula* to find the effective interest rate.

Formula:

$$r = \frac{2mI}{P\ (n + 1)}$$

Relating the foregoing data to this formula, we discover that high latent costs are buried in the financing plan.

$$r = \frac{2(12)\ (162)}{690\ (13)} = \frac{3{,}888}{8{,}970} = 0.4334 = 43.34\%$$

Equal Payments Throughout Investment Period

Solving problems in compounding, not restricted to finding effective interest rates, has produced formula variations to designate a future amount (F), an unknown principal (P), time period (n), or annual flow of payments or investments (A). The following example will illustrate how to find the latter, A, annual flow.

Consider a sales manager of the Mojave Paper Division, planning to retire in 6 years, who contemplates creation of an additional fund to supplement current savings and projected retirement income in order to bridge the retirement-adjustment gap and add some spice to life.

Formula:

$$F = A\frac{(1 + i)^n - 1}{i}$$

Example: Frank Wells, sales manager, discusses his situation with an investment counselor. Together they agree on an investment strategy that promises to yield about 8% compounded annually. Frank will make a series of 6 uniform payments of \$3,600 annually to purchase shares in a portfolio. What will be the value of Frank's investment when he retires at the end of 6 years?

$$F = \$3{,}600\frac{(1 + .08)^6 - 1}{.08}$$

$$= 3{,}600\frac{0.586874}{.08}$$

$$= 3{,}600\ (7.335925) = \$26{,}409.33$$

His efforts to sacrifice \$3,600 annually from his salary should reward him with a portfolio worth \$26,409.33 at the end of 6 years, given the assumptions.

Table III in the Appendix, an alternative to the preceding formula, shortens computation time. Table III, "Amount of 1 per Period Compounded for n Periods," records those factors which are equivalent to the uniform payment of \$1 per period, at *end* of each period, for n intervals. For the Frank Wells problem, under the 8% column, 6th row, we discover the factor 7.335929 $(F/A_{i,n})$; multiply this factor by the amount of the annuity (\$3,600) to determine future value (F).

$$F = P\ (F/A_{i,n})$$

$$F = \$3{,}600\ (7.335929)_{8\%,6} = \$26{,}409.34$$

Tables I and III, along with other tables in the Appendix provide for a more profitable use of time since time-consuming calculations, by formula, to fit most situations have been furnished as a convenience to the reader.

Compounding More Frequently

So far, cases have dealt with compounding annually, semi-annually, or quarterly, but the same formulas and tables can as easily handle situations where sums are compounded more frequently—monthly, weekly, daily, or hourly. As sums are converted faster, m, the effective rate, r, rises. (See Figure 1-2.) The larger m, the greater is r until reaching the situation of continuous compounding discussed at the end of this chapter.

Figure 1-2

	m	*r*
Annually	1	6.0000%
Semi-annually	2	6.0900%
Quarterly	4	6.1364%
Monthly	12	6.1678%
Weekly	52	6.1800%
Daily	365	6.1831%

Example: For example, what is the effective annual rate when an investment is compounded monthly at 6.3%? r = unknown; m = 12; j = 6.3%; $i = \frac{j}{m}$ $= \frac{0.063}{12} = 0.00525$

The formula is familiar:

$$r = \left(1 + \frac{j}{m}\right)^m - 1$$

and since $\frac{j}{m} = i$, we can write it

$$r = (1 + i)^m - 1$$

which puts it into a more familiar form. Substituting,

$$r = (1 + 0.00525)^{12} - 1$$

Obviously, as frequency of conversion increases, multiplication consumes more time, so let's look for a quicker way to solve this type of problem.

A Faster Method: Interpolation

If it just happens to correspond with an entry in Table I, then the solution unfolds quickly; however, we can still use Table I to *approximate* the effective rate, r, if we *interpolate.* To interpolate means to estimate a value that exists between two known values.

In this example Table I records values for ½% and 1% when n = 12. The first step: locate these two values from the table and subtract.

$$\left.\begin{array}{l}(F/P_{½\%,12}) = 1.06168 \\ (F/P_{1\%,12}) = 1.12683\end{array}\right\} = 0.0615 \text{ (difference)}$$

Since 0.00525 is 0.00025 ths between 0.005 and 0.010 we can say that it covers about 5% of the distance; that is, 0.00525 is 5% of the distance between ½% and 1%. The second step: pinpoint 5% of the above difference:

$$0.0615 \times 0.05 = 0.00326$$

The last result corresponds to the 0.00025 part of i = 0.00525. The third step: add 0.00326 and 1.06168 and, finally, solve the equation.

$$r = (1.06168 + 0.00326) - 1$$
$$= (1.06494) - 1 = 0.06494 = 6.49\%$$

Any two values in the table may be interpolated—between per cent columns or between n rows—to approximate the desired result.

OTHER QUICK-CUT SOLUTIONS

Three principal streamline methods reign here—the first quickly interprets compounded growth rate of a company's earnings, the second introduces logarithms. Logarithms, a very practical tool in financial computations, will crop up from time-to-time throughout this handbook, but alternative solutions will also be shown. The third method, punch, press and pray, should not be totally ignored for simplest calculations.

Three Methods to Determine a Firm's Compound Growth Rate

Statements like "a firm's income rose by 315% over the past decade" provide little basis for comparison with other businesses because the base period and time span selected significantly influence results. But expressing growth performance in terms of compounded annual rate of increase furnishes a means to secure uniformity among firms, a means to compare the data.

Case Study: At what rate has Dun & Bradstreet's earnings grown?

To illustrate, the following table registers earnings per share (EPS) over a 10-year span. Earnings of Dun & Bradstreet and its subsidiaries climbed about 1.9 times, approximately 86 per cent (Figure 1-3). That fact alone says little. Or to state that earnings grew an average 8.6 per cent per year for 10 years misleads. A closer *approximation* is the compounded growth rate. Here are three methods for computing this rate.

Figure 1-3

Earnings per Share, Dun & Bradstreet

Year	0	1	2	3	4	5	6	7	8	9	10
EPS	0.85	0.85	0.90	0.92	1.02	1.08	1.16	1.31	1.47	1.50	1.58

Source: Dun & Bradstreet Companies, Inc., Annual Report.

(A) The first method relies on *Table I* in the *Appendix*. The steps are:

(a) Find number of times earnings have increased (decreased).

(b) Along the appropriate n row (10 in this case) locate the factor in the table closest to the result from (a).

(c) Interpolate if a closer estimate is desired.

(d) Read final result as a per cent, the annually compounded growth rate.

Applying these steps to Dun & Bradstreet data we have:

$$\text{(a)}\ \frac{1.58}{.85} = 1.8588$$

$$\text{(b)}\ (F/P_{6\%,10}) = 1.7908$$

$$(F/P_{7\%,10}) = 1.9672$$

$$\text{(c)}\ r = \left[\frac{(1.8588 - 1.7908)}{(1.9672 - 1.7908)} \times (7\% - 6\%)\right] + 6\%$$

$$= \left[\frac{680}{1{,}764} \times 1.0\%\right] + 6\% = [0.3855 \times 1.0\%] + 6\%$$

(d) $= 0.4\% + 6\% = 6.4\%$

(B) The second method adopts *logarithms,* which lessen labor for more complicated problems. The following example enlists *common* logarithms, or *Briggs'* system, which base is 10. (*Natural* logarithms, are discussed in the last section of this chapter. Six and seven-place mantissas are reproduced in Tables XXIV and XXV in the Appendix.) To find compounded growth rate, the formula is:

Formula:

$$\log \frac{\text{final year}}{\text{beginning year}} = N \log(1 + r)$$

Substituting:

$$\log \frac{1.58}{0.85} = 10 \log(1 + r)$$

$$\log 1.8588 = 10 \log(1 + r)$$

$$0.269238 = 10 \log(1 + r)$$

$$0.0269238 = \log(1 + r)$$

$$\text{antilog } 1.064 = 1 + r$$

$$r = 0.064 = 6.4\%$$

Also see Example (B) under the caption "More Uses of Logarithms."

If you compute the antilog of 0.0269238, notice that it falls slightly short of 1.064, lying between 1.063 and 1.064. Of course, one can interpolate. At the next level of accuracy, the answer 6.3955% emerges. For this degree of perfection one should employ continuous compounding which closely reflects steady inflows and outflows associated with investments.

(C) If tables for compound interest or six-place mantissas are not immediately available (more than one meter from your desk), then the third method, playing around with a hand calculator (also known as punch, press and pray), works as well.

More Uses of Logarithms

Logarithms are especially convenient for certain types of problems or where tables do not apply. (Tables XXIV and XXV in the Appendix are useful in the solution of these problems.)

Finding Effective Rate from Nominal Rate

For instance, what effective rate, r, equals the nominal annual rate, j, 6% compounded quarterly (m)? The formula is:

$$j = m\,[(1 + r)^{1/m} - 1]$$

which can also be written:

$$j = m\,[\sqrt[m]{(1 + r)} - 1]$$

because

$$\sqrt[m]{1 + r} = (1 + r)^{1/m}$$

Pressing logarithms into service to calculate the effective annual rate, given the nominal rate, the steps are:

(a) Determine the log of 1 plus the effective rate, or the ratio of conversion;
(b) Divide the log in (a) by the number of conversion periods;
(c) Find the antilog of the quotient (b) which results in 1 plus the nominal rate;
(d) Subtract 1; and
(e) Express the nominal rate as a per cent.

By the letters, we have:

(a) log 1.06 = 0.0253059
(b) 0.0253059 ÷ 4 = 0.0063265 log of conversion ratio
(c) antilog 0.0063265 = 1.01467
(d) 1.01467 − 1 = 0.01467 rate for one quarter
(e) 0.01467 × 4 (quarters) = 0.05868 = 5.87% = j

Finding Unknown Rate for More Than One Year

Suppose, however, that the interest period extends beyond one year. Principal, future value, and time period are known but the interest rate is unknown. If $1,000 amounts to $1,262.50 in 4 years, what is the interest rate compounded annually?

Formula:

$$i = \sqrt[n]{\frac{F}{P}} - 1$$

The annual interest rate is the n_{th} root of the future sum (F) divided by the original investment (P) minus one.

$$i = \sqrt[4]{\frac{\$1{,}262.50}{1{,}000.00}} - 1$$

(See also Method (B) in the Dun and Bradstreet case study.)

1,262.50 ÷ 1,000 = 1.2625 (compound amount of 1 for 4 years at rate i)

log 1.2625 = 0.1012314 ÷ 4 = 0.0253078

antilog 0.0253078 = 1.060

1.060 - 1 = 0.060 = 6.0% = i

Finding Time with Principal, Future Value, Rate Known

Assume same data as above: P = \$1,000.00; F = \$1,262.50; i = 6.0%; n = ?

The steps to solve for this unknown time (n), are:

(a) Divide the future amount by the original principal (P) to compute the compound amount of \$1.
(b) Look up the log of (a).
(c) Determine the log of i.
(d) Divide (b) by (c) to determine n.

Formula:

$$n = \frac{\log \frac{F}{P}}{\log (1 + i)}$$

To illustrate:

(a) 1,262.50 ÷ 1,000 = 1.2625

(b) log 1.2625 = 0.1012314

(c) log 1.06 = 0.0253059

$$n = \frac{\log \dfrac{1{,}262.50}{1{,}000.00}}{\log 1.06}$$

$$\text{(d) } n = \frac{0.1012314}{0.0253059} = 4.0 \text{ (years)}$$

Finding Effective Rate with Interest Compounded Weekly

Whether interest is compounded quarterly, monthly, or weekly, the same method applies. Which effective rate (r) corresponds to a nominal rate of 6% (j) converted 52 (m) times yearly (n)?

$$j = 0.06; m = 52; n = 1; r = ?$$

Formula:

$$\log(1 + r) = N \log\left(1 + \frac{j}{m}\right)$$

$$\log(1 + r) = 52 \log 1.0011538$$

$$\log(1 + r) = 52\,(0.0005008) = 0.0260416$$

$$1 + r = 1.0618 \text{ antilog}$$

$$r = 1.0618 - 1 = 0.0618 = 6.18\%$$

The value of r is correct to three significant digits. For interest problems a seven-place mantissa table such as Table XXV in the Appendix will furnish desired accuracy.

MIRACLE OF CONTINUOUS COMPOUNDING

More frequent conversion leads to higher effective rates. If a sum earns interest compounded weekly, m equals 52, daily, m equals 365 (or 366), or hourly, m equals 8,760, but if interest is compounded continuously, then m erupts—approaching infinity. Fortunately, others have worked out the mathematics so that we concern ourselves only with results of their labor and how to profit by it in financial computations. The easiest is last, and a short-cut trick or two will simplify calculations, save time.

Although continuous compounding seldom is called into play on loans, its frequent applicability to savings accounts has popularized this technique;

nevertheless, it is valuable and practical in investment analysis. Rates of return figured on investment compounded annually leaves a reality gap because investing in and wearing out capital goods emerge as continuing processes; continuous compounding (and discounting) more closely relate to actual conditions surrounding business decisions and practices.

In the basic formula $\left(1 + \frac{j}{m}\right)^m$, m takes on higher values as the nominal rate is converted faster, but as m approaches infinity it takes on a limiting value of e^j. Development of this formula requires some knowledge of limits of calculus—certainly beyond the scope of this handbook written *not* for mathematicians but for practical-minded persons to solve practical problems profitably.

That mathematical symbol e is only the base of natural, or "Napierian," logarithms. What is e? Calculus textbooks say that e = 2.71828182845 . . . . And we'll just take their word for it.

So here is the formula for continuous compounding of interest. A nominal rate, j, converted continuously, resolves into the corresponding effective rate (r):

Formula: $$r = e^j - 1$$

The nominal rate is called the *force of interest* equivalent to effective rate, r.

Recommendation. Some readers may fail to recall their high school logarithm days, especially since past textbook-styled problems seemed unrelated to future occupations. Nevertheless, logarithms so greatly simplify many of these calculations that two or three hours in review will be rewarding.* To ease your burdens, the common log of e, the same for all these problems, is:

$$\log e = 0.434294481901$$

Example: Although we already know the answer, for practice, let's determine the effective rate, r, corresponding to a nominal rate, j, of 6% converted continuously. Rearranging the above formula, we have:

$$1 + r = e^j$$

$$1 + r = e^{0.06}$$

*Cf.: Thomas M. Simpson, et al, *Mathematics of Finance,* 4th ed. (Englewood Cliffs, N.J.: Prentice-Hall, Inc., 1969), chap. 9. Six and seven-place mantissas appear in the Appendix of this handbook.

Taking logarithms of both sides produces:

Formula:

$$\log(1 + r) = j \log e$$

$$\log(1 + r) = 0.06 \times \log e$$

$$= 0.06\,(0.4342945) = 0.0260577$$

Finding the antilog results in

$$1 + r = 1.061837$$

$$r = 1.061837 - 1 = 0.061837 = 6.1837\%$$

Of course, the above procedure applies whether you want to compute the effective rate of 3.5%, 22.13%, or 75% converted continuously, and log e remains unchanged for all operations. (Cf. Table XV in the Appendix.) The process is reversible as well.

Example: Suppose you desire to know the force of interest, the equivalent value of j converted continuously corresponding to an effective rate, r, of 6%. The formula, $r = e^j - 1$, can also be solved with logarithms.

Formula:

$$j = \frac{\log r}{\log e}$$

$$j = \frac{\log 1.06}{\log e} = \frac{0.0253059}{0.4342945} = 0.058269$$

$$j = 5.827\%$$

In other words, a nominal rate, j = 5.827%, converted continuously, corresponds to an effective rate, r, of 6.000%; both will yield the same compound sum at the end of one year. (Vide Table XIV in the Appendix.)

Short-Cut

If you do not have a conversion table handy, do not require accuracy to several decimal places, are working with low rates, the following short-cut substitutes.

(a) Determine the effective yield of the nominal rate compounded monthly (m = 12), which is rapidly achieved with any inexpensive hand calculator.

(b) Carry the result, r, expressed as a decimal, to five decimal places.

(c) Now round according to these rules:

(i) For 1% through 6%, if the 5th digit is less than 5, add + 3 to the 4th digit; if the 5th digit is 5 or more, add + 2 to the 4th digit.

(ii) For 7% through 12%, if the 5th digit is less than 5, add + 4 to the 4th digit; if the 5th digit is 5 or more, add + 3 to the 4th digit.

(d) Express answer as per cent. The result should be accurate to the first decimal place and close on the second. As rates climb, the error will carry over into the first decimal and eventually into the whole number.

Here is how it works. Compounded monthly, 6% results in 0.061678. Since the fifth place digit, 7, exceeds 5, add + 2 to 6, which equals 0.0618, or 6.18%. That turns out identical with the continuously converted rate if it were rounded to two places.

For 9%, the monthly equivalent rate is 0.09380. Since 0, the fifth digit, is less than 5, add + 4 to 8, which results in 0.0942 or 9.42%. The continuous rate, by logarithms, is 9.417%, or 9.42%. The error shows up in the third decimal place.

But error increases with 12% nominal rate, which yields 0.126824 compounded monthly. Since 2 is less than 5, add + 4 to 8, which equals 0.1275%. The continuous rate is 12.75%.

Too, tables reflecting continuous compounding of $1 invested at the *beginning* of each period are provided in the Appendix to save the reader's time. Two convenient reference tables relate to chapter one: Table VII, "Amount of 1 at Continuously Compounded Nominal Interest Rates," and Table IX, "Amount of 1 per Period for n Periods at Continuously Compounded Nominal Interest Rates." Enlisting concepts from this chapter, we can now experiment with their profitable application.

Case Study: Did Austin Federal Savings tell all?

During a presidential election year, Austin Federal Savings distributed a flyer which advertised: "Six Ways to Make Money Grow! 5¼% passbook combines complete flexibility with the highest interest allowed by law on insured passbook savings. Interest compounded daily and paid from date of deposit to withdrawal. Yields 5.39% annually."

From material in this chapter we have sufficient formulas, mathematical techniques, and tables to analyze Austin Federal Savings claims. They claim to compound daily, to credit interest earned quarterly. With the daily formula, m equals 366 days in a leap year. To convert nominal to effective interest we have:

$$r = \left(1 + \frac{j}{m}\right) - 1$$

$$= \left(1 + \frac{0.0525}{366}\right)^{366} - 1$$

$$\log(1 + r) = 366 \log(1 + 0.0001434426)$$
$$= 366 \log(1.0001434426)$$
$$= 366\,(0.000062292) = 0.02279889$$
$$1 + r = 1.053899 \text{ antilog*}$$
$$r = 1.053899 - 1 = 0.053899 = 5.39\%\text{*}$$

The answer, 5.39%, corresponds to the advertised effective yield when interest is compounded daily.

Austin's certificates of deposit (CDs) require a minimum $1,000 deposit. One advertised option promises a 6.81% effective return on a 6½% CD carrying a one year maturity. Although the flyer does not inform us how interest develops, the high rate points toward continuous conversion.

$$\log(1 + r) = 0.0650(0.4342945) = 0.0282291$$
$$1 + r = 1.067159 \text{ (found by interpolating)}$$
$$r = 1.067159 - 1 = 0.067159 = 6.7159\%$$

Continuous compounding generates the highest effective rate; 6.81% significantly outreaches 6.7159%; a daily compounded rate yields 6.71%. Is there a misprint in the literature? The clue lies in reversing the Banker's Rule mentioned earlier in this chapter.

RATES HIGHER THAN CONTINUOUS CONVERSION

If interest is compounded continuously, how can effective rates higher than that be realized? Recall that with the Banker's Rule interest is figured on a 360-day year but charged daily against a 365-day year so that the banker ends up with a little extra interest on loans. The same principal operates here only the saver now garners the additional benefit. The diurnal interest rate, calculated on a 360-day year, is paid daily for 365 days (or 366 days in leap years). We may call this the *Reversed Banker's Rule.*

Formula: $r = \left(1 + \frac{j}{m}\right)^{m^*} - 1$, but $m \neq m^*$

and, $m = 360$

$m^* = 366$ (for leap years)

---

*If seven-place tables are used and interpolated, rounding results in a lower 5.382%.

so that,

$$\log (1 + r) = 366 \log (1.0001806)$$
$$= 366 (0.0000782) = 0.0286212$$
$$1 + r = 1.068123 \text{ antilog}$$
$$r = 1.068123 - 1 = 0.6812 = 6.812\%$$

Why is this (and others) financial institution so circumlocutory when they actually pay their depositers more than bargained for? The fault inheres partly with a nescient public but essentially with government restrictions which have prevented savings and loans associations from competing effectively in money markets when interest rates climb. If they lose deposits, they must reject loan requests. Smaller savers, especially, are penalized by these restrictive governmental practices because limited investment alternatives minimize interest income.

In order to cede its customers maximum rates on insured deposits, within limits established by the Federal Reserve Board, these financial institutions base their rates on acceptable practices, the 360-day year, and then pay interest daily for 365 or 366 days. Better than continuous conversion!

The next chapter raises the curtain on still another reversal—the other side of compounding.

CONTENTS

Chapter Two: Seventeen Time-Saving Techniques to Calculate Present Values

PAGE

TWO

Seventeen Time-Saving Techniques to Calculate Present Values

In Central America an apothegm, "A bird in hand is worth a thousand flying," sounds like our, "A bird in hand is worth two in the bush," only more so. The first maxim suggests that Central Americans place an even higher value than we on money in-hand today over vague future promises—perhaps with good reason; but that, too, is the nature of the present value concept.

With *compounding,* a present sum of money multiplies to produce some *future* sum—looking forward into the future from the present. With *present value* concepts, a future sum of money *discounted* at an appropriate rate determines its equivalent present sum—looking from the future back to the present. Of course, the same factors operate to determine present values as well as future values, but present value techniques have wide-spread use, especially in capital budgeting, in comparing investment alternatives. The present chapter will explain the mechanics of calculating present values and develop a variety of useful formulas for personal and business situations; Chapters Three and Four will exhibit further operation of present value techniques in diverse investment situations.

A BIRD IN HAND

Discounting is compounding in reverse. It sets down future values in today's terms. In compounding an invested principal grows faster at higher interest rates, and the accumulated sum increases the longer funds are kept invested and compounded; while present worth (or discounted value) of future accumulations becomes progressively smaller with higher interest rates and time.

Underlying theory of discounting is the *time preferences* of individuals. It is human nature to place a higher value on the present than on the future. An interest rate represents a *ratio of exchange* between today and tomorrow, and the higher value we place on today, the higher the interest rate. Suppose, for example, that you know with a high degree of probability (due to health, war, or execution) that your earthly existence will end in 30 days. What value do you place on today, and each of the next 30 days, compared with next year? Relationship between this last month and an unknowable next year approaches infinity.

Use of time can be rearranged by lending and borrowing resources. Greater demand for resources today raises interest rates, which really denote premiums for impatience, so that interest rates (or *discount factors*) reduce the larger inflow of money tomorrow to the lower outflow of money today. We can rely on this positive relationship because more people seem impatient than patient. Therefore, interest rates emerge to bring this one-sided relationship into balance; hence, the time value of money, which reflects time preferences of lenders and borrowers.

The compounding formula in Chapter One resolves this question: How much will sum, P, invested today at interest rate, i, for years n, be worth in the future, F? Or, $F = P(1 + i)^n$.

Discounting resolves this issue: What is the value today, V, of a future sum F, that is invested for years n, at interest, i, compounded annually? The present value (PV) formula restates the compound interest formula.

Formula:

$$V = \frac{F}{(1 + i)^n}$$

Which reads that the present value (V) equals an accumulated future amount (F) divided by 1 plus the interest rate (i) raised to the number of years (n) the sum is invested.

Example: A sum invested today at 10% compounded annually for 2 years will result in $2,057 at the end of the second year. What is today's value (the present value) of $2,057, which sum will not materialize until the end of 2 years?

$$V = \frac{\$2,057}{(1 + 0.10)^2} = \frac{2,057}{1.21} = \$1,700$$

In other words, a bird in hand, $1,700, matches two in the bush, $2,057. *only when* the interest rate (or *discount rate*) equals 10% compounded annually for 2 years.

Fast Technique

For most problems present value tables offer the fastest and simplest means to solve these problems. To understand creation of present value tables return to the compound formula, $F = P(1 + i)^n$. In present value problems, with future amounts known, solve for P, the original investment, or outlay today.

Formula: $P = F(1 + i)^{-n}$

Although both of the above formulas are essentially identical, restated in the second fashion highlights efficacy of tables. Table II in the Appendix records present values of $1 at different discount rates for various time periods (n). The quantity $(1 + i)^{-n}$, the *discount factor,* is the present value of 1 at compound interest. To determine any sum other than 1, multiply that sum by the discount factor found in Table II, "Single Payment Present Value of 1 at Compound Interest." In the above formula, multiply F, the future sum, times the discount factor, $(1 + i)$, to obtain its present worth.

Present Value Tables

What is the present value of $4,300 received at end of 20 years if 14% is an appropriate discount rate? In Table II, in the Appendix, find the 14% column; run your finger down to the 20-year row and read 0.072762; then multiply this factor by $4,300.

$$P = \$4{,}300\ (1 + 0.14)^{-20}$$

$$P = \$4{,}300\ (0.072762) = \$312.88$$

The sum \$312.88 in-hand today is just as good as \$4,300 in 20 years when the discount rate is 14%. Or we can say that \$312.88 invested today at 14% compounded annually will yield \$4,300 by the end of the 20th year.

To check computations, apply the formula $F = P\ (1 + i)^n$: $F = \$312.88\ (1 + 0.14)^{20} = \$312.88\ (13.743490) = \$4{,}300.06$ (error due to rounding).

Note: If a present value table is not readily available, compute discount factors by taking the inverse of data found in a compound interest table for the comparable interest rate and time period.

Interpolation

Since most tables do not cover all possibilities, interpolate to estimate quickly value between two *discount rates* or two *time periods.*

(a) To discover the present value of \$4,300, received in 20 years, applying a rate of 14½%, interpolation furnishes an approximate factor. Using Table II:

i = 14%, n = 20 = 0.07276172
i = 16%, n = 20 = 0.05138546
0.02137626 difference

Since 14½% is one-fourth between 14% and 16%, multiply,

$$0.02137626 \times \tfrac{1}{4} = 0.00534407$$

and subtract this result from the factor for 14%:

0.07276172
0.00534407
0.06741765 factor, i = 14½%, n = 20 years.

Multiply:

$$0.06741765 \times \$4{,}300 = \$289.90$$

Because 14½% exceeds 14%, the present value of an identical future sum diminishes further.

(b) To discover the present value of $4,300, discounted at 14% for 20½ years, interpolate between 20 and 21 years.

$$\begin{aligned} i = 14\%, n = 20 &= 0.07276172 \\ i = 14\%, n = 21 &= \underline{0.06382607} \\ & 0.00893565 \end{aligned}$$

Since 20½ years lies half way between 20 and 21, multiply,

$$0.00893565 \times \tfrac{1}{2} = 0.00446783$$

and subtract above result:

$$\begin{aligned} &0.07276172 \\ &\underline{0.00446783} \\ &0.06829389 \text{ factor, } i = 14\%, n = 20\tfrac{1}{2} \text{ years.} \end{aligned}$$

Multiply:

$$0.068294 \times 4{,}300 = \$293.66$$

Because 20½ years lengthens the waiting period, the present value of a future sum declines.

Logarithms

Logarithms offer an alternative method. (Please refer to Chapter One for further details on logarithm application.) To solve, $P = F(1 + i)^{-n}$, apply this formula:

Formula: $\text{Log } P = \text{Log } F - n \log (1 + i)$

Example: To illustrate, find the present value of $1,000 due in 18 years if money is worth 7.29%. (Use Tables XXIV and XXV in the Appendix.)

$$\text{Log P} = \log \$1{,}000 - 18 \log 1.073$$

$$\text{(Use 7-place mantissa Table XXV.)} = 3.000000 - 18(0.0305592)$$

$$= 3.000000 - 0.5500656 = 2.449934$$

$$\text{(Finding antilog from Table XXIV) P} = \$281.80$$

Of course, the problem can also be estimated interpolating Table II. Margin of error between the two methods will be slight.

Real Value of Money

The interest rate on an interest-bearing debt does not necessarily reflect the real value of money. Interest rates do, or should, reflect *time preference, risks,* and, *inflation,* but these factors can change during the life of the debt or the negotiated *nominal interest rate* does not necessarily correspond to the *real rate.*

The maturity value of a $10,000 obligation due in 8 years bearing 9% interest converted annually is:

$$F = P(1 + i)^n = \$10{,}000\,(1 + 0.09)^8$$

$$= \$10{,}000\,(1.9925626) = \$19{,}925.63$$

If money is worth 9% effective, today's value of $19,925.63, 8 years from now, equals $10,000. They parallel each other when the discount rate is 9%. But if money is worth 11% effective, the present value of $19,925.63, equivalent debt at maturity, is $8,646.26—a substantial loss in real terms if inflation rates, for example, rise! (Refer to Chapter Fifteen on price-level accounting.)

WORTH OF PRESENT VALUE ANALYSIS

Knowing the distance between Earth and Ceres becomes a useful fact only when it relates to a practical problem. Of what practical value, if any, are techniques discussed in Chapter Two? Here are a few types of problems that can be solved or analyzed with these techniques.

(a) How do timing and size of cash flows relate to investment decisions?

(b) Which investment proposal should a firm undertake, given its scarce resources?

(c) If Lisa requires Y dollars in X years, how much should she invest each year to achieve her goal?

(d) Is a particular annuity plan a good deal? What interest rate corresponds to the investment?

(e) Peter weighs the advantages of graduate study, trade school, in-house company training. Which flow of estimated future income has the highest present value?

(f) What is the maximum amount that is reasonable to pay for an income-producing property?

(g) What is the value of anticipated future receipts?

(h) How can a rate of return be determined on income that will begin 3 years after initial investment and will vary from year-to-year?

(i) What is the worth of salvage value in investment decisions?

(j) What is the benefit-cost ratio of a project—with stipulated minimum attractive rate of return used as interest rate?

(k) Comparing various outflows of funds without regard for inflows—a question of relative economy—which option appears best?

A BIRD IN HAND EVERY YEAR

The preceding situation discussed payments that are received only once, at the end of the nth period. In most investment decisions, however, the investment will produce a stream of income over its life. That income flow may be continuous, discrete, or vary in size. To calculate the value of a steady inflow in which payments are equal each and every period, the following formula is expedient.

Formula:

$$V = F \frac{1 - (1 + i)^{-n}}{i}$$

This formula pinpoints the present value of $1 recruited each and every year for n years. If $1 accrues *once* at the *end* of the third year, discounted at 6%, the present value is $1 (0.83961928) = $0.84. If $1 is credited at the end of *every* year for 3 years, the present value of this stream of income is:

$$V = \frac{1 - (0.83961928)}{.06} = \$2.6730 = \$2.67$$

Training Program at Credit Card Center

For instance, management of a credit card accounting center considers a new program, proposed by a consulting firm, to efficiently train inexperienced key punch operators. Proposing a five-year project, the consultants claim the credit card firm will save more than $10,000 a year. The initial cost of the program, including fees, amounts to $20,000. To maintain the program *additional* annual training expenses will aggregate to $4,000. Should the company sign a contract with the consulting firm on these terms? (The company uses 8% annual interest for cost comparisons.)

F (savings are treated as annual inflow since they add to net income) = annual savings - annual costs

$$= \$10,000 - \$4,000 = \$6,000$$

To be acceptable the present value of the annual inflow ($6,000) must exceed the initial outlay ($20,000) for the proposal.

$$V = \$6,000 \left[\frac{1 - (1 + .08)^{-5}}{.08} \right]$$

Table IV in the Appendix, "Present Value of 1 per Period Received for n Periods," substitutes for that portion of the formula in brackets. In Table IV, find the 8% column, 5-year row, and multiply that factor by $6,000.

$$\$6,000\ (3.99271) = \$23,956.26$$

Because the present value of this $6,000 stream of annual savings exceeds the initial outlay of $20,000, the proposal comes under serious consideration.

Data in Table IV are the summation of factors from Table II. Find the 8% column, 3-year row in Table II. Now add together the three factors from Table II, 8% column, and n = 1, 2, and 3. This total matches the same factor in Table IV, 8%, n = 3.

We could have computed the present value of the last problem from Table II in four steps by determining the present value of $6,000 at the end of each year and then summing the results, which would have equalled the result of the one-step procedure from Table IV. In some problems, however, where income flows vary both tables may be utilized.

SIMPLE DISCOUNT

Probably the best-known forms of simple discounts relate to bank loans where interest is prepaid. A $2,000 discounted loan bearing 10% simple interest due in 9 months is calculated:

$2,000 X 10% = $200 X ¾ = $150 interest for 9 months;

$2,000 - 150 = $1,850 net loan proceeds.

This is not, of course, a loan bearing a true interest rate of 10%. Because only $1,850 is available for use on which is paid $150 interest for 9 months, the true interest rate exceeds 10%.

What, then, is the present value at 10% simple interest on $2,000 due in 9 months?

Formula:

$$V = \frac{F}{(1 + iT)}$$

In the above formula T denotes a fraction of year expressed in days, or, as in this case, in months, where $T = 9/12 = 3/4$; F symbolizes the amount due at the end of 9 months, $2,000; and i, 10%, designates the simple interest rate expressed in annual terms.

$$V = \frac{\$2{,}000}{1 + 0.10\,(3/4)} = \frac{\$2{,}000}{1 + 0.075} = \$1{,}860.47$$

In this example the borrower acquires and controls $1,860.47 for 9 months and pays a *true* discount of:

$$X(\text{true discount}) = F - V$$

$$= \$2{,}000 - 1{,}860.47 = \$139.53$$

To check whether the borrower, in fact, pays a true rate of 10%, compute interest for 9 months on $1,860.47 at 10% per annum.

$$\$1{,}860.47 \times 0.10 \times 3/4 = \$139.53$$

Equivalent Interest and Discount Rates

From the above examples, obviously, discount and effective interest rates do not necessarily equate, parallel to nominal and effective rates discussed in Chapter One. Here is an example to find interest rate, r, equivalent to a discount rate i.

To ascertain r, when i is 7% for 3 months, assuming F = 1, the three steps are:

$$\text{(i) } P = F\,(1 + iT)$$
$$= 1\,[1 - .07\,(1/4)]$$
$$= 1 - \frac{.07}{4} = \frac{3.93}{4}$$

$$\text{(ii) } P = \frac{F}{1 + rT}$$
$$= \frac{1}{1 + r\,(1/4)} = \frac{4}{4 + r}$$

$$\text{(iii) } \frac{3.93}{4} = \frac{4}{4 + r}$$

$$3.93\,(4 + r) = 16$$
$$3.93r = 16 - 15.72 = 0.28$$
$$r = .0712 = 7.12\%$$

Discounting Promissory Notes

A promissory note may be discounted and rediscounted several times during its brief life. For example, Krystal Lake, a beauty operator, opened a new five-woman beauty salon, "Le Boule de Cristal," in the new Woodhaven Mall. For certain supplies and materials she gave a promissory note to her supplier, Feinstein's Fine Line, for $3,500 due in 9 months bearing 10% interest. Three months later Feinstein discounted the note to a distributor, American Rose Distributing Corp., at 12%. What were the proceeds of the sale 6 months before due date?

(i) Interest on $3,500 for 9 months @ 10% is $3,500 (0.10) (3/4) = $262.50

(Maturity Value) F = P + I = $3,500 + $262.50 = $3,762.50

(ii) Period of discount, 6 months.

Discount on $3,762.50 for 6 months @ 12% is

$3,762.50 (0.12) (1/2) = $225.75

Proceeds to Feinstein are:

$3,762.50 - 225.75 = $3,536.75

At maturity, American Rose will collect \$3,762.50 on a note for which they paid \$3,536.75, an effective return of 6.4% for 6 months, a 12.8% annual rate. On the other hand, Feinstein collected \$36.75 in interest (3,536.75 - 3,500.00) on a note he held for 3 months, which yielded him a 4.2% annual rate for his troubles and assumed risks. Foregone interest income expresses Feinstein's time preference and need for money now instead of waiting six months until the note matures.

ANNUAL PAYMENTS REQUIRED TO REACH SPECIFIC SUM

Another type of question: How much must I invest annually in order to have a desired sum at some future date? This, too, reverses compounding because the future sum is known, but unknown are various interim payments at some interest rate, required to reach the targeted goal.

Jerry Krisolofski's Retirement Fund

Like Frank Wells, mentioned in Chapter One, Jerry Krisolofski, credit manager of Mojave Paper Division, also nears retirement, but he approaches his problem different from Wells. Kris and his wife plan to travel after his retirement and to purchase a condominium in Pompano Beach for a maintenance-free home base. Altogether Kris calculated that a new life style in seven years will necessitate \$22,000 additional to present savings and projected retirement income. He figures he can safely count on a 7.0% return compounded annually but needs to know how much to contribute each year to his self-styled investment portfolio to achieve his objective.

Formula:

$$A = \frac{Fi}{(1 + i)^n - 1}$$

Solution:

$$A = \$22{,}000 \left[\frac{0.07}{(1 + 0.07)^6 - 1} \right]$$

$$= \$22{,}000\ (0.1397958) = \$3{,}075.51$$

A = amount of annual contribution (payment) = unknown.

F = future desired sum = \$22,000.

i = annual interest rate = 7.0%

n = number of years interest is compounded = 6.

If other data turn out as expected, Kris will end up with $22,000 if he invests $3,075.51 annually, withdraws nothing from the fund in the interim, and leaves interest to compound at 7.0% annually for 6 years.

A Quick Solution

Rather than work out computations with the formula, Table VI in the Appendix, "Sinking Fund Factor of 1," furnishes a fast-cut solution. For the Krisolofski problem, locate the factor in Table VI corresponding to i = 7.0%, n = 6. This factor (0.13979580) relates to the bracketed portion above. Multiply the known future amount of the annuity, $22,000, times this factor, to ascertain the sum invested annually.

$$A = \$22{,}000\ (0.13979580) = \$3{,}075.51$$

A Variant: Interpolation

In the same problem, if Krisolofski had estimated a 7.4 per cent annual return instead of 7.0 per cent, Table VI still applies.
Interpolation:

$$(A/F_{7\%,6}) = 0.13979580$$
$$(A/F_{8\%,6}) = \underline{0.13631539}$$
$$0.00348041 \text{ difference}$$

Since 0.4 is 40% between 7% and 8% = .4 × 0.00348041 =

$$0.001392164 \text{ subtract from } (A/F_{7\%,6}) \text{ above, and}$$
$$(A/F_{7.4\%,6}) = 0.13840364\text{; therefore,}$$
$$A = \$22{,}000\ (0.13840364) = \$3{,}044.88$$

At a higher interest rate (7.4%), a smaller sum ($3,044.88) is required for annual investment to reach the $22,000 goal.

To check the result, refer back to Table III in the Appendix, "Amount of 1 per Period Compounded for n Periods." Again interpolate between 7 and 8 per cent.

$$(F/A_{8\%,6}) = 7.33592904$$
$$(F/A_{7\%,6}) = \underline{7.15329074}$$
$$0.18263830 \text{ difference}$$

$$40\% = 0.07305532 \text{ Add to } (F/A_{7\%,6})$$

$$(F/A_{7.4\%,6}) = 7.22634606$$

$$F = \$3{,}044.88\ (7.22634606) = \$22{,}003.36$$

Funding Debt

Winelovers International, Ltd. has a \$10,000 obligation due in one year and opts to make monthly deposits, beginning at the end of the second month, in an account which yields 8% compounded monthly. How much should the firm deposit monthly in order to reach the desired \$10,000 by the end of one year?

Formula:

$$A = \frac{F\left(\frac{j}{m}\right)}{\left(1 + \frac{j}{m}\right)^{m} - 1}$$

Applying the above data, the solution is:

$$A = \frac{10{,}000\left(\frac{.08}{10}\right)}{\left(1 + \frac{.08}{10}\right)^{10} - 1}$$

$$= \frac{80}{1.083 - 1} = \frac{80}{0.083} = \$965$$

Note—In the above, n = 10 rather than 11 or 12 because the first payment was deferred for two months so that interest on the first payment is compounded 10 months, on the second payment 9 months, etc.

PRESENT VALUE OF VARIABLE CASH FLOWS

Essentially, in above examples, we assume either cash receipts (or disbursements) occur once at the end of a period for n years or a constant (uniform) cash flow. Situations with variable cash flow frequently arise. These present value calculations, no more complicated than preceding solutions, require additional repetitive steps.

Uneven Income Flow

Scientific Explorations Incorporated decides to undertake an investment which will involve an initial outlay of $10 million, have an economic life of 10 years, and equipment will have a salvage value of $1 million. Throughout first year start-up, the firm will generate no income but an anticipated annual $0.5 million during years 2, 3, 4, $1 million for the next 3 years, and $0.5 million during the last 3 years. What is the present value of this income stream assuming a discount rate of 26%?

Year	*Flow (in millions)*
0	($10) outflow
1	$0
2, 3, 4	$0.5 per year
5, 6, 7	$1.0 per year
8, 9, 10	$0.5 per year
10	$1.0 sale of used equipment

We can solve for each year individually using Table II alone, but elements of the problem shorten computations with use of Table IV in the Appendix. Present value of year 1 is zero since there is no income, but $0.5 million is common to the remaining 9 years; therefore, we can treat this sum as a continuous flow and multiply by the factor from Table IV. (We assume cash inflows occur at year-end to simplify calculations.) In the table, the factor for n = 10 and i = 26% is 3.46480609, but no income materializes in year 1 so we subtract that factor:

Table IV:

$$(P/A_{26\%,10}) = 3.46480609$$

$$(P/A_{26\%,1}) = \underline{0.79365079}$$

$$2.67115530 \text{ factor for years 2 through 10.}$$

$$*(\$5 \times 10^5)(2.67115530) = \$1{,}335{,}577.70$$

(Present Value of $0.5 million flow, years 2–10)

*$0.5 million may also be written $5 × 10^5 so that it can be entered on small, inexpensive hand calculators with scientific notation capabilities to handle large numbers: $5 × 10^5 is the same as $500,000 where 10^5 signals to move the decimal point 5 places to the right. If the notation had been $5 × 10^{-5}, the "–5" requires shifting the decimal point 5 places to the left, which would be $0.00005.

Now determine Present Value of \$0.5 million for years 5, 6, 7. (We have already accounted for \$0.5 million of this flow above.)

Table II:

PV of \$1 received at end of year 5 (i = 26%) = 0.31488159

PV of \$1 received at end of year 6 (i = 26%) = 0.24990603

PV of \$1 received at end of year 7 (i = 26%) = 0.19833812

PV factor for years 5, 6, 7 (i = 26%) = 0.76312574

*(\$5 × 10^5) (0.76312574) = \$381,562.88

(Present Value of \$0.5 million for years 5, 6, 7.)

Salvage value, a partial return on investment, is treated as one-time inflow of cash in year 10.

Table II:

(n = 10, i = 26%) = 0.09915042

(\$1 × 10^6) (0.09915042) = \$99, 150.42

Summing the three sets of present values, we have

	\$1,335,577.70
	381,562.88
	99,150.42
PV of cash inflow	\$1,816,291.00

In the next chapter we will see why the time value of money underlies capital budgeting. The following, a variation of the preceding illustration, explicates two techniques.

Deferred Annuity (Two Solutions)

Beginning November 11, in Year 5, Ronny Lemieux will receive five yearly payments of \$4,200 from the Freedom Foundation through November 11, Year 12. For an *annuity deferred* 5 years, what is the present value of this stream of payments on November 11, Year 0 (today) when A = \$4,200, n = 5, and i = 10%?

Solution (A)–The annuity begins November 11, Year 5 with first payment made on November 11, Year 6. From today's viewpoint, the annuity is deferred 5 years. One method is to refer again to Table IV in the Appendix for the factor which relates to a continuous flow of income in years 6 through 10.

Factor (n = 10, i = 10%) = 6.144567

Factor (n = 5, i = 10%) = 3.790787

Factor for years 6, 7, 8, 9, 10 = 2.353780 (by subtraction)

$4,200 X 2.353780 = $9,885.88

(present value of this future stream of benefits.)

Solution (B)–This solution combines Tables II and IV first by looking at the annuity from the standpoint of Year 5, then from today (Year 0).

Table IV Factor (Year 5) n = 5, i = 10% = 3.790787

Table II Factor (Year 0) n = 5, i = 10% = 0.620921

Multiplying:

3.790787 X 0.620921 = 2.353780 X $4,200 = $9,885.88

This solution treats the present value of the 5-year continuous flow as though it were received in one lump sum and then computes the present value of the single payment. To convert the resulting factor, 2.353780, for $1, to the correct annual sum, multiply by $4,200. Both results state that at a given discount rate of 10%, $9,885.88 is just as good in-hand today as a 5-year deferred flow paying out a total of $21,000 divided among five equal installments. A third example is a familiar type problem.

Finding Interest Rates

Suppose that Washington C. Brown Financial Enterprises made this offer: "Give us $50,000 today and we will return to you a guaranteed annual income of $5,000 a year for 20 years to you and your heirs." Would you accept this 2-for-1 offer? The dollar return sounds suitable, but this question illustrates the importance of timing flows from investments. It is *good* to have cash flowing sooner than later. It is *better* to have more, sooner, rather than later. It is *best* to have it all now.

To start with this illustrative example, estimate the expected rate, the unknown. While a formula can apply for accurate results, the short-cut solution with tables provides a close approximation.

P = \$50,000; A = \$5,000; n = 20; i = ?

The first step is to convert this into a factor (X) that will relate to Table IV in the Appendix.

$$5{,}000X = 50{,}000$$
$$X = 10.0000$$

Next, in Table IV, along row n = 20, find the factor (f) closest to 10.0000: 7% = 10.59401425 and 8% = 9.81814741. Therefore, by inspection we know the answer lies about three-fourths between 7% and 8%, or about 7¾%. This may furnish an estimate close enough for your requirements—to reject or accept the offer.

If a better estimate is desired, then interpolate:

$(P/A_{7\%,20})$ =	10.59401425	10.59401425
$[(P/A_{i,20})$ =		10.00000000
$(P/A_{8\%,20})$ =	9.81914741	
Differences (X)	0.77486684 (Y) =	0.59401425

Let i = unknown; i = 7%; i = 8%

Formula:

$$i = \left[\frac{(Y)\,(i_2 - i_1)}{X}\right] + i$$

Substituting values:

$$i = \left[\frac{(0.59401425)\,(0.080 - 0.070)}{0.77486684}\right] + 0.070$$
$$= \left[\frac{0.00594014}{0.77486684}\right] + 0.070$$
$$= 0.00766601 + 0.070 = 0.07767$$
$$= 7.767\%$$

Electronic Hand Calculator Solution

If you use an electronic "slide-rule" type hand calculator programmed for algebraic method of entry, you may enter mathematical sequences in the same order as stated in the above formula.

DISCOUNT RATE DETERMINATION

Discount rates, like interest rates, encapsulate the time value of money, risks (measurable uncertainties), and inflation (or any other government-induced factor, such as anticipated changes in a tax rate, that can affect future values)—all of which hinge on interpretation of the future and given alternative investments available. Discount rates, therefore, are products of anticipated future events and present outlays of money, time, and energy.

$$\text{Discount Rate} = \frac{\text{Expected future results - Present costs}}{\text{Present costs}}$$

Rearranging the formula, we have:

$$\text{Present Value} = \frac{\text{Expected future results}}{(1 + \text{Discount rate})}$$

which really says that present value and present costs are the same.

Case Study: Why did the Arnold Syndicate agree to a higher purchase price?

(1) For example, properties of a financially troubled firm are being liquidated. Our first assumption is that the Arnold Syndicate will purchase, from the liquidating firm, a nearly completed and fully equipped restaurant and real estate for $275,000. The investors estimate that another $25,000 will render the restaurant operable and vendible within 4 to 6 months and further anticipate that within one year, after 6 months of regular operation, the restaurant and real estate can be marketed for $345,000.

$$\text{Discount rate} = \frac{345{,}000 - 300{,}000}{300{,}000} = 15\%$$

(2) Or we can examine the decision in this manner. The syndicate figures that location, size, and condition of the restaurant should bring $345,000 on a fairly quick sale, and, that given risks of market price fluctuations plus a standard minimum return demanded on all selected ventures, the syndicate's management requires 20% return. Arnold Syndicate's management estimate that $25,000 additional to purchase price will be required. How much will they bid for the property?

$$V = \frac{345{,}000}{(1 + 0.20)} = \$287{,}500$$

$287,500 - $25,000 = $262,500 (maximum price offered for restaurant property)

The Arnold Syndicate makes an offer of $262,500, but finally agrees to a purchase price of $285,000 on these terms: $125,000 when deed of ownership is transferred; $74,000 in 6 months; $85,000 in one year; zero interest paid on the deferred payments.

(a) From the seller's viewpoint, how much will they receive in terms of money today if they value money at 10%? (Figure 2-1.)

Figure 2-1

Period	*Amount*	X	*PV Factor*	=	*Present Value*
1 (today)	$125,000		1.000000		$125,000.00
2 (6 months)	75,000		0.952381		71,428.57
3 (1 year)	85,000		0.907029		77,097.51
	TOTAL PRESENT VALUES				$273,526.08

Formula:

$$^{*}\Sigma V = \frac{F_1}{\left(1 + \frac{j}{m}\right)^{mn}} + \frac{F_2}{\left(1 + \frac{j}{m}\right)^{mn}} + \frac{F_3}{\left(1 + \frac{j}{m}\right)^{mn}}$$

Data on the deal:

$$^{*}\Sigma V = \frac{125{,}000}{1} + \frac{75{,}000}{\left(1 + \frac{0.10}{2}\right)^{1\cdot 1}} + \frac{85{,}000}{\left(1 + \frac{0.10}{2}\right)^{2\cdot 1}}$$

$$= 125{,}000 + \frac{75{,}000}{(1 + 0.5)} + \frac{85{,}000}{(1 + 0.5)^2}$$

$$= 125{,}000 + 71{,}428.57 + 77{,}097.51 = \$273{,}526.08$$

By agreed terms of sale the sellers arrived fairly close to their target figure of $275,000, and could have improved upon the sum which they will receive

*The Greek letter sigma, Σ, denotes "sum of."

not by negotiating for a larger amount (which can kill a sale) but by bargaining for earlier payment of the deferred portion.

(b) From the buyer's viewpoint, how much did they really pay for the property? (Figure 2–2.) Remember that management of Arnold Syndicate eventually assigned a discount rate of 20% to the project.

Figure 2–2

Period	*Amount* ×	*PV Factor* =	*Present Value*
1 (today)	$125,000	1.000000	$125,000.00
2 (6 months)	75,000	0.909090	68,181.82
3 (1 year)	85,000	0.826447	70,247.93
	TOTAL PRESENT VALUES		$263,429.75

$$\Sigma V = \frac{125{,}000}{1} + \frac{75{,}000}{(1 + 0.10)} + \frac{85{,}000}{(1 + 0.10)^2}$$

$$= 125{,}000 + 68{,}181.81 + 70{,}247.93 = \$263{,}429.75$$

The negotiated final arrangements resulted in a price very close to the focal $262,500 calculated by Arnold Syndicate. They, too, walked away from the bargaining table happy.

How is it possible that both buyers and sellers negotiate a price that not only seems equitable to both sides but both parties to the transaction are convinced they arranged a good deal? The answer pivots on subjective evaluation of the future. Each viewed the future differently, each had different objectives, each evinced a different scale of time preferences. If it had been otherwise no transaction would have been possible. This is the logic and essence of a free market system whereas in another system the exchange of "ownership" still might have occurred but only by force or through subsidies.

NUMBER OF PAYMENTS TO REPAY DEBT

This type of problem concerns an interest-bearing debt of a fixed sum which will be repaid in annual installments. The formula below determines the present value of a uniform series of payments when the amount of each payment is unknown.

Formula:

$$A = P\left[\frac{i\,(1 + i)^n}{(1 + i)^n - 1}\right]$$

In this formula we want to determine the amount of each payment (A), given the original debt, or principal, (P), which bears an annual interest rate (i) during the life of the obligation in years (n).

(A) Annual Installments of Real Estate Holding Company

Amstel Lake Company, a real estate holding company, speculates on likely direction of suburban expansion and purchases a tract of land for future townhouses for $35,000 cash and a note for $195,000 bearing 8.75% interest for 5 years. What is the required annual payment to liquidate the note plus interest as agreed?

$$A = \$195{,}000 \left[\frac{0.0875\ (1 + 0.0875)^5}{(1 + 0.0875)^5 - 1}\right]$$

$$= \$195{,}000 \left[\frac{0.13309274}{0.52105994}\right]$$

$$= \$195{,}000\ (0.25542694) = \$49{,}808.25$$

The answer, $49,808.25, denotes the amount Amstel Lake Company must repay at the end of each year for 5 years to cover principal plus interest. (Instead of the formula, the bracketed portion of the solution can also be developed from Table V in the Appendix.) As a means of checking computations, apply the formula:

$$V = \frac{1 - (1 + i)^{-n}}{i}$$

which gives us the present value of a continuous stream of annual payments ($49,808.25) for 5 years, discounted at 8.75%.

$$V = \$49{,}808.25\ \frac{1 - (1 + 0.0875)^{-5}}{0.0875}$$

$$= \$49{,}808.25\ \frac{0.34256371}{0.0875}$$

$$= \$49{,}808.25\ (3.9150139) = \$194{,}999.99$$

(B) Monthly Installments of Pizza Parlor

Giovanni's Pizza Parlors, Inc. has opted to purchase a fleet of delivery vans. Management has calculated they can comfortably meet monthly installments of $700 and have been able to secure funds for a 4½-year term at 9.15% interest. Giovanni's has approximately $12,000 cash available in additional funds; each fully equipped van will run about $6,000; how many vans can management plan to purchase?

Modifying the annual continuous flow present value formula:

Formula:

$$V = F\left[\frac{1 - \left(1 + \frac{j}{m}\right)^{-mn}}{\frac{j}{m}}\right]$$

Where m = 12, n = 4½, j = 9.15%, $i = \frac{j}{m}$, we have:

$$V = \$700\left[\frac{1 - \left(1 + \frac{0.0915}{12}\right)^{-12 \times 4.5}}{\frac{0.0915}{12}}\right]$$

$$= \$700\left(\frac{0.3364746}{0.007625}\right)$$

$$= \$700\ (44.127816) = \$30{,}889.47$$

Available funds to Giovanni's, total about $42,889 ($12,000 + $30,889), allow them to consider purchasing seven equipped vans at approximately $6,000 each. Monthly note payments will be $700.

Check the above calculations with the formula:

$$A = P\left[\frac{\frac{j}{m}\left(1 + \frac{j}{m}\right)^{mn}}{\left(1 + \frac{j}{m}\right)^{mn} - 1}\right]$$

$$A = \$30{,}889.47 \left[\frac{\frac{0.0915}{12}\left(1 + \frac{0.0915}{12}\right)^{12 \times 4.5}}{\left(1 + \frac{0.0915}{12}\right)^{12 \times 4.5} - 1} \right]$$

$$= \$30{,}889.47 \left[\frac{0.0076\,(1.0076)^{54}}{(1.0076)^{54} - 1} \right]$$

$$= \$30{,}889.47\,(0.02266144) = \$700$$

Quick method–A substitute for an unavailable factor or to carry calculations to more decimal places than present value tables record, the following short-cut with a hand calculator will provide an entire series of Table II (Appendix) factors as rapidly as you can read them. An inexpensive electronic hand calculator will suffice.

Let's assume that you require present value factors for i = 23.5% and n = 13 years. One method is to start with the highest n (13 in this case) and calculate the PV factor for \$1 using the formula $V = (1 + 0.235)^{-13}$. To obtain the next lowest factor, multiply the result by (1 + 0.235) which yields n = 12, i = 23.5%. To save time, enter 1.235 with a constant (k) key and subsequent efforts will only require pressing the = key without entering further data.

The second method reverses the first one. Instead of multiplying, enter the divide function and the constant 1.235 and press the = key twice to obtain the PV factor for i = 23.5%, n = 1. Each subsequent factor, for n = 2, 3, 4, 5, etc., is obtained by pressing the = key once without entering more data.

For calculations by hand, the desk calculator method is superior to interpolating a series of factors from a table. Of course, where all is fed into a computer, one becomes separated from the input and results. It is always nice to know what the computer is up to.

INTEREST FACTORS FOR A UNIFORM CHANGE IN VALUES

While one common type of problem solves for an unknown where there are equal periodic payments, another usual type of problem focuses on an equal change (decrease or increase) in payments (outflow or inflow). The same yearly increase or decrease is known as a *uniform arithmetic gradient.* Interest tables for a uniform gradient series have been developed–Table XIII in the Appendix, "Factors to Convert a Gradient Series to Equivalent Uniform Series."

In the following formula, G represents the dollar amount of equal changes in payments from year-to-year for n years. For example, if payments rise by the same amount every year, this amount of increase, change, is G. The purpose of the formula is to convert the *gradient series* to a *uniform series* of amount A_g. *Gradient,* of course, means the change in value for each time period.

Formula:

$$A_g = G\left[\frac{1}{i} - \frac{n}{(1+i)^n - 1}\right]$$

G = amount of uniform change.

i = interest rate.

n = number of interest periods.

This type of formula may relate to increasing maintenance costs of equipment. For example, if maintenance costs of a machine for the first year is $1,000, for the second year $1,100, for the third year $1,200, etc., then the uniform annual flow of costs is $1,000 (A) per year plus $100 increase per year (G) beginning with the second year. To simplify the problem the gradient series is converted to a uniform flow of amount A_g. This conversion allows us to then employ formulas which require an even flow of cash during the economic life of the project. Tables for these factors, too, are available so that we designate $A_g = G(A/G_{i,n})$.

$$(A/G_{i,n}) = \left[\frac{1}{i} - \frac{n}{(1+i)}\right]$$

Once the gradient (G) is known ($100 in the above illustration), then it is multiplied by the factor in the table to find A_g, or the problem can be worked by the formula. Table XIII in the Appendix registers uniform gradient series factors for several interest and time periods.

Purchasing a De-nationalized Business

A country which has ousted a socialist regime begins to de-nationalize government-owned industries. One firm is sold to a group of local businessmen on a time-payment schedule of $100,000 the first year with payments increasing by $25,000 a year for the next 4 years. Total disbursements equal $600,000. The purchasers must deposit a sum initially, drawing 10% interest compounded annually, sufficiently large to guarantee the planned payment schedule. Assuming a 10% after-tax return, how much must the businessmen deposit?

$$A = \$100{,}000;\ G = \$25{,}000;\ i = 10\%;\ n = 5;\ A_g = G\left[\frac{1}{i} - \frac{n}{(1+i)^n - 1}\right];$$

The *equivalent uniform series* $A^* = A + A_g$; $P = A^*\left[\frac{1-(1+i)^{-n}}{i}\right]$

The steps are:

(1) convert the gradient series to a uniform series of amount A_g at the end of the first year;

$$A_g = G\left[\frac{1}{i} - \frac{n}{(1+i)^n - 1}\right] = G(A/G_{i,n}) \text{ Table XIII}$$

$$= \$25{,}000\ (1.810126) = \$45{,}253.15$$

(2) find A*, the equivalent uniform series, \$100,000 plus \$45,253.15 = \$145,253.15;

(3) solve for P, the initial investment:

$$P = A^*\left[\frac{1-(1+i)^{-n}}{i}\right] = (P/A_{i,n}) \text{ Table IV}$$

$$= \$145{,}253.15\ (3.7907869) = \$550{,}623.72$$

The sum, \$550,623.72, signifies the amount which the buyers will deposit initially to effectuate the terms of agreement.

PRESENT VALUE OF A GRADIENT SERIES

Finding the present value of a *gradient series* means to bring future *increments* back to the present according to the discount rate chosen. Since future values are changing in a gradient series, although in a uniform manner, the easiest way to handle this type of problem is to convert future increments into an equivalent uniform flow so that we may apply stated formulas in the manner achieved in the previous exhibit. To calculate the present value of a gradient series, multiply the factors resulting from two previously expressed formulas for a given discount rate and for a given time period. Because these factors are available already in the Appendix, the complete formula will not be developed but rather the rule to derive the present value factor of a gradient series, which is represented by $(P/G_{i,n})$.

Formula: $(P/G_{i,n}) = (A/G_{i,n}) \times (P/A_{i,n})$

The present value of a gradient series for a given i and n results from multiplying the gradient factor times the present value factor of $1 received every year for n years. In other words,

$$(P/G_{i,n}) = \text{Table XIII} \times \text{Table IV}$$

Whether Table XIII or Tables XIII times IV applies depends upon whether we solve for A or for P. An example will clear up questions.

Rising Maintenance Costs

Certain construction equipment will cost $28,000 new and will be fully depreciated by the end of 5 years. Estimated maintenance, taxes, insurance, fuels and lubrication costs are $3,000 the first year, increasing about $700 per year each subsequent year. Assuming a 10% interest rate, what is the present value of the annual outlays?

$$A = \$3{,}000;\ G = \$700;\ i = 10;\ n = 5;\ A_g = ?\ P = \$28{,}000.$$

PV = Present Value

$$\Sigma PV = PV \text{ of } P + PV \text{ of } A + PV \text{ of } G$$

To solve, sum present values of initial equipment cost, first year's costs, and uniform gradient series. The first expression is uncomplicated because the present value of $1 today equals $1; therefore, the present value of $28,000 expended in the initial period is $28,000.

To calculate the present value of $3,000 in annual costs, employ Table IV $(P/A_{10\%,5})$ in the Appendix. Multiply $3,000 by the factor that corresponds to i = 10%, n = 5.

Table IV:

$$PV_a = \$3{,}000\ (P/A_{10\%,5}) = 3{,}000\ (3.7907868) = \$11{,}372.36$$

$$PV_g = G\ (A/G_{10\%,5})\ (P/A_{10\%,5})$$
$$= \$700\ (1.8101260)\ (3.7907868)$$
$$= \$700\ (6.861802) = \$4{,}803.26$$

$$\Sigma PV = PV_p + PV_a + PV_g$$
$$= 28{,}000.00 + 11{,}372.36 + 4{,}803.26 = \$44{,}175.62$$

Sometimes annual increments are not uniform. If these estimated periodic fluctuations can be expressed as a uniform gradient series, it simplifies computations and permits utilization of formulas developed in the first four chapters of this handbook.

CONTINUOUS DISCOUNTING

One argument contra these mathematical techniques is that cash flows occur at *discrete* (noncontinuous) intervals, such as monthly mortgage payments, whereas many investments produce continuous outflows of cash. In compounding, the answer to this objection lies in continuous compounding which was discussed and demonstrated at the end of Chapter One. Its counterpart is continuous discounting. Mathematical techniques have been developed to reflect this reality.

For example, to find the future sum (F_c) of an amount (P) compounded continuously for one year at nominal rate j, the formula is:

Formula: $$F_c = Pe^j$$

Find the accumulated sum of $5,000 (P) invested for one year at 18.5% (j) compounded continuously.*

$$F_c = (\$5{,}000)\,(2.7182818)^{0.185}$$
$$= (5{,}000)\,(1.2032184) = \$6{,}016.09$$

Note: The effective rate is 20.32% when the nominal rate is 18.5% compounded continuously.

For periods exceeding one year,† the above formula need only be modified to accommodate n years:

Formula: $$F_c = Pe^{jn}$$

---

*With an electronic calculator having natural logarithm functions (base e) and e^x, simply punch 0.185 and press inverse lnx or e^x; or without e^x punch 2.7182818 and press exponential key raising it to the 0.185 power.

By natural logarithms, the steps are:

$$\ln F_c = \ln 5{,}000 + 0.185 \ln e \ [\ln e = 1]$$
$$[\text{From natural log table}]\ \ln F_c = 8.5171932 + 0.185 = 8.7021932$$
$$[\text{Taking anti-log}]\ F_c = \$6{,}016.09$$

†Pierre Masse, *Optimal Investment Decisions: Rules for Action and Criteria for Choice,* trans. by Scripta Technica. Inc. (Englewood Cliffs, N.J.: Prentice-Hall, Inc., 1962). Pp. 16–17.

If \$1,000 (P) is invested for 7 years (n) at 6% (j) compounded continuously, the future value (F_c) of this investment will be:

$$F_c = \$1{,}000\,(2.7182818)^{0.06 \times 7}$$
$$= 1{,}000\,(2.7182818)^{0.42}$$
$$= 1{,}000\,(1.5219616) = \$1{,}521.96$$

To check the result we already know that 6% compounded continuously (from Chapter One) by the formula equals 6.1837%. (Also refer to Table XV in the Appendix.) Raising this to the 7th power results in 1.52197 times \$1,000 equals \$1,521.97 (error due to rounding). (Also, vide Table XVI, "Continuously Compounded Rates Equivalent to Nominal Rates.")

Present Value of a Continuously Compounded Amount

Therefore, with continuous compounding, the single payment factor is e^{jn}. To determine the present value of an amount compounded continuously and paid once at the end of that period, the factor is e^{-jn}, and the formula of the present value of a single payment is:

Formula:

$$V_c = F_c\, e^{-jn}$$

F_c = future amount.

$e = 2.7182818285$

j = rate continuously compounded.

n = number of years.

e^{-jn} = present value factor at continuous compounding.

Reversing the above problem, what is the present value (V_c) of a sum that has been compounded continuously at 6% nominal rate (j) for 7 years (n) which yields \$1,521.96 at the end of the period?

$$V_c = \$1{,}521.96\,(2.7182818)^{-.42}$$
$$= 1{,}521.96\,(0.6570468) = \$1{,}000.$$

Underlying these computations is the assumption that interest is computed and added to principal an infinite number of intervals during the year. While it is rare to encounter loan transactions based on continuous compounding, the concept is well adapted to analyze an investment which produces a continuous flow at a uniform rate throughout the observed period. (For "Exponential Functions," e^x and e^{-x}, Table XXIII in the Appendix will be helpful.)

Rate of Return per Period

To calculate the rate of return per period for a single payment due n periods from now, under the assumption of continuous compounding, the formula is:

Formula:

$$j = \frac{\ln F - \ln P}{n}$$

The above formula employs natural logarithms; that is, base e, because of their use in continuous compounding and continuous discounting. Working with the same data, find j, the continuous nominal rate, when \$1,000 invested today will yield \$1,521.96 at the end of 7 years.

$$j = \frac{\ln 1521.96 - \ln 1{,}000}{7}$$

$$= \frac{7.3277543 - 6.907753}{7}$$

$$= \frac{0.419990}{7} = 6.0\%$$

An Annuity Continuously Discounted

Where future cash flows are known (or estimated), assumed to flow continuously throughout the periods, these future flows can be expressed in today's terms by continuous discounting.

Note—Do not confuse this concept with one discussed earlier in the chapter; viz., the present value of a future flow of income compounded periodically (annually in the earlier example) does not produce the same result as the case of continuous discounting. Comparison of the two results will follow.

Formula:

$$V_a = F_a \left[\frac{e^{jn} - 1}{je^{jn}} \right]$$

Subscripts "a" above denote a continuously discounted cash flow per period; j symbolizes the nominal rate; n represents the number of periods (years); and e = 2.7182818. Notice that this formula is for continuous discounting of cash flow rates period.

Continuously Discounted Cash Flow

For further evidence, posit that cash flows \$1,000 per year for 3 years; employing a discount rate of 8%, compute the present value of this cash flow by continuous discounting.

$$V_a = \$1{,}000 \left[\frac{(2.7182818)^{0.08 \times 3} - 1}{0.08\ (2.7182818)^{0.08 \times 3}} \right]$$

$$= 1{,}000 \left[\frac{0.27124915}{0.10169993} \right]$$

$$= 1{,}000\ (2.6671517) = \$2{,}667.15$$

Comparison of Discrete and Continuous Results

Comparing the present value found above with the present value formula for \$1,000 generated at the end of every year for 3 years, using Table IV,

$$V = \$1{,}000\ (P/A_{8\%,3}) = 1{,}000\ (2.577097)$$

$$= \$2{,}577.10$$

a smaller sum manifests because of different underlying assumptions. Nevertheless, the discrete (noncontinuous) approximation procedure functions as a rough check on results.

Let us also compare these outcomes with the present value of a single payment of \$3,000 at the end of 3 years. Recall the formula:

$$V_c = F_c e^{-jn}$$

$$V_c = \$3{,}000\ (2.7182818)^{-0.08 \times 3}$$

$$= 3{,}000\ (0.7866279) = \$2{,}359.88$$

It produces an even lower result. These three sets of calculations serve as a reminder of differences in these formulas.

To aid in calculations involving continuous compounding, Tables VII through XII plus Table XXIII in the Appendix are especially useful. For problems illustrated in Chapters One and Two, we have relied on data appearing in: Table VII, "Amount of 1 at Continuously Compounded Nominal Interest Rates;" Table VIII, "Present Value of 1 at Continuously Compounded Nominal Interest Rates;" Table IX, "Amount of 1 per Period for n Periods at Continuously Compounded Nominal Interest Rates;" and Table X, "Present Value of 1 per Period for n Periods at Continuously Compounded Nominal Interest Rates." Other useful tables include: Table XI, "Capital Recovery Factor of 1 at Continuously Compounded Nominal Interest Rates," and, Table XII, "Sinking Fund Factor of 1 at Continuously Compounded Nominal Interest Rates."

If it is not necessary to interpolate, using factors from one of these tables in the Appendix provides a quick-cut solution to many problems. With fractional interest rates and time periods, substituting values in one or more of the above formulas and solving with an electronic hand calculator may offer a preferred alternative. Solving operational problems in the next two chapters will draw upon mathematics, formulas, and tables thus far developed.

CONTENTS

Chapter Three: Sixteen Prize-Giving Methods to Determine Rate of Return

THREE

Sixteen Prize-Giving Methods to Determine Rate of Return

Before applying present value techniques illustrated in the preceding chapter, and before undertaking any new investment, the logical order is first to define whether a project is sound and second to study how to carry it out. All decisions, of course, involve deciding between alternatives even though only one investment possibility is under consideration. To go ahead or not go ahead with a single proposal embraces at least two possibilities, for by not acting an individual must bear consequences of a negative decision or indecision.

In financial and economic analysis, or operations research, or industrial engineering, or planning and budgeting, to establish criteria for making decisions, a criterion such as rate of return on investment, is essential. Why? All managers should employ financial and economic analysis to pinpoint most desirable capital expenditures in order to improve profits, to study alternative plans for future operations that pertain to marketing, manufacturing, taxation, defensive ploys, as well as financing, to decide leasing or buying, or buying or making decisions, for example, or to evaluate proposed mergers and acquisitions.

Rates of return vary among industries, among firms, among individual projects within an organization. Because of differences in risk, external policies (government, for example), pricing in various markets, or shifting demand for products and services, business growth occurs with a capital investment mix that depends upon objectives and inherent differences on return of individual projects which, together, add up to management's ability to maintain an acceptable growth pattern. The method to evaluate one investment opportunity where high probability of nationalization without compensation in five years exists will be weighed by criteria different from an objective of market penetration in a slowly growing but politically stable market.

Therefore, alternative sets of evaluation techniques evolve in this chapter. *Rules-of-Thumb* techniques are generally simpler to use and easier to present and explain than *discounted cash flows* methods, and situations may dictate preference for a rule-of-thumb, such as "payback period." Payback, a simple measure of risk or liquidity, establishes a *minimum* payout period. But with expanding business what passes for a *maximum* payback period? Shortcomings of the *payback method* also inhere in other rules-of-thumb.

Too, there are specialized tools used in mining, namely, *Hoskold's Method,* or the *undiscounted benefit-cost ratio,* or *equal-cost analysis,* as well as other techniques employed in all types of operational problems. One group, "Accounting Rates of Return," traditionally measure financial benefits of a capital expenditure. These usually relate cash flows to book value of the firm's investment. An approximate measure, lacking precision, it is not sensitive to the shape and size of the cash flow pattern.

On the other hand, *present value techniques* acknowledge that more dollars sooner is preferable to a large cash flow late in the economic life of an investment. Present value exercises worked out in the preceding chapter clearly expose effects of size of the discount rate on cash flows and how present value of a future cash flow rapidly diminishes the longer the waiting time. Present value analysis not only spotlights importance of *timing* of receipts and disbursements but focuses on *cash flows.* Capitalization accounting and resulting book depreciation have little significance for capital decisions because cash flows are the important element. Also, present value techniques allow that *income taxes* so greatly influence timing and size of cash flows that anticipated investment projects must include this variable.

RATE OF RETURN ON INVESTMENT

Rate of return on investment (ROI), or rate of return on assets, links the investment decision to estimated demand for the firm's products; that is, ROI formally entwines business investment in assets to output of goods and services.* This statement clearly suggests that a firm's investment decisions depend not only on internal conditions of the business but on external ones as well.

The classical financial statement approach to determination of ROI couples users of funds to suppliers of those funds via financial statements. To determine ROI, by this approach, add Net Working Capital (current assets minus current liabilities) to plant, equipment, and other fixed assets to designate total invested capital in the enterprise. Divide total invested capital by net profits after taxes (EAT) to specify ROI.

However, let us enlarge upon that definition to stress relationships between profits and sales, and sales and investment, and create the following accounting identity:

$$\text{ROI} = \left(\frac{\text{profits}}{\text{sales}}\right) \times \left(\frac{\text{sales}}{\text{assets}}\right)$$

(Profits/sales), the *profit margin,* gauges relative efficiency with which a firm produces its output. (Sales/assets), the *turnover ratio,* measures relative efficiency of using the firm's plant and equipment. Simplified even further the above identity reads:

$$\text{ROI} = \frac{\text{profits}}{\text{assets}}$$

Too, we can create other identities which appraise rate of return (r) on equity:

$$r = \frac{\text{profits}}{\text{net worth}}$$

*For more on this topic the reader is referred to: Ralph Badger, Harold Torgerson, and Harry Guthman, *Investment Principles and Practices* (Englewood Cliffs, N.J. Prentice-Hall, Inc., 1969), chaps. 4, 5.

or an identity which evaluates rate of return on total capital:

$$r = \frac{\text{profits}}{\text{liabilities + net worth}}$$

Capital budgeting focuses on allocation of the firm's resources among many demands placed on these scarce means of production by available market opportunities begging exploitation. To evaluate an investment opportunity means comparing expected future inflows of receipts that result from expected present and future outflows (investment expenditures). Presumably investors prefer larger to smaller cash inflows and prefer to have these inflows occur sooner rather than later.

To employ formulas which appear on the following pages, we should begin with an understanding of cash flow. *Gross cash flow* for each period consists of profits (earnings) after taxes (EAT) plus accounting depreciation charges. (Of course, for firms which persistently sustain losses, depreciation charges generate no cash.) The flow of the firm's pool of funds can be classified either as sources or as uses of funds. *Sources of funds* relate to any transactions which increase liabilities or increase net worth or reduce asset values. A new bond issue, sale of equipment or plant, or increase in retained earnings obviously provide funds. *Uses of funds* relate to transactions which increase asset values or reduce liabilities or net worth. An increase in accounts receivable, new plant, note repayment diminish further availability of funds to the firm.

RULES-OF-THUMB

In this category of nondiscounted rules-of-thumb approaches to business investment decisions are included Plowback, Putback, and Payback methods. Except in a few cases these approaches are generally inferior to discounted cash flows techniques because they frequently provide wrong answers to right questions. Nevertheless, these rules are still used in business decisions.

Plowback Method

A common rule-of-thumb, the *Plowback Method,* restricts investment to internal availability of funds; that is, paid-in capital and surplus retained earnings furnish nearly the entire source of funds for investment decisions. For one thing, these funds are frequently (and sometimes erroneously) thought to be the cheapest source. Borrowing may be cheaper when risk-sharing, real interest rates, foreign exchange exposure, and debt-equity ratio of the firm are taken stock of. Besides, limitation of retained earnings restricts the firm's ability to seize upon investment opportunities.

The principal difficulty with this approach is lack of specific criteria to measure and compare expected returns on investment proposals. It precludes purposive action associated with policy. It restricts the range of management decisions because at times yes decisions are made when no decision at all should have been made (poor timing), or an investment opportunity is lost when it should not have been. It ties tomorrow's decisions to yesterday's profits. However, debt itself is not especially meritorious. The author does not cheer indebtedness but rather encourages the best, most efficient, use of the firm's resources. Management may have a policy: "No debt." That policy is not under criticism. The decision-making question here centers on a means to compare satisfactorily investment decisions whether investment funds originate entirely internally or from a mixture of internal and external sources.

Putback Method

The *putback method* is on equal footing with the plowback method. One investment decision (or several) is "put back" on the shelf because of an "emergency" arising elsewhere. This method, too, partially takes control out of management's hands and places it in the hands of circumstances not always favorable to intermediate and long range planning. We could just as easily call this the "crisis method" or "state of urgency method" or "degree of necessity method." Here is how it works.

The emergency may well be one that demands immediate attention. Five bombs explode in Quincy causing severe damage to an air-compressor factory disrupting productive capacity. Does this emergency justify a quick investment decision by management? Yes, it certainly does! Consequently, other investment decisions are put back on a lower level of priority unless, of course, relocation of the Quincy facility has already been programmed which still means the emergency decision puts planning out of phase. Or the case of a steam boiler blowing up at U.S. Steel's plant near Fairless Hills, which disrupts operations at a locomotive shop, necessitates an urgent investment decision. However, consequences of even an emergency decision should be measured in terms of benefits and costs.

On the other hand, suppose that a firm's financial vice president urges an early 18-month start on a planned investment project because of an anticipated rise in interest costs. Certainly the matter of higher interest rates and scarcer capital is an urgent one, but the urgency criterion lacks objectivity and may imply an influence struggle occurring between groups within an organization. If an investment decision is wrapped up earlier than planned, what other decisions are put back on the shelf? Which criteria prevail for ranking investment decisions?

Payback Method

The *payback method,* being more specific, at least reduces investment alternatives to some comparability. This method focuses on how long it will take to recover an investment outlay. Practitioners of this method concern themselves little with economic life of the investment beyond recovery period or with cash flow during recovery. If five years is the cutoff date, then investments requiring more than five years to pay for themselves are outright rejected, while those which generate fastest recovery are preferred. The formula for determining the rate of return under the payback method is:

Formula:

$$r = \frac{\bar{A}}{P}$$

which states that the rate of return (r) is the average annual flow ($\bar{A}$) of funds divided by the original investment (P).

For example, an investment of \$25,000,000 promises to return \$6,875,000 annually. What is the rate of return by this method?

$$r = \frac{6{,}875{,}000}{25{,}000{,}000} = 0.275 = 27.5\%$$

This answer is not quite correct because it assumes perpetual income. We must also evaluate the time span of expected income.

The reciprocal of this rate, 1/r, tells us the number of years to recover the initial outlay of \$25,000,000. In this example, 1/0.275 = 3.6364 years, or about 3 years, 7 months, 19 days. If a firm prefers that no recovery period should exceed 5 years, then r is the reciprocal of 5, or $\frac{1}{5}$ = 20%. All other opportunities are rejected.

Sometimes a firm will modify this formula to include their in-house rule that recovery includes the initial investment plus another 22% return on investment; that is, P plus 0.22P, which we can write in the general form (P + K), giving us:

Formula:

$$r = \frac{\bar{A}}{P(1 + K)}$$

Substituting the same data into the formula results in:

$$r = \frac{6{,}875{,}000}{25{,}000{,}000\,(1 + 0.22)} = \frac{6{,}875{,}000}{30{,}500{,}000} = 22.54\%$$

The reciprocal of 22.54% is 4.436 years, or about 4 years, 5 months, 7 days to recover the original outlay (P) plus an additional 22% (K) on investment. If the firm's policy is 20%, then this investment falls within policy limits.

We agree that to bag a bird now is preferred to chasing the phoenix but this formula places no importance on when money accumulates. Funds received earlier will produce a higher rate of return than funds generated later simply because funds acquired now can be employed in other profitable endeavors. The method states nothing on how long these funds will flow after the initial recovery period. And the calculated rate of return is inaccurate. Additionally, the method overemphasizes liquidity as a capital expenditure goal; it overstates the value of flows during the recovery period; and it ignores efficient resource use.

Russian planners like this method. They call it the *recoupement-period.* With their record of failures we may well want to take a second look at any method praised by government planners. Nevertheless, the payback method is still popular among many corporate planners because of its simplicity and ease to calculate.

Certainly this method is justifiable for very risky investments. A firm interpreting an investment possibility in Rhodesia during a high-risk period may well assign a 60% or 80% rate of return as an acceptable minimum because of immediate political uncertainties. The calculated rate of return will give a correct reading for very short-lived investments of, say, one year; or if the investment has a very long life of, say, 75 or 100 years, the calculated rate of return provides a very rough approximation to the Internal Rate of Return discussed later in this chapter. Finally, in some instances, the method may substitute in initial screening of proposals if analysis is backed up by sounder methodology.

UNDISCOUNTED BENEFIT-COST RATIO

Similarly, the undiscounted benefit-cost ratio (UBCR) does not take into account timing of cash inflows. It, too, an approximate method, does not discount the future or risks. It may be expressed in gross terms (UGBCR) or net terms (UNBCR). Compare the two investment proposals in Figure 3–1.

Figure 3-1

	Project A			*Project B*		
Year	*Cash Flow*	*Deprecia-tion Charges*	*Net Income*	*Cash Flow*	*Deprecia-tion Charges*	*Net Income*
1	+50,000	-65,000	-15,000	+100,000	-65,000	+35,000
2	+75,000	-65,000	+10,000	+200,000	-65,000	+135,000
3	+100,000	-65,000	+35,000	+80,000	-65,000	+15,000
4	+125,000	-65,000	+60,000	+75,000	-65,000	+10,000
5	+150,000	-65,000	+85,000	+75,000	-65,000	+10,000
6	+100,000	-65,000	+35,000	+70,000	-65,000	+5,000
TOTALS	+600,000	-390,000	+210,000	+600,000	-390,000	+210,000

Initial investment for *both* projects A and B = $390,000 each. Straight line depreciation; zero salvage value at end of 6 years.

The undiscounted gross benefit-cost ratio (UGBCR) formula is:

Formula:

$$\text{UGBCR} = \frac{\sum_{t=1}^{n} A_t}{P}$$

Which states that the UGBCR embodies the sum of (Σ) the cash flow (A) generated from a project in year (t) divided by the original outlay (P). Substituting values from the table above, the solution is

$$\text{UGBCR}_a = \frac{600{,}000}{390{,}000} = 1.54$$

$$\text{UGBCR}_b = \frac{600{,}000}{390{,}000} = 1.54$$

Both investments will return slightly more than 1½ times original investment during the expected life of 6 years. The reciprocal of the ratio is 0.65, or 65%, which, in itself, has only vague significance.

The undiscounted net benefit-cost ratio subtracts out depreciation charges to furnish a net income figure. Total depreciation charges equal initial investment in these illustrative examples. The undiscounted net benefit-cost ratio (UNBCR) formula is:

Formula:

$$UNBCR = \frac{\sum_{t=1}^{n} A_t}{P} - 1$$

Solving for projects A and B, we have,

$$UNBCR_a = \frac{600{,}000}{390{,}000} - 1 = 0.54$$

$$UNBCR_b = \frac{600{,}000}{390{,}000} - 1 = 0.54$$

Acceptability of these two projects centers on total flows during the period without regard for timing. Even cursory examination of the above table will suggest that present values of cash flows for Project B will significantly exceed present values of cash flows for Project A, and that A is preferred over B, other things being equal.

ENGINEERING METHOD

Another approximate approach, *Hoskold's Method,* traditionally used in mining to determine rate of return, specifies that uniform annual payments are deposited in a conservatively invested sinking fund that earns a low rate. At the end of the asset's life cycle, value of the fund equals replacement cost of investment. To determine rate of return, divide the amount of original investment into cash remaining after accounting for the sinking fund deposit.

Formula:

$$r = \frac{\bar{F} - A}{P}$$

In this formula, $\bar{F}$ is the average annual cash flow, minus A, the annual sinking fund payment, while P represents original investment. To illustrate, assume that Freihofer Mines decides to add $700,000 (P) in new equipment in a mine that has a 12-year life remaining. Equipment will be abandoned at the end of 12 years and, consequently, has no salvage value. The investment is expected to produce an annual cash flow of $160,000.

First determine annual payments into a sinking fund which yields 5.5% compounded annually. A sinking fund formula and table is explained below, but we can work with knowns and find the sinking factor by taking the inverse of the factor found in Table III (Appendix), compound amount of an equal payment series, when i = 5.5% and n = 12. Found by interpolation,

$$\begin{aligned} A &= P\,(F/A_{5.5\%,12}) - 1 \\ &= \$700{,}000\left(\frac{1}{16.38559065}\right) = \$700{,}000\,(0.06102923) \\ &= \$42{,}720.46 \end{aligned}$$

The sinking fund deposits, $42,720.46, can now be substituted into the formula to solve for r, the rate of return.

$$r = \frac{160{,}000 - 42{,}720.46}{700{,}000} = 0.16754 = 16.75\%$$

According to *Hoskold's Method,* this proposal promises a return of 16.75%. Actually Freihofer Mines weighed two separate proposals which aggregate 16.75%. One proposal is an investment in a *sinking fund* which yields 5.5%. The other investment is $700,000 in *mine equipment* which promises to return $160,000 annually. Correctly analyzed by *compound interest methods,* the latter yields 20.4% rate of return if all turns out as forecasted. The combination of these *two separate investments* produces the 16.75% rate.

Sinking Fund Factor

A new term introduced in the above solution, a sinking fund factor, is easily and quickly explained. A *sinking fund,* a fund created to yield a specified amount at the end of a given time period, grows with a series of periodic payments deposited into it throughout the given time period. In the above mining example, the firm wanted to recover its original investment over 12 years. Since each deposit earned 5.5% interest compounded annually, the firm needed to deposit less than $58,333 annually (700,000 ÷ 12). To determine the exact annual deposit required, the final desired value of the fund (F, same as P in the preceding formula, but now F becomes a future desired sum) is multiplied by a *sinking fund factor,* that portion of the formula below set off in brackets.

Formula:

$$A = F\left[\frac{i}{(1+i)^n - 1}\right]$$

F = future sum.

i = applicable interest rate.

n = number of years fund is to exist.

Again, substituting the same values, we calculate that annual payments into the Freihofer sinking fund should be:

$$A = 700{,}000\left[\frac{0.055}{(1+0.055)^{12} - 1}\right]$$

$$= 700{,}000\ (0.06102923) = \$42{,}720.46$$

In the mining problem, we inverted the annuity factor, 16.38559065, from Table III. Table VI in the Appendix exhibits sinking fund factors $(A/F_{i,n})$ which, when located in the table, multiplied by the future desired sum, produces the amount of annual payments required. Either interpolation or solving by formula with a hand calculator will cover the range of interest rates and time periods not shown in Table VI.

ACCOUNTING RATES OF RETURN

Three variations of accounting rates of return used to relate investment profitability to capital are: original book method, average book method, year-by-year book method. These popular methods, simple, easy to apply, give rise to inconsistent rankings of investment priorities especially when cash flows fluctuate widely and/or are accompanied by substantial risk. Greater risk means higher probability that actual flows will deviate significantly from anticipated flows. Data for the following are from Figure 3–1 in the "Undiscounted Benefit-Cost Ratio" section of this chapter.

Original Book Method

To compute rate of return under the *original book method,* divide average annual *net* income by original cost of investment. *Net income* consists of average annual cash flow less annual depreciation charges. For Project A, in Figure 3–1, total net income for 6 years totals \$210,000; average net income ($\bar{F}^*$) equals \$210,000 divided by 6, or \$35,000, the same for Project B. The original investment cost is the book value, which is \$390,000 (P) for both Projects A and B. To compute rate of return (r):

Formula:

$$r = \frac{\bar{F}^*}{P}$$

$\bar{F}^*$ = average net income.

P = original investment.

Plugging in values, the result for Project A is

$$r = \frac{35{,}000}{390{,}000} = 0.0897 = 8.97\%$$

Of course, the rate of return for Project B is identical.

Average Book Method

To compute the rate of return under the *average book method,* begin with the same average annual net income but this time subtract salvage value (L) from the original outlay and divide that result by two in this manner:

Formula:

$$r = \frac{\bar{F}^*}{\frac{P - L}{2}}$$

$\bar{F}^*$ = average net income

P = initial outflow (investment)

L = salvage value

Obviously, the larger the salvage value (L) at the end of the asset's useful span, the smaller the denominator, and the larger will be the rate of return. In Projects A and B, the terminal value of the asset has a nominal, or zero for practical purposes, value; we will expect r to be lowest.

$$r_a = \frac{35{,}000}{\frac{390{,}000 - 0}{2}} = 0.17948 = 17.95\%$$

Once again data for Project B are identical and will render the same rate of return.

Year-by-Year Book Method

To compute the rate of return under the *year-by-year method* requires more calculations, essentially a repetition of the first formula for every year of the project's life. Net income for each year is divided by the total value of the investment. Each year, or time period, is denoted t, t + 1, t + 2, etc. Net income in this case is not average annual income but net income generated in a particular year. If net income fluctuates sharply from year-to-year so will the calculated rate of return.

Formula:

$$r_{a,t} = \frac{F^*_t}{P}$$

$r_{a,t}$ = rate of return for project A in year t.

F^*_t = net income for year t.

P = initial investment.

By the same token, rate of return for Project A in the second year will be:

$$r_{a,t+1} = \frac{F^*_{t+1}}{P}$$

For example, the rate of return for Year *1* of Project *A* is

$$r_{a,1} = \frac{-15{,}000}{390{,}000} = -0.03846 = -3.85\%;$$

while the rate of return for Year *6* of Project *B* is

$$r_{b,6} = \frac{5{,}000}{390{,}000} = 0.01282 = 1.28\%$$

The difficulty with all three above methods is that they will usually either overstate or understate the rate of return, and observation indicates that the same data will produce conflicting rates of return. Which rate of return is correct? With answers about 9% apart in the first two methods there really is no reconciliation or approximation. The average book method attempts to account for declining book value by taking an average value but it does not allow for reinvestment of recovered funds. Shortcoming of the first and last methods centers on the assumption that amount of reinvestment remains unchanged during its useful life. When several projects are compared, outcomes by any of the above methods will show inconsistent ranking. While no measurement produces perfect answers, discounted cash flow (DCF) techniques discussed below improve on the above by establishing investment priorities on the basis of rates of return; however, DCF methods rank below present value methods.

DISCOUNTED CASH FLOWS

The purpose of discounting is to compare equivalent amounts. Scuppernong grapes and cactus pears are not equivalent values until reduced to a common denominator–fruit. And \$100 in 3 years is not equivalent to \$100 in 2 years; therefore, any analysis will contain errors until variables are expressed in comparable terms. The following methods are first steps toward that objective.

Present Value of Dividend Growth—A Short-Cut

While the following formula is about as useful as price-earnings ratios* in evaluating stock investments, the present value method offers the advantage of pinning down investors' assumptions regarding estimates of quality, rate, and growth of dividends. Too, the technique decreases margin of error if a stock (equity) is evaluated from the viewpoint of a large group of potential and current investors. Validity of results depends upon a realistic estimate of a company's growth potential, a discount rate that appropriately reflects risk, the growth cycle of competing and complementary investments, and a great deal about investor psychology.

The following simple formula approximates the present value of *perpetual* dividend growth at a given discount rate.

Formula:

$$V = \frac{D}{\left[\frac{(1+i)}{(1+g)}\right] - 1}$$

D = dividends beginning of period

i = appropriate discount rate

g = growth rate of dividends

---

*For a concise critique of predictive value of P/E ratios see: Thomas J. Holt, *Total Investing* (New Rochelle, N.Y.: Arlington House Publishers, 1976), esp. Ch. 7.

Since this formulation averages out errors better when a group of stocks are analyzed, such as those that may comprise one of today's popular indices, suppose that your favorites yield an average \$2.80, that for as far into the future you care to look dividends will grow, on average, 5% a year, and that common stock investors demand an 11% rate of return to compensate for risks and unknowns.

$$V = \frac{2.80}{\left[\dfrac{(1+0.11)}{(1+0.05)}\right]-1} = \frac{2.80}{0.05714} = 49$$

How does 49 correspond to an actual value of your favorite index?

A short-cut method for finding the denominator is to subtract: (1 + i) - (1 + g) = (1.11) - (1.05) = 0.06, which may be reasonably close for estimations.

Minimum Life

The *minimum life* method, also known as *present value payback,* improves on the *minimum payback* approach illustrated earlier and focuses on risk involved in a project—an amended version of the simple payback. Its purpose is to determine the minimum economic life necessary to meet the rate of return norm established by the firm's management. At the point where present values of cash outflows and inflows equate, the project will pay out. The simplest illustration is one in which a project produces uniform inflows over the minimum period. The following example will be examined from two viewpoints.

To solve this problem will require a simple computation and use of Table IV in the Appendix. The first step: calculate the present value factor of an annuity, dividing outlay by annual inflow, on the assumption that an investment outflow precedes annual revenues. The second step: locate the factor (P/A) in Table IV nearest to the result, interpolate if necessary. The third step: evaluate results.

Formula:

$$(P/A_{i,n}) = \frac{P}{A}$$

Assume that an \$118,500 investment (P) will produce an annual inflow (A) of \$30,000. What is the minimum life that this proposal must have if the firm employs a 22% rate of return?

$$(P/A_{22\%,n}) = \frac{118{,}500}{30{,}000} = 3.950$$

Now look in Table IV, under the 22% column, for the closest n value which corresponds to 3.950. The answer is 10. In order for this investment to pay itself out and achieve an economic rate of return of 22%, the investment must be economically viable for 10 years.

If the firm has established a 5-year maximum payout on investments, it must either reject this investment opportunity or accept a lower rate of return. What rate of return corresponds to a maximum payback period of 5 years? This time, return to Table IV, follow along to the n = 5 row. As long as the factor exceeds 3.950, payback will fall within the established 5 years. Interest rates through 8% qualify. That is, a 5-year payback corresponds to an 8% return. To achieve higher rates, a longer minimum life must be accepted.

Internal Rate of Return

The *internal rate of return* (IRR), or *discounted cash flow* (DCF), expresses the same results found in the minimum life formula, but here it focuses on rate of return rather than number of years. Once again, Table IV simplifies calculations when annual flow is uniform. By definition the internal rate of return is that discount rate which reduces to equality present values of expected cash outflows to present values of expected cash inflows. In solving these problems we again assume a normal investment pattern, that is, a cash outflow followed by a series of cash inflows. When cash flows are not uniform, Table IV may not readily apply and results may not be entirely accurate; while a uniform cash flow not only produces more reliable results but can be quickly solved with factors found in Table IV. In the following case study, the economic life of the investment is given for the investor; we search for a discount rate which equates outflow with inflows. If cash flows were more complex, the discount rate would have to be discovered through trial-and-error.

Case Study: What rate of return did EZ Rent-to-All's proposal promise?

The owner of EZ Rent-to-All, a rental outlet of all types of power tools and appliances for short-term consumer use, mentioned to his friend, Caldwell Bridges, that he wanted to add several steam carpet cleaners but lacked funds to buy equipment and that he would sign a long-term lease if an outside investor showed interest. Caldwell Bridges grabbed the opportunity.

After some discussion C.B. signed an agreement with EZ in which he consented to purchase 4 steam carpet cleaners at $2,400 each, a total investment of $9,600. In turn, EZ consented to guarantee C.B. an annual lease income of $600 per machine for 5 years, maintain the equipment as long as it was rented a minimum of 100 full-time equivalent days per year, and after 5 years lease income would cease and ownership of the machines revert to

EZ. If rental income falls below 100 equivalent full days, then prorated main-tenance cost is deducted from C.B.'s lease income the following year. However, EZ's owner assured C.B. that this possibility was unlikely to occur given present projected demand; furthermore, once a total 500 equivalent full days are reached, then C.B. will no longer be subject to this provision. C.B. quickly computed his rate of return (2,400 ÷ 9,600) at 25% (notice that he employed the original book method), assented to the proposition, and for the next several days C.B.'s eyes sparkled with $s—the lazy man's way to riches.

Should C.B. have accepted the proposal? First, discount cash flows; second, compare this opportunity with alternative possibilities; third, allow for risk, the chance that C.B. will have to share in maintenance costs which will reduce his income. To verify the *internal rate of return* (IRR), divide outflow by annual inflow to express the result in terms of $1 so that Table IV applies.

$$\text{Factor} = \frac{9{,}600}{2{,}400} = 4.0000$$

Next, in Table IV, locate the factor nearest 4.0000 along the 5-year row. The answer lies between 7% and 8%, but closer to 8%; a more precise answer issues from interpolation.

$$7\%, 5 = 4.1001974$$

$$i, 5 = 4.0000000$$

$$8\%, 5 = 3.9927100$$

$$i = \frac{(4.1001974 - 4.0000)\,(0.08 - 0.07)}{(4.1001974 - 3.9927100)} + 0.07$$

$$= \frac{(0.1001974)\,(0.01)}{0.1074874} + 0.07$$

$$= \frac{0.00100197}{0.10748740} + 0.07 = 0.00932 + 0.07 = 0.07932 = 7.93\%$$

Bridges will earn 7.93%, not 25%, *if* rental demand is consistently lucrative during the entire period.

The IRR is inadequate for ranking projects. In this example, where Bridges makes an accept/reject decision on one proposal and inflow is expected to be fairly uniform during the economic life of the investment, this method will furnish satisfactory results. But where two or more propositions are under consideration, the IRR is inadequate as a single criterion. Which do you prefer: 50% of $3.75 or 4% of $375?

Suppose that you have $100,000 to invest and evaluate three proposals: (1) $50,000 returns 30%; (2) $100,000 returns 20%; and (3) $50,000 returns 6%. Assume no difference in risk or type of investment. Obviously, two Number 1 investments will maximize return on $100,000, but there may be only *one* Number 1 investment available—Liberia wants only one razor blade factory. Then the remaining $50,000 can only be employed in Number 3; Numbers 1 + 3 yield $18,000 annually, while Number 2 produces $20,000, the preferred alternative.

Another shortcoming of this method centers on life of the investment. Numbers 1 and 2 may have an economic life of 2 years, while Number 3 may have an economic life of 15 years. Preference depends upon many conditions, one of which is: At what rate can funds be reinvested? The IRR does not account for future changes. Decisions pivot on terminal value: How much will accrue by the end of n years? For that answer we need to explore further present value techniques.

PRESENT VALUE TECHNIQUES

In forecasting outflow, one should account for opportunity costs, economic loss of any alternative, or opportunity foregone, when an alternative decision is favored over another. The opportunity cost of planting a field in soybeans is income lost from other alternatives given up, which may include planting other crops, constructing apartments, a motel, overnight camper sites, or museum, or leasing or selling the land to others and employing the cash in some other endeavor. While investment combinations can be almost infinite, opportunities analyzed are those known and acceptable to the firm or investor and within range of financial and technological capabilities.

The other tricky issue focuses on the term "economic life." When a machine is worn out and scrapped, there is no question that its *economic life* for its original purpose has expired. But other factors determine useful life of a project; e.g., technological improvements, more efficient techniques of production, changing factor costs (labor and natural resources, for example) or their availability, changes in governmental policies (labor laws, tax writeoffs, nationalization), a change in demand for product or service produced, maintenance costs rising too fast relative to benefits. In general terms we can call the economic life of a project or investment that span of time in which the inflow of economic benefits exceeds feasible alternatives. The following examples illustrate use of present value analysis in investment decision-making.

Net Present Value

The *net present value* (NPV) technique attempts to compare present values of outflows and inflows given some discount rate that management employs as a standard at which funds can/should be invested or the rate may be referred to as the "cost of capital" detailed in Chapter Four. This rate, a long-run opportunity rate, in present value analysis indicates judgement of earnings power of a firm's investments.

Net present value analysis, a tool superior to DCF approaches, explicitly recognizes reinvestment of cash generated by a project, while the DCF method zeroes in on the profitability of the unrecovered investment in the original project, a constant rate of return. The NPV method tests attractiveness of an opportunity by calculating whether present values of cash inflows exceed present values of cash outflows when discounted at a standard, or minimum, rate of return. If NPV exceeds zero, then the DCF rate must be higher than the minimum acceptable rate. When the NPV equals zero, the investment will just yield the required minimum DCF rate. A negative NPV means that net cash inflow is inadequate to repay outstanding investment while providing the required minimum rate of return.

Formula:

$$NPV = \sum \frac{P_n}{(1+r)^n} + \sum \frac{A_n}{(1+r)^n}$$

NPV = Sum of (Σ) present values of cash outflows + Sum of (Σ) present values of cash inflows.

To illustrate present value analysis, refer back to the table on Projects A and B in this chapter (Figure 3-1). Since cash inflows vary considerably, present values are computed year-by-year. However, in Figure 3-2, a 9.5% continuously compounded rate is assumed; that is, more realistically, it is presumed that cash inflows occur continuously throughout the year. A 10% effective rate is equivalent to a nominal rate of 9.5310%. (Refer to Tables XIV and XV in the Appendix.*) Investment sequence is an outflow of $390,000 followed by a series of 6 annual inflows.

By the formula, the net present value of Project A is:

$$NPV_a = \frac{-390{,}000}{(1+0.10)^0} + \frac{50{,}000}{(1+0.10)^1} + \frac{75{,}000}{(1+0.10)^2} + \frac{100{,}000}{(1+0.10)^3} + \frac{125{,}000}{(1+0.10)^4} + \frac{150{,}000}{(1+0.10)^5} + \frac{100{,}000}{(1+0.10)^6}$$

$$= -390{,}000 + 417{,}532.13 = +27{,}532.13$$

*By restating 9.5310%, nominal rate continuously discounted, into an equivalent effective rate of 10%, a shift from Table VII to Table II in the Appendix can pare the number of calculations.

(N.B. Any number raised to a zero power equals 1:

$$\frac{-390{,}000}{(1 + 0.10)^0} = \frac{-390{,}000}{1} = -390{,}000)$$

Figure 3-2

PRESENT VALUE ANALYSIS BY PERIOD
(r = 10%, n = 6)*

Period	PV Factor @ 10%*	PROJECT A Flows	PROJECT A Present Values	PROJECT B Flows	PROJECT B Present Values
0	1.000000	-390,000	-390,000.00	-390,000	-390,000.00
1	0.909091	+ 50,000	+ 45,454.55	+100,000	+ 90,909.10
2	0.826447	+ 75,000	+ 61,983.53	+200,000	+165,289.40
3	0.751315	+100,000	+ 75,131.50	+ 80,000	+ 60,105.20
4	0.683014	+125,000	+ 85,376.75	+ 75,000	+ 51,226.05
5	0.620922	+150,000	+ 93,138.30	+ 75,000	+ 46,569.15
6	0.564475	+100,000	+ 56,447.50	+ 70,000	+ 39,513.25
NET		+210,000	+27,532.13	+210,000	+ 63,612.15

*See Table VII in the Appendix for continuously discounted factors, assuming payments made at year end; ergo, when r = 10%, j = 9.5310%; and see Table II for equivalent single payment present values.

Notice that both projects require the same original investment and both generate identical incomes during their respective economic lives, also assumed identical. Nevertheless, because of differences in timing of flows, the NPV of B substantially exceeds that of A. If 10% represents the standard employed, then both projects are acceptable, both yield a positive return, where inflow returns the original investment plus 10% continually reinvested. This positive difference provides excess value, an economic gain beyond standard earnings, to cushion any margin of error bound to occur in any investment analysis. A higher minimum rate reduces the cushion for both projects, and at some higher rate Project A will exhibit a negative NPV, an unacceptable alternative, while Project B remains acceptable. If we raise the required earnings hurdle to 15%, both projects will yield negative values and be unacceptable.

Observe the effect of economic life on a project. In Figure 3-3, present values cumulate for Project B. Notice how long it takes for a proposal to break even. At the 4-year interval, accumulative NPVs are still negative but turn positive in year 5; at 10% Project B pays out in 4½ years, while Project A requires another year to break even at the standard rate. The reader may want to check computations on present values of Project A.

Figure 3-3

PRESENT VALUE ANALYSIS OF PROJECT B
(r = 10%, n = 6)

Period	*Present Values*	*Accumulative Present Values*
0	-390,000.00	-390,000.00
1	+ 90,909.10	-299,090.90
2	+165,289.40	-133,801.50
3	+ 60,105.20	- 73,696.30
4	+ 51,226.05	- 22,407.25
5	+ 46,569.15	+ 24,098.90
6	+ 39,513.25	+ 63,612.15

Present Value Indices

The *present value index* (PVI) is also known by other tags: *Profitability Index* or *Gross Discounted Benefit-Cost Ratio.* The index employs the same data as in the NPV method above but expresses the results as an index. It is found by dividing the sum of present values of *total* cash inflows by present values of cash outflows.

Formula:

$$PVI = \frac{\Sigma A_n (1 + r)^{-n}}{\Sigma P_n (1 + r)^{-n}}$$

This index weighs, relative to amounts and timing of earnings, flows according to the periods in which they occur. A profitability, or present value, index of 1.000 or more suggests that the investment may be considered among acceptable alternatives, while an index of less than 1.000 is rejected.

Using the same data for Projects A and B, we have

$$PVI_a = \frac{417{,}532.13}{390{,}000.00} = 1.071$$

$$PVI_b = \frac{453{,}612.15}{390{,}000.00} = 1.163$$

Both NPV and PVI methods favor Project B. The PVI method will generate acceptable conclusions on accept/reject type investment decisions. When there are two or several projects, however, ranking them will indicate the most desirable one. In this example, Project B ranks higher, but frequently ranking will produce conflicting outcomes. The present value index reflects *relative* profitability. The net present value approach expresses *absolute* magnitudes, the expected net contribution of a project. The consistency of results from above examples are due to similar costs and flow patterns. In these examples, too, remember that r, 10%, represents a continuously discounted nominal rate of 9.531%.

Too, like the undiscounted net benefit-cost ratio, there is a discounted net benefit-cost ratio which is simply the gross rate (or PVI) minus 1.

Formula:

$$\text{DNBCR} = \frac{\Sigma\, A_n\, (1 + r)^{-n}}{\Sigma\, P_n\, (1 + r)^{-n}} - 1$$

Substituting values for Projects A and B into the formula,

$$\text{DNBCR}_a = \frac{417{,}532.13}{390{,}000.00} - 1 = 0.071$$

$$\text{DNBCR}_b = \frac{453{,}612.15}{390{,}000.00} - 1 = 0.163$$

For indices that resolve into negative values, the project is rejected; positive indices are ranked to select the best alternative; a zero value means that the minimum selected return has just been met without cushion for marginal errors.

Annualized Net Present Value

Annualized net present value approaches the *target cash flow* requirement of an investment; that is, given the amount of investment, opportunity rate, and estimated economic life of a project, the following formula approximates cash flows stipulated to meet criteria.

Formula:

$$\text{TCF} = \frac{P}{(P/A_{i,n})}$$

The formula asks: Which cash flow will satisfy conditions of opportunity rate and time span, given original investment? The target cash flow (TCF) equals original outlay (P) divided by the factor from Table IV which corresponds to a selected rate (i) and economic life (n) of the project.

Return to the case study involving Caldwell Bridges and EZ Rent-to-All. Suppose that Caldwell had approached the problem in this manner. Given original outlay (P) of $9,600 for 4 machines, which uniform annual cash flow will generate a 15% rate of return (r) during 5 years (n)? Plugging in values of the given investment and the factor, from Table IV, which corresponds to i = 15% and n = 5, then:

$$TCF_{15\%,5} = \frac{9{,}600}{3.3522} = \$2{,}863.79$$

Of course, this figure must be adjusted for any investment tax credits to arrive at the minimal pretax cash flow. One advantage of this technique is that comparison among investment alternatives with different economic lives can take place. Too, the approach is quick and practical to approximate cash flows during early stages of planning investments.

Net Terminal Value

With the net present value method, funds flowing from an investment are assumed to be reinvested at the same rate, the minimum standard established by the company or, frequently, the minimum rate is considered the cost of capital to the firm. However, during the project's economic life, actual results may vary substantially from anticipated outcomes. Funds generated during early phases of an investment may not find the same lucrative reinvestment opportunities later and may have to be reinvested in lower yielding combinations, or the situation may offer a new array of higher return options previously not available (new acquisitions, new products, new markets, for example).

The NPV method can be adapted to discount each flow at a different rate and still obtain the NPV of the set of cash flows. Sometimes NPV results will signal an incorrect accept/reject signal. An alternative approach, *net terminal value* (NTV), combines cash inflows from an investment with outflows of its investment source, which accumulate to a net terminal value at expiration of a project's economic life.

If the NTV is positive, this affirms an acceptable alternative because it adds something to the firm's total wealth after accounting for repayment of investment at some interest rate. Net terminal value comparisons also provide a means of ranking two or more projects; but if their economic lives are unequal, then a common denominator must be found among projects so that all results are expressed for the same corresponding periods. For example, if one project has an anticipated economic life of 8 years, another 12 years, the common denominator is 24. Obvious problems include the formidable task of projecting reinvestment rates and future capital costs.

The following formula, stated to embrace three flows, can be generalized to accommodate as many flows and as many changing reinvestment rates as required.

Formula:

$$NTV = A_1 (1 + r_1)^n + A_2 (1 + r_2)^n - A_3$$

A_1, A_2, A_3 = flows 1, 2, and 3.

r_1, r_2 = different rates, 1, 2.

The above expression, relating to the following problem, states that the net terminal value issues from addition of various cash inflows (A_1, A_2) at different times (n) and interest rates (r_1, r_2) and cash outflows ($-A_3$).

Tomorrow's opportunities depend upon financial decisions made today. Tomorrow's yields depend upon cash flows generated today from investments. Suppose that a sum, borrowed for three years, invested, produces a first cash inflow (A_1) which returns 30% effective (r_1) the first year but reinvested returns only 8% effective (r_2) for the next two years plus a second cash flow (A_2) in the second year which returns 8% effective (r_2) for two years; both 8% returns are under the 10% nominal cost of capital. Although part of the cash inflow is reinvested below the cost of capital, the overall investment produces a net return in excess of 10%, the cost of capital. (See Figure 3-4.)

Figure 3-4

FLOWS	t_0	t_1	t_2	t_3
A_1		+1,000		
A_2			+1,000	
A_3				-2,000

In this exhibit, funds are borrowed at 10% nominal rate, invested in time period t_0, and the total amount repaid, outflow in period t_3, is \$2,000 (A_3). At the beginning of period t_1, flow A_1 of \$1,000 arises. During the first period this flow generates a 30% effective return compounded continuously, but this sum is reinvested during periods t_2 and t_3 at the lower 8% effective rate compounded continuously. Flow A_2 produces an 8% effective rate compounded continuously during two periods, t_2 and t_3.

$$\begin{aligned} \text{NTV} &= \$1{,}000\,(1+0.30)\,(1+0.08)^2 + \$1{,}000\,(1+0.08)^2 - \$2{,}000 \\ &= 1{,}000\,(1.516) + 1{,}000\,(1.166) - 2{,}000 \\ &= 1{,}516 + 1{,}166 - 2{,}000 = +\,\$682 \end{aligned}$$

Net terminal value (NTV) is positive. Other things being equal, this project is acceptable because it does provide a return above cost of capital, and, in fact, holding risk and other variables constant, it pays the firm to continue borrowing and investing in projects down to the point where rate of return equals cost of capital. (Marginal financing is explained in Chapter Six.) Determining cost of capital, however, can be troublesome, especially in situations of multi-projects and multi-sources of investment capital. A firm may simply apply a weighted average of all capital sources as a minimum rate of return criterion.

CONTENTS

Chapter Four: Calculating Cost of Capital to Maximize the Firm's Worth

FOUR

Calculating Cost of Capital to Maximize the Firm's Worth

In the preceding chapter cost of capital cropped up in the application of present value techniques without reference to sources of these funds. Funds derived from a specific source, in some cases, may be described as "out of pocket" costs, but, more exact, the *specific cost of capital* measures the cost of capital derived from a single source; the *average cost of capital* refers to a schedule which includes capital from all sources–internal and external–available to the firm; the *marginal cost of capital* (more about marginal concepts in Chapter Six) refers to incremental costs associated with raising additional funds. It may result that in a particular project funds are indeed secured from a single source, but, then, how will funds obtained from one source affect cost of funds raised subsequently from other sources? At some point, of course, highly levered (see Chapter Five) firms will face sharply rising cost schedules.

Also, in Chapter Three, an "opportunity cost" concept, a quantitative estimate of returns that might have been earned in opportunities foregone, substituted for a required rate of return; that is, the investment project selected must yield a higher return than alternatives passed up.* Sometimes this opportunity cost supplants the cost of capital used for investment purposes. Rather than resist we surrender on this point to avoid confusion.

Too, examples in Chapter Three made some implicit assumptions about risks and taxes. A higher required rate of return is thought to account for risk elements; a lower rate of return may represent an after-tax return. However, this chapter, and the next, deals more explicitly with taxes and risk. It focuses on specific costs of long-term funds (funds coming from a single source) and finally on the average weighted cost of capital.

FINANCING WITH LONG TERM DEBT

Debt, frequently a preferable way to finance operations, tends to shift some risk from a firm's owners to lenders, raise returns to invested capital, offer a cheaper source of funds; and in most situations interest costs are treated as deductible expenses by tax authorities as long as the firm is profitable. The cost of capital on most forms of indebtedness may be calculated by the following formulas; one variation pertains to a Canadian case. Cost of financing a particular project should not relate exclusively to one source of funds because a change in the debt structure may alter costs for *all* forms of debt (and equity). Further, the cost of capital from an operational viewpoint means cost of funds obtained from all sources, external and internal.

Implied in the preceding chapter, the cost of capital is the rate of return which must be earned on investment so that the value of common stock remains unchanged; that is, present value computations employ a minimum, or acceptable, rate of return. This does not necessarily imply that a project must earn a return always greater than the cost of funds; if an investment lowers overall risk exposure of a firm, management acts to maximize the long run value of the enterprise. Specific discussion on risk exposure will be postponed; discussion of the calculation of the weighted average cost of capital will follow sections on individual components of capital cost determination. The following formulas apply to bonded indebtedness as well as most other forms of long-term debt—capital notes, debentures, mortgages—

*At this point the reader will find interesting and appropriate the discussion on explicit costs in: James T. S. Porterfield, *Investment Decisions and Capital Costs* (Englewood Cliffs, N.J.: Prentice-Hall, Inc., 1965), pp. 42-64.

except preferred stock, which is treated separately because of its dual owner/debtor nature and because of its dual tax treatment.

Although a bond is really a promissory note, bond terminology differs. The terms, *par value, face value, denomination* refer to the principal sum named in the contract, the bond. The nominal interest rate may be called a *coupon rate* or *bond rate,* based on the face value, which does not fluctuate with other interest rates nor with prices in the bond market. Nevertheless, bond prices respond to changes in interest rates to produce a *yield* that reflects changes in interest rates. Therefore, intervention in the money markets by the Federal Reserve or Treasury can create substantial losses to investors. At the end of the bond's contract period, at some specified future date, called the *maturity date,* or *redemption date,* the obligation is redeemed for a specific sum called *redemption value,* which may or may not equal the face value of the bond. A *discount* means bonds are sold under their face value and raises the cost of capital, while a *premium* means the borrower receives more than the face value and the yield to the investor is lower. Bonds are generally issued as long-term debt, that is, more than 10 years, although an intermediate term (5-to-10 years) is certainly practical in periods of great uncertainty and wide interest rate fluctuations.

There are many types and hybrids of bonds. If a bond is unsecured, it is usually called a *debenture* which closely ties an issue to the general credit standing of the borrower. A common type, *mortgage bonds,* requires that a firm pledges certain assets. Interest payments on *income bonds* is contingent on earnings the firm generates. Bonds secured by marketable securities of other corporations are *collateral trust bonds. Convertible bonds* provide that the lender may have the option of converting to the borrower's common or preferred stock at a stated relationship. But with *equipment trust bonds* actual title to equipment remains with a trustee, which provides added safety to lenders. While other types can, do, and should arise, the above list comprises some of the more common varieties.

Generalizing, we can state that the cost of debt (K) is:

$$\text{Cost of debt} = \frac{\text{Interest}}{\text{Principal}},$$

so that interest payments of \$100,000 on principal of \$1.2 million results in a cost of debt of:

$$k = \frac{1}{P} = \frac{100{,}000}{1{,}200{,}000} = 8.33\%$$

This is not exactly correct because we have not accounted for taxes and flotation costs. The real cost of borrowing to the corporation is its after-tax cost which means the before-tax cost must be adjusted by the applicable tax rate.

After-Tax Cost of Debt

After-tax cost of debt (%) equals (before-tax cost) times (one minus tax rate).

Formula: $$k = i(1 - h)$$

If i = 8.33% (found above) and the effective tax rate is 45% (h), then, the real cost of capital to the firm is:

$$k = 0.0833\,(1 - 0.45) = 0.0833\,(0.55) = 0.0458 = 4.58\%$$

Short-Cut Method

So let's begin with a short-cut method and then proceed to finer points. In this chapter k refers to cost of capital and various subscripts, b, e, p, simply refer to the type of capital under examination, bonds, equity, preferred, etc., and i or r still retain their designations of nominal or effective rates. A bond may carry a nominal rate of 8% but its effective rate may be above or below 8% depending upon whether it sells at a discount or premium to par. The effective rate, r, can equal k, but not necessarily. Furthermore, convention dictates the use of k. Net proceeds are the only significant sums to a borrower (designated Q) during the life of the loan while principal (P) represents the amount to be repaid. Flotation costs (K) may be small in direct borrowings, larger or substantial in publicly funded issues, but nevertheless represent a deduction from available funds, so that Q = (P – K), where Q connotes actual funds available to invest. Periodic payments (bond coupon, for example) R are dollar amounts which signify the price of using borrowed funds. Here is the *short-cut* formula to determine cost of debt:

Formula: $$k = \frac{(1 - h)\,R}{Q}$$

Using the same example again where R = \$100,000 and Q = \$1.2 million, then

$$k = \frac{(1 - 0.45)\,100{,}000}{1{,}200{,}000}$$

$$= \frac{55{,}000}{1{,}200{,}000} = 4.58\%$$

This formula, actually one used for perpetual bonds, provides only a crude approximation to the cost of borrowed funds. Matters of sinking fund requirements, timing of cash flows, maturity date will significantly alter computations.

Bonds Sold at Prices Different from Par

Bonds frequently sold at prices not equal to the face value of indebtedness due at maturity means that the firm has less funds (discount) available for investment and remaining funds must work that much harder to repay indebtedness plus interest, which raises the effective cost to borrowers, or the firm has more funds (premium) available than the par value of indebtedness which lowers the cost of debt to borrowers and reduces yield to lenders. For U.S. income tax purposes the discount or premium is amortized over the life of indebtedness; however, in those countries where they are not applicable, a modified, alternative formula appears below.

In the following formula, the same symbols apply, where h is the tax rate, R is the amount based on the coupon rate, P is the face value of the bond, and Q is the net amount available to the borrower.

Formula:

$$k_b = \frac{(1 - h)\left[R + \frac{1}{n}(P - Q)\right]}{\frac{Q + P}{2}}$$

This formula only approximates* the cost of bonded indebtedness when

*James Mao offers the following formula for computing the effective interest rate on long-term debt to solve for r by estimated trial-and-error, where interest payments are regular. The first term of the right-hand side represents the present value of interest expenses (after taxes), the second, the present value of the principal repaid at maturity. Rather than gross financing, r can be calculated on a per bond basis. Symbols are: M = market price per bond; i = coupon rate; P = par value; n = number of periods from issue to maturity; m = number of periods since bond was issued; h = tax rate.

Formula:

$$M = \sum_{t=1}^{n-m} \frac{(Pi)(1 - h) + [(M - P) \div (n - m)]\,h}{(1 + r)^t} + \frac{P}{(1 + r)^{n-m}}$$

there is a premium or discount that varies substantially from par value; the denominator represents the average balance outstanding during the life of indebtedness. If sinking-fund payments arise, the formula must be revised because it does not account for annual compounding.

Where tax laws differ from the U.S., however, as in the case of Canada, C. D. Quirin suggests the following modification where Q* represents the price received before deducting issue expenses.

Formula:

$$k_b = \frac{(1 - h)\left[R + \frac{1}{n}(Q^* - Q)\right] + \frac{1}{n}(P - Q^*)}{\frac{Q + P}{2}}$$

k_b = cost of capital for a bond.

h = income tax rate.

R = annual interest payments.

n = term of debt.

Q* = gross price received by borrower.

Q = net proceeds from debt issue.

P = face value of bond.

Case Study: (A) What is the real cost of IEC's debt?

The International Energy Corporation (IEC) sold a $6 million issue of 8% bonds at 92, in 1979, due in 1999, with no sinking fund requirement. The firm's tax rate, based on income from all sources, is presently 43%. Management wants to compare the cost of debt financing with costs of funds from alternative sources.

$$k_b = \frac{(1 - 0.43)\left[8.00 + \frac{1}{20}(100 - 92)\right]}{\frac{92 + 100}{2}}$$

$$= \frac{4.788}{96} = 0.049875 = 4.9875\%$$

The cost of borrowed funds, then, is about 5% for IEC.

Sinking Fund Requirement

A sinking fund may be established in a variety of ways: *uniform annual payments, uniform increments, tied to income earned,* etc. To create a sinking fund in which funds are conservatively invested at a rate below the coupon rate of the bond issue suggests inefficient employment of funds. If the sinking fund earns 5% interest and bond interest is 8%, then the best use of funds is to retire some of the debt because it produces a higher yield. A sinking fund that calls for uniform payments in good years and bad ones may strain company finances in bad years and encourage overinvestment, without regard for debt retirement, in good ones. It may be better to relate fund payments to income generated from the borrower's viewpoint, while the lender prefers protection especially in later years when equipment or buildings have deteriorated and the borrower's cushion of safety has narrowed. An alternative, *serial maturities,* serve the same function as sinking funds, and offter distinct advantages where income flows can be reasonably predicted, as in the case of utilities, but may prove rather burdensome for firms that experience wide income fluctuations. Serial maturities especially protect lenders of funds to public entities (cities, counties, parishes, states) because it reduces the political temptation of expropriating funds reserved for future repayment for current political use. The following example illustrates the difference between results arising from application of above formulas and those found by the longer method.

The Saginaw Valley Land Development Corp. sold a $1.5 million issue of 7% bonds in 1977, due in 1987, at a net price of 94, which bears a sinking fund commitment of $100,000 yearly for the first 5 years and $200,000 annually the last 5 years. The applicable tax rate is 46%. (See Figure 4-1.) The steps to calculate the cost of this issue are:

(1) Add annual interest payments to sinking fund payments;
(2) Subtract tax credit on interest expense and amortization of discount;
(3) Determine the present values of cash flows resulting from (1) and (2) above;
(4) Interpolate to compute debt cost.

After computing cash flows for 10 years, next estimate present values of these flows. To find the ball park, approximate cost of capital.

$$k_b = \frac{(1 - 0.46)\left[7.00 + \frac{1}{10}(100 - 94)\right]}{\frac{94 + 100}{2}} = 4.231\%$$

Figure 4-1

			Less: Tax Credit (46%)			Present Values	
Year	*Sinking Fund Pay't*	*Interest Pay't*	*Interest*	*Amorti- zation**	*Cash Flow*	*4¼%*	*4¾%*
1978	100,000	105,000	48,300	4140	152,560	146,341	145,642
1979	100,000	98,000	45,080	4140	148,780	136,897	135,593
1980	100,000	91,000	41,860	4140	145,000	127,979	126,155
1981	100,000	84,000	38,640	4140	141,220	119,562	117,295
1982	100,000	77,000	35,420	4140	137,440	111,618	108,979
1983	200,000	70,000	32,200	4140	233,660	182,024	176,872
1984	200,000	56,000	25,760	4140	226,100	168,954	163,389
1985	200,000	42,000	19,320	4140	218,540	156,647	150,764
1986	200,000	28,000	12,880	4140	210,980	145,063	138,949
1987	200,000	14,000	6,440	4140	203,420	134,163	127,895
	TOTALS				-1,817,700	-1,429,248	-1,391,533
	Q (= $1.5 million X 0.94)				+1,410,000	+1,410,000	+1,410,000
	DIFFERENCE				- 407,700	- 19,248	+ 18,467

*Amortization of discount on straight-line basis.

A good guess, then, is that actual cost will lie between 4¼% and 4¾%, and that certainly it will exceed the ball park estimate of 4.231%. By interpolation, we find cost of borrowed funds, given above assumptions, to be 4.505%. The approximate method understates results because of differences in timing of flows. However, in defense of the approximate method, it is rather difficult to project accurately 5 years ahead let alone 10, 15, 20 or more. The tax rate may change, and does periodically, interest rates may fall, the firm's needs may change—all of which can influence results and make earlier calculations quite invalid. Cost of capital analysis, therefore, not one of historical costs, is structured on future anticipated results, an imperfectly anticipated future.

Looking for a *short-cut* method? Then, approximate cost and raise the outcome to align it with actual cost. Further out in time errors between estimated and actual results may range from 0.25% to 0.50%. For situations of 10 years or so, add 0.25% to the product found by the formula; for longer situations of 20 years or more, add 0.50% to the result; for in-between situations, accommodate accordingly. Although this may not be accurate as sin, at least modification has been made in the right direction. In the foregoing example, the estimated cost by the formula is 4.231%, plus 0.25% error adjustment, equals 4.481%, which is fairly close to 4.505% found by the longer method.

Purchase Price of a Bond (Three Methods)

Because the purchase price of a bond (either new or outstanding issue) likely differs from its face (or redemption) value, those mathematical factors which can be isolated—number of years to maturity, coupon rate, expected rate of return—are pooled in the following *short-cut* formulation in order to determine the purchase price of a bond.

Formula:

$$V_b = P^* + (Pi - P^*\,r)\left[\frac{1-(1+r)^{-n}}{r}\right]$$

Although P, face value of the bond, may equal P*, redemption value, the formula distinguishes between the two values. The bond's coupon rate, i, will unlikely match the investor's rate of return, r. The bracketed portion of the formula is familiar Table IV, which greatly facilitates hand calculations.

A bond purchaser obtains the right to receive a stream of income (interest payments) plus a single sum payable at bond's maturity, which means that the present value of a bond equals the sum of present values of these two flows. Suppose that a $1,000, 6% bond, interest payable semiannually, matures in another 14 years. Which purchase price will yield 8% converted semiannually? (P* = P, and n = 28)

$$V_b = 1{,}000 + [(1{,}000 \times 0.03) - (1{,}000 \times 0.04)]\ (P/A,4\%,28)$$

$$= 1{,}000 + (30 - 40)\,(16.66306)$$

$$= 1{,}000 - 166.63 = \$833.37$$

A *variation short-cut* of the above formula, which, too, only requires use of one table instead of two, will produce the same result:

Formula:

$$V_b = \frac{Pi}{r} + \left(P^* - \frac{Pi}{r}\right)[(1+r)^{-n}]$$

P = face value of bond.

P* = redemption value of bond.

i = bond's coupon rate.

r = investor's rate of return.

$(1 + r)^{-n}$ = single period present value of 1.

The bracketed portion, of course, refers to factors found in Table II in the Appendix. Let's now solve the equation with the same above data.

$$V_b = \frac{1{,}000\,(0.03)}{0.04} + \left[1{,}000 - \frac{1{,}000\,(0.03)}{0.04}\right](P/F_{4\%,28})$$

$$= 750 + 250\,(0.333477)$$

$$= 750 + 83.37 = \$833.37$$

The *third method* simply restates mathematically what a bond purchaser has acquired; viz., the right to a stream of income plus a single redemption amount.

Formula:

$$V_b = Pi\left[\frac{1 - (1 + r)^{-n}}{r}\right] + P^*\,[(1 + r)^{-n}]$$

Since the bracketed portions represent factors that can be located in the Appendix, Tables IV and II, we can rewrite the formula:

$$V_b = Pi\,(P/A_{r,n}) + P^*\,(P/F_{r,n})$$

To check results in this third formula, substitute data from the above example:

$$V_b = 1{,}000\,(0.03)\,(16.66306) + 1{,}000\,(0.333477)$$

$$= 499.89 + 333.48 = \$833.37$$

Bond Refunding

One aspect of the cost of debt is whether new debt can replace old debt at a lower cost; that is, *refunding,* if bonds are *callable.* However, all decisions have their costs and refunding means payment of a *call premium, flotation costs, overlapping interest expenses* when new bonds are issued before old ones are called, and consideration of income tax provisions that apply to refunding operations. J. C. T. Mao suggests one approach to this problem of comparing costs to determine savings:

(1) Determine cost of refunding (X).
(2) Compute annual net savings from refunding (Y).
(3) Calculate net present value (NPV) of refunding and accept if NPV exceeds zero (NPV > 0).

Formula: (1)

$$X = (bP - P)(1 - h) + \left(\frac{n_1}{n_2}\right)K_2 + \left(\frac{n_1}{n_2}\right)(i_2 P)\left(\frac{x}{12}\right)(1 - h) + (S_p - K_1)h$$

The foregoing formula is less unglamorous than it at first appears, especially since most symbols are already familiar from their earlier use in this chapter. Subscripts 1 and 2 refer to old issue (1) and new debt issue (2).

- b = redemption price determined as a percentage of face value.
- P = face value, outstanding debt.
- h = marginal tax rate.
- n = number of years to maturity.
- K = flotation (or issue) costs–for (1) this represents unamortized issue costs and for (2) the costs associated with a new issue.
- i = coupon rate.
- x = number of months required for advance redemption notice.
- S_p = unamortized bond premium.

To better understand the above formula, examine each term of the equation. The first term is the tax adjusted call premium, next the cost of issuing new bonds, then the tax adjusted overlapping interest expenses, and finally the current tax obligation on the difference between unamortized bond premium and the unamortized bond issue cost. Custom dictates bond maturities of 10, 20, 25, 30 or more years so that a new issue offers the advantage of lengthening debt maturity while lowering interest costs (if that objective is included). Therefore, only the fraction of $\frac{n_1}{n_2}$ relates to a reduction in interest expense and not total interest on the entire issue.

Formula: (2)

$$Y = (i_1 P - i_2 P)(1 - h) + \frac{S_p}{n_1}h + \left(\frac{K_2}{n_2} - \frac{K_1}{n_1}\right)h$$

This second formula necessary to the solution determines the annual net savings that would result from refunding. There are a great many ifs and what might have beens in these calculations. For one thing how long should the firm wait to refund its debt? Will interest rates be lower next year, or will it be cheaper to refinance when the present outstanding bonds mature?

We can only assume that the best decision is made given available information and management's interpretation of that data. Then, to determine the net present value of refunding the formula is:

Formula: (3) $$NPV = Y\,(P/A_{k,n}) - X$$

Assuming that management's objective is to maximize the net present value of the business, it should refund the old issue if NPV exceeds zero. The rationale for this set of formulations will become clearer with an example.

Refinancing Debt

The Everest Co. (manufacturer of sporting gear and recreational vehicles) with \$16 million, 8% bonds outstanding due in 15 years weighs the possibility of refunding this issue with 7½%, 25-year bonds. On the negative side management will face flotation costs estimated higher in relation to face value of the debt, double interest payments for 3 months, and a call premium of 1.05 as penalty for debt pre-payment. On the positive side annual interest expenses will be lowered by \$80,000, debt maturity will be lengthened, and the economic staff forecasts a rise in interest rates over the next several years. We assume with complete certainty that the entire new issue will be absorbed by the market. What action should management take?

P = \$16 million (face amount of outstanding debt).

n_1 = 15 years n_2 = 25 years

K_1 = \$30,000 (unamortized flotation costs).

K_2 = \$144,000 (flotation costs of new issue).

i_1 = 8% i_2 = 7½%.

x = 3 months (advance redemption notice).

h = 46% (marginal tax rate).

S_p = \$50,000 unamortized bond premium.

b = 1.05 redemption price (percentage of face value).

$k = (1 - h)\, i_2 = 0.0405$ cost of capital.

$$(1)\ X = [1.05\,(16 \times 10^6) - (16 \times 10^6)]\,(1 - 0.46) + \left(\frac{15}{25}\right)144{,}000$$

$$+ \left(\frac{15}{25}\right)0.075\,(16 \times 10^6)\left(\frac{3}{12}\right)(1 - 0.46) + (50{,}000 - 30{,}000)\,0.46$$

$$= 432{,}000 + 86{,}400 + 97{,}200 + 9{,}200 = \$624{,}800$$

$$(2)\ Y = [0.08\,(16 \times 10^6) - 0.075\,(16 \times 10^6)]\,(1 - 0.46)$$

$$+\left(\frac{50{,}000}{15}\right)0.46 + \left(\frac{144{,}000}{25} - \frac{30{,}000}{15}\right)0.46$$

$$= 43{,}200 + 1{,}533.33 + 1{,}729.60 = \$46{,}462.93$$

$$(3)\ NPV = 46{,}462.93\left[\frac{1 - (1 + 0.0405)^{-15}}{0.0405}\right] - 624{,}800$$

$$= 46{,}462.93\,(11.079616) - 624{,}800$$

$$= 514{,}791.42 - 624{,}800 = -\$110{,}008.58$$

Since NPV is less than zero, management should reject refunding operations based on current data and forecasts. However, they may want to consider selling preferred stock as an alternative source.

FINANCING WITH PREFERRED STOCK

Finding the net present value of preferred stock means to compare the present value of outflows with present value of inflows; however, preferred stock shares characteristics of both debt and equity participation and while neither it is both—"legally equity, behaviorally debt"—like being named an honorary citizen—you are and are not and yet are both. Preferred stock only rates preference when dividends are paid, usually a fixed dividend rate expressed as a percentage of par value—only it is not legal debt of the firm—and when the business liquidates, over common stockholders, but preferred claims are junior to creditors. Because the preferred contract may be written with any variation of provisions necessary to sell the issue, it may at times more closely resemble a debt issue rather than an equity one, or it may be a hybrid of debt and equity, being interest sensitive rather than earnings sensitive.

Cumulative dividends mean that if a preferred dividend is passed, nonpayment accumulates and remains an obligation of the firm; *noncumulative* means that a passed dividend is lost forever. Other possible contract features may include *participation* which permit shareholders to participate in income on a stipulated basis, a *stock purchase warrant* may make a new issue more vendible and permit some lowering of the dividend rate, and a *convertible* feature which allows preferred to be converted into common stock according to some conversion ratio. Most preferreds contain a *callable* option or provide for retirement through a sinking fund, but premium paid over par is not tax deductible. A *standard call* generally restricts redemption during the first 5 years to exchange for common stock at a premium, then at 5-year intervals redemption prices are scaled down for perhaps 20 years at which time redemption price parallels issue price. A *conventional call* permits redemption any time on a one or two month notice but at a substantially higher premium plus accrued dividends. Advantages of preferreds include flexibility of financing, certain tax advantages to corporate investors, reduction of risks and contingent liabilities. Some disadvantages are that dividends are not tax deductible as interest expense, sharing or dilution of ownership, restrictive covenants. In recent years most preferred stocks have been issued by utility companies.

Cost of Preferred Stock

The simplest case of finding the cost of capital arising from preferred stock financing is to treat it as a perpetual obligation. Such treatment may provide an adequate estimate in most cases. The cost of capital is the expected dividend per share divided by price per share. No after-tax consideration is necessary since preferred dividends must be paid out of corporate income left over after everyone else—debtors, bondholders, and governments are paid off; that is, from earnings after interest and taxes (EAT).

Formula:

$$k_p = \frac{D}{Q}$$

Remember that Q represents net proceeds to the corporation, after flotation costs (Q = P - K), and D denotes dividends (per share) on preferred stock.

If a firm sells a new issue of preferred at 100, paying \$7.00, on which flotation costs are \$0.75 per share, what is the cost of funds to the issuing firm?

$$k_p = \frac{D}{P - K} = \frac{7.00}{100.00 - 0.75} = \frac{7.00}{99.25} = 7.053\%$$

Yield-to-Call Method

Call provisions, briefly summarized on preceding pages, are important in transactions of new and seasoned preferred stock. In the following *yield-to-call formula,* the firm's obligation is not a fixed 100 as in the case of bonds but fluctuates according to time and the corresponding call provisions; therefore, P, five years after an issue, is not the same P ten years after issue but will fall towards par value with time. Of course, government intervention in the money markets, inflation, changes in interest rates naturally affect values of financial instruments. In this example, we assume a stable market.

Formula:

$$k_p = \frac{D - \frac{1}{n}(M - P)}{\frac{P + M}{2}}$$

In the above, P, then, represents the call price, while M is the market price of the original transaction and n the number of years the stock is held. The annual dividend may be expressed dP* where d is a rate (%) and P* the par value and D = dP*.

Louisiana Power & Energy Company sold a new issue of 8½% cumulative preferreds at a market price of $112 per share to provide a current yield of 7.589%. After 5 years the stock is redeemable at $107. D = $8.50; n = 5; M = $112; P = $107. By the approximate yield-to-call method, the cost of capital solution is:

$$k_p = \frac{8.50 - \frac{1}{5}(112 - 107)}{\frac{107 + 112}{2}}$$

$$= \frac{7.50}{109.50} = 6.849\%$$

After-Tax Method

As of the time of writing the federal tax code allows taxable corporations to deduct 85 per cent of dividend income derived from investments in taxable corporations. To calculate the after-tax yield of a preferred stock investment, the formula is:

Formula:

$$k_p = \frac{D\,[1 - (h\,(1 - b))]}{M}$$

Once again D is the annual dividend, h the applicable tax rate, and M the purchase price or cost base. To ascertain the taxable rate on dividends, multiply the tax rate times (1 - b), where b equals the 85% allowable exemption on dividend income.

For example, assume that preferred stock pays an annual dividend of $7.75, purchased at 101, that the marginal tax rate is 48%, and that corporate dividend exemption rate is 85%.

$$k_p = \frac{7.75\ [1 - (0.48\ (1 - 0.85))]}{101}$$

$$= \frac{7.192}{101} = 7.121\%$$

Whether operations are financed with debt or preferred stock, the objective is to increase return to owners' equity (risk reduction through diversification of investments also increases "return" to owners' equity), but owners' equity in the form of common stock and retained corporate earnings, too, have a cost.

FINANCING WITH COMMON STOCK

There is probably no entirely satisfactory method for determining with complete accuracy the cost of either external or internal funds although various estimating techniques provide guidelines in management decisions. Common stock valuation is subject to even greater errors in dynamic situations, in spite of corrective formulations provided by the following three methods, because it is impossible to incorporate all significant variables into any model with any degree of confidence. The stock market exists apart from company operations and even if a stock's price fell to zero on the exchange the company remains a healthy, viable entity, although one model below binds book value to market price of stock. Capital market fluctuations, accounting procedures, cycles, cash flow, indirect operating expenses, investor psychology, economic and monetary forecasts, and many other factors affect both present valuations and future expectations. Nevertheless, the three methods below are quickly applicable in hand calculations, easy to understand, and furnish a reasonable short-cut to computations when coupled with common sense and knowledge of general economic conditions.

Calculations are on a per share basis, such as earnings per share (EPS), dividends per share (D), market price (M), or book value of common stock (P), rate of growth (%) on dividends or earnings (g), or rate of payout of earnings (1 - b); but it is also recognized that many of these variables can only be represented by approximations or estimates of their values. The starting point for computing the cost of equity capital (k_e) is to divide EPS by the market price (M) of the stock:

$$k_e = \frac{EPS}{M}$$

The reciprocal of k_e, that is, $\frac{1}{k_e}$, is the price-earnings (P/E) ratio, a rule-of-thumb approach that substitutes for analysis.* The first modification below considers the possibility of constant growth.

Gordon-Shapiro Method

About 20 years ago, a method, that probably originated over 100 years ago, has been refined and is referred to as the Gordon-Shapiro (G-S) growth stock model which assumes that a firm (this model especially fit several utility firms in the 1960s) continues to pay dividends (D) into an indefinite future and that earnings retained in the firm are invested at rate r to produce an annual growth rate g. The market price (M) of the stock will be:

$$M = \frac{D}{k_e - g}$$

The cost of capital, then, where k_e is treated as a dependent variable, is:

Formula:

$$k_e = \frac{D}{M} + g$$

Suppose that anticipated dividends of Redwood Leisure Furniture Co. are \$2.56 per share, that shares currently sell at \$32, and that the firm expects to maintain annual growth rate of 4%. What is the cost of equity funds?

$$k_e = \frac{2.56}{32.00} + 4\% = 8\% + 4\% = 12\%$$

One difficulty with this model is that in a high-growth situation where g exceeds k_e, the market price cannot be calculated. For example, if k_e is 8%, the market price of stock will be \$256 when growth rate g is 7%, but \$512 when g rises to 7½%, and (?) when g equals k_e. Another limitation arises from random market fluctuations which make it not a reliable analytical tool, because there is no dependable link between cause and effect of price changes. Too, the method assumes that all variables grow at a perpetual uniform rate, which became particularly significant for stocks that broke out of their patterns established in the previous decade.

On the positive side, the method assumes reinvestment of retained earnings at a positive rate of return plus capitalization of dividends. It encom-

*For a critical analysis of P/E ratios, vide: Thomas J. Holt, *Total Investing* (New Rochelle, N.Y.: Arlington House Publishers, 1976), especially Chapter 7.

passes anticipated dividend streams that rise in an approximate geometric pattern. Too, the price of stock depends upon expectations with regard to future growth of earnings and dividends. Of course, it is an extremely popular technique because it is easy to apply. Where new capital must be raised to finance a new project or management evaluates retirement of its own stock as an investment alternative, the method is particularly valuable.

New Issue Method

To develop cost of capital raised from a new stock issue, essentially the same as the G-S technique, explicitly account for flotation and underpricing costs which may range from 5 to 30 per cent. Management works with funds received regardless of how much purchasers paid for new common stock. Because of complex relationships between the firm's capital structure and capital markets which may severely discount the future, especially where markets are thin or limited for a specific issue, together with the expenses of obtaining funds, the cost of capital formula below employs Q, net proceeds to the firm, as an alternative.

Formula:

$$k_e = \frac{D}{M - K} + g, \text{ or, } k_e = \frac{D}{Q} + g$$

This method approximates the cost of new equity capital after deducting flotation costs (K) from the market price (M), which may have severely discounted the future, and adding a reasonable estimate of future growth prospects.

If Alu-Screen, Inc., a small manufacturer of aluminum door and window screens pays a 25-cent dividend per share per year, issues new stock for plant expansion at a market price of \$6.25, incurs flotation costs equal to 20% of the issue price (\$1.25), and 5% growth is projected, the cost of capital is:

$$k_e = \frac{0.25}{6.25 - 1.25} + 5\% = 5\% + 5\% = 10\%$$

However, if the market price of stock is linked to its book value, then the following method is of interest.

Lerner-Carleton Method

Expanding the G-S formulation, the Lerner-Carleton (L-C) method focuses on the relationships between market value (M) and book value (P) of common stock, where:

$$\frac{M}{P} = \frac{r - rb}{k_e - rb}$$

The rb (equals g in the G-S model) is the rate at which EPS, dividends per share, and book value are growing; (1 - b) is the dividend payout ratio, where b represents the percentage of earnings per share retained in the corporation.

Formula:

$$k_e = \frac{(1 - b)\, rP}{M} + rb$$

The problem with this method is that the r in the numerator is the rate of return on book value, that is, an average based on historical values; while the r in the denominator apparently represents a marginal rate of return on expected investment, the most important variable that relates to capital budgeting. Too, other limitations in the whole area of estimating values apply here as well. On the plus side, the method does link market value and book value per share, which are seldom identical because of separation of markets.

By way of illustration, we can utilize data from Redwood Leisure Furniture Co. in which the market price was $32. Let's say that the dividend payout ratio is 50%, book value is $40 per share, and rate of return on book value of equity is 12.8%.

$$k_e = \frac{(1 - 0.50)\, 0.128\, (40)}{32} + 0.128\, (0.50)$$

$$= \frac{2.56}{32} + 0.064 = 14.4\%$$

To check results and correct application of the formula, notice that when (r - rb) exceeds (k_e - rb), the market price (M) will be greater than book value (P) per share. Since (0.128 - 0.64) is less than (0.144 - 0.064), then the market price should be under book value, which it is. Of course, changes in k_e take place continually and independent of r, and dividend policy may be adjusted until they are equal, which is supposed to be the point where the price of a share is maximized, *ceteris paribus.* As long as the firm can generate a return on its funds (r, the rate of return on book value) greater than the cost of equity funds (k_e) calculated on the market price, then the market price will rise; i.e., if $r > k_e$, then M will rise, and if $r < k_e$, M will fall. Where $r > k_e$, the policy suggestion is that the firm should increase its investments (assuming no change in risk) which will pressure the marginal return downward.

Mean Annual Yields Method

This technique focuses on the average annual yields of common stock. (The technique can also be applied to preferred stock or bonds.) The first step in the *mean annual yields method* is to find the short-term k_e, say, for a period of one year; i.e., what are the historical annual yields over some period of time? The second step is to calculate the geometric means of these short-period rates. The major limitation of this approach is that past performance is an inadequate guide for tomorrow's performance. A second limitation is that data from five or more years, preferably more, should enter into calculations.

To begin, the first step is to compute short-term yields:

Formula:

$$k_e = \frac{D + M_2}{M_1} - 1$$

To calculate average annual yields, employ year-end prices. However, where annual price fluctuations are not great, the annual mean price may be substituted. Opening and closing prices are preferable and will produce substantially divergent results where prices have moved widely and wildly between opening and closing periods. If year-end market prices are employed, the market price at the end of the second year, M_2, is added to the annual dividend per share. This sum is divided by the market price at the end of the first year, M_1, minus 1, to give k_e (expressed in per cent). The yield may be positive or negative.

For example, assume that the market price of Rogue River Travel Trailer stock at the end of the first year (which is the same as the beginning of the second year) is 57, and 65 a year later; the annual dividend is \$2; the arithmetic is:

$$k_e = \frac{2 + 65}{57} - 1 = 17.54\%$$

But if price had fallen, not risen, by more than the amount of dividend, the result would be negative. The purpose of averaging several years, 5, 10, or more, is to smooth out these sharp changes that may occur with stock prices in the market.

In the accompanying table, Figure 4-2, exhibiting data on Southern Natural Resources, Inc., for years 6 through 15, to find annual yield (column 3), add the average year 7 stock price ($39\frac{7}{8}$) to year 7 dividends (1.30). For this first calculation we will need year 6 average price ($30\frac{1}{8}$)

Figure 4-2

MEAN ANNUAL YIELDS AND STANDARD DEVIATION
SOUTHERN NATURAL RESOURCES, INC.

Year	*Dividends (1)*	*Annual Mean Price* (2)*	*Annual Yield (%) (3)*	*Column (3) Less Mean (10.364%) (4)*	*Column (4) Squared (5)*
6		30⅛			
7	1.30	39⅞	+36.680	+26.316	692.53186
8	1.40	46⅞	+21.066	+10.702	114.53280
9	1.40	44¾	- 1.547	-11.911	141.87192
10	1.40	48⅞	+12.346	+ 1.982	3.92832
11	1.40	49¼	+ 3.632	- 6.732	45.31982
12	1.45	54	+12.589	+ 2.225	4.95063
13	1.50	54⅜	+ 3.472	- 6.892	47.49966
14	1.58	41⅜	-21.002	-31.366	983.82596
15	1.65	50½	+26.042	+15.678	245.79968
	TOTALS		+93.278		2280.2607

Average = 93.278 ÷ 9 = 10.364%
Variance = 2280.2607 ÷ 9 = 253.362%
Standard deviation (σ) $\sqrt{253.362}$ = 15.917%

*Instead of using beginning of and end of year prices, as recommended, calculations were based on calendar year mean price adjusted to nearest one-eighth.

which is divided into the above. From this result, subtract 1, which yields 0.36680, or 36.680%. Annual yields in years 9 and 14 are negative because the annual average stock market price dipped more than the dividend paid in each of those years.

Then, to designate a single figure that represents a 9-year average, add data in column 3 (both positive and negative), which is 93.278 in this example, divide by 9 to obtain the mean of 10.364%.

Each figure in column 4 is found by subtracting the mean (10.364%) from the corresponding number in column 3. Column 5 figures are column 4 ones squared. Add column 4 results, divide by 9, to obtain the variance. The square root of 253.362% gives us the desired *historical cost of capital,* 15.917%.

The method can be applied to any historical study—bonds, preferred or common stocks—if history is relevant to the future or as a means of checking on past decisions, and, too, it incorporates risk measurement, an advantage over alternative methods. So far, of course, we have concentrated on the cost of external funds. Internal savings, also, represent a source of funds.

FINANCING WITH RETAINED EARNINGS

Retained earnings, certainly not a free gift of nature, should serve common stockholders, residual owners of the business. Essentially there are only two decisions with respect to net earnings generated by a firm—either pay them out as dividends or retain them for reinvestment in new assets or reduction of obligations or outstanding stock. The opportunity cost (discussed more fully in Chapter Six) represents opportunities foregone from the stockholders' viewpoint. If use of retained earnings by the firm does not measure up to alternatives available to individual investors, then investors will sell their holdings to invest proceeds in more lucrative opportunities. Enough sales will depress prices. Nevertheless, there are tax differentials which complicate decisions. Except for minor exclusions, dividends are taxable at the marginal tax rate of the investor, while capital gains resulting from reinvested retained earnings result in a lower tax rate (still applicable at the date of writing). This differential works out to about 10% for the "average" investor, which, in turn, provides the firm with a margin favoring retention of earnings. But investor psychology does change and current preferences tilt toward higher current income from dividends in spite of the tax disadvantage.

Actually it is not necessary to separately compute the cost of retained earnings from profits earned in previous periods because historical results are already included in the price of existing common stock, and future expectations have already been discounted in the market. Previous formulas projected future dividends and growth. Growth partially results from reinvested earnings, reflected in stock prices. Nevertheless, for the individual stockholder he must confront his personal tax situation and make his peace with local, state, federal, and foreign governments. Therefore, the following formula treats income received from dividends (D) at the personal tax rate (h_p) and income derived from capital gains at a different tax rate (h_c), and M remains the market price.

Formula:

$$k_r = \frac{(1 - h_p)\,D}{(1 - h_c)\,M}$$

For example, an investor owns stock in Western Ride Company, manufacturer, importer, and distributor of equestrian paraphernalia, which trades locally at \$25 per share and pays \$1.50 dividend. The investor's marginal tax rate on ordinary income is 40% and 20% on capital gains (long-term). Before taxes, the cost of retained earnings is 6.0% (or to a tax-exempt investor the cost is, also, 6.0%). The required rate of return for an investor in the 40% bracket ($h_p = 0.40$) is:

$$k_r = \frac{(1 - 0.40)\,1.50}{(1 - 0.20)\,25.00} = \frac{0.90}{20.00} = 4.5\%$$

which is a "cutoff" rate for capital budgeting purposes but it does not signal whether funds should be reinvested. To solve the dilemma between the tax exempt investor and the one in a high income tax bracket, the solution is to opt to meet minimum requirements of the tax exempt investor so that he will be no worse off while all other investors will be better off.

To account for growth, the formula can be modified:

Formula:

$$k_r = k_e \frac{(1 - h_p)}{(1 - h_c)}$$

Return to data in the Alu-Screen, Inc. example where D = 25¢, M = \$5, and g = 5%; k_e = 10%. Still assuming that h_p = 40%, and h_c = 20%,

$$k_r = 0.10 \frac{0.60}{0.80} = 7.5\%$$

If the firm retains and reinvests its earnings at an adequate rate, the price of the stock should rise. There are, however, other available financing instruments.

FINANCING WITH RIGHTS

With the special case of *rights* offerings, where stock is offered only to existing stockholders, a privileged subscription, if all existing shareholders acquiesce then their prorata participation in the business remains unchanged. In order for the market price of the stock not to drop, capitalized earnings from new funds must increase the market value of new funds to match pre-offering earnings conditions. The appropriate cost of funds equals that which was derived for the general common stock instance; and this analysis would be true whether rights are sold (owners are selling part of their equity) or not. For the case where some rights are sold, James Mao suggests this formulation:

Formula:
$$k_{er} = \frac{N_0 N_2}{(N_0 + N_1)(N_1 + N_2)} i \frac{M_0}{M'} + \frac{N(N_1 M' - N_2 a M_r)}{(N_0 + N_1)(N_1 + N_2) M'} i$$

If one can keep his Ms and Ns from melding, the formula presents no difficulty.

N_0 = number of existing shares

N_1 = number of new shares sold to existing shareholders

N_2 = number of new shares sold to new investors

N = total number of shares—old (N_0) plus new ($N_1 + N_2$)

M_0 = current market price of stock per share on-right

M' = subscription price of new shares

M_r = value of one right

a = the subscription ratio

i = rate of return required by shareholders

To understand the computations, assume that a non-growth company has 10 million shares outstanding (N_0) whose shareholders demand a 12% return (i) and proposes to issue 1 million shares ($N_1 + N_2$) in new stock. Current shareholders have the preemptive right to subscribe to new shares on a proportionate basis of 1 new for each 10 of old (a = 10) at a subscription price of \$42 (M). Assume that existing owners decide to purchase N_1, or 50%, of new shares (= 500,000), and sell remaining rights so that N_2 (500,000) shares are bought by outsiders. Because the current *on-right* market price is \$53, the value of each right (M_2) is \$1.

$$M_r = \frac{M - M'}{a + 1} = \frac{53 - 42}{10 + 1} = \$1$$

Summarizing, the values are:
N_0 = 10,000,000 shares; $N_1 + N_2$ = 1,000,000; N_1 = 500,000; N_2 = 500,000; N = 11,000,000; M_0 = \$53 (on-right); M' = \$42 (subscription price); M_r = \$1; a = 10; i = 12%. Substituting values into the formula,

$$k_{er} = \frac{(10{,}000{,}000)\,(500{,}000)}{(10{,}000{,}000 + 500{,}000)\,(500{,}000 + 500{,}000)}\,0.12\,\frac{53}{42}$$

$$+ \frac{11{,}000{,}000\,[(500{,}000 \times 42) - (500{,}000 \times 10 \times 1)]}{(10{,}000{,}000 + 500{,}000)\,(500{,}000 + 500{,}000)\,42}\,0.12$$

$$= 4.7619 \times 10^{-1}\,(0.1514) + 3.9909 \times 10^{-1}\,(0.12)$$

$$= 7.2095 \times 10^{-2} + 4.7891 \times 10^{-2} = 0.12 = 12\%$$

FUNDING WITH DEPRECIATION

In addition to rights, another situation concerns depreciation and non-cash expenses. These provide a source of funds in profitable situations but do not exhibit separate costs because these funds originate from a mixture of sources already discussed. If this conclusion bothers the reader, it is reasonable to assume that the cost of capital from depreciation funds equals the overall cost of capital; ergo, it need not be calculated separately. But to tally the cost of capital from all sources, the favored technique is to consider the proportion of capital contributed by each category of sources.

FINDING WEIGHTED AVERAGE COST OF CAPITAL

To measure the cost of capital, it is not practical to simply calculate the cost of a component linked to a particular investment simply because rates fluctuate and would signal a rather erratic investment process. On the other hand, an unweighted arithmetic mean would only give correct results if the proportion of funds from each source were equal. The problem is that all financing must begin from some equity base. One of the first questions a banker wants answered: How much of the risk are you assuming? No rational investor wants to assume more risk without participating in benefits and all would like the enviable position of governments which share in benefits without accepting risks (i.e., taxation). The issue of risk and leverage are discussed in more detail in the following chapter; at this juncture we simply want to learn the weighting procedure in order to calculate the cost of capital from all sources. Rather than construct a lengthy and complicated formula, the computational steps are more quickly grasped in tabular form. For this we will return to the example of the International Energy Corporation.

Case Study: (B) What is IEC's weighted average cost of capital?

Recall that International Energy Corporation sold \$6 million of 8% bonds at 92, in 1979, due in 20 years, on which we calculated the after-tax cost of bonds at 4.9875%. Other bonds outstanding are \$4 million in 6%

mortgage bonds issued in 1970, due in 1990, which currently trade at 84. A summary of all long-term liabilities and equity appear in Figure 4-3.

Figure 4-3

Capital Structure (Source of funds)	*Balance Sheet Figures \$ (000)*	*Market Value (per unit)*	*Proportion (%)*	*After-tax Component Cost (%)*	*Weighted Cost (%)*
6% Mortgage Bonds (due 1990)	4,000	84	10.26	4.480	0.460
8% Bonds (due 1999)	6,000	92	15.38	4.988	0.767
7½% Preferred Stock	1,000	97	2.56	7.732	0.198
Common Equity	28,000	21	71.80	13.762	9.881
TOTAL	\$39,000		100.00%		11.306%

Due to its multinational operations, the current marginal tax rate is 43%. Although present and anticipated near-term dividends are only \$1 per share, analysts peg the combination of management, technology, and subsidies to turn investors' dollars into 9% annual growth.

The method to calculate the weighted average cost of capital (k_w) is to compute first individual components of the capital structure, which results appear in the next-to-last column in Figure 4-3. These results are multiplied by the percentage contribution of each component to total capital structure to reflect weighted costs of each. Totaling weighted costs render an average weighted cost of capital derived from all sources of 11.306%.

Caveat

The widely applied capital budgeting decision rule is to accept an investment alternative if its after-tax rate of return is not less than the firm's weighted average cost of capital. It is further thought that minimization of the weighted average cost of capital will result in an optimal financing structure. But, in practice, k_w should serve as a guide post, not an automatic decision-maker. Decisions, and responsibility for success or failure of undertakings, originate with individuals, reflecting human action taken in a given situation according to incomplete data, faulty estimates, and imperfect foreknowledge available.

Cost of capital is based on estimates, inadequate interpretation of past, present, and future events, definitions (assumptions), and activities beyond direct influence of the firm's management. Differences between the weighted average cost of capital and the true cost may result from divergence of market and book values, proportional changes in capital structure, or a new set of risk characteristics. And certainly before-tax methods will lead to a capital structure different from after-tax methods, neither of which may produce an optimal finance mix.

All debt financing must be built on some equity base. If employment of funds acquired from alternative sources did not raise yield to common stockholders' equity, then decision-rules would be less complicated. After all, common stockholders' interests should be paramount, and investments undertaken should contribute at least toward maintaining the minimum return required by shareholders. At the same time in seeking higher yield opportunities, management is also faced with increasing risk to common stockholders. Cost of equity funds may well be broken down into three components: a *risk-free rate* (i), a premium for *business risk* (β), a premium for *financial risk* (ϕ).

Formula:

$$k_e = i + \beta + \phi$$

If a business aggressively pursues projects which significantly raise marginal risk, the cost of capital is directly affected and both equity and nonequity costs will rise. Similarly, the method chosen to finance additional projects increases or decreases risk to a firm's operations. Although a highly leveraged firm may appear to meet common stockholders' minimum financial objectives, increasing the proportion of debt-to-equity raises other issues, the possibility of other consequences.

CONTENTS

Chapter Five: Converting Debt to Profit–A Sensible Approach to Leverage and Risk

PAGE

FIVE

Converting Debt to Profit-
A Sensible Approach
to Leverage and Risk

Behind "precise" calculations developed in these chapters are data evolved from estimates, guestimates, and imprecisely interpreted information about the past, present, and an imperfectly known future. "The Past is like a funeral gone by, The Future comes like an unwelcome guest."* Frequently, rate of return and cost of capital computations encompass an average of opinions which evince varying reliabilities and wide range of probabilities; that is, these computations may be subject to a high degree of uncertainty, which means that forecasted earnings can widely miss projected targets. In spite of this fuzziness, decisions must be made, a financing mix decided upon.

---

*Edmund Gosse, *May-Day*.

The technique of production and combination of debt and equity selected add more or less risk to the project's possible outcomes. When sales, costs, and demand estimates point toward a high return, the decision-maker needs to know explicitly which risks he undertakes and which additional ones he assumes with various financing possibilities. *Business risk* is the dispersion of operating income. *Financial risk* covers not only variability of earnings to common shareholders but also risk of ruin, the chance of insolvency. A firm expanding lease commitments, proportion of debt, and preferred financing, also swells its fixed charges. Are sales and earnings appraisals sufficiently accurate to cover these charges even with the worst possible outcome? Can a business influence its cost of capital and total valuation by changing its finance mix, the degree of leverage?

This chapter zeroes in on leveraging for profits rather than chancey high-flying. The *leverage ratio* is measured by the rate of growth in earnings available to common stock equity to the rate of growth of earnings before interest and taxes. In other words, if total capitalization is not altered but the amount of fixed or limited charge securities is varied relative to the proportion of equity capital employed in financing, how are earnings per share of common stock affected? What additional risks do owners assume? Pearson Hunt proposes that we define *trading on the equity* as "the use of fixed (or limited) charge securities in the capitalization of a company, measured by the ratio of (1) the rate of return on the existing common-stock equity to (2) the rate of return on the entire capitalization as it would have been if there were only common stock outstanding."* In theory, management should finance with debt until reaching an optimal capital structure to equate marginal real cost of debt to equity. In practice, this chapter aims toward the best capital structure according to best information available to management.

LEVERAGING FOR MORE PROFITS

Leverage (or "trading-on-equity" or "gearing") provides the means to obtain more mileage out of equity. To lever implies that a firm, or investor, employs borrowed funds at a rate higher than their cost with the objective of raising return on investment and total value of the enterprise. Interest on borrowing, generally touted as a cheaper source of funds, is a tax deductible expense; to a point, increasing the corporation's debt will lower overall cost of capital (discussed in Chapter Four). In the past 10-to-15 years firms have felt pressure from powerful institutional investors to push up the proportion of debt to equity as a means to improve earnings per share. Too, a low-debt firm has tended to attract leveraged-minded managers of conglomerates so

---

*Pearson Hunt, "A Proposal for Precise Definitions of 'Trading on the Equity' and 'Leverage'," *Journal of Finance* 16 (Sept., 1961), p. 379.

that a low-leveraged firm has invited takeover attempts—the price of cautiously minding one's own business. On the other hand, excessive leverage breeds risk, the risk of insolvency. Sooner or later, accumulating more debt will no longer raise the firm's income, and its traded value, but will actually reduce total worth of the business. More recent trends suggest that with increased uncertainty of the future, and predicted erratic income behavior, management has restored financial conservatism, reduced leverage, and tended to rely on internally generated or equity funds for capital expansion. This section of the chapter spotlights two aspects of leverage—operating and financial leverage—and then returns to further comments on the risk of ruin.

Operating Leverage

Although most operations can proceed with one of several possible combinations of labor services and capital investment, concerns tend to opt for that theoretical least-cost combination of inputs which depends not only on costs of factor inputs but also on various risks associated with operations, stock-outs of inventories, unforeseen contingencies too manifold to account for individually, customer reactions to products in different marketing areas, cash flows, scheduling, etc.—all of which add something to costs, explicit or implicit, so that the best combination of resource employment may well be any of several possible acceptable alternatives. Here let us grapple with the division between fixed and variable costs and probabilities of achieving different sales levels and earnings per share.

Let's assume that Klammath Falls Mfg. Co., Inc. studies the possibility of *additional* investment that will churn out a product that can be sold for $15 per unit. *Variable costs* vary directly with output; the more the firm produces, the higher variable costs will climb. *Fixed costs* do not change with output; they remain constant, in a fixed amount, regardless of production between zero and capacity. Obviously, at low outputs not all costs are covered but as production expands it reaches a break-even point where income meets expenditures. By formula, the break-even point is: Divide total fixed costs by the difference between price per unit and variable cost per unit.

Formula:

$$\text{BEP} = \frac{C_f}{p - c_v}$$

C_f = Total fixed costs (TFC).

p = price of each unit of product sold.

c_v = variable cost per unit of product produced.

Fixed costs provide the advantage of additional leverage to operational profits; i.e., the presence of fixed investment may yield higher earnings per share than otherwise. However, always recalling that everything bears a cost, fixed investment carries with it additional responsibilities, risks of illiquidity. Therefore, a firm that accelerates fixed investment because of technology, higher wages which result in labor substitution, or some other reason, induces a variance in net operating income that exceeds the variance in sales. Of course, the above break-even formula also indicates that no operating leverage or break-even point arises without fixed costs. For example, if a firm has fixed costs of $10,000 (which are constant at all outputs) and variable costs per unit of $3 on a product that sells for $5 each, the break-even point of operations is:

$$\text{BEP} = \frac{10{,}000}{5 - 3} = 5{,}000 \text{ units}$$

Returning to the Klammath Falls Mfg. Co., Inc. example, how many additional units can it sell at $15 each? Predicting (guessing at) the future may be approached with a simple probability distribution. There is a 25% chance that only 100,000 units of product will sell, a 50% possibility that buyers will purchase 150,000 units, or a 25% likelihood that the market will absorb as many as 200,000 units. In other words, we don't know precisely what the final outcome will be. But we figure the firm can market 150,000 units, given 50/50 odds.

To finance this additional investment, let's conjecture that the business acquires 100% of the needed $2,000,000 from the sale of 100,000 shares of common stock at $20 per share so that there are no interest costs. The Table in Figure 5–1 summarizes three sales levels. Notice that variable costs rise with sales; fixed costs remain a constant $250,000 in case A. Case A depicts low operating leverage; i.e., fixed investment is low, while variable per unit costs are high. If the firm should suddenly close down case A operations, most of its costs would disappear.

In Figure 5–1, earnings before taxes (EBT) is derived by subtracting variable and fixed costs from sales revenue. From EBT, taxes (T), calculated at 48%, are deducted. Earnings after taxes (EAT) are divided by the number of additional shares outstanding to determine earnings per share (EPS). The best possibility of earning $3.90 per share exceeds the least likely one ($1.30) by only three times. Compare these calculations with Figure 5–2. Case B exhibits higher operating leverage. Earnings vary considerably more, ranging from a low likelihood of $0.52 per share to a high of $4.68.

This greater variance, which ranges considerably outside of the possibilities in case A, emanates from nearly three times as much investment in fixed assets, from $250,000 in case A to $700,000 in case B. If, by some chance,

Figure 5-1

OPERATING LEVERAGE
(100% equity)
(Case A)

Probability of Sales	*0.25*	*0.50*	*0.25*
Volume (units)	100,000	150,000	200,000
Sales (@ $15 per unit)	+$1,500,000	+$2,250,000	+$3,000,000
Variable Costs (@ $10 per unit)	- 1,000,000	- 1,500,000	- 2,000,000
Total Fixed Costs	- 250,000	- 250,000	- 250,000
Earnings Before Taxes (EBT)	+$ 250,000	+$ 500,000	+$ 750,000
Taxes (T) (48%)	- 120,000	- 240,000	- 360,000
Earnings After Taxes (EAT)	+$ 130,000	+$ 260,000	+$ 390,000
EPS (100,000 shares)	$1.30	$2.60	$3.90

EPS = earnings per share

sales dipped much below 100,000 units, say, to 80,000 units, the firm would lose money in the high operating leverage situation (B) while sales would have to drop below 50,000 units before losses spring up in the low operating leverage (A) situation. In other words, a smaller safety margin cushions

Figure 5-2

OPERATING LEVERAGE
(100% equity)
(Case B)

Probability of Sales	*0.25*	*0.50*	*0.25*
Volume (units)	100,000	150,000	200,000
Sales (@ $15 per unit)	+$1,500,000	+$2,250,000	+$3,000,000
Variable Costs ($7 per unit)	- 700,000	- 1,050,000	- 1,400,000
Total Fixed Costs	- 700,000	- 700,000	- 700,000
EBT	+$ 100,000	+$ 500,000	+$ 900,000
T (48%)	- 48,000	- 240,000	- 432,000
EAT	+$ 52,000	+$ 260,000	+$ 468,000
EPS (100,000 shares)	$0.52	$2.60	$4.68

possible errors in case B. But higher risks also suggest greater possibility of larger profits. The best estimate of earnings per share in case B exceeds the worse estimate nine times.

Now let's apply the above formula to calculate break-even points.

$$BEP_a = \frac{250{,}000}{15 - 10} = 50{,}000 \text{ units}$$

$$BEP_b = \frac{700{,}000}{15 - 7} = 87{,}500 \text{ units}$$

We want to know the rate of change in net operating income in relation to a change in sales. By how much will net operating income increase if sales rise by some per cent? This ratio is called the *degree of operating leverage* (DOL).

Formula:

$$DOL = \frac{N}{N - BEP}$$

The degree of operating leverage at some specific output (N) is the ratio of the percentage change in net operating income divided by the percentage change in sales. Since we have already calculated break-even points for each case, let us now determine the degree of operating leverage at an output of 100,000 units.

$$DOL_{a,100{,}000} = \frac{100{,}000}{100{,}000 - 50{,}000} = 2$$

$$DOL_{b,100{,}000} = \frac{100{,}000}{100{,}000 - 87{,}500} = 8$$

What do these figures connote? Assuming linear relationships, the DOL equals 2 means that a 10% increase in sales will bring about a 20% rise in net operating income, a relationship of 2-to-1; while 8 signifies that a 10% upsurge in sales will produce an 80% jump in net operating income. The degree of operating leverage is significantly higher in case B over case A, which was already apparent from above tables. When output in B-type operations mounts from sales of $1,500,000 to $2,250,000, an advance of 50%, the DOL equals 8 suggests that net operating income ascend about 400%, which it does.

Imagine, however, that the break-even point has not been derived. What is the formula for calculating the degree of operating leverage (DOL) at output N?

Formula:

$$DOL_N = \frac{N(p - c_v)}{N(p - c_v) - C_f}$$

The symbols stand for the same as above: a given output (N); price per unit (p); variable cost per unit (c_v); total fixed costs (C_f). Substituting values from case B, output of 100,000 units, we have

$$DOL_{b,100,000} = \frac{100{,}000\,(15 - 7)}{100{,}000\,(15 - 7) - 700{,}000} = 8$$

Now observe what occurs at higher outputs. Moving away from the break-even point lowers the degree of operating leverage; i.e., the higher the output the less each further increase in sales will magnify net operating income. Staying with case B, look at what happens to the DOL when output shifts further away from the break-even point of 87,500 units to sales of 150,000 units.

$$DOL_{b,150,000} = \frac{150{,}000\,(15 - 7)}{150{,}000\,(15 - 7) - 700{,}000} = 2.4$$

At this point of operations, less can be squeezed out of the situation because a 10% advance in sales will now only result in a 24% ascent in net operating income instead of 80%. And at an even higher production of 200,000 units, the DOL will decline to 1.78 for case B. If the firm wants to achieve even wider swings in income, then the return to common stockholders pivots on debt financing.

Financial Leverage

Financial leverage refers to some mix of debt and equity.* A highly leveraged firm relies on debt financing as long as the cost of borrowed funds is

---

*For a discussion on leverage and the MM model, vide: Alexander A. Robichek and Stewart C. Myers, *Optimal Financing Decisions* (Englewood Cliffs, N.J.: Prentice-Hall, Inc., 1965), pp. 20–50.

less than yield to common stockholders so that return on equity rises. To illustrate the effects of financial leverage, let us continue with the same above examples and present results again in tabular form, Figure 5-3.

Financing with Bonds

Instead of new investment financed entirely with equity capital, assume a financial mix of 50% equity and 50% bonded indebtedness. The company now issues 50,000 shares of common stock (instead of 100,000 shares as before) at $20 per share for one-half the needed $1,000,000, and sells 9%, 20-year bonds, at par, to raise the other $1,000,000. Fixed charges now climb by the amount of annual interest payments due on the bonds; namely, $90,000.

Figure 5-3.

FINANCIAL LEVERAGE–I
(50% debt)
(Case A)

Probability of Sales	*0.25*	*0.50*	*0.25*
Volume (Units)	100,000	150,000	200,000
Sales ($15 per unit)	$1,500,000	$2,250,000	$3,000,000
EBIT	+$ 250,000	+$ 500,000	+$ 750,000
I (9% bonds)	- 90,000	- 90,000	- 90,000
EBT	+$ 160,000	+$ 410,000	+$ 660,000
T (48%)	- 76,800	- 196,800	- 316,800
EAT	+$ 83,200	+$ 213,200	+$ 343,200
EPS (50,000 shares)	$1.66	$4.26	$6.86

EBIT = earnings before interest and taxes (same as EBT from preceding tables).
I = Interest.
EBT = earnings before taxes.
T = taxes.
EAT = earnings after taxes.
EPS = earnings per share.

In Figure 5-3 (case A), earnings before interest and taxes (EBIT) correspond to earnings before taxes (EBT) in earlier tables, except that now, to arrive at EBT, fixed interest charges of $90,000 ($1,000,000 X 9%) are subtracted from EBIT. The applicable tax rate remains 48%. Obviously, earnings after taxes (EAT) will now be lower at all sales levels, but earnings per share (EPS) rise because there are only one-half as many new shares outstanding. Dividing EAT by number of shares (50,000) results in EPS. The expected EPS must promise to surpass that offered to creditors in order to compensate common shareholders for additional risk assumed through funding operations. Bondholders, in part, are compensated for their risk-bearing function by being granted priority on claims on both income and assets. The essence of obtaining some funds at a fixed annual cost is that shareholders reap financial benefits from debt employment.

Figure 5-4

FINANCIAL LEVERAGE–I
(50% debt)
(Case B)

Probability of Sales	*0.25*	*0.50*	*0.25*
Sales ($15 per unit)	$1,500,000	$2,250,000	$3,000,000
EBIT	+$ 100,000	+$ 500,000	+$ 900,000
I	- 90,000	- 90,000	- 90,000
EBT	+$ 10,000	+$ 410,000	+$ 810,000
T (48%)	- 4,800	- 196,800	- 388,800
EAT	+$ 5,200	+$ 213,200	+$ 421,200
EPS (50,000 shares)	$0.10	$4.26	$8.42

With case B, Figure 5-4, the lower estimate comes dangerously close to generating just sufficient earnings to cover interest costs. The high opinion promises to supply earnings to common stockholders more than 80 times the lower end of the scale. As the firm becomes more highly leveraged, the possibility of bigger profits, of course, prevail, but variance among possible outcomes also gains ground until results become boundless, bouncing beyond limits of reason, with additional injections of hyperactive leverage. With results of case B available, we can now compute the *degree of financial leverage* (DFL) by applying a simple formula.

Formula:

$$DFL = \frac{EBIT}{EBIT - I}$$

Which states that the degree of financial leverage equals earnings before interest and taxes (EBIT) divided by earnings after payment of interest (I) and before payment of taxes. For A and B, at outputs of 100,000 units, the degree of financial leverage is:

$$DFL_{a,100,000} = \frac{250,000}{250,000 - 90,000} = 1.56$$

$$DFL_{b,100,000} = \frac{100,000}{100,000 - 90,000} = 10.00$$

If interest charges rise (which decreases the denominator) relative to net operating income, the degree of financial leverage increases. Relating this to a times-interest coverage ratio (more on ratios in Chapter Twelve), the more that interest payments are covered the lower the degree of financial leverage. As long as EBIT outpace fixed charges, then any change in the rate of return on total capitalization can be converted into a change in the rate of return on the equity portion of capitalization. To accomplish this conversion, multiply the rate of return on total capitalization by $\frac{1}{b}$ (where b represents percentage of equity). For example, if the first rate advances from 8% to 10%, and the equity ratio is 50%, then the ratio $\frac{\text{Residual}}{b}$ will gain by 4% (where residual represents earnings available to common shareholders).

However, these examples actually employ two types of leverage—operating and financial—which directs us to combined effects of these production and financing possibilities. The combined effect (CE) formula at a specific output (N) ties in information already given:

Formula: $$CE_N = \frac{N(p - c_v)}{N(p - c_v) - C_f - I}$$

N = number of units sold.

p = price per unit.

c_v = variable cost (per unit).

C_f = total fixed costs.

I = total dollar amount of interest paid on debt.

Calculations of the combined effect from above examples are:

$$CE_{a,100,000} = \frac{100,000\,(15 - 10)}{100,000(15 - 10) - 250,000 - 90,000} = 3.13$$

$$CE_{b,100,000} = \frac{100,000\,(15 - 7)}{100,000(15 - 7) - 700,000 - 90,000} = 80$$

$$CE_{b,150,000} = \frac{150,000\,(15 - 7)}{150,000(15 - 7) - 700,000 - 90,000} = 2.93$$

The degree of leverage depends on not only the combination of factors of production employed and amount of fixed charges but also point of analysis. With case B the full effect of leverage cannot be realized at low levels of output, and degree of leverage declines sharply when output rises by 50%.

Financing with Preferreds

From the viewpoint of improving return to common stockholders, little difference may stand between financing investments with debt or preferred stock, although discussions in the preceding chapter set forth differences in explicit costs.

If operations are financed by a mix of debt, preferred and common stock, the formula for finding the degree of financial leverage is:

Formula:

$$DFL = \frac{EBIT}{EBIT - \left[I + \left(\frac{D_p}{(1 - h)} \right) \right]}$$

Modifying the case A (50% debt) illustration above, posit that interest charges (I) are now $45,000, annual dividends payable to preferred owners (D_p) equals $45,000, the tax rate is 48% (h), while EBIT remain at $250,000.

$$DFL = \frac{250,000}{250,000 - \left(45,000 + \frac{45,000}{0.52}\right)} = 2.11$$

Figure 5-5 data sum up effects on earnings per share if 7% cumulative preferreds are substituted for bonded debt. For case A possibilities behavior of EPS projections varies only slightly from debt financing; with leverage magnified in case B, results are volatile.

Without interest payments, earnings before taxes (EBT) corresponds to

Figure 5-5

FINANCIAL LEVERAGE–II
(50% preferred)

Probability of Sales	*0.25*	*0.50*	*0.25*
Sales Volume (units)	*100,000*	*150,000*	*200,000*
Sales ($15 per unit)	*$1,500,000*	*$2,250,000*	*$3,000,000*

	Case A		
EBT	+$ 250,000	+$ 500,000	+$ 750,000
T (48%)	- 120,000	- 240,000	- 360,000
EAT	+$ 130,000	+$ 260,000	+$ 390,000
D_p	- 70,000	- 70,000	- 70,000
Residual	+$ 60,000	+$ 190,000	+$ 320,000
EPS (50,000 shares)	$1.20	$3.80	$6.40

	Case B		
EBT	+$ 100,000	+$ 500,000	+$ 900,000
T (48%)	- 48,000	- 240,000	- 432,000
EAT	+$ 52,000	+$ 260,000	+$ 468,000
D_p	- 52,000*	- 70,000	- 70,000
Residual	–0–	+$ 190,000	+$ 398,000
EPS (50,000 shares)	$0.00*	$3.80	$7.96

D_p = dividends on preferred (7% cumulative*)
Residual = amount of earnings available to common shareholders

EBIT used previously. The tax rate is still 48%. However, 7% preferred dividends (D_p) are paid from earnings after taxes (EAT), a sum of $70,000 annually. Because preferred dividend obligations cumulate, notice that in the first column under case B only $52,000, instead of $70,000, are paid out due to inadequate earnings. The remaining $18,000 accrues to the following year imposing further obligations on the firm unless sales increase by about 2,300 units at the going price. If the first situation under case B had arisen with the debt issue, we would show EPS as -$0.36; but preferred dividends are not obligations in the same manner as interest. Common stock owners have a right to participate in residual earnings in the form of dividends (if any) or capital gains.

EFFECTS OF OPERATING AND FINANCIAL LEVERAGE

For quick comparison of the effects of operating and financial leverage, six graphs in Figure 5-6 abstract cases A and B, in which 100% equity funds, 50% debt and 50% equity, and 50% preferred and 50% equity are proposed financing alternatives, first with three possibilities in situations of low operating leverage, then with three possibilities in situations of high operating leverage. While the graphs add nothing to information already developed from previous tables, they allow rapid assimilation of concept of *variance* in each option.

The greatest variance (risk) evinces in the combination of high operating and high financial leverage. The lowest variance results from low operating leverage and no financial leverage. To restate it, with a low risk option, possible sales results fall within a fairly narrow range. While management will not set the world on fire, golden touch wunderkinder, neither are they likely to swamp the firm's operations with the new undertaking. A speculator may sleep better under option I(1) but, at the extreme, *if* he's so lucky, will eat better under option II(2). Striking a compromise may imply selection of either option I(2) or I(3). The safest course to follow depends upon variables, not included here for obvious reasons, which fluctuate not only according to the firm, and industry within which it functions, but also according to economic times and forecasts of expected changes.

That is, the analysis of financial leverage conveys that a firm should raise its capital in the cheapest sources, usually debt, as long as the expected return from investment exceeds not only explicit costs but implicit ones as well. For example, a fall in the price/earnings ratio of common stock may have resulted from excessive financial leverage. Such implicit costs should not be excluded from analysis.

INDIFFERENCE POINTS

When choosing between two (or more) finance mixes, what amount of earnings before interest and taxes (EBIT) will produce the same earnings per share (EPS)? In the case of 100 per cent equity financing versus a mix of equity and debt, the *indifference point* signals that at a certain EBIT either method of financing will result in the same EPS (but not necessarily the same degree of risk). Indifference points may be computed by formulas. For *common* stock versus *bonds,* the formula is:

Formula: $$\frac{X(1-h)}{N_c} = \frac{(X-I)(1-h)}{N_{cb}}$$

Figure 5-6
Graphical Representations of Alternative Effects of Operating and Financial Leverage

I. LOW OPERATING LEVERAGE

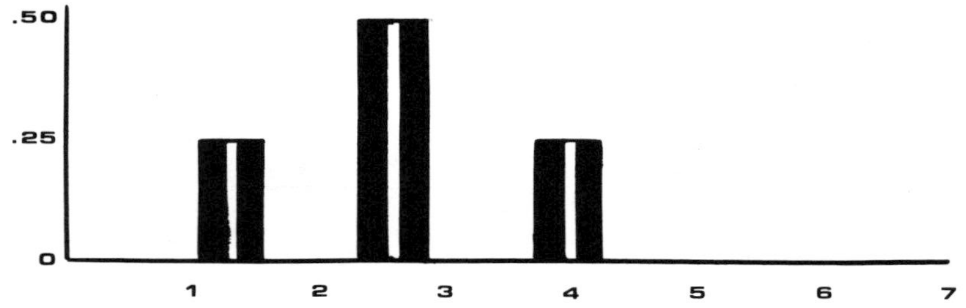

.50
.25
0
1 2 3 4 5 6 7

1. NO FINANCIAL LEVERAGE
(100% equity)

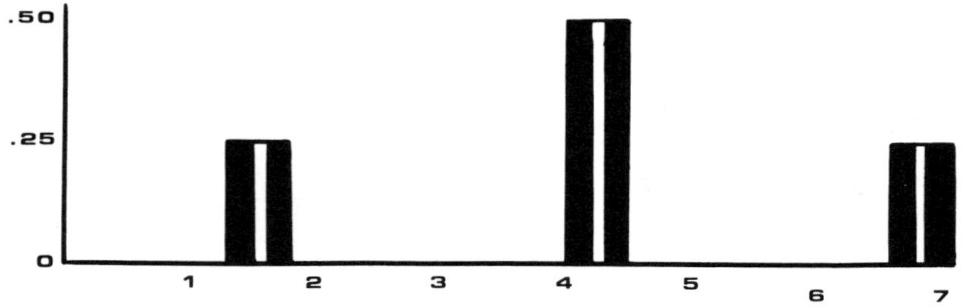

.50
.25
0
1 2 3 4 5 6 7

2. HIGH FINANCIAL LEVERAGE
(50% debt)

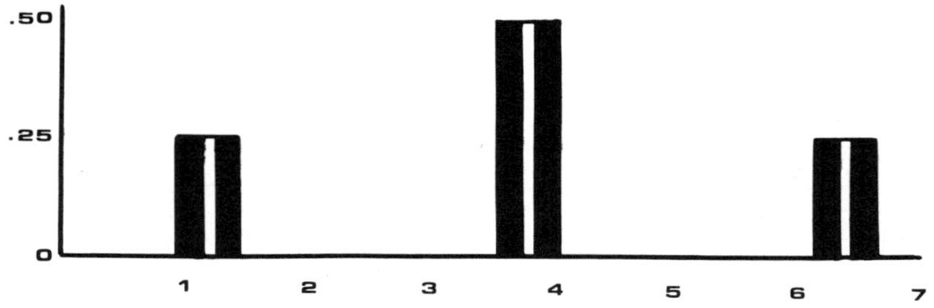

.50
.25
0
1 2 3 4 5 6 7

3. HIGH FINANCIAL LEVERAGE
(50% preferred)

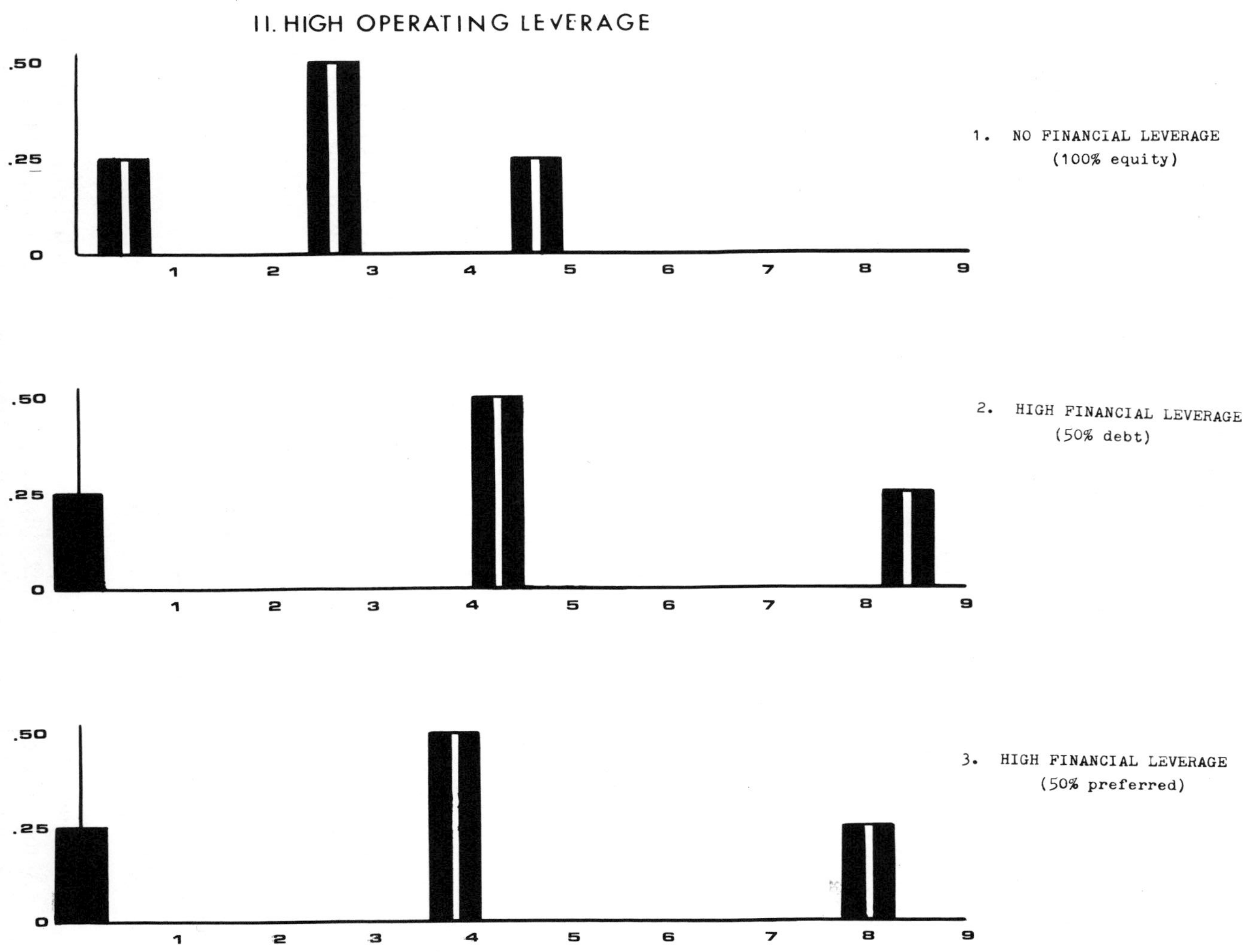
II. HIGH OPERATING LEVERAGE
1. NO FINANCIAL LEVERAGE
(100% equity)
2. HIGH FINANCIAL LEVERAGE
(50% debt)
3. HIGH FINANCIAL LEVERAGE
(50% preferred)
.50
.25
0
1
2
3
4
5
6
7
8
9

X = EBIT at the indifference point, the sum to be determined.

h = applicable tax rate.

I = dollar amount of interest on debt.

N_c = number of outstanding shares if only common stock is issued.

N_{cb} = number of outstanding common shares if both common and bonds enter into the finance mix.

Referring back to the same example, the tax rate (h) is 48%; interest (I) on $1,000,000 of 9% bonds is $90,000 annually; the number of shares of common (N_c) with 100% equity financing is 100,000 and with 50% equity financing (N_{cb}) is 50,000 shares. Solving:

$$\frac{X(1 - 0.48)}{100{,}000} = \frac{(X - 90{,}000)(1 - 0.48)}{50{,}000}$$

$$X = \$180{,}000 \text{ EBIT}$$

Finding the indifference point between common and preferred employs essentially the same formula with modification to take into account that preferred dividends are paid out of EAT.

Formula:

$$\frac{X(1 - h)}{N_c} = \frac{X(1 - h) - D_p}{N_{cp}}$$

Symbols signify the same as above except that D_p represents total preferred dividends payable and N_{cp} denotes the number of shares of common when both common and preferred stock are issued. With the same data above, the indifference point is:

$$\frac{X(1 - 0.48)}{100{,}000} = \frac{X(1 - 0.48) - 70{,}000}{50{,}000}$$

$$X = \$269{,}231 \text{ EBIT}$$

The graph in Figure 5-7 illustrates the same relationships among the three financing alternatives. In the graph, line A represents 100% equity financing, line B 50% equity and 50% debt, line C 50% equity and 50% preferred. The intersection of lines purports the same information calculated by

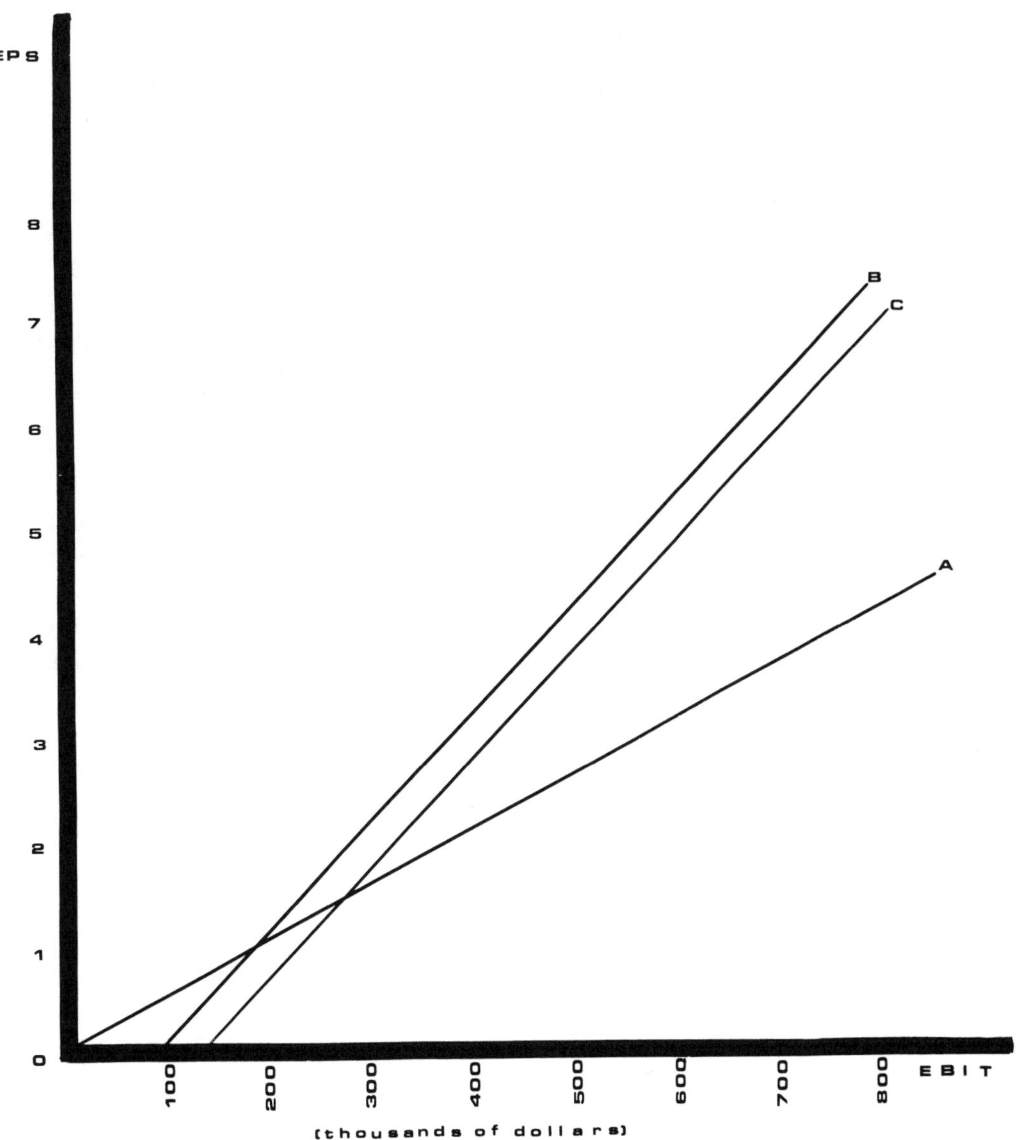

Figure 5-7

formula; i.e., the indifference point between common and bonds is at EBIT of $180,000, and between common and preferred at $269,231 EBIT. Recall, at the outset, that we assumed a linear relationship. Therefore, the graph diagrammatizes various sales and earnings possibilities beyond specific ones indicated in case A situations under three financing alternatives.

EBIT are registered on the horizontal axis; the intercepts with the horizontal axis represent annual before-tax costs of each financing option, which is zero for the all-equity option, $90,000 for the debt option, and $134,615 for the preferred option. That is, residual earnings of common shareholders would be zero at each of these EBITs, and higher fixed costs raise the point at which EPS will be exactly zero.

Beyond this break-even point, the greater the slope of each line in the graph, the greater the absolute increase in EPS for a given increase in EBIT. If earnings advance from $300,000 to $400,000, earnings per share (EPS) will rise most sharply with the 50% debt option, least sharply with 100% common stock financing. This chart's usefulness, its graphic detail on the appropriate capital structure, aids in analyzing the degree of financial leverage under each alternative.

VALUATION OF EARNINGS

Can a business affect its total valuation and cost of capital by varying its finance mix? What happens when the degree of leverage is altered? The table in Figure 5-8 brings together two case A alternatives at the 150,000 unit output level; the first alternative assumes no debt, 100% equity financing; the second assumes 50% equity and 50% debt financing, using the same figures from previous examples.

Figure 5-8

CASE A AT 150,000 UNIT OUTPUT

	No Debt	*50% Debt*
EBIT	+$ 500,000	+$ 500,000
I	- –0–	- 90,000
EBT	+$ 500,000	+$ 410,000
T (48%)	- 240,000	- 196,800
EAT	+$ 260,000	+$ 213,200
Add: I	+ –0–	+ 90,000
Total Income to All Security Holders	+$ 260,000	+$ 303,200
After-tax Capitalization Rate (10%)	0.10	0.10
E	+$2,600,000	+$3,032,000
M_b	- –0–	- 1,000,000
M_e	+$2,600,000	+$2,032,000

E = total value of firm.
M_b = market value of debt
M_e = market value of stock

In Figure 5–8, earnings before interest and taxes (EBIT) of $500,000, presumed in both alternatives, correspond to the 150,000 unit output described early in the chapter. After finding earnings after taxes (EAT), to this amount add the annual interest payment (I) back into EAT, which result is the total income available to *all* security holders. In this example, an after-tax capitalization rate of 10% is proposed. Total income to all security holders is then capitalized at the 10% rate which underlies E, the total value of the enterprise. With the debt option the higher E value derives from leverage. The market value of debt (M_b) varies but in this example we assert that the face value and market value are the same $1 million. The market value of debt subtracted from the total value of the firm leads to the market value of common stock (M_e).

Because of this deductibility of interest payments, the overall cost of capital (k_o) will be lower on a before-tax basis. Under certain restrictive premises, then, the business can reduce its weighted average cost of capital while total value increases with leverage. The formula for computing the overall cost of capital is:

Formula:

$$k_o = \frac{i_o - h\,(i_b)\left(\frac{M_b}{E}\right)}{(1 - h)}$$

$\frac{M_b}{E}$ = ratio of market value of debt to total value of firm.

i_b = yield on (perpetual) debt (bonds).

i_o = after-tax capitalization rate.

k_o = overall capitalization rate for firm (the weighted average cost of capital).

Applying this formulation to the 50% debt alternative in the above table, we have:

$$k_o = \frac{0.10 - (0.48)\,(0.09)\left(\frac{1{,}000{,}000}{3{,}032{,}000}\right)}{(1 - 0.48)}$$

$$= \frac{0.085752}{0.52} = 16.49\%$$

Within a narrow range of possibilities this analysis proposes that the greater the leverage the greater the total value of the firm. However, at some point of excessive leverage, cost of capital soars due to added financial risk, so that the optimal capital structure is one of maximum debt.

Nevertheless, if stockholders believe that management is aggressive, up to a point, they may ignore the risk of a highly leveraged firm for prospects of even greater growth. A short-sighted analyst may misinterpret signals, that a favorable effect on the price/earnings ratio does not necessarily result from high leverage but simply reflects investor psychology, the bandwagon effect. The emergent analysis may deceive if all significant variables are not accounted for.

TRADING ON THE EQUITY

Trading on the equity ratio (TER) compares rate of return on common stock equity to rate of return on total capitalization. The following formula requires application of the proportion of equity capital to total capitalization (b) in addition to inputs on earnings before interest and taxes (EBIT) and the dollar value of interest charges (I).

Formula:

$$TER = \frac{1}{b}\left(\frac{EBIT - I}{EBIT}\right)$$

Still using a case A (50% debt) illustration, with equity equal to 50% of total capitalization, EBIT of \$250,000, and I of \$90,000, the solution is:

$$TER_a = \frac{1}{0.50}\left(\frac{250{,}000 - 90{,}000}{250{,}000}\right) = 1.28$$

By employment of debt, return on equity is about one-fourth better than if investment had been financed entirely by common stock. If there had been no internal risk, so that b equals unity and fixed charges disappear, the trading on equity ratio would be one.

But if preferred stock had been issued along with debt, the above formula is adjusted to reflect the before-tax burden, where D_p denotes an annual preferred dividend obligation and h the tax rate.

Formula:

$$TER' = \frac{1}{b}\left[1 - \frac{1}{EBIT}\left(I + \frac{D_p}{(1 - h)}\right)\right]$$

Using above material imagine that all data remain unchanged except that a preferred issue partly displaces debt so that I drops to \$45,000 and D_p becomes \$45,000, and h equals 48%.

$$\text{TER}' = \frac{1}{0.50}\left[1 - \frac{1}{250{,}000}\left(45{,}000 + \frac{45{,}000}{(1 - 0.48)}\right)\right] = 0.95$$

The effect of trading on the equity is modified by the proportion of fixed charges to total earnings. In this last illustration the burden of preferred dividend payments decrease the return to common.

RISK OF RUIN

The above analyses have indicated that as long as earnings before interest and taxes exceed interest charges, profits will be greater in a leveraged firm than in one financed entirely by equity. On the other hand, excessive leverage raises the real risk of bankruptcy, and since there are very real costs associated with this possible outcome, excessive leverage can reduce total value of the firm. Businesses with predictable, relatively stable income flows—such as highly regulated monopolies perpetuated by government legislation, or firms with long term contracts, for example—can tolerate more leverage because of less variance in anticipated earnings. Firms with riskier income streams will find the marginal cost of capital rising as debt expands. In spite of tax advantages of debt, excessive leverage will eventually more than offset these gains and endanger the total value of the enterprise.

The risk of ruin is the prospect of having insufficient funds to meet fixed obligations. Both amount and term of obligations affect size of fixed charges—interest plus principal repayment—and before taking on new debt, management must carefully examine expected future cash flows to avoid danger of financial insolvency. Future flows are predicated on not only internal competition for funds and adequate market projections but on general economic conditions as well. How will a business or economic recession affect cash flows?

Formula: $$S_r = A_o + F_r$$

The amount of funds available at some point during a recessionary period (S_r) is the sum of cash at the beginning of the period (A_o) plus the expected flow generated during the recession (F_r).

Suppose a problem does develop. What sources of funds attract notice during adverse years? (1) One obvious but painful source, liquidation of equity—reduction in fixed assets—will pay accruing fixed charges. (2) More commonly, liquidation of current assets—inventory reduction, tighter receivable control, or delaying tactics in paying current obligations—may enable the firm to survive for a while without further complications. (3) But if the business has operated successfully for a number of years, earning profits, even a highly leveraged firm with loss carry-back and tax refunds can pay off fixed charges for several years. Resting on this cushion of safety may encourage management in the direction of excessive leverage.

One doorway to reckoning future flows (F_r) may be to derive a probability distribution of potential values in the manner that data in this chapter have been developed; i.e., sales were scaled on less likely low and high volumes and on a most likely middle ground. By developing a contingency plan for most adverse circumstances, management is less likely to sink the firm. Certainly gambling that results will always trail along the upper end of the range of forecasts encouraging insolvency, sooner or later, when sales fall short of projections and the business fails to generate enough funds in adverse years to meet fixed obligations.

WARRANT LEVERAGE

Another financing postern, *warrants,* an option written by a corporation, usually on its own stock, grants the buyer the right to purchase a share of its common stock at a fixed exercise price during a set time span. (Do not confuse warrants with rights mentioned in Chapter Four.) There are two advantages to the issuing corporation. In adverse financial periods, an uncompromising market for secondary financial issues and public financing may cruelly discount or reject an issue, but a corporation with outstanding warrants may be able to force financing. If a stock sells for anything over the warrant exercise price, to cover transaction costs, surely warrants will be exercised and the firm will obtain a cash inflow sans underwriting costs. If a stock sells below the warrant exercise price, the firm can always lower the exercise price for a brief stint to encourage conversion. The other advantage is to aid a merger undertaking. On the other hand, a disadvantage of warrants outstanding is that they dilute earnings per share.

Investors are attracted to warrants because of leverage, the chance that the value of warrant will rise faster than the value of the common stock. How can the degree of warrant leverage (DWL) be measured?

Formula:

$$DWL = \frac{\dfrac{M_w^* - M_w}{M_w}}{\left(\dfrac{M_c^* - M_c}{M_c}\right) + \dfrac{D}{M_c}}$$

M_w^* = expected future price of the warrant when common stock sells at M_c^* per share.

M_w = current price of the warrant.

M_c^* = expected future price of common stock per share.

M_c = current price of common stock.

D = value of dividend per share (if any) issued during time warrant is held.

For example, grant that Delta Consolidated's stock sells at exercise price \$20 (M_c) and that the warrant goes at \$5 (M_w). If the price of stock advances to \$30 (M_c^*) and the warrant trades at \$9 (M_w^*), what is the degree of warrant leverage (DWL) if no dividends are paid out during the observed period?

$$\text{DWL} = \frac{\dfrac{9 - 5}{5}}{\dfrac{30 - 20}{20}} = 1.6$$

When stock prices climb 50%, the warrant's value jumps 80%, which encourages speculation in warrants issued by the corporation. However, as stock prices continue to mount and expiration date of warrants nears, the degree of warrant leverage will shift. Notice, too that the last expression $\left(\frac{D}{M_c}\right)$ drops out of the calculations when no dividends are emitted during the period which the warrant is held. If dividends are paid out, this raises the denominator and reduces leverage. For example, a 50-cent dividend inflates the denominator to 0.525, and the DWL falls to 1.5.

In this chapter issues have dealt with opportunity costs and marginal costs implicitly; the next chapter focuses specifically on these topics.

CONTENTS

Chapter Six: Applying Marginal, Opportunity, Sunk Costs to the Profit Concept

SIX

Applying Marginal, Opportunity, Sunk Costs to the Profit Concept

If cost of capital and risks did not increase with leverage then only availability of profitable opportunities to exploit would limit debt financing; but additions to debt will eventually raise costs and risks. On the other hand, failure to contract debt may mean that unexploited opportunities have been sacrificed. This chapter, then, will examine more closely the methodology of measuring additions to costs, opportunities not taken, and relevance of past investments.

By definition, *marginal cost* is the change in total cost associated with a shift in business activity such as variability in output, resource replacement or use, quality of merchandise, industrial technology, product mix, etc. Of course, all decisions are made at the margin with costs just one aspect of it. Mainly developed by Carl Menger, marginal analyses with respect to revenue, time, productivity offer further possibilities of the impressive application of this practical postulate. The *opportunity cost* concept, evoluted in the same historical period by Frederich von Weiser, requires measurement of sacrifices, of alternatives that could have been implemented but were not. If a decision requires no sacrifice, it is cost free; but, unfortunately, everything has its price in this life. The last notion touched upon in this chapter, *sunk costs,* relates to decisions already executed and acted upon, irrelevant in future decision-making. What has been done, is done, and no present or future measures can alter past transactions, good or bad. "In the past nothing can be altered and in the present little, but the future is ours and capable of raising life's intensity to its highest pitch."*

MARGINAL COSTS

The marginal cost concept may be tagged "incremental cost" in managerial economics or "differential cost" in accounting, and a few accountants have added to the confusion by employing the term "relevant costs" to transmit a similar impression. The word "marginal," frequently employed in popular parlance to express "unprofitable" such as a marginal (high cost) operation, may confuse. Here marginal is synonymous with "additional." Marginal cost means additional cost, or additions to cost. Of course, incremental and differential convey the same thought. Specifically, to the economist marginal characterizes those costs that attend the production of *one more unit.* By definition, marginal cost is the change in total cost brought about by a one-unit change in total production. Later, this idea is slightly modified for expediency, but marginal analysis is not only practical and proper but underlies decisions—from drinking an extra cup of coffee to investing an extra $250 million in refining operations.

Modifying business activity recasts costs. Whether or not the production shift occurs usually does not coincide with conventional accounting costs because change may not only influence the endeavor under consideration but other activities as well. Additionally, altering production infects prices. Significantly increased output can only be marketed at lower prices so that marginal decisions also encompass changes in revenues as well as in costs. If a particular option raises income more than costs, or if it decreases some costs more than it raises others, then the plan will contribute to profits. In any event, the decision takes place at the margin, not by including all past or total investment, whether that investment is in capital goods, technology, or time.

---

* C. G. Jung, *Psychological Reflections* (N.Y.: Harper & Row, 1961), p. 264.

Average Versus Marginal Costs

Because most calculations arise at the margin,* average costs are less significant for decision-making, unless, of course, by coincidence the two costs are about the same over a narrow range of possibilities. Most accounting costs are historical averages which are not very useful in decision-making because (1) the figures are averages and (2) the data are historical. Investment judgments focus on prospective differences among *future* alternatives rather than on *past* receipts and disbursements. The following simple, but commonly encountered, illustration demonstrates how past averages will trigger unprofitable signals for future courses of action.

Incremental Cost of Electricity

Assume that an individual ponders whether or not to install a humidifier. After weighing all factors, his final action hinges on operating costs; namely, electricity consumption. Averaging electric usage for the previous twelve months, he finds that he consumes 400 kwh per month. At the 400 usage level, the cost of each kwh is 3.225 cents. He calculates that during Fall and Winter months the humidifier will consume an average 100 kwh per month, or, according to the calculations, an additional $3.23 of electricity per month. If he should happen to decide correctly, but for wrong reasons, sloppy decision-making will not always work out so well, and especially in recessionary times, when management ability counts more than ever, the decision-maker will eventually have to pay the piper for unprofitable guesses. The individual in this illustration erred several times; we will focus on only two.

Electricity costs are usually based on a *discrete scale* with rates inverse to quantity consumed. Assume the following residential charge schedule applies.

Basic Service Charge	$0.85
First 30 kwh @ 6½¢ per kwh	1.95
Next 60 kwh @ 4½¢ per kwh	2.70
Next 100 kwh @ 3¼¢ per kwh	3.25
Next 200 kwh @ 2¢ per kwh	4.00
Next 110 kwh @ 1½¢ per kwh	1.65
Next 500 kwh @ 1¼¢ per kwh	6.25

*An example of marginal analysis applied to leverage concepts is available in: John J. Hampton: *Financial Decision Making: Concepts, Problems and Cases* (Reston, Va: Reston Publishing Company, Inc., 1976). pp. 212–13.

The first problem with averages is the high-low range. If this individual disposes of 200 kwh some months and 600 kwh other months, although usage will average to 400 kwh, his monthly bills will range from \$8.95 (for 200 kwh) to \$15.50 (for 600 kwh). But if he typically consumes 400 kwh each month, his cost will be \$12.90.

Basic	\$ 0.85
30 kwh @ 6½¢	1.95
60 kwh @ 4½¢	2.70
100 kwh @ 3¼¢	3.25
200 kwh @ 2¢	4.00
10 kwh @ 1½¢	0.15
TOTAL	\$12.90

To solve this challenge, the first question to answer is whether Fall and Winter usage are close to the annual average. If so, then the cost of absorbing an additional 100 kwh is *not* the average 3.225 cents per kwh but the *additional* charge. The additional expense of each kwh beyond 400 kwh and up to 500 kwh is not 3.225 cents but 1.50 cents. That extra 100 kwh will cost the user an additional \$1.50, the *marginal* cost, and not \$3.23, the *average* cost. The marginal figure is the relevant one in decision-making.

Although marginal pricing of electricity rates usually discounts per unit charges to large residential users, and industrial consumers receive better price breaks than a commercial consumer, also, penalties or premiums for high usage may be introduced into the pricing system so that marginal rates may not necessarily be lower but higher. Peak load pricing variations such as a *Hopkinson* type of rate or *Wright* type of demand rate may "penalize" industrial users, or the subsidy method for low residential users employed in Puerto Rico, and similarly, in California, suggests some complications in calculations but the technique of marginal analysis remains the same. Sometimes, too, it is not convenient to compute marginal costs as the cost of using or producing one more unit as set forth in the next example.

Marginal Costs of Manufacturing Firm

Although marginal costs are defined as the cost of using or producing one more unit of product or service, many types of operations do not lend themselves to such minute calculations. The management of Colorado Plastex, Inc., manufacturer of plastic containers, considers minimum variations of 100,000 units of output. For practical purposes the difference between the cost of producing unit number 434,000 and unit number 434,001 is meaningless even if computations can be derived. The solution, to determine an "average marginal cost" (c_m), can be accomplished by dividing the change in total cost (ΔC) by the change in output (ΔX).

Formula:

$$c_m = \frac{\Delta C}{\Delta X}$$

All marginal costs in Figure 6–1 are found by this formula. Colorado Plastex, represented by these data, operates with a fixed capacity but modifies production by changing variable factor inputs (labor, overtime pay, raw materials, utilities, etc.) so that while total fixed costs remain unaltered at all outputs between zero and capacity, variable costs ascend with production. Total costs, therefore, increase throughout relevant outputs between 100,000 and 900,000 units, from $195,000 to $306,000.

Figure 6–1

	TOTAL			*AVERAGE*			
Production (units)	*Fixed Costs*	*Variable Costs*	*Costs*	*Fixed Costs*	*Variable Costs*	*Total Costs*	*Marginal Costs*
100,000	$180,000	$ 15,000	$195,000	$1.800	$0.150	$1.950	
200,000	180,000	29,000	209,000	0.900	0.145	1.045	$0.14
300,000	180,000	42,000	222,000	0.600	0.140	0.740	0.13
400,000	180,000	52,000	232,000	0.450	0.130	0.580	0.10
500,000	180,000	58,000	238,000	0.360	0.116	0.476	0.06
600,000	180,000	60,000	240,000	0.300	0.100	0.400	0.02
700,000	180,000	70,000	250,000	0.257	0.100	0.357	0.10
800,000	180,000	88,000	268,000	0.225	0.110	0.335	0.18
900,000	180,000	126,000	306,000	0.200	0.140	0.340	0.38

Average costs have been broken down into three columns. *Average fixed costs* are simply total fixed costs ($180,000) divided by various outputs. The divers *total variable costs* are divided by the corresponding outputs (e.g., $238,000 ÷ 500,000 = $0.116). *Average total costs* can be found either by adding together average fixed and variable costs or dividing total costs by the corresponding output; that is, average total costs encompass all costs and all output up to the point analyzed. Notice the *asymptotic relationship* of average fixed costs, which, continuously diminishing, never reaches, but approaches, zero. Average variable costs decline to 10 cents per unit at production of 600,000 and 700,000 units of plastic containers, rising to 11 cents at 800,000 units, and jumping sharply to 14 cents at 900,000 containers.

But total variable costs do not bottom out until an output of 800,000 units. What happens is that the 3-cent fall in average fixed costs when production was increased from 700,000 to 800,000 more than offsets the slight increase of 1 cent per unit of variable costs. Which sales level is best for this manufacturing concern–600,000, 700,000, 800,000 containers, or some other volume?

To get a better handle on this issue turn to *marginal costs.* Marginal costs tell us how much it will cost to manufacture that *last* container, or the last batch of containers, while average costs reflect total costs and total production. The marginal decision is the relevant one because it asks: By how much will costs rise with a given increase in volume? At 600,000 containers, the cost of an additional output beyond 500,000 is 2 cents each; while progressing from 700,000 to 800,000 means adding 18 cents to the cost of each container produced. Where costs alone are pivotal in the decision processes, then the important figure is the marginal one. Where income weighs against costs, then the significant data are marginal revenue versus marginal costs.

Marginal Revenue

Like marginal costs, *marginal revenue* is the amount of income added by the sale of one more unit of product or service. Also, like costs, except for big ticket items, higher sales revenue usually results from a lump increase in production, or the purchase of lots, carload deliveries, or based on annual contracts. While the purpose of this chapter is not to examine the complicated process of pricing policy, it should be recognized that any significant expansion in sales usually must be accompanied by lower prices whether in the form of discounts, liberal credit arrangements, extra services, or bonus plans. By formula, then, marginal revenue (y_m) is the change in total revenue (ΔY) divided by the change in sales volume (ΔX).

Formula:

$$y_m = \frac{\Delta Y}{\Delta X}$$

Decisions at the margin pit additions to income against additions to cost. If build-up in costs is less than increments to revenue, then profits rise. The following example and case study illustrate the point.

Manufacturer of Plastic Containers

To continue with the preceding example, the cost schedule of Colorado Plastex, the plastic container manufacturer, tells nothing about possible income from different sales levels. If management seeks to minimize costs, then production should occur where marginal costs are minimized between outputs of 500,000 and 600,000; but when income is estimated, then a least-cost combination may not necessarily render the best financial results.

What should management maximize? Total income? If it chooses to maximize total revenue, then an output of 900,000 containers will result in the largest possible income. Price per unit? If it chooses to obtain the highest selling price, then it will sell 100,000 units at $1.00 each. Profit per unit? If per unit profits are maximized, then production and sales of 600,000 containers will be selected. If management wants to minimize costs or maximize total income, per unit price, or per unit profit, then it will have to decide among various production alternatives: 100,000, 500–600,000, 600,000, or 900,000. Which one of these will yield the best financial results? The most favorable financial results may signal to minimize losses or it may mean to maximize profits.

Since all decisions are marginal ones, we must analyze marginal data remembering that additional benefits also carry with them supplemental costs. If any chosen production contributes more to costs than it does to gains, the firm's losses mount. If any volume adds more to income than it does to costs, operations expand profits. Therefore, sales option of 900,000 containers is eliminated from considerations. By the same token, several more production levels become possible alternatives. (Refer to Figure 6–2.)

Figure 6-2

Production (units)	*Total Costs*	*Price (per unit)*	*Total Revenue*	*Net Revenue*	*Marginal Revenue ($ per unit)*	*Marginal Cost ($ per unit)*
100,000	$195,000	$1.00	$100,000	-$95,000		
					$0.60	$0.14
200,000	209,000	0.80	160,000	- 49,000		
					0.54	0.13
300,000	222,000	0.68	204,000	- 18,000		
					0.44	0.10
400,000	232,000	0.62	248,000	+ 16,000		
					0.37	0.06
500,000	238,000	0.57	285,000	+ 47,000		
					0.27	0.02
600,000	240,000	0.52	312,000	+ 72,000		
					0.10	0.10
700,000	250,000	0.46	322,000	+ 72,000		
					0.06	0.18
800,000	268,000	0.41	328,000	+ 60,000		
					0.05	0.38
900,000	306,000	0.37	333,000	+ 27,000		

The proper solution lay in an understanding of marginal concepts. Because production in this example occurs in batches of 100,000 units, the "average marginal revenue", that is, the income contributed by the sale of *one more unit,* between 100,000 and 200,000 containers, is $0.60 for each one sold; while the "average marginal cost," that is, the cost of producing *one more unit,* between 100,000 and 200,000 containers, is $0.14 for each unit produced. Therefore, we must conclude that manufacturing up to 200,000 containers, each one will add more to income (60¢) than it will to costs (14¢). By analogy, we conclude that production should be augmented to that level at which profits are no longer being improved, to that point where marginal revenue and marginal cost equal each other, or an output between 600,000 and 700,000. Somewhere in this range will yield best financial results given cost and income estimates. Beyond 700,000 units notice that marginal costs exceed marginal revenues which worsen rather than improve financial results.

Therefore, the general rule tells us that favorable financial outcomes occur at those volumes which equate marginal revenue and marginal cost. If production is curtailed at 300,000 units, then the firm's management is failing to increase profits which it can do by raising output and sales. If production is sustained at 900,000 to meet customer demand or competition, then the firm's management has chosen to add more to costs than to income thereby worsening the immediate financial outcome. On the other hand, it is possible to select an output which does not cover fully allocated costs and still add to profits. The Continental Air Line case study elucidates this mystery.

Case Study: Should Continental Air Lines fly a money-losing route?

This case deals with Continental Air Lines, Inc.* when it suffered losses due to a poor load factor. To increase the load factor, Continental could have eliminated 5% of its runs and raised its load factor significantly. However, management decisions do not spotlight load factors exclusively but profits. If decisions focus on fully allocated costs, the alternative selected may reduce profits rather than strengthen them. Using simplified data, here is how marginal analysis signals the best approach.

Suppose that the fully allocated cost of flying from Tri-City to Mid-City is $49,500; marginal (out-of-pocket) costs are $24,200; and marginal (addition to) revenue is $34,100. While the data on costs are fairly accurate, based on information developed in every operating department, revenue projections are marketing estimates for new, and even existing, routes. Obviously, accounting points toward a loss if the existing run is not dropped.

---

*Adapted from Leonard S. Silk and Daniel B. Moscowitz, "Airline Takes the Marginal Route," *Business Week* (April 20, 1963), reprinted in Robert P. Vichas (ed.) *Coeval Economics* (McCutchan Publishing Co., 1970), pp. 146–8.

Full Costing:

Marginal income	+$34,100
Total costs	- 49,500
LOSS	-$15,400

The question here is what costs must the airline sustain if the flight is cancelled? Because of fixed investment in planes, equipment, and buildings, plus fixed salaries and other costs, the concern will bear outlays of $25,300, whether the flight takes place or not. What matters are marginal costs. Which costs are marginal ones? Any cost that is incurred directly as a consequence of flying (fuel, service, salaries) represents additions to operational charges. Suppose that a service crew is already on hand because of another flight departure, then salaries of the service crew do *not* represent an addition to cost because they are on duty whether there is a flight to Mid-City or not. And if some costs are eliminated because of the flight (hangar crew costs, for example), then these eliminated charges must be deducted from marginal costs to arrive at a correct out-of-pocket cost. The question boils down to improving profits and not of covering fully allocated costs.

Marginal Analysis:

Addition to income	+$34,100
Addition to costs	- 24,200
Addition to Profits	+$ 9,900

Marginal pricing underlies the touchy issue of discriminatory pricing policies. Not only early-only rates, but group tours, special packages, and age, occupation, time of year and class exceptions to the general tariff make sense only when marginal analysis applies. Naturally, in the totality, all costs must be covered or a business will bankrupt. But once an investment has been made (see the section on "Sunk Costs") then marginal analysis comes into play and expansion of sales (and profits) may well depend upon price discrimination where permitted. While dumping, in international trade, is frowned upon by local competing firms, consumers benefit from lower prices, and exporting concerns add to profits by selling below fully allocated costs but above marginal costs.

Marginal Contribution per Hour

While "time" is not normally counted as a factor input in productive processes, it, nevertheless, enters into decisions. Electricity generated at 9:00

A.M. and not sold is lost forever. The two-thirds empty flight from Tri-City to Mid-City represents revenue lost forever. Inefficient use of productive facilities signals productive time lost. One method of measuring dollar efficiency of products competing for use of facilities is suggested by D. W. Wycoff in which the marginal contribution of a product is measured on a time scale. The technique for gauging marginal dollars per hour (MDH) is to divide the marginal contribution (Y) of each unit sold by the number (or fraction) of hours (X) required to produce it. In the case of simultaneous multi-stage productive processes, the worst time is used rather than a summation.

Formula:

$$\mathrm{MDH} = \frac{\mathrm{Y}}{\mathrm{X}}$$

Profitability Measurement

Assume that a firm produces three distinct products, all of which require three-step production techniques of times expressed in a fraction of an hour in the table below:

	PRODUCTS		
Steps	*A*	*B*	*C*
1	0.25*	0.10	0.10*
2	0.10	0.20	0.10
3	0.15	0.30*	0.10

In completing calculations below, the longest time factor (designated by * above) is employed because within the production cycle the worst time factor controls the production schedule and determines the rate of final output. Applying the above formula to data below, the plant can determine the most profitable product; that is, the most efficient use of time-facilities.

	PRODUCTS		
	A	*B*	*C*
Sales Price (per unit)	$ 90	$135	$ 75
Variable Cost	50	75	50
(Y) Marginal Contribution (dollars)	$ 40	$ 60	$ 25
(X) Hours (worst production time)	0.25	0.30	0.10
(MDH) Margin Dollars per Hour	$160	$200	$250

In terms of total dollars consigned to marginal revenue, Product B shines forth. However, when it turns to using plant capacity to expand sales of, say, product B at the expense of diminishing output and sales of products A and C, then product C ranks as the best nomination. Assuming that the market will absorb increased output at the going price, then it pays the firm to train its facilities on product C because they can churn out three units of C while manufacturing one of B. Additional revenue will be \$75 (\$25 X 3), while the cost of an opportunity foregone (lost sale of B) will be \$60, a net gain of \$15 by switching.

Increasing Efficiency

Suppose, however, that the plant efficiency can be improved by 22% for product B, so that it now requires only 0.234 hours of production time per unit. B's contribution of \$256.41 margin dollars per hour exceeds C's by \$6.41. To determine annual gain by now switching from C to B, multiply number of facility hours by the gain per hour. Again calculations hold good at the margin rather than overall production time.

Marginal Cost of Time

Up to now we have explored multifarious management decisions that can affect output and income. We have varied combinations of factor inputs, the finance mix, and income possibilities at different outputs, all of which can produce a combination of costs and revenues that are more or less favorable to operations, but we need to expand on time relations in production schedules to account for those decisions in which times and dates of inputs can be staggered to shade cost patterns. Too, in processes that mature slowly—Christmas trees, timber, coffee, vanilla beans, wines and whiskys, cheese, ginseng root, etc.—the question is not only *how much* output and input but also *when* that output shall be marketed. Time, then, becomes a factor in decision-making, which the following case study illustrates.

Case Study: When is the best time to sell scotch whisky?

Most scotch whiskies consist of a blend of about 80% grain and the remainder normally a secret combination of malt whiskies. Relative prices of malt and grain, world demand, availability of supplies are some factors that influence the price any specific lot of whisky will bring. Scotch whisky is not bottled until it has aged at least three years in oak barrels, although the United States government stipulates that it must age four years before being imported into this country. Older scotch whiskies retail at substantially higher prices so that one would expect to pay considerably more for 25-year old scotch over a 4-year blend, but because the interaction of demand and supplies determines prices, the price relationship between 4, 8, 12, 25, or 30-year whiskies is neither stable nor constant. While older whiskies are more expensive no rule emerges that requires a 25-year brand to sell at 6 times a 4-year blend. Time, a factor, alone does not determine final prices. At any given point in time, the absolute quantity of oldest whiskies in existence can be estimated, but the amount of 3 or 4 or 6-year whisky depends not only on production decisions made 3, 4, or 6 years ago, but this quantity can be expanded by combining, say, 8-year whiskies as long as labeling conforms to the youngest whisky in the blend. Therefore, near-term supplies tend to fluctuate more.

Suppose that Klaus Oberg, an investor, speculates on new grain whisky by investing $40,000, which includes prepaid storage and insurance costs for the first 8 years of aging. How does the investor know whether he should undertake the investment? When should he sell? In other words, how can Oberg maximize net income from this investment? By applying the basic principle, he will *maximize net income* at that point where *marginal cost of time* equates to *marginal revenue of time.* To properly approach this perplexing situation, Oberg should have some knowledge of the whisky market, unless he has managed to obtain a forward agreement, past, present, and anticipated prices based on a study of estimated supplies and projected demand, so that he may develop some basis for decision-making.

The table in Figure 6–3 consolidates these projections. Total cost, easiest to derive, begins with initial outlay, compounded annually at 12%, an *opportunity cost* (discussed in the next section) assigned by the investor. After developing a number of income possibilities, the speculator picks most likely ones and enters them as "anticipated income," which reflects that time alone, aging, will make his whisky investment more valuable. Net income is the difference between rows (1) and (2) in Figure 6–3. If he decides to maximize net income, then he will likely sell his whisky in the 7th and 8th years of aging.

However, Oberg opts to discount future income streams at a 12% rate to determine their present values, which results indicate he should sell out during the 6th and 7th years, and perhaps to *hedge* somewhat against risk of price decline he may even prefer to reduce his holdings beginning in the 5th year, say, one-fourth in the 5th year, one-third in the 6th year, and the remaining five-twelfths in the 7th year. Because the investor has doubts about his decision-making basis, he adds rows (5) and (6)—*cost differences* and *income differences.*

Cost difference (5) is the algebraic difference between each time period from row (1) figures (44,800 - 40,000 = 4,800, and 50,175 - 44,800 = 5,375, etc.). *Income difference* is derived from row (2) in the same manner (44,800 - 33,000 = 11,880). Row (5) we might call the *marginal cost of time* and row (6) the *marginal revenue of time.* To maximize net income, the investor

Figure 6-3

AGING OF SCOTCH WHISKY

YEAR:	*0*	*1*	*2*	*3*	*4*	*5*	*6*	*7*	*8*
1. Total Cost	$40,000	$44,800	$50,175	$56,197	$62,941	$70,494	$ 78,953	$ 88,427	$ 99,039
2. Anticipated Income	33,000	44,880	53,312	66,640	79,968	95,162	107,533	120,437	131,049
3. Net Income	$ (7,000)	$ 80	$ 3,137	$10,443	$17,027	$24,668	$ 28,580	$ 32,010	$ 32,010
4. No. 3 Discounted	$ (7,000)	$ 71	$ 2,500	$ 7,433	$10,821	$13,997	$ 14,480	$ 14,480	$ 12,928
5. Cost Differences		$ 4,800	$ 5,375	$ 6,022	$ 6,744	$ 7,553	$ 8,459	$ 9,474	$10,612
6. Income Differences		$11,880	$ 8,432	$13,328	$13,328	$15,194	$12,371	$12,904	$10,612
7. Rate of Cost Rise		12%	12%	12%	12%	12%	12%	12%	12%
8. Rate of Income Rise		36%	19%	25%	20%	19%	13%	12%	8.8%

should hold his scotch until the two equate. He should sell between the 7th and 8th years.

But the investor does *not* want to maximize net income. This is the "bird in hand" argument of Chapter Two. A smaller net income sooner is better than a larger one later if it can be reinvested at a rate of return acceptable to the investor. For this analysis turn to rows (7) and (8) in Figure 6–3, in which rates of change are recorded to tell us where the *discounted marginal revenue* is at a maximum. The rate at which total costs rise in a given year is the *rate of cost increment* in row (7) found by dividing the *absolute increase in total cost* between two years by the *total cost* of the earlier year. In this case, the rate of cost rise is 12% a year, the rate of return employed by the investor. The rate of income advance is the absolute change between two years divided by the total income of the earlier year: for years 0 to 1, 11,880 ÷ 33,000 = 36%; years 1 to 2, 8,432 ÷ 44,880 = 19%, etc.

In this table, the discounted net revenue is maximized where the *rate* of income expansion matches the *rate* of cost increase; that is, where both are 12%. The investor, therefore, chooses to sell his whisky inventory between the 6th and 7th years. As a general principle, we can state that discounted net revenue is at a maximum when growth in income equates to the expected rate of return on investments (or the rate of interest). To arrive at this 12%, the investor employed an opportunity cost principle first elaborated by Friedrich von Weiser.

OPPORTUNITY COSTS

One way of looking at *opportunity costs* is a sacrifice, the opportunity lost by not marrying the boss's daughter. In the above case study, what rate of return did the investor forego by putting his money in scotch whisky? He employed a 12% rate because had he not invested in scotch he would have earned 12% per annum in another endeavor. Opportunity costs may be counted as profits from alternative uses of limited facilities, or funds, that are given up when a particular option is chosen, a sacrificed alternative. Earlier emphasis was placed on the necessity of including not only explicit costs (those that enter into accounting data) but implicit ones as well. What a concern does *not* do is just as critical as what it does with its investments. The following simplified example illustrates this importance.

A New Business Venture

Roberto Flores decided to quit his $18,000 a year job as plant foreman to begin his own small business producing couplers. His sole proprietorship was financed by long-term equipment loans; for working capital he sold his stocks to raise $30,000 plus another $20,000 loaned interest-free from his mother-in-law; the rest he borrowed at interest. His wife had inherited some acreage and he converted the existing building into a shop and office. At the end of his second full year of operations he bragged to an economist friend, Ludwig, that he had earned $24,000, better than he could have done as plant foreman. "Are you sure you really earned $24,000?" asked Ludwig.

"Well, my accountant says I did. And I paid taxes on $24,000 income," answered Roberto.

"Where the IRS is concerned, might may not make right but it certainly is an advantage in extracting tribute. You didn't make a $24,000 profit from your business operations. You actually lost money. Here, I'll show you why." And economist Ludwig proffered the following explanation.

"When you sold your stock to raise $30,000, how much were your dividends and capital gains averaging every year?"

"Ten per cent."

"Your mother-in-law loaned you $20,000 'interest-free.' Weren't those savings earning money for her some place?"

"She had some 6% certificates of deposit," answered Roberto, "but I don't have to pay her any interest, just the principal after five years."

"Think of all the uses your wife could have put that land to and bring in an income. You could lease it, plant it, sell it and invest the money elsewhere. If she leased the property, what do you think it'd bring?" asked Ludwig.

"Probably $400 a month without much trouble," Roberto volunteered.

After several suspenseful minutes of calculating, Ludwig presented these figures to Flores.

Salary lost (former employment)	$18,000
Rent foregone	4,800
Interest sacrificed:	
a) Stocks ($30,000 × 10%)	3,000
b) Subsidy from mother-in-law ($20,000 × 6%)	1,200
	$27,000

"You lost $3,000 last year," said Ludwig. "If this business had to make a go of it entirely on its own, you would be $3,000 worse off than if you had stayed with your former job, not counting lost retirement and other benefits capitalized at some rate, say, 10%. I'm not saying a man shouldn't strike out on his own, but he should not delude himself about costs. Maybe it's worth $3,000 just to be on your own, and after a couple of more years you'll have that loss more than made up. In the meantime, recognize that for that 'privilege' of paying more in taxes, and being your own boss, everyone–you, your wife, and your mother-in-law–have all had to take a little less, some losses.

These are the opportunity costs of your business, the opportunities that were sacrificed, given up, when you opted for your own manufacturing business."

"I see what you mean." Roberto pondered. "I wonder if the IRS has ever heard of opportunity costs."

Processing Costs

Measurement of opportunity costs occurs in different ways according to what results are being weighed. While underlying principles do not change, the method of deriving the desired data will. When a single input is processed to yield two or more outputs, this creates the phenomenon of joint costs and the question of how to measure them. The question: Is total income originating from the sale of these several outputs sufficient to cover all additional costs of inputs? Total income depends upon the price at which each output can be sold. After an undertaking is judged profitable, the question arises on how far processing should be carried. Should a coconut palm grower simply sell the raw material or should he extract oil and sell both oil and pulp, or should the oil be processed into soap?

A Fruit Orchard

As an illustrative example, consider a large apple grower who can retail apples of mixed grades for $3.00 per bushel in his farm store or he can press these apples into apple cider. Can the sale value of the product be raised by more than incremental processing costs? The question is not what the apples cost to grow; these *sunk costs* no longer enter into the analysis. In determining the "profit" on apple cider, the cost of producing apples is not the relevant figure but the revenue from alternative uses (sales) is. The *opportunity cost* is that sum which could have been realized from sale of apples in the normal course of business. If these apples can be marketed at $3.00 per bushel, then that is income foregone by diverting them to the cider press and the relevant cost in deciding whether to press on or not.

Market Value of Apple Cider		$5.00
Less:		
Market value of apples	$3.00	
Additional costs	1.15	
		-4.15
Addition to Profits		$0.85

This technique applies in selecting new customers, approving an order quantity, utilizing productive capacity, allocating storage space, pricing new products, or replacing equipment, for example.

Minimizing Costs

Correct equipment replacement analysis should also encompass opportunity costs. In earlier chapters, the worth of an investment usually centered on whether the value of future inflows exceeded the cost of cash outflows; however, many alternatives focus not on maximizing profits but on minimizing costs and such an analysis emanates entirely from the viewpoint of costs without reference to revenues. *Replacement cost* decisions should also include a review of existing operations within the business along with possible alternatives; for example, replacement of an asset does not necessarily mean that an asset is worn out. A decade ago many Third World countries complained bitterly that they had become the "junkyard" of used American equipment. Obviously exported machinery still had some useful life left. Whether equipment is replaced because of technological, competitive, or cost reasons, the net cash outlay attributable to the investment evaluation should be considered as the sacrificed net salvage value if the activity or asset is not sold or scrapped. The following illustration outlines the type of opportunity cost reasoning a firm faces when it must choose between rebuilding existing facilities or building a new hotel.

Case Study: Should CIT build a new hotel or remodel an old one?

Crichton Investment Trust (CIT) found itself in possession of a rather ancient, but well-situated, 100-room hotel of sound structure but with 70-year old decor, plumbing and heating. The question they face is whether to renovate the old hotel or sell out and apply those funds toward construction of a new one. The consulting economist assembled the following estimates.

OLD		*NEW*	
(E) Book value	$ 600,000	Cost (new)	$6,000,000
(L) Market (salvage) value	$ 500,000		
(K) Rehabilitation cost	$1,000,000		
(k) Cost of capital	12%	Cost of capital	12%
(h) Tax rate	48%	Tax rate	48%
(C) Operating costs of bldg. per year	$1,000,000	Annual operating costs of bldg.	$ 400,000
(n) Estimated life (after remodeling)	40 years	Estimated life	40 years

In analyzing these two mutually exclusive alternatives, Crichton's staff elects to minimize costs rather than attempt to project future income from hotel operation. Further, to simplify initial calculations in the planning stages, it is assumed that the new hotel will be purchased for cash. Instead of relying on reconstruction costs alone, the staff applies the concept of opportunity costs, on the advice of the economist, to the old building; i.e., the investment base includes not only renovation outlays but the market (or salvage) value sacrificed if the old building is retained as well as tax savings given up on the book loss. Here is how calculations began on the old hotel.

First, the tax gain foregone is calculated. The tax gain foregone (TGF) is the book value (E) of the investment less its salvage value (L) times the applicable tax rate (h).

Formula: TGF = (E - L) h

TGF = ($600,000 - 500,000) 0.48 = $48,000

Next the investment base is derived. (For the new hotel the investment base is simply its cost of $6,000,000.) The investment base (IB) for the old building is its salvage value (L) plus the tax gain foregone (TGF) plus reconstruction costs (K).

Formula: IB = L + (TGF) + K

IB = $500,000 + 48,000 + 1,000,000 = $1,548,000

The third set of data concern depreciation, which is initially computed on a straight-line basis. For the new hotel, the depreciation base is its cost; for the old one, it is its book value plus revamping costs (E + K), $600,000 plus $1,000,000 or $1.6 million. Annual depreciation charges are 2½% calculated by dividing 40 (years) into the depreciation base, which equals $40,000 annually for the rehabilitated hotel and $150,000 yearly for the new alternative. (Please refer to Chapter Seven for further discussion on depreciation.)

With these figures available, the staff now calculates future operating costs and finally comparative total costs. (See Figure 6–4.)

Total costs, then, consist of the present values of outflows: the investment base (IB) in time period 0 (the present) plus the present value of a flow of costs occurring over a 40-year period. To facilitate the exposition of financial data of this case and to illustrate the significance of opportunity costs in these calculations, data were simplified but this does not affect the basis for decision-making. In cases where differences are not so apparent, absence of opportunity costs will give false signals. For example, if reconstruction costs

Figure 6-4

	OLD	*NEW*
Tax gain foregone	$ 48,000	$
Investment base	1,548,000	6,000,000
Annual depreciation	40,000	150,000
Future operating costs:		
(C) Operating costs	1,000,000	400,000
+ Annual depreciation	40,000	150,000
	$1,040,000	$ 550,000
(H) Tax at (h) 48%	499,200	264,000
(C) Operating costs	$1,000,000	$ 400,000
- (H) Tax saved	499,200	264,000
Actual cash flow	$ 500,800	$ 136,000
$(P/A_{12\%,40})$ (Present Value Factor)	X 8.243777	X 8.243777
Present Value of outflow	$4,128,484	$1,121,154

To determine which option offers the best advantages, total costs are computed by summing the investment base to the present value of outlays.

TOTAL COSTS:		
(IB) Investment base	$1,548,000	$6,000,000
PV of cash outflow	4,128,484	1,121,154
TOTAL	$5,676,484	$7,121,154

had been near $3,000,000, the new hotel option would be chosen if opportunity costs are included, but if only explicit cash costs had been included analysis would have signalled retaining the old hotel. On the other hand, once an outlay has been made, marginal decisions no longer refer to these historical costs.

SUNK COSTS

All decisions are made at the margin; they concern incremental outlays measured against incremental revenues. If option A is selected, in addition to explicit costs, opportunities foregone by not choosing alternatives B, C, and D enter into the decision-making process. *Sunk costs* have no meaning in these elections. They are *historical,* past, done with, and nothing we can do either now or later will undo what has been acted upon in the past. Choices are concerned with the future–future costs, future incomes–those cash flows which are anticipated to occur, or not occur, according to actions taken today.

Suppose that Bahgat Abdallah buys a used boat for $20,000, paying $2,000 down, the balance $300 monthly, with title changing hands after principal is paid. Default results in loss of all payments made but failure to pay releases the buyer from his obligation without penalty. After two years and $9,200 later, a severe recession depresses the boat market and Abdallah, the buyer, is offered another boat of the same size and age and similar condition for $8,000. If Abdallah continues making remaining payments totaling $10,800, he will at least conserve his $9,200 investment to date–or is that important? ***Sunk costs are not important.*** That $9,200 has been spent forever and his options now are the same as though he were considering two new investments: buy boat A for $10,800, or buy an identical boat B for $8,000.

If a person holds 10 December corn contracts in the commodity futures market on which he has lost already $5,000, should his decision to buy 10 more contracts pivot on losses already accrued? Or suppose that he has a $4,000 profit on those first 10 corn contracts, should he sell out and take his profit because "it never hurts to take a profit?" The answer is *no* in both situations. *The past is past.* Tomorrow depends upon what we do today, but by tomorrow today's actions will be irrevocable. Forecasting tomorrow's price moves in the futures market has nothing to do with the amount of losses or profits accumulated.

Cost of Driving Automobile

Let's apply the sunk cost concept to determining how much it costs to operate an automobile. Figures mostly range between 10-to-40 cents per mile, with a few estimates outside this range. Writing off the original cost of the automobile over some period based on time, mileage, or combination of time and mileage is an accounting entry and has no influence on the car's operational costs. Certainly direct costs–gasoline, oil–are relevant plus those which relate to the vehicle's wear–tires, battery, belts, etc. To the extent that use affects its market value is significant, but depreciation based on historical costs is not. Consider the following exposition.

Capital Recovery Costs

A firm purchased a small delivery van two years ago for $7,500, which is depreciated by the straight-line method over 5 years with a salvage value of $500. Its present book value is $4,700, market value, $3,000. Should the firm keep the vehicle two more years or sell it now and rent one when the need arises? If the concern uses it one more year the resale value will drop to

\$2,100 and by the end of two more years to \$1,300. Rate of return (interest) is calculated at 10%. The *capital recovery cost* of extending vehicle use another two years is the decrease in market value plus interest foregone on the sale price if it were sold today.

Capital Recovery Factor

To discover capital recovery costs, we begin by developing a capital recovery factor. (Also refer to Chapter Two.) The capital recovery formula is:

Formula:

$$(A/P_{i,n}) = P\left[\frac{i\,(1+i)^n}{(1+i)^n - 1}\right]$$

The bracketed portion in the above formula is called the capital recovery factor, which is equal to the sinking fund factor plus the interest rate. These factors for various interest rates and n periods are available in Table V in the Appendix.

The proper approach to capital recovery costs on any asset is to base it on present net realizable value. What is it worth if sold? By the end of another two years the van's market value will have dropped to \$1,300, a decrease of \$1,700. Proceeds from the sale are then available for use at the stated 10% rate.

Formula:

$$CRC = (M_t - M_{t+n})\,(A/P_{i,n}) + (M_{t+n})\,(i)$$

The capital recovery cost (CRC) equals the market value of the asset in time period t (M_t) less its market value in a future time period (M_{t+n}) multiplied by the appropriate capital recovery factor ($A/P_{i,n}$) plus the last resale value times the interest rate (i).

$$CRC = (\$3{,}000 - 1{,}300_2)\,(0.5761905) + (1{,}300)\,(0.10)$$

$$= 979.52 + \$130 = \$1{,}109.52$$

Another Way

The next method may be slightly longer but perhaps easier to digest.

Step One:

$$CRC_{t+1} = (3{,}000 - 2{,}100) + 3{,}000\,(0.10) = \$1{,}200$$

$$CRC_{t+2} = (2{,}100 - 1{,}300) + 2{,}100\,(0.10) = \$1{,}010$$

Step Two:

$$\text{PV of } \$1{,}200 = \$1{,}200\,(0.909091) = \$1{,}090.91$$

$$\text{PV of } \$1{,}010 = \$1{,}010\,(0.826446) = \underline{\quad 834.71}$$

$$\Sigma\text{PV} \qquad \$1{,}925.62$$

Step Three:

$$\text{CRC} = \$1{,}925.62\,(0.5761905) = \$1{,}109.52$$

The answer, of course, the same capital recovery cost of retaining the van for an additional two years, is based on estimated resale values and a 10% interest rate. Notice that in these calculations the original outlay of $7,500 does not enter into computations. This is a sunk cost, past history. Neither does current book value or rate of depreciation affect data. The analysis focuses on the money difference between selling a used asset now and selling it later. Its current book value is just as irrelevant as future depreciation charges. Nevertheless, tracking depreciation charges is especially important in tax calculations and cash flows measurements.

CONTENTS

Chapter Seven: Twenty-Six Formulas on Depreciation, Depletion, and Investment Credit for Capital Replacement and Growth

SEVEN

Twenty-Six Formulas on Depreciation, Depletion, and Investment Credit for Capital Replacement and Growth

However, once an opportunity is selected and incremental investments undertaken, how should these sunk costs be allocated against income for tax purposes? While sunk costs are historical, recoverable only by exhausting these assets, converting them into something vendible, or reselling them, from an accounting viewpoint they are important in taxable income or valuation calculations, and the depreciation method chosen hinges more on what Washington, D.C. does than on any measure of practicality.

Depreciating an asset, an accounting practice of making periodic charges against income to "recover" an investment outlay, may be *straight line* in which "recovery" proceeds *pari passu* or accelerated during the asset's life. As a management tool, depreciation functions to increase after-tax cash by reducing taxable income and to improve corporate savings by restricting cash income and to improve corporate savings by restricting cash income distribution to stockholders. Joel Dean writes: ". . . depreciation accounting is too crude a device to be managerially useful in our dynamic economy of changing technology, geographic mobility, rapid growth and rising price levels. As a neatly computed but fictitious cost, book depreciation obscures managerial analysis more than it enlightens." As the last chapter emphasized, previous financial outlays do not, or at least should not, affect present and future decisions. *Incremental investment* should be weighed against *expected return* that it will generate, and the proper focus of management is to earn a rate of return at least as great as stockholders could have acquired in some other alternative with adequate adjustment for differences in *risk* and *time.*

Before 1954, most businesses enlisted straight line depreciation expedient both for tax accounting and financial reporting purposes, but after the Internal Revenue Code of 1954 allowed a faster write-off for tax accounting many large firms switched to *accelerated depreciation* for financial reporting as well as tax purposes. However, a decade later, T.R. Archibald discovered that a number of large firms began switching back to straight line depreciation for financial reporting while employing an alternative measure for tax accounting. Why? Certainly some enterprises had isolated reasons. For example, management employing full costing accounting found they were underbid by contractors who resorted to straight line. In the main, however, the objective to paint a rosier picture to stockholders and potential investors (and creditors) and a gloomier one to the tax collector prevails. In fact, an analysis of several concerns demonstrates that both net income and profits improve in the magnitude of 1-to-23 per cent with the switch to straight line for financial reporting. The fullest effect manifests during transition years before the switch ceases to benefit new assets depreciated on a straight line basis. Of course, the pattern of investment, the life of the asset, and the rate of investment growth prior to and following the reporting switch influence the degree of benefit.*

Although most of this chapter assembles major *depreciation* remedies, the mathematics of figuring *depletion allowances* and *investment tax credits* merit a niche with appropriate examples on profitable administration of these techniques.

---

*For general comments on depreciation, see: Robert M. Parker, *Mathematics of Finance* (Englewood Cliffs, N.J.: Prentice-Hall, Inc., 1956), pp. 85 ff.

STRAIGHT TIME METHOD

The procedure in this category, *straight line depreciation,* about the only technique employed 50 years ago, still is popular, especially in heuristic models, because the arithmetic appears easy to understand and calculate. In practice, however, depreciation accounting, necessitated by tax laws and enforcement, requires diversion of resources from more productive endeavors, and in this context no accounting appliance is "simple," but costly. The device may be defensible if an asset wears out, *pari passu,* at an even rate; but suppose that overtime, or an extra shift, is added, do not assets simply break down quicker? The approach is criticized mainly because it does not encompass the *time value of money* in its calculations. In the following formula, annual depreciation is constant and applies an economic concept of the asset's estimated life.

Formula:

$$A = \frac{(P - L) + K}{n}$$

A = annual depreciation charge.

P = present value of asset at time zero (the purchase price).

L = salvage value (a future value) at the end of the asset's economic life, which is zero if the asset is abandoned at no cost, negative if removal costs exceed value, or positive if the asset has a resale value.

K = repair or rehabilitation costs during the asset's life.

n = economic life (in years).

A saw mill operator purchases a planer for $70,000 (including installation expenses) which has an economic life of 8 years. Repair costs will be an estimated $20,000, salvage value about $10,000. With the straight line method of depreciation, annual charges will be:

$$A = \frac{(\$70{,}000 - 10{,}000) + 20{,}000}{8} = \$10{,}000$$

The economic life, not necessarily the same as service life or ownership life, is the number of years of utilization "that minimizes the equivalent annual cost of holding" the asset. For this reason, depreciated machinery may be pressed into service for years after sale by the original owner. In this example, the annual $10,000 depreciation expense represents charges against taxable income as well as cash flow if operations are profitable.

From these data we can calculate the book value at the end of any given number of years (t). By formula, the book value (E) of the asset at the end of year t is:

Formula:
$$E_t = (P + K) - \left(\frac{P - L + K}{n}\right)t$$

For example, what is the book value of the planer at the end of the fifth year (t)?

$$E_5 = (70{,}000 + 20{,}000) - \left(\frac{70{,}000 - 10{,}000 + 20{,}000}{8}\right)5$$

$$= 90{,}000 - 50{,}000 = \$40{,}000$$

Of course, the above presentation inadequately treats repair costs which occur unevenly throughout the asset's life and may tend to accelerate toward the end of its functional life (but not necessarily). *Accelerated time methods* account for this erratic flow more satisfactorily.

Capital Recovery Factor—A Short-Cut

For those who open the handbook here and are unfamiliar with compound interest techniques and with the development of the capital recovery factor (CRF) in Chapters Two and Six, the following approximation represents capital recovery with straight line depreciation plus average annual interest. Within a narrow range of interest rates and time periods, margin of error is not too serious.

Formula:
$$CRF = \frac{1}{n} + \frac{i\,(n + 1)}{2n}$$

To illustrate, assume that interest rate (i) is 9% and time span (n) is 7 years, the result is:

$$CRF = \frac{1}{7} + \frac{0.09\,(7 + 1)}{2(7)} = 0.19428571$$

as compared to the Table V (Appendix) or actual application of the correct formula which gives 0.19869052.

Figure 7-1 profiles an interpretation of this factor when yearly capital recovery is homogeneous. The factor (0.19869052) bears upon the initial outlay, $42,000, and year-by-year, each line in the table exhibits how the investor recovers his capital during the economic life of the asset (7 years) and returns to him 9% interest on outstanding investment.

Figure 7-1

Year	*Balance Left at Beginning of Year (1)*	*Annual Net Receipts (2)*	*9% Interest on Balance in Col. (1) (3)*	*Portion of Net Receipts Available to Reduce (1) (4)*	*Unrecovered Balance at End of Year (5)*
1	$42,000.00	$ 8,345	$ 3,780.00	$ 4,565.00	$37,435.00
2	37,435.00	8,345	3,369.15	4,975.85	32,459.15
3	32,459.15	8,345	2,921.31	5,423.68	27,035.47
4	27,035.47	8,345	2,433.19	5,911.81	21,123.66
5	21,123.66	8,345	1,901.13	6,443.87	14,679.79
6	14,679.79	8,345	1,321.18	7,023.82	7,655.97
7	7,655.97	8,345	689.04	7,655.96	–
	TOTAL	$58,415	$16,415.00	$41,999.99	

The first step, to derive the equivalent uniform annual series multiply initial outlay of $42,000 by the CRF $(A/P_{9\%,7})$:

$$(\$42{,}000)\,(0.19869052) = \$8{,}345$$

Multiplying the column (1) entry by 9%, annual return on the unrecovered portion of the investment determines column (3). Subtracting column (3) from column (2) yields figures in column (4), annual cash flow from recovery minus an assignable return on the outstanding value of the investment for any given year. This sum, then, in column (4), being subtracted from column (1), results in the unrecovered balance at the end of the year (5), the same as the balance remaining in the following year (1). Figure 7-1, therefore, discloses the rationale behind proper treatment of a capital recovery factor in which an investor recovers his original investment plus a 9% return *pari passu.* In this sense depreciation represents capital recovery (which is included in the CRF) but is ignored as a separate element of cost; i.e., *cash flows,* rather than accounting entries, are relevant data in an economy study. But accelerating depreciation does not alter present values of cash flows.

ACCELERATED TIME METHODS

The advantage of accelerating accounting entries of depreciating assets is to reduce tax payments in early years of the economic life of an investment, postpone payment of taxes as long as possible, and hope that a favorable change in tax laws occurs in the near future. The rationale proferred, of course, is that repair and maintenance expenses are heaviest during the latter part of an asset's life and that to balance expenses with depreciation charges an accelerated method is preferred. Naturally, technological obsolescence or shifts in product demand (actual or induced by governmental regulations) encourage an early write-off of assets. The 1954 revision of the Internal Revenue Code supported application of the accelerated method for tax purposes, but for financial reporting the trend points to straight line depreciation. Two basic accelerated depreciation methods, along with several possible variants, prevail.

Sum-of-the-Years' Digits Method

One wide-spread treatment, sum-of-the-years' routine of accelerated depreciation, bears little, if any, relationship to the rate of expiring economic life of the investment, but in their infinite wisdom (?) the Internal Revenue Service approves of the technique. Suppose that an asset is depreciable over five years. Adding together 1 + 2 + 3 + 4 + 5 equals 15, *sum of the years' digits.* Depreciation for the first year absorbs $5/15$ (or $1/3$) of original investment (minus salvage value, if any), $4/15$ for the second year, $3/15$ for the third year, $2/15$ for the fourth year, and $1/15$ for the fifth year at which time the asset is totally depreciated. By formula the approach is:

Formula:

$$A_t = \frac{2(n - t + 1)}{n(n + 1)}(P - L)$$

A = annual depreciation.

n = economic life (in years).

N = number of years of depreciated use.

P = original outlay (present value of asset at time zero).

L = the future value (salvage value) at the end of the asset's useful life.

An asset purchased for \$1,900,000, having an economic life of 7 years and a salvage value of \$500,000, for the first year will carry a depreciation cost of:

$$A_1 = \frac{2(7 - 1 + 1)}{7(7 + 1)} (\$1{,}900{,}000 - 500{,}000)$$

$$= \frac{7}{28} (\$1{,}400{,}000) = \$350{,}000$$

And for the fifth year depreciation charges will be:

$$A_5 = \frac{2(7 - 5 + 1)}{7(7 + 1)} (\$1{,}900{,}000 - 500{,}000) = \$150{,}000$$

What is the book value of the investment at the end of any given year? The book value (E) is the original investment minus depreciation plus salvage value, or:

Formula:

$$E_t = \frac{(n - t)(n - t + 1)(P - L)}{n(n + 1)} + L$$

Let's solve, by formula, for the book value at the end of year 5.

$$E_5 = \frac{(7 - 5)(7 - 5 + 1)(\$1{,}900{,}000 - 500{,}000)}{7(7 + 1)} + 500{,}000$$

$$= \$650{,}000$$

Time Value Equivalence

When interest costs are included in the two approaches, *straight line depreciation and sum-of-the-years' digits* (SYD), so that both the equivalent opportunity costs of unrecovered investment and yearly recovery from depreciation are discounted back to the present, the sum of present values equate, as Figure 7–2 specifies first straight line, then SYD.

Data in the first two columns originate from beginning of year values, while depreciation is treated as an end of year phenomenon. Column (2) figures are a what-might-have-been approach, the return (computed at 9%) on book value at the onset of each year. Column (2) added to column (3), depreciation expenses for that year, yields column (4), capital recovery plus a return at 9%. These yearly flows in column (4) are multiplied by the appropriate present value factor from Table II in the Appendix. (Derivation and significance of present value factors are developed in Chapter Two.) Summing discounted payments in column (6) produces the same total with both modes of depreciation. Had this comparison been applied to the *declining balance or sinking fund* arrangement, results would have been the same. The significance of this introduction is that it allows us to develop a short-cut formula later in this chapter that serves regardless of the depreciation tactic exercised.

Figure 7-2

Year (N)	*Book Value Beginning of Year (1)*	*Return on Unrecovered Capital at 9% Interest (2)*	*Yearly Depreciation Charge (3)*	*Capital Recovery plus Return (2) + (3) (4)*	$(P/F_{9\%,n})$ *(5)*	*Present Value of Payments (4) × (5) (6)*
			Straight Line ($000)			
1	$1,900	$171	$200	$371	0.917431	$ 340.37
2	1,700	153	200	353	0.841680	297.11
3	1,500	135	200	335	0.772183	258.68
4	1,300	117	200	317	0.708425	224.57
5	1,100	99	200	299	0.649931	194.33
6	900	81	200	281	0.596267	167.55
7	700	63	200	263	0.547034	143.87
					ΣPV =	$1,626.48
			SYD (000)			
1	$1,900	$171.00	$350	$521.00	0.917431	$ 477.98
2	1,550	139.50	300	439.50	0.841680	369.92
3	1,250	112.50	250	362.50	0.772183	279.92
4	1,000	90.00	200	290.00	0.708425	205.44
5	800	72.00	150	222.00	0.649931	144.28
6	650	58.50	100	158.50	0.596267	94.51
7	550	49.50	50	99.50	0.547034	54.43
					ΣPV =	$1,626.48

Declining Balance Method

A second method, *declining balance,* amortizes an investment at a higher rate during the early portion of its economic life by applying a fixed rate to the net asset balance. As the asset's value declines, therefore, amount of depreciation decreases. Without a positive salvage value the depreciation rate would be 100 per cent, which would result in the asset being fully depreciated during its first year of use, and that would not pass muster with the powers that be.

The depreciation rate is sensitive to the size of terminal value, and small changes in salvage value reflect significant shifts in the depreciation rate (b).

Formula:

$$b = 1 - \sqrt[n]{\frac{L}{P}}$$

All symbols, other than b, were encountered in preceding formulas. Referring again to the previous example, if an asset costing $1,900,000 (P) has a salvage value of $500,000 (L) and an economic life of 7 years (n), the depreciation rate under the declining balance device will be:

$$b = 1 - \sqrt[7]{\frac{500{,}000}{1{,}900{,}000}} = 1 - 0.82636853 = 17.36\%$$

If salvage value had been decreased to $400,000, then rate of annual depreciation would have risen to nearly 20%; that is, changes in salvage value inversely affect the depreciation rate. The table in Figure 7-3 summarizes annual depreciation of this investment.

Figure 7-3

Year	*Asset Value Beginning of Year (1)*	*Annual Depreciation (@ 17.36%) (2)*	*Asset Value End of Year (3)*
1	$1,900,000.00	$ 329,840.00	$1,570,160.00
2	1,570,160.00	272,579.78	1,297,580.22
3	1,297,580.22	225,259.99	1,072,320.30
4	1,072,320.30	186,154.80	866,165.49
5	886,165.49	153,838.33	732,327.16
6	732,327.16	127,132.00	605,195.17
7	605,195.17	105,061.88	500,133.29
	TOTAL	$1,399,866.80	

However, suppose that salvage value were zero, or suppose a firm wanted to narrow the range between high and low annual depreciation charges; does an alternative formula exist? Yes! (Or else I would not have brought up the matter.)

Formula:

$$X_{db} = P + \frac{(1 - b)^n P - L}{1 - (1 - b)^n}$$

This formula solves for a depreciation base (X_{db}) while an arbitrary depreciation rate (b) is preselected. Salvage value (L) may or may not be zero. To operate this formula, let's choose arbitrarily a depreciation rate of 17%, a constant rate applied in the same way as in the above example only this time the depreciation base no longer represents the asset's true value but is simply a base figure from which annual depreciation expenses are charted.

$$X_{db} = \$1{,}900{,}000 + \frac{(1 - 0.17)^7 (\$1{,}900{,}000) - 500{,}000}{1 - (1 - 0.17)^7}$$

$$= \$1{,}900{,}000 + 21{,}389 = \$1{,}921{,}389 \text{ (depreciation base)}$$

During the economic life of this asset, by the revised formula, annual depreciation will be calculated at the rate of 17% of the adjusted depreciation base. Annual depreciation charges appear in Figure 7–4.

Figure 7–4

Year	*Depreciation Base Beginning of Year (1)*	*Annual Depreciation (@ 17%) (2)*	*Depreciation Base End of Year (3)*
1	$1,921,389.00	$ 326,636.13	$1,594,752.87
2	1,594,752.87	271,107.99	1,323,644.88
3	1,323,644.88	225,019.63	1,098,625.25
4	1,098,625.25	186,766.29	911,858.96
5	911,858.96	155,016.02	756,842.94
6	756,842.94	128,663.30	628,179.64
7	628,179.64	106,790.54	521,389.10
	TOTAL	$1,399,999.99	

Notice that total depreciation charges for the economic life of the asset roughly match, but not the difference between first and last years which exhibits a narrowing of range. Any differences are adjusted through the end value (salvage) of the investment.

Book value (E) can also be approximated for any year (t) with the following formula:

Formula:

$$E_t = P \sqrt[n]{\left(\frac{L}{P}\right)^t}$$

For example, to estimate (rounding contributes to errors) the book value for the fifth year in the first example:

$$E_5 = \$1{,}900{,}000 \sqrt[7]{\left(\frac{500{,}000}{1{,}900{,}000}\right)^5}$$

$$= \$732{,}187.75$$

Double Declining Balance Method

A variation of the preceding, *double declining balance,* allowed by the revised Income Tax Code of 1954, which popularity exceeds the former, for tax purposes is limited to new assets, which may not be depreciated faster than double the straight line rate assuming zero salvage value. That is, the annual depreciation rate (b) is:

Formula:

$$b = \frac{2}{n}$$

If an asset has an economic life of 7 years, the straight line rate is:

Formula:

$$A_t = \frac{2}{n}\left(1 - \frac{2}{n}\right)^{t-1} P$$

Staying with the same data, find depreciation charges for year 5 (t) of an asset that cost new \$1,900,000 and has an economic life of 7 years.

$$A_5 = \frac{2}{7}\left(1 - \frac{2}{7}\right)^{5-1} (\$1{,}900{,}000)$$

$$= \frac{2}{7}(0.2603082)\ \$1{,}900{,}000 = \$141{,}310.17$$

Similarly, book value of the investment is found by:

Formula:

$$E_t = \left(1 - \frac{2}{n}\right)^t P$$

What is the asset's book value at the end of the fifth year?

$$E_5 = \left(1 - \frac{2}{7}\right)^5 \$1{,}900{,}000 = \$353{,}275.42$$

Combined Tax-Deferral Method

With the double declining balance method figures do not work out evenly so that at the end of the economic life there is an undepreciated balance. If the book value exceeds the salvage value, the difference may be written off as a loss; but, frequently, after midpoint in the asset's life, depreciation plans are changed from double declining balance to straight line if the salvage value is zero or later if the salvage value is greater than zero. Formulas affecting this conversion appear below; Figure 7-5 summarizes the familiar asset depreciated at an annual rate of 28.6% under the DDB method for years 1 through 4, and at 33.3% for years 5 through 7, fully depreciating the asset during its economic life.

Figure 7-5

Year	*Asset Value Beginning of Year (1)*	*Annual Depreciation (2)*	*Asset Value End of Year (3)*
1	$1,900,000.00	$543,400.00	$1,356,000.00
2	1,356,000.00	387,987.60	968,612.40
3	968,612.40	277,023.15	691,589.25
4	691,589.25	197,794.53	493,794.73
5	493,794.73	164,598.24	329,196.49
6	329,196.49	164,598.24	164,598.24
7	164,598.24	164,598.24	–

Why was the switch made to straight line method in year 5 instead of year 4 or 6? This could have been determined by trial and error. But the *short-cut* method for *profitably* combining the two techniques lies in these two formulas.

Formulas:

$$A)\ t_o = \frac{n}{2} + 1\tfrac{1}{2}$$

$$B)\ t_e = \frac{n}{2} + 2$$

If the asset has an economic life ending in an odd digit, as in our example, and the salvage value is zero, formula (A) reports when the switch should be made from DDB to straight line based on the remaining value of the asset.

$$t_o = \frac{7}{2} + 1\tfrac{1}{2} = 3\tfrac{1}{2} + 1\tfrac{1}{2} = 5\text{th year}$$

If the asset's life ends in an even digit, then, of course, apply formula (B) to determine the year of switch.

In the above table a DDB rate of 28.6% was applied to depreciate the first four years of the asset's life. At the beginning of the fifth year, the remaining book value of the investment amounted to $493,794.73. Since three years remain, this sum is divided by 3, or, we can say that the remaining life of the asset, based on the book value at the start of year 5, will be depreciated at an annual rate of 33.3%.

1.25 Declining Balance Method

Not all assets may be depreciated at twice the straight line rate. For some the maximum is 1.5 times the straight line rate, for others 1.25. For pre-owned residential rental property acquired after July 24, 1969, with an anticipated functional life of less than 20 years, 1.0 times the straight line rate is the maximum allowable, but with an economic life exceeding 19 years the referential limit is 1.25 times the straight line rate. The advantage of starting with a 1.25 rate and switching to straight line at an optimum point is demonstrated in Figure 7-6 based on these circumstances.

The Pryor Real Estate Holding Co., Inc. purchased a 15-year old small apartment building for $900,000, which will be depreciated over 20 years taking advantage of the permissible accelerated arrangement. The terminal (resale) value is estimated at less than 10 per cent of the purchase price and for accounting and tax purposes the nominal sum counts as zero. In the first panel of figures, the building is depreciated at a straight line rate of 5%,

Figure 7-6

Year	Value Beginning of Year	Annual Depreciation (5%)	Value Beginning of Year	Annual Depreciation	SL Depreciation Beginning in Year ___
1	$900,000	$45,000	$900,000	$56,250	5%
2	855,000	45,000	843,750	52,734	5.26%
3	810,000	45,000	791,016	49,439	5.56%
4	765,000	45,000	741,577	46,349	5.88%
5	720,000	45,000	695,228	43,452	6.25%
6	675,000	45,000	651,776	43,452	6.67%
7	630,000	45,000	608,324	43,452	7.14%
8	585,000	45,000	564,872	43,452	7.69%
9	540,000	45,000	521,420	43,452	8.33%
10	495,000	45,000	477,968	43,452	9.09%
11	450,000	45,000	434,516	43,452	10.00%
12	405,000	45,000	391,064	43,452	11.11%
13	360,000	45,000	347,612	43,452	12.50%
14	315,000	45,000	304,160	43,452	14.29%
15	270,000	45,000	260,708	43,452	16.67%
16	225,000	45,000	217,256	43,452	20.00%
17	180,000	45,000	173,804	43,452	25.00%
18	135,000	45,000	130,352	43,452	33.33%
19	90,000	45,000	86,900	43,452	50.00%
20	45,000	45,000	43,448	43,448	100.00%

1.0 Straight line depreciation: $\Sigma PV = \$281,670$
1.25 Straight line depreciation: $\Sigma PV = \$295,941$

$45,000 per year, until the asset is fully depreciated at the end of 20 years. At the present value of this flow, discounted at 15%, the minimum rate of return (opportunity rate) expected by Pryor on such holdings, is $281,670.

In the second panel of data, Pryor combines two methods, switching from 1.25 to 1.0 times the straight line rate at an optimal point for the remaining 15 years of the asset's life. The optimal switching point is where the straight line rate equals or exceeds the accelerated rate.

For illustrative purposes an additional column on the right of the table records the pertinent straight line depreciation rate relevant to any given year in which the switch occurs. If the switch transpires in the first year, the property is depreciated over its remaining years at an equal rate of 5% of the original investment per annum. If the switch materializes after the end of the tenth year, the straight line rate is 11.11% of the book value at the beginning of the eleventh year and remains constant for the last ten years of the asset's life. Since 1.25 times the straight line rate is 6.25%, the point of indifference issues forth in the fifth year and for the remaining 15 years of the estate's life it is depreciated at 6.67% of the beginning of the sixth year's value of $651,776, which yields a constant depreciation charge of $43,452 annually. The building will be fully depreciated at the end of the twentieth year.

The sum of the present values under the straight line method is $281,670, and the higher $295,941 under the optimal switching technique. The second stream produces a present value greater by $14,271. As a percentage of investment, the before-tax incremental yield is 1.586% under the second option. Assuming a 47% marginal tax rate, the present value of the depreciation tax shield is 0.745% (1.586% X 47%), certainly less than 1% of the original investment in the apartment building.

Taxes, Capital Structure, and Depreciation

While the degree of leverage has been ignored in these calculations, certainly the amount of debt and interest payments, and the depreciation device selected will influence amount paid in taxes and return to common stockholders. Repayment of debt principal, interest and taxes, tie in with declining book value of the holding. With accelerated depreciation the impact on rate of return to common shareholders is unfavorable because of required higher rate of repayment. Debt financing, mostly cheaper than equity, in a highly leveraged firm will tend to produce a lower return to equity as before-tax cash flows rise during the latter years of the asset's life. As long as the tax rate continues constant, accelerated depreciation defers this tax obligation, which is reduced by interest expense. Therefore, careful evaluation may lead management to select straight line depreciation to maximize return on equity.

COMPOUND INTEREST METHODS

Some authors suggest that with property having economic lives exceeding eight years that the sum-of-the-years' digits takes precedence when salvage is zero and cost of capital ranges between 10 and 20%. Others prefer methods that explicitly encompass an interest rate.

Sinking Fund Method

If depreciation charges amass in a fund, then at the end of the asset's life the accumulation should match the total amount of depreciation after n years and the yearly increase of this depreciation fund will equal the depreciation charge for the related year. The purpose of this technique does not focus on asset replacement but pivots on cost allocation to measure income. Mostly linked to regulated industries (utilities, for example) it appears to offer little suitability to most nonregulated industries. The depreciation fund parallels a sinking fund first mentioned in Chapter Three. (Enlist Table VI in the Appendix to find $(A/F_{i,n})$.)

The equal annual contributions (A) for n periods grow in a fund at a given rate i, creating an ordinary annuity (P – L).

Formula: $$A = (P - L)(A/F_{i,n})$$

A business purchases an auxiliary generator for \$673,000 (P), which will have a terminal value of \$100,000 (L) at the end of its economic life of 10 years (n). The depreciation fund is expected to earn an average 6½% during its existence. How much are depreciation charges? (See Figure 7-7).

$$A = (\$673{,}000 - 100{,}000)(0.07410469) = \$42{,}462$$

The depreciation charge, \$42,462, for any given year equals the increase in the depreciation fund at the end of any given year.

Figure 7-7

End of Year	*Book Value of Asset*	*Annual Contribution*	*Interest due on Fund @ 6½%*	*Increase in Fund*	*Fund Value (cumulative)*
0	$673,000.00	$ –	$ –	$ –	$
1	630,538.00	42,462	–	42,462.00	42,462.00
2	585,315.97	42,462	2,760.03	45,222.03	87,684.03
3	537,154.51	42,462	5,699.46	48,161.46	135,845.49
4	485,862.55	42,462	8,829.96	51,291.96	187,137.45
5	431,236.62	42,462	12,163.93	54,625.93	241,763.38
6	373,060.00	42,462	15,714.62	58,176.62	299,940.00
7	311,101.90	42,462	19,496.10	61,958.10	361,898.10
8	245,116.52	42,462	23,523.38	65,985.38	427,883.48
9	174,842.09	42,462	27,812.43	70,274.43	498,157.91
10	99,999.83	42,462	32,380.26	74,842.26	573,000.17

Figure 7-7 condenses the depreciation schedule of an asset under the sinking fund method. Accrued annual payments of \$42,462 plus interest earned (at 6½%) on the previous period's accumulation will mount up to the depreciated value of the asset at the end of its economic life. Book value of the generator decreases until it matches salvage value at the end of the tenth year.

To find the book value at the end of any given year, determine the depreciation fund at the end of the year in question and subtract that amount from the original cost of the generator. The difference is the book value. Although payment into the fund is constant, because of interest earned depreciation charges rise. The book value formula is:

Formula: $E_t = P - (P - L)(A/F_{i,n})(F/A_{i,t})$

$(A/F_{i,n})$ = sinking fund factor, Table VI in the Appendix.

$(F/A_{i,t})$ = compound amount of annuity, Table III in the Appendix

$(P - L)$ = depreciation base (cost minus salvage value).

To solve for the book value at the end of year 5, recall that $i = 6.5\%$, $n = 10$, and $t = 5$, while $P = \$673{,}000$ and $L = \$100{,}000$.

$$E_5 = \$673{,}000 - (673{,}000 - 100{,}000)(0.07410469)(5.693641)$$

$$= \$673{,}000 - 241{,}763.31 = \$431{,}236.69$$

This result matches rather well the figure in Figure 7–7. With the sinking fund scheme, book values exceed those of the straight line pattern and this difference will increase with a higher interest rate.

Composite Life Method

This formulation consolidates the composite life of the entire enterprise, or a portion of it, when it encompasses various holdings of differing values and economic lives in order to express the business life in terms of a single figure. A mortgagor may want to know the composite life of a concern if assets of the entire operation are pledged. To protect the lender's interests the mortgage term should be less than the composite life of the business. This system is more comprehensible in the proximate profile, Figure 7–8.

In this example, investment in the enterprise is divided into four categories, indicated in the first column. The next three columns establish the depreciation base (P – L) for each group of assets and their estimated economic life (n). Annual depreciation contribution is determined by the sinking fund blueprint in which the interest rate is pegged at 7% and n varies

Figure 7-8

Investment	*Original Cost (P)*	*Salvage Value (L)*	*Depreciation Base (P - L)*	*Economic Life (n)*	*Annual Contribution (A)*
		($000)			
I	1,000	120	880	20 (years)	21.47
II	10,000	2,000	8,000	8	779.74
III	18,000	3,000	15,000	7	1,733.30
IV	6,000	–	6,000	12	335.41
TOTALS	35,000	5,120	29,880		2,869.92

according to the life expectancy of the investment. (Sinking fund factors are available in Table VI in the Appendix.) The next step is to find the value of an annuity of $1.

Formula:

$$(F/A_{i,n}) = \frac{(P - L)}{A}$$

Plugging in above values into this formulation gives us:

$$(F/A_{7\%,n}) = \frac{35{,}000 - 5{,}120}{2{,}869.92} = 10.41144$$

To discover the nearest n value turn to Table III in the Appendix. Under the 7% column, locate the nearest factor to the above and read the n value. The closest n is 8 years. The composite life of this concern is 8 years.

Annuity Method

Depreciation charges in this model are equal each year as each year's depreciation charges encompass part of the asset cost plus a return on the amount invested. This variation of preceding procedures equates the present value of the outflow in time period 0 to present values of inflows of annual depreciation plus salvage value. Annual depreciation (A) remains to be calculated.

Formula:

$$A = \frac{P - L\,(P/F_{i,n})}{(P/A_{i,n})}$$

(The reader should consult Chapter Two for an explanation of these factors. The factor in the numerator turns up in Table II in the Appendix; for the factor in the denominator regard Table IV.)

To illustrate this strategy refer again to the sinking fund problem in which P = \$673,000, L = \$100,000, n = 10, and i = 6½%.

$$A = \frac{673{,}000 - 100{,}000\,(0.53272603)}{7.1888303}$$

$$= \frac{619272.40}{7.1888303} = \$86{,}207$$

For comparison and contrast with the sinking fund rule a similar schedule emerges in Figure 7-9 with data similar to the earlier table.

In Figure 7-9, the constant annual depreciation charge was derived by formula. Interest income, based on net book value at the end of the preceding year, is calculated at 6½%. The difference between annual depreciation charge and interest income applies to the accumulated depreciation column. Notice that in both tables book value and accumulated depreciation work out equally. Interest, however, ebbs because it derives from decreasing book value. Nevertheless, net expenses under both schemes match.

Figure 7-9

End of Year	*Book Value*	*Annual Contribution*	*Interest on Book Value*	*Increase in Depreciation*	*Accumulated Depreciation*
0	\$673,000.00	\$ –	\$ –	\$ –	\$ –
1	630,538.00	86,207	43,745.00	42,462.00	42,462.00
2	585,315.97	86,207	40,984.97	45,222.03	87,684.03
3	537,154.51	86,207	38,045.54	48,161.46	135,845.49
4	485,862.55	86,207	34,915.04	51,291.96	187,137.45
5	431,236.62	86,207	31,581.07	54,625.93	241,763.38
6	373,060.00	86,207	28,030.38	58,176.62	299,940.00
7	311,101.90	86,207	24,248.90	61,958.10	361,898.10
8	245,116.52	86,207	20,221.62	65,985.38	427,883.48
9	174,842.09	86,207	15,932.57	70,274.43	498,157.91
10	99,999.83	86,207	11,364.74	74,842.26	573,000.17

A PROFITABLE, TIME-SAVING SHORT-CUT METHOD

Earlier in the chapter we compared straight line and sum-of-the-years' digits techniques to illustrate that time values of the depreciation stream were identical. If we had worked out data for the same asset under the declining balance method or sinking fund notion the same present values would have resulted, which leads us to a *short-cut formula.* Because of this *time value equivalency,* one formula will perform extra duty to account for *capital recovery* returns on any investment.

Formula: $CRD = (P - L)\,(A/P_{i,n}) + L\,(i)$

Capital recovery depreciation (CRD), the annual payment to recover the depreciable portion of the asset (P – L) during its economic life (n) plus an acceptable rate of return (i) plus return on the terminal resale value (L) if those funds had been available for alternative uses, is, of course, a restatement of the preceding but in an expediential form.

To solve with same data from the section on SYD: P = \$1,900,000; L = \$500,000; n = 7; i = 9%; and the capital recovery factor $(A/P_{9\%,7})$ is located in Table V in the Appendix. (Problem solution expressed in thousands of dollars.)

$$CRD = (1{,}900 - 500)\,(0.19869052) + (500)\,(0.09)$$
$$= \$287.17 + \$45.00 = \$323.17$$

Is this determination equal to the present values in earlier tables? To prove this, multiply the above result by $(P/A_{9\%,7})$ the factor for the present value of an annuity from Table IV in the Appendix.

$$V = \$323.17\,(5.03295) = \$1{,}626.50$$

This \$1,626.50 corresponds to the present values found under the longer measures, the present value of capital recovery plus return, which necessitates using only one formula for capital recovery depreciation in comparing time value alternatives regardless of the depreciation accounting instrument employed.

SERVICE LIFE METHODS

Service life remedies, really a variation of above methods, especially straight line treatment of assets, instead of depreciating property at a constant or accelerated rate of time, imply that a machine or asset is serviceable as long as it can economically produce; that is, the physical life of the property ranks more important and the faster it is exhausted the shorter its depreciable life. Four variations are explored here very briefly.

Service Hours

Service hours refer to the time an asset functions so that a one-shift operation will result in three times the life expectancy of three-shift wear. On a straight line basis in the formula n years now become T time measured in hours, the expected number of hours of service from a machine.

Formula:

$$a = \frac{(P - L) + K}{T}$$

An engine that costs \$400,000 (P) will have a nominal scrap value (assume L = 0) and absorb about \$50,000 (K) in repair over its estimated useful life of 250,000 hours (T). What is the rate of depreciation (a) per hour?

$$a = \frac{(400{,}000 - 0) + 50{,}000}{250{,}000} = \$1.80$$

The book value (E) at the end of any time period (t) is found by a known formula modified to fit a service-hour situation.

Formula:

$$E_t = (P + K) - \left(\frac{P - L + K}{T}\right)t$$

At the end of 100,000 hours of use, the book value will be:

$$E_{100{,}000} = (400{,}000 + 50{,}000) - \left(\frac{450{,}000 - 0 + 50{,}000}{250{,}000}\right)100{,}000$$

$$= 450{,}000 - 200{,}000 = \$250{,}000$$

Productive Output

A similar mechanism links economic life of an investment to its estimated total output. Depreciation charges correspond to per unit (or batch) of output instead of time and fluctuate according to production and sales.

Formula:

$$a = \frac{(P - L) + K}{N}$$

A cutter purchased for \$100,000 (P) will have an estimated residual (terminal) value of \$16,000 (L) after an output of 1,200,000 (N) production units. (K = 0) What is the depreciation expense per unit of output (a)?

$$a = \frac{100{,}000 - 16{,}000 + 0}{1{,}200{,}000} = \$0.07$$

Too, an accelerated strategy serves by adapting previously discussed formulas to hours or production units rather than time so that holdings depreciate faster when investment is new and requires less repair expenses. Investments in natural resources lend themselves to a production model.

Depletion

In natural resource investments not all equipment necessarily has the same life expectancy as the supply of natural elements, although when coal, iron, gas, petroleum, trees, etc. are depleted the economic life of at least some equipment, too, has terminated. Depletion, of course, refers to exhausting natural resources. The productive output logic is acceptable in accounting, the percentage rule below is not.

A coal mine, having an estimated productive output of 40 million tons, is developed at a cost of \$8 million. During its second year of operation 300,000 tons are mined and 250,000 tons are sold. Here we have two charges to consider: one to operating income and one to inventory. Annual depreciation expenses (A) is the cost per unit of production (a) times output (x). $(A = a \cdot x)$

Formula:

$$A = \frac{(P - L) + K}{N}(x)$$

In this example, L and K disappear, so that annual depreciation costs against operating income are:

$$A = \frac{8{,}000{,}000}{40{,}000{,}000}(250{,}000)$$

$$= \$0.20\ (250{,}000) = \$50{,}000$$

The depletion charged to inventory is: $0.20 × 50,000 = $10,000.

Percentage of Gross Income

The government has granted certain industries preferred status so that recovery of investments can be effectuated at a higher rate. The Internal Revenue Code establishes depletion allowances ranging upwards from 5%; this constant percentage (b) then reduces *gross income* (Y_g) produced by investment in a natural resource. However, the depletion allowance is limited to one-half of net revenue $\left(\frac{Y_n}{2}\right)$.

Formula:

$$A = Y_g\,(b), \quad \left(\text{if } A \leqslant \frac{Y_n}{2}\right)$$

Say that a domestic oil well yields 1,000,000 barrels annually which are sold at $11 per barrel to yield gross income (Y_g) of $11,000,000. Production costs are $4 a barrel ($Y_n$ = $7,000,000), the depletion rate is 22% (b). By what amount can taxable income be reduced, not to exceed $3,500,000?

$$A = (\$11{,}000{,}000)\,(0.22) = \$2{,}420{,}000$$

Since this sum is less than $\frac{Y_n}{2}$, or $3,500,000, the permitted depletion allowance, the full $2,420,000, decreases taxable income by that figure. Notice that this artifice is biased against high cost, low volume producers and discourages investment in secondary and tertiary extraction methods which are higher cost techniques. This tends to promote abandonment of resources and discourages new, speculative firms from competing with low cost, high volume operations.

INVESTMENT TAX CREDIT METHOD

Ever since fruitful effects with the Internal Revenue Act of 1962, investment tax credits have been resurrected as the *sine qua non* of reviving an economy already made sick by over-injections of taxes and inflation. The purpose is to encourage investment by permitting additional credits up to a certain percentage of acquisition costs of tangible assets applied against income taxes—a strategem akin to but not as spectacular as depletion allowances. The flow-through model uses full investment credit in the year in which credit is granted. The deferred scheme spreads tax credit over estimated life of the asset. If the second method is utilized for an investment costing \$100,000 with an economic life of 7 years and allowable tax credit of 7%, then income taxes are reduced by \$1,000 a year $\left(\frac{\$100{,}000 \times 7\%}{7} = \$1{,}000\right)$.

To tie in depreciation, depletion, and tax credits explicated in this chapter, the following three formulas solve for income taxes due (H_t), net income after taxes (Y_{nh}) and cash flow (F_t). Any inappropriate (equal to zero) term in the expressions drops out of computations.

Formula:

$$H_t = [Y_n - (C + A_d + A_a)]\, h - v$$

Formula:

$$Y_{nh} = [Y_n - (C + A_d + A_a)]\, (1 - h) + v$$

Formula:

$$F_t = (Y_n - C)\,(a - h) + A_d\,(h) + A_a\,(h) + v$$

H_t = income taxes (dollar amount) in year t.

Y_n = net income.

C = expenses before deduction of depreciation and depletion.

A_d = depreciation expense.

A_a = depletion allowance.

h = income tax rate.

v = investment tax credit.

Y_{nh} = net income after taxes.

F_t = cash flow in year t.

The question, however, not limited to amount of depreciation and depletion allowances plus available tax credits, is how to maximize the long run worth of the business, which means not only when will investment occur and what kind of technology, but how it will be financed, the degree of operating and financial leverage, risk on not only the new undertaking but the change in risk on the entire investment portfolio, the cost of financing and the effect on overall costs of the enterprise. Or will it be best not to invest at all but lease?

CONTENTS

Chapter Eight: Leasing, Buying or Borrowing for Funds and Profits

EIGHT

Leasing, Buying or Borrowing for Funds and Profits

While property owners can deflate taxable income with depreciation expense deductions, lease payments, also deductible expenses, become more attractive as tax rates rise. Nevertheless, leases entail future commitments as much as, or more than, ownership, and as an alternative financing source alter capital structure and degree of leverage of the corporation. Wherein *financial leases* predominate in the firm's operations, these obligations should inhere in trading-on-the-equity ratio computations discussed in Chapter Five. In the formula, page 190, the proportion of common stock in total capitalization (b) should reflect leases to properly assess leverage and risk.

This chapter excludes short-term arrangements such as rentals, cancellable leases, generally, any contract that runs less than three years (an optional, not obsolute cutoff) or any lease that does not involve a fixed future commitment. Such leases are termed *operating leases.* A *nonpayout lease,* one in which the asset rents for some period less than its useful life, accumulates to less than the asset's purchase cost. The lessor bears risks of obsolescence and loss, maintains and repairs equipment, covers costs of insurance, taxes and license fees. Of course, the final user in the end must pay for these outlays; the point here rests on how they are paid.

On the other hand, a *financial lease* represents the type of long term irrevocable commitment that will run most, if not all, of the asset's economic life and lease payments exceeding the item's purchase price. Terms of contract may accord renewal at reduced rate, sanction penalty for early cancellation, or convey title to the asset at some fixed figure at the end of the lease period. Variations are almost endless. The lessee usually bears maintenance and operating costs, the lessor property taxes, although these, too, enter into cost calculations.

Basic financial lease amalgams produce hybrids such as the *full maintenance lease* in which the lessor maintains, repairs, and replaces worn equipment but the lessee may end up paying more than if he had assumed this responsibility in the first place. The *tax shelter lease,* or *leveraged lease,* corresponds to the situation where the lessor (frequently an individual or group), in a higher tax category than the lessee, passes along some tax advantages and investment credits (if available) in the form of lower lease payments. Two other terms which crop up are: *net lease,* a financial lease where operating expenses and taxes are paid by the lessee; *gross lease,* where the lessor incurs these obligations.

CHECKLISTS OF OWNERSHIP VERSUS LEASING

Everything written about pride of ownership and other intangibles are usually only marginally important when the decision between buying and borrowing and leasing is close, otherwise leasing strikes out as an acceptable alternative. The main economic factors, generally quantifiable ones, conform to some measurable comparability. The following checklists, a cross-section of experiences and opinions, adumbrate useful guidelines in analysis.

Advantages in Owning

1. For utilities and price regulated businesses, property owned becomes part of the rate base.

2. Owned property, especially buildings, always have some value at the end of their depreciated life even assuming 100 per cent depreciation.

3. If assets are financed with long term debt or preferred stock in a high interest period, obligations may be refinanced at lower interest rates in a future period, while a lease represents a fixed obligation in all periods.

4. An asset, equipment or building, no longer needed for operations may be sold or disposed of but an unwanted lease is dead weight.

5. Ownership provides possibility of capitalizing costs of future alterations to property.

6. The enterprise may be able to take advantage of business tax credits or other subsidies.

7. In periods of rising prices resulting from inflation, some company assets may appreciate in value but that protection does not revert to lessees.

8. Owning may be cheaper than leasing.

9. Owning does not establish a fixed commitment in the same way a lease does.

10. Interest on borrowing and accelerated depreciation may be more attractive financially than leasing.

11. Owning may decrease pressure of loss in hard times while a lessee may lose an income-producing asset.

12. There may exist greater flexibility in use and disposal of owned property.

*Advantages in Leasing**

1. There may be no alternative to leasing; e.g., the ideal location can only be acquired by lease or a foreign government will lease but not sell.

2. The lessee may be able to structure the transaction to defer taxes.

3. As a financing alternative, leasing may be cheaper than auto-financing (leveraged lease, for example), decrease costs (in a period of rising prices with a fixed lease payment), offer long term financing without diluting ownership or control, or permit 100 per cent financing.

4. Leasing avoids restrictive covenants in loan agreements, leaves alternative financing sources (line of bank credit) still untouched, and generally is easier to negotiate.

5. Lease payments figure in before-tax rather than after-tax earnings; leases free working capital for other endeavors.

6. A lease arrangement allows cost-cutting equipment to be installed immediately.

7. Leases establish only a restricted, not general, obligation in the case of bankruptcy or reorganization.

8. Lease obligations create a permissible cost under government contracts.

9. Leases shift some risks, especially risk of obsolescence.

10. Lease contracts assure prompter, better servicing of equipment than what might be available to an owner of the same equipment.

---

*For a brief discussion on advantages of leasing, refer to: James C. van Horne, *Fundamentals of Financial Management,* 2nd ed. (Englewood Cliffs, N.J.: Prentice-Hall, Inc., 1974), pp. 360–2.

11. With leasing a firm can increase leverage and alter its capital structure in a manner not always available during periods of an unfriendly financial market.

12. The lease contract may more closely conform to the firm's needs; it avoids the problems associated with selling unwanted equipment; a lessee can "borrow" in smaller units than with direct debt.

Leasing, if thought of as simply another price, a price which may represent either a premium or discount to owning, is less complicated, and should not be paired with an alternative finance source such as 100 per cent debt in capital budgeting decisions. Leases, when capitalized, do, in fact, alter capital structure as much as a new issue of preferred stock, and these long term commitments represent risk to other categories of debtors and owners. Once leasing becomes an alternative to consider, then, which analytical process will yield the best answer?

LEASE OR BUY

Of several following techniques analyzing the buy-lease-borrow decision, this one is preferable because it excludes explicit financing costs from the capital budgeting decision process, while other models encapsulate financing charges in the analysis of cash flows, to avoid double counting. Recall that discussion in earlier chapters did not link necessarily a specific project with a specific financing source because capital decisions are made not in isolation of one another, that waves and ripples caused by one decision undulates the entire pool of assets and liabilities. Cost of capital consists of explicit costs as well as implicit ones, risks borne by owners, and this overall cost, or discount rate, specifies the investment's present value. In the following buy or lease formulation, two rates reflect degree of risk associated with various flows. Where certainty of outcome is less predictable, such as operating costs and salvage value, the higher cost of capital discount rate substitutes for those after-tax flows, such as lease payments and tax shield, which are discounted at the lower after-tax borrowing rate of the firm.

The results balance the net present value of the purchase alternative against net present value of flows associated with leasing. The net present value of flows related to buying the asset is the sum of the present values of the asset's net after-tax cash operating profits, plus the discounted after-tax residual value, less initial cost of the asset. The net present value of flows pertaining to the leasing option is the present value of the net after-tax cash operating profits minus after-tax present values of lease payments, the lease payments and tax savings being discounted at a rate reflecting lower risk (greater certainty).

Rather than compute these flows separately, R. W. Johnson and W. G.

Lewellen suggest eliminating common elements in these formulas, combining them to determine differences, because it is change in net present value (ΔNPV) that interests us. The change in net present value equals the net present value of the buying option minus the net present value associated with leasing.

Formula:

$$\Delta NPV = \sum_{t=1}^{n} \frac{h(A_t) - K_t(1 - h)}{(1 + k)^t} + \frac{(1 - h_v)(L - E)}{(1 + k)^n} - P + \sum_{t=1}^{n} \frac{s_t(1 - h)}{(1 + r)^t}$$

h = applicable tax rate on ordinary income.

A = annual depreciation charge (for owned assets).

t = a specific time period (or year).

K = additional annual operating costs from owning asset (including property taxes, maintenance, repair, insurance, etc.).

k = after-tax cost of capital for the enterprise.

L = terminal (residual) value of asset.

h_v = applicable tax rate on gains or losses from sale of asset.

E = expected book value of asset at termination of its economic life.

n = economic life (years).

P = cash purchase price of asset.

s = annual before-tax lease payment.

r = after-tax interest rate on business's recent borrowings.

While other models may approach the decision-making process on the assumption of 100 per cent borrowing to finance the asset's purchase, this measure does not. This rule assumes that leasing is another purchase price considered in the decision process, a price that may not necessarily be higher than outright purchase. Too, the formulation does not encompass some non-quantifiable advantages of buying or leasing listed at the beginning of this chapter and elsewhere. These factors may be of substantial importance in the final analysis but no method exists to generalize these elements which subjectively may be added to or subtracted from calculable change in net present value computed from numerical data.

To interpret results of this formulation, a negative change in net present value suggests that leasing is preferable to buying; a positive change in net present value favors purchasing over leasing. If the purchase price, less tax savings from depreciation, is less than the burden of lease payments, then a buy signal emerges from the positive change in NPV. If the net salvage value is less than the additional costs of owning, then a negative change in NPV triggers a lease decision. To better comprehend this model, examine the following illustration.

Buy or Lease Metal Detection Equipment

A firm decides to invest in additional metal detection equipment at a cost of \$52,500 (P), which will have a residual value of \$5,000 (L) at the end of its economic life of 6 years (n), with an anticipated applicable tax rate of 30% (h_v) on gain issuing from sum-of-the-years' digits method of depreciation which produces zero residual book value (E = 0). If metal detection equipment is leased, the annual fixed lease payment will be \$13,500 (s). Incremental pre-tax operating costs of owning are \$1,000 yearly (K). The applicable tax rate on ordinary income is 50% (h); overall cost of capital is 15% (k); the pre-tax rate on recent borrowings is 8% (r = 4%). An annual profile in Figure 8-1 facilitates quick grasp of the problem.

Figure 8-1

Year	*Tax Saving on Depreciation* $h(A)$ *(1)*	*After-Tax Added Operating Costs* $(1-h)K$ *(2)*	*Salvage Value Net of Taxes* $(1-h_v)(L-E)$ *(3)*	*After-Tax Lease Payment* $(1-h)s$ *(4)*	*Present Value of (1) - (2) + (3) @ 15% (5)*	*Present Value of (4) @ 4% (6)*
1	0.50(15,000)	0.50(1,000)	–	0.50(13,500)	6,087	6,490
2	0.50(12,500)	0.50(1,000)	–	0.50(13,500)	4,348	6,241
3	0.50(10,000)	0.50(1,000)	–	0.50(13,500)	2,959	6,000
4	0.50(7,500)	0.50(1,000)	–	0.50(13,500)	1,858	5,770
5	0.50(5,000)	0.50(1,000)	–	0.50(13,500)	994	5,548
6	0.50(2,500)	0.50(1,000)	0.70(5,000)	0.50(13,500)	1,837	5,335
					\$18,083	\$35,384

ΔNPV = 18,083 - 52,500 + 35,384 = +967

Conforming to established criteria, the emergent positive change in net present value betokens that buying takes precedence over leasing if a firm decision to acquire detection equipment exists, but this may not necessarily be the focal point. Suppose that the firm has requested bids on equipment. It may, after evaluating lowest bids, still decide not to accept the alternative investment when ranked alongside other company priorities. Consider the lease offer as just another bid for the company's business. Other things being equal, the lease option is dismissed as too costly in terms of expected benefits and alternatives such as labor-intensive search techniques or contracting with an outside enterprise for services. By the same token, the firm may also reject purchasing equipment for the same reasons; that is, both prices and buying or leasing are too high.

Nevertheless, because of the possibility of spreading tax obligations an individual investor may offer to lease equipment for $12,500 yearly.

[*An Example:* A leaser of equipment can lease it for less than what a purchaser pays for it as arranged between Flexi-Van Corp. and the Bank of America. Flexi-Van Corp. ordered $23 million of truck trailers, assigned the order to Bank of America, let the bank pay for the trailers, and then leased them from the bank. *Payments totaled less than what the bank paid* for the trailers. Flexi-Van Corp. traded tax reduction benefits—depreciation expenses and investment tax credits—for lower costs. Additionally, the bank forgave interest on the lease. Consequently, both parties benefited more from the combined transactions than if either had acted independently without cooperating.]

Applying the above formula meets with a negative change of −1,653 to net present value which signals that leasing is cheaper than buying and now may make investment decidedly desirable because of an upgrade in ranking on the scale of priorities.

Timing of lease payments similarly affects NPV. In this illustration it was assumed that lease payments began after equipment had been installed and used for one year with equal annual payments thereafter. Of course, payments may neither be equal nor annual but this does not change the method of calculation. (See "Solutions to Other Problems" at end of chapter.) Too, payments may start at the beginning of the lease period amounting to advance payments so that in this example, the lease would have been paid out at the end of the sixth year. Had lease payments been required at the beginning of each year in an equal sum, the positive change in NPV would have been +2,382 instead of +967, which, in effect, substantially raises the lease price vis-à-vis the outright purchase price.

LEASE OR BORROW

While the first technique appropriately interprets leasing versus buying, without reference to the source of financing, the next three methods center on acquisition by borrowing mostly up to 100 per cent of the purchase price.

Discounted Cash Flow

Another, popular but less desirable, technique compares cash flows arising from leasing against borrowing either 100 per cent or a combination of equity and debt–both flows being discounted at the same cost of capital (k) rate. The objective is to match discounted cash flows with the lesser being more desirable; i.e., a discounted present value cost of lease financing (V_r) less than the discounted present value cost of debt financing (V_d) advertises leasing, while a V_d less than V_r signals debt financing as the better bet.

Of course, one objects to violation of principle that a capital investment decision should be evaluated without reference to a singular method of financing and without including finance charges *sui generis.* Cost of capital computations discussed in Chapter Four encompassed not only explicit finance charges–interest costs, dividend payments, etc.–but implicit ones, risk for example, as well. The following illustration does indeed utilize a 15% cost of capital (k) rate but the formulations, in dealing with the debt option, employs an additional interest rate i (8% in this example) applied against the borrowed portion of the financing arrangement. That clearly involves double counting. The costs computed in the example reflect an intermixture of tax savings effects and amount of funds provided, and the technique misleads management from making a more accurate comparison on leasing versus borrowing costs.

The procedure, easiest explained by the application of two formulas, then compares results. Under debt financing, the company seeks to borrow Q amount of funds at the onset after a down payment of (1 – Q). Interest (I) and depreciation (A), annually deducted to reduce taxable income, minimizes cash outflow by the applicable tax rate (h). The other outflow associated with the investment decision, debt reduction payment (S), is assumed yearly. These adjusted outflows are discounted at rate k, the firm's marginal investment return, the yield which protects the value of owners' investment in each time period t.

Formula:

$$V_d = \sum_{t=1}^{n} \frac{S_t - (I_t + A_t)\,h}{(1+k)^t} + (1 - Q)$$

Lease financing, somewhat easier to calculate since rental payments are fully deductible, in most cases, in the year paid out with the tax shield depending upon the marginal tax rate applicable at the time, results in:

Formula:

$$V_r = \sum_{t=1}^{n} \frac{s_t(1 - h)}{(1+k)^t}$$

n = economic life of asset (in years).

t = a specific time period (year in this case, $t = 1, 2, \ldots n$).

S_t = payment in year t to reduce principal plus interest $(p_t + I_t)$.

I_t = dollar amount of interest payable in year t.

A_t = annual asset depreciation.

h = applicable income tax rate.

k = marginal investment return for the enterprise.

Q = initial borrowing to finance asset purchase.

$(1 - Q)$ = down payment at time of acquisition when purchase is financed by a combination of equity plus debt.

s_t = lease payment in year t.

V_r = discounted present value of lease financing.

V_d = discounted present value of debt financing.

Carefully observe differences between these formulas and the preceding one in which two discount rates reflected relative predictability of outcomes without double counting. Too, the above does not easily account for possibility of disparities in operating costs which may increase or diminish total outflow under each alternative.

Modifying the previous example, still assume a lease or borrow alternative to finance acquisition of \$52,500 detection equipment, which has an economic life of 6 years (n) and can either be leased for \$12,500 yearly (s_t) or purchased with a down payment of \$10,500 (1 - Q) and the balance of \$42,000 (Q) financed for 6 years at a true interest rate of 8% with principal (p) and interest (I) payable in the sum of \$9,085 (S_t) at the end of each year. (The 11½% equivalent lease option is a 3¼% premium over the borrowing rate.) Additionally, the marginal investment rate, 15% (k), tax rate 50% (h), and SYD depreciation are still valid. Should the company lease or borrow?

In Figure 8–2, the table records steps in the discounted cash flow method with each column's designation keyed to symbols appearing below the formulas. Because $V_d < V_r$, the operation points toward borrowing rather than leasing. Although the problem is slightly modified, compare this result with that found in the previous section in which leasing for \$12,500 annually was a decided improvement over the buy option.

Dissimilarities emerge not only from departures in approach but also in data. The decision: to lease or to borrow. Previously we rallied on whether to lease or buy without specifying the finance plan because discount rates already mirror these costs (whether equity or debt). With the second method

Figure 8-2

A. PV After-Tax Cost of Debt Alternative

$P = 52{,}500$

$(I - Q) = 10{,}500$

$Q = 42{,}000 = q_1$

Year (t)	q_t*	S_t	I_t	p_t	A_t	$(I_t + A_t)$	$(I_t + A_t)h$	$S - (I_t + A_t)h$	$\frac{S - (I_t + A_t)h}{(1+k)^t}$
1	42,000	9,085	3,360	5,725	15,000	18,360	9,180	- 95	- 83
2	36,275	9,085	2,902	6,183	12,500	15,402	7,701	1,384	1,047
3	30,092	9,085	2,407	6,678	10,000	12,407	6,204	2,881	1,894
4	23,414	9,085	1,873	7,212	7,500	9,373	4,687	4,398	2,515
5	16,202	9,085	1,295	7,790	5,000	6,295	3,148	5,937	2,952
6	8,412	9,085	673	8,412	2,500	3,173	1,587	7,498	3,242
									$11,567
						+ (1 - Q)			10,500
						ΣPV			$22,067

*Balance at beginning of year.

B. PV After-Tax Cost of Financial Lease

Year (t)	s_t	$s_t(1-h)$	$\frac{s_t(1-h)}{(1+k)^t}$
1	12,500	6,750	5,870
2	12,500	6,750	5,104
3	12,500	6,750	4,438
4	12,500	6,750	3,859
5	12,500	6,750	3,356
6	12,500	6,750	2,918
		ΣPV	$25,545

and data input, lease would occur only with a marked increase in the corporate tax rate. But in the previous technique a shift in k or r or both revises the picture while recasting k in the present mechanism scales both V_d and V_r in the same direction. Naturally, manipulating outflows revamps results, but this does not influence application of these techniques. To isolate the tax consequence in lease or borrow decisions, R. F. Vancil has put together the following procedure.

Basic Interest Rate

To reduce combined effects of financial leverage to only the tax savings denouement, the *basic interest rate* (BIR) approach developed by R. F. Vancil bears upon tax savings ascribed to the noninterest constituent of lease disbursements. This procedure, assumes 100 per cent financing, credits lease remittances with a tax saving in an amount that exceeds tax savings on interest charges that would be payable on an equivalent loan. The tax shield from interest recompense allows for the amount of financing provided by a given plan; that is, 100 per cent debt, which method is inconsistent with the normative framework of capital budgeting.

As in the previous mechanism, this one, too, relies on the development of two formulas–one, the present value of tax savings arising from the noninterest segment of lease installments; another, the present value of tax savings from depreciation generated from ownership–to differentiate results in deciding whether to lease or borrow. The cost of leasing amounts to the equivalent cash price of the asset (P) less the sum of present values emanating from the noninterest portion of lease payments. The cost of debt financing emerges with the cash purchase price minus the sum of present values issuing from annual depreciation charges.

Imputed interest expenses in leasing is rq_t, the firm's borrowing rate times the balance outstanding at the beginning of each year t. The remaining portion of the lease payment $(s_t - rq_t)$ is a surrogate for repayment of principal, the noninterest division of each lease installment. To eliminate the difference in the amount of financing furnished by leasing or borrowing, this model identifies tax savings on the $(s_t - rq_t)$ share of lease contributions. Therefore, the formula for finding present value of the concomitant tax saving from leasing is:

Formula:

$$V_r = P - \sum_{t=1}^{n} \frac{(s_t - rq_t)\,h}{(1+k)^t}$$

The present value of depreciation, the only deductible expense under ownership is found by:

Formula:

$$V_d = P - \sum_{t=1}^{n} \frac{A_t(h)}{(1+k)^t}$$

P = equivalent cash purchase price of asset.

n = economic life of asset.

t = the specific year under analysis.

s_t = lease payment in year t.

rq_t = imputed interest expense for year t.

$(s_t - rq_t)$ = noninterest integrant of each lease disbursement (corresponding to principal repayment of loan).

h = applicable income tax rate.

k = marginal return on firm's investments.

A_t = depreciation in year t.

Referring again to the same example, notice narrowing of inequalities between the two outcomes and what emerges in the lease-borrow decision. The detection equipment costs \$52,500 (P). It is depreciated by sum-of-the-years' digits method (A_t) over its economic life of 6 years (n). Assume 100 per cent financing so that the original surrogate loan balance is \$52,500 (Q) and the corresponding lease expenditure of \$12,500 annually (s_t) defrays interest charges calculated at 8% (r) on the outstanding balance at the beginning of each year (q) and the remainder of the lease fee ($s_t - rq_t$) serves to reduce the "loan" principal. The income tax rate is still 50% (h), k is 15%. The accompanying table consolidates pertinent calculations. (See Figure 8–3.)

Notice that the difference between present values under the DCF method was \$3,514, while the present model shows only a \$150 margin in the opposite direction. Under the DCF mechanism, buying was definitely favored. Under the BIR rule, the decision affirms leasing. Recall, too, that the NPV remedy decidedly favored leasing at a lease price of \$12,500 annually, the same assumption employed in these last two examples. The superiority of the NPV system has already been attested to; possible shortcomings of the DCF and BIR strategies spring up. Asymmetry between the last two approaches centers on what is included. Both interest and noninterest elements of lease subscriptions are deductible, but to eliminate financial leverage dominance and focus on the tax savings sequela, the BIR modification of assumptions will naturally produce disparity of results. The question on which blueprints to discard has led some businesses to adopt a simplistic rule of thumb.

Figure 8-3

A. PV of Tax Savings on Noninterest Portion of Lease Payments.

Year (t)	q_t*	rq_t	$(s_t - rq_t)$	$(s_t - rq_t)h$	$\frac{(s_t - rq_t)h}{(1+k)^t}$
1	52,500	4,200	8,300	4,150	3,609
2	44,200	3,536	8,964	4,482	3,389
3	35,236	2,819	9,681	4,841	3,183
4	25,555	2,044	10,456	5,228	2,989
5	15,099	1,208	11,292	5,646	2,807
6	3,807	305	12,195	6,098	2,636
				ΣPV	-$18,613
				P	+ 52,500
					$33,887

*Balance at beginning of year.

B. PV Cost of Ownership.

Year (t)	A_t	$A_t(h)$	$\frac{A_t(h)}{(1+k)^t}$
1	15,000	7,500	6,522
2	12,500	6,250	4,726
3	10,000	5,000	3,288
4	7,500	3,750	2,144
5	5,000	2,500	1,243
6	2,500	1,250	540
		ΣPV	-$18,463
		P	+ 52,500
			$34,037

Rule of Thumb—A Short-Cut

This short-cut approach, certainly not a recommended one, is sometimes known as the "Envy Rule" or "Beat-the-Middleman System" because its initial premise is that if A leases to B and makes a profit doing so, then why not eliminate A and let B keep the profits? The quick procedure relies on analogical interest charges. If B pays 7 per cent on its borrowings to purchase equipment but lease fees are a correlative 12 per cent interest, then to borrow and buy is cheaper than to lease and let the other fellow make all the profit. Let's see how this works with the same example.

Still assuming that annual rental disbursements on $52,500 worth of equipment is $12,500 and that the firm can borrow funds at 8%, what is the parallel interest rate attributed to leasing over a six-year period? The first step is to determine the matching interest rate. Several formulas surface in Chapter One to find r, the interest rate. One device is to divide 52,500 by 12,500, which yields 4.2. Now referring to Table IV in the Appendix, along the n = 6 row, we learn that 4.2 rests between 11% and 12% and by interpolation judge the corresponding interest rate to be 11¼%.

Therefore, the corporate decision may follow this line. "Since we can borrow funds at 8% to buy the equipment which we will then own, why pay a leasing firm 11¼% comparable interest and not own the equipment? Therefore, we will not lease."

If we kept score, out of four methods developed, although assumptions have been modified in each instance, the count is two for leasing, two against. This rule of thumb does not, of course, substitute for sound economic analysis. While it is a cheap way to arrive at a decision, the quality of the decision does not reflect sound management appraisal. Objections met in Chapter Two again crop up. Size and timing of cash flows affect present value of cash outlays, and the Arnold Syndicate case provides a clear example on this matter. Too, the rule of thumb ignores dissimilarities in expenses between owning or leasing and opportunity costs. The matter of risk is overlooked. The procedure violates the rationale behind capital budgeting decision-making. The shortcomings evidenced here also prevail in the next short-cut rule of thumb.

LEASE CAPITALIZATION

Because leasing arrangements have grown rapidly in the past couple of decades and because lease undertakings represent substantial long term commitments for many firms, accounting for leases moves up from the footnotes into the balance sheet. Of course, competent financial analysts have long accounted for lease installments, although some have taken an ostrich stance, usually in the direction of overstatement. Two instruments of analysis appear below.

Rule of Thumb—A Short-Cut

While the following technique evinces its share of faults, once basic information is accumulated and generalizing assumptions made, the three-step approach will at least interpret capitalized value of long term lease engagements. For the outsider, information to ascertain or verify these obligations will always be incomplete; for the insider, the scheme in the next section is preferable.

STEP ONE: To the extent possible assemble all pertinent data on leases—minimum annual rentals, amounts paid, remaining terms of leases, types of leases, when agreements were entered into and then calculate a weighted average of the remaining terms of leases.

STEP TWO: Multiply this average by the factor which reflects life and average interest rate built into leases; i.e., treat leases in the same manner as loan pledges.

STEP THREE: Register the capitalized value of lease indebtedness.

To determine the extent of lease liability, the formula is:

Formula:

$$P = s_t(b)$$

To find factor (b):

Formula:

$$b = \frac{(1 + i)^n - 1}{(1 + i)^n \, (i)}$$

Or it can be located by reference to Table IV in the Appendix.

For example, an 8% loan payable over 8 years requires a level annual pay-out of around 17.4%. Taking the reciprocal of 17.4% yields 5.75, which can be found by the above formula. Multiplying 5.75 times annual lease contributions will result in the total value of lease expenditures. The importance of this procedure in analyzing a firm's capital structure manifests in the table in Figure 8–4.

Figure 8–4

	CAPITAL STRUCTURE ($000,000) *No Lease Value*		*5.75 × Annual Rents*	
	A	*B*	*A*	*B*
Long Term Debt	15	25	15	25
Lease Commitments	–	–	40	10
Total Obligations	15	25	55	35
Stockholders' Equity	75	65	35	55
Total Investment	90	90	90	90
Owners' Participation	5.00	2.60	0.64	1.57

Here we have two large retailers: A is a major discount chain which has expanded rapidly by leasing its stores; B is a well-known chain which owns a substantial proportion of its stores. The discount chain has annual lease encumbrances of $6,960,153, while the department store chain pays out around $1,740,038 in lease expenses. Analyzed from the viewpoint of no debt or contingent liability in the financial statement, both firms exhibit stockholders' equity exceeding several times the amount of debt with store A in the stronger position. Multiplying lease payments by the factor 5.75 not only reverses the position of stores A and B but the equity-to-debt ratio of A is decidedly unfavorable with "debtors' contributing more than owners to the firm's operations. The analysis reveals that A's indebtedness jumped more than 3½ times, while B's indebtedness rose less than 1½ times. That is, in the first instance it appears as though A has unused debt capacity when in reality it has employed substantial leverage.

Nevertheless, this method forces the analyst to substitute judgment for data and, therefore, conclusions will not be consistent from firm to firm. For example, the imputed average interest rate is subject to wide variances, and, too, in the absence of complete or accurate information there may be error on the remaining life of lease ties. (Which terminal data should be used?) Rental data may mislead if it accommodates taxes, maintenance, insurance, and other expenses. However, from the inside these informational errors should at lease be minimized.

The Penney Method

The J. C. Penney Company in 1969 developed a blueprint to measure long term lease liabilities, albeit a conservative one, in response to the wide-ranging results circulated in analysts' reports. The interesting nature of Penney's leases dramatizes the arduousness of reconciling many types of nearly 2,500 leases which have characterized the business's operations. While the following steps appear to simplify the notion, the perplexity lies in accumulating accurate data and then sifting it for relevant details. The steps in the Penney Procedure are:

STEP ONE: Evaluate structure of leases and admit only those which typify long term affirmations. The first criterion is to embrace only those which elapse three years or more from date of analysis. Deny entry to leases that originally exceeded three years but expire in less than three years from time period t.

STEP TWO: Irreversibility validates a firm commitment so that the first cancellation year predicates the extent of fixed responsibility; a new investment decision must be made again at that time; data on leases with less than three years until the first cancellation option are treated the same as in Step

One and are rejected. But renewing a lease counts as a new contract beginning in time period (t + 1).

STEP THREE: Any lease contingent upon some other operation of the firm, such as straight percentage leases dependent upon sales, are excluded.

STEP FOUR: Only the equivalent "net lease" commitment enters into calculations; i.e., on gross leases executory expenses are deducted. Project these expenses for the life of the lease as defined above.

STEP FIVE: Determine the effective interest cost paid by lessor and treat this figure as the effective interest rate paid by lessee. (This rate depends upon the prevailing interest rates at the time the contract was signed, the type of investment financed, and the lessor dealt with.)

STEP SIX: Calculate the present value of the net commitment for each year of the lease.

STEP SEVEN: The sum of present values, then, represents the total value of lease commitments.

Figure 8-5

Year	*Minimum Lease Payment*	*Executory Expenses*	*Net Commitment*	*Present Value*
1	$300,000	$55,000	$245,000	$ 226,852
2	300,000	57,000	243,000	208,333
3	300,000	59,000	241,000	191,314
4	300,000	61,000	239,000	175,672
5	300,000	63,000	237,000	161,298
6	300,000	65,000	235,000	148,090
7	300,000	67,000	233,000	135,953
8	300,000	69,000	231,000	124,802
			ΣPV	$1,372,314

For example, Figure 8-5 records the procedure for finding the value of a lease which has a remaining life of 8 years. Executory expenses may include insurance, real estate taxes, maintenance, and related disbursements which are subtracted from the minimum annual rental fee to derive net charges for each year. Executory outlays may remain constant, decline, or increase, according to assumptions based upon recent experiences. In this example, an 8 per cent rate appears reasonable so that the appropriate factor from Table II in the Appendix is multiplied by the net commitment to arrive at the present value for each year. The sum of present values renders the value of this lease; the same steps would then have to be repeated for all other operative leases to determine the total figure for the company. Such a procedure contributes to financial planning internally and externally provides interested parties with better insight into the lessee's capital structure. But are there other risks?

RISK AND OPPORTUNITY LOSS

At the beginning of this chapter risk of obsolescence was suggested as an advantage to leasing. Since risk can never be excluded, it can only be shifted from one party to another regardless of guarantees from individuals either in private or public sectors. Any risks apparently shifted from lessee to lessor are ultimately borne by the final consumer unless, of course, the game of musical chairs leaves the financier or lessor without profit. The lessor carries other risks as well, the uncertainty of a lessee bankrupting, failing to pay, or unilaterally cancelling the lease (defaulting) before the asset's economic life expires. Or changes in corporate tax rates alter the buy-borrow decision. Too, the lessee risks acquiring equipment for longer than needed.

Risk: Lease or Borrow

An earlier rule-of-thumb indicated that if the comparable interest rate embodied in the lease exceeds the firm's borrowing rate, then the company should not lease but buy. The example below identifies a case in which the cognate lease interest rate exceeds the loan rate by 4½ percentage points, and it still may be better to lease; but the disparity could have been even greater and still countenance leasing under certain circumstances. Size and timing of cash flows depend largely upon legal contracts surrounding lease or debt payments except for depreciation which is fixed, within limits, by tax law.

Suppose that an enterprise requires construction equipment costing \$105,000 (P) with an economic life of 6 years (n) and depreciated by the SYD method which results in zero terminal value. If equipment is no longer needed at the end of any year (t), it can likely be sold for its residual value (L_t) in year t, that is, its book value (E_t), so that $L_t = E_t$. Since the before-tax borrowing rate is 8% (i), and the applicable tax rate is 50% (h), the effective after-tax rate is 4% (r). Of course, the cost of this equipment depends upon the length of time its use is required and, therefore, annual costs of owning will vary. The decision incorporates this uncertainty.

Alternatively, the construction equipment may be leased for \$26,000 annually (s_t) during the entire 6 years. Cost to lessee is (h) (s_t), or \$13,000, in each time period assuming no change in tax rate. The firm's analysts calculated that the correlative interest rate on leasing the entire 6 years is 12.6%, considerably higher than recent borrowing costs. The lease may be canceled without penalty after 3 years. The lessor may not cancel. Results of borrowing (owning) versus leasing appear in Figure 8-6.

Figure 8-6

Year (t)	*PV Tax Shield Depreciation SYD (1)*	*PV Residual Value (2)*	*NPV Costs (3)*	*Probabilities (4)*	*Expected PV (Buying) (3 X 4) (5)*	*PV Leasing (6)*	*Expected PV (Leasing) (4 X 6) (7)*
1	14,423	72,115	18,462	0.05	923	12,500	625
2	25,980	46,228	32,792	0.10	3,279	24,519	2,452
3	34,870	26,670	43,460	0.20	8,692	36,076	7,215
4	41,281	12,822	50,897	0.20	10,179	47,189	9,438
5	45,391	4,110	55,499	0.35	19,425	57,874	20,256
6	47,366	0	57,634	0.10	5,763	68,148	6,815
	TOTALS			1.00	$48,261		$46,801

Column (1), the present value of the tax shield from depreciation based on sum-of-the-years' digits for year t, is:

Formula:

$$V_{syd} = \frac{(A_t)(h)}{(1 + r)^t}$$

Tax shield from depreciation for year 1 is $\frac{6}{21}$ (105,000), (A_t), times the tax rate 50%, (h), or $15,000. Its present value is:

$$V_1 = \frac{15{,}000}{(1 + 0.04)^1} = \$14{,}423$$

For year 2:

$$V_{1+2} = \$14{,}423 + \frac{(25{,}000)(0.50)}{(1 + 0.04)^2} = \$25{,}980$$

The present value of the salvage value, assumed to equal the book value for any given year, is:

Formula:

$$V_t = \frac{P - \sum_{t=1}^{n} A_t}{(1 + r)^t}$$

For the second year:

$$V_2 = \frac{105{,}000 - 55{,}000}{(1 + 0.04)^2} = \$46{,}228$$

NPV costs, Column (3), are P minus columns (1) plus (2).

The present value of the tax benefit from leasing, column (6), is the annual lease payment (s_t) times the tax rate (h) divided by $(1 + r)^t$ for any given year t. Lease payments are $26,000 annually.

The rule of thumb, comparative loan rate method, points in the direction of buying (8% against 12.6%). Keeping the construction equipment for the full 6 years, its economic life, again highlights that buying and borrowing is cheaper than leasing. But what are the chances that the equipment will not be needed for the entire 6 years?

Comparative present values of flows lean either toward buying or leasing in different time periods. Paring columns (3) and (6) tells us that using the asset through year 4 endorses leasing as the cheaper source. Working the asset 4 years carries no cancellation premium and the present value of leasing ($47,189) is less than the present value of borrowing and buying ($50,897). In fact, buying is preferred only if the asset will be held for 5 or 6 years.

One approach to this dilemma is to assign probabilities, the likelihood that the asset will be needed only t number of years. Project analysis and management discussion reveals there is 1 chance in 20 the equipment will be required only 1 year, and probabilities for subsequent years appear in column (4) which indicate that odds are highest that equipment will be used through year 5. If we pick the fifth year, then the decision is to borrow and buy. But we cannot ignore there will be a need for possibly only 3 or 4 years. The technique? Derive expected values accomplished in columns (5) and (7). Summing expected present values of buying (5) versus leasing (7) definitely applauds the cheaper leasing option, a difference of $1,460.

Opportunity Loss

Figure 8-7 projects the amount by which the cost of one alternative exceeds the cost of the other. This excess cost is what H. Bierman calls the *opportunity loss.* Probabilities are carried forward from the preceding table. The opportunity loss states that if we bought when we should have leased, then the *additional* cost of owning is an opportunity cost, the incremental loss incurred by not selecting the cheaper alternative.

Referring to the preceding table, for each year subtract the datum in column (6) from column (3). If the result is positive, enter it under the column, "buying opportunity loss." If the difference is negative, change its sign and enter the result under the column, "leasing opportunity loss."

For example, in year 1, if the asset were bought, the present value of the loss is \$298, the additional cost incurred from an opportunity foregone. In the 6th year, if the asset were leased, the additional cost accompanying this decision is \$1,052. For each figure entered, multiply it by the corresponding probability to derive expected values for each alternative. The opportunity loss of buying exceeds leasing by \$145; ergo, leasing is preferred.

Figure 8-7

		Buying		*Leasing*	
Year (t)	*Probability*	*Opportunity Loss*	*Expected Value*	*Opportunity Loss*	*Expected Value*
1	0.05	298	15		
2	0.10	827	83		
3	0.20	1,477	295		
4	0.20	741	148		
5	0.35			831	291
6	0.10			1,052	105
TOTALS	1.00		541		396

SOLUTIONS TO OTHER PROBLEMS

In the foregoing material, examples were simplified to illustrate various techniques. Lease payments were assumed to occur annually and at the end of each period whereas payments may be required more frequently and at the beginning of the period. This presents no difficulty except that extra computations may be involved. The following four problems specify rapid solutions to modify any of the procedures in this chapter.

Finding i for End of Month Lease Payments

What is the nominal interest rate (i) when lease installments come about monthly at the end of each month? Assume that a trailer costs \$81,352 (P) which is leased at \$2,000 (s) monthly (m = 12) for 5 years (n = 5); that is, for 60 periods (mn), and at the end of its economic life, salvage value (L) will be nominal. To find the nominal interest rate on this lease, first we will need to determine the factor (f) for $1 in order to utilize Table IV in the Appendix.

Formula: $f = \frac{P}{s}$

In this example, the factor (f) is $\frac{81{,}352}{2{,}000} = 40.676$.

By trial and error, reading along line 60 of Table IV, we find the factor 40.676. At the heading of the corresponding column, the interest rate, i, is 1.375%, or annually, j, 16½% (found by interpolation).

When the factor works out between two columns in the table, then interpolation, discussed earlier in this Handbook, will furnish a close approximation.

Finding i for Beginning of Month Lease Payments

This problem, essentially the same as above, requires that each monthly lease payment is due in advance, which means that the lessor has use of money 30 days sooner while the lessee loses 30 days use of funds. Assuming the same set of data, what is the nominal interest rate in this case?

The first step: Determine the present value of the first lease contribution; i.e., the present value of $1 today is 1.000.

The second step: For the remaining 59 disbursements, again find the factor in Table IV for the nearest interest rate, $\frac{j}{m}$. When j equals 16½% and mn 59, the factor is 40.235294.

$$\begin{array}{r} 1.000000 \\ \underline{40.235294} \\ 41.235294 \end{array}$$

Since the summation exceeds 40.676000, we know that when $2,000 exchanges transpire at the start of each month that the nominal interest rate exceeds 16½%. For 18%, the result is:

$$\begin{array}{r} 1.000000 \\ \underline{38.970972} \\ 39.970972 \end{array}$$

Interpolation produces an estimated interest rate of 17.16%.

Finding Monthly Lease to Be Paid at Start of Month

The unknown in this problem, not the interest rate, spotlights monthly lease charges. Suppose that an organ costs \$8,000 (P), has an economic life of 6 years (n), is expected to earn 12% (j) on investment, and carries a zero salvage value. How much should periodic charges be for the 72-month lease span?

Formula:

$$s = \frac{P}{f}$$

By the same method as above, the present value factor is 1.000000 plus 50.661895 (when mn = 71 and i = 1%), or 51.661895 (f). Dividing this factor into the asset's cost yields the monthly lease payment:

$$\frac{8{,}000}{51.6619} = \$154.85 \text{ (monthly)}$$

Finding Unpaid Principal on Lease

What is the unpaid principal (Q) on a lease after X number of installments have passed?

Formula:

$$Q = (f)\,(s)$$

Assuming the same data in the preceding problem but now that only 30 payments of \$154.85 (s) each have transpired, what is the unpaid principal on the remaining 42 payments?

PV of next payment		1.000
PV of following 41 disbursements		35.500
	f =	36.500

Q = (36.500) (154.85) = \$5,652 (unpaid principal)

Similarly, with nonleased assets such as inventories, the problem is how to minimize costs and maximize profits.

CONTENTS

Chapter Nine: Pinpointing Profit Factors in Inventory Management

$$\text{Formula: } Y^* = c\,(LOQ)\left[\frac{\sum_{1}^{n} T_{ht}}{\sum_{1}^{n} T_a^*}\right] \qquad 298$$

NINE

Pinpointing Profit Factors in Inventory Management

A former Dun and Bradstreet vice president wrote that there are three psychological spark plugs which influence management decisions. "These three spark-plugs are the expected volume of sales in the months ahead, the expected profits in the months ahead, and the expected level of prices of raw materials or finished products which a business uses in its daily operation. Decisions, policies, and budgets are based fundamentally by managements on these three expectations."* Inventory management is just as important for small retailers as giant manufacturers. If expected sales fail to materialize then inventories accumulate and businesses have involuntarily increased investment in inventories—known as *unplanned investment*—resulting in a rapid rise in liabilities. One benefit of leasing is release of scarce funds for

*Roy A. Foulke, *Inventories and Business Health* (N.Y.: Dun and Bradstreet, Inc., 1960), p. 8.

other current and more lucrative alternatives, but if released funds simply finance an oversize, slow-moving, or obsolete inventory which increases storage and clerical expenses, then management effectiveness is blunted.

Of course, a wide range of formulations, techniques, and procedures crop up to control what might become an unwieldy investment in inventory. Too, problems originating in loose scheduling, uneconomical lot sizes, transportation difficulties, poor supplier relationships, etc., not purely financial in origin, certainly are mirrored in the bottom line. Much that has been developed on inventory control refers to production planning, engineering, quantitative controls, and security measures that only indirectly relate to the finance function. Consequently, selection of formulas and procedures that most closely adhere to the objectives of this Handbook are included with due recognition of the complexity of surveillance of multi-item inventories and of industrial engineering techniques that contribute to effective control, flow, and maintenance of inventories.

Essentially inventories are classified as *raw materials, work-in-process,* and *finished goods* for manufacturers; *work-in-process* and *finished products* for assemblers; and *finished merchandise* for distributors and retailers. Whatever the breakdown, overinvestment in superfluous items, obsolete or defective material, means funds tied up in less productive endeavors. If management assumes additional risks of speculator, as frequently occurs, then this extraneous contingency can bring a business to its knees just as readily as excessive lease commitments. Of course, correct anticipation of price changes can make a hero of the speculator, but so can correct anticipation of market demand or of a competitor's weakness. This chapter zeroes in on minimizing inventory investment in order to maximize profits.

ECONOMIC LOT SIZE MODEL

How much stock should be ordered? Enough—but not too much! Enough to forestall stockouts and production down-time or customer loss but at the same time minimize costs associated with ordering and carrying inventories.

A Simple Model

The objective of the first model is to determine total annual inventory cost (C_i) by this formula:

Formula:

$$C_i = \frac{a\,C_s}{J} + 0.5\,(c)\,(b)\,J + ac$$

a = annual demand in units (units per year).

C_s = set-up costs (dollars per lot).

J = economic lot size (units per lot).

$\frac{J}{2}$ = average inventory carried per period.

c = unit cost (for manufactured items this includes the sum of direct material, labor and overhead costs).

b = total carrying charges expressed as a percentage of the cost of items carried annually in inventory.

The formula advertises that total annual inventory costs (C_i) consist of set-up outlays plus the yearly expenditure of carrying inventory plus the value of inventory. However, to minimize inventory disbursements determine the economic lot size (J). One approach, trial and error in tabular form, is illustrated in Figure 9–1.

Figure 9–1

Lots (per year) (1)	*J (units)* (2)	$\frac{a\,C_s}{J}$ (3)	+	$0.5(c)(b)J$ (4)	+	*a c* (5)	=	C_i (6)
1	250,000	$ 175		$16,350		$272,500		$289,025
2	125,000	350		8,175		272,500		281,025
3	83,334	525		5,450		272,500		278,475
4	62,500	700		4,088		272,500		277,288
5	50,000	875		3,270		272,500		276,645
6	41,667	1,050		2,725		272,500		276,275
7	35,715	1,225		2,336		272,500		276,061
8	31,250	1,400		2,044		272,500		275,944
9	27,778	1,575		1,817		272,500		275,892
10	25,000	1,750		1,635		272,500		275,885
11	22,728	1,925		1,486		272,500		275,911
12	20,834	2,100		1,363		272,500		275,963

Suppose that an electronics manufacturer wants to calculate the economic quantity of metal cases for its pager. Since the firm requires 1,000 units daily, and operates 250 days annually, yearly demand aggregates to 250,000 units (a) which cost $1.09 each (c) to produce. Set-up costs equal $175 a lot ($C_s$). The ensemble of interest, taxes, insurance and other related costs works out to 12% (b) of unit cost.

The first column of the Figure 9–1 table records number of times per year lots are made up (or ordered)—from once yearly to monthly in this case.

Dividing annual usage of 250,000 units by column (1), rounding the result to the next highest whole number, results in quantity of units per lot. Column (3), cost of preparation for production, rises in equal installments of \$175. The outlay of carrying inventory, column (4), consists of the average inventory on hand during the year times cost per unit multiplied by the carrying charge percentage of part cost. In column (5) the value of inventory equals annual consumption times unit cost. Totaling columns (3), (4), and (5) expresses total annual inventory disbursement, column (6).

Observe that column (6) sums first fall sharply, then decrease by smaller amounts, and finally rise. Why? While carrying charges in column (4) decrease, set-up expenditures rise, column (3). When production preparation expense additions more than offset the drop in carrying costs, it no longer pays to produce items in smaller lot sizes. Therefore, available data indicate that turning out about 25,000 cases 10 times a year will tend to minimize corresponding inventory outlays.

Classical Model—A Short-Cut

Although the above mechanism is cumbersome, costly, and complex, restating the formula to solve for J above, the economic order quantity (EOQ), reduces annual total costs compared with a rule-of-thumb that does not adequately account for rate of sales, unit cost, and set-up expenditures.

Formula:

$$EOQ = \sqrt{\frac{2\,a\,C_s}{bc}}$$

a = annual demand in units.

C_s = production preparation outlays or order expenses if purchased from a supplier.

c = unit cost (either purchase price or manufactured cost).

b = total carrying charges expressed as an annual percentage.

Assume that a bicycle manufacturer markets 400,000 bicycles yearly. The firm buys certain components, namely, wheels, for \$3 a piece (c) from a supplier and estimates that ordering expenses—documentation, unloading, checking, clerical, processing, etc.—total about \$110 per order (C_s). Carrying charges—interest, taxes, insurance, storage—add 20% (b) to costs. What is the economic order quantity?

$$EOQ = \sqrt{\frac{2\,(800{,}000)\,(110)}{0.20\,(3)}}$$

$$= \sqrt{2.933 \times 10^8} = 17{,}127 \text{ units}$$

Naturally, accuracy of results from this formula depends upon reliability of data. Actual usage will most likely deviate from estimates so that periodic inventory adjustments become mandatory. Too, even if all data are dependable, discounts, custom, regularity of reorder cycle will diverge from the specific EOQ. In this case, the company's books show actual orders of 17,400 wheels each time.

Order Cycle

How frequently should inventory be replenished under conditions of certainty? In this simple illustration of a single item, the solution is uncomplicated.

Formula:

$$N = \frac{a}{EOQ}$$

In this example,

$$N = \frac{800{,}000}{17{,}127} = 46.7 \text{ times per year,}$$

or about every 8 days. In practice, 17,400 units were ordered every 8 days.

Safety Stock

However, to account for possible delay in transportation resulting from weather, strikes, or misrouted shipments, the enterprise stocked an additional lot of wheels, a *safety stock,* to prevent disruption of the production schedule. For example, say that normal processing and shipping time is 24 days. Under certainty, management places an initial order for 17,400 wheels when inventory level drops to 52,500 units to assure a continuous supply and an average inventory level of 8,700 wheels. But if shipment does not arrive by the 24th or 25th day, the plant will have to suspend productive operations. For a safety cushion, management allows an extra 8 days when ordering so that the initial *order point* becomes 69,900, a rounded 70,000 wheels in practice. Naturally, this safety stock raises costs of carrying inventory because it doubles average inventory on hand. Total inventory costs equal carrying costs plus ordering costs.

Quantity Discounts

Another factor that affects the economic order quantity, *volume discounts,* can be calculated from the basic EOQ mechanism. Savings from quantity purchases equal the discount per unit times usage. On the other hand, cost arises from additional carrying outlays less saving on ordering expenses.

Formula:

$$\Delta C = \left[\frac{(J^* - J)\,bc}{2}\right] - \left[\frac{a\,C_s}{J} - \frac{a\,C_s}{J^*}\right]$$

ΔC = change in costs resulting from a change in order quantity.

J = original EOQ.

J* = revised lot size.

bc = carrying costs per unit per period.

a = total usage per period (year).

C_s = ordering costs.

Staying with the wheel problem of 800,000 (a) annual usage, ordering costs of $110 ($C_s$), and carrying expenses per unit of $0.60 (bc), ordering 46 times yearly the order size was 17,400 (J). However, assume that a per unit discount of $0.01 (v) is offered if the bicycle manufacturer will order 40,000 wheels (J*) each time. The first question to answer: What is the net increase in costs (ΔC)? In the above formula, the first expression refers to the additional carrying expenditures resulting from the increased order size; the second bracketed portion relates to the saving in ordering disbursements.

$$\Delta C = \left[\frac{(40{,}000 - 17{,}400)\,0.60}{2}\right] - \left[\frac{(800{,}000)\,(110)}{17{,}400} - \frac{(800{,}000)110}{40{,}000}\right]$$

$$= 6{,}780 - 2{,}857 = \$3{,}923 \text{ net increase in costs.}$$

On the benefit side, the firm saves from a lower purchase price; viz., per unit discount (v) times consumption (a).

Formula: Savings = (v) (a)

Savings = ($0.01) (800,000) = $8,000

Therefore, the net advantage (8,000 – 3,923 = $4,077) favors expanding order size to 40,000 wheels, paying additional storage expenses, and ordering 20 times yearly which lowers ordering costs. This alternative, of course, is not the cheapest one, for if wheels could be bought in any quantity for $2.99, the economic lot size would be nearly unchanged (actually 17,127 wheels). The issue here is whether the benefit of lot size discounts dictated by the supplier exceeds, the cost of deviating from present inventory policy. In this example such a net advantage exists.

Cost of Capital

In the classical model above, "b" represented total carrying charges (expressed as an annual percentage) including interest. To call attention to interest as part of the cost of financial decisions, b may be separated into two components: b which represents all costs except interest rate and i, the interest rate charged to average capital tied up in inventory. Rewritten, the revised formula will be:

Formula:

$$EOQ_1 = \sqrt{\frac{2\,a\,C_s}{c\,(b + i)}}$$

The foregoing bicycle example allowed for annual carrying costs of 20% of cost per unit of inventory (c). If the revised b is now computed at 12% and i at 8%, the economic order quantity (EOQ_1) remains the same; but if carrying charge calculations had previously omitted interest costs, then (b + i) would equal 28%, and the revised EOQ_1 would be 14,475 units rather than 17,127.

Classical Model with Rising Prices

The classical model explicated above assumes no price change, or if prices do change they do not influence the EOQ, whereas in reality prices of some commodities do shift resulting from changing demand-supply interrelationships or because of inflation (see Chapter Fifteen on "Inflation Accounting") average prices (the price level) rise. With predictable price increases, inventory hedging (also, refer to Chapter Fourteen) provides an alternative use of surplus funds. Prices may rise steadily or may reflect stair-step increases as new catalogs are issued, new contracts negotiated, or new models unveiled. The two formulas below* revise the classical model to account for price increases.

Steady Price Rise

If prices rise at a steady rate g—whether that rate is a high or low one—the adjusted economic order quantity (EOQ_2) can be ascertained from the

---

*These formulas appeared in: L. Pack. *Optimale Bestellmenge und Optimale Lossgröbe–Zu einigen Problemen ihrer Ermittlung.* Wiesbaden, 1964. Cited in: Bernard A. Lietaer. *Financial Management of Foreign Exchange* (Cambridge, Mass.: The M.I.T. Press, 1971), p. 87.

following formula:

Formula:

$$EOQ_2 = \sqrt{\frac{2\,a(C_s + K)}{c\left[\frac{K_1}{c} - 2g + \left(1 + \frac{K_2}{c}\right)i\right]}}$$

- a = annual demand in units.
- C_s = order costs per order independent of order size.
- K = fixed cost to maintain inventory for one year.
- c = cost (price) per unit produced (or purchased).
- K_1 = variable inventory cost—varies with quantities and storage time.
- K_2 = variable inventory cost as function of order size but not storage time (e.g., loading, shipping documents, checking, etc.).
- g = percent of steady price increase.
- i = annual interest rate on funds tied up in inventory.

As long as the price increase is known (say, pegged to an index), solution of the formula relies on obtaining sufficient data on other components. Alternatively, g can be based on g*, an anticipated rate of price increase, to adequately increase the EOQ.

Step Price Rise

On the other hand, prices may rise discretely, rather than continuously, in stair-step fashion with substantial periodic price increases. Naturally, before a forthcoming price rise of w (%), anticipation ordering justifies an economic order quantity (EOQ_3) of:

Formula:

$$EOQ_3 = \sqrt{\frac{2\,a\,(C_s + K)}{c\left[i\left(1 + \frac{K_2}{c}\right)(1 + w) + wX + \frac{K_1}{c}\right]}} + \frac{a\,w}{i\left(1 + \frac{K_1}{c}\right)(1 + w) + wX + \frac{K_1}{c}}$$

a = annual demand in units.

C_s = order costs per order independent of order size.

K = fixed cost to maintain inventory one year.

c = cost per unit of inventory.

w = per cent of price increase in one step.

i = annual interest rate on funds invested in inventory.

X = inventory losses (measured in units per year).

K_1 = inventory cost varying with quantities and storage time.

K_2 = inventory cost varying with quantities but not time.

Since w frequently depends upon future expectations, the actual rate of step price rise may result in an economical quantity smaller or larger than actually required. Nevertheless, this last formula provides the best results. The classical formula is unaffected by price changes so that the EOQ will be unchanged even under conditions of high inflation rates. According to model simulation (consult Chapter Sixteen for comments on "simulation") executed by Bernard Lietaer, EOQ_2 deviates only marginally from the basic classical formula at yearly price change rates less than 25%; beyond that rate EOQ_2 results diverge substantially from those of the standard formula and demonstrate marked rates of departure when prices double annually. Discrete price changes most significantly affect inventory policy even at low rates of price changes.

Continuous Product Flow

The foregoing examples assume that items, produced or ordered, arrive all at once, but the enterprise may receive units of product continuously during some time period. That is, produced items may flow into inventory one at a time instead of in a batch size. In this case, the formula for determining the optimum production run (J) is:

Formula:

$$J = \sqrt{\frac{2\,a\,C_s}{bc} \cdot \frac{y}{y - a}}$$

a = usage per period.

b = total carrying charge per period expressed as a percentage of unit cost.

c = unit cost.

C_s = set-up costs.

y = production per period.

Note: All variables should be expressed in terms of the same period.

Assume that annual consumption of a product is 30,000 units (a), that set up costs are $250 ($C_s$), and that carrying charges per unit per year is $10 (bc). Production capacity of 360 units daily must be expressed in yearly terms to correspond with other data. Assuming a 250-day work year, annual production equates to 90,000 items (y). Therefore, the optimum production run (X) is:

$$X = \sqrt{\frac{2(30{,}000)250}{10} \cdot \frac{90{,}000}{(90{,}000 - 30{,}000)}}$$

$$= \sqrt{1{,}500{,}000 \cdot 1.5} = \sqrt{2{,}250{,}000} = 1{,}500 \text{ units}$$

PRODUCTION CYCLED AMONG SEVERAL PRODUCTS

Although illustrations in the preceding section assumed the simple case of determining the lot size of *one* inventory item in isolation of other inventoried units, this problem begins with several items, produced one after another on the same equipment, on a regular cycle, such as a paper mill going from finer to coarser grades of paper on the same machinery. This approach resembles the above technique. But in this case a period is defined as one cycle, a time period sufficiently long to run through *all* products.

Formula:

$$N = \sqrt{\frac{\Sigma\, a_1\,(bc)\left(1 - \frac{a_1}{y_1}\right)}{2\, C_s}}$$

N = total number of cycles.

a_1 = usage per period for product 1.

bc = carrying cost per period.

y_1 = production per period of product 1.

C_s = set-up costs for one cycle.

To illustrate, assume the following data in Figure 9–2 prevail:

Figure 9-2

Product	*a* (*per year*)	*bc* (*per item*)	*y* (*per day*)
1	70,000	\$0.30	1,000
2	80,000	0.15	2,000
3	100,000	0.032	1,250
4	40,000	0.005	1,600

First designate usage (a) and production (y) for the 4 products in common units. The common element may be hours, days, weeks, etc. of production. In this example, consumption, production and carrying costs are denoted in production-days per year so that the production sequence may be calculated for an entire cycle. (Figure 9–3).

Figure 9-3

Product	*a*	*y*	*bc*
1	70	250	\$300
2	40	250	300
3	80	250	40
4	25	250	8
	215		

In Figure 9–3, the production rate is the same for all products. But how many production cycles yearly will minimize operational expenditures? To minimize carrying costs of inventory emerges as one problem. More frequent change-overs raise production outlays due to set-up expenses (C_s) and create a second problem. Applying data in Figure 9–4 to the preceding formula results in the most economical number of cycles.

Therefore, frequency of production runs is 6; i.e., the minimum-cost option is 6 runs per year, each lasting 36 days, so that one-sixth of sales requirements are fulfilled each cycle.

Figure 9-4

Product	$1 - \frac{a}{y}$ (1)	abc (2)		$abc\left(1 - \frac{a}{y}\right)$ (1) × (2) (3)	C_s (4)
1	0.72	21,000		15,120	200
2	0.84	12,000		10,080	230
3	0.68	3,200		2,176	45
4	0.90	200		180	125
			Σ =	27,556	400

$$N = \sqrt{\frac{27{,}556}{2 \cdot 400}} = \sqrt{34.445} = 5.87 \text{ or 6 cycles per year}$$

MONEY-SAVING INVENTORY REDUCTION REMEDIES

Because inventories have so frequently been a major factor in business failures and liquidations, they have been called the "graveyard of American business." Certainly *unplanned inventory investment* may result from inaccurate sales projections, but inventories also accumulate from lack of an adequate control policy and often consist of an assortment of obsolete goods, or poorly selected or unbalanced items. Dun and Bradstreet, Inc. has documented that heavy inventories "are the primary cause of tens of thousands of voluntary business discontinuances each year." Funds tied up in inventory are unavailable for other immediate and more productive needs. Scrap and obsolete inventories unproductively tie up funds. Slow-moving merchandise unproductively tie up funds. Excessive stocks and slow-moving work-in-progress unproductively tie up funds. Warehouse space and person-hours accounting for accumulated inventories unproductively tie up funds. The obvious, but painful, solution is to take the cash loss now rather than postpone it, convert undesirable inventory into cash, and employ these funds more productively. Which mathematical measures will assist in making inventory reduction decisions?

Productivity Ratio

Work-in-progress that is slow-moving may result from poor scheduling but it costs the business money in unproductive operations—security, storage, transportation, accumulation—and, consequently, reduces profits. In a job-shop situation, management needs to examine the ratio (f) of productive-to-nonproductive stages in order to pinpoint profit opportunities in inventory management.

Formula:

$$f = \frac{\sum_{1}^{n} T_x}{\sum_{1}^{n} t_x}$$

T_x = operating time for a sample of x lots.

t_x = manufacturing interval for a sample of x lots.

Assume the following hypothetical case summarized in Figure 9-5.

Figure 9-5.

Lot (number)	*Labor (hours)*	*Cycle Time (weeks)*
1	50	13
2	53	14
3	49	12
4	51	13
5	48	11
6	49	12
	300	75

After accumulating data on item number 1 above, substitute into the formula to obtain the ratio of productive-to-nonproductive time:

$$f_1 = \frac{300}{(75 \times 50)} = \frac{300}{3{,}750} = 0.08 = 8\%$$

Which states that only 8% was working time for item number 1. Therefore, the other 92% of time should be scrutinized for tying up funds unproductively in slow-moving work-in-progress.

Flow-Shop Situation

While the above formula is relevant to a job-shop facility, the next formula more appropriately fits into a flow-shop situation.*

Formula:

$$f_x = \frac{\left(\sum_{x=1}^{n} T_1\right)\left(\sum_{x=1}^{n} G\right)}{\left(\sum_{x=1}^{n} X_p\right)(T_h)}$$

T_1 = labor content of line's output for a sample of N days.

T_h = time measured in hours per day.

G = production per time period.

X_p = work-in-progress (inventory).

To illustrate, imagine the following situation in Figure 9-6.

Figure 9-6

Day	*Hours (per day)*	*Line Inventory*	*Output (per day)*	*Labor Content (in hours)*
1	8	7,000	400	8.00
2	8	5,000	450	7.75
3	8	5,300	500	7.00
4	8	5,650	500	7.00
5	8	6,050	450	7.25
	Σ =	29,000	2,300	37.00

Solving for productive time versus nonproductive time by formula:

$$f_1 = \frac{(37)(2{,}300)}{(29{,}000)(8)} = \frac{85{,}100}{232{,}000} = 36.7\%$$

Of course, ratios are inconclusive because other factors relevant to the

*G. W. Plossl and O. W. Wight, *Production and Inventory Control: Principles and Techniques* (Englewood Cliffs, N.J.: Prentice-Hall, Inc., 1967), pp. 293–6.

case may surface. Nevertheless, they do indicate a need for further investigation to specify trouble spots, reduce costs, and increase profits.

Productivity-Value Ratio

Let's suppose several items interest us. The technique here is to compare the *productivity ratio* (mentioned earlier) with the *productivity-value ratio* (f_v) below to determine whether higher-value items in the inventory are moving rapidly enough.

Formula:

$$f_v = \frac{\sum_{x=1}^{n} T_x c_x}{\sum_{x=1}^{n} t_x c_x}$$

T_x = operating time for item x.

t_x = cycle time for item x.

c_x = value of item x.

The procedure: Calculate both the productivity ratio and productivity-value ratio. If the productivity ratio exceeds the productivity-value ratio, turnover of higher value items is too slow. (See Figure 9–7.)

Figure 9-7

Item	*T*	*t*	*c*	*Tc*	*tc*
1	6	30	2.50	15	75
2	10	50	4.00	40	200
3	5	13	7.00	35	91
4	4	32	1.50	6	48
5	12	20	8.00	96	160
6	8	40	3.00	24	120
Σ	45	185		216	694

The productivity ratio is:

$$f = \frac{45}{185} = 0.243$$

The productivity-value ratio is:

$$f_v = \frac{216}{694} = 0.311$$

Since the productivity-value ratio exceeds the productivity ratio, apparently management recognizes the profitability of rapid nonretention of high value items. And the higher f_v is to f, the better the inventory turnover. That is, management in this illustration should ask: Can clearance of items 3 and 5 be accelerated? Suppose management reduces cycle time of item 3, to 10, and of item 5, to 15, while flow through of both items 1 and 4 rise to 35. Does an improvement evince?

The new cycle value (tc), 650, ratifies a 6.3% reduction of work-in-progress inventory, a bettered inventory turnover. The revised productivity-value ratio is:

$$f_v = \frac{216}{650} = 0.332$$

Perhaps not a spectacular change but small transformations enhance the possibility of profits.

The Scrap Decision

When obsolete inventory or scrap materials, similar to work-in-progress, accumulate, management deprives current operations of funds and sacrifices profits. If scrap has no value to current operations convert it into cash. Do the same with obsolete items. Surplus inventory, on the other hand, may be perfectly acceptable merchandise but it gathers dust, not profits. Should it be sold for its salvage value or held for future demand?

Formula:

$$f = \frac{\rho\,(c\,J)}{k\,(L\,J)}$$

ρ = probability of sale within a given time period (e.g., one year).

c = selling price per item.

J = number of items in inventory.

k = marginal investment rate.

L = salvage value per item in an immediate transaction.

For example, Rahja Kapur, an importer, discovers a surplus inventory of 10,000 (X) Mexican ceramic pots which normally sell for $0.80 (c) each. A present quick sale would bring in about $0.25 (L) each. The chance (probability) that she can unload the surplus inventory within a year is 20% (ρ). The firm's marginal investment rate is 18% (k). The question: Sell now at a loss of $0.15 per unit and reinvest these funds at 18% or hold the pots on a 25% chance that all can be sold at $0.80?

$$f = \frac{0.20(0.80)10{,}000}{0.18(0.25)10{,}000} = \frac{1{,}600}{450} = 3.56$$

The general rule is that if $f > 1$, hold and sell at the higher price. If $f < 1$, sell now to salvage whatever materializes. In this example, the importer opts to wait and hopes her estimates are reasonable.

LOT-SIZE INVENTORY MANAGEMENT INTERPOLATION TECHNIQUE

Known by its acronym LIMIT, this procedure evaluates a group of items handled by a single buyer, department, or common manufacturing facilities.* The LIMIT technique, uncomplicated in its application, relates the EOQ model to a specific situation and signals what action must be taken to ameliorate profits. Unlike EOQ, LIMIT encapsulates aggregate data with respect to ordering and carrying expenditures and inventories to highlight investment alternatives available to management.

The prescribed steps of this technique are:

1. Calculate trial economic lot sizes with the EOQ formula.
2. Compare total set-up hours required for present lot sizes to set-hours of TOQ (from No. 1) lots.
3. Calculate new "LIMIT" order quantities which equate present total set-up hours to new lot sizes. (The objective is to reduce investment in stock without altering operating conditions.)
4. Study available alternatives to lower costs and raise profits.

Note: The limitation need not be hours or number of persons available but may be a limited number of orders or whatever constraint is selected.

To begin with step 1, certain data will have to be acquired and ordered (tabulated in Figure 9-8) in order to calculate production preparation hours

---

*For further analysis of constrained multiple item problems, vide: G. Hadley and T. W. Whitin, *Analysis of Inventory Systems* (Englewood Cliffs, N.J.: Prentice-Hall, Inc., 1963), pp. 304-7.

per year currently employed for each manufacturing order. The formula for annual set-up hours (T_a) is:

Formula: $$T_a = \frac{a\,T_h}{J}$$

in which annual usage (a) multiplied by set-up hours per order (T_h) is divided by the quantity order (J).

Figure 9-8

Item	*a*	T_h	*c*	*J*	T_a	*c J*
1	36,000	10	4.90	6,000	60	29,400
2	8,000	7	3.00	2,670	21	8,010
3	16,000	7	8.00	2,670	42	21,360
4	4,000	6	2.50	2,000	12	5,000
5	30,000	5	0.75	10,000	15	7,500
				Σ =	150.0	$71,270

a = annual usage (units).
T_h = set-up hours per order (hours).
c = cost per unit (dollars per unit).
J = present order quantity (units).

T_a = present LIMIT set-up hours per year $= \frac{a\,T_h}{J}$ (hours).

For later reference:
cJ = investment in inventory (dollars).

Now prepared for step 1, we can compute trial order quantities (TOQ), using the EOQ formulation, from foregoing data. Set-up costs are established at $40 per hour ($C_s = T_h \times \$40$) and carrying charges estimated at 20% (b) of unit price (c). For example:

$$\text{TOQ} = \sqrt{\frac{2 \cdot 36{,}000 \cdot (10 \cdot 40)}{0.20(4.90)}} = 5{,}421 \text{ units}$$

In order to complete step 2 of the procedure, we need to determine set-up hours under TOQ results (T_{ht}).

Formula:

$$T_{ht} = a \frac{T_h}{TOQ}$$

$$T_{ht} = 36{,}000 \frac{10}{5{,}421} = 66.4$$

To proceed with step 3, we need to know which LIMIT order quantities (LOQ) are most economical given the constraint of time–set-up hours. In other words, without changing the number of set-up hours, how can lot sizes be rearranged more efficiently?

Formula:

$$LOQ = TOQ \left[\frac{\sum_{1}^{n} T_{ht}}{\sum_{1}^{n} T_a} \right]$$

$$LOQ = 5{,}421 \left[\frac{163.2}{150.0} \right] = 5{,}898 \text{ units}$$

Results of computations, trial order quantities (TOQ), trial set-up hours (T_{ht}), LIMIT order quantities (LOQ), and other data, appear in the next table, Figure 9–9.

Figure 9-9

Item	*TOQ*	T_{ht}	*LOQ*	T_{al}	*c*	*c(LOQ)*
1	5,421	66.4	5,898	61.0	4.90	28,900
2	2,733	20.5	2,974	18.8	3.00	8,922
3	2,366	47.3	2,574	43.5	8.00	20,592
4	1,960	12.2	2,132	11.3	2.50	5,330
5	8,944	16.8	9,731	15.4	0.75	7,298
	Σ =	163.2		150.0		$71,042

Checking, to learn whether we have violated the given constraints of 150 set-up hours (T_a), the fifth column is added for revised LIMIT set-up hours (T_{al}). The formula for T_{al} is identical to T_a except to substitute LOQ for J. The first computation works out to:

$$T_{al} = \frac{a\,T_h}{LOQ} = \frac{36{,}000(10)}{5{,}898} = 61.0$$

Summing T_{al}, we find that $\sum_{1}^{5} T_a = \sum_{1}^{5} T_{al}$, and, therefore, we have rearranged production schedules more efficiently within the cost limitation of 150.0 set-up hours.

To better grasp the significance of these calculations, let's translate them into dollars and profits. The last columns of both tables summarize inventory investment from present lot sizes (cJ) and the new LIMIT order quantity (c • LOQ). A $228 improvement can be significant based on an average inventory, $\frac{J}{2}$, carried per period. It represents a decrease in inventory investment with no increase in operating expenses.

Step 4 suggests an examination of alternatives. Which alternatives are there? Set-up time can be changed. Are the entire round of calculations necessary to develop other options? No, if only $\Sigma\, T_a$, for example, is modified, say, from 150.0 to 170 set-up hours ($\Sigma\, T_a{*}$), multiply the LIMIT inventory value times the new ratio to obtain the new inventory value, (Y*).

Formula:

$$Y^* = c\,(LOQ)\left[\frac{\sum_{1}^{n} T_{ht}}{\sum_{1}^{n} T_a{*}}\right]$$

In this example, the revised inventory value, with a change in set-up hours, would be:

$$Y^* = \$71{,}042\left[\frac{163.2}{170.0}\right] = \$68{,}200$$

In other words, two sets of alternatives manifest. In the first instance, holding total yearly set-up time constant, rearranging LIMIT order quantities will produce different total annual inventory values. In the second instance, order quantities are held constant while set-up time is varied. The example posits that an increase in production preparation hours from 150 to 170 will raise set-up outlays but the value of average inventory carried declines. An inverse relationship between set-up expenses and inventory investment evince. If one value rises, the other falls, but not necessarily at equal rates.

Earlier in this chapter Dun and Bradstreet's warning of overinvestment in inventory as a cause of business discontinuances was noted. Too, we should recall that Dun and Bradstreet also cautioned that a sale is never complete until the money is collected.

CONTENTS

Chapter Ten: Monitoring Receivables for Liquidity and Profit

TEN

Monitoring Receivables for Liquidity and Profit

"Current assets are those which are reasonably expected to be transformed into cash or to be sold or consumed during the normal operating cycle of the business."* In many businesses inventories are largest among current assets and their improper care and feeding has driven more than just a few concerns to dissolution—voluntary or otherwise. But turning an inventory into receivables may seem like a charitable operation if receivables are not properly monitored, controlled, and kept within safe limits. "Receivables are stated as the net amount expected to be collected after providing for estimated uncollectibles, discounts, returns, and price allowances."* In this chapter we reconsider interest and discounts on receivables—notes or ac-

*Charles T. Horngren, *Accounting for Management Control: An Introduction* (Englewood Cliffs, N.J.: Prentice-Hall, Inc., 1965), p. 48.

counts receivable—how best to keep track of them and collect them—always aiming to improve profits.

INTEREST ON RECEIVABLES

Extending credit encompasses more than a sales tool adjunct. Because of the "banking" aspect, carrying receivables creates additional costs which should not exceed marginal profits. Similarly, discounts offered should encourage sales rather than discourage financial gains, and from the buyer's viewpoint, discounts lost represent income foregone. Money not received represents an opportunity loss, a real cost to the firm. Too, "order costs" parallel inventory ordering costs, recognized in the preceding chapter, due to clerical, preparatory, and computer time expenses.

Equivalent Interest Rates

Trade discounts tend to encourage a greater percentage of advance collections. Between the discount period and net due date, while usually only a matter of days, it represents, at times, substantial equivalent annual interest. To find the approximate annual equivalent rate, the difference between the discount period and net period is divided into 360 days and multiplied by the proferred discount.

Formula: $$j^* = im$$

j^* = approximate equivalent annual interest rate.

i = discount rate expressed as a percentage of receivable.

$m = \frac{360}{T}$, where T is the number of days between the end of discount period and end of net period, and based on a 360-day year.

For example, on terms of 2/10, net 30, $i = 2\%$ and $m = \frac{360}{20}$, so that,

$$j^* = 2\% \times 18 = 36\%$$

Substantial discounts encourage debtors to seek their own source of funds rather than rely on creditors banking their operations. Creditors offer these discounts with expectations that lower prices, resulting from discounted invoices, will sufficiently raise volume and profits. A partial table of approximate equivalent annual interest rates appears in Figure 10–1.

Figure 10-1

Terms	j^*
1% 10 days, net 30 days	18% per annum (19.6%)
1% 10 days, net 60 days	7.2% per annum (7.4%)
2% 10 days, net 30 days	36% per annum (42.8%)
2% 10 days, net 60 days	14.4% per annum (15.3%)
2% 30 days, net 60 days	24% per annum (26.8%)
2½% 10 days, net 30 days	45% per annum (56.0%)
3% 10 days, net 30 days	54% per annum (70.2%)
4% 10 days, net 30 days	72% per annum (102.6%)
5% 10 days, net 30 days	90% per annum (140.7%)
5% 20 days, net 45 days	72% per annum (101.9%)
5% 20 days, net 60 days	45% per annum (55.1%)
5% 10 days, net 60 days	36% per annum (42.1%)

The figures in parentheses represent a compounded rate.

Discounts—A Sales Tool

Although discounts lower the sales price to customers who accept them, as a collection and sales tool they may improve liquidity and profits not only by encouraging prompter payment but also expanded sales. Whether sales rise by any appreciable quantity depends upon the *elasticity of demand* at current prices. If demand is sufficiently elastic, then lower prices resulting from a prompt payment discount will raise total sales and possibly enhance profits. Naturally, both seller and buyers benefit. The objective of this exercise is to compare pre-discount profits with post-discount profits (actual or expected).

The formula for determining profits resulting from revised credit policy is:

Formula:

$$\pi^* = MX\ [(1 - y) + y(1 + f)(1 - i)]$$
$$- cX\ [1 - y)(1 + k^*) + y(1 + f)(1 + bk^*)]$$

π^* = profit after offering new credit terms.

M = market price of good (per unit).

X = total initial sales volume under old credit policy (in units).

y = customers taking discounts (%).

$(1 - y)$ = customers not taking discounts but assumed to pay promptly.

i = discount expressed as a rate per period (%).

f = increase in sales resulting from lower price (%).

c = cost of good per unit (in dollars).

k^* = carrying cost of receivables per period, an opportunity cost (%).

b = fraction of a period (the base period expressed in k^*) during which receivables are carried for y customers taking discounts (a ratio).

An example will clear up any confusion. Suppose that Vickers & Co., which sells 2,000 units of product monthly on terms of net 30, decides to promote a discount on terms of 2½% 10 days, net 30 days. About 75% of customers are expected to snatch up the discount and because of the lower price will increase purchases by 10%. Sales price of the item is $10 per unit, costs $6 each, credit carrying charge per month amounts to 1½%; but for customers annexing discounts the credit carrying charge will be for only one-third of a month $\left(b = \frac{10}{30}\right)$, assuming that most discounting customers will appropriate the full 10 days. In summary, we have these data: m = $10 per unit; X = 2,000 units (original sales); c = $6 per unit; y = 75% of original sales; f = 10% increase of y; i = 2½% discount; k* = 1½% per month; b = 10/30 = 0.33 of k*.

$$\begin{aligned}\pi^* &= 10 \cdot 2{,}000\ [(1 - 0.75) + 0.75(1 + 0.10)(1 - 0.025)] \\ &\quad - 6 \cdot 2{,}000\ [(1 - 0.75)(1 + 0.015) + 0.75(1 + 0.10)(1 + 0.33 \cdot 0.015)] \\ &= 21{,}088 - 12{,}994 = \$8{,}094.\end{aligned}$$

Notice that the first bracketed portion represents revenue from one-fourth of original sales at $10 per unit plus income from 82.5% of initial sales base at a net price of $9.75 per unit. Deducted from net sales income are costs. Outlays consist of unit cost of $6 on all sales (assuming that a 7.5% increase neither raises nor lowers production and sales expenses at these outputs) plus credit carrying charges based on cost figures. For one-fourth of the customers who pay at the end of 30 days, the carrying charge of 1½% is applied. For the remaining customers who pay within 10 days, this expense is reduced to 0.50%. The last step in the analytical process is to evaluate total profits arising from the new credit policy.

This formulation is predicated on prompt payments, but if we add bad debts and delinquent accounts, then costs rise. These costs can be accounted for with the formula by designating some proportion of sales as potential delinquents, or they may be figured separately and deducted from revised profits. Over-aged accounts cost more not only because of increased credit carrying charges but additional collection efforts and nonroutine handling of accounts plus attorney fees, court costs, and eventual write-offs further discount profits. On the other hand, interest-bearing notes sometimes substitute for accounts receivable or are used to consummate a large sale.

Interest on Receivables

In this illustration Hy-Fly, Inc. values a building on its books at $800,000, that it sells for $1,500,000. Terms of sale include $100,000 cash payment plus a note receivable for the balance, $1,400,000, payable in equal end-of-year installments over 7 years. The note bears no interest. The problem in computing the note's present value arises from treatment for tax purposes different from the value recorded in the firm's books. Since the note carries no interest, an imputed interest rate of 5% for tax purposes diverges from an 11% rate that more logically reflects true interest and risk associated with the transaction.

The table in Figure 10–2 summarizes steps required to determine the present value of the note under both conditions–5% and 11%–with interest figured at a rate compounded semi-annually. In reverse order, columns (1) and (4) register the present values of years 7 through 1 recorded as years 1 through 7. The sums of columns (1) and (4) equal present values of the note. Inequality between the collected $200,000 in each period and amount recorded in columns (1) and (4) appears in columns (2) and (5), the discounts on the note. The numbers in columns (3) and 6 originate in the present values of the note minus the present values of principal collections on a year-by-year basis.

The price of the building equals the cash down payment plus the present value of the note. For tax purposes, the value of the building is $1,254,657. For reporting purposes, the value of the building is $1,033,298, a smaller gain. (Refer to Chapter Two for present value discussion.)

Timing Difference

The timing difference is simply calculated. After reducing comparative values by the book value of the building ($800,000 in this example), it is the difference between gain in sale by the tax computations minus the book gain or $1,254,675 less $1,033,298 equals $221,359.

Income Taxes

Assume in this example that the tax rate on capital gains (h_c) is 30%. The rule for computing taxes is to multiply the tax rate by the timing difference.

Figure 10–2

Year	Annual Collections	*Present Values @ 5%**			*Present Values @ 11%**			*Timing Effect*	
		Principal (1)	*Interest (2)*	*PV of Note (3)*	*Principal (4)*	*Interest (5)*	*PV of Note (6)*	*(5) – (2) (7)*	*30% × (7) (8)*
1	200,000	141,545	58,455	1,154,657	94,514	105,486	933,298	47,031	14,109
2	200,000	148,711	51,289	1,013,112	105,196	94,804	838,784	43,515	13,055
3	200,000	156,240	43,760	864,401	117,086	82,914	733,588	39,154	11,746
4	200,000	164,149	35,851	708,161	130,320	69,680	616,502	33,829	10,149
5	200,000	172,459	27,541	544,012	145,049	54,951	486,182	27,410	8,223
6	200,000	181,190	18,810	371,553	161,443	38,557	341,133	19,747	5,924
7	200,000	190,363	9,637	190,363	179,690	20,310	179,690	10,673	3,202
		1,154,657	245,343		933,298	466,702		221,359	66,408

*Compounded semi-annually.

(See columns (7) and (8) in Figure 10-2.) The effect, of course, shifts income from gain into interest and influences timing of the tax obligation because income has been spread over the life of the note.

CONTROL OF RECEIVABLES

Receivable control implies keeping accounts within some range of reasonableness, given sales objectives and cost structure of the firm. Whether receivables are indeed out of line depends upon the accuracy of the measuring device. Although some conventional approaches crop up below, unfortunately, they tend to register false signals as sales trends shift. A superior method, offered at the end of this section, relates receivables to the appropriate sales period in which they originally occur.

Aging of Receivables

Traditional accounting techniques call for arranging accounts receivable according to age relative to terms of sale. The objective is to segregate, first of all, current accounts from past due ones, and, secondly, to categorize delinquent receivables in order to (1) implement an adequate collection procedure and (2) to direct receivable management toward bulges in the schedule. The more delinquent accounts delay payment the greater the odds of not collecting. On terms of net 30 days, accounts more than 90 days past due usually represent a serious credit problem, and, in fact, by that time, collection efforts internally should be exhausted and accounts placed for collection with an outside agency if no satisfactory payment plan has been worked out. But we all live on hopes. We try not to offend customers even though we bank their operations, and collection agencies will likely receive the account after a year or so has passed on which expected miracles infrequently materialize. A sample schedule appears in Figure 10-3.

Each column heading is self-explanatory. Accounts receivable for each month, column (3), are classified according to age, columns (4), (5), (6), (7). Terms are net 30 days. Therefore, accounts receivable under column (4) correspond to sales made within the last 30 days and not yet due. Scanning these data alone makes it difficult to realize whether a danger spot is building up because rising sales will generate more receivables.

One signalling device relates average daily sale per period (month) to total accounts receivable in order to determine how many days sales are outstanding. Column (2) results from dividing each column (1) figure by 30 (days). Then column (2) is divided into column (3) to compute the days sales outstanding (DSO) in column (8). These figures are available on both a monthly and quarterly basis. This single indicator supposedly reveals the extent to which receivables build up or effectiveness of management's monitor-

Figure 10-3

AGING OF ACCOUNTS RECEIVABLE IN YEAR t

Month	*Monthly Credit Sales (1)*	*Average Sales per Day (2)*	*Accounts Receiv-able (3)*	*Current (4)*	*31 - 60 Days (5)*	*61 - 90 Days (6)*	*91 - 120 Days (7)*	*DSO (8)*
July	1,050	35	1,615	1,000	290	210	115	46
Aug.	1,020	34	1,525	980	320	150	75	45
Sept.	1,110	37	1,593	1,065	303	170	55	43
Qtr. I	3,180	35.33	4,733	3,045	913	530	245	44.7
Oct.	1,500	50	2,015	1,440	330	170	75	40
Nov.	1,740	58	2,380	1,690	445	185	60	41
Dec.	1,860	62	2,601	1,800	500	240	61	42
Qtr. II	5,100	56.67	6,996	4,930	1,275	595	196	41.2
Jan.	1,710	57	2,585	1,650	560	280	95	45
Feb.	1,620	54	2,489	1,560	527	310	92	46
Mar.	1,800	60	2,616	1,721	508	287	100	44
Qtr. III	5,130	57.00	7,690	4,931	1,595	877	287	45.0
Apr.	1,770	59	2,563	1,705	506	260	47	43
May	1,410	47	2,289	1,356	530	304	99	49
June	1,110	37	1,877	1,071	420	280	106	51
Qtr. IV	4,290	47.67	6,729	4,132	1,456	844	297	47.1

DSO - days sales outstanding.
Firm's fiscal year begins July 1, ends June 30.

ing and collection procedures. In this hypothetical example, it seems that during the first two quarters management has succeeded in reducing the volume of outstanding receivables relative to current sales. But the picture changes. Beginning with 40 days of sales outstanding in October, receivables accumulate steadily to 51 DSO by the end of June of the current accounting year, which runs from July 1st to June 30th. This trend suggests that management should tighten up in the third and fourth quarters should such a pattern persist.

Past Due Index

Another simple device lumps together all past due customer obligations and compares them with total receivables outstanding at the end of each period—which may be weekly, monthly, quarterly, etc. The formula for the past due index (PDI) is:

Formula:

$$PDI = \frac{F_{pd}}{F_{ar}}$$

in which F_{pd} represents the aggregate of past due accounts and F_{ar} total accounts receivable for the current period.

For example, to use data from the preceding table, quarterly computations are:

$$PDI_{I} = \frac{1{,}688}{4{,}733} = 0.357$$

$$PDI_{II} = \frac{2{,}060}{6{,}996} = 0.295$$

$$PD_{III} = \frac{2{,}759}{7{,}690} = 0.359$$

$$PD_{IV} = \frac{2{,}597}{6{,}729} = 0.386$$

These indices point toward the same trend indicated by the DSO; viz., that second quarter improvement is short-lived and that third and fourth quarter delinquent accounts exceed the ratio of the first half of the year. Does a problem really exist?

Moving Average Rule

Perhaps you object to measuring past due accounts, which result from previous months' sales, to either current sales or total receivables which encompass mostly current accounts. Possibly a moving average will render better results. With net 30-day terms and 120 days required for all collectible accounts to materialize into cash, it will require 150 days to complete the cycle from the first day a sale transpires until the last day the last dollar is collected. Instead of finding average daily sales based on current income, sales for the most recent 150 days are averaged, column (3) of Figure 10–4. To keep the average moving, add the current month to the total, drop the last month of the series, and divide by 150.

A new DSO (days sales outstanding) is then developed, column (4), by dividing column (3) into column (2) figures. Comparing the bottom portion of the table (year t) with Figure 10–3 data, the smoothing out procedure

Figure 10-4

Month	*Credit Sales ($00)* *(1)*	*EOM A/R ($00)* *(2)*	*150-day Moving Average (Daily Sales)* *(3)*	*EOM DSO* *(4)*	*Distribution, by Age, of Outstanding Receivables (in days)* *0 - 30* *(5)*	*30 - 60* *(6)*	*60 - 90* *(7)*	*90 - 120* *(8)*
(Year t - 1)								
July	810	1,443	45.4	31.8	17.4	6.1	6.2	2.1
Aug.	720	1,213	39.0	31.1	18.1	6.7	4.3	2.1
Sept.	900	1,313	33.4	39.3	25.8	7.2	4.5	1.8
Oct.	1,410	1,825	31.6	57.8	42.7	9.3	4.1	1.6
Nov.	1,770	2,348	37.4	62.7	45.4	11.9	4.2	1.3
Dec.	1,590	2,403	42.6	56.4	36.4	12.9	5.6	1.5
Jan.	1,470	2,335	47.6	49.1	30.5	10.2	6.3	2.1
Feb.	1,590	2,400	52.2	46.0	30.1	8.6	5.3	2.0
Mar.	1,830	2,650	55.0	48.2	32.7	8.6	4.5	2.3
Apr.	1,800	2,673	55.2	48.4	31.7	10.0	5.0	1.8
May	1,320	2,240	53.4	41.9	24.0	10.3	5.8	1.9
June	990	1,740	50.2	34.7	19.0	7.6	6.0	2.1
(Year t)								
July	1,050	1,615	46.6	34.7	21.5	6.2	4.5	2.5
Aug.	1,020	1,525	41.2	37.0	23.8	7.8	3.6	1.8
Sept.	1,110	1,593	36.6	43.5	29.1	8.3	4.6	1.5
Oct.	1,500	2,015	37.8	53.3	38.1	8.7	4.5	2.0
Nov.	1,740	2,380	42.8	55.6	39.5	10.4	4.3	1.4
Dec.	1,860	2,601	48.2	54.0	37.3	10.4	5.0	1.3
Jan.	1,710	2,585	52.8	49.0	31.3	10.6	5.3	1.8
Feb.	1,620	2,489	56.2	44.3	27.8	9.4	5.5	1.6
Mar.	1,800	2,616	58.2	44.9	29.6	8.7	4.9	1.7
Apr.	1,770	2,563	58.4	43.9	29.2	8.7	4.5	1.6
May	1,410	2,289	55.4	41.3	24.5	9.6	5.5	1.8
June	1,110	1,877	51.4	36.5	20.8	8.2	5.4	2.1

Sales for year t - 2, in reverse order, are: $900, $1,680, $1,740, $1,680.

produces a wider range of DSOs. In Figure 10–3 the days sales outstanding range from 40 to 51, but for the same period, in Figure 10–4, they range from 35 to 55. Analyzing the year t trend, receivables seem to build up from July 1 to the end of the year, then decline for the next six months. That is, a seasonal trend evinces. How does this trend compare with a previous year?

For year t - 1 in Figure 10–4, a similar flow manifests. Receivables relative to sales accumulate, peak in November, then decline, the same as year t. Where is the trouble spot?

Columns (5) through (8) break down each month's outstanding receivables according to four categories listed by number of days outstanding. The sum of these four columns necessarily equals column (4). The greatest fluctuation surfaces in current accounts, 0 - 30 days, followed by a narrower range of variations as we move to the right. Column (5) does indicate some interesting results in which up to 45 days sales stand out in current receivables on items sold on net 30-day terms. However, deciphering is a vertical maneuver, not a horizontal one, and management is curiously helpless to strengthen collections on accounts not yet due on existing terms of sale. Most effort apparently should be directed toward 30 - 60 day delinquents, although even a significant improvement will produce only modest changes on DSO. In spite of three monitoring tools, the course is not clearly set nor the problem, if any, definitely defined.

The Best Approach

The difficulty is that when sales rise and fall, whether a seasonal trend, evidenced each year in the preceding tables, or a growing firm, also suggested by foregoing data, changing sales pattern produces a shifting base. High sales in one month will undoubtedly influence delinquent receivables in subsequent months as a natural course of business. But if higher receivables resulting from high sales in the preceding period are compared with current period low sales, the number of days receivables uncollected will rise and so will the proportion of delinquent accounts. And someone gets blamed for being lax. But if the reverse occurs, where lower receivables, resulting from previous low sales, are matched against current higher sales, then the DSO will fall and our man on the spot is a hero for effectuating an efficient collection policy. By any preceding measure several signals spring up to either tighten or relax credit policy, and, like most fine tuning, management may teeter when it should totter or tilt, or even remain neutral. (Refer to Figure 10–5.)

In other words, the problem is mismatching and aggregation. Aggregation makes it impossible to detect shifts in payment patterns. Aging of accounts receivable have a potentially proper use if sales are stable without seasonal and yearly swings. Columns (1) through (4) present another format of aging accounts receivable by percentages. Each line must add up to 1.000 since each column represents the subdivided proportion of total accounts. There is no way of discerning whether receivables are indeed out of control because of aggregation and because each category is not appropriately identified with the month's sales which give rise to those receivables. Even being aware of these defects does not adequately communicate the direction and nature of receivable policy. Column (1) ranges from 57% to 74%, a 30% divergence from low to high values. The other columns register an even higher percentage change, which means that partners may be changed more frequently than necessary.

An effective tool for monitoring accounts receivable is exhibited in Figure 10–5. Disaggregation is achieved by using the same sales and receivable data but receivables relate to original sales which gave rise to the account. How are data in columns (5) through (8) developed?

Formula:

$$PU_t = \frac{F_t}{MX_t}$$

The percentage uncollected (PU) is the ratio of receivables in time period t (F_t) to sales in time period t (MX_t), and in period t - 1, it is the ratio of receivables originating in time period t - 1, to sales of that same period. Consequently, with terms of net 30 days, receivables 31 - 60 days old relate to last month's sales so that if last month's sales were higher than usual, then 31 - 60 days receivables will loom larger in the pattern.

Examine carefully columns (5) through (8). First observe that these data do not sum to 1.000. Why? The sales base (MX) changes, therefore, output conforms to a percentage of sales for each period whereas figures in columns (1) through (4) all originate from the same common denominator, the same total receivables for each period.

We have, logically, apportioned receivables in such a way that seasonal sales fluctuations, and year-to-year swings, do not fog up the analysis. We can clearly discern the pattern and spot problems from deviations in that pattern. For example, we have used the same data throughout this section and monitoring tools reveal that a variable credit and collection policy will furnish funds required in business operations. But scan column (5). Notice that the relationship of current receivables, not yet due, to current sales exhibits a rather stable pattern throughout the observed two-year period. The high-low divergence is less than three percentage points. Compare this stability of experience with that indicated in column (1) which signals action to be taken when, in fact, none is required. Similarly, columns (6), (7), and (8), indicate that same collection stability with widest variation observed in t - 3 accounts. It appears that a norm of 0.960, 0.300, 0.160, and 0.060 prevails.

Examining the second six-month period of 30 - 60 day outstanding accounts, column (2), of year t - 1, by the traditional aging method the percentage of receivables range from less than 18 per cent to more than 24 per cent, while column (6) comparisons suggest that very little fluctuation did occur and that which did show up in column (2) resulted mostly from sales first increasing, then declining, during the semi-annual span.

Figure 10-5

			Distribution of Outstanding A/R by Age (%)							
Month	*Credit Sales ($00)*	*Accts. Rec. ($00)*	*0 - 30 (1)*	*30 - 60 (2)*	*60 - 90 (3)*	*90 - 120 (4)*	*t (5)*	*t - 1 (6)*	*t - 2 (7)*	*t - 3 (8)*
(Year t - 1)										
July	810	1,443	0.549	0.191	0.195	0.066	0.978	0.306	0.167	0.055
Aug.	720	1,213	0.581	0.214	0.138	0.066	0.979	0.321	0.187	0.048
Sept.	900	1,313	0.657	0.184	0.114	0.046	0.958	0.321	0.185	0.067
Oct.	1,410	1,825	0.740	0.162	0.071	0.027	0.957	0.328	0.181	0.062
Nov.	1,770	2,348	0.723	0.190	0.066	0.021	0.959	0.316	0.173	0.069
Dec.	1,590	2,403	0.645	0.229	0.100	0.026	0.975	0.311	0.170	0.070
Jan.	1,470	2,335	0.621	0.208	0.128	0.043	0.986	0.305	0.169	0.071
Feb.	1,590	2,400	0.654	0.188	0.115	0.044	0.987	0.306	0.173	0.059
Mar.	1,830	2,650	0.679	0.178	0.094	0.048	0.984	0.297	0.170	0.081
Apr.	1,800	2,673	0.655	0.206	0.103	0.034	0.972	0.301	0.173	0.067
May	1,320	2,240	0.571	0.246	0.138	0.045	0.970	0.306	0.169	0.063
June	990	1,740	0.549	0.218	0.172	0.060	0.965	0.288	0.167	0.057
(Year t)										
July	1,050	1,615	0.619	0.180	0.130	0.071	0.952	0.293	0.159	0.064
Aug.	1,020	1,525	0.643	0.210	0.098	0.049	0.961	0.305	0.152	0.057
Sept.	1,110	1,593	0.669	0.190	0.107	0.035	0.959	0.297	0.153	0.056
Oct.	1,500	2,015	0.715	0.164	0.084	0.037	0.960	0.297	0.167	0.071
Nov.	1,740	2,380	0.710	0.187	0.078	0.025	0.971	0.297	0.167	0.059
Dec.	1,860	2,601	0.692	0.192	0.092	0.023	0.968	0.287	0.160	0.055
Jan.	1,710	2,585	0.638	0.217	0.108	0.037	0.965	0.301	0.161	0.063
Feb.	1,620	2,489	0.627	0.212	0.125	0.037	0.963	0.308	0.167	0.053
Mar.	1,800	2,616	0.657	0.194	0.110	0.038	0.956	0.314	0.168	0.054
Apr.	1,770	2,563	0.665	0.197	0.101	0.036	0.965	0.281	0.161	0.054
May	1,410	2,289	0.592	0.232	0.133	0.043	0.963	0.299	0.169	0.061
June	1,110	1,877	0.571	0.224	0.149	0.056	0.965	0.298	0.158	0.059

An Oscillator

To better track flows over time and to create a device which parallels traditional systems of monitoring receivables, an oscillator furnishes instant visual comparison. The oscillator registers whether obligations are running above or below the established norm. Let's say that the standard for t (current) accounts is 0.960, for t - 1 accounts 0.300, for t - 2 accounts 0.160, and for t - 3 accounts 0.160. Two methods are suggested; only one is illustrated.

The first step is to record data as it appears in Figure 10–6. Each column corresponds to columns (5) through (8) of the preceding table. The procedure is to subtract *from* the standard, 0.960 in the case of the first column, the first entry in column (5) of Figure 10–5, 0.978, which produces a difference of minus 18 points (–18). If the column (5) figure is below the normal 0.960, as in line 3, then the resultant plus number (+2) is recorded in Figure 10–6. These computations can be derived for as far back as desirable in order to establish a pattern, although only the most recent six months will be scrutinized for action and, possibly, the most recent 18 months for management effectiveness.

When should action be taken? That depends upon circumstances, company policy, and some common and analytical sense. A 10 per cent deviation either way probably would not be considered excessive. Column (1) data diverge less than 3 per cent (30 points) from the norm of 0.960 and most of the time less than 1½ per cent. With rare exception both columns (2) and (3) fall within the 10 per cent range. Because of dealing with such small percentages, column (8) figures of the preceding table appear to fluctuate within a narrow range, but oscillating data in the next table reveal occasional call for action when accounts shift more than 6 or 7 points away from the standard 0.060. Most recent six-month experience, however, seems quite satisfactory at all levels.

A variation of this procedure, to smooth out data, a moving average of, say, 4 or 6 months of Figure 10–5 inputs might be maintained to compare with experiences of two and three years previously and also with data in a similar stage of a previous business cycle. Although seasonality has been factored out by this method, it is usually better to compare matching periods of different years. With this information, receivable balances can be predicted from the sales forecast, and funding operations will be subject to errors at fewer points in the estimating process. The best approach accompanied with an indicator of the type in this section, easily constructed from existing information, provides a more reliable reading of receivables.

COLLECTION OF RECEIVABLES

Because a sale is not complete until an item works itself up the scale of assets finally reaching that most liquid of all, money, accounts receivable tie

Figure 10-6

Month	*0.960* *t* *(1)*	*0.300* *t - 1* *(2)*	*0.160* *t - 2* *(3)*	*0.060* *t - 3* *(4)*
(Year t - 1)				
July	-18	-06	-07	+05
August	-19	-21	-27	+12
September	+02	-21	-25	-07
October	+03	-28	-21	-02
November	+01	-16	-13	-09
December	-15	-11	-10	-10
January	-26	-05	-09	-11
February	-27	-06	-13	+01
March	-24	+03	-10	-21
April	-12	-01	-13	-07
May	-10	-06	-09	-03
June	-05	+12	-07	+03
(Year t)				
July	+08	+07	+01	-04
August	-01	-05	+08	+03
September	+01	+03	+07	+04
October	00	+03	-07	-11
November	-11	+03	-07	+01
December	-08	+13	00	+05
January	-05	-01	-01	-03
February	-03	-08	-07	+07
March	+04	-14	-08	+06
April	-05	+19	-01	+06
May	-03	+01	-09	-01
June	-05	+02	+02	+01

up funds. The longer a past-due obligation goes unpaid the greater are the collection costs, loss of profit, and loss of potentially more sales to the same customer. At different points collection efforts must be evaluated; the old saw about throwing good money after bad is a legitimate policy.

Probability of Collection

Suppose that an account has run the gamut of the internal collection procedure and management now ponders whether to spend more in collection efforts either internally or with an outside collection agency. Let's say that an Irish firm in Limerick owes \$890, now one year past due, and that further collection efforts will cost the American concern another \$160. Should another \$160 be invested to collect \$890? It depends upon the probability of collection. While a subjective measurement, probability exercises are an effort to quantify results based on an assessment of the debtor firm, its ability to work itself out of a financial problem, and past experience in similar situations.

Assume the following probability distribution represents the best judgements of management concerned with this account:

Probability of Collection	*Amount Collected*	*Expected Value*
0.10	\$ 00	\$00
0.50	100	50
0.20	175	35
0.10	200	20
0.05	300	15
0.05	400	20

The expected value of results, \$140, hardly suggests that spending \$160 more is worth it. The firm is better off employing \$160 elsewhere and redirect its human energy into more productive endeavors. The formula for expected value is:

Formula:

$$V_e = \rho F^*_{pd}$$

Multiply the stated probability (ρ) by the anticipated amount to be collected (F^*_{pd}) to derive the expected value (V_e). The general rule applied to marginal collection efforts: If additional collection costs exceed the expected value of anticipated collections, then discontinue efforts and write-off the account.

Sales Expansion Through Credit

Sometimes bad debt write-offs are deliberately increased in order to stimulate total sales. Loosening credit reins must be traded off against anticipated profits. Expected profits are matched with the required rate of return on additional investment caused by carrying receivables a longer period brought about by extended credit terms. If new credit terms equally affect present business as well as expected new sales, then these extra costs and calculated losses must also be included in the analysis. In the following example, markets are segregated so that terms offered to different groups do not overlap and unused plant capacity makes supplementary investment in equipment and storage space unnecessary. The marginal analysis focuses strictly on new accounts activities.

Assume that a firm currently sells \$800,000 worth of merchandise at \$50 per unit, a total of 16,000 units of product. Average fixed costs are \$23; average variable costs are \$22; average total costs are \$45. Terms currently are net 30 days. All sales, present and projected, are for credit. Management contemplates two policies to increase sales by relaxing credit terms with the following presumed outcomes:

	Present Policy	*Program A*	*Program B*
Increased Demand	0	12½%	25%
Net Terms (in days)	30	60	90
Bad Debt Losses	1¼%	4%	8%

Sales will advance to \$900,000 under policy A and to \$1,000,000 under policy B. Figure 10-7 features the upshot of the analysis.

Figure 10-7

	Program A	*Program B*
(1) Additional Volume (units)	2,000	4,000
(2) Additional Sales	\$100,000	\$200,000
(3) Bad Debt Loss	\$ 4,000	\$ 16,000
(4) Cost of Bad Debt Loss	\$ 1,760	\$ 7,040
(5) Profitability of Additional Sales	\$ 54,240	\$104,960
(6) Extra Investment in Accts. Rec.	\$ 88,000	\$264,000
(7) Required Return (A @ 16%; B @ 20%)	\$ 14,080	\$ 52,800

Line (2) equals line (1) multiplied by \$50, the sales price. The bad debt loss arises from earlier estimates calculated as a percentage of marginal sales. If new sales spill over into present ones, then subsidiary bad debt losses should be accounted for. The cost of bad debt losses (CBDL), line (4), is derived from the following formula:

Formula:

$$CBDL = (BDL)\frac{C_m}{M}$$

The cost of bad debt losses amounts to bad debt losses (BDL) from line (3) multiplied by the ratio of marginal costs (C_m), \$22 in this case, to the selling price (M) of \$50 per unit. Since fixed costs are already covered by present sales, double counting is avoided by including only those costs that are directly related to increased output and sales. (See Chapter Four for further details on this point.)

Profitability of additional sales, line (5), is gross profit minus bad debt losses. Supplementary investment in accounts receivable arise not from fixed investment but tying up funds for an extra 30 or more days, the result of a relaxed credit policy. These funds, like all others, must earn a return. The rate of return on policy A is figured at the lower 16% since it is believed that policy B will carry with it a higher degree of risk. The solution points toward the more profitable policy A as the better choice under existing conditions.

An alternative method of presenting this case appears in Figure 10-8.

Figure 10-8

Policy A			*Policy B*		
Pay't Rec'd at End of: (days)	*p*	*Anticipated Collections*	*Pay't Rec'd at End of:*	*p*	*Anticipated Collections*
60	0.75	$ 75,000	90	0.65	$130,000
90	0.10	10,000	120	0.15	30,000
120	0.06	6,000	150	0.06	12,000
150	0.04	4,000	180	0.04	8,000
180	0.01	1,000	210	0.02	4,000
Bad Debt	0.04	4,000	Bad Debt	0.08	16,000
	1.00	$100,000		1.00	$200,000

The probability distribution encompasses all accounts instead of singling out each one as presented in the preceding section. But the cycle never ends—from receivables to cash and then start again to decide how to reallocate the firm's available resources among available alternatives.

CONTENTS

Chapter Eleven: Managing Cash Efficiently to Maximize Return on Idle Balances

ELEVEN

Managing Cash Efficiently to Maximize Return on Idle Balances

Up the liquidity scale from inventory and receivables to cash and near-cash assets—plus an item not appearing in the balance sheet, the firm's line of credit—these together determine the degree of liquidity; but liquidity names its costs. This chapter focuses on minimization of those costs to free liquid assets for more profitable employment in noncash uses. *Liquidity,* of course, refers to the firm's ability to meet current obligations on time, while *profitability* means using all assets optimally. Therefore, holding excessive cash balances, not only difficult to justify in the short run, holds certain apparent dangers—a symptom that acquisition finders, corporate control raiders, and professional dissident stockholders search out. On the other hand, preparing for likely forthcoming tight money situations, business and political uncertainties, and myriad contingencies may mean seeking innovative and imaginative avenues other than ordinary cash build-ups. Formulations and techniques advanced in this chapter contribute to such advantageous decision-making.

Commonly, management, in analyzing cash float, has sought to minimize it; nevertheless, artifices such as lock boxes, frequent deposits, wire transfers, delaying payments on accounts, utilization of isolated non-par banks for payroll, tight controls, and timing of payments to gain an extra two or three days of float reach a *ne plus ultra.* These techniques call for close supervision to avoid errors and even criminal penalties. Additionally, efficacious management of accounts receivables and inventory, discussed in Chapters Ten and Nine, a factor in both liquidity and profitability, may be enervated, even garroted, by inflation, price controls, and shortages. Unfortunately, risk of government interference increases costs of doing business; therefore, recommended procedures must be adapted to the times and likely changes.

Money management rallies on innovation both in short term markets and long term financing. For instance, *repurchase agreements* allow for a guaranteed repurchase of securities at a fixed price and interest rate, which shifts the burden of price-change risk to the bank. *Doughnut loans,* commercial paper with a guaranteed takeout during the course of the loan, permit the lender to repossess funds for special purposes. For intermediate financing the *mini-bond* may attract inflation-shy investors. Too, in *link financing* a third party supplies the bank, the lender, with funds. *Segmental financing* was proposed to decentralize the firm's capital structure. And *Employee Stock Ownership Trusts* (ESOTs) offer a special situation of tapping long term capital sources.

The objective, *liquidity flexibility,* infers that an independent listing of all possible (even unusual and unlikely) money sources be ranked in terms of speed and dependability for supplying funds. From there let imagination take over.

Rather than aim at how or where to obtain funds, this chapter converges on means to estimate cash flows, minimize cash balances, and maximize return on liquid assets. Techniques discussed range from inventory-type models to a simple rule-of-thumb to assist financial management in a dynamic firm in liquidity subvention.

INVENTORY MODELS

The following models, not perfect in any absolute sense, in a rudimentary form aid in cash balance optimization. They assume a periodicity and certainty, seldom realized in practice, and tie in analyses with near-liquid investments, marketable securities, which provide a potential pool of available cash.

Baumol Approach

The first model derives from the EOQ inventory mechanism developed in Chapter Nine, in which a stock of cash parallels an inventory of goods and this stock must be replenished, but at a cost. The cost may embody a broker's fee (transactions costs) when converting a financial asset to cash, clerical expenses, or opportunity costs (see Chapter Six), the income foregone by transforming income-paying assets into nonincome-producing cash balances. In its simplest form, the model assumes near-perfect information, lack of uncertainty, and ease of exchange. The subject is to discover the optimum "order size" of cash (COOS).

Formula:

$$\text{COOS} = \sqrt{\frac{2\,Q\,C_c}{k}}$$

Q = demand for cash in the period under analysis.

C_c = average transaction cost to obtain cash.

k = cost of carrying cash inventory.

For example, management of Hept and Bes Frog Legs, Inc. figure they need about $3 million per year (Q) in cash. Average fixed cost of obtaining cash is $15,000 ($C_c$). The difference between the cost of capital and return on short term securities is (15% – 6%) 9% (k). What is the *optimum cash order size* (COOS)?

$$\text{COOS} = \sqrt{\frac{2\,(3{,}000{,}000)\,(15{,}000)}{0.09}} = \$1{,}000{,}000$$

According to the above result, the financial manager will hasten to the market three times a year to raise $1,000,000 and invest surplus cash in short term securities yielding 6% in this example.

Consider the problem in two parts. Suppose that the firm acquires $1,000,000 in a capital market each time. Since no immediate need for the entire sum arises, the temporary surplus is placed in short term bills so that every conversion into cash from bills costs a flat $49. How much cash should be drawn each time from this reserve? The same formula applies.

$$\text{Cash} = \sqrt{\frac{2\,(3{,}000{,}000)\,(49)}{0.06}} = \$70{,}000$$

Withdrawals from this reserve, made in lumps of $70,000, minimize costs and maximize benefits under conditions of certainty. To learn how often these transactions will occur refer again to the inventory formulas.

Formula:

$$N = 52 \div \frac{Q}{\text{Cash}}$$

Or, in this instance, the result is 52 ÷ 3,000,000/70,000 = 1.2 weeks. Uncertainty or uneven flows may be compensated for with larger temporary reserves, which, of course, increases total cost of holding cash. Presumably, offsetting benefits (or negative costs) exceed costs associated with uncertainty when higher balances are maintained.

Miller-Orr Approach

Another method allows for *random cash flows* and adjusts balances according to the deficit or surplus generated without reference to a specific time period. This model focuses on the flow of cash into or out of marketable securities. Cash limits are established by management according to preferences, forecasts, or terms fixed by the lending agent (bank). The lower limit sets a *target cash balance* and whenever discretionary balances hit zero, it triggers a flow from securities into cash in order to restore this minimum level. Whenever cash balances reach a maximum level, then surplus funds are drained off to the lower limit level and placed in income-yielding securities. Between these limits, cash balances change randomly over time both in amount and direction without triggering any further responses. In other words, there are three cash levels stipulated: the *zero level, target level* (minimum balances) and *maximum level.* Lower and upper limits are *optimal values.* The probability that cash balances will swing in either direction is 50/50. Employing the same terminology as in the Baumol approach, the formula is:

Formula:

$$TL = \sqrt[3]{\frac{3\,C_c\,Q^2 t}{4k}}$$

TL = target level.

3 TL = maximum level.

C_c = average transaction cost between cash and securities.

Q = demand for cash in period under analysis.

t = number of operating cash transactions per day.

Q^2t = variance of cash balance changes.

k = daily interest rate.

The opportunity cost of holding cash is usually taken as the long term interest rate. Too, the model is subject to certain limitations and assumptions. The practice of maintaining many cash accounts may obscure results. Negotiated compensating balances, while not always closely adhered to, may distort values in the computations. Nevertheless, the model significantly improves upon a rule-of-thumb approach which arbitrarily fixes minimum and maximum levels not necessarily optimal.

MARKETABLE SECURITIES

During short run periods of surplus cash, the firm will want to place excess funds in marketable securities, disregarding expected interest rate changes, for a period of time sufficiently long to overcome transaction costs in order to provide a net positive rate of return. Otherwise, the effort is self-defeating. Although *U.S. Treasury bills* represent the main outlet for these funds, other acceptable possibilities include *tax anticipation notes, time certificates of deposit, repurchase agreements, securities of government agencies, commercial and finance company paper.* From the money manager's viewpoint *marketability, liquidity, safety, and risk of interest rate changes* (price fluctuations) are of considerable importance and one or most of these investment alternatives may be eliminated in practice for many concerns.

To estimate net return on the investment vehicle chosen, the following formula reigns:

Formula: $$\pi = N_d \, P \, i_d + G_c^* - 2c$$

π = net gain resulting from investment in marketable securities.

N_d = number of days funds are invested.

P = amount invested.

i_d = daily interest rate.

G_c^* = expected capital gain on date of sale

c = cash cost per transaction—buy or sell.

Although i_d, the daily interest rate, may not necessarily be independent of N_d, the number of days funds are invested, the formula assumes so for simplicity. Too, in some instances expected capital gain (G_c^*) may equal zero. Where prices of securities do fluctuate in a predictable pattern the money manager may increase his net return (π) by careful planning and timing of encashment. Transaction costs are particularly important for very short term commitment of funds or where the sum is small relative to minimum transaction charges. If temporarily idle funds exist, the interest rate may be unimportant; but the possibility of adverse price fluctuations, or transaction expenses excessive relative to invested principal, may point toward a market that can be hedged or else forego entirely the chance of any income and choose cash as the better option.

UNCERTAIN CASH FLOWS

Predicting cash flows, especially in the face of new investment, a new marketing program, or uncertainties external to the firm's operations, may require a set of answers expressed in *probabilistic terms.* The advantage of this method is that it offers more visible detail. That is its disadvantage as well because input may require more information than the money manager can readily evaluate. For the following explications, assume these data (in Figure 11-1) on the Tar Heel Transportation Co.

Figure 11-1

Outcome	*Probability of Outcome*	*Cash Flow* 1	2	3
a	0.2	-1,000	500	200
b	0.2	-1,200	400	650
c	0.3	-1,000	750	450
d	0.2	-1,000	800	0
e	0.1	-1,000	300	900
	1.0			

Summary data in Figure 11-1 indicate cash flows that would occur in each of five possible decisions limited to a three-year period for simplicity. Probability of each occurrence is estimated. How can these data be efficiently handled and presented?

Weighted Average

To calculate the *weighted average,* the expected cash flows for each period, multiply each outcome by its probability of occurring; i.e., each outcome is weighted by the chance of its occurrence in Figure 11-2.

Figure 11-2

Outcome	*Probability of Outcome*	*Expected Cash Flows*		
		1	*2*	*3*
a	0.2	-200	100	40
b	0.2	-240	80	130
c	0.3	-300	225	135
d	0.2	-200	160	0
e	0.1	-100	30	90
Weighted Average		-1,040	595	395

Although cash decisions may be limited to this type of presentation, further analysis is useful.

Period Analysis

Arranging data on a *period-by-period basis* begins with the above weighted average but additional information furnishes further insight into the issue.

Figure 11-3

	Periods		
	1	*2*	*3*
Expected Cash Flow	-1,040	+595	+395
Optimistic Cash Flow	-1,000	+800	+900
Pessimistic Cash Flow	-1,200	+300	0

With the addition of optimistic and pessimistic cash flows we now have a rough idea of upper and lower limits of possible results—the best outcomes and worst outcomes according to estimates of chance occurrences. That is, this measure of *variability,* the *range,* supplies an approximate indication of the range of *dispersion* of possible outcomes. An extreme value may have small chance of occurrence. To judge the closeness of an estimate, we need to know something about variability.

The *sample range* is the difference between the extremes. For period 2, in Figure 11-3, the range of results is 800 − 300 = 500. Although the range is easy to calculate and perceive, it does not always provide the best measurement of variation because, being based on extremes of estimates of cash flows, it does not indicate dispersion of data between upper and lower estimates.

Standard Deviation

A better measurement of dispersion of results, *standard deviation,* indicates whether results are widely scattered from the mean or whether the dispersion is closely bunched around the mean. Naturally, the greater the dispersion the greater the risk that cash flows will not fall within the expected level. Greater risk suggests that a greater reserve of liquidity is necessary to forestall consequences of cash shortages and associated costs. Therefore, a more liquid position raises the cost of operations and these costs arising from risk or variability of cash flows must be compared with risks and costs of cash shortages. Standard deviation calculations are developed in Figure 11–4.

Figure 11–4

	(1)	*(2) Cash Flow Minus Expected Cash Flow*			*(3) Squared Deviations*			*(4) (1) X (3)*		
		1	2	3	1	2	3	1	2	3
a	0.2	-40	-95	-195	1,600	9,025	38,025	320	1,805	7,605
b	0.2	160	-195	255	25,600	38,025	65,025	5,120	7,605	13,005
c	0.3	-40	155	55	1,600	24,025	3,025	480	7,208	908
d	0.2	-40	205	-395	1,600	42,025	156,025	320	8,405	31,205
e	0.1	-40	-295	505	1,600	87,025	255,025	160	8,703	25,503
						Variances		6,400	33,726	78,226
						Standard Deviation		$80	$183.65	$279.69

The first step, in Column (2) of Figure 11–4, is to record differences between cash flow and expected cash flow utilizing same data presented previously. Flow 1 figures are bunched together, suggesting little dispersion, while Flow 3 data indicate a rather large dispersion, or variability, of results. Of course, to average these deviations from the mean is not useful because the sum of deviations from the mean always equals zero.

Our interest focuses on the *magnitude of deviations,* which means we must eliminate the negative signs. One way to do it is square all figures grouped in Column (2), which results appear under Column (3).

Because we deal with a set of possible cash flows whose chance of occurrence is estimated in Column (1), multiply Columns (1) times (3). The *variance,* then, is computed by squaring each deviation and finding the expected value of squared deviations; that is, the weighted average of squared deviations from the mean.

But what does the *variance* tell us? It is a measurement of variation. Unfortunately, the variance is not stated in the same units as the original data on cash flows so that our measurement can be improved by taking the square root of variances to yield standard deviations.*

Outcome Analysis

Still another method to distill and analyze above information is to summarize cash flows for each outcome and then calculate *net present value.*** Relying on preceding data and employing a discount rate of 6%, Figure 11-5 results are:

Figure 11-5

Possible Outcomes	*Probability of Outcome*	*Net Present Values @ 6%*	*Expected NPV*
a	0.2	-350.30	-70.06
b	0.2	-244.14	-48.83
c	0.3	108.05	32.42
d	0.2	-245.28	-49.06
e	0.1	84.02	8.40
			-127.13

Results, of course, are not favorable since a negative net present value surfaces. As an additional element, the *standard deviation of net present value* appears in Figure 11-6.

*For further explanations of standard deviation, vide: John E. Freund and Frank J. Williams, *Elementary Business Statistics: the Modern Approach* (Englewood Cliffs, N.J.: Prentice-Hall, Inc., 1964), especially pp. 50-4.

**See Chapter Three for additional discussion on net present value.

Figure 11-6

Possible Event	*Probability (1)*	*Net Present Value Minus Expected Net Present Value (2)*	*Squared Deviation (3)*	*(1) X (3) (4)*
a	0.2	-223.17	49,804.85	9,960.97
b	0.2	-117.01	13,691.34	2,738.27
c	0.3	235.18	55,309.63	16,592.89
d	0.2	-118.15	13,959.42	2,791.88
e	0.1	211.15	44,584.32	4,458.43
		Variance		36,542.44
		Standard Deviation		$ 191.16

CASH BUDGETS

However, the problem of how to reasonably predict future cash flows to determine cash needs remains. One estimating technique, the *cash budget,* relies heavily on accurate sales projections to plan liquidity and financing needs. Although cash budgets may encompass any time period, short term forecasts are essentially monthly to account for seasonal fluctuations. As a rule, greater sales volatility favors more frequent projections to hedge these variations. The following example illustrates that this widely employed tool is mechanically uncomplicated; the cost of preparation is in obtaining reliable data input which means that information from various sources within the firm must be scrutinized and screened carefully.

Actual and estimated sales for The Lampton Company are shown below. Last year's sales are actual (rounded to simplify presentation); current year's sales (January - August) are estimates derived largely from previous years' patterns coupled with management's intuitive projections for this year.

September	$300,000	March	$350,000
October	400,000	April	225,000
November	500,000	May	275,000
December	600,000	June	200,000
January	300,000	July	280,000
February	250,000	August	235,000

In preparing the cash budget the following assumptions prevail.

–Prices and costs remain constant.
–Sales are 20% for cash and 80% on credit terms, N 30.
–Collections are:
80% First month after sale
10% Second month after sale
6% Third month after sale
4% Fourth month after sale.
(Bad debt write-offs are negligible and ignored.)
–Cost of goods sold equals 60% of sales price; stock is ordered one month in advance for following month's anticipated sales; accounts payable are liquidated the month in which sales occur.
–Variable expenses equal 20% of sales.
–Fixed expenditures are $70,000 monthly.
–Interest on long term obligations due at end of each quarter in the amount of $30,000.
–Tax payments due in April, $50,000, and in July, $40,000.
–Cash balance at January 1 is $145,000; minimum desired range, $125–150,000.
–Outstanding short term note of $175,000 owing in January.

The objective now is to compress data into a readily comprehensible tabular form such as that disclosed in Figure 11-7. While estimates herein have been simplified for heuristic purposes, the format followed by The Lampton Company coincides with that preferred by many firms of this size.

The upper portion of the cash budget consolidates cash receipts arising from cash transactions on current sales plus turnover of receivables from previous months' sales. The middle section brings together disbursements. Cash payments regularly consist of payment of expenses and overhead plus previous months' purchases. Less frequent transactions include payments for taxes, interest, and other short term obligations.

At the bottom of the cash budget monthly results appear. If cash receipts exceed cash disbursements then the positive cash balance is added to cash on hand at the beginning of the month. A net cash outflow reduces cash on hand at the end of the month. Since cash balances remain within the acceptable range through June, The Lampton Company makes no new short term working capital loans. July's balance is below the desired cash level which means that management will prepare well in advance to secure adequate funds. Apparently the firm will remain indebted for cash needs the remaining of the year due to seasonal inventory build-up.

Although the orthodox cash budget is widely used it has distinct disadvantages. The forecast is based on single valued estimates for cash inflows

Figure 11-7

CASH BUDGET
($000)

	Jan.	*Feb.*	*March*	*April*	*May*	*June*	*July*
Sales	*300*	*250*	*350*	*225*	*275*	*200*	*280*
Collections:							
Cash Sales	60	50	70	45	55	40	56
Accounts Receivable–previous month	384	192	160	224	144	176	128
Accounts Receivable–2nd previous month	40	48	24	20	28	18	22
Accounts Receivable–3rd previous month	19.2	24	28.8	14.4	12	16.8	10.8
Accounts Receivable–4th previous month	9.6	14.4	16	19.2	9.6	8	11.2
CASH RECEIPTS	512.8	328.4	298.8	322.6	248.6	258.8	228
Cash Payments:							
Variable Expenses	60	50	70	45	55	40	56
Fixed Costs	70	70	70	70	70	70	70
Note Payment	175	–	–	–	–	–	–
Interest	–	–	30	–	–	30	–
Taxes	–	–	–	50	–	–	40
Purchases	180	150	210	135	165	120	168
TOTAL	485	270	380	300	290	260	334
NET CASH GAIN (LOSS)	27.8	58.4	(81.2)	22.6	(41.4)	(1.2)	(106)
CUMULATIVE CASH (OR REQUIRED FINANCING)	172.8	231.2	150	172.6	131.2	130	24 (125)

and outflows. One problem is uncertainty. Actual results may vary considerably from forecasted ones. In other words, there are risks. Greater dispersion of result signals the need for larger safety stocks of cash in the absence of better estimates and forecasting techniques. Excessive safety stocks of cash results in higher costs to the concern because of low or zero productivity of cash balances and also because of higher total borrowing costs resulting from average borrowing above the optimum level. And unless all costs associated with borrowing are analyzed, the firm may pay an exceptionally higher rate than it supposes.

CREDIT COSTS

Because companies enter into formal credit agreements with banks or arrange lines of credit total borrowing costs may encompass commitment fees, compensating balances plus interest charges so that the cost of credit needs to be carefully calculated. The following short cut approach illustrates the technique.

The Maize Tortilla Co., Inc. has negotiated a $2 million credit arrangement which requires a 0.5% *commitment fee* charged on the unused portion of the credit limit, an 8½% *interest cost* on borrowings, a 15% *compensating balance* against borrowed funds, and a 10% compensating balance on the unused segment of the *credit limit.* Average annual borrowings have been $1 million over a recent 12-month period; normal account balances average $40,000. What is the cost of credit to this enterprise?

Figure 11-8

Dollar Costs:	
Interest on average borrowing (8½% X $1 million)	$ 85,000
Commitment fee (0.5% X $1 million)	5,000
TOTAL COSTS	$ 90,000
Available Funds:	
Average borrowing	$1,000,000
Less:	
15% compensating balance on $1 million	(150,000)
10% compensating balance on $1 million	(100,000)
	$ 750,000
Plus: Normal account balance	40,000
AVERAGE AVAILABLE FUNDS	$ 790,000

$$\text{Interest rate} = \frac{\text{Dollar costs}}{\text{Average available funds}} = \frac{90{,}000}{790{,}000} = 11.4\%$$

The steps illustrated in Figure 11–8 are:

A. To calculate dollar costs:

1. Determine average borrowings for the period (annual in this example).
2. Multiply borrowings times period interest rate to specify interest costs on actual debt.
3. Multiply commitment fee rate times unused portion of agreed credit limit.
4. Add together (2) and (3) to obtain total dollar costs.

B. To calculate average available funds:

5. Enter the figure found in (1) above.
6. Subtract compensating balance on (a) borrowings and (b) unused portion of credit limit.
7. Add usual (or average) account balance to find average amount of funds available during the period.

C. To calculate the effective interest rate divide dollar costs (A) by average available funds (B).

Maize Tortilla Co., Inc., instead of paying an effective interest rate of 8½% actually paid 11.4% for use of funds. Added costs reflect commitment fee plus compensating balances. Of course, if the firm normally maintains a bank balance of $250,000 or more (which may be an inefficient utilization of funds) then a lower interest rate cost arises because the full $1 million borrowed is available rather than $790,000; i.e., the effective interest rate would be 9.0%. If we were to compare performances of two money managers, a just comparison would not focus only on comparative effective borrowing rates because efficiency encompasses total money management including size of the cash safety stock.

Figure 11-9 depicts various credit options which demonstrate advantages of carefully estimated credit requirements and terms on which credit lines are negotiated. Preparing such information in tabular form provides a better grasp of money management alternatives.

By formula, average available funds (Y) can be calculated as long as the compensating balance requirement exceeds the concern's average bank balance.

Formula: $$Y = (1 - a + b)\,\bar{S} - b\,v + \bar{Q}$$

$\bar{S}$ = average borrowings.

$\bar{Q}$ = average bank balances.

Figure 11-9

Credit Limit ($000)	Average Available Funds ($000)	Compensating Balance on Borrowing (%)	Compensating Balance on Unused Credit (%)	Commitment Fee on Unused Credit (%)	Interest Rate on Borrowings (%)	Average Borrowing ($000)	Cost of Available Funds (%)
2	790	15	10	0.5	8.5	1,000	11.4
2	560	20	10	0.5	8.5	800	13.2
2	740	20	10	0.5	8.5	1,000	12.2
2	640	30	10	0.5	8.5	1,000	14.1
3	2,740	10	10	0.0	8.5	3,000	9.3
3	1,690	15	5	0.5	8.5	2,000	10.4
3	1,690	15	5	0.1	8.5	2,000	10.7
3	1,640	15	10	0.1	8.5	2,000	11.0
3	1,540	20	10	0.5	8.5	2,000	11.4
3	1,540	20	10	0.5	9.5	2,000	12.7
3	1,360	20	10	0.5	8.5	1,800	11.7
3	1,090	20	10	0.5	8.5	1,500	12.4
3	940	30	10	0.1	8.5	1,500	15.2
3	640	20	10	0.1	8.5	1,000	16.4

v = credit limit established by agreement.

a = compensating balance requirement (%) on borrowings.

b = compensating balance requirement (%) on unused portion of credit limit.

Applying the formula to the previous problem, we have:

$$Y = (1 - 0.15 + 0.10)\$1{,}000{,}000 - 0.10(\$2{,}000{,}000) + \$40{,}000$$
$$= \$790{,}000 \text{ available funds.}$$

The dollar costs of credit (I) are:

Formula: $$I = i_1\bar{S} + i_2(v - \bar{S})$$

i_1 = interest rate on average borrowings.

i_2 = commitment fee rate on unused portion of credit limit.

v = credit line.

$\bar{S}$ = average borrowings.

Using the same example results in:

$$I = 0.085(\$1{,}000{,}000) + 0.005(\$2{,}000{,}000 - 1{,}000{,}000)$$
$$= \$90{,}000 \text{ dollar costs of credit.}$$

The effective interest rate (r) is:

Formula: $$r = \frac{I}{Y}$$

I = total dollar costs of credit.

Y = average available funds.

Checking once again, we find that

$$r = \frac{90{,}000}{790{,}000} = 11.4\%$$

Too, by rearranging, we can determine average borrowings ($\bar{S}$):

Formula:

$$\bar{S} = \frac{Y + bv - \bar{Q}}{(1 - a + b)}$$

Y = average available funds.

$\bar{Q}$ = average bank balances.

a = compensating balance requirement (%) on borrowings.

b = compensating balance requirement (%) on unused credit.

v = credit limit.

The lesson of the above method is to emphasize the real cost of credit. Financial executives may pay two or even three times the interest rate on debt because the price of liquidity insurance, shifting risk of illiquidity to a financial institution, is not free. The problem is less high interest rate and more ability to plan.

RULE-OF-THUMB

The rule-of-thumb approach reflects differences in organizational structure, money market conditions, expectations, and, to some extent, custom established within the firm or even the industry. The rationale behind a rule-of-thumb concept is to minimize some costs of hard planning and thinking in terms of liquidity management. Certainly, where sales and production patterns exhibit narrow random fluctuations and volatility, a rule-of-thumb technique may be acceptable for concerns operating under these predictable conditions.

The formula offered below encompasses more than desired cash balances; it defines the liquidity position of the enterprise as consisting of cash plus marketable securities plus its credit line. Credit line may include access to the commercial paper market and even long term markets to cover permanent cash needs. For smaller businesses, however, liquidity is defined as cash or cash plus near-cash assets.

Formula:

$$Y^* = \frac{Q^* + E_1 + v}{Y_s}$$

Y^* = desired liquidity position of the firm.

Q^* = desired cash balances.

E_1 = near-cash assets.

v = credit line.

Y_s = sales.

The credit line (v) as seen by the firm may differ from the bank's, lender's, or market's view. While management may believe it can borrow a certain sum, changing money market and business conditions may make the cost of those obligations prohibitive or unavailable. Although this formula states that the desired liquidity position is linked to sales, the actual sales used may be lagged by one or more periods or the ratio may be tied in to projected sales. That is, such a rule-of-thumb focus, although popular, need not be mechanically or rigidly applied in the absence of better planning guides. Naturally, the cash position ultimately taken influences both liquidity and profitability ratios.

CONTENTS

Chapter Twelve: Sixty Measures to Plan for Profit and Growth with Financial Analysis

TWELVE

Sixty Measures to Plan for Profit and Growth with Financial Analysis

The previous chapter focused on liquidity. This chapter ties together relationships in the firm's financial structure.

Ratios, important profit tools in financial analysis, are measures, guides, in planning for greater profitability, liquidity, advantageous reordering of the financial structure, leverage and interest coverage, as well as providing lead indications of potential problem areas; that is, ratios mostly report on past performances, but they are predictive, too.

Presented here, they have been subdivided into eight working categories: income, profitability, liquidity, working capital, bankruptcy, long term analysis, coverage, and leverage. These subcategories, which simplify cognizability and future reference to them, certainly overlap, and occasionally a ratio is reidentified in more than one category.

For illustrative purposes, a year-end balance sheet and income statement appear on pages 346 and 347 and many of the ratios explained in terms of

HUZZAH HOSSIER HOSIERY MILLS, INC.
Balance Sheet at Year End
($000)

ASSETS	
Cash	832
Marketable Securities	430
Accounts Receivable (net)	4,621
Inventory	10,066
Prepaid Expenses	8
TOTAL CURRENT ASSETS	15,957
Plant and equipment (net)	8,247
Buildings (net)	3,200
Land (at cost)	3,000
Patients and Intangibles	2,850
TOTAL FIXED AND INTANGIBLE ASSETS	17,297
TOTAL ASSETS	33,254
LIABILITIES	
Accounts Payable	7,051
Notes Payable	1,000
Accrued Expenses	46
Long Term Debt (current portion)	675
TOTAL CURRENT LIABILITIES	8,772
1st Mortgage (7½% matures in 24 years)	4,600
2nd Mortgage (12% matures in 2 years)	475
20-Year Bonds (8% due in 10 years) (No sinking fund)	4,000
Debentures (9%, subordinated, due in 3 years)	1,000
Preferred Stock ($8 non-cumulative)	500
Retained Earnings (Earned Surplus)	11,947
Common Stock	1,960
TOTAL LIABILITIES AND EQUITY	33,254

these data will resolve most questions concerning their application. Nevertheless, the fun of completely analyzing this enterprise's condition, a hosiery manufacturer, is reserved to the reader.

INCOME RATIOS

Although income and profitability ratios are spots on the same leopard, dividing them into two sections facilitates presentation. The long run success of the business depends upon profitability and profits derive from income. Loss of them may originate at any point in the income statement; therefore, income ratios reveal more when compared over several periods expressed as

HUZZAH HOOSIER HOSIERY MILLS, INC.
Income Statement at Year End
($000)

Sales	46,308
Cost of Goods Sold	39,217
GROSS MARGIN	7,091
Less:	
Administrative and Selling Expenses	871
General Expenses	2,626
Depreciation	1,331
Other Expenses	42
INCOME FROM OPERATIONS	2,221
OTHER INCOME (LOSS), NET	15
EARNINGS BEFORE INTEREST AND TAXES (EBIT)	2,236
Interest Expense	892
EARNINGS BEFORE TAXES (EBT)	1,344
Provision for Income Taxes	630
EARNINGS AFTER TAXES (EAT)	714
Current Dividends on Preferred Stock	40
EARNINGS AVAILABLE TO COMMON SHAREHOLDERS	674
Average Number of Shares Outstanding	1,960
Earnings Per Share on Common Stock (EPS)	0.344

NOTE:
Recent selling price of common stock $2.00 per share.
Recent selling price of preferred stock $100.00 per share.

trend indices. Data for HHHM, Inc. illustrate application of ratios rather than analysis for which we would need comparative balance sheets and income statements.

Turnover of Total Operating Assets

Sales-to-investment in total operating assets, the turnover of total operating assets, tracks overinvestment in operating assets. Obviously, sales expansion will necessitate more operating assets at some point, but within a given range sales may rise without additional investment. Or inadequate sales volume may call for reduced investment. Although this ratio does not measure profitability, overinvestment may result in a lack of adequate profits.

$$\text{Turnover} = \frac{\text{Net Sales}}{\text{Total Operating Assets}} = \frac{46{,}308}{30{,}404} = 152\%$$

Total operating assets consist of total assets less long term investments and intangible assets. Without comparative date, the 152% for HHHM, Inc. does not provide much clue on efficiency. Financial statements for the past ten years disclose direction of change.

Net Sales to Tangible Net Worth

The ratio of net sales-to-tangible net worth indicates whether investment is adequately proportionate to sales and whether a potential credit problem or management problem exists. Tangible net worth equals owners' equity less intangible assets.

$$\text{Ratio} = \frac{\text{Net Sales}}{\text{Tangible Net Worth}} = \frac{46{,}308}{11{,}557} = 4.01 \text{ times}$$

Undertrading, most commonly encountered, is a management problem that stems from underutilization of investment and perhaps lack of ingenuity, skill, or aggressiveness of the management team. Overtrading, while it may indicate considerable management skill, also presents a potential problem for creditors. To overtrade, that is, excessive sales volume transacted on a thin margin of investment, means that outside creditors furnish more funds to carry on daily operations. Since Dun and Bradstreet monitors this ratio by industry groupings, we find the HHHM, Inc. compares favorably with the industry median of 3.19 and upper quartile of 4.6.*

Gross Margin on Net Sales

The ratio, gross margin on sales-to-net sales, highlights average spread between costs of goods sold and selling price. Gross margin is the difference between net sales and cost of goods sold.

$$\text{Gross Margin Ratio} = \frac{\text{Gross Margin}}{\text{Net Sales}} = \frac{7{,}091}{46{,}308} = 15.3\%$$

Comparing this figure over several years will indicate whether to examine closely company policies relating to credit extension, markups (or markdowns), purchasing, or general merchandising (where applicable). An increase in gross margin may result from higher sales, lower cost of goods sold, some combination of these variables, or an increase in the proportionate volume of higher margin products.

**Key Business Ratios* (N.Y.: Dun & Bradstreet, Inc., 1975), p. 9.

Operating Ratio

Relating operating income to net sales reveals profitableness of sales resulting from regular conduct of business, the buying, selling, manufacturing operations.

$$\text{Operating Ratio} = \frac{\text{Operating Income}}{\text{Net Sales}} = \frac{2{,}221}{46{,}308} = 4.8\%$$

Operating income derives from ordinary business operations and excludes other revenue (losses), extraordinary items, interest on long term obligations, and income taxes. A 15–25% range seems normal for most manufacturing entities, hosiery manufacturers excepted.

Operating Expense Ratio

Total operating expenses-to-net sales reflects management's ability to adjust expense items to changing sales. Trending each category of expenses will readily spotlight areas out of line.

$$\text{Operating Expenses Ratio} = \frac{\text{Total Operating Expenses}}{\text{Net Sales}} = \frac{44{,}087}{46{,}308} = 95.2\%$$

Total operating expenses include cost of goods sold plus selling, administrative, and general expenses associated with operations. The higher the ratio the more sales are being absorbed by expenses.

Maintenance and Repairs to Net Sales

This example of expense ratios by expenditure category is only important for certain types of manufacturing.

$$\text{Sum Spent on Repairs per Dollar of Sales} = \frac{\text{Maintenance \& Repair Expenses}}{\text{Net Sales}}$$

Certainly these expenses vary according to the age of plant and property, rate of use of equipment, maintenance policy, tax credits and availability of replacements, relationship between labor and capital charges, cost of closing down operations for repair. (Illustrative figures not accessible for HHHM, Inc.)

Maintenance and Repairs to Fixed Assets

Relating expenses to fixed assets gives some indication of management attitude toward maintaining property. This ratio is studied along with the preceding one.

$$\frac{\text{Sum Spent on Repairs per}}{\text{Dollar of Fixed Assets}} = \frac{\text{Maintenance \& Repair Expenses}}{\text{Gross Tangible Fixed Assets - Land}}$$

Gross value of fixed assets excludes intangible items and land as well as long term investment but does include accumulated depreciation. When maintenance and repairs do not vary directly with sales, the significance of this ratio is increased.

Similarly, ratios for depreciation charges can be related to sales or to fixed assets (adjusted as above) according to whether depreciation more closely ties in with sales or fixed assets. Too, depreciation method, age of property, and composition of fixed assets affect these ratios.

Acceptance Index

A high sales volume transacted with two or three major accounts is riskier than the same volume derived from a large number of customers. Losing one out of three major accounts is disastrous; replacing one out of 150 is routine. A growing firm that endures may spread this risk of dependency through active sales and promotion, discounts, or an active credit department, for example. Although quality of customers originates in general management policy, quantity of new accounts opened reflects sales and credit publicity.

$$\text{Acceptance Index} = \frac{\text{Applications Accepted}}{\text{Applications Submitted}}$$

Naturally, this index of effectiveness does not apply to every line of endeavor.

PROFITABILITY RATIOS

Closely linked with income ratios, profitability ratios provide the final answer on overall effectiveness of management ranked by returns generated on sales and investment.

Gross Profit on Net Sales

(See "Gross Margin on Net Sales" in the section on Income Ratios.)

$$\text{Gross Profit Rate} = \frac{\text{Net Sales - Cost of Goods Sold}}{\text{Net Sales}}$$

The percentage of gross profit on net sales discloses whether the average markup on goods will normally cover expenses and result in a profit. A deterioration in this rate signals problems that will show up on the bottom line; ergo, rates compared over several years will identify the trend of a particular business. However, this rate will vary widely even among concerns within the same industry, according to sales, location, size of operations, and intensity of competition.

Net Operating Profit Ratio

(See "Operating Ratio" in the section on Income Ratios.) This ratio zeroes in on management's ability, skill, and resourcefulness to operate successfully the business's main function.

Net Profit to Net Sales

Sales, pivotal in reaching the break-even point, are needed to rise as far as possible above the break-even point of operations, because once basic expenses are covered profits rise disproportionately greater than sales above this point. Sales expenses may be substituted out of profits for other costs to generate even more sales—and profits.

$$\text{Net Profit Rate} = \frac{\text{Earnings after Taxes}}{\text{Net Sales}} = \frac{714}{46{,}308} = 1.54\%$$

This ratio serves as a guide to particular operations. Since it is another Dun and Bradstreet key business ratio, comparing HHHM, Inc. with the industry we discover that a net profit rate of 1.54% lies between the median rate of 0.84% and upper quartile rate of 1.83%.

Net Profit to Tangible Net Worth

A second, complementary, important appraisal of net profits, related to investment, sizes up the ability of management to earn a return. Sound management policies will result in consistent profits over the long haul.

$$\text{Net Profit Rate} = \frac{\text{Earnings after Taxes}}{\text{Tangible Net Worth}} = \frac{714}{11{,}557} = 6.18\%$$

This is another D & B key ratio. HHHM, Inc. exceeds the industry median of 2.32% and approaches the upper quartile figure of 7.95%. Adequate profits provide for dividends and future growth. Profits furnish the incentive for greater efficiency and better use of resources, and signal expansion or contraction of investment within a firm and reallocation of funds among industries. Taxing them impinges on the constitutional basis of property rights, limits capital formation, and destroys productive employment of labor and resources.

Turnover Ratio

(Consult "Turnover of Operating Assets" under Income Ratios.) A gauge of asset use, the turnover ratio designates the efficiency with which assets are employed to produce an output expressed in sales data.

Net Operating Profit Rate of Return

Because net profit-to-net worth is influenced by the method of financing, this ratio employs earnings before interest and taxes (EBIT) rather than earnings after taxes (EAT).

$$\text{Net Operating Profit Ratio} = \frac{\text{EBIT}}{\text{Tangible Net Worth}} = \frac{2{,}236}{30{,}404} = 7.35\%$$

The ratio of net profit-to-tangible net worth is "somewhat inappropriate, inasmuch as profits are taken after interest is paid to creditors. As these creditors provide means by which part of the total assets are supported, there is a fallacy of omission. When financial charges are significant, it is preferable, for comparative purposes, to compute a net operating profit rate of return instead of return on assets ratio."*

Rate of Return on Common Stock Equity

Instead of focusing on total assets, this ratio takes a reading on the rate of return (RR) on stockholders' equity.

$$\text{RR} = \frac{\text{Earnings after Taxes} - \text{Preferred Stock Dividends}}{\text{Tangible Net Worth} - \text{Par Value of Preferred Stock}} = \frac{714 - 40}{11{,}557 - 500} = 6.10\%$$

---

*James C. van Horne, *Financial Management and Policy* (Englewood Cliffs, N.J.: Prentice-Hall, 1968). p. 520.

Based on book value rather than market value of owners' equity, this rate of return is most useful when compared with other similar firms within the industry.

Management Rate of Return

Another profitability ratio compares operating income to operating assets which are defined as the sum of tangible fixed assets plus net working capital.

$$RR = \frac{\text{Operating Income}}{\text{Fixed Assets + Net Working Capital}} = \frac{2{,}221}{14{,}447 + 7{,}185} = 10.27\%$$

This rate, which may be calculated on a divisional or operational basis or company wide, quantifies efficient use of assets compared with a target rate of return.

Earning Power

The earning power ratio combines asset turnover with the net profit rate; that is, net sales-to-operating assets (see Income Ratios) times net profit on net sales (see ratio above).

$$\text{Earning Power} = \frac{\text{Net Sales}}{\text{Tangible Assets}} \times \frac{\text{EAT}}{\text{Net Sales}} = \frac{46{,}308}{30{,}404} \times \frac{714}{46{,}308} = 2.35\%$$

Earning power can be increased by trading heavier on assets or decreasing costs (or lowering the break-even point) or increasing sales faster than the accompanying rise in costs. Sales, however, hold the key.

Earnings per Share

Earnings per share (EPS) conveniently demonstrate to individual shareholders company earnings (EAT) available for each share of common stock outstanding.

$$EPS = \frac{\text{EAT - Preferred Dividends}}{\text{Average No. of Shares Outstanding}} = \frac{714 - 40}{1{,}960} = \$0.344$$

Although income earned does not necessarily imply income distributed, legally common owners have a residual interest in the firm's assets in the event of dissolution; therefore, earnings retained and reinvested at a satisfactory rate will influence stock prices.

Price-Earnings Ratio

The price-earnings (P–E) ratio really tells nothing except to express a mathematical relationship between market price and EPS.

$$\text{P-E Ratio} = \frac{\text{Market Price of Common Stock}}{\text{Earnings per Share}} = \frac{2.000}{0.344} = 5.8 \text{ times}$$

Its inverse registers a kind of "rate of return" on corporate earnings, not an appropriate investment guide, which does reflect what stock purchasers feel about the concern.

LIQUIDITY RATIOS

Continuing with short term analysis, liquidity ratios are most important to short term creditors—suppliers and bankers—and to financial managers who must meet obligations to suppliers of credit plus tributes to various governments. Liquidity ratio analyses help point out any weaknesses in the financial position of the enterprise.

Current Ratio

A test of solvency, popular since the turn of the century,* balances current assets against current liabilities. Current assets are net of contingent liabilities on notes receivable, and current liabilities include all debt due within one year of statement data. The current ratio will disclose balance sheet changes that net working capital will not.

$$\text{Current Ratio} = \frac{\text{Current Assets}}{\text{Current Liabilities}} = \frac{15{,}957}{8{,}772} = 1.82 \text{ times}$$

The current ratio signifies the firm's ability to meet its current obligations but it should be supplemented with other ratios listed below. Compared with other hosiery manufacturers, HHHM, Inc. ranks in the lower quartile (1.76

*For an interesting survey of the historical development of this popular ratio, vide: Roy A. Foulke, *Practical Financial Statement Analysis,* 4th ed., (New York: McGraw-Hill Book Company, 1957), Chap. VI.

in D & B's *Key Business Ratios*), well below the median of 2.45. The next step is to look for the cause of this low ratio.

Quick Ratio

A subsidiary test developed after the current ratio, the acid-test or quick ratio, specifies whether those current assets that could be quickly converted into cash are sufficient to cover current liabilities. Until recent years, a current ratio of 2:1 was considered standard, and a firm that additionally had sufficient quick assets available to creditors was believed sound.

$$\text{Quick Ratio} = \frac{\text{Cash + Marketable Securities + Accounts Receivable (net)}}{\text{Current Liabilities}}$$

$$= \frac{832 + 430 + 4{,}621}{8{,}772} = 0.67$$

HHHM, Inc. can quickly cover about two-thirds of its current liabilities with this test. However, this ratio assumes that all assets are of equal liquidity, and although receivables are one step closer to liquidity than inventory, "a sale is never complete until the money is collected."

Absolute Liquidity Ratio

Therefore, a subsequent innovation in ratio analysis eliminates any unknowns surrounding receivables and tests short term liquidity in terms of cash and marketable securities only.

$$\text{Absolute Liquidity} = \frac{\text{Cash + Marketable Securities}}{\text{Current Liabilities}} = \frac{832 + 430}{8{,}772} = 14.4\%$$

If 50% coverage is an acceptable norm, then this very low ratio for HHHM, Inc. suggests closer examination of other current assets.

Basic Defense Interval

For how many days can the concern cover its cash expenses without additional financing should all revenues suddenly cease? The basic defense interval (BDI) approaches this issue.

$$\text{BDI} = \frac{365\ (\text{Cash} + \text{Receivables} + \text{Marketable Securities})}{\text{Operating Expenses} + \text{Interest} + \text{Income Taxes}}$$

$$= \frac{365\ (832 + 430 + 4{,}621)}{44{,}087 + 892 + 630} = 47 \text{ days}$$

This roughly explains the concept proposed by G. Sorter and G. Benston.*

Receivables Turnover

Another indicator of liquidity and how efficiently management employs those funds invested in receivables is the turnover ratio. Net credit sales, while preferable, may be replaced with net total sales for industry-wide comparison.

$$\text{Receivables Turnover} = \frac{\text{Total Credit Sales}}{\text{Average Receivables Owing}} = \frac{46{,}308}{4{,}621} = 10.0 \text{ times}$$

Closely monitoring the ratio, monthly or quarterly, quickly underscores any change in collections.

Average Collection Period

Akin to receivables turnover, the average collection period (ACP) further attests to the quality of receivables expressed by the length of the collection period.

$$\text{ACP} = \frac{365\ (\text{Accounts} + \text{Notes Receivable})}{\text{Annual Net Credit Sales}} = \frac{365\ (4{,}621)}{46{,}308} = 37 \text{ days}$$

D & B business ratios record net sales since a breakdown of credit versus cash sales is not always accessible for an entire industry. One rule states that outstanding receivables should not exceed credit terms by 10-to-15 days. On net 30-day terms, HHHM, Inc. fares well. The hosiery industry median is 44 days, the upper quartile 31 days. If credit transactions vary, such as a retail outlet selling both on open credit and installment, then the ACP must be calculated separately for each category. Too, discounted notes which create contingent liabilities must be added back into receivables.

---

*Charles T. Horngren, *Accounting for Management Control: An Introduction* (Englewood Cliffs, N.J.: Prentice-Hall, Inc., 1965), p. 114.

Collection Index

A similar credit control device, the collection index, exhibits the same fundamental relationships.

$$\text{Collection Index} = \frac{\text{Collections Made During Period}}{\text{Accounts Receivable Owing at Start of Period}}$$

On net 30-day terms a collection index of 75% connotes that only three-fourths of accounts due paid up during the month. Dividing this index into the net credit period approximates the average collection period. In this example, $30 \div 0.75 = 40$ days outstanding.

Past Due Index

This is an index of the proportion of past due receivables relative to total outstanding accounts.

$$\text{Past Due Index} = \frac{\text{Total Amount Past Due}}{\text{Total Sum Uncollected}}$$

Its main purpose is trending. Computed over several periods, the resulting indices will reveal any deterioration (or improvement) in collection policies and procedures. (Also, consult Chapter Ten for further discussion on this index.)

Bad Debt Loss Index

For internal evaluation the bad debt loss index (BDLI) may be calculated on credit sales but for comparative purposes again reliance on total net sales is practical.

$$\text{BDLI} = \frac{\text{Bad Debt Losses}}{\text{Total Credit Sales}}$$

An increase in this index is not necessarily an evil to avoid if a more lax credit policy produces more sales and profits than losses. (See "Sales Expansion Through Credit" in Chapter Ten.)

Net Sales to Inventory

Other than receivables the important current asset to monitor is inventory. (Chapter Nine outlines how to pinpoint profit factors with proper inventory management.) A low ratio, that is, slow-moving inventory, may result from obsolescent merchandise, old or outmoded, overcommitment of investment, poor purchasing policy, or perhaps planned stockpiling due to impending price controls or government intervention. Nevertheless, excessive inventories are a major cause of business failure.

$$\text{Net Sales-to-Inventory} = \frac{\text{Net Sales}}{\text{Inventory}} = \frac{46{,}308}{10{,}066} = 4.6 \text{ times}$$

According to Dun & Bradstreet ratios, 4.6 times is about right for the average firm in the hosiery industry. Of course, the method of inventory evaluation and changing that system induce inconsistencies in these ratios over time.

Inventory Turnover Ratio

From a practical standpoint, net sales-to-inventory figures are most easily obtainable for comparative purposes, but this is not an inventory ratio. The turnover ratio calculation requires information on cost of goods sold and average inventory.

$$\text{Inventory Turnover} = \frac{\text{Cost of Goods Sold}}{\text{Average Inventory}} = \frac{39{,}217}{10{,}066} = 3.9 \text{ times}$$

In other words, this concern replenishes its stock an average of every three months. A better figure than the balance sheet inventory would have been average monthly inventories.

WORKING CAPITAL RATIOS

Gross working capital, developed from the turn-of-century term, "current and working assets," describes current assets; while *net working capital,* which Moody's Investors Service has listed since 1922, consists of current assets minus current liabilities. Although more sales tend to solve many business problems, sales must be built upon sound policies surrounding other current assets and sufficient working capital. Inadequate working capital can be corrected by lowering sales or increasing current assets through internal savings (retained earnings) or external savings (sale of stock). The following ratios center on some tests related to net working capital.

Working Capital Ratio

(See "Current Ratio" in the section on Liquidity Ratios.) This extensively applied ratio has been particularly valuable in determining a concern's ability to meet current liabilities. This ratio and others appear periodically in the magazine, *Dun's Review*.

Working Capital Turnover

Another D & B key ratio, the net sales-to-net working capital ratio helps to ascertain whether an enterprise is top-heavy in fixed or slow assets. This ratio complements net sales-to-tangible net worth.

$$\text{Working Capital Turnover} = \frac{\text{Net Sales}}{\text{Net Working Capital}} = \frac{46{,}308}{7{,}185} = 6.45 \text{ times}$$

Overtrading may precipitate a high ratio; a high ratio may also indicate that the business requires additional funds to support a financial structure top-heavy with fixed investment. The median for hosiery manufacturers is 4.40, the upper quartile 8.50—about the same level where net sales-to-tangible net worth ratio puts the firm. Results call for further analysis.

Current Asset Turnover

The turnover of current assets ticks off the number of times current assets are used in paying costs and expenses.

$$\text{Current Asset Turnover} = \frac{\text{CGS + Expenses + Interest + Taxes - Depreciation}}{\text{Average Current Assets}}$$

$$= \frac{39{,}217 + 4{,}870 + 892 + 630 - 1{,}331}{15{,}957} = 2.8 \text{ times}$$

(CGS equals cost of goods sold.) If depreciation must be included, the turnover will be slightly less accurately stated. This ratio is most valuable deciphering trends in turnover and profitability of current assets.

Inventory to Net Working Capital

Even though inventory turnover is pivotal to profits, this relationship must be supplemented with a fairly fixed cognation; net working capital provides a firmer linkage than fluctuating sales.

$$\text{Inventory-to-NWC} = \frac{\text{Inventory}}{\text{Net Working Capital}} = \frac{10{,}066}{7{,}185} = 140.1\%$$

Overstocking, one of the worst evils that a business suffers, can lead to inability to meet obligations and bankruptcy. This homolog, an additional sign of inventory balance, normally should not exceed 80%. The hosiery industry median is 87% and lower quartile 130%. Whereas other ratios implied happy results for HHHM, Inc., we seem to have located a potentially very saturnine problem with inventory.

Current Liabilities to Inventory

Still another inventory flag matches total current debt to inventory. It affirms the extent to which an enterprise relies on funds from sale of accumulated inventories in order to meet its current obligations.

$$\text{Current Debt-to-Inventory} = \frac{\text{Current Liabilities}}{\text{Inventory}} = \frac{8{,}772}{10{,}066} = 87.1\%$$

The industry median is 71, lower quartile 116. For HHHM, Inc., this ratio is expectedly on the low side.

Net Working Capital to Total Assets

(Refer to the next section on Bankruptcy Ratios for an explanation of this ratio.) The working capital ratio, quick ratio, and net working capital-to-total assets have proved most valuable in liquidity tests.

Cash Available to Finance Operations

(See "Basic Defense Ratio" in the section on Liquidity Ratios.) This turnover ratio roughly gauges the adequacy of cash to finance current operating needs. Since depreciation is not a cash drain, we can modify the basic defense ratio by subtracting depreciation from the denominator which alters results only slightly.

Net Profits on Net Working Capital

Current assets in excess of liabilities represents the provisionary cushion to carry inventories and receivables and finance ordinary operations of the business. Divide earnings after taxes (EAT) by net working capital (NWC) to develop this copula.

$$\text{Net Profits-to-Net Working Capital} = \frac{\text{EAT}}{\text{NWC}} = \frac{714}{7{,}185} = 9.94\%$$

Compared with other hosiery manufacturers, HHHM, Inc. is on the high side. The industry median is nearly 4%, the upper quartile over 12%.

Current Debt to Net Worth

This ratio measures the proportion of funds current creditors contribute to operations. A business concern should not have debt in excess of invested capital.

$$\text{Current Debt-to-Net Worth} = \frac{\text{Current Liabilities}}{\text{Tangible Net Worth}} = \frac{8{,}772}{11{,}557} = 75.9\%$$

HHHM, Inc. falls quite low in the industry. D & B ratios indicate an industry median around 45% and lower quartile of 72%. Ordinarily, problems begin for smaller firms when this relationship exceeds 60–65% and for larger firms when it exceeds 75–80%.

Funded Debt to Net Working Capital

Funded debt, long term liabilities, consists of all obligations due more than one year from the balance sheet date.

$$\text{Funded Debt-to-Net Working Capital} = \frac{\text{Long Term Debt}}{\text{Net Working Capital}} = \frac{10{,}075}{7{,}185} = 140.2\%$$

The maxim is that long term liabilities should not exceed net working capital.

The hosiery industry median is 56%, lower quartile 85%. In this illustration, long term debts are out of proportion.

BANKRUPTCY RATIOS

With ratios can we predict a possible bankrupt course in sufficient time for the business to take corrective action or at least for some creditors to reduce potential losses? Several studies suggest this possibility, which aid in tracking the concern's regression, but with effort any future can be altered so that predictions are not inevitable future outcomes. Edward I. Altman has discovered that the first five following ratios can detect potential problems up to three years prior to bankruptcy. The sixth ratio below, according to William Beaver, is the best single predictor of failure.

Working Capital to Total Assets

Of liquidity ratios this one is the most valuable and best indicator of ultimate discontinuance of business. It records net liquid assets relative to total capitalization.

$$\text{Working Capital-to-Total Assets} = \frac{\text{Net Working Capital}}{\text{Total Assets}} = \frac{7{,}185}{33{,}254} = 21.6\%$$

Consistent operating losses will cause shrinking current assets relative to total assets. A negative ratio, resulting from negative net working capital, presages serious problems. Although HHHM, Inc. does not fit this category, the rather low ratio points toward immediate corrective action.

Retained Earnings to Total Assets

This ratio designates cumulative profitability. Obviously, new firms will exhibit a low ratio, but the incidence of failure is highest among firms less than three years in existence.

$$\text{Retained Earnings-to-Total Assets} = \frac{\text{Retained Earnings}}{\text{Total Assets}} = \frac{11{,}947}{33{,}254} = 35.9\%$$

HHHM, Inc. is in a satisfactory middle range. A negative figure once again definitely portends thorny issues. However, manipulated retained earnings (earned surplus) data can distort numerical results.

EBIT to Total Assets

Earnings before interest and taxes (EBIT)-to-total assets expresses productivity of a firm's assets. Asset values derive from earning power, and, therefore, whether or not liabilities exceed the true value of assets (insolvency) depends upon earnings generated.

$$\text{EBIT-to-Total Assets} = \frac{\text{EBIT}}{\text{Total Assets}} = \frac{2{,}236}{33{,}254} = 6.72\%$$

Despite a rather low proportion for HHHM, Inc., degenerative problems would not unravel until the ratio became negative. Of course, maximizing rate of return on assets does not match maximizing return on equity because different degrees of leverage (consult Chapter Five) affect conclusions.

Sales to Total Assets

(Also, see "Turnover Ratio" under Profitability Ratios.) This calculation does not exclude intangible assets as previously but throws light on management's ability to function in competitive situations.

$$\text{Sales-to-Total Assets} = \frac{\text{Total Sales}}{\text{Total Assets}} = \frac{46{,}308}{33{,}254} = 139.3\%$$

For HHHM, Inc. the ratio is on the low side. Notwithstanding its importance, alone the ratio is inconclusive; but taken together with the other three it confirms whether a firm has imminent agonies. Generally, a relative position of 200% is preferable to one nearer 100%.

Equity to Debt

The *market value* of common and preferred stock divided by current plus long term debt delimits by how much the concern's assets can decline in value before the business becomes insolvent.

$$\text{Equity-to-Debt} = \frac{\text{Market Value of Common + Preferred}}{\text{Total Current + Long Term Debt}}$$

$$= \frac{3{,}920 + 500}{8{,}772 + 10{,}075} = 23.5\%$$

A small drop in value will render HHHM, Inc. insolvent. A safer range exceeds 200%.

Cash Flow to Debt

(Also, refer to "Debt-Cash Flow Coverage Ratio" under the section on Coverage Ratios.) Cash flow consists of net income plus depreciation. Because of varying depreciation accounting practices this ratio serves better for comparative statements within the firm rather than industry-wide comparison.

$$\text{Cash Flow-to-Debt} = \frac{\text{Net Income + Depreciation}}{\text{Total Debt}}$$

Too, debt does not materialize as a liquidity problem until its due date so that the closer to maturity the greater liquidity should be. Other than above-mentioned ratios, others useful in predicting insolvency include total debt-to-total assets (see Leverage Ratios) and current ratio (see Liquidity Ratios).

LONG TERM ANALYSIS

Bankruptcy ratios rally on not only longer term but near term liquidity as well. Long term analysis centers on the firm's capitalization, debtors and owners, to the extent of long run profitability and short term ability to meet current obligations so as not to impair the position of long term creditors and residual owners and for the firm to be able to attract new owners and arrange its debts advantageously.

Current Assets to Total Debt

More net working capital protects short term creditors. This ratio marks off the degree of protection linked to short and long term debt. A high ratio, significantly above 100%, signals that if liquidation losses on current assets are not excessive, long range debtors can be paid in full out of working capital.

$$\text{Current Assets-to-Debt} = \frac{\text{Current Assets}}{\text{Current + Long Term Debt}} = \frac{15{,}957}{18{,}847} = 84.7\%$$

Long run debtors of HHHM, Inc. are not in the best position.

Effective Cost of Debt

(Also, review Chapter Four on cost of capital.) Effective cost of debt (r) means the amount of interest payable during the life of debt related to net proceeds received by the borrower. The following formula is only an approximate method.

$$r = \frac{iP + \dfrac{(P - M)}{n}}{\dfrac{P + M}{2}}$$

i = contractual interest rate.

P = face value of debt at maturity.

M = market value (sales price) of debt instrument; i.e., net proceeds to the borrower.

(P - M) = discount from face value, if P > M, or premium, M - P, if M > P.

n = number of years to maturity.

Stockholders' Equity Ratio

Owners' equity-to-total assets approximately records relative financial strength and long run liquidity. A low ratio portends difficulties. A high ratio suggests less difficulty in meeting fixed interest charges and maturing debt obligations.

$$\text{Equity Ratio} = \frac{\text{Stockholders' Equity}}{\text{Total Assets}} = \frac{14{,}407}{33{,}254} = 43.3\%$$

Subtracting this result from 100% highlights the percentage of assets supplied by creditors—56.7% in this example—while stockholders supply 43.3%.

Fixed Assets to Net Worth

Because bills cannot be paid with bricks, mortar, and superchic office appointments, the proportion of funds invested in fixed assets influences depreciation charges and net working capital and flexibility in financing current operations.

$$\text{Fixed Assets-to-Net Worth} = \frac{\text{Fixed Assets(net)} - \text{Intangibles}}{\text{Tangible Net Worth}} = \frac{14{,}447}{11{,}557} = 125\%$$

Comparing HHHM, Inc. with D & B industry averages, we find a median of 47% and lower quartile of 67%; ergo, 125% blazons excessive investment in fixed assets. As a general rule, smaller firms should show a ratio under 65%, larger businesses under 75%.

Total Debt to Net Worth

Rarely should total liabilities of an enterprise exceed its tangible net worth because creditors will be assuming more risk than stockholders.

$$\text{Total Debt-to-Net Worth} = \frac{\text{Current + Deferred Debt}}{\text{Tangible Net Worth}} = \frac{18{,}847}{11{,}557} = 163.1\%$$

In hosiery manufacturing it is common for creditors' equity to approach or match stockholders' equity (a ratio of 100%), but HHHM, Inc. falls below the lower quartile figure of 153%. Certainly a business handicapped with heavy interest charges gives its better-financed competitors an edge.

Return on Residual Equity

(Consult "Rate of Return on Common Stock Equity" under Profitability Ratios.) Creditors are not the only ones concerned about a firm's success. Stockholders, too, explore the dollar amount of corporate earnings theoretically available; i.e., is management attaining profit objectives of the company's owners?

Dividend Payout Ratio

Whereas residual owners have a claim on all residual income, dividends represent the portion they actually receive.

$$\text{Payout Ratio} = \frac{\text{Dividends per Share}}{\text{Earnings per Share}}$$

The dividend payout ratio is simply the percentage of earnings received by the stockholder in each period.

Dividend Yield Ratio

Another ratio which converges on income and dividends per share is the dividend yield.

$$\text{Dividend Yield Ratio} = \frac{\text{Common Dividends per Share}}{\text{Average Market Price of Common}}$$

A high ratio attracts investors who seek high cash returns now.

COVERAGE RATIOS

Notwithstanding the arbitrary division between long term analysis and coverage ratios, an analyst, creditor, or debtor will concentrate on that area of the balance sheet of immediate interest. Coverage ratios assist in this type of inquiry.

Current Liabilities to Tangible Net Worth

(See appropriate heading under Working Capital Ratios.)

Debt Cash Flow Coverage Ratio

This one and the next two ratios emphasize cash flow analysis first brought out under Bankruptcy Ratios. The debt-cash flow coverage ratio (CFC_d) determines the number of times interest on debt plus sinking fund payments (adjusted for taxes) are covered by cash flow.

$$CFC_d = \frac{EBIT + A_d}{I + \frac{s_f}{1 - h}}$$

EBIT = earnings before interest and taxes.

A_d = annual depreciation charges.

I = dollar amount of interest payments.

s_f = sinking fund payments on debt.

h = applicable income tax rate.

Preferred Stock Cash Flow Coverage Ratio

By how many times will annual cash flow cover preferred dividends and sinking fund requirements? Because of preferred stock's low priority, as a potential creditor in the event of liquidation, ranking lower than other creditors, the denominator will include interest as well as sinking fund payments on debt in addition to items associated with preferred stock.

$$CFC_p = \frac{EBIT + A_d}{I + \frac{s_d}{1 - h} + \frac{D_p}{1 - h} + \frac{s_p}{1 - h}}$$

EBIT = earnings before interest and taxes.

A_d = annual depreciation expense.

I = dollar interest payments.

s_d = sinking fund payments on debt.

s_p = sinking fund requirements on preferreds.

D_p = preferred dividend payments.

h = applicable income tax rate.

Common Stock Cash Flow Coverage

The method for common stock cash flow coverage (CFC_c) is essentially identical with preferred coverage calculations above except that common stock dividends are added to the formula.

$$CFC_c = \frac{EBIT + A_d}{I + \frac{s_d}{1 - h} + \frac{D_p}{1 - h} + \frac{s_p}{1 - h} + \frac{D_c}{1 - h}}$$

All symbols have the same meaning as above except:

D_c = dividend payment on common stock.

Times Interest Earned

This ratio answers the question: How many times will earnings cover fixed interest payments on long term debt?

$$\text{Times-Interest-Earned} = \frac{\text{EBIT}}{\text{I}} = \frac{2{,}236}{812} = 2.75 \text{ times}$$

EBIT = earnings before interest and taxes.

I = dollar amount of interest payable on debt.

Total Coverage Ratio

Because debt obliges the borrower to pay not only interest but repay principal periodically, this ratio improves on times-interest-earned.

$$\text{Total Coverage Ratio} = \frac{\text{EBIT}}{\text{I} + \dfrac{s}{1 - h}}$$

I = interest payments.

s = payment on principal figured on income after taxes (1 - h).

Total Fixed Charge Coverage

Besides interest a business must sustain other fixed charges even though income suddenly drops. Other fixed costs include any contractual obligations such as lease payments (see Chapter Eight), rent, insurance, taxes, certain salaries, debt reduction, and similar obligations.

$$\text{Fixed Charge Coverage} = \frac{\text{EBIT}}{\text{I} + s_r + \dfrac{s_f}{1 - h} + C_f}$$

I = interest expense.

a_r = lease (or rental) payments.

s_f = sinking fund payments adjusted for taxes (1 - h).

C_f = other fixed costs (rent, taxes, etc.).

Cumulative Deduction Method

In calculating number of times interest on various debt issues is covered, we must account for debt seniority. If debt B is junior to debt A, then times-interest-covered for B must encompass priority awarded A. For example, compare the first (7½%) and second (12%) mortgages of HHHM, Inc.

$$\text{First Mortgage Coverage} = \frac{\text{EBIT}}{I_{7\frac{1}{2}\%}} = \frac{2{,}236}{345} = 6.48 \text{ times, but}$$

$$\text{Second Mortgage Coverage} = \frac{\text{EBIT}}{I_{7\frac{1}{2}\%} + I_{12\%}} = \frac{2{,}236}{345 + 57} = 5.56 \text{ times.}$$

In other words, obligations accumulate rather than are computed separately.

Preferred Dividend Coverage

Preferred stock, a hybrid owner-debt issue, receives dividends before common owners but after payment of all other expenses including taxes. Although preferred stock may be counted as an issue junior to all other debt, the following formula more accurately describes the position of preferred owners. (Chapters Four and Thirteen discuss financing with preferreds.)

$$\text{Preferred Coverage} = \frac{\text{EAT} + I}{D_p + I(1 - h)} = \frac{714 + 812}{40 + 812(1 - 0.46875)} = 3.24 \text{ times}$$

EAT = earnings after taxes.

I = dollar interest cost on debt.

D_p = preferred dividend payment.

h = applicable income tax rate.

The ratio conveys the probability of preferred owners receiving the agreed upon dividend.

LEVERAGE RATIOS

Leverage ratios indicate proportionate contributions of owners and creditors to an enterprise. (Refer to Chapter Five for further details on leverage and risk.) Naturally, creditors look to participation by owners for their margin of safety, but from management's viewpoint debt offers greater opportunity for risk shifting and multiplying return on equity. Although leverage magnifies earnings, in reverse, it exaggerates losses.

Equity Ratio

The ratio of common stockholders' equity, including earned surplus, to total capital of the business tells what share of total capitalization derives from owners.

$$\text{Equity Ratio} = \frac{\text{Common Shareholders' Equity}}{\text{Total Capital Employed}} = \frac{13{,}907}{24{,}482} = 56.8\%$$

Of total capitalization, residual owners of the concern supply slightly more than one-half.

Debt and Preferred Ratio

Mirroring the above equity ratio, the kinship of long term debt plus preferred contributions-to-total capital reveals the extent of financing contributed by creditors and preferred owners.

$$\text{Debt and Preferred Ratio} = \frac{\text{Long Term Debt + Preferred Funds}}{\text{Total Capital Employed}}$$

$$= \frac{10{,}075 + 500}{24{,}482} = 43.2\%$$

Of course, the sum of these last two ratios equal 100% capitalization.

Debt to Equity Ratio

This ratio highlights relative positions of owners and creditors.

$$\text{Debt-to-Equity} = \frac{\text{Long Term Debt + Preferred}}{\text{Common Stockholders' Equity}} = \frac{10{,}075 + 500}{13{,}907} = 76.0\%$$

A high ratio means less protection for creditors, while a low ratio indicates a wider safety cushion; i.e., owners' funds are regarded by creditors as a source to absorb possible losses of income and capital.

Total Debt to Tangible Net Worth

(See "Total Debt-to-Net Worth" under Long Term Analysis.) Tracking this ratio in a growth firm will provide some insight into the distributive source of funds used to finance expansion.

Debt Ratio

Total debt-to-total assets measures the percentage of total funds provided by creditors. Although creditors tend to prefer a lower ratio, management may prefer to lever operations which produces a higher ratio.

$$\text{Debt Ratio} = \frac{\text{Current + Long Term Debt}}{\text{Total Assets}} = \frac{8{,}772 + 10{,}075}{33{,}254} = 56.7\%$$

More than one-half of financing originates from creditors' sources; this firm would be hard pressed to secure more funds in an emergency. For most manufacturers this ratio is ordinarily under 35–40%.

Times Interest Earned

(Refer to Coverage Ratios in the preceding section.)

Planning for and awareness of a situation are essential to successful financial management. Ratios provide one tool to aid comprehension of complex events. Types of ratios employed depends upon the viewpoint, creditor, debtor, or owner, and line of business. Certainly candidates for mergers and takeovers are scrutinized with ratio analysis as one step in the inquisitional process.

CONTENTS

Chapter Thirteen: Crucial Valuation Factors in Acquisition Analysis

THIRTEEN

Crucial Valuation Factors in Acquisition Analysis

Merger and acquisition analysis invites implementation of an array of analytical tools, including financial ratios, in order to strike a bargain acceptable to both parties in the transaction. Although no guaranteed, sure-fire method has ever been discovered, a crucial step in analysis centers on ability to determine the value of potential acquisitions and probable value of merged firms both in near and intermediate terms. Formulas and guidelines developed in this chapter offer a range of profitable valuation analysis for any number of situations encountered. Final judgment, however, rests with the evaluator as he assesses factors not readily quantifiable in addition to application of many financial tools and profitable ideas presented throughout this handbook.

PURPOSES OF VALUATIONS

A valuation is little more than an expressed opinion of the worth of an enterprise, albeit an informed one developed through training and/or experience. (Actually all transactions originate with subjective valuations.) In this chapter emphasis, through examples, is on acquisition of a firm, but analysis is equally important in dispositions and other property transfers whether for an entire concern or only certain assets. For example, some purposes valuations serve include:

1. acquisition or disposal of an entire business or subsidiary;
2. purchase or sale of certain assets or interests only;
3. business mergers;
4. determination of the market value of securities such as common stock, bonds, or rights, whether privately exchanged or traded in an active market;
5. valuation for tax, inheritance, or transfer purposes, or for capital gains or losses;
6. valuation of earning power to determine the worth of good will or other intangible assets;
7. conversion of a proprietorship or partnership into a corporate entity;
8. claims against government for property acquired through nationalization, condemnation, or other methods of expropriation such as eminent domain proceedings.

FORMS OF COMBINATIONS

Mergers and acquisitions are sometimes a means to accelerate corporate growth. Or, everyone likes a bargain, and acquiring another business at a good price substitutes for expansion via sales and profits (internal growth), especially a going concern because it eliminates most start-up costs. External growth means that one business takes over another because underutilized assets offer immediate cash inflow, or economies of scale result either with expansion of volume or displacement of duplicative plant and equipment, or there is risk reduction associated with new product introduction or with learning new processes, for example. Too, risk reduction may result with diversification of market, operations, and sales related to predictable cyclical fluctuations. Instability from short life cycles of products may be offset through a business combination.

When two or more companies combine assets in exchange for securities, where only one concern survives, this form of transaction, called a *merger,* may occur in one of several ways. There may be an exchange of common stock for stock or stock for assets or there may be an outright purchase of common stock. Also, B may buy assets of S, leaving S with a corporate shell.

Three major types of mergers are identified. A *vertical merger* is the combination of firms engaged in different steps of the production or distribution of a product or service. For example, a medical clinic purchases a funeral home and a pharmacy. A *horizontal merger* is the combination of firms in the same line of business. An unlikely example is Ford Motor Co. and General Motors combining into a single structure. A *conglomerate merger* results from a combination of firms with activities unrelated either horizontally or vertically.

If two or more firms combine to form a third and new corporation, a *consolidation* unfolds. The new corporation survives, absorbing perhaps assets and liabilities of the dissolved entities. Frequently no distinction is made between mergers and consolidations.

Another alternative, a *holding company,* is a corporation that owns controlling interest in the voting stock of subsidiaries. Both parent company and subsidiaries survive. Controlling interest may mean 51% ownership, or, in the situation of stock widely-held by inactive or disinterested stockholders, as little as 10% ownership may suffice to control and influence management decisions in a firm. One attraction of this form of organization is leverage. A subsidiary may be highly leveraged, and if 25% controlling stock is owned by a levered holding company, the latter can greatly increase its return on investment and, also, via the subsidiary, gain control indirectly over other businesses by dispensing the subsidiary's funds. Another important advantage is that this arrangement allows the holding company to operate in many states without the necessity of registering in each as a foreign corporation and to be subject to possibly higher taxes and certainly more paper work. Too, we cannot overlook the advantage of diversification and ease of ownership.

Another form is the *nontaxable reorganization* of enterprises. There are three types. A *statutory merger* occurs in strict compliance with state statutes and which form permits the acquiring company to give substantial amounts of cash, bonds, or nonvoting stock. An exchange of *stock for stock* is when one corporation acquires stock of another entirely in exchange for voting stock. An exchange of *stock for assets* takes place when the acquired business exchanges at least 70–90% of its assets for voting stock in the surviving entity.

BUSINESS VALUATIONS

What is a firm worth? Acquisition of an enterprise essentially verifies the rights of owners to streams of income generated in the form of interest, dividends, or profits. Evaluating the worth of a concern, basically an expression of informed opinion, pivots on the type of acquisition and corresponding rights which inure to the benefit of owners, and method of valuation employed. Various approaches appear below.

Earning Power Approach

Especially where tangible assets represent an insignificant portion of the purchase price, the earnings stream, reflected in goodwill, an intangible asset, evaluated and capitalized, fixes the value of the enterprise. Such an approach assumes that the going concern will continue to produce this income stream and places a present value on estimated futures earnings, assumed to continue indefinitely in the absence of restraints and risk of their not being realized in future periods. When earnings form the basis for evaluation, the steps are:

1. Forecast future earnings considering tax factors.
2. Assess risk (probability of not receiving anticipated earnings) and time elements.
3. Develop a capitalization rate.

Going Concern Value

An operator of a small business, Buckeye Enterprises, that prints computerized charcoal-style photos and imprints T-shirts has realized a net annual income (after owner's salary) averaging $32,000 (F) for the past 4 years with favorable prospects into an indefinite future. Capitalized at 16% (i), considered a fair rate of return, the value of the firm (E) is:

Formula:

$$E = \frac{F}{i}$$

$$E = \frac{\$32,000}{0.16} = \$200,000$$

Goodwill (or badwill) registers the difference between the above value (E) and worth of tangible assets.

Intrinsic Value

The *intrinsic value* of a stock is computed by two methods based on earnings per share (EPS) and its price-earnings (P–E) ratio. Assume that stock of Bryce Canyon Service Co. currently earning $3.10 per share (EPS) is anticipated to begin generating $3.50 per share (EPS*) in subsequent periods. What is the value per share of stock (V_c) if the capitalization rate is 10% (i)?

Formula:

$$V_c = \frac{EPS^*}{i}$$

$$V_c = \frac{3.50}{0.10} = \$35$$

Alternately, we can multiply EPS* times the price-earnings ratio (P–E)–10 in this example.

Formula:

$$V_c = \text{EPS*} \times \text{P-E}$$

$$V_c = \$3.50 \times 10 = \$35$$

If the P–E relationship rises to 14, the stock will be valued at $49, without any further change in earnings forecast.

Weighted Average Value

The following example applies the foregoing principle to an acquisition made by an exchange of stock based on capitalization of the weighted average of earnings over the preceding 4 years. Nathan Hale Furniture Makers, Inc. plans to acquire the Feather-Rest Mattress Co. Net incomes of previous 4 years (-4 = 4 years ago, -1 = 1 year ago) are shown in Figure 13–1.

Figure 13–1

Year	*Nathan Hale*	*Feather-Rest*
-4	$720,000	$109,000
-3	756,000	181,000
-2	777,000	114,000
-1	802,000	135,000

The price-earnings ratio for Nathan Hale is 8.7 times, for Feather-Rest 15.6. It was decided to weight the most recent year's earnings 4 times earnings of 4 years ago. (See Figure 13–2.)

Nathan Hale has 450,000 shares outstanding, Feather-Rest 150,000. Capitalized EPS will be:

Nathan Hale	Feather-Rest
$\frac{\$6{,}760{,}770}{450{,}000} = \$15.02$	$\frac{\$2{,}110{,}680}{150{,}000} = \$14.07$

Figure 13-2

Year	Weights	Weighted Sales	
		Nathan Hale	*Feather-Rest*
-4	1	720,000	109,000
-3	2	1,512,000	362,000
-2	3	2,331,000	342,000
-1	4	3,208,000	540,000
	10	7,771,000	1,353,000
Weighted Average		777,100	135,300
Capitalized Value of Earnings		6,760,770	2,110,680

What will be the exchange ratio of shares based on the *earning power* approach to valuation?

$$\frac{15.02}{14.07} = 1.0675$$

One share of Nathan Hale will exchange for 1.0675 shares of Feather-Rest. The exchange rate reflects differences in growth rates, absolute level of earnings, and number of outstanding shares.

Adjustments from this figure can be arranged according to the value of surplus assets or cost to replace worn or obsolete equipment to overcome some of the disadvantages of this technique. Generally, the earning power approach is criticized because it does not adequately account for different productivity of assets, growth rates, the time value of money.

Asset Value Approach

Another traditional technique focuses on the net asset value instead of earnings. Essentially three approaches prevail. Under the *book value method,* the value of a firm is the excess value of assets over liabilities derived from the accounting worth registered on the company's books. Book value may result from tangible assets alone or coupled with intangible values which derive from location, trade or manufacturing secrets, superior management and organization, special privileges or grants from government. Intangible values require an arbitrary adjustment of asset appraisals. *Going concern valuation* originates in replacement costs of assets at current prices. *Liquida-*

tion values are what a forced or discontinuance sale of assets will bring on the market.

The book value per share (B_{ps}) is the excess value of assets divided by the number of common shares issued and outstanding.

Formula:

$$B_{ps} = \frac{E - Z}{N}$$

E = total assets of the business.

Z = total debt of the business.

N = number of outstanding common shares.

The Constant Companion Casket Company has assets of $4,110,900, liabilities of $985,400, and 125,000 shares out.

$$B_{ps} = \frac{4{,}110{,}900 - 985{,}400}{125{,}000} = \$25$$

Book value per share fails to account for future asset productivity which price appreciation of stock or cash dividends reflect. Too, different accounting procedures will result in different book values. Reproduction costs partially escape this issue. Liquidation values are significant in mergers if some assets will be sold after acquisition.

Quoted Investment Approach

When adequate market data exist for both parties of a prospective merger, quoted prices on a national stock exchange may tend to reflect a reasonable standard of value and provide the basis for reaching agreement on an exchange ratio. (Dilution is discussed later in this chapter. The relationship between the P–E ratio of the prospective purchaser and firm to be acquired determines whether there will be dilution and whether the stock exchange favors the surviving entity.)

In spite of efforts of mathematicians and statisticians, value remains a subjective concept. Obviously, most parties to a transaction must each believe they gain from the exchange—a positive gain or minimization of hardships or losses amount to a gain—or else commerce will not occur. (Compare the Arnold Syndicate example in Chapter Two.) What exactly constitutes value depends on individual preferences and individual evaluations of the market. The recorded market price of a stock represents a consensus, an average, which does *not* imply that all investors in a particular stock are identical. To some the price is only marginally favorable; to others it may appear to be a super bargain. Therefore, we can generalize and state that the value of a concern (V) is the product of the market price per share of common stock (M) times the number of shares outstanding (N).

Formula: $$V = M \cdot N$$

Nevertheless, other factors do influence stock prices and value in mergers: dividend policy, publicity, volume of transactions, number of shares outstanding, manipulation, economic conditions, expectations, government interference.

Dividend Payout Approach

The dividend payout capacity of a potential acquisition pivots on potential rather than historical experience and is useful in analyzing companies with a stable dividend-paying history. Although this method interests stockholders, it is not a particularly adequate model for companies growing through acquisitions.

Formula: $$M = \frac{(1 - h)(1 - b)\, r \frac{E}{N}}{k - (1 - h)br}$$

M = price of stock.

h = income tax rate.

b = retention rate on earnings.

(1 - b) = dividend payout rate.

r = rate of return on assets = $\frac{EBIT}{E}$

EBIT = earnings before interest and taxes.

E = value of total assets.

N = total number of common shares outstanding.

(1 - h) (1 - b)rE = dollar amount of dividends paid to shareholders.

k = discount rate.

(1 - h)br = growth rate (g) of assets.

With this valuation equation, assuming no debt, price per share of stock

(M) depends upon two management decisions—retention rate (b) and income generated on assets employed (r)—while income tax (h) and discount (k) rates and total assets (E) remain unchanged.

Assume that Limoges Arts, Inc. has total assets valued at $15,000,000 (E), no debt, and 291,777 (N) shares of common stock outstanding. Retention rate is 50% (b), dividend payout rate 50% (1 - b), tax rate 45% (h), rate of return on assets 20% (r), growth rate of assets 5.5% (g), and discount rate 12% (k).

$$M = \frac{(1 - 0.45)\,(1 - 0.50)0.20\left(\dfrac{15{,}000{,}000}{291{,}777}\right)}{0.12 - (1 - 0.45)0.50(0.20)} = \$43.50$$

Of course, a constant share price of $43.50 can be maintained by any number of combinations of r and b, and even if r were negative or b zero, stock would still yield a positive price.

Expected P-E Approach

This Robichek-Bogue formula centers on the expected value of the price-earnings ratio at some future date.

Formula:

$$\text{P-E}^* = (b^* - 1) + \text{P-E}\,\frac{(1 + k)}{(1 + g^*)}$$

P-E = price-earnings ratio at the present time.

P-E* = expected price-earnings ratio in a future time.

b* = expected retention ratio.

k = the discount rate.

g* = expected growth rate of earnings per share in the future.

What this formula states is that the expected price-earnings ratio in the future depends upon the expected retention ratio and expected growth rate of earnings in the future, current price-earnings relationship, and the discount rate.

To illustrate, imagine that Joy-of-Life Calendar Corporation's stock currently sells at a P-E ratio of 15 (P-E), expected growth rate of earnings is 5.5% (g*), future retention rate is anticipated at 38% (b*), and the discount rate is 12%. What will be the future price-earnings ratio (P-E*)?

$$\text{P-E*} = (0.38 - 1.00) + 15\,\frac{(1 + 0.120)}{(1 + 0.055)} = 15.3$$

Naturally, changes in the dividend payout ratio, discount rate, or future growth rates, and errors resulting from predicting future trends, will alter outcomes.

Weighted Exchange Ratio Approach

One solution to the pitfalls of preceding methods is to combine them when evaluating a potential merger situation. Should each category be assigned equal value? Certainly the agreed upon ratio of exchange depends upon hard bargaining, but a reasonably fair basis to begin negotiations is represented by a *weighted ratio* illustrated in Figure 13-3.

Figure 13-3

Item	*X/Y*	*Weight*	*Weighted Ratio*
ASSET VALUE PER SHARE:			
X = $35 Y = $25	1.40	0.10	0.1400
EARNINGS PER SHARE:			
X = $5.60 Y = $2.24	2.50	0.25	0.6250
MARKET PRICE:			
X = $60 Y = $37.50	1.60	0.40	0.6400
GROWTH RATE:			
X = 6.75% Y = 9.00%	0.75	0.25	0.1875
			1.5925

The weighted exchange ratio technique results in 1.00 share of X traded for 1.5925 shares of Y. Had weights been shifted so that EPS were 0.20 and growth rate 0.30, the exchange rate would have resulted in 1:1.5. Weights can be approximated with reference to industry averages or of similar firms.

Unquoted Investment Approach

Investment possibilities for which no market quotations are available require essentially the same close examination that quoted investments necessitate. (Also, refer to "New Issue Method" in Chapter Four.)

1. An investigation of management—experience, reputation, capabilities, and plans for future activities.

2. A study of the concern's operations to root out any problems (or potential ones) and to determine whether plant and equipment are being efficiently utilized.

3. An analysis of annual reports and supplementary financial data to discover trends in costs, sales, income, and pertinent ratios.

4. An examination of the capital structure and ability to meet obligations, to learn of special rights or preferential treatment of various classes of debt and equity and whether the capital structure may be rearranged advantageously.

5. An assessment of the firm's marketing possibilities, growth potential, and effect on competition within the industry.

These five steps formulate minimum investigation and information requirements in evaluating the business either on an asset or earnings basis tempered by data and discovery compiled during initial analysis. Another valuations approach compares the unquoted investment with quoted ones if a fairly active market for those traded stocks exists. However, for the potential purchaser, the advantages of buying an established firm may outweigh the costs of creating a new entity, which factor is also mirrored in the final negotiated price.

OTHER VALUATION ISSUES

Because mergers may also mean raising additional capital, valuation of bonds, preferred shares, and stock rights are briefly reviewed here. The money value of a security is anchored to a given point in time.

Bonds

In determining today's value of a bond redeemable at some future date, first, we need to state future interest payments in today's terms and, second, we need to account for today's worth of the future redemption value of the financial instrument. Suppose that a 7½% bond is redeemable at face value in 6 years. Considering all factors and alternative investment possibilities, a discount rate of 8% seems more than reasonable. What is the bond worth today?

Formula: $V_b = F\,(P/A_{r,n}) + P\,(P/F_{r,n})$

F = annual interest payments flow.

$(P/A_{r,n})$ = factor from Table IV in the Appendix, where r = 8% and n = 6 years

P = redemption value of bond at par.

$(P/F_{r,n})$ = factor from Table II in the Appendix, where r = 8% and n = end of 6th year.

V_b = \$75(4.62288) + \$1,000(0.63017) = \$976.89

Because the discount rate exceeds the interest rate on the bond, the instrument will sell at a discount. The value of bonds with conversion rights depends upon the soundness of the enterprise coupled with the probability that conversion will occur. (See section on "Stock Rights" below.)

Preferred

Preferred stock valuation may be treated similarly to bonds, having a definite and knowable life, or as income (dividends) received in perpetuity. Even preferreds with a *call feature,* when that call date is unknown or unpredictable, are easiest analyzed as an endless stream of future dividends discounted to the present.

Formula:

$$V_p = \frac{D_p}{k}$$

If the Printer's Hall Book Company pays \$7 preferred dividends annually, but the capitalization rate (k) is 10%, which encompasses a risk factor—the possibility that dividends may, at times, cumulate—then the current value per share is:

$$V_p = \frac{\$7}{0.10} = \$70$$

Another method to develop k depends upon a rate parallel to what evinces from issues of other and similar companies. (Additional formulas are developed in Chapter Four under "Financing with Preferred Stock.")

Stock Rights

When stockholders receive a preemptive right to buy additional shares of common stock at a stated price to aid in further financing of the enterprise, the value of this right, which enables the stockholder to maintain his proportional share of ownership, can be determined. (Also, see formula in Chapter Four, "Financing with Rights.")

Posit that one right is issued for each of the 1,000 shares of common stock, previously selling at $50 a share, but that 5 rights are required to purchase an additional share at $45. *Cum rights* the common stock sells at $60. What is the value of shares *ex rights?*

Value of one share cum rights	$60
Cash required to exercise one right (1/5)	9
Total investment in 1 1/5 shares ex rights	$69
Value of one common share ex right (69 ÷ 1 1/5)	$57.50
Current value of one share cum rights	60.00
Value of stock right	$ 2.50

DILUTION PROBLEMS

The price-earnings ratio of the acquiring firm, the exchange ratio of the potential acquisition, and, of course, general conditions of the stock market dominate an analysis of merging two publicly traded concerns.

Price-Earning Multiple

Any dilution in earnings resulting from the merger must be considered in two time frames. Short run dilution that is more than offset by future earnings may not be a serious matter; if earnings per share decrease because of a higher price paid for an investment, then dilution occurs. The price-earnings multiple largely determines whether earnings dilution will result. Dilution crops up when one business acquires another at a higher price-earnings multiple.

Figure 13-4

	Case #1		*Case #2*		*Case #3*	
	P	*Q*	*P*	*Q*	*P*	*Q*
EAT	$2,800	$2,000	$2,800	$2,000	$2,800	$2,000
Shares Outstanding	400	400	400	400	400	400
EPS	$ 7	$ 5	$ 7	$ 5	$ 7	$ 5
Exchange P-E	14:1	14:1	10:1	14:1	14:1	10:1
Exchange Price	$ 98	$ 70	$ 70	$ 70	$ 98	$ 50
Exchange Ratio	1:1.4		1:1		1:2	

Three possibilities are summarized in Figure 13–4 in which Pyro-Fax (P) plans to acquire Quix-Top (Q). Earnings after taxes (EAT) remain unchanged in each case but the price-earnings multiple varies to illustrate no dilution (#1), dilution (#2), and a gain in earnings (#3). Consequently, the exchange ratio of P-to-Q changes according to the P–E multiple variation. To purchase firm Q, P issues common stock in different amounts according to data in Figure 13–5.

Figure 13-5

	Firm Pyro-Fax (P) issues:		
	286 New Shares	*400 New Shares*	*200 New Shares*
EAT	$4,800	$4,800	$4,800
Shares Outstanding	686	800	600
EPS	$ 7	$ 6	$ 8

Issuing 286 new shares in case #1 is adequate to acquire 400 outstanding shares of Q's stock at an exchange ratio of 1:1.4. Since the P–E exchange multiples match, earnings per share before and after acquisition remain at $7. Dilution occurs in case #2 when the P–E multiple of the acquiring firm is lower than that of the acquired one resulting in a drop of EPS from $7 to $6 for firm P. In case #3, where P's P–E multiple exceeds that of the acquired business, P's earnings per share rise from $7 to $8.

This analysis misleads by placing singular emphasis on initial dilution. The new combination may well result in faster growth to more than offset disadvantages of initial dilution. Too, the combined P–E ratio cannot be pin-pointed beforehand with complete accuracy; the market may evaluate the combination more favorably than the acquired concern alone. For example, with dilution in case #2, the new P–E ratio may range anywhere from 10:1 to 14:1. At 10, the new stock price will be $60, down from P's old price of $70. A mid-ratio of 12 will result in a new price of $72, a slight gain over $70. But at 14, stockholders decidedly gain at a new price of $84 after the merger, in spite of apparent initial dilution.

Earn Out

Suppose that Quix-Top's management is reluctant to sell at $50 or $70 or even $90 per share because they are developing a new product which, when marketed, will substantially raise earnings per share and possibly influence favorably the price-earnings multiple so that the stock's price may rise sharply. Further assume that Pyro-Fax's management is inclined to agree with that assessment.

Pyro-Fax may propose a two-part settlement to the acquisition. First issue 286 new shares and acquire Q at the going market price of $70. The second part of the agreement calls for the emission of additional P shares to Q stockholders as Q's earnings rise as forecasted by the introduction of the new product line. How many new shares should P issue?

Formula:

$$N_{ns} = \frac{(\Delta EAT)\,(P\text{-}E_o)}{M}$$

N_{ns} = number of new shares to be issues.

ΔEAT = increase in earnings over the base period.

$P\text{-}E_o$ = original agreed upon multiple.

M = current market price of common stock.

Let's say that EAT of Q, now a subsidiary of P, rises from $2,000 to $2,700, a change (increase) of $700. The original P–E multiple agreed upon is 14:1 and is still applicable as part of the original settlement contract. Therefore, P will issue shares in a number that allows Q stockholders to realize $700 capitalized to reflect current market prices. Suppose that the stock now sells for $140.

$$N_{nsp} = \frac{(700)\,(14)}{140} = 70$$

P will now issue 70 new shares to Q stockholders so that they receive a multiple of the increase in earnings, namely, $9,800. If stock sold for less than $140, then a larger number of shares will be issued for a total market value of $9,800. A higher market price per share will yield fewer new shares. This arrangement is tagged an *earn out.*

The two-tier deal allows Q stockholders to participate in future growth. With an earn out the buyer acquires the selling firm cheaper, in current terms, with a higher selling price actually paid from income generated by the seller, certainly a low-risk agreement for the larger acquiring enterprise.

A VALUATION MODEL

In evaluating the worth of an acquisition, we began with the premise that the acquiring firm is purchasing an income stream and that it will pay more for an investment the higher the after-tax earnings coupled with the chance (risk) that actual earnings will not match anticipated ones. Another factor is whether the acquisition can be levered.

Formula:

$$V_1 = \frac{EBIT\,(1 - h)}{k_h} + h\,Z$$

V_1 = value of levered firm.

EBIT = earnings before interest and taxes.

h = income tax rate.

EBIT(1 - h) = expected after-tax net operating income.

k_h = after-tax discount rate for unlevered firm.

Z = total amount of debt.

The objective of this formulation is to calculate estimated market value of the enterprise. Earlier in the chapter a method to estimate earnings appears. Taxes are exogenous. Determination of a discount rate is uncomplicated.

Formula:

$$k_h = \frac{\dfrac{EBIT(1 - h)}{N}}{\dfrac{V}{N}}$$

EBIT(1 - h) = operating income after taxes.

N = number of shares of common stock outstanding.

EBIT(1 - h)/N = earnings per share.

V = value of an unlevered enterprise.

V/N = market price (M) per share of stock.

One method of determining the after-tax discount rate of an unlevered firm (k_h) is to examine other similar firms within the same industry and relate their earnings per share to the stock's market price. Then adjust the resulting discount rate according to relative risk associated with the potential acquisition. Of course, if we deal with levered firms then we must account for business and financial (consult Chapter Five) risk and for long term debt (Z) in the formula.

Formula:

$$k_h = \frac{EBIT\,(1 - h)}{V_1 - h\,Z}$$

Assume the following data:

EBIT = earnings before interest and taxes = \$900,000.

h = income tax rate = 40%.

V_1 = capitalization (at market value) of levered firm: = \$7,000,000

market value of debt (Z) \$2,000,000

market value of common stock \$5,000,000

$$k_h = \frac{900\ (1 - 0.40)}{7{,}000 - (0.40 \times 2{,}000)} = 8.7\%$$

Estimating the market value pivots on approximations developed from an examination of the market. How much debt can the potential acquisition sustain safely? Looking at comparable firms in the industry affords some notion of capacity to service debt. Suppose that \$2,000,000 of debt seems reasonable. What is the market value of the levered firm? Assume:

EBIT = \$1,200,000

h = 46%

Z = \$2,000,000

k = 8.7% = 9%

$$V_1 = \frac{\$1{,}200\ (1 - 0.46)}{0.09} + 0.46\ (2{,}000) = \$8{,}120{,}000$$

Working from this figure adjustments, with regard to excess assets, intangibles, can be made. Although this method is hardly "scientific" it provides a framework within which analysis can originate. If there are 500,000 shares outstanding, then the approximate market value of common stock is 16¼.

Valuation methods explained in this chapter principally focused on protecting one's interests and at least to keep from doing something foolish. However, there is no guarantee of results because risks associated with possible errors cannot be shifted elsewhere. Nevertheless, a technique exists in which some risks can be shifted to speculators who are eager to absorb them.

CONTENTS

Chapter Fourteen: Winning Techniques to Shield Transactions and Investments Against Devaluations

FOURTEEN

Winning Techniques to Shield Transactions and Investments Against Devaluations

Because acquisition programs are no longer entirely domestic operations, the profit-conscious executive must learn to hedge another type of risk, adverse rate changes in foreign exchanges, to defend his business assets against losses arising from exports, imports, short term and long term investments, and even if he never engages in foreign transactions he must know how to protect himself from losses issuing from careless customers who have foreign exchange exposure. This chapter explains how to do it with examples.

Why should any enterprise concern itself with such complicated matters as hedging and arbitrage? Isn't that something only banks deal in—the experts? The Lugano branch of the Swiss Credit Bank erred and lost $110 million in foreign exchange transactions. The manager of the foreign exchange department of an American branch bank in Belgium lost millions of dollars for his bank; he subsequently turned to another vocational interest—gardening. Three American giant multinationals together lost hundreds of millions because they failed to properly protect foreign exchange exposure over a period of several years.

In transnational transactions, new winners and losers crop up every accounting period. For example R. J. Reynolds Industries Inc. sold $186 million in D-mark designated bonds. Four years later, with an appreciating German currency, and after having made $59 million in repayments, the company refinanced about $160 million with Eurodollar notes—at a loss of nearly $25 million. Or the case of Burlington Industries Inc., in which the firm floated $55 million in bonds designated in Swiss francs, where losses still remain to be counted, provides another illustration of unhedged exchange rate risks. And then there is Firestone Tire & Rubber Co.'s $150 million Swiss franc loan made at 0.2500 in the early 1970s. By mid-1977, the Swiss franc had risen to 0.4000 against the U.S. dollar and to 0.5400 by mid-1978. In another area, currency translations, described in this chapter and the next, produced bookkeeping losses of nearly $2 million per year two years running for Avery International. On the success side, NL Industries Inc. borrowed CD$10 million in Canada, converted the proceeds into U.S. dollars at 0.9910, and when the Canadian dollar slumped to about 0.9000, repaid the loan at a handsome $1 million profit (in U.S. dollars).

On the other hand, many U.S. firms have gained enough insight into foreign exchange operations to save their stockholders millions of dollars in dividends that would otherwise have been lost through devaluations and revaluations. The present era of fluctuating exchange rates makes it imperative that management at least has a basic understanding of options available to protect investments while taking advantage of profitable foreign markets. Hedging, of course, is not restricted to foreign exchange operations discussed in this chapter, although the technique is essentially the same in other markets.

FOREIGN EXCHANGE MARKETS

In the United States there are two markets to hedge against risk of loss from *foreign exchanges*:* The Interbank Foreign Exchange Market and the

*Foreign exchanges (plural) refers to international transfers and means of payment in which currencies are converted into each other; foreign exchange (singular) is the system or process of converting one currency into another. Cf. Paul Einzig, *A Textbook on Foreign Exchange,* 2d ed. (N.Y.: St. Martin's Press, 1969), p. 237.

International Monetary Market (IMM) of the Chicago Mercantile Exchange. Advantages and disadvantages of either market depend upon what the hedger wants to achieve. Learning to utilize these markets shields corporate assets from excessive losses induced by exchange rate adversities.

The Interbank Foreign Exchange Market is not organized like the IMM, but if we define "market" in the abstract as a means for buyers and sellers to be systematically in contact with each other for the purpose of commercial intercourse, then the Interbank Market qualifies. Although the Interbank Market exists for transactions among banks domestically or with foreign banks or foreign exchange dealers abroad, the purpose of this market is for banks to hedge their own foreign exchange exposure which originates in contracts with their own customers. Banks engage in *spot* (cash) and *forward* (contract to be completed on a specific future date) market interchanges. A spot transaction occurs when an individual or firm wants to purchase a foreign currency. A traveler acquires, say, French francs at an exchange rate applicable at the time of day purchase is consummated, or a larger transaction may mean the domestic bank issues a check drawn against its account with the Banque Nationale de Paris.

If a corporation knows exactly when it will receive or make payments in foreign exchanges it can enter into a *forward contract* that matures on the date required to conclude the transaction. The price of a forward contract is the exchange rate determined at time of negotiation. Forward markets are independent of spot markets although an obvious link creates opportunities for arbitrage which tends to keep both markets together. When a bank enters into an agreement with a business, the consequence is to shift the risk of foreign exchange losses (and, of course, the opportunity of gains as well) from the corporation to the bank. If the bank does not want overexposure in any one currency, it will seek to offset its position by locating another institution willing to accept the other side of the transaction. The bank's income derives from the spread between bid and offer. The *bid* is what the bank will pay for foreign exchanges; the *offer* is the bank's selling price. In a stable, heavily traded market, the bid-offer divergence tends to narrow but widens in thinner, higher risk markets. Principal U.S. markets are in New York City and Chicago with secondary markets in Boston, Philadelphia, Detroit, and San Francisco. However, contact with any market is the price of a telephone call. Most business in the United States occurs through the Interbank Market, possibly averaging $15 billion daily, compared with the $50 million or so done on the International Monetary Market. Nearly all forward transactions of the Interbank Market, about 95%, result in actual physical delivery of currency.

On the other hand, the opposite outcome crops up on the International Monetary Market in which more than 95% of the trades are *offset* (cancelled) before delivery data so that few physical deliveries are executed; i.e., actual delivery of currency is unnecessary to transfer risk of price changes from hedger to speculator. The IMM began operations in May, 1972, in response to floating exchange rates. While the Interbank Market deals in any contract size for forward delivery, the IMM futures contract is standardized, restricted to a few major currencies, and contract termination dates (*settlement dates*) are fixed by the exchange rather than by agreement between buyer and seller. Furthermore, daily price (exchange rate) fluctuations are limited by the IMM and all prices of foreign currencies are stated in dollar terms, whereas on the Interbank Market no limits to daily price fluctuations arise and rates can be expressed in terms of any currency. Transaction costs are frequently cheaper for the hedger on the IMM.

For major currencies, at least, markets are worldwide and adjustments to exchange rate differentials take place rapidly because of continuous communication links via telephone, cable, telex. In the London market, much communication occurs over private lines between foreign exchange departments and brokers. Since 1974, the IMM has fallen under control of the federal Commodity Futures Trading Commission and about the same time the Bank of England initiated tighter regulations over London commodity markets although the Bank has had authority to name authorized foreign exchange dealers since post-war resumption in 1951. In Switzerland the market is made among banks since there are no brokers; principal market is in Zurich. Other major markets are situated in Paris, Milan, Tokyo, and Frankfort with secondary markets in numerous locales. Although speculative activity is important to the maintenance and smooth functioning of these markets, the volume of corporate foreign exchange transactions has far greater impact on rates.

HEDGING FOREIGN TRANSACTIONS*

The process of *hedging* means to transfer certain risks from one party to another. Whenever an enterprise deals in foreign transactions in which it must either buy or sell a foreign currency at some future date, a risk element additional to usual business and financial risks is introduced; namely, the possibility that the future price of the foreign currency will diverge from its present value. The risk of price (exchange rate) fluctuations may be borne, shifted to the other party in the commercial transaction, or transferred for a cost to a third party, bank, speculator, or another hedger who will accept the opposite position in a foreign exchange.

For example, if an American exporter invoices a Brazilian importer in dollar terms, the exporter has established his costs and transferred risk of losses resulting from a depreciating cruziero to the importer. In a competitive

---

*Parts of this section are developed from: Robert Vichas, *Getting Rich in Commodities, Currencies, or Coins* (New Rochelle, N.Y.: Arlington House Publishers, 1975), Chapter 18.

market, the exporter may find it more lucrative to bill the importer in the buyer's currency. Then the American exporter may prefer to buy some insurance against exchange rate fluctuations that could wipe out a profit rather quickly; the insurance premium is the cost of hedging.

Exporting Equipment

Let's say that the Wyoming Tool, Screw, and Die Corporation exports products billed at £10,000 to Brighton Iron Works, Ltd. due in 30 days. Wyoming Tool cannot accurately predict the future cash exchange rate when it receives payment in British pounds in 30 days. It can hedge by selling £10,000 forward 30 days. Suppose that the spot rate of one British pound equals 1.7199 dollars—and the 30-day forward rate is 1.7154. Here are the options Wyoming Tool faces.

(a) Do nothing. If the exchange rate in 30 days is still 1.7199, the company can trade £10,000 for $5,814. If the rate depreciates (from Wyoming Tool's viewpoint) to 1.7500 in 30 days the firm can acquire only $5,714 with its pounds, a loss of $100 resulting from a change in the price of pounds for dollars. On the other hand, if the dollar rate of pounds rises to 1.6910, the firm can purchase $5,914, a speculative gain of $100 derived from the foreign exchange transaction rather than from ordinary conduct of business.

(b) Sell £10,000 forward 30 days at a rate of 1.7154. When Wyoming Tool receives its £10,000, it honors its forward contract for which it is guaranteed to receive $5,830, regardless of what happens to the spot rate. If the spot (cash) rate did in fact turn out to be 1.6910, then it lost the chance of generating an additional $84 in speculative profit; and if the spot rate were 1.7500, the cost of hedging insurance was cheaper than potential speculative losses.

Many firms do, of course, speculate on exchange rate fluctuations either with an eye to outguessing the market or because they anticipate small change in rates and avoid additional costs associated with hedges. When a money manager attempts to outguess a major price swing he will either be a momentary hero or unemployed. But hedging frees the firm's resources to concentrate on its principal line of business and leaves foreign exchange matters to the experts—or foolhardy.

Importing Clocks

Now let's reverse the above example. Assume that Opportunity Mail Order, Inc. imports Black Forest clocks from Freiburg Uhrmacher, G.m.b.H. valued at DM 100,000 due in 90 days. If there is a chance of *revaluation* (an upward change in the exchange rate) from the current rate of 0.4200, Opportunity (OMO) might end up disbursing substantially more than the $42,000 it expected to pay for imports. If OMO buys in June to remit in September, and locks in the expected profit from anticipated resale of the merchandise, it may acquire a futures contract on the International Monetary Market (IMM), because if the exchange rate in 90 days should happen to fall against the dollar (rise in terms of D-marks) from 0.4200 to 0.4500, OMO will expend an additional $3,000 to purchase needed D-marks to pay its obligations to Freiburg Uhrmacher.

Deutschemark contracts on the IMM are fixed in multiples of DM 125,000; therefore, OMO will be *overhedged* since the enterprise requires only DM 100,000. However, OMO is willing to speculate, a little, on the chance of an upward movement in rates, and if management errs the loss on DM 25,000 will not likely be excessive. So OMO buys one September contract (it could just as well purchase a December contract because OMO does not plan to take delivery of D-marks but offset the contract prior to settlement date) on the IMM at a price of 0.4275.

At the end of 90 days, Opportunity Mail Order, Inc. need not wait to accept delivery of D-marks through the IMM (actually effectuated via the Continental Illinois Bank) if it is inconvenient or if the contract's expiration data does not coincide with payment date. The main function of the IMM is not to sell foreign exchanges but to provide a vehicle for transference of price fluctuations. For sake of illustration, posit that the exchange rate falls against the dollar to 0.4425 when OMO sells its Deutschemark contract on the IMM. (Selling what it had previously bought cancels out its obligation and wipes out its position with the International Monetary Market.)

In summary, OMO bought one D-mark contract in June at 0.4275 and sells it in September at 0.4425. Because each contract consists of DM 125,000, stated in dollar terms OMO paid $53,437.50 and sold it for $55,312.50, a gross profit of $1,875 minus about $45 in commissions. Before OMO has cause to celebrate its knowledgeable foresight (or good luck), we must carry the transaction through to completion because the bill to Freiburg Uhrmacher, G.m.b.H. remains unpaid. Now Opportunity Mail Order, Inc. must purchase in the spot market DM 100,000 at a rate of, say, 0.4415, a total cost of $44,150. Instead of paying $42,000 for the merchandise, OMO must ante up $44,150, a loss of $2,150 offset by the $1,875 profit on the IMM trade, or a net loss of $275, which seems better than a net loss of $2,150 had OMO not hedged. If OMO had originally insisted on being billed in dollars, then Freiburg Uhrmacher would have taken the opposite position in the German foreign exchange market.

Building New Plant

Since much foreign exchange risk relates to owning or acquiring foreign assets, the following example explains how to protect them. Suppose that The Miletus Society decides to construct its new European headquarters in

Interlaken, Switzerland. Construction costs of about $800,000 (SFr 2,000,000) must be covered in 10 months in Swiss francs. The Miletus Society, a Christian separatist organization, has laid aside necessary funds but does not want to risk the possibility of additional costs issuing from exchange rate depreciation of the dollar. A *buying hedge* offers some protection against unfavorable rate changes. The Society realizes that at current rates of 0.3990, construction costs will be $798,000; however, it has analyzed inflationary programs of the President and Congress and calculates there is a 30% chance that the dollar may depreciate as much as 10% vis-à-vis the Swiss franc and a 50% chance it will depreciate only 3%. Even a 3% drop in 10 months would cost The Society an additional $22,000 or more. Therefore, the trustees vote to purchase 16 Swiss franc futures contracts, one year ahead, a total value of SFr 2,000,000. Transactions completed at an average price of 0.4042 equal a dollar value of $808,400. Here are the results 10 months later.

The 16 contracts are offset at an average price of 0.4102 (an equivalent $820,400), which yields a gross gain of $12,000 (minus about $720 in commissions), and profit after commissions of $11,280. Meanwhile, The Miletus Society had purchased with its $800,000 building fund interest-bearing financial instruments, which returned another $29,520 in interest income. In the cash market they bought SFr 2,000,000 at a favorable rate of 0.4098, or a cost of $819,600. Without interest income, the building cost $808,320—more than originally planned but less than if they had not hedged the contract. With interest income added, total cost of building drops to $778,800.

The Society had at least two other options. It could have pre-paid the cost of the structure and perhaps have even negotiated a lower total contract price due to early payment, but that alternative would have left the Society vulnerable and perhaps stranded with an unenforceable contract. Another course would have been to buy Swiss francs initially at the lower 0.3990 rate, which would have cost them $798,000 guaranteed. However, the interest rate on short term securities, substantially lower in Switzerland, would have yielded only SFr 30,000 in interest income (or $11,970 at 0.3990), and total building costs of $786,030 (if based on a rate of 0.3990). If we use the conversion rate of 10 months later, their interest income of SFr 30,000 will translate into $12,294, and total plant construction costs will equal $785,706—still above the plan activated by the trustees.

Too, other possibilities exist in the *Eurodollar market.* After buying the initial SFr 2,000,000, instead of investing funds in Switzerland for the short term, they could have opened a Swiss franc account in, perhaps, Belgium and earned a slightly higher return of possibly SFr 40,000, but even at an exchange rate of 0.4098, total costs would have been $781,608. If taxation had been a consideration in each case, the last possibility would have produced the most desired outcome.

Using Foreign Funds

Firms or organizations may not always hold liquid assets in dollars, and quite possibly an enterprise may own a number of currencies in reserve and in transferring funds from one point to another for temporary employments, possibility of changes in exchange rates should not be ignored. Applying the above example again, suppose that instead of owning dollars The Miletus Society holds certain financial assets denominated in Swiss francs. Still assuming that construction of new headquarters is underway, costing SFr 2,000,000 due in 10 months, posit that The Society, instead of holding dollars, owns a SFr2,000,000 deposit in Switzerland, but that it will require temporary use of those funds in dollars. Instead of borrowing, The Society converts francs into dollars and requests that funds be wire transferred to its American depository.

Assume that the transfer rate on September 1 is 0.3990, equal to $798,000. Due to likely exchange rate depreciation, The Society purchases on the IMM 16 Swiss franc contracts, September the following year; i.e., they simultaneously sell Swiss francs spot and buy Swiss francs forward at a rate of 0.4042. At the end of 10 months the transactions are reversed so that The Miletus Society is back again in Swiss francs. They offset 16 futures contracts at 0.4102 and purchase Swiss francs in the cash market at 0.4098. (The figures are identical with those above in the original example.) Figure 14-1 recaps the flows.

Figure 14-1

Spot Market		*Futures Market*	
September 1:		September 1:	
Sell SFr 2,000,000		Buy 16 futures contracts	
@ 0.3990	= $798,000	@ 0.4042	= $808,400
July 1:		July 1:	
Buy SFr 2,000,000		Sell 16 futures contracts	
@ 0.4098	= $819,600	@ 0.4102	= $820,400
LOSS	($ 21,600)	GAIN	$ 12,000
RESULT: Loss ($9,600)			

In this illustration, risks were partly shifted to others; and although a loss of $9,600 materializes, it is less than the $21,600 potential loss if the transaction had not been covered. Is this procedure practical and profitable? With a perfect hedge, no loss at all surfaces. Unless transaction costs are excessive, such an operation will reduce losses or even produce speculative profits. With too narrow a difference possibly transaction costs will exceed any savings afforded by the technique. Whatever happens to the Swiss franc-dollar exchange ratio—up or down—the eventual cost of Swiss francs has been predetermined because gains in the futures market are annulled by losses in the spot market—or losses in futures are counterbalanced by gains in the cash market.

The other point: Could not The Miletus Society have borrowed in dollars and not worried about exchange rate risks? Cancelling out foreign exchange transaction costs and losses are gains in interest income from the Swiss franc deposit plus local cost of borrowing about $800,000 in dollars. It may also be necessary to compute comparative tax rates. Ignoring tax implications, an 8% domestic borrowing rate against a 3% interest income rate favors transfer of funds over borrowing. Too, hedging may not necessarily produce a $21,600 loss. If The Society has sufficient confidence in its ability to predict the direction of rates, then it may *overhedge* by, say, 10%, which avers that the total transaction is mostly hedging, partly speculative. The factor to include in this alternative is whether the futures market has already discounted anticipated rises in the Swiss franc rate. But the principal function of hedging is to reduce, or even eliminate, losses arising from foreign exchange transactions; i.e., to safeguard against indefinite and indirect exchange risk arising from assets or liabilities whose values are apt to be altered by exchange rate movements.

Hedging Others' Transactions

Management which never deals in foreign markets, whose business is strictly local, may be surprised to learn that through its customers it may expose its operations to hazards of foreign exchange rate adversities. Nevertheless, this situation lends itself to protection by hedging. Although names and products have been altered, the following case illustrates losses sustained from the devaluation of the Mexican peso.

The Sapphire Engine Company sold diesels to a producer and exporter of locomotives, Free Wheeler, Inc., an open account. Free Wheeler owed Sapphire nearly $4,000,000 in receivables and normally paid about 30 days slow; however, their past due obligations now rose to 45 days late. Free Wheeler reproved the Mexican government, nearly 90 days past due on a $15,000,000 shipment of locomotives sold on open account billed in Mexican pesos, which rebutted that a couple of blocks cracked caused by a sudden freeze at high altitudes when engines were left unprotected. Nevertheless, Free Wheeler informed Sapphire that it expected payment from Mexico soon and that they would clean up their account as soon as funds arrived.

Although Sapphire had never dealt in foreign markets, the company treasurer, concerned about growing rumors of a peso devaluation before the symbolic change of presidential power, convinced Sapphire's management that it would be prudent to hedge the Mexican peso exposure of their customer since Free Wheeler's management was unconvinced of the necessity. In that way, reasoned Sapphire's treasurer, if the peso should be devalued by 50%, for example, Free Wheeler would not receive enough pesos to pay off all their dollar obligations; no exchange rate risk clause appeared in Free Wheeler's contract with the Mexicans.

Sapphire decided that as a minimum they should hedge the $4,000,000 of outstanding receivables since liquidation depended upon Free Wheeler's ability to promptly collect from Mexico. On the other hand, if Sapphire hedged the entire $15,000,000 they could bail out Free Wheeler, Inc. with a loan and prevent bankruptcy of a customer. Management finally compromised on a hedge of $8,000,000 at a cost of $8,000 for 6 months. Five months later, with Free Wheeler's bill still unpaid, the treasurer became hero number one when profits alone from short sales of Mexican pesos nearly covered Free Wheeler's indebtedness. Free Wheeler, Inc. reorganized under Chapter 11. Had the treasurer miscalculated, the mounting pressures on the peso still justified cost of hedging—a cheap insurance policy under the circumstances.

MATHEMATICS OF SWAP ARRANGEMENTS

Foreign currency swapping can benefit any firm which needs to exchange its local currency for other currencies. Recognizing that present value techniques presented in Chapter Two are superior in evaluating investment alternatives, the emphasis here is on single period analysis to illustrate different effects of swap or no swap in defending foreign investments against exchange depreciation or devaluation.

Investing with Swap

Assume that expansion of Industrias Nacionales, S.A., the Spanish subsidiary of Liberty Consolidated, Inc., can generate an approximate 40% rate of return on incremental investment, but a likely chance prevails that the Spanish peseta will be devalued 20% before the end of the investment period. Liberty Consolidated decides *not* to arrange a *currency swap* with its domestic commercial bank for the amount of investment, $3,000,000, because of high costs of the arrangement. The current spot rate of pesetas, in terms of dollars, is 0.0130.

Liberty Consolidated exchanges dollars for pesetas. During the time funds are invested, Liberty's investment, profits, interest, and dividends are exposed to foreign exchange risk. The question arises whether an investment under these additional risk variables is worthwhile undertaking.

Formula:

$$\pi = P\left[\frac{f_1^*}{f_o}(1 + r_f^*) - (1 + i)\right]$$

π = profitability of foreign investment.

P = initial investment.

f_1^* = projected spot rate at end of investment period.

f_o = spot rate at time of initial investment (when rate is expressed as price of foreign currency in terms of domestic money).

r_f^* = anticipated rate of return on foreign investment.

i = domestic borrowing or opportunity cost rate.

Although the concern reasonably projects its anticipated rate of return, additional unknown variables and influence of governmental intervention in foreign exchange markets add to the difficulty of anticipating future exchange rates. To the extent that actual deviates from projected rates, anticipated profits (or losses) are misjudged. But for the sake of illustration, suppose that actual spot rates at the end of the investment period do reflect a 20% decline in the value of the peseta, or 0.0104 to the dollar. Furthermore, assume that the opportunity cost rate (i) is 15%. Should Liberty expose itself to foreign exchange risks? Will profits materialize?

$$\pi = \$3{,}000{,}000\left[\frac{0.0104}{0.0130}(1 + 0.40) - (1 + 0.15)\right]$$
$$= -\$90{,}000 \text{ (loss)}$$

If the actual devaluation rate exceeds the expected rate, loss will be even greater. Since the investment is otherwise acceptable and desirable, management must seek a way to reduce costs associated with an unfavorably changing exchange rate. If roles were reversed—a Spanish firm investing in the U.S.—the Spanish concern would purchase more pesetas at time of repatriation of profits and investment after a devaluation of the peseta and realize speculative profits additional to business profits.

Investing Without Swap

For Liberty Consolidated, Inc., a *foreign currency swap,* in which it makes available through its commercial bank a hard currency credit, reduces risk substantially. Of course, there is a cost; the swap rate exceeds the cash market rate. Whether such arrangement is profitable depends partly upon the extent of anticipated devaluation.

Formula:

$$\pi_s = P_{oc}\left[\frac{f_1^*}{f_{os}}(r_f - i_f) + 1 - (1 + i_d)\right]$$

π_s = profitability of foreign investment with swap.

P_{oc} = initial hard currency credit (value of investment) expressed in terms of domestic currency.

f_1^* = projected spot rate at end of investment period.

f_{os} = swap rate at beginning of investment period.

$P_{oc} \times f_{os}$ = value of investment in terms of foreign currency.

r_f = rate of return calculated on foreign investment proposal.

i_f = interest rate payablè on foreign currency credit.

i_d = domestic borrowing or opportunity cost rate.

Applying the same previous data between Liberty Consolidated, Inc. and its Spanish subsidiary, Industrias Nacionales, S.A., Liberty makes available \$3,000,000 (P_{oc}) credit to its domestic commercial bank which translates into pesetas at the *swap rate* 0.0156 (f_{os}), set 20% above current spot rate, or 192,310,000 pesetas ($P_{oc} \times f_{os}$). The future spot rate still reflects a projected 20% devaluation, 0.0104 (f_1^*) and the Spanish investment is anticipated to return 40% (r_f) as stated before. Industrias Nacionales pays 12% interest (i_f) on the peseta loan; the *opportunity cost* of funds to Liberty Consolidated remains 15% (i_d). Without the *swap* arrangement, the investment will hatch a \$90,000 loss, stated in dollars, if the peseta indeed is devalued by 20%. While it definitely fixes costs and profits (if any), the 20% higher swap rate over current spot rate consumes profits–a high price risk premium.

$$\pi_s = \$3{,}000{,}000\left[\frac{0.0104}{0.0156}(0.40 - 0.12) + 1 - (1 + 0.15)\right]$$

$$= \$110{,}000 \text{ (profit)}$$

One risk, a depreciating exchange rate, is eliminated at high cost. This technique, not exactly a hedge, still exposes assets to further exchange rate depreciation. The model assumes fairly accurate predictions.

INTERNATIONAL ARBITRAGE

Although all manner of arbitrage situations surface, three types of exchange arbitrage that are an integral part of foreign exchange transactions are: *time arbitrage, space arbitrage, interest arbitrage.* An example will clearly illustrate how a firm's management, international organization, or individual investor can profitably engage in interest arbitrage. Paul Einzig defines *arbitrage* as the "simultaneous buying and selling of foreign exchanges . . . or between interest rates prevailing at the same time in different centres or in different currencies."*

Time Arbitrage

Most businesses will not be interested in *time arbitrage* which takes advantage of divergences between forward margins of different maturities. In other words, a systematic relationship exists among *forward rates* (30, 60, 90 days, for example) and when this linkage appears to be too far out of line, then buying one maturity, simultaneously selling another one, may yield a profit. This can only be accomplished successfully by those close to the market, and the *arbitrageur* contributes to a smoothly functioning market, an economic benefit to corporations. Contrary to popular opinion, his role in international markets results in small, smooth adjustments rather than sharp rate fluctuations.

Space Arbitrage

Space arbitrage serves to keep rates between or among markets orderly with small, swift adjustments rather than disorder frequently observed by massive government interventions. *Two-point arbitrage* is between two markets. For example, if pound rate of dollars in London diverges too far from the dollar rate of pounds in New York, arbitrageurs will sell dollars against pounds in one market and sell pounds against dollars in the other market until rates in both markets tend to merge and possibility of further profits disappears. Again we see that arbitrageurs furnish an important economic function to keep market rates orderly internationally. *Three-point arbitrage* is based on cross rates, the ratio between the quotation of two foreign exchanges in relation to each other in a third market. Even *four-point arbitrage* is possible but complicated because it relies on swift action and an arbitrageur may not be able to place all buy and sell orders close enough together to protect his profit. It depends upon market activity and volume.

*Interest Arbitrage***

Short term funds which flow from one currency to another to take advantage of interest rate differentials describes what occurs under *interest*

---

*Paul Einzig, *A Textbook on Foreign Exchange,* 2nd ed. (N.Y.: St. Martin's Press, 1969), p. 233.

**The example in this section is based on data from: Robert Vichas, *Getting Rich in Commodities, Currencies, or Coins* (New Rochelle, N.Y.: Arlington House Publishers, 1975), pp. 267–8.

arbitrage. Interest arbitrage may be *covered* in which case the lender covers his exchange exposure in the forward market, paying a premium for this insurance. *Uncovered interest rate arbitrage* means that the profit derived is the gross differential between yields on short term securities, but the transaction is not sheltered against exchange rate shifts. Actually, with uncovered interest arbitrage, there is an element of speculation additional to investment.

The First Fidelity Arbitrage Fund invests exclusively in short term securities principally in the United States, Canada, and England, and occasionally elsewhere. If interest rates on one-year certificates of deposit are higher in Canada than in the United States, First Fidelity will invest in Canadian deposits but *cover* the associated exchange rate risk. In a hypothetical situation, First Fidelity learns that one-year certificates now return 7.0% in Toronto compared with 6.0% in New York.

On December 15, First Fidelity purchases 93,500 Canadian dollars (CD) at the spot rate of 0.9500, paying US$ 88,825 for CD$ 93,500, which it places in a time deposit at 7.0% due in 12 months, because First Fidelity does not want to expose assets to possible adverse exchange rate fluctuations it opts to cover. It buys one December (next year) futures contract on the International Monetary Market at a rate of 0.9465, or US$ 94,650. (One contract equates to CD$ 100,000.)

During this one year period, interest accumulates on the Canadian deposit in the sum of $6,545, and at the end of one year First Fidelity collects principal of CD$ 93,500 plus interest CD$ 6,545, and delivers this sum against the futures contract for which it pays a commission of $45. The transaction is summarized in Figure 14-2.

Figure 14-2

SPOT		*FUTURES*	
		December 15, Year 1	
Buy CD$ 93,500 @ 0.9500	= US$ 88,825	Sell 1 Dec. futures contract of CD$ @ 0.9465	= US$ 94,650
		December 15, Year 2	
Collect:			
Principal	CD$ 93,500	Deliver CD$ 100,000 against Dec. futures contract.	
+ interest	6,545		
- Fees	45		
	CD$100,000		
		ORIGINAL INVESTMENT	US$ 88,825
		GROSS PROFIT	US$ 5,825
		EFFECTIVE INTEREST RATE	6.56%

Had the US$ 88,825 not been invested in Canadian funds, a comparable U.S. investment would have yielded US$ 5,329.50 (based on 6.0%), while the higher return of US$ 5,825 yielded 6.56% after payment of commissions. Although most traders would not deliver funds against the short sale on the IMM, First Fidelity used the IMM in the same way it would have dealt in the forward market. It might have been possible for First Fidelity to offset its contract on the IMM, by simply buying a Canadian dollar contract, and have realized a larger profit if the spot rate one year hence had been above the December futures rate.

There is another aspect to interest arbitrage for corporate borrowers. A firm with a subsidiary in Belgium will weigh interest rates in Belgium versus domestic interest rates and borrow in the cheaper market, risk and inflation rates considered. Or it may resort to third-market financing of its transactions. Eurocurrency rates tend to influence many such decisions.

ACCOUNTING FOR FOREIGN EXCHANGE

Accounting for foreign exchange gains and losses not only is costly for multinational corporations to compute but also difficult to determine with complete accuracy in fluctuating exchange markets. Furthermore, in controlled exchange markets greater uncertainty pertaining to values always arises. In fact, different accounting methods will render diverse results. The purpose behind such translation is to express all accounts in the same terms—dollars, francs, pesos. Of course, every account could be expressed in terms of gold for universality, and among other benefits, a return to a gold coin standard might render multinational corporate accounting easier as well. The main difference among the following methods centers on timing rather than magnitude of gains or losses resulting from exchange rate changes.

The Current Rate Method

Widely employed by British firms, this method requires that all assets, liabilities, income and expenses are translated at the current exchange rate, and the full translation gain or loss arises in the period in which exchange rate changes—devaluation, revaluation, depreciation, appreciation—take place. Advantages of this technique are simplicity and practicality. Regardless of what the rate was fifteen years ago when an asset was acquired, at which price it will translate into domestic currency today decides its efficacy as an investment alternative. Like a receivable, the sale is not completed until the receivable is converted into an exchangeable asset. The term *conversion* applies when one currency is actually converted into another currency. *Translation* means to restate account balances from one currency into equivalent value in another; no actual exchange transaction arises.

The Current/Noncurrent Method

While the above method guides British accountants, American ones have influenced their companies in the current/noncurrent direction, a rather straight-forward, uncomplicated method to administer. All foreign subsidiary current assets and current liabilities are translated into headquarter's money at the current exchange rate; all noncurrent assets and liabilities are translated at their historic rates, the apposite exchange rate at time asset was acquired or liability assumed. If its foreign subsidiary maintains a positive net working capital position, the parent concern will register a translation loss with foreign currency devaluation and a gain with revaluation.

The income statement may be translated at an average exchange rate, or a weighted average if business is seasonal, with the exception of noncurrent related items, such as depreciation, which are translated at the same rate germane to the corresponding balance sheet item.

The Monetary/Nonmonetary Method

This method, being promoted with moderate success in the United States, has its counterpart in inflation or price-level accounting. Undeniably, the two phenomena, *inflation* and *exchange depreciation,* are linked. When all currencies in which a multinational enterprise retains investments are inflated, the business, helot of an inflation tax, *forfeits purchasing power.* If all currencies were inflated equally (employing a weighted average) world-wide, then exchange rates would tend to hang together, but anyone holding financial assets loses because of a transfer of real wealth and income to governments which impose the *inflation tax.* Depreciating currencies reflect relative values among each other largely due to differing effective rates of inflation. Both *absolute levels* (sacrifice of purchasing power) of various currencies and *relative changes* of a depreciating currency are levies on corporate entities and consumers. The monetary/nonmonetary method focuses on relative changes among currencies, while the next chapter centers on loss of purchasing power of a single currency.

Monetary assets and liabilities include:

Monetary Assets	*Monetary Liabilities*
Cash	Accounts Payable
Marketable Securities	Notes Payable
Accounts Receivable	Tax Liability Reserves
Notes Receivable	Bonds
Prepaid Insurance and Taxes	Preferred Stock

The technique dictates that monetary assets and liabilities be translated at current exchange rates, while nonmonetary assets and liabilities–inventory, fixed assets, long term investments–are translated at the rate prevailing at time of acquisition.

To ascertain the decay resulting from devaluation of foreign currency in which a firm's subsidiary deals, determine the value of net monetary assets–monetary assets minus monetary liabilities–and multiply the outcome times the difference in exchange rates between two periods.

Formula:

$$\text{Loss} = (E_m - Z_m)(f_o - f_1)$$

E_m = value of monetary assets.

Z_m = value of monetary liabilities.

f_o = exchange rate at beginning of period.

f_1 = exchange rate at end of period.

The foreign subsidiary may opt to borrow a sum locally equal to net monetary assets to finance nonmonetary assets in order to offset monetary set-backs caused by exchange rate changes. The expense of this safeguard is the additional burden of borrowing funds.

Formula:

$$K = \frac{i_f (E_m - Z_m)}{f_1}$$

K = cost of shielding assets.

i_f = interest rate on foreign loan.

$(E_m - Z_m)$ = net monetary assets.

f_1 = exchange rate at end of period (assuming that the then spot rate is used to translate the cost into parent company currency).

The benefit of achieving monetary balance is to hedge anticipated exchange rate depreciation of the foreign currency vis-à-vis the domestic currency. The effect is to cancel losses arising from monetary assets with gains credited to new monetary liabilities (the borrowings).

The Other Methods

In practice, however, businesses exercise a variety of methods and hybrids of the above. A popular system assigns the current rate to all balance sheet items except property with other exceptions dedicated to inventory, debt, and goodwill. Some firms prefer an assortment of rates to reflect varying conditions or simply convenience to show a more or less favorable balance sheet and income statement. The *modified monetary method* calls for inventory translation at current rates with all other nonmonetary categories unchanged. The advantage (or disadvantage) of this modified technique is to increase monetary assets relative to monetary liabilities. Obviously, a highly levered firm will prefer a method different from one whose fixed investment relative to other assets reigns high and unlevered; ergo, a devaluation or revaluation may give rise to either translation increments or decrements with the same set of data according to the accounting method employed.

While gains or losses unfold among its foreign subsidiaries, occasioned by exchange rate changes, the parent organization must concern itself with dispossession brought about by depreciating domestic currency; viz., the expropriation of purchasing power caused by monetary inflation.

CONTENTS

Chapter Fifteen: Using Price-Level Accounting Advantageously During Inflationary Times

FIFTEEN

Using Price-Level Accounting Advantageously During Inflationary Times

Although a firm can more readily defend its assets against currency depreciation and devaluation losses, there is less defense against the cruelest of all taxes—the universally applied governmental *inflation tax*. Unfortunately, income taxes must be paid on ersatz profits artificially induced by inflationary budgets. While no escape from the inflation tax applied by most countries of the world is totally possible for any active firm or investor, rearranging the construct of assets and liabilities can shift some inflation losses to others. This chapter explains how to monitor financial statements with inflation, or general price-level, accounting.

Fully adjusted financial statements highlight effects of changing currency values on debtor and creditor; adjusted statements also reveal losses or gains resulting in ownership of monetary items such as cash, receivables, payables, etc. Creditors, too, will have a better idea of the safety cushion behind their claims. Stockholders can ascertain whether invested capital has been increased or decreased as a result of financial policies of the corporation, and, also, whether dividends were paid out of capital or earnings adjusted for price-level changes. With rising costs and income taxes, coupled with an inflation tax, adjusted income statements will indicate whether income taxes do, indeed, exceed pretax earnings in real terms. And for future employment of funds, the adjusted information will aid in calculation of a more reliable rate of return, and, consequently, better allocation of resources.

INFLATION AND PRICE-LEVEL CHANGES

Improper usage of several important terms have crept into popular parlance. We speak of inflation as a rise in prices. This is incorrect. *Inflation* is an increase in the purchasing media, for example, dollars.* Inflation is itself an act of expropriation of assets, even if no verifiable price-level increase ensues, because printing or creation of money by any agency, private or governmental, means acquiring fruits of others' labor by deception without offsetting productive efforts. Inflation, then, distends the supply of *purchasing media* without expanding production, that is, a counterfeit issue is added to existing money supply.

What results? One outcome is redistribution of resources and wealth. Sooner or later higher prices emerge, which means that those who have honestly acquired money and monetary assets discover that their values decline. The worth of money derives from what it will exchange for, goods or services, in the market place; but money is held for reasons other than *transaction purposes,* viz., *portfolio diversification.* Money, the numeraire in most transactions, ranks highest on the liquidity scale; ergo, diversification of investment portfolio may mean holding some assets in a money or near-money form. Since other *monetary assets*—time deposits, equity, bonds, cash value of life insurance, notes, receivables, etc.—are expressed in money terms, their values rise or fall with changes in the price level to produce gains occasionally, losses usually. In other words, one consequence of inflation is a *rising price level.*

*The term "dollars" likewise is incorrect, which, according to constitutional definition, are monetary units, used in exchange, backed by gold and silver. Our present *fiat issues* are supported by more printed paper of the same; therefore, they are correctly termed *Federal Reserve Notes* (FRN), not dollars. Money, of course, is an asset which facilitates exchanges among other assets; however, purchasing media, as a broader concept, encompasses not only money but near-money substitutes such as current account deposits and similar liquid assets. Interestingly American FRNs are popularly called pesos in Puerto Rico and Balboas in Panama; they are worth as much.

Price-level changes, usually monitored with some type of index, cannot accurately be reflected statistically. Because the set of transactions of each entity is dissimilar, purchasing power changes may be likened to different foreign exchange transactions; in this case each entity, individual or firm, is the separate "foreign country" and purchasing power losses emanating from inflationary policies of governments act on each entity differently. Nevertheless, with time, and increasing rate of deterioration of purchasing power, a real transfer of income and wealth does occur. To borrow from the physicists, the half-life of money can be determined easily.

Formula:

$$\text{Half-life} = \frac{\log 2}{\log (1 + w)}$$

The above formula sets forth how many years will pass before the worth of money falls to one-half its purchasing power from some base period given a constant, annually compounded price rise of w. To conceptualize the disastrous consequence of even low rates of inflation, Figure 15–1 records after how many years and days purchasing power is halved at various rates of price-level increases.

Figure 15-1

1%	69 years, 241 day(s)	6%	11 years, 327 days
2%	35 " , 1 "	7%	10 " , 89 "
3%	23 " , 164 "	8%	9 " , 2 "
4%	17 " , 246 "	9%	8 " , 16 "
5%	14 " , 75 "	10%	7 " , 99 "

"In Germany between the world wars, a man died. His family made application for payment of the life insurance for which he had paid premiums nearly all his life. Those premiums were hard to meet at times but he had never begrudged them, for they would give his family financial security when he was gone. When the money came from the insurance company, it was just enough to pay the wreath hung on his door."* The government had taxed away the rest of the insurance value via inflation. And so it has been throughout history—as long as governments control the money supply—whether it is "printing press inflation" of the German type or "controlled inflation" of U.S. and French varieties.

Sometimes confusion arises over differences between relative price

*Norman F. Dacy, *What's Wrong with Your Life Insurance* (N.Y.: Macmillan Publishing Co., Inc., 1963), p. 245.

changes and price-level change. *Relative prices* among goods and services constantly vary because of shifting demand and supply relationships; but a *price-level change* signifies transformation of the *absolute price level* so that, on average, prices of everything together shift upwards. The impact of price-level changes depends upon acquisitions during the period and composition of assets and liabilities.

General price-level accounting techniques translate assets and liabilities into comparable terms expressed either in terms of the base period or in today's terms. We saw expressions of this idea in compounding and present values in Chapters One and Two and in foreign exchange hedging in Chapter Fourteen. Here we must rely on price indices in spite of their obvious shortcomings.

Suppose that the *price index* is expressed in terms of a base period 1, 100, that the index rises to 125 in period 2, and again to 160 in period 3. In period 1, $10,000 will exchange for $10,000 worth of goods and for $8,000 worth in period 2; but posit that we are interested in changes from period 2 to period 3. In period 2, for example, $100,000 will buy that amount of capital equipment but in period 3, when prices have slipped to 78% of period 2's purchasing power, that same $100,000 will buy only $78,125 (0.78125 X $100,000) worth of equipment. Or, phrased another way, to buy the same amount of equipment in period 3 will now require $128,000 (1.28 X $100,000), a $28,000 loss in purchasing power. This is essentially the idea behind price-level accounting.

Any index may be used to adjust financial statements to current price levels; however, the Financial Accounting Standards Board recommends the *Implicit Price Deflator* for Gross National Product, which is no worse than any other index. In Tables XVIII through XX in the Appendix appear Implicit Price Deflators for base years 1958 and 1972.

STATEMENTS FOR ILLUSTRATION

Once again employing financial statements of Huzzah Hoosier Hosiery Mills, Inc. from Chapter Twelve, year-end income statement and comparative balance sheets, coupled with appropriate notes, are reproduced in Figures 15-2 and 15-3 and will be adjusted principally according to procedures systematized by Sidney Davidson, Clyde P. Stickney, and Roman L. Weil.* As a matter of interest the reader may desire to recalculate key ratios summarized in Chapter Twelve based on adjusted financial statements developed herein.

*Procedures applied herein were largely developed by: Henry W. Sweeney, *Stabilized Accounting*. N.Y.: Harper & Brothers, 1936.

Figure 15-2

HUZZAH HOOSIER HOSIERY MILLS, INC.
Income Statement at Year End
($000)

Sales	46 308
Cost of Goods Sold	39 217
GROSS MARGIN	7 091
Less:	
Administrative and Selling Expenses	871
General Expenses	2 626
Depreciation	1 331
Other Expenses	42
INCOME FROM OPERATIONS	2 221
OTHER INCOME (LOSS), NET	15
EARNINGS BEFORE INTEREST AND TAXES (EBIT)	2 236
Interest Expense	892
EARNINGS BEFORE TAXES (EBT)	1 344
Provision for Income Taxes	630
EARNINGS AFTER TAXES (EAT)	714
Current Dividends on Preferred Stock	40
EARNINGS AVAILABLE TO COMMON SHAREHOLDERS	674
Average Number of Shares Outstanding	1 960
Earnings per Share on Common Stock (EPS)	0.344

NOTE:
Recent selling price of common stock $2.00 per share.
Recent selling price of preferred stock $100.00 per share.

ADJUSTED INCOME STATEMENT

To adjust an income statement stated in *nominal values* for price-level changes, the estimating procedure will advance step-by-step covering major points on Huzzah Hoosier Hosiery Mills, Inc.'s (HHHM, Inc.) income statement followed by adjustments to comparative balance sheets. For reference, the adjusted income statement appears in Figure 15-4. The form presented differs from the original to focus on categories of adjusted figures.

Generally, the adjustment process classifies all items as monetary or nonmonetary. *Monetary items,* already stated in nominal terms, are not adjusted; e.g., one Federal Reserve Note ($1) today will buy $1 worth of goods and services and, consequently, cash balances are not adjusted. Similarly, any

Figure 15-3

HUZZAH HOOSIER HOSIERY MILLS, INC.
Comparative Year-End Balance Sheets ($000)

	Year t	*Year t - 1*
ASSETS:		
Cash	832	970
Marketable Securities	430	–
Accounts Receivable	4 621	5 150
Inventory	10 066	9 781
Prepaid Expenses	8	9
TOTAL CURRENT	15 957	15 910
Plant & Equipment (Net)	8 247	} 12 778
Buildings (Net)	3 200	
Land (Cost)	3 000	3 000
Patents, Intangibles	2 850	2 850
TOTAL NONCURRENT	17 297	18 628
TOTAL ASSETS	33 254	34 538
LIABILITIES:		
Accounts Payable	7 051	6 809
Notes Payable	1 000	1 500
Accrued Expenses	46	34
Long Term Debt (current portion)	675	830
TOTAL CURRENT	8 772	9 173
1st Mortgage (7½%)	4 600	4 800
2nd Mortgage (12%)	475	715
Bonds (8%)	4 000	4 000
Debentures (9%)	1 000	1 000
Preferred Stock (8%)	500	500
Retained Earnings	11 947	12 450
Common Stock	1 960	1 900
TOTAL LIABILITIES & EQUITY	33 254	34 538

NOTES: Inventories calculated 75% LIFO assumption, 25% FIFO. If FIFO had been used, value on LIFO portion would have been $1,705 more or ending inventory of $11,771 under FIFO. Accumulated depreciation of plant, equipment, and buildings at end of year t equals $7,150.

Figure 15-4

HUZZAH HOOSIER HOSIERY MILLS, INC.
Price-Level Adjusted Income Statement
($000)

	Adjusted Amounts	*Unadjusted Amounts*
Revenues	47 368	46 308
Cost of Goods Sold (CGS)	40 234	39 217
Expenses:		
Depreciation	1 864	1 331
Income & Other Taxes	644	630
Interest	912	892
Other Costs & Expenses	3 620	3 539
TOTAL EXPENSES & COST OF GOODS SOLD	47 274	45 609
Other Income	15	15
Income Before Gain on Monetary Items	109	714
Gain on Monetary Items	637	–
NET INCOME	746	714
Less: Preferred Dividends	41	40
Income to Common Stockholders	705	674

item labeled as money-value assets or liabilities requires no adjustment—cash, short term marketable securities, accounts receivable, prepaid expenses, most liabilities except certain contingency items, and preferred stock (a borderline situation). Everything else is *nonmonetary;* all revenues and expenses likewise are nonmonetary.

Sales Revenues

In all of these calculations an appropriate adjustment factor must be agreed upon and quarterly and/or annual GNP Implicit Price Deflators for a period long enough to cover all items in financial statements must be available. For HHHM, Inc., income from sales is assumed to flow fairly evenly throughout the year. From Table XX in the Appendix, using 1972 as the base year for indices, we read that the rate of price increase during base year plus 4 years was 4.6%. (Assume that HHHM, Inc.'s current reporting year—*year t*—ends December 31, base year + 4.) More specifically, we can compute this rate of 12-month change by:

Formula:

$$w = \frac{W_t}{W_{t-4}} - 1$$

where the rate of price change (w) equals the deflator for the current quarter (W_t) divided by the deflator for four quarters earlier (W_{t-4}), minus one.

$$w = \frac{136.30}{130.27} - 1 = 4.629\%$$

Since some revenues arise prior to midyear and some afterwards, not all income loses purchasing power *pari passu.* Revenues generated earlier in the year will lose more in purchasing power during inflationary periods. Therefore,

Formula:

$$w_{\frac{1}{2}} = \left(\frac{W_t}{W_{t-4}}\right)^{\frac{1}{2}} - 1 = \sqrt{\frac{W_t}{W_{t-4}}} - 1$$

$$= \sqrt{1.04629} - 1 = 2.288\%$$

This half-year factor, for most computations of revenues and expenses, compounds to 4.629% (or $(1.02288)^2 - 1 = 0.04629$).

Why are five quarters necessary for this calculation? Because quarterly indices approximate mid-quarter products (November 15th, August 15th, etc.), relating November 15, year t - 1 to November 15, year t, casts a 12-month change.

Due to losses of purchasing power for income received throughout the 12-month period, annual sales of $46,308 (all figures for HHHM, Inc. are stated in thousands) will not actually command that amount of goods and services by year-end. To maintain level purchasing power, $47,368 are now needed:

$46,308 × 1.02288 = $47,368 (in thousands)

Cost of Goods Sold

Adjusting cost of goods sold compels extra calculations because the firm employs both First-in-First-Out (FIFO) and Last-in-Last-Out (LIFO) methods of inventory valuations. The LIFO assumption, a substantial nisus toward price-level adjustments, embodies 75% of the inventory; the remaining 25% is valued basis FIFO.

FIFO Adjustment

The first step in adjusting the FIFO segment of cost of goods sold (CGS) is to ascertain purchases for the year (assumed to flow steadily throughout the period).

Formula: $\text{Purchases} = (\text{CGS} + E_e) - E_b$

That is, subtract beginning inventory (E_b) from the sum of ending inventory (E_e) and cost of goods sold to find yearly purchases.

$$\text{Purchases} = (39{,}217 + 10{,}066) - 9{,}781 = \$39{,}502$$

Nevertheless, the complexity of the issue is this. Not all current year (t) purchases enter into cost of goods sold; a fraction of beginning FIFO inventory must be adjusted for previous year's price changes (t – 1) or rather that share of goods purchased last year (t – 1) which enter into current year's cost of goods sold.

Before proceeding, we need to know what proportion of cost of goods sold originate in last year's purchases; Figure 15-5 facilitates understanding of calculations.

Figure 15-5

	Percent		*Amounts in Thousands*		
	LIFO	*FIFO*	*LIFO* +	*FIFO* =	*TOTAL*
Beginning Inventory	75%	25%	7,335.8	2,445.2	9,781
Purchases	78.63%	21.37%	31,060.4	8,441.6	39,502
Stock Available	–	–	38,396.2	10,886.8	49,283
Less: Ending Inventory	75%	25%	7,549.5	2,516.5	10,066
Cost of Goods Sold	–	–	30,846.7	8,370.3	39,217

From a footnote to financial statements of HHHM, Inc., we learn that if FIFO had been employed exclusively, then 100% of the inventory would have been worth \$11,771; that is, the LIFO share of ending inventory would have been valued \$1,705 higher. Since the FIFO fraction of adjusted ending inventory equals \$2,516 (25% of \$11,771), the FIFO part is 21.37% (2,516 ÷ 11,771) of total adjusted year-end inventory, and, therefore, LIFO is represented by 78.63%, as indicated in Figure 15-5; i.e., of total purchases of \$39,502, 21.37% are valued basis FIFO or \$8,441.6 (still stated in thousands), and the LIFO balance represents \$31,060.4.

Total inventory available for sale, beginning inventory plus purchases during year t, consists of FIFO and LIFO segments described in Figure 15-5. Ending inventory of \$10,066 embraces, according to footnotes to financial statements of HHHM, Inc., 25% FIFO, 75% LIFO, also appropriately recorded in Figure 15-5. The FIFO quota of cost of goods sold is \$8,370.3. Notwithstanding, the work is unfinished for we still need to adjust for last year's price changes which encompasses a fraction of FIFO plus FIFO purchases modified by this year's price changes.

Formula:

$$(\hat{t} - 1)_{FIFO} = \left(1 - \frac{CGS - E_b}{Purchases}\right) 0.50$$

$(\hat{t} - 1)_{FIFO}$ = portion of FIFO affected by last year's price change.

CGS = cost of goods sold.

E_b = beginning inventory.

Purchases = FIFO portion of total purchases.

Solving for this example, $(\hat{t} - 1)_{FIFO} = \left(1 - \frac{8{,}370.3 - 2{,}445.2}{8{,}441.6}\right) 0.50$ = 14.905% which equals about 60% of the fourth quarter of last year $\left(\frac{0.14905 \times 12}{3} = 59.620\%\right)$.

Formula:

$$w_{\hat{t}} = \left(\frac{W_t}{W_{t-1}}\right)^t$$

Applying the formula to the instant problem, the rate of price change for the fourth quarter ($w_{\hat{t}}$) is the price index of the fourth quarter (W_t) divided by the price index of the third quarter (W_{t-1}) raised to the power (t) which represents the aliquant part of the quarter, 0.59620 in this case.

$$w_{\hat{t}} = \left(\frac{130.27}{128.07}\right)^{\frac{0.14905 \times 12}{3}} - 1 = \left(\frac{130.27}{128.07}\right)^{0.59620} - 1 = 1.021\%$$

With these figures in hand—the fraction of last year's price change and the current year's price change calculated earlier—we can adjust the FIFO subgroup of beginning inventory (E_b).

Formula: $$\text{Adj. } E_{b,FIFO} = E_{b,FIFO}\,(w_t \times w_{\hat{t}})$$

The adjusted beginning FIFO inventory is the unadjusted FIFO fragment of beginning inventory multiplied by the price change for the current year times the price change for the affected proportion of the previous year.

$$\text{Adj. } E_{b,FIFO} = \$2{,}445.2\,(1.04629 \times 1.01021) = \$2{,}585$$

The next step in this process of deciding the adjusted cost of goods sold basis FIFO is to establish equivalent purchases which accommodate FIFO calculations, or CGS - E_b = 8,370.3 - 2,445.2 = \$5,925.1, adjusted for the average number of months carried in inventory:

$$\left(\frac{5{,}925.1 \times 12}{8{,}370.3}\right)0.50 = 0.354 \text{ of a year or } 4.247 \text{ months}$$

after January 1st of the current year, about May 8th, represents average purchase date of FIFO inventory.

If, on average, FIFO merchandise was acquired on May 8th, then it was carried 7.753 months (12 - 4.247) or the last 64.608% of the year. Since price change for the entire current year was 4.629%, adjusting for the last 64.608% of the year ($w_{t/n}$) will result in a price change of:

$$(1.04629)^{0.64608} - 1 = 2.967\%$$

Now we are prepared to compute the adjusted FIFO cost of goods.

Formula: $$\text{Adj. } CGS_{FIFO} = [E_{b,FIFO} \times (w_t \times w_{\hat{t}})] + [(CGS - E_b)_{FIFO} \times w_{t/n}]$$

$\text{Adj. } CGS_{FIFO}$ = price-adjusted FIFO cost of goods sold.

$E_{b,FIFO}$ = beginning FIFO inventory

w_t = price change for current year.

$w_{\hat{t}}$ = proportionate price change of previous year.

$(CGS - E_b)_{FIFO}$ = cost of goods sold minus beginning inventory, FIFO data.

$w_{t/n}$ = proportionate price change for current year.

Combining and utilizing above FIFO data plugged into the last formula, the adjusted FIFO cost of goods sold is:

$$\begin{aligned}\text{Adj. CGS}_{\text{FIFO}} &= [2{,}445.2 \times (1.04629 \times 1.01021)] \\ &+ [(8{,}370.3 - 2{,}445.2) \times (1.04629)^{0.64608}] \\ &= \$8{,}685.4 \text{ (in thousands)}\end{aligned}$$

LIFO Adjustment

Because the firm in our example employs both FIFO and LIFO inventory valuation, the adjusted cost of goods sold must also reflect adjusted price-change values for the LIFO category as well. Last-in-First-out assumes that most recently bought goods sell first. What ratio of LIFO purchases (x) enter into the cost of goods sold during the current year?

Formula:

$$x = \frac{\text{CGS}_{\text{LIFO}}}{\text{Purchases}_{\text{LIFO}}}$$

Referring to Figure 15–5 data, we find that

$$x = \frac{30{,}846.7}{31{,}060.4} = 99.312\%;$$

and to determine the average acquisition date, we learn that (0.99312 X 12) 0.50 = 0.497 of a year or 5.959 months, about July 2nd.

The rate of price change since July 2nd of the current year equals:

$$(1.04629)^{0.497} - 1 = 2.274\%$$

At this point we have garnered sufficient information to figure adjusted cost of LIFO goods sold.

Formula: $\text{Adj. CGS}_{\text{LIFO}} = (E_b - E_e + \text{Purchases})_{\text{LIFO}} \times (w_t)^{t/n}$

$\text{Adj. CGS}_{\text{LIFO}}$ = price-level adjusted LIFO costs of goods sold.

$(E_b - E_e + \text{Purchases})_{\text{LIFO}}$ = LIFO cost of goods sold.

w_t = current year price change.

t/n = proportionate period of current year.

$\text{Adj. CGS}_{\text{LIFO}}$ = $\$30{,}846.7 \times (1.04629)^{0.497} = \$31{,}548.2$ (in thousands)

Combined CGS

Combining FIFO and LIFO cost of goods sold adjusted for respective changes in price levels presents no difficulty since we have separately calculated results. Summing, we have:

Combined CGS = 8,685.4 + 31,548.2 = $40,234 (in thousands)

Do results justify the effort? Certainly in periods of slowly changing price levels outcomes will deviate less than in periods of rapid inflation. Additionally, the structure of assets and liabilities, seasonality, and accounting assumptions influence the degree of departure from nominal figures. In this example of HHHM, Inc., the price-level adjusted costs of goods sold exceeds reported unadjusted costs of goods sold by 2.593%. In periods of hyperinflation, quarterly adaptations will be inadequate, calling for monthly, even weekly or daily, alterations. Of course, by the time inflationary price-level shifts reach these levels, more resources are diverted to the question of inflation survival rather than inflation accounting.

Expenses

Following suppositions similar to those affecting revenues—that is, assuming that both revenues and expenses occur fairly evenly during the year—general, administrative, selling, and miscellaneous expenses can most easily be accommodated on the same basis; i.e., employ a rate that, compounded semi-annually, will match the annual rate of price change. In this illustration we discovered previously that a half-year rate of 2.288% applies. Therefore, expense adjustments for price-level changes will be:

Expenses:		
Administrative and Selling	$871 × 1.02288 =	$891
General	2,626 × 1.02288 =	2,686
Other	42 × 1.02288 =	43
TOTAL EXPENSES		$3,620 (in thousands)

It may be argued that supplies should be reconciled in a manner similar to cost of goods sold, and certainly the quest for exactitude (to the extent that this technique portends precision) requires the added calculations. However, for many firms, supply inventories are relatively small items in the balance sheet and frequently are consumed *pari passu* with sales. Should this not be the case or where supply stockpiling evinces, then expenditure of additional mathematical labors may be justified.

Depreciation

For fidelity, depreciation alignments must proceed item-by-item, but such detailed data, not always available, are not altogether necessary for external analysis of an enterprise. Price-level computations for Huzzah Hoosier Hosiery Mills, Inc. are fairly uncomplicated because sufficient detail turns up and straight line depreciation applies. Estimating average life of assets under more complicated accelerated depreciation methods is discussed at the end of the chapter. (Also, consult Chapter Seven for additional comments on depreciation methods.) From a footnote to the HHHM, Inc. statement we learn that accumulated depreciation amounts to $7,150; from that we can discern the average age of depreciable assets on a straight-line basis (N).

Formula:

$$N = \frac{A_{t+n}}{A_t}$$

N = average age of depreciable asset (straight line) in number of years.

A_{t+n} = accumulated depreciation.

A_t = annual depreciation.

The greater the denominator, reflecting increased annual depreciation charges, the newer equipment and buildings. Older assets will reflect higher accumulated depreciation in the numerator. For HHHM, Inc., the average age of depreciable assets is:

$$N = \frac{7{,}150}{1{,}331} = 5.372 \text{ years}$$

Still assuming for sake of illustration that the current statement ends December 31, year t, then an age of 5.372 years suggests that average asset acquisition relates to the middle of the third quarter of year t – 5.

In terms of base year dollars, the price rise during the period assets have been held is:

$$\left[136.30 \div \left(\frac{142.03}{145.92} \times 100\right)\right] - 1 = 40.033\%^*$$

*To transform an index from one base year to another base year, divide the index calculated on the old base by the index for the desired year as the new base. In the above calculations the index under the 1958 base year is divided by 145.92 to approximate a 1972 base year. *(See rest of footnote at bottom of facing page.)*

Depreciation standardized for price-level changes is the stated annual depreciation for the most recent year times the index expressing price rise since average asset purchase.

$$\text{Adj. Depreciation} = \$1{,}331 \times 1.40033 = \$1{,}864 \text{ (in thousands)}$$

This sum is entered in the adjusted income statement, Figure 15–4.

Other Items

Remaining items in the unadjusted income statement will be recast for half-year price changes on the assumption that other income and expenditures occur at a steady pace throughout the year so that about one-half of income and expenditures materialize before mid-year, the other one-half after mid-year. Therefore, the same 2.288% rate applies.

Other Income

$$\$15 \times 1.02288 = \$15 \text{ (in thousands)}$$

Actual answer is 15.34, but rounding to nearest thousand leaves the adjusted answer unchanged from the unadjusted one.

Interest Expense

$$\$892 \times 1.02288 = \$912 \text{ (in thousands)}$$

Income Taxes

$$\$630 \times 1.02288 = \$644 \text{ (in thousands)}$$

Taxes may require different treatment depending on how and when they

---

Since indices are calculated at mid-quarter, no further adjustment is necessary in this illustration. Alternatively, the result for the 4th quarter can be multiplied by the applicable proportion of the 3rd quarter. (4th quarter index = $\frac{142.70}{145.92} \times 100 = 97.99$; 3rd quarter index = $\frac{142.03}{145.92} \times 100 = 97.33$). $\left(\frac{136.30}{97.99}\right) \times \left(\frac{97.99}{97.33}\right)^{\frac{0.372-0.250}{0.250}} - 1 = 39.55\%$.

are paid. Certainly *prepaid taxes* represent a *monetary loss* since taxes would be paid in dearer currency when postponement of payment would mean paying them in cheaper currency (that is, money of lower purchasing power).

Preferred Stock Dividends

$$\$40 \times 1.02288 = \$41 \text{ (in thousands)}$$

The same assumptions apply to *preferred stock dividends;* but if all dividends are paid out at the end of the last quarter, then no adjustment is necessary because dividends are paid from current dollars. Or if the dividends are paid at the end of 6 months and again after 12 months, then one-half of dividend payments would be transfigured for one-half year price change.

Gains or Losses on Monetary Items

A distinction arises between monetary and nonmonetary items in rectifying price-level variations. "A 'monetary' item is one the *amount* of which is fixed by statute or contract, and is therefore not affected by a change in the price level."* This definition does not imply that the *value* of the contract is permanent but that the number of units of currency required to liquidate the obligation remains sustained regardless of what happens to the value of purchasing media. Referring to the balance sheet of Huzzah Hoosier Hosiery Mills, Inc., all current assets, except inventories, are monetary items (cash, accounts receivable, marketable securities, prepaid expenses excluding supplies) which, consequently, are subject to depreciation in value as price levels rise. All liabilities, except retained earnings and common stock, are monetary items—accounts and notes payable, accrued expenses, long term obligations and preferred stock—and, therefore, are a possible source of gain to the debtor firm because repayment of debt will be in cheaper media than received at time of borrowing. Of course, creditors are aware of this and reset interest rates upward to account for *anticipated* price-level rises within constraints of competition. (As explained in an earlier chapter, the cost of credit or interest rate consists of payment for time, risk of default, and anticipated rise in the price level.) Everything else in the balance sheet encompasses nonmonetary items; namely, merchandise and supply inventories, fixed assets, and common stockholders' equity.

The issue here is to determine the net monetary position of the enter-

---

**Reporting the Financial Effects of Price-Level Changes,* Accounting Research Study No. 6 (N.Y.: American Institute of Certified Public Accountants, Inc., 1963), p. 138.

prise. Typically, businesses are *deficit spending units,* that is, net debtors, which suggests that, as debtors, theoretically they gain. (Actually, no one gains from inflation except inflators, but to the extent borrowers can shift risk of loss to creditors, not offset by higher interest rates, then some gain may transfer to debtors. Most of it is illusory, however.)

Adding together all liabilities, from which we subtract common stockholders' equity, for current year t, monetary liabilities aggregate to $19,347 and for the previous year t - 1, $20,188 (both counted in thousands). Monetary assets, consisting of current assets less inventory, are, respectively, $5,891 and $6,129 (in thousands).

	t	*t - 1*
Monetary Liabilities	19,347	20,188
Monetary Assets	5,891	6,129
Net Monetary Liabilities	13,456	14,059

To determine average outstanding *net monetary liabilities* for the present year, t, add together year-end net monetary positions for years t and t - 1 and divide by 2: (13,456 + 14,059) ÷ 2 = 13,757.5. The gain in being net debtor derives from price-level mutation during year t.

Formula:

$$\text{Gain on NML} = w_t\left(\frac{Z_{nm,t} + Z_{nm,t-1}}{2}\right)$$

w_t = rate of price-level change in current year.

$Z_{nm,t}$ = net monetary liabilities in current year.

$Z_{nm,t-1}$ = net monetary liabilities in previous year.

The gain on net monetary liabilities for HHHM, Inc. for year t is:

$$\text{Gain on NML} = 0.04629 \times \$13{,}757.5 = \$637 \text{ (in thousands)}$$

We now have sufficient data to construct a price-level adjusted income statement for HHHM, Inc. (which appears in Figure 15-4). Because of gains from being net debtor, the firm shows a higher current dollar profit than otherwise. In the chapter on ratios, it was observed that HHHM, Inc. fared not too well, and, at best, was a borderline case.

ADJUSTED BALANCE SHEET

Revising a balance sheet for price-level metastasis allows for comparison because amounts shown in balance sheets of earlier years are not comparable to current sums. Why? One may as well try to compare pesos to yen; without the key—the applicable rate of exchange between pesos and yen—to state all terms in some common denominator, there can be no translatable relationship. Or, for example, linking a statement in Canadian dollars to U.S. dollars is not possible even though both countries have and employ dollars. Their respective values differ. Similarly, U.S. dollars of 1958 and 1978 are not comparable until they are stated in relatable terms. Price-level translations of balance sheets attempt to reduce all statements to analogical terms, viz., to nominal dollars of today, or most recent statement date. This can mislead as will be pointed out below. Examples of all adjustments are drawn from original balance sheets of Huzzah Hoosier Hosiery Mills, Inc. and appear in Figure 15-6 in unadjusted and adjusted columns. The crucial distinction between monetary and nonmonetary items, adumbrated in the previous section, remains.

Cash

The purpose of recasting comparative balance sheets for price-level changes centers on translating all statements to today's money terms. Prior statements conform to price changes. In current statements nonmonetary items are adjusted; monetary ones are not. Money, or cash, being the numeraire for all other items in the balance sheet, is not adjusted because money today will exchange today at the current value of money. Similarly, monetary assets, a restatement of money, are unadjusted in the current period. Therefore, in the HHHM, Inc. balance sheet, cash for year t is invariable.

Nevertheless, cash in the year t - 1 balance sheet must be updated. It is reconciled because cash a year ago had a greater value (in times of rising price levels) than purchasing power of the same amount today. Consequently, cash of a year ago must be restated into today's terms. For illustrative purposes, assume that end of year t is December 31, base year + 4 and year t - 1, December 31, base year + 3 so that implicit price deflators for those periods correspond in the same manner as in adjusting HHHM, Inc.'s income statement.

$$\$970 \times \frac{136.30}{130.27} = \$1{,}015 \text{ (in thousands)}$$

This restatement does not imply that the firm now has $45,000 more

Figure 15-6

HUZZAH HOOSIER HOSIERY MILLS, INC.
Price-Level Adjusted Balance Sheets
(at year end in $000)

	Unadjusted		*Adjusted*	
	t	*t - 1*	*t*	*t - 1*
ASSETS				
Cash	832	970	832	1 015
Marketable Securities	430	–	430	–
Accounts Receivable	4 621	5 150	4 621	5 388
Inventory	10 066	9 781	11 851	12 612
Prepaids	8	9	8	9
TOTAL CURRENT	15 957	15 910	17 742	19 024
Noncurrent Assets	17 297	18 628	24 226	26 090
TOTAL ASSETS	33 254	34 538	41 968	45 114
LIABILITIES				
TOTAL CURRENT	8 772	9 173	8 772	9 597
Long Term Debt	10 075	10 515	10 075	11 001
Preferred Stock	500	500	500	523
Common Stockholders Equity	13 907	14 350	22 621	23 993
TOTAL LIABILITIES & EQUITY	33 254	34 538	41 968	45 114
RATIOS*				
Rate of return on equity	6.10%		3.79%	
Earning power	2.35%		1.96%	
Net profit-to-sales	1.54%		1.57%	
Current assets-to-debt	84.67%		94.14%	
Debt-to-total capital	56.67%		44.91%	
Earnings per share	$0.344		$0.360	
Price-earnings ratio (times)	5.81		5.56	

*For definitions, see Chapter Twelve.

but means that $970 a year ago parallels $1,015 today when the annual rate of price change is 4.629% (136.30 ÷ 130.27 - 1 × 100). The objective is to compare $832 in statement of year t with equivalent purchasing power of cash of year t - 1—a means of bringing everything forward in time. Undoubtedly, this restatement misleads one into sensing that more cash somehow materialized. To focus upon actual losses in purchasing power, we could state that if the cash balance of $970 at the beginning of year t had been held for one year, to the end of year t, it would have depreciated in value to a purchasing power level of $927—a very real loss to the firm in an equivalent amount of $43, the inflation tax on one asset alone. Unfortunately, the price-level translation technique discussed herein glosses over this alarming situation.

Marketable Securities

A marketable security, like cash, is a monetary item and requires no metastasis for the current year t. Had there been marketable securities at the end of year t - 1, these would have been treated in the same manner as cash above.

Accounts Receivable

Similarly, accounts receivable presents no modification problems. Like cash and marketable securities, this monetary item is not adjusted for the current year, but the previous year's receivables are restated into today's terms by the same annual index.

$$\$5{,}150 \times \frac{136.30}{130.27} = \$5{,}388 \text{ (in thousands)}$$

Inventories

Inventories under First-in-First-out (FIFO) assumptions are fairly easily qualified; inventories under Last-in-Last-out (LIFO) assumptions present more difficulty. According to footnotes, about 25% of ending inventories, a nonmonetary item, are valued on FIFO basis and 75% LIFO. In this illustration we will start with year t - 1.

Referring to Figure 15-5, we see that the FIFO portion of ending inventory (beginning inventory year t) is $2,445.2 (25% of $9,781). Adjusting for annual price-level change,

$$\$2{,}445.2 \times \frac{136.30}{130.27} = \$2{,}558.4 \text{ (in thousands)}$$

(The underlying assumption is that FIFO inventory was purchased in the fourth quarter.)

LIFO calculations require that original purchase date (or date of change to LIFO) of inventories be ascertained because the accounting supposition is that last items bought are first ones whose costs are computed, and the residual value of the inventory is based on time-receding values. In other words, the bulk of the \$7,335.8 LIFO share of inventory (year t - 1) was obtained when the business was acquired over 5 years ago. Subsequently, as inventories build up, the LIFO segment of inventories increased. Later acquisitions are subject to smaller price-level changes than earlier ones.

Assuming that a 75/25 relationship was maintained throughout the 5 plus years of business operations and that LIFO inventories grew at an approximate rate of 3% per year, then we estimate that LIFO inventories in year t - 5 amounted to \$6,517, and that subsequent additions equaled \$200 annually, more or less. The fourth quarter index for 1971 (t - 5) was 97.79 (1972 = 100), 101.44 for t - 4, 109.05 for t - 3, 121.60 for t - 2, 130.27 for t - 1, and 136.30 for year t. Therefore, the restated value of t - 5 FIFO inventory, in terms of year t, is:

$$\$6{,}517 \times \frac{136.30}{97.79} = \$9{,}083 \text{ (in thousands)}$$

Applying the appropriate price-level index for each subsequent addition to LIFO inventory, the LIFO division of year t - 1 inventory, stated in year t terms, will approximate \$10,054 (in thousands). Summing the LIFO and FIFO portions of inventories for year t - 1, their combined restated value will be:

LIFO	\$10,054
FIFO	2,558
TOTAL	\$12,612 (in thousands)

For year t, the FIFO part of inventory, \$2,516.5, was purchased during the last quarter of the present year and requires no adjustment. The LIFO lot can also be determined by the method explicated above; however, the following *short-cut method* is available when detailed inventory data are not.

The first step is to compute purchases, which we did previously, represented in Figure 15-5. Purchases consist of cost of goods sold minus beginning inventory plus ending inventory, or \$39,502. The next step is to figure value of ending inventory under implied FIFO conditions. In this case we have complete information in a footnote to the financial statement of HHHM, Inc., which signals a FIFO equivalent inventory of \$11,771.

The third step is to find the proportion (f) of year affected by calculations.

Formula:

$$f_t = 0.50\left(\frac{E^*_{e,FIFO}}{Purchases}\right)$$

$E^*_{e,FIFO}$ = FIFO equivalent ending inventory.

Purchases = total purchases for year t.

$$f_t = 0.50\left(\frac{11{,}771}{39{,}502}\right) = 14.90\%$$

The fourth step is to discover rate of price change for the relevant part of the year (f) derived from the annual rate of price change (w), and to multiply the result times the equivalent value of FIFO inventory.

Formula:

$$\text{Adj. } E_e = (1 + w_t)^f \times E^*_{e,FIFO}$$

w = annual rate of price-level change.

f = proportion of year relating to inventory purchases.

$E^*_{e,FIFO}$ = FIFO equivalent ending inventory.

$$\text{Adj. } E_{e,t} = (1 + 0.04629)^{0.1490} \times 11{,}771 = \$11{,}851 \text{ (in thousands)}$$

Since the rate of price change for year t is 4.629%, the price change for 14.90% of the year is 0.68%. The ending inventory for year t, altered for price-level variations, is $11,851 (in thousands), which figure is entered in the financial statement in Figure 15-6.

Prepaid Expenses

Exclusive of supplies, prepaid expenses are a monetary item (although some authors disagree). Hence, for year t no adjustment supervenes. For year t - 1, the regulation procedure parallels other monetary items.

$$\$9 \times \frac{136.30}{130.27} = \$9 \text{ (in thousands)}$$

(Actually, the result $9.4, rounded to the nearest thousand, imposes no modification in the rectified statement.)

Plant, Equipment, Buildings

These fixed assets were acquired in the third quarter of year t - 5 (determined earlier in this chapter) at a cost of $18,600. Confirmed net book value hinges on accumulative depreciation rated for price-level mutations since date of acquisition (presumed third quarter of base year – 1 for illustration). The index for the third quarter of year t – 5 is figured at 97.33 (1972 = 100).

For year t – 1, the steps are:

Cost:	$\$18{,}600 \times \frac{136.30}{97.33} =$	\$26,047
Accumulated Depreciation:	$5{,}819 \times \frac{136.30}{97.33} =$	8,149
Adjusted Net Book Value$_{t-1}$:		\$17,898 (in thousands)

For year t, the process is coincident:

Cost:	$\$18{,}600 \times \frac{136.30}{97.33} =$	\$26,047
Accumulated Depreciation:	$7{,}150 \times \frac{136.30}{97.33} =$	10,013
Adjusted Net Book Value$_t$:		\$16,034 (in thousands)

Land

This translation is congruent for year t and year t – 1 since the objective is to restate all values in today's terms.

$$\$3{,}000 \times \frac{136.30}{97.33} = \$4{,}201 \text{ (in thousands)}$$

Patents, Intangibles

As with land, these items, too, are nonmonetary ones subject to a one-step correction for both years under analysis.

$$\$2{,}850 \times \frac{136.30}{97.33} = \$3{,}991 \text{ (in thousands)}$$

Notice that the last two calculations employed the same index, 97.33, which represents the year of acquisition, t – 5.

Current Liabilities

This group of items is monetary. Consequently, no adaptation is demanded for current year t, but for year t - 1 all are multiplied by the same index $\left(\frac{136.30}{130.27}\right)$.

Accounts Payable	6,809 X 1.04629 = $7,124
Notes Payable	1,500 X 1.04629 = 1,569
Accrued Expenses	34 X 1.04629 = 36
L. T. Debt (current)	830 X 1.04629 = 868
Adjusted Current Liabilities	$9,597 (in thousands)

Long Term Liabilities

Long term debt, treated no differently than current debt, invites no adjustment for year t; enlist the same index for year t - 1 $\left(\frac{136.30}{130.27}\right)$.

First Mortgage	$4,800 X 1.04629 = $ 5,022
Second Mortgage	715 X 1.04629 = 748
Bonds	4,000 X 1.04629 = 4,185
Debentures	1,000 X 1.04629 = 1,046
Adjusted Long Term Debt	$11,001 (in thousands)

Preferred Stock

This entry, considered monetary because it is carried at par value rather than market value which, presumably, would otherwise reflect price-level shifts, calls for no adjustment for year t. For year t - 1,

$$\$500 \times \frac{136.30}{130.27} = \$523 \text{ (in thousands)}$$

Stockholders' Equity

Retained earnings and common stock, although they are nonmonetary items, need no restatment because they are treated as residual entries, that is, the adjusting entry that balances the balance sheet.

The results, then, appear in Figure 15–6, and comparative balance sheets restated in current terms highlight strengths and weaknesses of individual items in the firm's finances. At the bottom stand out several ratios which suggest either further deterioration or improvement over ratio analysis in Chapter Twelve. Obviously, some ratios will not be sensitive to price-level changes; others will flash different signals depending upon assumptions.

OTHER ADJUSTMENT ISSUES

Neither are all situations dealt with in the example nor adequately handled within the framework of this chapter, but two general cases are touched on below: accelerated depreciation and replacement cost accounting.

Accelerated Depreciation

In the illustration HHHM, Inc. employed straight line depreciation; we found the average age of assets dividing accumulated depreciation by annual depreciation. Had the firm used an accelerated method of depreciation such as sum-of-the-years'-digits (SYD) or double declining balance (DDB), the straight line technique would have overstated estimated age of depreciable assets. Davidson and Weil* have developed tables with age-reducing factors, reproduced in Tables XXI and XXII in the Appendix, to translate, in three steps, asset age from straight line to accelerated depreciation.

The first step is to approximate asset age assuming straight line method of depreciation. Suppose that accumulated depreciation equals 43,410, current year charges 6,394; the average age is $\frac{43{,}410}{6{,}394} = 6.789$ years.

The second step is to ascertain the growth rate (g) of assets approximated by:

Formula:

$$g = \sqrt[n]{\frac{A_t}{A_{t-n}}} - 1$$

A_t = depreciation charges for current year.

A_{t-n} = depreciation charges for n years ago.

n = year closest to average age found under straight line calculations.

For example, posit that current year depreciation expenses (A_t) amount to

---

*Sidney Davidson and Roman L. Weil, "Inflation Accounting: What Will General Price Level Adjusted Income Statements Show?" *Financial Analysts Journal* (Jan./Feb., 1975), 70–1.

6,394 and 7 years ago (n), nearest to 6.789 years, is 3,852. The approximate growth rate of assets is:

$$g = \sqrt[7]{\frac{6{,}394}{3{,}862}} - 1 = 7.5\%$$

The third step is first find the corresponding factor in the tables. (Assume DDB method.) In Table XXI, one-half the distance between 5% and 10%, when n equals 7, is 0.8079. Next multiply this factor (f) times number of years found above.

Formula: Average Age of Assets = f X n

= 0.8079 X 6.789 = 5.485 years

To adjust for depreciation expenses employ the quarterly price index applicable 5.485 years ago and correct depreciation charges by the same technique illustrated earlier in the chapter.

Replacement Cost Accounting

Principles of accounting, as well as most other areas of endeavor and investigation, based on a set of assumptions, are useful as long as assumptions are strictly stated, understood, and adhered to. General price-level accounting, useful within named restrictions, presumes additional suppositions as well. Certainly there are shortcomings, the principal one of which is it ignores opportunity costs (see Chapter Six) and alternatives that a manager faces in decision-making. Because different assumptions render divergent results, price-level accounting is not totally reliable for comparative purposes. Like normal accounting, data derived from historical figures are simply restated in current year's terms. One suggested alternative is replacement cost accounting.

Replacement cost accounting restates nonmonetary items in terms of their current replacement costs. (LIFO represents such a restatement.) However, this method, which has limited support outside of government circles, led Texas Instruments, Inc. to add to their annual report: "In the opinion of management the above information [based on replacement cost accounting] does not reflect all the effects of inflation, other economic factors or the company's operating philosophy and, accordingly, is of limited if any usefulness," which about sums up the criticisms.

There are several criticisms. One is that it causes distortions, because replacing total capacity with new equipment not only involves a highly unlikely managerial decision (see "Marginal Analysis" in Chapter Six) but is physically impossible. Too, replacement cost accounting ignores changes in values of monetary items, which are at least covered in price-level accounting. Again we see that different results emerge under alternative sets of assumptions making industry-wide comparison not feasible. Similarly, if old equipment is replaced, there are other issues involving improvement in efficiency and productivity and lowering of costs and taxes. In other words, the outcome is expensively produced information of potentially misleading and dubious value.

On the positive side, industries with rapidly developing technology are less affected than those with stagnant technology because equipment is newer. In some industries information generated is comparable where companies have similar assets and have closely coordinated their approach to cost replacement valuations. Some examples include: railroads, utilities, textiles, retail, automotive, trucking, airline, cement, lodging, aerospace. Alternatively, all financial statement items, domestic and foreign, could be stated in terms of grains of gold at time of acquisition and final figures restated at the free market price of gold on statement date. Somehow it seems to improve on using inflated currencies as the numeraire.

CONTENTS

Chapter Sixteen: Programming the Computer to Maximize Gains, Minimize Losses

SIXTEEN

Programming the Computer to Maximize Gains, Minimize Losses

The first 15 chapters centered on profitable methods to aggregate, evaluate, analyze, and interpret data for more beneficial financial analysis and decision-making by successful investors and managers. This last chapter focuses on how to do it faster.

Electronic data processing in business involves repetitive cycles. For management decisions, where time horizons influence profits, larger quantities of data processed within a shorter span of time can be evaluated to answer specific questions, prepare tables, control processes, or to simulate outcomes under different probable conditions. Twenty years ago it was widely believed that computers would replace employees, handle routine decisions, and free top management from making intuitive judgements so that they could rely entirely on "pure facts." Whether facts are pure or not, these science-fiction fantasies imparted powers to computers which did (and do) not match reality. Nevertheless, computers efficiently assist in solving most financial problems discussed in previous chapters of this handbook, where quantities of output are more quickly handled by machine rather than by hand. Although a financial manager will not need be programmer, or mathematician, to enjoy advantages springing from computer use, this chapter simply explains fundamentals of certain basic techniques to increase profitable utilization of computers.

AUTOMATED DECISION-MAKING

Electronic data processing deals with systems and processes; decision-making, too, is a systematized procedure that follows about the same logic each time.

Step 1: Recognition that a problem exists or that a decision must be made.

Or what today is widely referred to as awareness. There are two prominent hurdles in the decision-making process—the first step and next-to-last step. Decision-making is not restricted to actions of chief operating officers, divisional managers, or even to businesses and financial institutions. Moreover, the first step for individual or committee decisions must be adequately dealt with or control over the decision will shift to others. Notice that the problem does not disappear but that if the individual is now aware of it, his failure to act in his favor grants someone else the opportunity to take over the decision process. Occasionally computers can signal pending difficulties through model-building and simulation by highlighting possible bottlenecks or low payoff options.

Step 2: Accumulation and evaluation of data and information surrounding the problem (or issue).

In some instances Step 2 may be part and parcel of Step 1 especially if the issue emerges initially from data sifting. Nevertheless, arrogation of additional facts and opinions are ancillary to study of the problem. Where data are scattered and inputs originate in many departments at different levels (cash budgets, for example), such information can be sorted and stored in the computer while Step 3 action takes place.

Step 3: Evaluation of other feasible options and alternative strategies.

That is, not an initial yes-or-no at Step 1 or 2, but: What other options are available to us? Step 3 requires repetition of Step 2 for each alternative examined, then sort, store and evaluate the data, which leads to Step 4.

Step 4: Perception of risk—the chance that actual future results will deviate by some amount from predicted ones.

Risk analysis deals in probabilities and data inputs are usually more opinion than fact when confronting the future so that the computer's efficiency really becomes evident at this point as each strategy is evaluated according to perceived risks at each stage in the process and a probability distribution of each possible outcome links each option with Step 5.

Step 5: Selection of a strategy or alternative.

Choosing an alternative does not necessarily imply a final decision because other variables may affect timing and implementation of the chosen alternative as well as coordination with other activities of the enterprise, or Step 5 and 6 may combine.

Step 6: Action.

Without action expensive planning and wise analysis of information lead to nowhere. This hurdle has led managers of households, investment portfolios, speculators, businesses, institutions, and other enterprisers to downfall because Step 6 cannot be avoided. Inaction is a negative form of action. Inaction implies a decision has been made—a decision to not act positively in a certain direction. On the other hand, inaction *can be* a form of positive action when done purposefully and assertively. Although a computer will probably not be programmed to perform Step 6 (it can be, of course), the instrument is valuable in Step 7.

Step 7: Reevaluation of action taken in 6.

Step 7 may be omitted, and frequently is when decisions turn sour (How many can bear the pain of reviewing failures?), but successful managers review both good and bad experiences to extract whatever lessons are relevant to future situations. Once again, the computer is a money-saving resource to quickly rerun stored data and to even reevaluate successful decisions to ascertain whether an even more profitable course could have been foreseen and followed. Computers can be employed to trace interrelationships of hundreds of thousands of possibilities faster than any hand calculations to at least eliminate least profitable alternatives.

So what happened to predictions of two decades or more ago? More data, *more employees* in the aggregate—and the myth of massive technological unemployment is exploded (if history is accurately perceived). Making routine decisions has triggered research of further simplification of business processes which, contrary to popular belief, has encouraged more hiring of *less skilled,* less educated, while demand for employees with 4-to-6 years of college has diminished relative to projections. And the intuition criticism? Intuition seems not to have disappeared from the decision-making process when dealing with unquantifiable unknowns.

Certainly some decision-making can be adequately accommodated by automated processes. The formulas, tables, and techniques contribute to achieving better, faster, more profitable decisions at a higher level of sophistication. For a small quantity of data, analyzed on a one-time basis, the hand calculator may still be the cheapest approach. On the other hand, if data covering most topics and decisions brought out in this handbook can be automated, then why bother referring to any handbook? Or if the company mathematician, statistical economist, and computer programmer will supply technical abilities, why even be concerned with this chapter on computers?

Of course, no successful manager will be asking these questions. The unsuccessful ones will not even have this volume within reach (physical or mental). Naturally, individuals who deal directly with material highlighted in this book are aware of its usefulness. But others, who have only occasional need to check out a topic in these pages will soon recognize, as they successfully reach for their goals, that even fractional knowledge of a concept enhances grasp of significance of data. To those individuals the remainder of this chapter is aimed.

LINEAR PROGRAMMING

Linear, of course, means arranged in a line, or described mathematically by terms of the first degree. *Linear programming* is a method to *maximize* or *minimize* a given linear function on a set defined by a system of linear inequalities usually requiring non-negative variables. In other words, it is a field of mathematics that deals with simple, straight line relationships (although there may be numerous relationships) which can be evaluated by a computer, that is, a technique for model-building or simulation; however, not all linear programs have solutions.

Simulation is a technique to work out many possible results under hypothetical conditions; the computer furnishes a cheaper means of manipulating factors, expressed in sets of linear equations, to observe possible outcomes within constraints of the model. The purpose of linear programming is to derive *optimum* solutions to problems such as minimization of costs or maximization of output or profits given limited resources (time, capital, labor, land, etc.). The optimum, or best, solution overrides all other possibilities because no other solution produces lower costs or higher profits, for example. Linear programming aids in discovering the optimum solution without the necessity of evaluating every possible solution. The following graphic solution illustrates operation of linear programming logic.

Graphic Solution

In a simplified demonstration, posit that a manufacturer of children's furniture, Tot-N-Toddlers, Inc. discovers that excess capacity exists for short periods every week so that equipment must either set idle for brief periods or be employed in alternative endeavors. For short periods, when machinery and labor services are not directed to the main line of operations, productive facilities can produce either table-top book cases or spice racks (or some combination of these two items). Manufacturing facilities are substitutable for output of one product or the other although time required for each step in the manufacturing process of each item is not identical.

The four basic steps to manufacture either wooden book holders or spice racks are: cutting, assembling, finishing, packaging. Produced and packaged in units of one gross, time required (in minutes for completion of each step) for production of one unit (one gross) is summarized in Figure 16-1. Each unit of book holders contributes $10.50 to profits; each unit of spice racks contributes $14 to profits. That is, after covering direct manufacturing costs, marginal analysis (see Chapter Six for a discussion of marginal analysis) indicates that the foregoing contribution figures are appropriate within present range of sales.

Figure 16-1

	Production Time per Unit (in minutes)			
Process	*Books*	*Spices*	*Ratio*	*Time Available per Week (in minutes)*
#1 Cut	8	14	1.75:1	112
#2 Assemble	20	24	1.20:1	240
#3 Finish	12	14	1.17:1	168
#4 Package	12	12	1.00:1	180

In Figure 16–1, to assemble one unit (one gross) of book racks requires 20 minutes of production time; to assemble one unit of spice racks requires 24 minutes. That is, in a given 24-minute interval, an equivalent 1.2 units of book racks can be assembled for each unit of spice racks. In fact the firm is more efficient in every step of the process in book rack production; on the other hand, spice racks contribute more to profits. Because varying amounts of time are available for each process, the solution calls for finding the best combination of output given constraints of time with the objective of profit maximization.

The graph in Figure 16–2 depicts various production possibilities of process #1, cutting, which assumes a constant rate of resource substitution of 1.75:1. The vertical axis of the graph registers units of book rack production; the horizontal axis records spice rack output. At one extreme, given the time restriction of 112 minutes available, Tot-N-Toddlers, Inc. (TNT) can turn out 14 units of unassembled book racks per week but 0 production of spice racks, designated point P in the diagram. At the other extreme, if all spare resources turn to spice rack production, then 8 spice racks and 0 book racks are cut per week, point Q. That is, weekly cutting within a time constraint of 112 minutes range from 0 to 14 units of book racks, 0 to 8 units of spice racks, some intermediate combination of book and spice racks such as point R, or none of each.

Moreover, output is not limited to some point along the line PRQ; production can occur at any point on or to the left of the line (represented by the shaded area), such as point S. Anywhere along the line or to the left of it represent production possibilities; i.e., the line signals extreme points possible within the time constraint. Any place to the right of the line, such as point T, exemplifies an unattainable goal within the 112-minute time limitation. Point T is not a viable alternative; likewise point S, and all other combinations to the left of the line are rejected as inadequate production levels or inefficient uses of resources. In other words, point R overrides point S if the same amount of time is involved in producing either a smaller (less efficient) output at S or the greater (more efficient) volume at R. Or, if resources are efficiently employed in both cases, then at point S, unutilized capacity remains, and points PRQ are preferable combinations which will contribute more to profits.

Which production possibility is desired? Since there are three suppletory processes necessary before the finished products hit the streets, these are added to the diagram, Figure 16–3, by the same logic as process #1. Two problems appear. One is that each process demands different times to completion, and, two, the amount of free time bears no direct relationship to need in each step. Whatever viable product combination is selected there will be unused capacity somewhere in the plant. Although some combination along production possibilities curve #4 is desired, insufficient capacity (time) in steps #1, 2, and 3 make this an uneconomical or impractical alternative.

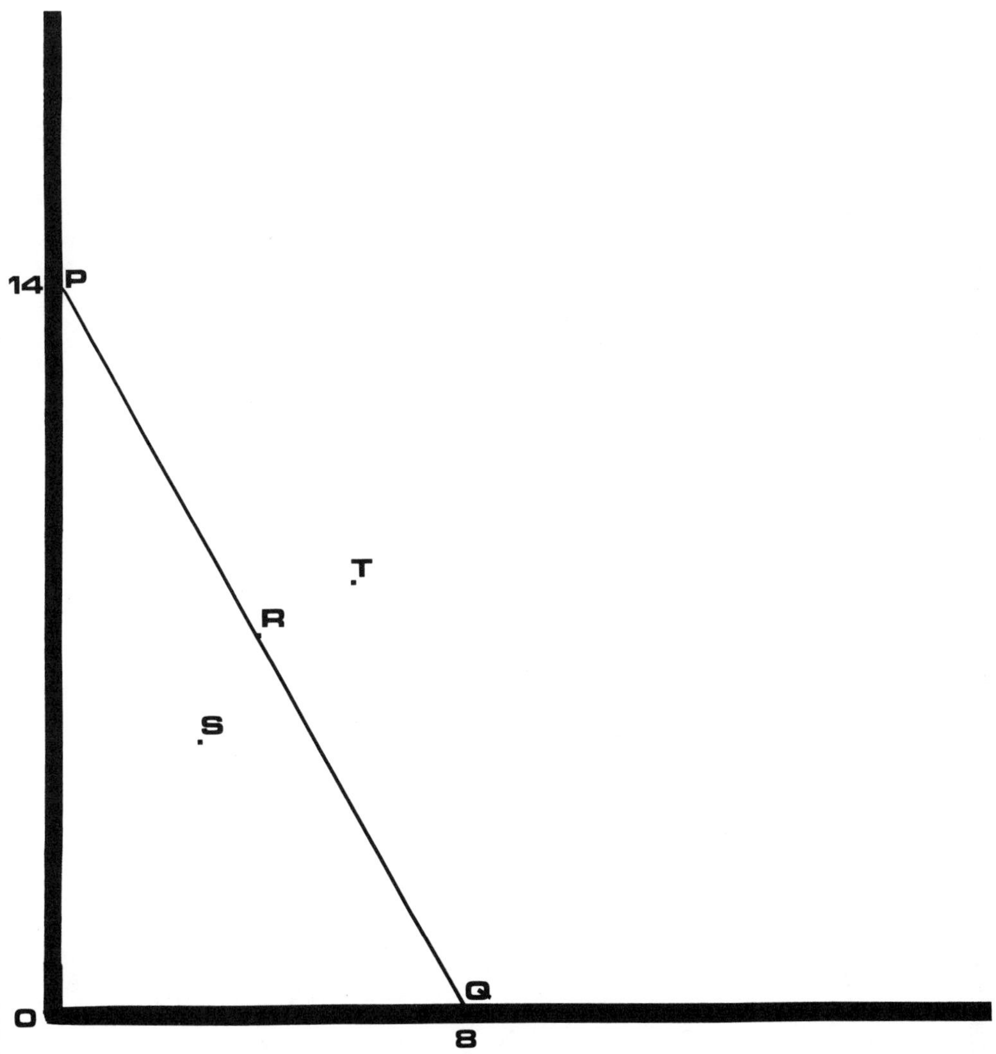

Figure 16-2

Before proceeding to Figure 16–4, let's examine the "profit line" designated in Figure 16–3. This profit line, while fictitious, denotes the exchange relationship between book and spice racks, viz., $10.50-to-$14. If 15 units of spice racks are available for sale, each unit contributing $14, total addition to profit will be $210. To draw a constant profit line, we ask: How many units of book racks will aggregate $210 at $10.50 each? Twenty units, of course, provide the second point, on the vertical axis. The connecting line concatenates various sales combinations that will yield a constant $210.

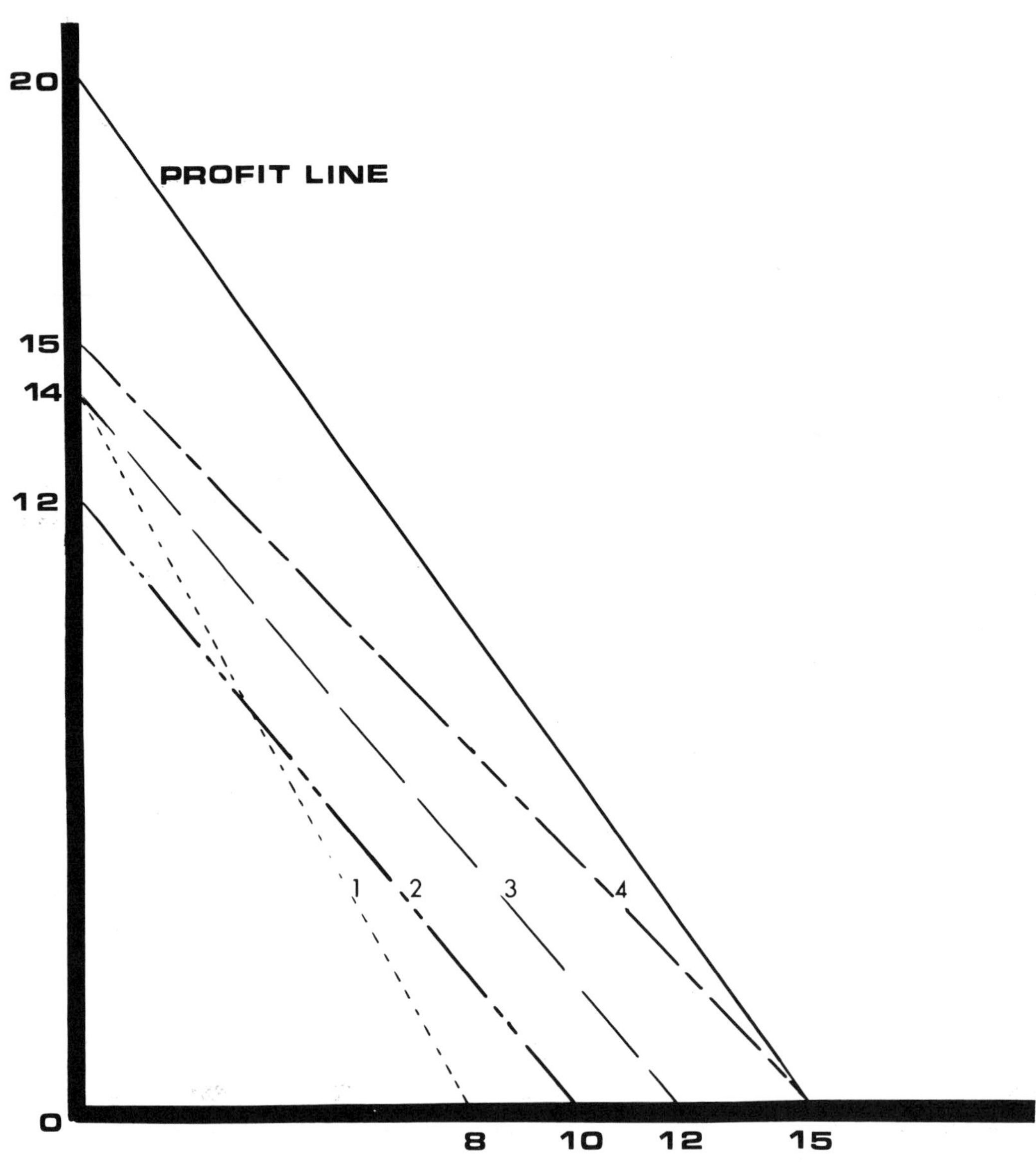

Figure 16-3

Naturally, this profit level is unattainable. Because the ratio of book-to-spice racks remains constant over the production range under consideration, the appropriate profit line will parallel and be drawn to the left of the hypothetical one.

In examining Figure 16–4, notice that a heavy solid line traces part of process line #2 and continues downward along line #1. The set of possible

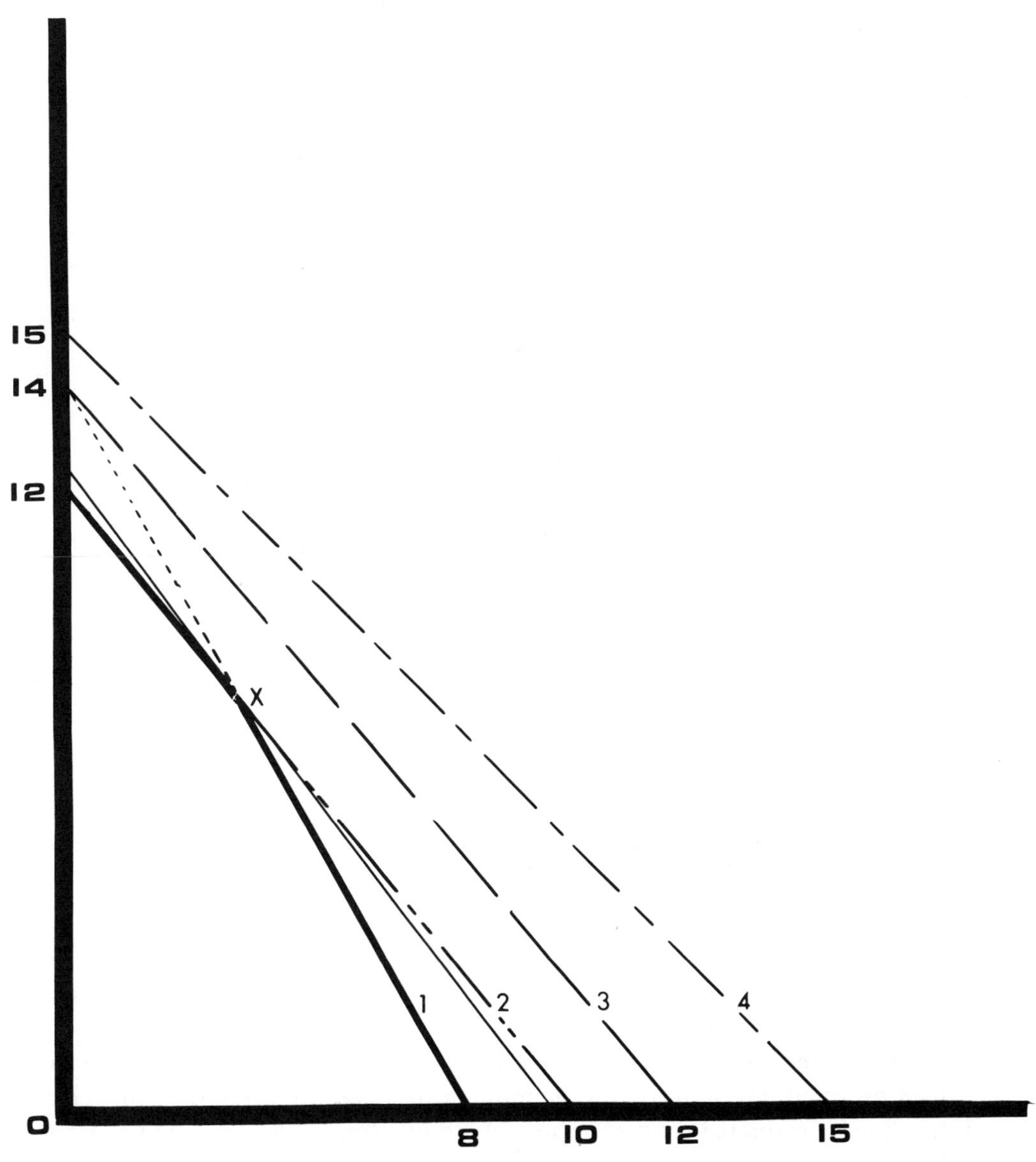

Figure 16-4

solutions, given the time restraint, lay within the enclosed area. The most efficient combinations lie along this frontier which defines the extremities of this set. The final question focuses on that combination which *maximizes* contribution to profits. We already know that the preferred solution lies along this curve, but some combinations are more profitable than others.

Drawing a new, parallel profit line so that it is tangent to the efficiency frontier of feasible combinations, it touches point X, which suggests an output of book racks in the 7-to-8 range and of spice racks in the 4-to-3 range. (We assume the acceptable answer must be in whole, not broken, units.) If 8 units of book racks and 3 of spice racks are sold, the contribution to profits will be:

$$\begin{aligned}\pi_c &= 8B + 3S \\ &= 8(\$10.50) + 3(\$14) = \$126.\end{aligned}$$

A combination of 7B and 4S will yield:

$$\pi_c = 7(\$10.50) + 4(\$14) = \$129.50$$

the better result.

Of course, every time we add 1S and drop 1B, results will improve by $3.50, but the rate of substitution between book and spice racks is not constant 1-to-1. If it were, then 6B and 5S would be even better:

$$\pi_c = 6B + 5S = \$133.$$

But such combination falls beyond the range of possibilities unless steps #1 and 2 are eliminated in the productive process, while production of 7 book and 4 spice racks (allowing for slight margin of favorable error) is possible and yields the highest contribution to profits, given the price relationships of $10.50-to-$14 per unit.

Mathematical Programming

This problem can be solved by trial-and-error, or graphically, but even with 3 products and 4 processes the number of possibilities rapidly multiply. More than 3 products becomes impossible to illustrate in a graph, and solving for 6 or 10 products would require an enormous amount of time for calculations. High speeds of computers fractionalize evaluation time once the program is established and relationships remain linear.

Linear programming indicates that given a number of unknowns subject to linear inequalities, find the nonnegative value that maximizes (or the objective may be to minimize in other cases) a linear function of the objective function within conditions stated.

Setting our objectives and limitations in mathematical terms, the relevant set of expressions are:

Maximize $\$10.50\ B + \$14.00\ S = \pi_c$ (profit contribution)

Subject to

$$8\ B + 14\ S \leqslant 112 \text{ (cutting)}$$

$$20\ B + 24\ S \leqslant 240 \text{ (assembling)}$$

$$12\ B + 14\ S \leqslant 168 \text{ (finishing)}$$

$$12\ B + 12\ S \leqslant 180 \text{ (packaging)}$$

$$B \geqslant 0$$

$$S \geqslant 0$$

The above set of expressions describes a mathematical *model* that relates to the weekly production of book and spice racks within constraints of time. Through linear programming we can manipulate these expressions in such a way so as to maximize contribution to profits. In a linearly programmed model, cost information is sometimes called *shadow prices.* Each constraint has a shadow price that mirrors the cost of not relaxing the constraint. The cost of time restrictions on steps #1 and 2 in the production process is output foregone and, consequently, not sold. If more time is allowable to steps #1 and 2, without negatively affecting regular plant operations, a higher output and profit contribution become possible.

Using linear programming in portfolio analysis, typical constraints include yield, price-earnings ratio, risk, amount of funds available for investment. For example, assume that an optimum portfolio of Wolverine International, S.A. has an expected return of 15%, risk constraint is set at 10% of current market value. Each constraint has a shadow price; i.e., what is the cost of *not* relaxing the constraint? Suppose, in this case, the shadow price of the risk constraint is 4. If risk level is permitted to rise to 11%, expected performance of the portfolio would rise by 4%, to 19%. The value of this technique is to pinpoint restrictions which are too costly to entertain. A yield-to-risk tradeoff of 4-to-1, suggests that diversification limits on the investment portfolio may be advantageously revised.

FLOW CHARTING

Planning and management of resources, requiring frequent assessment of alternatives, is aided through model-building provided that (a) the model replicates reasonably well real world situations and (b) it is remembered that the model is an abstraction constructed on a set of assumptions. The model then can be programmed to simulate various outcomes as assumptions are changed. A model is not predictive but sets forth what will happen if real world conditions approximate those of the model.

For example, earlier chapters in this handbook discussed investment options under varying cost and benefit conditions. In Chapter Fourteen a new dimension to risk was added to multinational operations—devaluations and revaluations. Under various cost and profit conditions, net asset exposure can be computed. Multiplying net exposure times the devaluation results in calculated devaluation losses. Flow charts, a diagram of the sequence by which various steps in a program are executed, define the problem to facilitate computer programming and for future reference record the nature of the program.

Various standard symbols for flow charting facilitate communications by normalizing readily recognizable shapes. These are described in Figure 16-5.

Figure 16-5

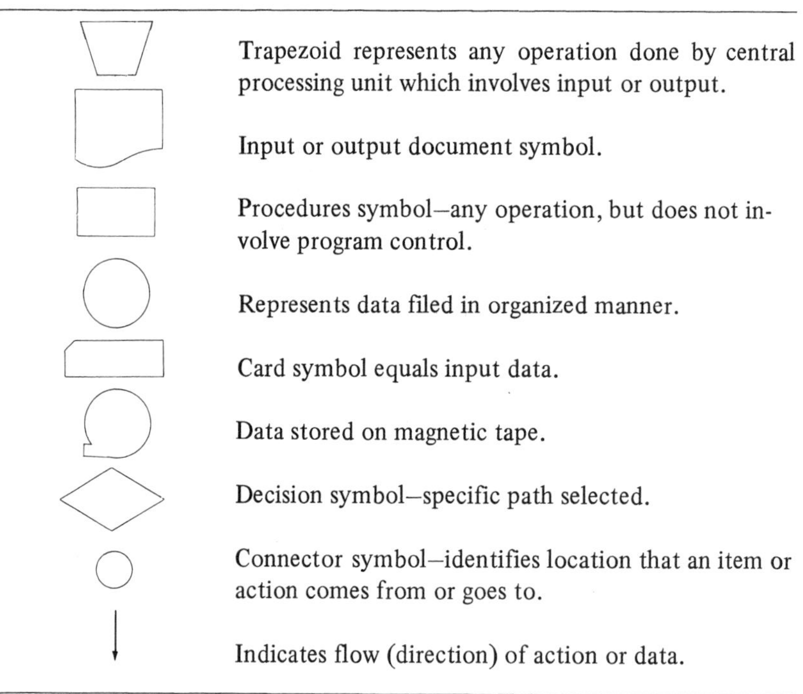

DECISION TABLES

An alternative and/or companion to flow charts, *decision tables* attempt to overcome any deficiencies of flow charts in systems designs. Procedures preciously and subsequently illustrated are *computational* and require some comprehension of mathematical notations to visualize steps within procedures. *Logical* information procedures, before the advent of modern computers, abutted on the vernacular for expression. Decision tables rely on a "if . . . then" approach. *If* the weather forecaster predicts rain, *then* operate rule #1 (carry an umbrella). That is, if it rains, activate rule #1, if it snows rule #2 applies, but if the sun shines exercise rule #3. In creating a decision table, list *conditions* vertically and *actions* horizontally. The table layout in Figure 16–6 illustrates a simple case of rule application in which "0" designates a no reaction and "1" yes, except where reference is made to other tables or procedures. Reading across, if merchandise is sold for cash then do what rule #1 requires . . . but do not do what rule #2 states, or if it is a credit sale from an established account rule #3 applies. New account transactions are handled according to procedure #7. Followed by an asterisk it means to complete procedure #7, then return to the next line in the table. The last line of each rule ties in with the number of the next table.

This simple decision table demonstrates that conditions and actions remain separate. Additionally, the set of conditions specified by each rule must avoid ambiguity; i.e., *equivalent* sets of conditions cannot lead to different actions but *different* conditions can reasonably lead to the same action. Naturally, proliferation of redundant rules is inefficient.

Figure 16–6

Item	*Rule 1* *Cash*	*Rule 2* *Cash*	*Rule 3* *Credit*	*Rule 4* *Credit*
Merchandise Sales	1	0	1	0
New Accounts	P 7*	P 7*	P 7*	P 7*
Tax on Local Sales (mdse.)	0	1	0	1
Tax on Labor Services (local)	1	0	1	0
Tax on Out-of-State Labor	0	0	0	1
Government Contracts	0	0	1	0
Exports	P 8	P 8	P 9	P 9
Go to Table	3	3	3	3

Parallel testing denotes that all conditions within a rule are tested at once to discern whether the rule bears upon a specific situation in the data. However, rules need not be executed in the 1-2-3-4 sequence indicated.

Decision tables were organized as a logical method for problem solving but they can also be used as a programming language. The *if* statement can order the computer to *perform* certain functions or encompass a *go to* statement to send program control to any decision table. A perform statement means that all data are processed under decision rules relating to a particular table; and program control can be sent to another table, then returned to the main program. Routine matters can be evaluated and processed while others are diverted for special handling, cost factors notwithstanding.

OTHER TECHNIQUES OF PROGRAMMING

Although linear programming is the most widely used tool of analysis and evaluation, other techniques, discussed cursorily below, exist.

Nonlinear Programming

A great many business and financial problems can be adapted for solution by linear programming. Nevertheless, stochastic models are practical for a number of problems dealing with *random variables.* A random variable, also known as stochastic or chance variable, can assume a number of values with given probabilities. *Stochastic programming* is an attempt to optimize random variables. Another technique, *dynamic programming,* is employed in analysis of sequential decision problems.

A number of portfolio models employ *quadratic programming* to find optimal solutions whenever X^2 appears in the problem. The objective of these models is to maximize portfolio return subject to a risk constraint. Risk is defined as variance, a quadratic, of return. (Review Chapter Five on risk and variance.) Riskier investments exhibit higher variances; i.e., the uncertainty of achieving expected return is greater. Defining risk in mathematical terms allows use of a mathematical model that explicitly embodies risk in optimization computations.

Parametric Programming

The levels of constraints fix maximum range of solutions. In the above portfolio return vs. risk example, relaxing the risk constraint means that additional or riskier (higher variance) investments raise the potential expected return on portfolio. With *parametric programming* relationships between levels of constraints and yield, for example, can be systematically explored.

Integer Programming

A special form of linear programming that would have lent itself well to the book and spice rack problem is *integer programming,* where values of the variables must be integers (i.e., whole numbers). In the TNT problem, solution called for whole lots (fractional lots being uneconomical). If the solution under linear programming had simply been rounded up, the less favorable result of 8 book and 3 spice racks would have been printed. Desiring optimum fruits from labor, the integer requirement must be built into the problem (rather than approximated after the fact); hence, the value of integer programming emerges. While this approach may have less application in investment portfolio research, it can be profitably applied in *personnel selection* and deployment, resource, *research* and development *allocations, capital budgeting,* for example.

PERT

When applicable historical inputs are unavailable for prediction, comparison information can be generated by projection methods such as *Program Evaluation and Review Technique* (PERT), which sunders a project into subgroups, i.e., a system for planning and control of interrelated activities. Referring again to the TNT problem, management might ask: When should we begin process #1 (cutting) for it to be completed before process #2 (assembling) begins since #2 depends upon completion of #1, and process #2 must be completed before #3 (finishing) and, subsequently, #4 (packaging) can start.

PERT expresses the interrelationships of these different processes necessary for final output with the use of a *network,* a pictograph of activities and estimated time to complete the project or achieve the final result. For example, in construction a contractor obviously will not engage certain subcontractors until the project reaches a certain stage. The pictograph highlights bottlenecks and minimum time necessary to bring sub-projects to fruition in order to maximize efficiency.

CPM

Closely related to PERT, the *Critical Path Method* (CPM), a mathematical approach to compare time and costs required to complete a project against time and costs of a crash program to achieve the same outcomes, refers to the path through the network which defines the shortest feasible time within which project completion can be accomplished.

COMPUTER REGRESSION PROGRAMMING

Regression analysis is used to develop equations needed to predict the *dependent variable* from values of the *independent variable,* or, how to express the relationship between two variables. In a simple case developing a straight line equation with one independent variable, Wolfcry Pet Accessories, Ltd. (WPA) wishes to predict next year's sales of hamster and gerbil food based on retail store sales of these rodents. A scatter diagram is developed in which historical rodent sales (lagged by 3 months) are measured on the horizontal axis and H & G food sales on the vertical axis. To develop a predictive model with a regression application, we need to establish a criterion for determining the best fit for the predicting equation, expressed in the general form:

$$y = a + bx$$

It is desirable that deviations between predicted values and values of dependent variables be minimal. One method of fitting an equation to data is the *least squares method,* which will determine the coefficients of the equation making the sum of the squares of deviations minimal.

A computer regression program* attempts to locate the linear combination of interactions of functions of independent variables that explains best the behavior of the dependent variable. Where interactions of variables are elevated only to the primal powers of independent variables, the program would attempt to fit a linear equation in the form:

$$y = b_o + b_1x_1 + b_2x_2 + \ldots + b_nx_n$$

or elevated to first and second powers in more complex cases:

$$y = b_o + b_1x_1 + b_2x_1^2 + b_3x_2 + \ldots + b_{2n}x_n^2$$

The program may specify powers and roots of independent variables or generate them randomly in the absence of other fundamental factors.

The problem now relates to determination of various b_1 values. For example, state interactions as Z_1, defined as:

$$Z_1 = x_1$$
$$Z_2 = x_2$$
$$Z_3 = x_1^2$$
$$Z_4 = x_1x_2^2 \text{ etc.}$$

To select the single Z_i that best predicts Y, calculate the correlation coefficient between Z_i and Y and choose the Z_i with the largest coefficient. For example, say that Z_4 is selected; ergo, the predicting equation takes the initial form:

*Cf. Wilbert Steffy, Thomas Zearley, and Jack Strunk. *Financial Ratio Analysis—An Effective Management Tool.* Ann Arbor: Institute of Science and Technology, University of Michigan, 1974.

$$Y = b_o + b_4 x_1 x_2^2$$

Compute the constant (b_o) and coefficient (b_4) so that the least squares criterion is satisfied.

After computing an important factor for each variable in the equation, the smallest factor is matched against the minimum level of importance necessary to keep the term in the equation. Then variables not already in the equation are evaluated and the potential importance factor is determined for each one. These factors signal the possible contribution of each variable to interpret any unexplained variance in the dependent variable. The largest factor is isolated and evaluated in terms of criteria established by the user.

For example, posit that Z_3 is the valid term. Other Z_s are examined to find the one with the highest potential importance factor. Assume that Z_4 is selected. The new predicting equation is:

$$Y = \overline{b_o} + \overline{b_3 x_1^2} + b_4 x_1 x_2^2$$

(Bars indicate new values of constants which satisfies the least squares criterion.)

Now with the new equation the same search and match process is repeated to bring forth new terms until all significant terms are included. At end of processing, the computer calculates and prints out the standard error of Y, coefficient of determination, multiple correlation coefficient, together with a table that relates actual and predicted values of Y for each set of data. These are some of the ways in which computers aid in profitable decision-making. End of program.

APPENDIX

CONTENTS

Sources

TABLES XVIII–XX:	Data provided by the Federal Reserve Bank of St. Louis
TABLES XXI–XXII:	Sidney Davidson, Clyde P. Stickney, and Roman L. Weil, *Inflation Accounting: A Guide for the Accountant and Financial Analyst* (New York: McGraw-Hill Book Company, 1976), pp. 126–7. © 1976. McGraw-Hill Book Company, by permission.
TABLES XXIV–XXV:	Simpson, Pirenian, Crenshaw, Riner, *Mathematics of Finance,* 4th edition, © 1969. Prentice-Hall, Inc., by permission.

Table I

SINGLE PAYMENT OF 1 AT COMPOUND INTEREST

n	⅛%	¼%	½%	7/12%	n
1	1.00125000	1.00250000	1.00500000	1.00583333	1
2	1.00250156	1.00500063	1.01002500	1.01170069	2
3	1.00375469	1.00751877	1.01507513	1.01760228	3
4	1.00500938	1.01003756	1.02015050	1.02353830	4
5	1.00626565	1.01256266	1.02525125	1.02950894	5
6	1.00752348	1.01509406	1.03037751	1.03551440	6
7	1.00878288	1.01763180	1.03552940	1.04155490	7
8	1.01004386	1.02017588	1.04070704	1.04763064	8
9	1.01130641	1.02272632	1.04591058	1.05374182	9
10	1.01257055	1.02528313	1.05114013	1.05988865	10
11	1.01383626	1.02784334	1.05639583	1.06607133	11
12	1.01510356	1.03041596	1.06167781	1.07229008	12
13	1.01637244	1.03299200	1.06698620	1.07854511	13
14	1.01764290	1.03557448	1.07232113	1.08483662	14
15	1.01891496	1.03816341	1.07768274	1.09116483	15
16	1.02018860	1.04075882	1.08307115	1.09752996	16
17	1.02146383	1.04336072	1.08848651	1.10393222	17
18	1.02274066	1.04596912	1.09392894	1.11037182	18
19	1.02401909	1.04858404	1.09939858	1.11684899	19
20	1.02529911	1.05120550	1.10489558	1.12336395	20
21	1.02658074	1.05383352	1.11042006	1.12991690	21
22	1.02786396	1.05646810	1.11597216	1.13650808	22
23	1.02914879	1.05910927	1.12155202	1.14313771	23
24	1.03043523	1.06175704	1.12715978	1.14980602	24
25	1.03172327	1.06441144	1.13279558	1.15651322	25

Table I—continued

SINGLE PAYMENT OF 1 AT COMPOUND INTEREST

n	1/8%	1/4%	1/2%	7/12%
26	1.03301293	1.06707247	1.13845955	1.16325955
27	1.03430419	1.06974015	1.14415185	1.17004523
28	1.03559707	1.07241450	1.14987261	1.17687049
29	1.03689157	1.07509553	1.15562197	1.18373557
30	1.03818769	1.07778327	1.16140008	1.19064069
31	1.03948542	1.08047773	1.16720708	1.19758610
32	1.04078478	1.08317892	1.17304312	1.20457202
33	1.04208576	1.08588687	1.17890833	1.21159869
34	1.04338836	1.08860159	1.18480288	1.21866634
35	1.04469260	1.09132309	1.19072689	1.22577523
36	1.04599847	1.09405140	1.19668052	1.23292559
37	1.04730596	1.09678653	1.20266393	1.24011765
38	1.04861510	1.09952850	1.20867725	1.24735167
39	1.04992587	1.10227732	1.21472063	1.25462789
40	1.05123827	1.10503301	1.22079424	1.26194655
41	1.05255232	1.10779559	1.22689821	1.26930791
42	1.05386801	1.11056508	1.23303270	1.27671220
43	1.05518535	1.11334149	1.23919786	1.28415969
44	1.05650433	1.11612485	1.24539385	1.29165062
45	1.05782496	1.11891516	1.25162082	1.29918525
46	1.05914724	1.12171245	1.25787892	1.30676383
47	1.06047117	1.12451673	1.26416832	1.31438662
48	1.06179676	1.12732802	1.27048916	1.32205388
49	1.06312401	1.13014634	1.27684161	1.32976586
50	1.06445291	1.1329717 1	1.28322581	1.33752283

Table I—continued

SINGLE PAYMENT OF 1 AT COMPOUND INTEREST

n	1/8%	1/4%	1/2%	7/12%
51	1.06578348	1.13580414	1.28964194	1.34532504
52	1.06711571	1.13864365	1.29609015	1.35317277
53	1.06844960	1.14149026	1.30257060	1.36106628
54	1.06978517	1.14434398	1.30908346	1.36900583
55	1.07112240	1.14720484	1.31562887	1.37699170
56	1.07246130	1.15007285	1.32220702	1.38502415
57	1.07380188	1.15294804	1.32881805	1.39310346
58	1.07514413	1.15583041	1.33546214	1.40122990
59	1.07648806	1.15871998	1.34213946	1.40940374
60	1.07783367	1.16161678	1.34885015	1.41762526
61	1.07918096	1.16452082	1.35559440	1.42589474
62	1.08052994	1.16743213	1.36237238	1.43421246
63	1.08188060	1.17035071	1.36918424	1.44257870
64	1.08323295	1.17327658	1.37603016	1.45099374
65	1.08458699	1.17620977	1.38291031	1.45945787
66	1.08594273	1.17915030	1.38982486	1.46797138
67	1.08730015	1.18209817	1.39677399	1.47653454
68	1.08865928	1.18505342	1.40375785	1.48514766
69	1.09002010	1.18801605	1.41077664	1.49381102
70	1.09138263	1.19098609	1.41783053	1.50252492
71	1.09274686	1.19396356	1.42491968	1.51128965
72	1.09411279	1.19694847	1.43204428	1.52010550
73	1.09548043	1.19994084	1.43920450	1.52897279
74	1.09684978	1.20294069	1.44640052	1.53789179
75	1.09822084	1.20594804	1.45363252	1.54686283

Table I—continued

SINGLE PAYMENT OF 1 AT COMPOUND INTEREST

n	1/8%	1/4%	1/2%	7/12%
76	1.09959362	1.20896291	1.46090069	1.55588620
77	1.10096811	1.21198532	1.46820519	1.56496220
78	1.10234432	1.21501528	1.47554622	1.57409115
79	1.10372225	1.21805282	1.48292395	1.58327334
80	1.10510191	1.22109795	1.49033857	1.59250910
81	1.10648328	1.22415070	1.49779026	1.60179874
82	1.10786639	1.22721108	1.50527921	1.61114257
83	1.10925122	1.23027910	1.51280561	1.62054090
84	1.11063778	1.23335480	1.52036964	1.62999405
85	1.11202608	1.23643819	1.52797148	1.63950235
86	1.11341611	1.23952928	1.53561134	1.64906612
87	1.11480788	1.24262811	1.54328940	1.65868567
88	1.11620139	1.24573468	1.55100585	1.66836134
89	1.11759665	1.24884901	1.55876087	1.67809344
90	1.11899364	1.25197114	1.56655468	1.68788232
91	1.12039238	1.25510106	1.57438745	1.69772830
92	1.12179287	1.25823882	1.58225939	1.70763172
93	1.12319511	1.26138441	1.59017069	1.71759290
94	1.12459911	1.26453787	1.59812154	1.72761219
95	1.12600486	1.26769922	1.60611215	1.73768993
96	1.12741236	1.27086847	1.61414271	1.74782646
97	1.12882163	1.27404564	1.62221342	1.75802211
98	1.13023266	1.27723075	1.63032449	1.76827724
99	1.13164545	1.28042383	1.63847611	1.77859219
100	1.13306000	1.28362489	1.64666849	1.78896731

Table I–continued

SINGLE PAYMENT OF 1 AT COMPOUND INTEREST

n	1/8%	1/4%	1/2%	7/12%
101	1.13447633	1.28683395	1.65490183	1.79940295
102	1.13589442	1.29005104	1.66317634	1.80989947
103	1.13731429	1.29327616	1.67149223	1.82045722
104	1.13873593	1.29650935	1.67984969	1.83107655
105	1.14015935	1.29975063	1.68824894	1.84175783
106	1.14158455	1.30300000	1.69669018	1.85250142
107	1.14301153	1.30625750	1.70517363	1.86330768
108	1.14444030	1.30952315	1.71369950	1.87417697
109	1.14587085	1.31279696	1.72226800	1.88510967
110	1.14730319	1.31607895	1.73087934	1.89610614
111	1.14873732	1.31936915	1.73953373	1.90716676
112	1.15017324	1.32266757	1.74823140	1.91829190
113	1.15161096	1.32597424	1.75697256	1.92948194
114	1.15305047	1.32928917	1.76575742	1.94073725
115	1.15454918	1.33261240	1.77458621	1.95205822
116	1.15593490	1.33594393	1.78345914	1.96344522
117	1.15737982	1.33928379	1.79237644	1.97489865
118	1.15882654	1.34263200	1.80133832	1.98641890
119	1.16027507	1.34598858	1.81034501	1.99800634
120	1.16172542	1.34935355	1.81939673	2.00966138
121	1.16317757	1.35272693	1.82849372	2.02138440
122	1.16463155	1.35610875	1.83763619	2.03317581
123	1.16608734	1.35949902	1.84682437	2.04503600
124	1.16754494	1.36289777	1.85605849	2.05696538
125	1.16900438	1.36630501	1.86533878	2.06896434

Table I—continued

SINGLE PAYMENT OF 1 AT COMPOUND INTEREST

n	⅛%	¼%	½%	7/12 %
126	1.17046563	1.36972077	1.87466548	2.08103330
127	1.17192871	1.37314508	1.88403880	2.09317266
128	1.17339362	1.37657794	1.89345900	2.10538284
129	1.17486037	1.38001938	1.90292629	2.11766424
130	1.17632894	1.38346943	1.91244092	2.13001728
131	1.17779935	1.38692811	1.92200313	2.14244238
132	1.17927160	1.39039543	1.93161314	2.15493996
133	1.18074569	1.39387142	1.94127121	2.16751044
134	1.18222162	1.39735609	1.95097757	2.18015425
135	1.18369940	1.40084948	1.96073245	2.19287182
136	1.18517902	1.40435161	1.97053612	2.20566357
137	1.18666050	1.40786249	1.98038880	2.21852994
138	1.18814382	1.41138214	1.99029074	2.23147137
139	1.18962900	1.41491060	2.00024219	2.24448828
140	1.19111604	1.41844787	2.01024340	2.25758113
141	1.19260494	1.42199399	2.02029462	2.27075036
142	1.19409569	1.42554898	2.03039609	2.28399640
143	1.19558831	1.42911285	2.04054808	2.29731971
144	1.19708280	1.43268563	2.05075082	2.31072074
145	1.19857915	1.43626735	2.06100457	2.32419995
146	1.20007737	1.43985802	2.07130959	2.33775778
147	1.20157747	1.44345766	2.08166614	2.35139470
148	1.2030794	1.44706631	2.09207447	2.36511117
149	1.20458329	1.45068397	2.10253484	2.37890765
150	1.20608902	1.45431068	2.11304752	2.39278461

Table I–continued

SINGLE PAYMENT OF 1 AT COMPOUND INTEREST

n	1/8%	1/4%	1/2%	7/12%
151	1.20759663	1.45794646	2.12361276	2.40674252
152	1.20910613	1.46159132	2.13423082	2.42078186
153	1.21061751	1.46524530	2.14490197	2.43490308
154	1.21213078	1.46890842	2.15562648	2.44910668
155	1.21364595	1.47258069	2.16640462	2.46339314
156	1.21516300	1.47626214	2.17723664	2.47776293
157	1.21668196	1.47995279	2.18812282	2.49221655
158	1.21820281	1.48365268	2.19906344	2.50675448
159	1.21972556	1.48736181	2.21005875	2.52137722
160	1.22125022	1.49108021	2.22110905	2.53608525
161	1.22277678	1.49480791	2.23221459	2.55087908
162	1.22430525	1.49854493	2.24337566	2.56575921
163	1.22583564	1.50229129	2.25459254	2.58072614
164	1.22736793	1.50604702	2.26586551	2.59578037
165	1.22890214	1.50981214	2.27719483	2.61092242
166	1.23043827	1.51358667	2.28858081	2.62615280
167	1.23197632	1.51737064	2.30002371	2.64147203
168	1.23351629	1.52116406	2.31152383	2.65688062
169	1.23505818	1.52496697	2.32308145	2.67237909
170	1.23660200	1.52877939	2.33469686	2.68796796
171	1.23814776	1.53260134	2.34637034	2.70364778
172	1.23969544	1.53643284	2.35810219	2.71941906
173	1.24124506	1.54027393	2.36989270	2.73528233
174	1.24279662	1.54412461	2.38174217	2.75123815
175	1.24435011	1.54798492	2.39365088	2.76728704

Table I—continued

SINGLE PAYMENT OF 1 AT COMPOUND INTEREST

n	1/8%	1/4%	1/2%	7/12%
176	1.24590555	1.55185488	2.40561913	2.78342954
177	1.24746293	1.55573452	2.41764723	2.79966622
178	1.24902226	1.55962386	2.42973546	2.81599760
179	1.25058354	1.56352292	2.44188414	2.83242426
180	1.25214677	1.56743172	2.45409356	2.84894673
181	1.25371195	1.57135030	2.46636403	2.86556559
182	1.25527909	1.57527868	2.47869585	2.88228139
183	1.25684819	1.57921688	2.49108933	2.89909469
184	1.25841925	1.58316492	2.50354478	2.91600608
185	1.25999227	1.58712283	2.51606250	2.93301612
186	1.26156726	1.59109064	2.52864281	2.95012538
187	1.26314422	1.59506836	2.54128603	2.69733444
188	1.26472315	1.59905604	2.55399246	2.98464389
189	1.26630406	1.60305368	2.56676242	3.00205431
190	1.26788694	1.60706131	2.57959623	3.01956630
191	1.26947180	1.61107896	2.59249421	3.03718043
192	1.27105864	1.61510666	2.60545668	3.05489732
193	1.27264746	1.61914443	2.61848397	3.07271755
194	1.27423827	1.62319229	2.63157639	3.09064174
195	1.27583107	1.62725027	2.64473427	3.10867048
196	1.27742586	1.63131839	2.65795794	3.12680440
197	1.27902264	1.63539669	2.67124773	3.14504409
198	1.28062142	1.63948518	2.68460397	3.16339018
199	1.28222219	1.64358390	2.69802699	3.18184329
200	1.28382497	1.64769285	2.71151712	3.20040404

Table I–continued

SINGLE PAYMENT OF 1 AT COMPOUND INTEREST

n	2/3%	3/4%	5/6%	11/12%
1	1.00666667	1.00750000	1.00833333	1.00916667
2	1.01337778	1.01505625	1.01673611	1.01841736
3	1.02013363	1.02266917	1.02520891	1.02775285
4	1.02693452	1.03033919	1.03375232	1.03711739
5	1.03378075	1.03806673	1.04236692	1.04668135
6	1.04067262	1.04585224	1.05105331	1.05627593
7	1.04761044	1.05369613	1.05981209	1.06595846
8	1.05459451	1.06159885	1.06864386	1.07572974
9	1.06162514	1.06956084	1.07754922	1.08559060
10	1.06870264	1.07758255	1.08652880	1.09554185
11	1.07582732	1.08566441	1.09558321	1.10558431
12	1.08299951	1.09380690	1.10471307	1.11571884
13	1.09021950	1.10201045	1.11391901	1.12594626
14	1.09748763	1.11027553	1.12320167	1.13626743
15	1.10480422	1.11860259	1.13256168	1.14668322
16	1.11216958	1.12699211	1.14199970	1.15719448
17	1.11958404	1.13544455	1.15151636	1.16780210
18	1.12704794	1.14396039	1.16111233	1.17850695
19	1.13456159	1.15254009	1.17078927	1.18930993
20	1.14212533	1.16118414	1.18054484	1.20021194
21	1.14973950	1.16989302	1.19038271	1.21121388
22	1.15740443	1.17866722	1.20030256	1.22231667
23	1.16512046	1.18750723	1.21030509	1.23352124
24	1.17288793	1.19641353	1.22039096	1.24482852
25	1.18070718	1.20538663	1.23056089	1.25623945

Table I–continued

SINGLE PAYMENT OF 1 AT COMPOUND INTEREST

n	2/3%	3/4%	5/6%	11/12%
26	1.18857857	1.21442703	1.24081556	1.26775498
27	1.19650242	1.22353523	1.25115569	1.27937607
28	1.20447911	1.23271175	1.26158199	1.29110368
29	1.21250897	1.24195709	1.27209517	1.30293880
30	1.22059236	1.25127176	1.28269596	1.31488240
31	1.22872964	1.26065630	1.29338510	1.32693549
32	1.23692117	1.27011122	1.30416331	1.33909907
33	1.24516731	1.27963706	1.31503133	1.35137414
34	1.25346843	1.28923434	1.32598993	1.36376174
35	1.26182489	1.29890359	1.33703984	1.37626289
36	1.27023705	1.30864537	1.34818184	1.38887863
37	1.27870530	1.31846021	1.35941669	1.40161002
38	1.28723000	1.32834866	1.37074516	1.41445811
39	1.29581153	1.33831128	1.38216804	1.42742397
40	1.30445028	1.34834861	1.39368611	1.44050869
41	1.31314661	1.35846123	1.40530016	1.45371336
42	1.32190092	1.36864969	1.41701099	1.46703906
43	1.33071360	1.37891456	1.42881942	1.48048692
44	1.33958502	1.38925642	1.44072625	1.49405805
45	1.34851559	1.39967584	1.45273230	1.50775358
46	1.35750569	1.41017341	1.46483840	1.52157466
47	1.36655573	1.42074971	1.47704539	1.53552243
48	1.37566610	1.43140533	1.48935410	1.54959805
49	1.38483721	1.44214087	1.50176538	1.56380270
50	1.39406946	1.45295693	1.51428009	1.57813755

Table I–continued

SINGLE PAYMENT OF 1 AT COMPOUND INTEREST

n	$^2/_3\%$	$^3/_4\%$	$^5/_6\%$	$^{11}/_{12}\%$
51	1.40336325	1.46385411	1.52689910	1.59260382
52	1.41271901	1.47483301	1.53962325	1.60720268
53	1.42213713	1.48589426	1.55245345	1.62193538
54	1.43161805	1.49703847	1.56539056	1.63680312
55	1.44116217	1.50826626	1.57843548	1.65180714
56	1.45076992	1.51957825	1.59158911	1.66694871
57	1.46044172	1.53097509	1.60485235	1.68222907
58	1.47017799	1.54245740	1.61822612	1.69764951
59	1.47997918	1.55402583	1.63171134	1.71321129
60	1.48984571	1.56568103	1.64530893	1.72891573
61	1.49977801	1.57742363	1.65901984	1.74476412
62	1.50977653	1.58925431	1.67284501	1.76075780
63	1.51984171	1.60117372	1.68678538	1.77689808
64	1.52997399	1.61318252	1.70084193	1.79318631
65	1.54017381	1.62528139	1.71501561	1.80962385
66	1.55044164	1.63747100	1.72930741	1.82621207
67	1.56077792	1.64975203	1.74371830	1.84295234
68	1.57118310	1.66212517	1.75824929	1.85984607
69	1.58165766	1.67459111	1.77290137	1.87689466
70	1.59220204	1.68715055	1.78767554	1.89409953
71	1.60281672	1.69980418	1.80257284	1.91146211
72	1.61350217	1.71255271	1.81759428	1.92898385
73	1.62425885	1.72539685	1.83274090	1.94666620
74	1.63508724	1.73833733	1.84801374	1.96451064
75	1.64598782	1.75137486	1.86341385	1.98251865

Table I—continued

SINGLE PAYMENT OF 1 AT COMPOUND INTEREST

n	2/3%	3/4%	5/6%	11/12%
76	1.65696107	1.76451017	1.87894230	2.00069174
77	1.66800748	1.77774400	1.89460016	2.01903141
78	1.67912753	1.79107708	1.91038849	2.03753920
79	1.69032172	1.80451015	1.92630839	2.05621664
80	1.70159053	1.81804398	1.94236096	2.07506530
81	1.71293446	1.83167931	1.95854731	2.09408673
82	1.72435403	1.84541691	1.97486853	2.11328252
83	1.73584972	1.85925753	1.99132577	2.13265428
84	1.74742205	1.87320196	2.00792015	2.15220361
85	1.75907153	1.88725098	2.02465282	2.17193214
86	1.77079868	1.90140536	2.04152493	2.19184152
87	1.78260400	1.91566590	2.05853764	2.21193340
88	1.79448803	1.93003339	2.07569212	2.23220946
89	1.80645128	1.94450865	2.09298955	2.25267138
90	1.81849429	1.95909246	2.11043113	2.27332087
91	1.83061758	1.97378565	2.12801806	2.29415964
92	1.84282170	1.98858905	2.14575154	2.31518944
93	1.85510718	2.00350346	2.16363280	2.33641201
94	1.86747456	2.01852974	2.18166308	2.35782912
95	1.87992439	2.03366871	2.19984360	2.37944255
96	1.89245722	2.04892123	2.21817563	2.40125411
97	1.90507360	2.06428814	2.23666043	2.42326560
98	1.91777409	2.07977030	2.25529926	2.44547887
99	1.93055925	2.09536858	2.27409343	2.46789576
100	1.94342965	2.11108384	2.29304420	2.49051814

Table I–continued

SINGLE PAYMENT OF 1 AT COMPOUND INTEREST

n	2/3%	3/4%	5/6%	11/12%
101	1.95638585	2.12691697	2.31215291	2.51334789
102	1.96942842	2.14286885	2.33142085	2.53638691
103	1.98255794	2.15894036	2.35084935	2.55963713
104	1.99577499	2.17511324	2.37043976	2.58310047
105	2.00908016	2.19144591	2.39019343	2.60677889
106	2.02247403	2.20788175	2.41011171	2.63067436
107	2.03595719	2.22444087	2.43019597	2.65478887
108	2.04953024	2.24112417	2.45044761	2.67912444
109	2.06319377	2.25793260	2.47086800	2.70368308
110	2.07694840	2.27486710	2.49145857	2.72846684
111	2.09079472	2.29192860	2.51222072	2.75347779
112	2.10473335	2.30911807	2.53315590	2.77871800
113	2.11876491	2.32643645	2.55426553	2.80418958
114	2.13289000	2.34388473	2.57555107	2.82989465
115	2.14710927	2.36146386	2.59701400	2.85583535
116	2.16142333	2.37917484	2.61865578	2.88201385
117	2.17583282	2.39701865	2.64047791	2.90843231
118	2.19033837	2.41499629	2.66248190	2.93509293
119	2.20494063	2.43310876	2.68466925	2.96199795
120	2.21964023	2.45135708	2.70704149	2.98914960
121	2.23443784	2.46974226	2.72960017	3.01655014
122	2.24933409	2.48826532	2.75234684	3.04420185
123	2.26432965	2.50692731	2.77528306	3.07210703
124	2.27942518	2.52572927	2.79841042	3.10026801
125	2.29462135	2.54467224	2.82173051	3.12868714

Table I—continued

SINGLE PAYMENT OF 1 AT COMPOUND INTEREST

n	$2/3\%$	$3/4\%$	$5/6\%$	$11/12\%$
126	2.30991882	2.56375728	2.84524493	3.15736677
127	2.32531828	2.58298546	2.86895530	3.18630930
128	2.34082040	2.60235785	2.89286326	3.21551713
129	2.35642587	2.62187553	2.91697046	3.24499271
130	2.37213538	2.64153960	2.94127854	3.27473847
131	2.38794962	2.66135115	2.96578920	3.30475691
132	2.40386928	2.68131128	2.99050411	3.33505051
133	2.41989507	2.70142112	3.01542498	3.36562181
134	2.43602771	2.72168177	3.04055352	3.39647334
135	2.45226789	2.74209439	3.06589146	3.42760768
136	2.46861635	2.76266010	3.09144056	3.45902742
137	2.48507379	2.78338005	3.11720256	3.49073517
138	2.50164095	2.80425540	3.14317925	3.52273358
139	2.51831855	2.82528731	3.16937241	3.55502530
140	2.53510734	2.84647697	3.19578385	3.58761303
141	2.55200806	2.86782554	3.22241538	3.62049949
142	2.56902145	2.88933424	3.24926884	3.65368740
143	2.58614826	2.91100424	3.27634608	3.68717953
144	2.60338924	2.93283677	3.30364897	3.72097868
145	2.62074517	2.95483305	3.33117937	3.75508765
146	2.63821681	2.97699430	3.35893920	3.78950929
147	2.65580492	2.99932176	3.38693036	3.82424645
148	2.67351028	3.02181667	3.41514782	3.85930205
149	2.69133369	3.04448029	3.44361441	3.89467898
150	2.70927591	3.06731390	3.47231119	3.93038021

Table I—continued

SINGLE PAYMENT OF 1 AT COMPOUND INTEREST

n	⅔%	¾%	⅚%	11/12%
151	2.72733775	3.09031875	3.50124712	3.96640869
152	2.74552000	3.11349614	3.53042418	4.00276744
153	2.76382347	3.13684736	3.55984438	4.03945947
154	2.78224896	3.16037372	3.58950975	4.07648785
155	2.80079729	3.18407652	3.61942233	4.11385566
156	2.81946927	3.20795709	3.64958418	4.15156600
157	2.83826573	3.23201677	3.67999738	4.18962202
158	2.85718750	3.25625690	3.71066403	4.22802689
159	2.87623542	3.28067882	3.74158623	4.26678380
160	2.89541032	3.30528392	3.77276612	4.30589599
161	2.91471306	3.33007354	3.80420583	4.34536670
162	2.93414448	3.35500491	3.83590755	4.38519923
163	2.95370544	3.38021196	3.86787344	4.42539689
164	2.97339681	3.40556355	3.90010572	4.46596303
165	2.99321945	3.43110528	3.93260660	4.50690102
166	3.01317425	3.45683857	3.96537833	4.54821428
167	3.03326208	3.48276486	3.99842315	4.58990624
168	3.05343883	3.50888560	4.03174334	4.63198038
169	3.07384038	3.53520224	4.06534120	4.67440204
170	3.09433265	3.56171625	4.09921904	4.71728924
171	3.11496154	3.58842913	4.13337920	4.76053106
172	3.13572795	3.61534235	4.16782403	4.80416926
173	3.15663280	3.64245741	4.20255589	4.84820748
174	3.17767702	3.66977584	4.23757719	4.89264938
175	3.19886153	3.69729916	4.27289034	4.93749867

Table I–continued

SINGLE PAYMENT OF 1 AT COMPOUND INTEREST

n	⅔%	¾%	⅚%	11/12%
176	3.22018728	3.72502891	4.30849776	4.98275907
177	3.24165519	3.75296662	4.34440190	5.02843436
178	3.26326623	3.78111387	4.38060525	5.07452834
179	3.28502134	3.80947223	4.41711030	5.12104485
180	3.30692148	3.83804327	4.45391955	5.16798776
181	3.32896762	3.86682859	4.49103555	5.21536098
182	3.35116074	3.89582981	4.52846084	5.26316846
183	3.37350181	3.92504853	4.56619802	5.31141417
184	3.39599182	3.95448639	4.60424967	5.36010213
185	3.41863177	3.98414504	4.64261841	5.40923640
186	3.44142265	4.01402613	4.68130690	5.45882107
187	3.46436546	4.04413133	4.72031779	5.50886026
188	3.48746123	4.07446231	4.75965377	5.55935815
189	3.51071097	4.10502078	4.79931755	5.61031893
190	3.53411571	4.13580843	4.83931187	5.66174686
191	3.55767649	4.16682700	4.87963947	5.71364620
192	3.58139433	4.19807820	4.92030313	5.76602129
193	3.60527029	4.22956379	4.96130565	5.81887649
194	3.62930543	4.26128551	5.00264987	5.87222162
195	3.65350080	4.29324516	5.04433862	5.92604484
196	3.67785747	4.32544449	5.08637477	5.98036691
197	3.70237652	4.35788533	5.12876123	6.03518694
198	3.72705903	4.39056947	5.17150090	6.09050950
199	3.75190609	4.42349874	5.21459675	6.14633916
200	3.77691880	4.45667498	5.25805172	6.20268060

Table I—continued

SINGLE PAYMENT OF 1 AT COMPOUND INTEREST

n	1%	2%	3%	4%
1	1.01000000	1.02000000	1.03000000	1.04000000
2	1.02010000	1.04040000	1.06090000	1.08160000
3	1.03030100	1.06120800	1.09272700	1.12486400
4	1.04060401	1.08243216	1.12550881	1.16985856
5	1.05101005	1.10408080	1.15927407	1.21665290
6	1.06152015	1.12616242	1.19405230	1.26531902
7	1.07213535	1.14868567	1.22987387	1.31593178
8	1.08285671	1.17165938	1.26677008	1.36856905
9	1.09368527	1.19509257	1.30477318	1.42331181
10	1.10462213	1.21899442	1.34391638	1.48024428
11	1.11566835	1.24337431	1.38423387	1.53945406
12	1.12682503	1.26824179	1.42576089	1.60103222
13	1.13809328	1.29360663	1.46853371	1.66507351
14	1.14947421	1.31947876	1.51258972	1.73167645
15	1.16096896	1.34586834	1.55796742	1.80094351
16	1.17257864	1.37278571	1.60470644	1.87298125
17	1.18430443	1.40024142	1.65284763	1.94790050
18	1.19614748	1.42824625	1.70243306	2.02581652
18	1.20810895	1.45681117	1.75350605	2.10684918
20	1.22019004	1.48594740	1.80611123	2.19112314
21	1.23239194	1.51566634	1.86029457	2.27876807
22	1.24471586	1.54597967	1.91610341	2.36991879
23	1.25716302	1.57689926	1.97358651	2.46471554
24	1.26973465	1.60843725	1.03279411	2.56330416
25	1.28243200	1.64060599	1.09377793	2.66583633

Table I–continued

SINGLE PAYMENT OF 1 AT COMPOUND INTEREST

n	1%	2%	3%	4%
26	1.29525631	1.67341811	2.15659127	2.77246978
27	1.30820888	1.70688648	2.22128901	2.88336858
28	1.32129097	1.74102421	2.28792768	2.99870332
29	1.33450388	1.77584469	2.35656551	3.11865145
30	1.34784892	1.81136158	2.42726247	3.24339751
31	1.36132740	1.84758882	2.50008035	3.37313341
32	1.37494068	1.88454059	2.57508276	3.50805875
33	1.38869009	1.92223140	2.65233524	3.64838110
34	1.40257699	1.96067603	2.73190530	3.79431634
35	1.41660276	1.99988955	2.81386245	3.94608899
36	1.43076878	2.03988734	2.89827833	4.10393255
37	1.44507647	2.08068509	2.98522668	4.26808986
38	1.45952724	2.12229879	3.07478348	4.43881345
39	1.47412251	2.16474477	3.16702698	4.61636599
40	1.48886373	2.20803966	3.26203779	4.80102063
41	1.50375237	2.25220046	3.35989893	4.99306145
42	1.51878989	2.29724447	3.46069589	5.19278391
43	1.53397779	2.34318936	3.56451677	5.40049527
44	1.54931757	2.39005314	3.67145227	5.61651508
45	1.56481075	2.43785421	3.78159584	5.84117568
46	1.58045885	2.48661129	3.89504372	6.07482271
47	1.59626344	2.53634351	4.01189503	6.31781562
48	1.61222608	2.58707039	4.13225188	6.57052824
49	1.62834834	2.63881179	4.25621944	6.83334937
50	1.64463182	2.69158803	4.38390602	7.10668335

Table I—continued

SINGLE PAYMENT OF 1 AT COMPOUND INTEREST

n	1%	2%	3%	4%
51	1.66107814	2.74541979	4.51542320	7.39095068
52	1.67768892	2.80032819	4.65088590	7.68658871
53	1.69446581	2.85633475	4.79041247	7.99405226
54	1.71141047	2.91346144	4.93412485	8.31381435
55	1.72852457	2.97173067	5.08214859	8.64636692
56	1.74580982	3.03116529	5.23461303	8.99222160
57	1.76326792	3.09178859	5.39165144	9.35191046
58	1.78090060	3.15362436	5.55340098	9.72598688
59	1.79870960	3.21669685	5.72000301	10.11502635
60	1.81669670	3.28103079	5.89160310	10.51962741
61	1.83486367	3.34665140	6.06835120	10.94041250
62	1.85321230	3.41358443	6.25040173	11.37802900
63	1.87174443	3.48185612	6.43791379	11.83315016
64	1.89046187	3.55149324	6.63105120	12.30647617
65	1.90936649	3.62252311	6.82998273	12.79873522
66	1.92846015	3.69497357	7.03488222	13.31068463
67	1.94774475	3.76887304	7.24592868	13.84311201
68	1.96722220	3.84425050	7.46330654	14.39683649
69	1.98689442	3.92113551	7.68720574	14.97270995
70	2.00676337	3.99955822	7.91782191	15.57161835
71	2.02683100	4.07954939	8.15535657	16.19448308
72	2.04709931	4.16114038	8.40001727	16.84226241
73	2.06757031	4.24436318	8.65201778	17.51595290
74	2.08824601	4.32925045	8.91157832	18.21659102
75	2.10912847	4.41583546	9.17892567	18.94525466

Table I–continued

SINGLE PAYMENT OF 1 AT COMPOUND INTEREST

n	1%	2%	3%	4%
76	2.13021975	4.50415216	9.45429344	19.70306485
77	2.15152195	4.59423521	9.73792224	20.49118744
78	2.17303717	4.68611991	10.03005991	21.31083494
79	2.19476754	4.77984231	10.33096171	22.16326834
80	2.21671522	4.87543916	10.64089056	23.04979907
81	2.23888237	4.97294794	10.96011727	23.97179103
82	2.26127119	5.07240690	11.28892079	24.93066267
83	2.28388390	5.17385504	11.62758842	25.92788918
84	2.30672274	5.27733214	11.97641607	26.96500475
85	2.32978997	5.38287878	12.33570855	28.04360494
86	2.35308787	5.49053636	12.70577981	29.16534914
87	2.37661875	5.60034708	13.08695320	30.33196310
88	2.40038494	5.71235402	13.47956180	31.54524163
89	2.42438879	5.82660110	13.88394865	32.80705129
90	2.44863267	5.94313313	14.30046711	34.11933334
91	2.47311900	6.06199579	14.72948112	35.48410668
92	2.49785019	6.18323570	15.17136556	36.90347094
93	2.52282869	6.30690042	15.62650652	38.37960978
94	2.54805698	6.43303843	16.09530172	39.91479417
95	2.57353755	6.56169920	16.57816077	41.51138594
96	2.59927293	6.69293318	17.07550559	43.17184138
97	2.62526565	6.82679184	17.58777076	44.89871503
98	2.65151831	6.96332768	18.11540388	46.69466363
99	2.67803349	7.10259423	18.65886600	48.56245018
100	2.70481383	7.24464612	19.21863198	50.50494818

Table I–continued

SINGLE PAYMENT OF 1 AT COMPOUND INTEREST

n	5%	6%	7%	8%
1	1.05000000	1.06000000	1.07000000	1.08000000
2	1.10250000	1.12360000	1.14490000	1.16640000
3	1.15762500	1.19101600	1.22504300	1.25971200
4	1.21550625	1.26247696	1.31079601	1.36048896
5	1.27628156	1.33822558	1.40255173	1.46932808
6	1.34009564	1.41851911	1.50073035	1.58687432
7	1.40710042	1.50363026	1.60578148	1.71382427
8	1.47745544	1.59384807	1.71818618	1.85093021
9	1.55132822	1.68947896	1.83845921	1.99900463
10	1.62889463	1.79084770	1.96715136	2.15892500
11	1.71033936	1.89829856	2.10485195	2.33163900
12	1.79585633	2.01219647	2.25219159	2.51817012
13	1.88564914	2.13292826	2.40984500	2.71962373
14	1.97993160	2.26090396	2.57853415	2.93719362
15	2.07892818	2.39655819	2.75903154	3.17216911
16	2.18287459	2.54035168	2.95216375	3.42594264
17	2.29201832	2.69277279	3.15881521	3.70001806
18	2.40661923	2.85433915	3.37993228	3.99601950
19	2.52695020	3.02559950	3.61652754	4.31570106
20	2.65329771	3.20713547	3.86968446	4.66095714
21	2.78596259	3.39956360	4.14056237	5.03383372
22	2.92526072	3.60353742	4.43040174	5.43654041
23	3.07152376	3.81974966	4.74052986	5.87146365
24	3.22509994	4.04893464	5.07236695	6.34118074
25	3.38635494	4.29187072	5.42743264	6.84847520

Table I—continued

SINGLE PAYMENT OF 1 AT COMPOUND INTEREST

n	5%	6%	7%	8%
26	3.55567269	4.54938296	5.80735292	7.39635321
27	3.73345632	4.82234594	6.21386763	7.98806147
28	3.92012914	5.11168670	6.64883836	8.62710639
29	4.11613560	5.41838790	7.11425705	9.31727490
30	4.32194238	5.74349117	7.61225504	10.06265689
31	4.53803949	6.08810064	8.14511290	10.86766944
32	4.76494147	6.45338668	8.71527080	11.73708300
33	5.00318854	6.84058988	9.32533975	12.67604964
34	5.25334797	7.25102528	9.97811354	13.69013361
35	5.51601537	7.68608679	10.67658148	14.78534429
36	5.79181614	8.14725200	11.42394219	15.96817184
37	6.08140694	8.63608712	12.22361814	17.24562558
38	6.38547729	9.15425235	13.07927141	18.62527563
39	6.70475115	9.70350749	13.99482041	20.11529768
40	7.03998871	10.28571794	14.97445784	21.72452150
41	7.391998815	10.90286101	16.02266989	23.46248322
42	7.76158756	11.55703267	17.14425678	25.33948187
43	8.14966693	12.25045463	18.34435475	27.36664042
44	8.55715028	12.98548191	19.62845959	29.55597166
45	8.98500779	13.76461083	21.00245176	31.92044939
46	9.43425818	14.59048748	22.47262338	34.47408534
47	9.90597109	15.46591673	24.04570702	37.23201217
48	10.40126965	16.39387173	25.72890651	40.21057314
49	10.92133313	17.37750403	27.52992997	43.42741899
50	11.46739979	18.42015427	29.45702506	46.90161251

Table I—continued

SINGLE PAYMENT OF 1 AT COMPOUND INTEREST

n	5%	6%	7%	8%
51	12.04076978	19.52536353	31.51901682	50.65374151
52	12.64280826	20.69688534	33.72534799	54.70604084
53	13.27494868	21.93869846	36.08612235	59.08252410
54	13.93869611	23.25502037	38.61215092	63.80912603
55	14.63563092	24.65032159	41.31500148	68.91385611
56	15.36741246	26.12934089	44.20705159	74.42696460
57	16.13578309	27.69710134	47.30154520	80.38112177
58	16.94257224	29.35892742	50.61265336	86.81161151
59	17.78970085	31.12046307	54.15553910	93.75654043
60	18.67918589	32.98769085	57.94642683	101.25706367
61	19.61314519	34.96695230	62.00267671	109.35762876
62	20.59380245	37.06496944	66.34286408	118.10623906
63	21.62349257	39.28886761	70.98686457	127.55473819
64	22.70466720	41.64619967	75.95594509	137.75911724
65	23.83990056	44.14497165	81.27286124	148.77984662
66	25.03189559	46.79366994	86.96196153	160.68223435
67	26.28349037	49.60129014	93.04929884	173.53681310
68	27.59766488	52.57736755	99.56274976	187.41975815
69	28.97754813	55.73200960	106.53214224	202.41333880
70	30.42642554	59.07593018	113.98939220	218.60640590
71	31.94774681	62.62048599	121.96864965	236.09491837
72	33.54513415	66.37771515	130.50645513	254.98251184
73	35.22239086	70.36037806	139.64190699	275.38111279
74	36.98351040	74.58200074	149.41684048	297.41160181
75	38.83268592	79.05692079	159.87601931	321.20452996

Table I–continued

SINGLE PAYMENT OF 1 AT COMPOUND INTEREST

n	5%	6%	7%	8%
76	40.77432022	83.80033603	171.06734066	346.90089236
77	42.81303623	88.82835620	183.04205451	374.65296374
78	44.95368804	94.15805757	195.85499832	404.62520084
79	47.20137244	99.80754102	209.56484820	436.99521691
80	49.56144107	105.79599348	224.23438758	471.95483426
81	52.03951312	112.14375309	239.93079471	509.71122101
82	54.64148878	118.87237828	256.72595034	550.48811869
83	57.37356322	126.00472097	274.69676686	594.52716818
84	60.24224138	133.56500423	293.92554054	642.08934164
85	63.25435344	141.57890449	314.50032838	693.45648897
86	66.41707112	150.07363875	336.51535137	748.93300808
87	69.73792467	159.07805708	360.07142596	808.84764873
88	73.22482091	168.62274050	385.27642578	873.55546063
89	76.88606195	178.74010494	412.24577558	943.43989748
90	80.73036505	189.46451123	441.10297988	1018.91508928
91	84.76688330	200.83238191	471.98018847	1100.42829642
92	89.00522747	212.88232482	505.01880166	1188.46256013
93	93.45548884	225.65526431	540.37011778	1283.53956494
94	98.12826328	239.19458017	578.19602602	1386.22273014
95	103.03467645	253.54625498	618.66974784	1497.12054855
96	108.18641027	268.75903028	661.97663019	1616.89019244
97	113.59573078	284.88457209	708.31499430	1746.24140783
98	119.27551732	301.97764642	757.89704390	1885.94072046
99	125.23929319	320.09630520	810.94983698	2036.81597809
100	131.50125785	339.30208352	867.71632557	2199.76125634

Table I–continued

SINGLE PAYMENT OF 1 AT COMPOUND INTEREST

n	9%	10%	11%	12%
1	1.09000000	1.10000000	1.11000000	1.12000000
2	1.18810000	1.21000000	1.23210000	1.25440000
3	1.29502900	1.33100000	1.36763100	1.40492800
4	1.41158161	1.46410000	1.51807041	1.57351936
5	1.53862396	1.61051000	1.68505816	1.76234168
6	1.67710011	1.77156100	1.87041455	1.97382269
7	1.82803912	1.94871710	2.07616015	2.21068141
8	1.99256264	2.14358881	2.30453777	2.47596318
9	2.17189328	2.35794769	2.55803692	2.77307876
10	2.36736368	2.59374246	2.83942099	3.10584821
11	2.58042641	2.85311671	3.15175730	3.47854999
12	2.81266478	3.13842838	3.49845060	3.89597599
13	3.06580461	3.45227121	3.88328016	4.36349311
14	3.34172703	3.79749834	4.31044098	4.88711229
15	3.64248246	4.17724817	4.78458949	5.47356576
16	3.97030588	4.59497299	5.31089433	6.13039365
17	4.32763341	5.05447029	5.89509271	6.86604089
18	4.71712042	5.55991731	6.54355291	7.68996580
19	5.14166126	6.11590905	7.26334373	8.61276169
20	5.60441077	6.72749995	8.06231154	9.64629309
21	6.10880774	7.40024994	8.94916581	10.80384826
22	6.65860043	8.14027494	9.93357404	12.10031006
23	7.25787447	8.95430243	11.02626719	13.55234726
24	7.91108318	9.84973268	12.23915658	15.17862893
25	8.62300807	10.83470594	13.58546380	17.00006441

Table I–continued

SINGLE PAYMENT OF 1 AT COMPOUND INTEREST

n	9%	10%	11%	12%
26	9.39915792	11.91817654	15.07986482	19.04007214
27	10.24508213	13.10999419	16.73864995	21.32488079
28	11.16713952	14.42099361	18.57990145	23.88386649
29	12.17218208	15.86309297	20.62369061	26.74993047
30	13.26767847	17.44940227	22.89229657	29.95992212
31	14.46176953	19.19434250	25.41044919	33.55511278
32	15.76332879	21.11377675	28.20559861	37.58172631
33	17.18202838	23.22515442	31.30821445	42.09153347
34	18.72841093	25.54766986	34.75211804	47.14251748
35	20.41396792	28.10243685	38.57485103	52.79961958
36	22.25122503	30.91268053	42.81808464	59.13557393
37	24.25383528	34.00394859	47.52807395	66.23184280
38	26.43668046	37.40434344	52.75616209	74.17966394
39	28.81598170	41.14477779	58.55933991	83.08122361
40	31.40942005	45.25925557	65.00086731	93.05097044
41	34.23626786	49.78518112	72.15096271	104.21708689
42	37.31753197	54.76369924	80.08756861	116.72313732
43	40.67610984	60.24006916	88.89720115	130.72991380
44	44.33695973	66.26400761	98.67589328	146.41750346
45	48.32728611	72.89048368	109.53024154	163.98760387
46	52.67674185	80.17953205	121.57856811	183.66611634
47	57.41764862	88.19748526	134.95221060	205.70605030
48	62.58523700	97.01723378	149.79695377	230.39077633
49	68.21790833	106.71895716	166.27461868	258.03766949
50	74.35752008	117.39085288	184.56482674	289.00218980

Table I–continued

SINGLE PAYMENT OF 1 AT COMPOUND INTEREST

n	14%	16%	18%	20%
1	1.140000	1.160000	1.180000	1.200000
2	1.299600	1.345600	1.392400	1.440000
3	1.481544	1.560896	1.643032	1.728000
4	1.688960	1.810639	1.938778	2.073600
5	1.925415	2.100342	2.287758	2.488320
6	2.194973	2.436396	2.699554	2.985984
7	2.502269	2.826220	3.185474	3.583181
8	2.852586	3.278415	3.758859	4.299817
9	3.251949	3.802961	4.435454	5.159780
10	3.707221	4.411435	5.233836	6.191736
11	4.226232	5.117265	6.175926	7.430084
12	4.817905	5.936027	7.287593	8.916100
13	5.492411	6.885791	8.599359	10.699321
14	6.261349	7.987518	10.147244	12.839185
15	7.137938	9.265521	11.973748	15.407022
16	8.137249	10.748004	14.129023	18.488426
17	9.276464	12.467685	16.672247	22.186111
18	10.575169	14.462514	19.673251	26.623333
19	12.055693	16.776517	23.214436	31.948000
20	13.743490	19.460759	27.393035	38.337600
21	15.667578	22.574481	32.323781	46.005120
22	17.861039	26.186398	38.142061	55.206144
23	20.361585	30.376222	45.007632	66.247373
24	23.212207	35.236417	53.109006	79.496847
25	26.461916	40.874244	62.668627	95.396217

Table I–continued

SINGLE PAYMENT OF 1 AT COMPOUND INTEREST

n	14%	16%	18%	20%
26	30.166584	47.414123	73.948980	114.475460
27	34.389906	55.000382	87.259797	137.370552
28	39.204493	63.800444	102.966560	164.844662
29	44.693122	74.008515	121.500541	197.813595
30	50.950159	85.849877	143.370638	237.376313
31	58.083181	99.585857	169.177353	284.851577
32	66.214826	115.519594	199.629277	341.821892
33	75.484902	134.002730	235.562547	410.186270
34	86.052788	155.443166	277.963805	492.223524
35	98.100178	180.314073	327.997290	590.668229
36	111.834203	209.164324	387.036802	708.801875
37	127.490992	242.630616	456.703427	850.562250
38	145.339731	281.451515	538.910044	1020.674700
39	165.687293	326.483757	635.913852	1224.809640
40	188.883514	378.721159	750.378345	1469.771568
41	215.327206	439.316544	885.446447	1763.725882
42	245.473015	509.607191	1044.826807	2116.471058
43	279.839237	591.144341	1232.895663	2539.765269
44	319.016730	685.727436	1454.816847	3047.718323
45	363.679072	795.443826	1716.683879	3657.261988
46	414.594142	922.714838	2025.686977	4388.714386
47	472.637322	1070.349212	2390.310633	5266.457263
48	538.806547	1241.605086	2820.566547	6319.748715
49	614.239464	1440.261900	3328.268525	7583.698458
50	700.232989	1670.703804	3927.356860	9100.438150

Table I—continued

SINGLE PAYMENT OF 1 AT COMPOUND INTEREST

n	22%	24%	26%	28%
1	1.22000	1.24000	1.26000	1.28000
2	1.48840	1.53760	1.58760	1.63840
3	1.81585	1.90662	2.00038	2.09715
4	2.21534	2.36421	2.52047	2.68435
5	2.70271	2.93163	3.17580	3.43597
6	3.29730	3.63522	4.00150	4.39805
7	4.02271	4.50767	5.04190	5.62950
8	4.90771	5.58951	6.35279	7.20576
9	5.98740	6.93099	8.00451	9.22337
10	7.30463	8.59443	10.08569	11.80592
11	8.91165	10.65709	12.70796	15.11157
12	10.87221	13.21479	16.01204	19.34281
13	13.26410	16.38634	20.17516	24.75880
14	16.18220	20.31906	25.42071	31.69127
15	19.74229	25.19563	32.03009	40.56482
16	24.08559	31.24259	40.35792	51.92297
17	29.38442	38.74081	50.85097	66.46140
18	35.84899	48.03860	64.07223	85.07059
19	43.73577	59.56786	80.73100	108.89036
20	53.35764	73.86415	101.72107	139.37966
21	65.09632	91.59155	128.16854	178.40596
22	79.41751	113.57352	161.49236	228.35963
23	96.88936	140.83116	203.48038	292.30033
24	118.20502	174.63064	256.38528	374.14442
25	144.21013	216.54199	323.04545	478.90486

Table I—continued

SINGLE PAYMENT OF 1 AT COMPOUND INTEREST

n	22%	24%	26%	28%
26	175.93636	268.51207	407.03727	612.99822
27	214.64236	332.95497	512.86696	784.63772
28	261.86368	412.86416	646.21236	1004.33628
29	319.47368	511.95156	814.22758	1285.55044
30	389.75789	634.81993	1025.92675	1645.50456
31	475.50463	787.17672	1292.66770	2106.24583
32	580.11565	976.09913	1628.76131	2695.99467
33	707.74109	1210.36292	2052.23925	3450.87317
34	863.44413	1500.85002	2585.82145	4417.11766
35	1053.40184	1861.05403	3258.13503	5653.91061
36	1285.15025	2307.70699	4105.25014	7237.00558
37	1567.88330	2861.55667	5172.61517	9263.36714
38	1912.81763	3548.33027	6517.49512	11857.10994
39	2333.63751	4399.92954	8212.04385	15177.10072
40	2847.03776	5455.91262	10347.17525	19426.68892
41	3473.38607	6765.33165	13037.44081	24866.16182
42	4237.53100	8389.01125	16427.17542	31828.68713
43	5169.78782	10402.37395	20698.24103	40740.71953
44	6307.14114	12898.94370	26079.78370	52148.12099
45	7694.71219	15994.69019	32860.52747	66749.59487
46	9387.54887	19833.41583	41404.26461	85439.48144
47	11452.80963	24593.43563	52169.37340	109362.53624
48	13972.42774	30495.86018	65733.41049	139984.04639
49	17046.36185	37814.86662	82824.09722	179179.57937
50	20796.56145	46890.43461	104358.36249	229349.86160

Table I—continued

SINGLE PAYMENT OF 1 AT COMPOUND INTEREST

n	30%	32%	34%	36%
1	1.3000	1.3200	1.3400	1.3600
2	1.6900	1.7424	1.7956	1.8496
3	2.1970	2.3000	2.4061	2.5155
4	2.8561	3.0360	3.2242	3.4210
5	3.7129	4.0075	4.3204	4.6526
6	4.8268	5.2899	5.7893	6.3275
7	6.2749	6.9826	7.7577	8.6054
8	8.1573	9.2170	10.3953	11.7034
9	10.6045	12.1665	13.9297	15.9166
10	13.7858	16.0598	18.6659	21.6466
11	17.9216	21.1989	25.0123	29.4393
12	23.2981	27.9825	33.5164	40.0374
13	30.2875	36.9370	44.9120	54.4510
14	39.3738	48.7568	60.1821	74.0534
15	51.1859	64.3590	80.6440	100.7126
16	66.5417	84.9538	108.0629	136.9691
17	86.5042	112.1390	144.8043	186.2779
18	112.4554	148.0235	194.0378	253.3380
19	146.1920	195.3911	260.0107	344.5397
20	190.0496	257.9162	348.4143	468.5740
21	247.0645	340.4494	466.8752	637.2606
22	321.1839	449.3932	625.6127	866.6744
23	417.5391	593.1990	838.3210	1178.6772
24	542.8008	783.0227	1123.3502	1603.0010
25	705.6410	1033.5900	1505.2892	2180.0814

Table I—continued

SINGLE PAYMENT OF 1 AT COMPOUND INTEREST

n	30%	32%	34%	36%
26	917.3333	1364.3387	2017.0876	2964.9107
27	1192.5332	1800.9271	2702.8974	4032.2786
28	1550.2933	2377.2238	3621.8825	5483.8988
29	2015.3813	3137.9354	4853.3225	7458.1024
30	2619.9956	4142.0748	6503.4522	10143.0193
31	3405.9943	5467.5387	8714.6259	13794.5062
32	4427.7926	7217.1511	11677.5987	18760.5285
33	5756.1304	9526.6395	15647.9823	25514.3187
34	7482.9696	12575.1641	20968.2963	34699.4735
35	9727.8604	16599.2166	28097.5170	47191.2839
36	12646.2186	21910.9659	37650.6728	64180.1461
37	16440.0841	28922.4750	50451.9015	87284.9987
38	21372.1094	38177.6670	67605.5481	118707.5982
39	27783.7422	50394.5205	90591.4344	161442.3336
40	36118.8648	66520.7670	121392.5221	219561.5736
41	46954.5243	87807.4125	162665.9796	298603.7402
42	61040.8815	115905.7845	217972.4127	406101.0866
43	79353.1460	152995.6355	292083.0330	552297.4778
44	103159.0898	201954.2388	391391.2642	751124.5698
45	134106.8167	266579.5953	524464.2940	1021529.4149
46	174338.8617	351885.0658	702782.1540	1389280.0043
47	226640.5202	464488.2868	941728.0864	1889420.8059
48	294632.6763	613124.5386	1261915.6358	2569612.2960
49	383022.4792	809324.3909	1690966.9519	3494672.7226
50	497929.2230	1068308.1960	2265895.7156	4752754.9027

Table I–continued

SINGLE PAYMENT OF 1 AT COMPOUND INTEREST

n	38%	40%	45%	50%
1	1.380	1.400	1.450	1.500
2	1.904	1.960	2.103	2.250
3	2.628	2.744	3.049	3.375
4	3.627	3.842	4.421	5.063
5	5.005	5.378	6.410	7.594
6	6.907	7.530	9.294	11.391
7	9.531	10.541	13.476	17.086
8	13.153	14.758	19.541	25.629
9	18.151	20.661	28.334	38.443
10	25.049	28.925	41.085	57.665
11	34.568	40.496	59.573	86.498
12	47.703	56.694	86.381	129.746
13	65.831	79.371	125.252	194.620
14	90.846	111.120	181.615	291.929
15	125.368	155.568	263.342	437.894
16	173.008	217.795	381.846	656.841
17	238.751	304.913	553.676	985.261
18	329.476	426.879	802.831	1477.892
19	454.677	597.630	1164.105	2216.838
20	627.454	836.683	1687.952	3325.257
21	865.886	1171.356	2447.530	4987.885
22	1194.923	1639.898	3548.919	7481.828
23	1648.994	2295.857	5145.932	11222.741
24	2275.611	3214.200	7461.602	16834.112
25	3140.344	4499.880	10819.322	25251.168

Table I—continued

SINGLE PAYMENT OF 1 AT COMPOUND INTEREST

n	38%	40%	45%	50%
26	4333.674	6299.831	15688.017	37876.752
27	5980.470	8819.764	22747.625	56815.129
28	8253.049	12347.670	32984.056	85222.693
29	11389.208	17286.737	47826.882	127834.040
30	15717.106	24201.432	69348.978	191751.059
31	21689.607	33882.005	100556.019	287626.589
32	29931.657	47434.807	145806.227	431439.883
33	41305.687	66408.730	211419.029	647159.825
34	57001.848	92972.223	306557.592	970739.737
35	78662.551	130161.112	444508.508	1456109.606
36	108554.320	182225.556	644537.337	2184164.409
37	149804.961	255155.779	934579.139	3276246.614
38	206730.847	357162.090	1355139.751	4914369.920
39	285288.568	500026.926	1964952.639	7371554.881
40	393698.224	700037.697	2849181.327	11057332.321
41	543303.550	980052.775	4131312.924	16585998.481
42	749758.899	1372073.885	5990403.740	24878997.722
43	1034667.280	1920903.439	8686085.423	37318496.584
44	1427840.846	2689264.815	12594823.863	55977744.875
45	1970420.368	3764970.741	18262494.602	83966617.313
46	2719180.108	5270959.038	26480617.173	125949926.000
47	3752468.548	7379342.653	38396894.901	188924889.000
48	5178406.597	10331079.714	55675497.606	283387333.430
49	7146201.104	14463511.600	80729471.529	425081000.146
50	9861757.523	20248916.240	117057733.717	637621500.221

Table II

SINGLE PAYMENT PRESENT VALUE OF 1 AT COMPOUND INTEREST

n	1/8%	1/4%	1/2%	7/12%	I
1	.99875156	.99750623	0.99502488	0.99420050	1
2	.99750468	.99501869	0.99007450	0.98843463	2
3	.99625936	.99253734	0.98514876	0.98270220	3
4	.99501559	.99006219	0.98024752	0.97700301	4
5	.99377337	.98759321	0.97537067	0.97133688	5
6	.99253270	.98513038	0.97051808	0.96570361	6
7	.99129359	.98267370	0.96568963	0.96010301	7
8	.99005602	.98022314	0.96088520	0.95453489	8
9	.99881999	.97777869	0.95610468	0.94899906	9
10	.98758551	.97534034	0.95134794	0.94349534	10
11	.98635257	.97290807	0.94661489	0.93802354	11
12	.98512117	.97048187	0.94190534	0.93258347	12
13	.98389130	.9680617[illegible]	0.93721924	0.92717495	13
14	.98266297	.96564759	0.93255646	0.92179779	14
15	.98143618	.96323949	0.92791688	0.91645182	15
16	.98021092	.96083740	0.92330037	0.91113686	16
17	.97898718	.95844130	0.91870684	0.90585272	17
18	.97776498	.95605117	0.91413616	0.90059922	18
19	.97654430	.95366700	0.90958822	0.89537619	19
20	.97532514	.95128878	0.90506290	0.89018346	20
21	.97410750	.94891649	0.90056010	0.88502084	21
22	.97289139	,94655011	0.89607971	0.87988815	22
23	.97167679	.94418964	0.89162160	0.87478524	23
24	.97046371	.94183505	0.88718567	0.86971192	24
25	.96925215	.93948634	0.88277181	0.86466802	25

Table II—continued

SINGLE PAYMENT PRESENT VALUE OF 1 AT COMPOUND INTEREST

n	1/8%	1/4%	1/2%	7/12%
26	.96804210	0.93714348	0.87837991	0.85965338
27	.96683355	0.93480646	0.87400986	0.85466782
28	.96562652	0.93247527	0.86966155	0.84971117
29	.96442100	0.93014990	0.86533488	0.84478327
30	.96321697	0.92783032	0.86102973	0.83988394
31	.96201446	0.92551653	0.85674600	0.83501303
32	.96081344	0.92320851	0.85248358	0.83017037
33	.95961392	0.92090624	0.84824237	0.82535580
34	.95841590	0.91860972	0.84402226	0.82056914
35	.95721938	0.91631892	0.83982314	0.81581025
36	.95602435	0.91403384	0.83564492	0.81107896
37	.95483081	0.91175445	0.83148748	0.80637510
38	.95363876	0.90948075	0.82735073	0.80169853
39	.95244820	0.90721272	0.82323455	0.79704907
40	.95125913	0.90495034	0.81913886	0.79242659
41	.95007154	0.90269361	0.81506354	0.78783091
42	.94888543	0.90044250	0.81100850	0.78326188
43	.94770080	0.89819701	0.80697363	0.77871935
44	.94651766	0.89595712	0.80295884	0.77420316
45	.94533599	0.89372281	0.79896402	0.76971317
46	.94415579	0.89149407	0.79498907	0.76524922
47	.94297707	0.88927090	0.79103390	0.76081115
48	.94179982	0.88705326	0.78709841	0.75639883
49	.94062404	0.88484116	0.78318250	0.75201209
50	.93944973	0.88263457	0.77928607	0.74765079

Table II–continued

SINGLE PAYMENT PRESENT VALUE OF 1 AT COMPOUND INTEREST

n	1/8%	1/4%	1/2%	7/12%
51	0.93827688	0.88043349	0.77540902	0.74331479
52	0.93710550	0.87823790	0.77155127	0.73900393
53	0.93593558	0.87604778	0.76771270	0.73471808
54	0.93476712	0.87386312	0.76389324	0.73045708
55	0.93360012	0.87168391	0.76009277	0.72622079
56	0.93243458	0.86951013	0.75631122	0.72200907
57	0.93127049	0.86734178	0.75254847	0.71782178
58	0.93010786	0.86517883	0.74880445	0.71365877
59	0.92894667	0.86302128	0.74507906	0.70951990
60	0.92778694	0.86086911	0.74137220	0.70540504
61	0.92662865	0.85872230	0.73768378	0.70131404
62	0.92547181	0.85658085	0.73401371	0.69724677
63	0.92431642	0.85444474	0.73036190	0.69320308
64	0.92316246	0.85231395	0.72672826	0.68918285
65	0.92200995	0.85018848	0.72311269	0.68518593
66	0.92085888	0.84806831	0.71951512	0.68121219
67	0.91970924	0.84595343	0.71593544	0.67726150
68	0.91856104	0.84384382	0.71237357	0.67333372
69	0.91741427	0.84173947	0.70882943	0.66942872
70	0.91626894	0.83964037	0.70530291	0.66554637
71	0.91512503	0.83754650	0.70179394	0.66168653
72	0.91398255	0.83545786	0.69830243	0.65784908
73	0.91284150	0.83337442	0.69482829	0.65403388
74	0.91170187	0.83129618	0.69137143	0.65024081
75	0.91056367	0.82922312	0.68793177	0.64646973

Table II–continued

SINGLE PAYMENT PRESENT VALUE OF 1 AT COMPOUND INTEREST

n	1/8%	1/4%	1/2%	7/12%
76	0.90942689	0.82715523	0.68450923	0.64272053
77	0.90829152	0.82509250	0.68110371	0.63899307
78	0.90715757	0.82303491	0.67771513	0.63528723
79	0.90602504	0.82098246	0.67434342	0.63160288
80	0.90489393	0.81893512	0.67098847	0.62793990
81	0.90376422	0.81689289	0.66765022	0.62429816
82	0.90263592	0.81485575	0.66432858	0.62067754
83	0.90150904	0.81282369	0.66102346	0.61707792
84	0.90038356	0.81079670	0.65773479	0.61349917
85	0.89925948	0.80877476	0.65446248	0.60994118
86	0.89813681	0.80675787	0.65120644	0.60640382
87	0.89701554	0.80474600	0.64796661	0.60288698
88	0.89589567	0.80273915	0.64474290	0.59939054
89	0.89477720	0.80073731	0.64153522	0.59591437
90	0.89366013	0.79874046	0.63834350	0.59245836
91	0.89254445	0.79674859	0.63516766	0.58902240
92	0.89143016	0.79476168	0.63200763	0.58560636
93	0.89031726	0.79277973	0.62886331	0.58221014
94	0.88920576	0.79080273	0.62573464	0.57883361
95	0.88809564	0.78883065	0.62262153	0.57547666
96	0.88698690	0.78686349	0.61952391	0.57213918
97	0.88587955	0.78490124	0.61644170	0.56882106
98	0.88477359	0.78294388	0.61337483	0.56552218
99	0.88366900	0.78099140	0.61032321	0.56224243
100	0.88256579	0.77904379	0.60728678	0.55898171

Table II–continued

SINGLE PAYMENT PRESENT VALUE OF 1 AT COMPOUND INTEREST

n	1/8%	1/4%	1/2%	7/12%
101	0.88146396	0.77710104	0.60426545	0.55573989
102	0.88036351	0.77516313	0.60125915	0.55251688
103	0.87926443	0.77323006	0.59826781	0.54931255
104	0.87816672	0.77130180	0.59529136	0.54612681
105	0.87707038	0.76937836	0.59232971	0.54295955
106	0.87597541	0.76745971	0.58938279	0.53981065
107	0.87488181	0.76554584	0.58645054	0.53668002
108	0.87378957	0.76363675	0.58353288	0.53356754
109	0.87269870	0.76173242	0.58062973	0.53047312
110	0.87160919	0.75983284	0.57774102	0.52739664
111	0.87052104	0.75793799	0.57486669	0.52433800
112	0.86943424	0.75604787	0.57200666	0.52129710
113	0.86834881	0.75416247	0.56916085	0.51827383
114	0.86726473	0.75228176	0.56632921	0.51526810
115	0.86618200	0.75040575	0.56351165	0.51227980
116	0.86510062	0.74853441	0.56070811	0.50930884
117	0.86402060	0.74666774	0.55791852	0.50635510
118	0.86294192	0.74480573	0.55514280	0.50341849
119	0.86186459	0.74294836	0.55238090	0.50049891
120	0.86078860	0.74109562	0.54963273	0.49759627
121	0.85971396	0.73924750	0.54689824	0.49471046
122	0.85864066	0.73740399	0.54417736	0.49184138
123	0.85756870	0.73556508	0.54147001	0.48898895
124	0.85649808	0.73373075	0.53877612	0.48615305
125	0.85542879	0.73190100	0.53609565	0.48333361

Table II–continued

SINGLE PAYMENT PRESENT VALUE OF 1 AT COMPOUND INTEREST

n	1/8%	1/4%	1/2%	7/12%
126	0.85436084	0.73007581	0.53342850	0.48053051
127	0.85329422	0.72825517	0.53077463	0.47774367
128	0.85222894	0.72643907	0.52813396	0.47497300
129	0.85116498	0.72462750	0.52550643	0.47221839
130	0.85010235	0.72282045	0.52289197	0.46947976
131	0.84904105	0.72101791	0.52029052	0.46675701
132	0.84798107	0.71921986	0.51770201	0.46405005
133	0.84692242	0.71742629	0.51512637	0.46135879
134	0.84586509	0.71563720	0.51256356	0.45868314
135	0.84480908	0.71385257	0.51001349	0.45602301
136	0.84375439	0.71207239	0.50747611	0.45337830
137	0.84270101	0.71029664	0.50495135	0.45074893
138	0.84164895	0.70852533	0.50243916	0.44813481
139	0.84059820	0.70675843	0.49993946	0.44553585
140	0.83954877	0.70499595	0.49745220	0.44295197
141	0.83850064	0.70323785	0.49497731	0.44038306
142	0.83745382	0.70148414	0.49251474	0.43782906
143	0.83640831	0.69973480	0.49006442	0.43528987
144	0.83536411	0.69798983	0.48762628	0.43276541
145	0.83432120	0.69624921	0.48520028	0.43025558
146	0.83327961	0.69451292	0.48278635	0.42776031
147	0.83223931	0.69278097	0.48038443	0.42527952
148	0.83120031	0.69105334	0.47799446	0.42281311
149	0.83016260	0.68933001	0.47561637	0.42036100
150	0.82912619	0.68761098	0.47325012	0.41792312

Table II–continued

SINGLE PAYMENT PRESENT VALUE OF 1 AT COMPOUND INTEREST

n	1/8%	1/4%	1/2%	7/12%
151	0.82809108	0.68589624	0.47089565	0.41549937
152	0.82705726	0.68418578	0.46855288	0.41308968
153	0.82602473	0.68247958	0.46622177	0.41069396
154	0.82499349	0.68077764	0.46390226	0.40831214
155	0.82396353	0.67907994	0.46159429	0.40594414
156	0.82293486	0.67738647	0.45929780	0.40358986
157	0.82190748	0.67569723	0.45701274	0.40124924
158	0.82088138	0.67401220	0.45473904	0.39892220
159	0.81985656	0.67233137	0.45247666	0.39660864
160	0.81883302	0.67065473	0.45022553	0.39430851
161	0.81781075	0.66898228	0.44798560	0.39202172
162	0.81678977	0.66731399	0.44575682	0.38974819
163	0.81577005	0.66564987	0.44353912	0.38748784
164	0.81475161	0.66398989	0.44133246	0.38524060
165	0.81373444	0.66233406	0.43913678	0.38300640
166	0.81271855	0.66068235	0.43695202	0.38078515
167	0.81170392	0.65903476	0.43477813	0.37857679
168	0.81069055	0.65739129	0.43261505	0.37638123
169	0.80967846	0.65575191	0.43046274	0.37419841
170	0.80867621	0.65411661	0.42832113	0.37202824
171	0.80765805	0.65248540	0.42619018	0.36987066
172	0.80664974	0.65085826	0.42406983	0.36772560
173	0.80564268	0.64923517	0.42196003	0.36559297
174	0.80463689	0.64761613	0.41986073	0.36347272
175	0.80363235	0.64600112	0.41777187	0.36136475

Table II—continued

SINGLE PAYMENT PRESENT VALUE OF 1 AT COMPOUND INTEREST

n	1/8%	1/4%	1/2%	7/12%
176	0.80262906	0.64439015	0.41569340	0.35926902
177	0.80162703	0.64278319	0.41362528	0.35718544
178	0.80062624	0.64118024	0.41156744	0.35511394
179	0.79962671	0.63958129	0.40951984	0.35305445
180	0.79862842	0.63798632	0.40748243	0.35100691
181	0.79763139	0.63639533	0.40545515	0.34897125
182	0.79663559	0.63480831	0.40343796	0.34694739
183	0.79564104	0.63322525	0.40143081	0.34493527
184	0.79464773	0.63164613	0.39943364	0.34293481
185	0.79365566	0.63007096	0.39744641	0.34094596
186	0.79266483	0.62849971	0.39546906	0.33896864
187	0.79167924	0.62693238	0.39350155	0.33700279
188	0.79068688	0.62536895	0.39154383	0.33504835
189	0.78969975	0.62380943	0.38959586	0.33310523
190	0.78871386	0.62225380	0.38765757	0.33117339
191	0.78772920	0.62070204	0.38572892	0.32925275
192	0.78674577	0.61915416	0.38380987	0.32734324
193	0.78576356	0.61761013	0.38190037	0.32544482
194	0.78478258	0.61606996	0.38000037	0.32355740
195	0.78380283	0.61453362	0.37810982	0.32168093
196	0.78282430	0.61300112	0.37622868	0.31981534
197	0.78184699	0.61147244	0.37435689	0.31796057
198	0.78087090	0.60994757	0.37249442	0.31611655
199	0.77989603	0.60842650	0.37064121	0.31428323
200	0.77892238	0.60690923	0.36879723	0.31246055

Table II–continued

SINGLE PAYMENT PRESENT VALUE OF 1 AT COMPOUND INTEREST

n	2/3%	3/4%	5/6%	11/12%
1	0.99337748	0.99255583	0.99173554	0.99091660
2	0.98679882	0.98516708	0.98353938	0.98191570
3	0.98026373	0.97783333	0.97541095	0.97299657
4	0.97377192	0.97055417	0.96734970	0.96415845
5	0.96732310	0.96332920	0.95935508	0.95540061
6	0.96091699	0.95615802	0.95142652	0.94672232
7	0.95455330	0.94904022	0.94356349	0.93812286
8	0.94823175	0.94197540	0.93576545	0.92960152
9	0.94195207	0.93496318	0.92803185	0.92115757
10	0.93571398	0.92800315	0.92036217	0.91279033
11	0.92951720	0.92109494	0.91275587	0.90449909
12	0.92336145	0.91423815	0.90521243	0.89628316
13	0.91724648	0.90743241	0.89773134	0.88814186
14	0.91117200	0.90067733	0.89031207	0.88007451
15	0.90513775	0.89397254	0.88295412	0.87208044
16	0.89914346	0.88731766	0.87565698	0.86415898
17	0.89318886	0.88071231	0.86842014	0.85630947
18	0.88727371	0.87415614	0.86124312	0.84853127
19	0.88139772	0.86764878	0.85412540	0.84082372
20	0.87556065	0.86118985	0.84706652	0.83318618
21	0.86976224	0.85477901	0.84006597	0.82561802
22	0.86400222	0.84841589	0.83312327	0.81811860
23	0.85828035	0.84210014	0.82623796	0.81068730
24	0.85259638	0.83583140	0.81940954	0.80332350
25	0.84695004	0.82960933	0.81263756	0.79602659

Table II—continued

SINGLE PAYMENT PRESENT VALUE OF 1 AT COMPOUND INTEREST

n	2/3%	3/4%	5/6%	11/12%
26	0.84134110	0.82343358	0.80592155	0.78879596
27	0.83576931	0.81730380	0.79926104	0.78163101
28	0.83023441	0.81121966	0.79265558	0.77453114
29	0.82473617	0.80518080	0.78610471	0.76749576
30	0.81927434	0.79918690	0.77960797	0.76052429
31	0.81384868	0.79323762	0.77316493	0.75361614
32	0.80845896	0.78733762	0.76677514	0.74677074
33	0.80310492	0.78147158	0.76043815	0.73998752
34	0.79778635	0.77565418	0.75415354	0.73326592
35	0.79250299	0.76988008	0.74792087	0.72660537
36	0.78725463	0.76414896	0.74173970	0.72000532
37	0.78204102	0.75846051	0.73560962	0.71346522
38	0.77686194	0.75281440	0.72953021	0.70698453
39	0.77171716	0.74721032	0.72350103	0.70056270
40	0.76660645	0.74164796	0.71752168	0.69419921
41	0.76152959	0.73612701	0.71159175	0.68789352
42	0.75648635	0.73064716	0.70571083	0.68164511
43	0.75147650	0.72520809	0.69987851	0.67545345
44	0.74649984	0.71980952	0.69409439	0.66931804
45	0.74155613	0.71445114	0.68835807	0.66323835
46	0.73664516	0.70913264	0.68266916	0.65721389
47	0.73176672	0.70385374	0.67702727	0.65124415
48	0.72692058	0.69861414	0.67143200	0.64532864
49	0.72210654	0.69341353	0.66588297	0.63946686
50	0.71732437	0.68825165	0.66037981	0.63365833

Table II–continued

SINGLE PAYMENT PRESENT VALUE OF 1 AT COMPOUND INTEREST

n	2/3%	3/4%	5/6%	11/12%
51	0.71257388	0.68312819	0.65492213	0.62790255
52	0.70785485	0.67804286	0.64950955	0.62219906
53	0.70316707	0.67299540	0.64414170	0.61654738
54	0.69851033	0.66798551	0.63881821	0.61094703
55	0.69388444	0.66301291	0.63353872	0.60539755
56	0.68928918	0.65807733	0.62830287	0.59989848
57	0.68472435	0.65317849	0.62311028	0.59444936
58	0.68018975	0.64831612	0.61796061	0.58904974
59	0.67568518	0.64348995	0.61285350	0.58369916
60	0.67121044	0.63869970	0.60778859	0.57839719
61	0.66676534	0.63394511	0.60276555	0.57314338
62	0.66234968	0.62922592	0.59778401	0.56793728
63	0.65796326	0.62454185	0.59284365	0.56277848
64	0.65360588	0.61989266	0.58794411	0.55766654
65	0.64927737	0.61527807	0.58308507	0.55260103
66	0.64497752	0.61069784	0.57826619	0.54758153
67	0.64070614	0.60615170	0.57348713	0.54260763
68	0.63646306	0.60163940	0.56874756	0.53767890
69	0.63224807	0.59716070	0.56404717	0.53279495
70	0.62806100	0.59271533	0.55938562	0.52795536
71	0.62390165	0.58830306	0.55476260	0.52315973
72	0.61976985	0.58392363	0.55017779	0.51840766
73	0.61566542	0.57957681	0.54563086	0.51369875
74	0.61158816	0.57526234	0.54112152	0.50903262
75	0.60753791	0.57097999	0.53664944	0.50440887

Table II–continued

SINGLE PAYMENT PRESENT VALUE OF 1 AT COMPOUND INTEREST

n	2/3%	3/4%	5/6%	11/12%
76	0.60351448	0.56672952	0.53221432	0.49982712
77	0.59951769	0.56251069	0.52781585	0.49528699
78	0.59554738	0.55832326	0.52345374	0.49078810
79	0.59160336	0.55416701	0.51912768	0.48633008
80	0.58768545	0.55004170	0.51483736	0.48191255
81	0.58379350	0.54594710	0.51058251	0.47753514
82	0.57992732	0.54188297	0.50636282	0.47319750
83	0.57608674	0.53784911	0.50217800	0.46889925
84	0.57227159	0.53384527	0.49802777	0.46464005
85	0.56848171	0.52987123	0.49391184	0.46041954
86	0.56471693	0.52592678	0.48982992	0.45623736
87	0.56097709	0.52201169	0.48578174	0.45209318
88	0.55726201	0.51812575	0.48176702	0.44798663
89	0.55357153	0.51426873	0.47778547	0.44391739
90	0.54990549	0.51044043	0.47383683	0.43988511
91	0.54626374	0.50664063	0.46992083	0.43588946
92	0.54264610	0.50286911	0.46603718	0.43193010
93	0.53905241	0.49912567	0.46218563	0.42800670
94	0.53548253	0.49541009	0.45836592	0.42411895
95	0.53193629	0.49172217	0.45457777	0.42026650
96	0.52841353	0.48806171	0.45082093	0.41644905
97	0.52491410	0.48442850	0.44709514	0.41266628
98	0.52143785	0.48082233	0.44340014	0.40891787
99	0.51798462	0.47724301	0.43973567	0.40520350
100	0.51455426	0.47369033	0.43610149	0.40152287

Table II–continued

SINGLE PAYMENT PRESENT VALUE OF 1 AT COMPOUND INTEREST

n	2/3%	3/4%	5/6%	11/12%
101	0.51114661	0.47016410	0.43249735	0.39787568
102	0.50776154	0.46666412	0.42892299	0.39426162
103	0.50439888	0.46319019	0.42537817	0.39068038
104	0.50105849	0.45974213	0.42186265	0.38713167
105	0.49774022	0.45631973	0.41837618	0.38361520
106	0.49444393	0.45292281	0.41491853	0.38013067
107	0.49116946	0.44955117	0.41148945	0.37667779
108	0.48791669	0.44620464	0.40808871	0.37325627
109	0.48468545	0.44288302	0.40471608	0.36986584
110	0.48147561	0.43958612	0.40137131	0.36650620
111	0.47828703	0.43631377	0.39805420	0.36317707
112	0.47511957	0.43306577	0.39476449	0.35987819
113	0.47197308	0.42984196	0.39150198	0.35660927
114	0.46884743	0.42664214	0.38826642	0.35337004
115	0.46574248	0.42346615	0.38505761	0.35016024
116	0.46265809	0.42031379	0.38187531	0.34697960
117	0.45959413	0.41718491	0.37871932	0.34382784
118	0.45655046	0.41407931	0.37558941	0.34070471
119	0.45352695	0.41099683	0.37248536	0.33760996
120	0.45052346	0.40793731	0.36940697	0.33454331
121	0.44753986	0.40490055	0.36635402	0.33150452
122	0.44457602	0.40188640	0.36332630	0.32849333
123	0.44163181	0.39889469	0.36032361	0.32550949
124	0.43870710	0.39592525	0.35734572	0.32255276
125	0.43580175	0.39297792	0.35439245	0.31962288

Table II–continued

SINGLE PAYMENT PRESENT VALUE OF 1 AT COMPOUND INTEREST

n	2/3%	3/4%	5/6%	11/12%
126	0.43291565	0.39005252	0.35146359	0.31671962
127	0.43004866	0.38714891	0.34855893	0.31384273
128	0.42720065	0.38426691	0.34567828	0.31099197
129	0.42437151	0.38140636	0.34282144	0.30816710
130	0.42156110	0.37856711	0.33998820	0.30536790
131	0.41876930	0.37574899	0.33717838	0.30259412
132	0.41599600	0.37295185	0.33439178	0.29984553
133	0.41324106	0.37017553	0.33162821	0.29712192
134	0.41050436	0.36741988	0.32888748	0.29442304
135	0.40778579	0.36468475	0.32616941	0.29174868
136	0.40508522	0.36196997	0.32347379	0.28909860
137	0.40240254	0.35927541	0.32080045	0.28647261
138	0.39973762	0.35660090	0.31814921	0.28387046
139	0.39709035	0.35394630	0.31551988	0.28129195
140	0.39446061	0.35131147	0.31291228	0.27873686
141	0.39184829	0.34869625	0.31032622	0.27620498
142	0.38925327	0.34610049	0.30776155	0.27369610
143	0.38667543	0.34352406	0.30521806	0.27121001
144	0.38411467	0.34096681	0.30269560	0.26874650
145	0.38157086	0.33842860	0.30019398	0.26630537
146	0.37904390	0.33590928	0.29771304	0.26388641
147	0.37653368	0.33340871	0.29525260	0.26148942
148	0.37404008	0.33092676	0.29281250	0.25911421
149	0.37156299	0.32846329	0.29039256	0.25676057
150	0.36910231	0.32601815	0.28799262	0.25442831

Table II–continued

SINGLE PAYMENT PRESENT VALUE OF 1 AT COMPOUND INTEREST

n	2/3%	3/4%	5/6%	11/12%
151	0.36665792	0.32359122	0.28561252	0.25211724
152	0.36422973	0.32118235	0.28325208	0.24982715
153	0.36181761	0.31879141	0.28091116	0.24755787
154	0.35942147	0.31641828	0.27858958	0.24530921
155	0.35704119	0.31406280	0.27628718	0.24308096
156	0.35467668	0.31172487	0.27400382	0.24087296
157	0.35232783	0.30940434	0.27173932	0.23868502
158	0.34999453	0.30710108	0.26949354	0.23651694
159	0.34767669	0.30481496	0.26726632	0.23436857
160	0.34537419	0.30254587	0.26505751	0.23223970
161	0.34308695	0.30029367	0.26286695	0.23013018
162	0.34081485	0.29805823	0.26069450	0.22803981
163	0.33855779	0.29583944	0.25854000	0.22596843
164	0.33631569	0.29363716	0.25640331	0.22391587
165	0.33408843	0.29145127	0.25428427	0.22188195
166	0.33187593	0.28928166	0.25218275	0.21986651
167	0.32967807	0.28712820	0.25009859	0.21786937
168	0.32749478	0.28499077	0.24803166	0.21589038
169	0.32532594	0.28286925	0.24598181	0.21392936
170	0.32317146	0.28076352	0.24394891	0.21198615
171	0.32103125	0.27867347	0.24193280	0.21006060
172	0.31890522	0.27659898	0.23993335	0.20815253
173	0.31679326	0.27453993	0.23795043	0.20626180
174	0.31469529	0.27249621	0.23598390	0.20438824
175	0.31261122	0.27046770	0.23403362	0.20253170

Table II–continued

SINGLE PAYMENT PRESENT VALUE OF 1 AT COMPOUND INTEREST

n	$2/3\%$	$3/4\%$	$5/6\%$	$11/12\%$
176	0.31054095	0.26845429	0.23209946	0.20069202
177	0.30848438	0.26645587	0.23018128	0.19886906
178	0.30644144	0.26447233	0.22827896	0.19706265
179	0.30441203	0.26250355	0.22639235	0.19527265
180	0.30239605	0.26054943	0.22452134	0.19349891
181	0.30039343	0.25860986	0.22266580	0.19174128
182	0.29840407	0.25668472	0.22082558	0.18999962
183	0.29642788	0.25477392	0.21900058	0.18827378
184	0.29446478	0.25287734	0.21719065	0.18656361
185	0.29251469	0.25099488	0.21539569	0.18486898
186	0.29057750	0.24912643	0.21361556	0.18318974
187	0.28865315	0.24727189	0.21185014	0.18152575
188	0.28674154	0.24543116	0.21009932	0.17987688
189	0.28484259	0.24360413	0.20836296	0.17824299
190	0.28295621	0.24179070	0.20664095	0.17662393
191	0.28108233	0.23999077	0.20493317	0.17501959
192	0.27922086	0.23820423	0.20323951	0.17342981
193	0.27737171	0.23643100	0.20155985	0.17185448
194	0.27553482	0.23467097	0.19989406	0.17029346
195	0.27371008	0.23292404	0.19824204	0.16874661
196	0.27189743	0.23119011	0.19660368	0.16721382
197	0.27009679	0.22946909	0.19497886	0.16569495
198	0.26830807	0.22776089	0.19336746	0.16418988
199	0.26653119	0.22606540	0.19176938	0.16269847
200	0.26476608	0.22438253	0.19018451	0.16122062

Table II—continued

SINGLE PAYMENT PRESENT VALUE OF 1 AT COMPOUND INTEREST

n	1%	2%	3%	4%
1	0.99009901	0.98039216	0.97087379	0.96153846
2	0.98029605	0.96116878	0.94259591	0.92455621
3	0.97059015	0.94232233	0.91514166	0.88899636
4	0.96098034	0.92384543	0.88848705	0.85480419
5	0.95146569	0.90573081	0.86260878	0.82192711
6	0.94204524	0.88797138	0.83748426	0.79031453
7	0.93271805	0.87056018	0.81309151	0.75991781
8	0.92348322	0.85349037	0.78940923	0.73069021
9	0.91433982	0.83675527	0.76641673	0.70258674
10	0.90528695	0.82034830	0.74409391	0.67556417
11	0.89632372	0.80426304	0.72242128	0.64958093
12	0.88744923	0.78849318	0.70137988	0.62459705
13	0.87866260	0.77303253	0.68095134	0.60057409
14	0.86996297	0.75787502	0.66111781	0.57747508
15	0.86134947	0.74301473	0.64186195	0.55526450
16	0.85282126	0.72844581	0.62316694	0.53390818
17	0.84437749	0.71416256	0.60501645	0.51337325
18	0.83601731	0.70015937	0.58739461	0.49362812
19	0.82773992	0.68643076	0.57028603	0.47464242
20	0.81954447	0.67297133	0.55367575	0.45638695
21	0.81143017	0.65977582	0.53754928	0.43883360
22	0.80339621	0.64683904	0.52189250	0.42195539
23	0.79544179	0.63415592	0.50669175	0.40572633
24	0.78756613	0.62172149	0.49193374	0.39012147
25	0.77976844	0.60953087	0.47760557	0.37511680

Table II–continued

SINGLE PAYMENT PRESENT VALUE OF 1 AT COMPOUND INTEREST

n	1%	2%	3%	4%
26	0.77204796	0.59757928	0.46369473	0.36068923
27	0.76440392	0.58586204	0.45018906	0.34681657
28	0.75683557	0.57437455	0.43707675	0.33347747
29	0.74934215	0.56311231	0.42434636	0.32065141
30	0.74192292	0.55207089	0.41198676	0.30831867
31	0.73457715	0.54124597	0.39998715	0.29646026
32	0.72730411	0.53063330	0.38833703	0.28505794
33	0.72010307	0.52022873	0.37702625	0.27409417
34	0.71297334	0.51002817	0.36604490	0.26355209
35	0.70591420	0.50002761	0.35538340	0.25341547
36	0.69892495	0.49022315	0.34503243	0.24366872
37	0.69200490	0.48061093	0.33498294	0.23429685
38	0.68515337	0.47118719	0.32522615	0.22528543
39	0.67836967	0.46194822	0.31575355	0.21662061
40	0.67165314	0.45289042	0.30655684	0.20828904
41	0.66500311	0.44401021	0.29762800	0.20027793
42	0.65841892	0.43530413	0.28895922	0.19257493
43	0.65189992	0.42676875	0.28054294	0.18516820
44	0.64544546	0.41840074	0.27237178	0.17804635
45	0.63905492	0.41019680	0.26443862	0.17119841
46	0.63272764	0.40215373	0.25673653	0.16461386
47	0.62646301	0.39426836	0.24925876	0.15828256
48	0.62026041	0.38653761	0.24199880	0.15219476
49	0.61411921	0.37895844	0.23495029	0.14634112
50	0.60803882	0.37152788	0.22810708	0.14071262

Table II–continued

SINGLE PAYMENT PRESENT VALUE OF 1 AT COMPOUND INTEREST

n	1%	2%	3%	4%
51	0.60201864	0.36424302	0.22146318	0.13530059
52	0.59605806	0.35710100	0.21501280	0.13009672
53	0.59015649	0.35009902	0.20875029	0.12509300
54	0.58431336	0.34323433	0.20267019	0.12028173
55	0.57852808	0.33650425	0.19676717	0.11565551
56	0.57280088	0.32990613	0.19103609	0.11120722
57	0.56712879	0.32343738	0.18547193	0.10693002
58	0.56151365	0.31709547	0.18006984	0.10281733
59	0.55595411	0.31087791	0.17482508	0.09886282
60	0.55044962	0.30478227	0.16973309	0.09506040
61	0.54499962	0.29880614	0.16478941	0.09140423
62	0.53960358	0.29294720	0.15998972	0.08788868
63	0.53426097	0.28720314	0.15532982	0.08450835
64	0.52897126	0.28157170	0.15080565	0.08125803
65	0.52373392	0.27605069	0.14641325	0.07813272
66	0.51854844	0.27063793	0.14214879	0.07512762
67	0.51341429	0.26533130	0.13800853	0.07223809
68	0.50833099	0.26012873	0.13398887	0.06945970
69	0.50329801	0.25502817	0.13008628	0.06678818
70	0.49831486	0.25002761	0.12629736	0.06421940
71	0.49338105	0.24512511	0.12261880	0.06174942
72	0.48849609	0.24031874	0.11904737	0.05937445
73	0.48365949	0.23560661	0.11557998	0.05709081
74	0.47887078	0.23098687	0.11221357	0.05489501
75	0.47412949	0.22645771	0.10894521	0.05278367

Table II—continued

SINGLE PAYMENT PRESENT VALUE OF 1 AT COMPOUND INTEREST

n	1%	2%	3%	4%
76	0.46943514	0.22201737	0.10577205	0.05075353
77	0.46478726	0.21766408	0.10269131	0.04880147
78	0.46018541	0.21339616	0.09970030	0.04692449
79	0.45562912	0.20921192	0.09679641	0.04511970
80	0.45111794	0.20510973	0.09397710	0.04338433
81	0.44665142	0.20108797	0.09123990	0.04171570
82	0.44222913	0.19714507	0.08858243	0.04011125
83	0.43785063	0.19327948	0.08600236	0.03856851
84	0.43351547	0.18948968	0.08349743	0.03708510
85	0.42922324	0.18577420	0.08106547	0.03565875
86	0.42497350	0.18213157	0.07870434	0.03428726
87	0.42076585	0.17856036	0.07641198	0.03296852
88	0.41659985	0.17505918	0.07418639	0.03170050
89	0.41247510	0.17162665	0.07202562	0.03048125
90	0.40839119	0.16826142	0.06992779	0.02930890
91	0.40434771	0.16496217	0.06789105	0.02818163
92	0.40034427	0.16172762	0.06591364	0.02709772
93	0.39638046	0.15855649	0.06399383	0.02605550
94	0.39245590	0.15544754	0.06212993	0.02505337
95	0.38857020	0.15239955	0.06032032	0.02408978
96	0.38472297	0.14941132	0.05856342	0.02316325
97	0.38091383	0.14648169	0.05685769	0.02227235
98	0.37714241	0.14360950	0.05520164	0.02141572
99	0.37340832	0.14079363	0.05359383	0.02059204
100	0.36971121	0.13803297	0.05203284	0.01980004

Table II–continued

SINGLE PAYMENT PRESENT VALUE OF 1 AT COMPOUND INTEREST

n	5%	6%	7%	8%
1	0.95238095	0.94339623	0.93457944	0.92592593
2	0.90702948	0.88999644	0.87343873	0.85733882
3	0.86383760	0.83961928	0.81629788	0.79383224
4	0.82270247	0.79209366	0.76289521	0.73502985
5	0.78352617	0.74725817	0.71298618	0.68058320
6	0.74621540	0.70496054	0.66634222	0.63016963
7	0.71068133	0.66505711	0.62274974	0.58349040
8	0.67683936	0.62741237	0.58200910	0.54026888
9	0.64460892	0.59189846	0.54393374	0.50024897
10	0.61391325	0.55839478	0.50834929	0.46319349
11	0.58467929	0.52678753	0.47509280	0.42888286
12	0.55683742	0.49696936	0.44401196	0.39711376
13	0.53032135	0.46883902	0.41496445	0.36769792
14	0.50506795	0.44230096	0.38781724	0.34046104
15	0.48101710	0.41726506	0.36244602	0.31524170
16	0.45811152	0.39364628	0.33873460	0.29189047
17	0.43629669	0.37136442	0.31657439	0.27026895
18	0.41552065	0.35034379	0.29586392	0.25024903
19	0.39573396	0.33051301	0.27650833	0.23171206
20	0.37688948	0.31180473	0.25841900	0.21454821
21	0.35894236	0.29415540	0.24151309	0.19865575
22	0.34184987	0.27750510	0.22571317	0.18394051
23	0.32557131	0.26179726	0.21094688	0.17031528
24	0.31006791	0.24697855	0.19714662	0.15769934
25	0.29530277	0.23299863	0.18424918	0.14601790

Table II–continued

SINGLE PAYMENT PRESENT VALUE OF 1 AT COMPOUND INTEREST

n	5%	6%	7%	8%
26	0.28124074	0.21981003	0.17219549	0.13520176
27	0.26784832	0.20736795	0.16093037	0.12518682
28	0.25509364	0.19563014	0.15040221	0.11591372
29	0.24294632	0.18455674	0.14056282	0.10732752
30	0.23137745	0.17411013	0.13136712	0.09937733
31	0.22035947	0.16425484	0.12277301	0.09201605
32	0.20986617	0.15495740	0.11474113	0.08520005
33	0.19987254	0.14618622	0.10723470	0.07888893
34	0.19035480	0.13791153	0.10021934	0.07304531
35	0.18129029	0.13010522	0.09366294	0.06763454
36	0.17265741	0.12274077	0.08753546	0.06262458
37	0.16443563	0.11579318	0.08180884	0.05798572
38	0.15660536	0.10923885	0.07645686	0.05369048
39	0.14914797	0.10305552	0.07145501	0.04971341
40	0.14204568	0.09722219	0.06678038	0.04603093
41	0.13528160	0.09171905	0.06241157	0.04262123
42	0.12883962	0.08652740	0.05832857	0.03946411
43	0.12270440	0.08162962	0.05451268	0.03654084
44	0.11686133	0.07700908	0.05094643	0.03383411
45	0.11129651	0.07265007	0.04761349	0.03132788
46	0.10599668	0.06853781	0.04449859	0.02900730
47	0.10094921	0.06465831	0.04158746	0.02685861
48	0.09614211	0.06099840	0.03886679	0.02486908
49	0.09156391	0.05754566	0.03632410	0.02302693
50	0.08720373	0.05428836	0.03394776	0.02132123

Table II—continued

SINGLE PAYMENT PRESENT VALUE OF 1 AT COMPOUND INTEREST

n	5%	6%	7%	8%
51	0.08305117	0.05121544	0.03172688	0.01974188
52	0.07909635	0.04831645	0.02965129	0.01827952
53	0.07532986	0.04558156	0.02771148	0.01692548
54	0.07174272	0.04300147	0.02589858	0.01567174
55	0.06832640	0.04056742	0.02420428	0.01451087
56	0.06507276	0.03827115	0.02262083	0.01343599
57	0.06197406	0.03610486	0.02114096	0.01244073
58	0.05902291	0.03406119	0.01975791	0.01151920
59	0.05621230	0.03213320	0.01846533	0.01066592
60	0.05353552	0.03031434	0.01725732	0.00987585
61	0.05098621	0.02859843	0.01612834	0.00914431
62	0.04855830	0.02697965	0.01507321	0.00846695
63	0.04624600	0.02545250	0.01408711	0.00783977
64	0.04404381	0.02401179	0.01316553	0.00725905
65	0.04194648	0.02265264	0.01230423	0.00672134
66	0.03994903	0.02137041	0.01149928	0.00622346
67	0.03804670	0.02016077	0.01074699	0.00576247
68	0.03623495	0.01901959	0.01004392	0.00533562
69	0.03450948	0.01794301	0.00938684	0.00494039
70	0.03286617	0.01692737	0.00877275	0.00457443
71	0.03130111	0.01596921	0.00819883	0.00423558
72	0.02981058	0.01506530	0.00766246	0.00392184
73	0.02839103	0.01421254	0.00716117	0.00363133
74	0.02703908	0.01340806	0.00669269	0.00336234
75	0.02575150	0.01264911	0.00625485	0.00311328

Table II–continued

SINGLE PAYMENT PRESENT VALUE OF 1 AT COMPOUND INTEREST

n	5%	6%	7%	8%
76	0.02452524	0.01193313	0.00584565	0.00288267
77	0.02335737	0.01125767	0.00546323	0.00266914
78	0.02224512	0.01062044	0.00510582	0.00247142
79	0.02118582	0.01001928	0.00477179	0.00228835
80	0.02017698	0.00945215	0.00445962	0.00211885
81	0.01921617	0.00891713	0.00416787	0.00196190
82	0.01830111	0.00841238	0.00389520	0.00181657
83	0.01742963	0.00793621	0.00364038	0.00168201
84	0.01659965	0.00748699	0.00340222	0.00155742
85	0.01580919	0.00706320	0.00317965	0.00144205
86	0.01505637	0.00666340	0.00297163	0.00133523
87	0.01433940	0.00628622	0.00277723	0.00123633
88	0.01365657	0.00593040	0.00259554	0.00114475
89	0.01300626	0.00559472	0.00242574	0.00105995
90	0.01238691	0.00527803	0.00226704	0.00098144
91	0.01179706	0.00497928	0.00211873	0.00090874
92	0.01123530	0.00469743	0.00198012	0.00084142
93	0.01070028	0.00443154	0.00185058	0.00077910
94	0.01019074	0.00418070	0.00172952	0.00072138
95	0.00970547	0.00394405	0.00161637	0.00066795
96	0.00924331	0.00372081	0.00151063	0.00061847
97	0.00880315	0.00351019	0.00141180	0.00057266
98	0.00838395	0.00331150	0.00131944	0.00053024
99	0.00798471	0.00312406	0.00123312	0.00049096
100	0.00760449	0.00294723	0.00115245	0.00045459

Table II–continued

SINGLE PAYMENT PRESENT VALUE OF 1 AT COMPOUND INTEREST

n	9%	10%	11%	12%
1	0.91743119	0.90909091	0.90090090	0.89285714
2	0.84167999	0.82644628	0.81162243	0.79719388
3	0.77218348	0.75131480	0.73119138	0.71178025
4	0.70842521	0.68301346	0.65873097	0.63551808
5	0.64993139	0.62092132	0.59345133	0.56742686
6	0.59626733	0.56447393	0.53464084	0.50663112
7	0.54703424	0.51315812	0.48165841	0.45234922
8	0.50186628	0.46650738	0.43392650	0.40388323
9	0.46042778	0.42409762	0.39092477	0.36061003
10	0.42241081	0.38554329	0.35218448	0.32197324
11	0.38753285	0.35049390	0.31728331	0.28747610
12	0.35553473	0.31863082	0.28584082	0.25667509
13	0.32617865	0.28966438	0.25751426	0.22917419
14	0.29924647	0.26333125	0.23199482	0.20461981
15	0.27453804	0.23939205	0.20900435	0.18269626
16	0.25186976	0.21762914	0.18829220	0.16312166
17	0.23107318	0.19784469	0.16963262	0.14564434
18	0.21199374	0.17985879	0.15282218	0.13003959
19	0.19448967	0.16350799	0.13767764	0.11610678
20	0.17843089	0.14864363	0.12403391	0.10366677
21	0.16369806	0.13513057	0.11174226	0.09255961
22	0.15018171	0.12284597	0.10066870	0.08264251
23	0.13778139	0.11167816	0.09069252	0.07378796
24	0.12640494	0.10152560	0.08170498	0.06588210
25	0.11596784	0.09229600	0.07360809	0.05882331

Table II–continued

SINGLE PAYMENT PRESENT VALUE OF 1 AT COMPOUND INTEREST

n	9%	10%	11%	12%
26	0.10639251	0.08390545	0.06631359	0.05252081
27	0.09760781	0.07627768	0.05974197	0.04689358
28	0.08954845	0.06934335	0.05382160	0.04186927
29	0.08215454	0.06303941	0.04848793	0.03738327
30	0.07537114	0.05730855	0.04368282	0.03337792
31	0.06914783	0.05209868	0.03935389	0.02980172
32	0.06343838	0.04736244	0.03545395	0.02660868
33	0.05820035	0.04305676	0.03194050	0.02375775
34	0.05339481	0.03914251	0.02877522	0.02121227
35	0.04898607	0.03558410	0.02592363	0.01893953
36	0.04494135	0.03234918	0.02335462	0.01691030
37	0.04123059	0.02940835	0.02104020	0.01509848
38	0.03782623	0.02673486	0.01895513	0.01348078
39	0.03470296	0.02430442	0.01707670	0.01203641
40	0.03183758	0.02209493	0.01538441	0.01074680
41	0.02920879	0.02008630	0.01385983	0.00959536
42	0.02679706	0.01826027	0.01248633	0.00856728
43	0.02458446	0.01660025	0.01124895	0.00764936
44	0.02255455	0.01509113	0.01013419	0.00682978
45	0.02069224	0.01371921	0.00912990	0.00609802
46	0.01898371	0.01247201	0.00822513	0.00544466
47	0.01741625	0.01133819	0.00741003	0.00486131
48	0.01597821	0.01030745	0.00667570	0.00434045
49	0.01465891	0.00937041	0.00601415	0.00387540
50	0.01344854	0.00851855	0.00541815	0.00346018

Table II—continued

SINGLE PAYMENT PRESENT VALUE OF 1 AT COMPOUND INTEREST

n	14%	16%	18%	20%
1	0.87719298	0.86206897	0.84745763	0.83333333
2	0.76946753	0.74316290	0.71818443	0.69444444
3	0.67497152	0.64065767	0.60863087	0.57870370
4	0.59208028	0.55229110	0.51578888	0.48225309
5	0.51936866	0.47611302	0.43710922	0.40187757
6	0.45558655	0.41044225	0.37043154	0.33489798
7	0.39963732	0.35382953	0.31392503	0.27908165
8	0.35055905	0.30502546	0.26603816	0.23256804
9	0.30750794	0.26295298	0.22545607	0.19380670
10	0.26974381	0.22668360	0.19106447	0.16150558
11	0.23661738	0.19541690	0.16191904	0.13458799
12	0.20755910	0.16846284	0.13721953	0.11215665
13	0.18206939	0.14522659	0.11628773	0.09346388
14	0.15970999	0.12519534	0.09854893	0.07788657
15	0.14009648	0.10792701	0.08351604	0.06490547
16	0.12289165	0.09304053	0.07077630	0.05408789
17	0.10779969	0.08020735	0.05997992	0.04507324
18	0.09456113	0.06914427	0.05083044	0.03756104
19	0.08294836	0.05960713	0.04307664	0.03130086
20	0.07276172	0.05138546	0.03650563	0.02608405
21	0.06382607	0.04429781	0.03093698	0.02173671
22	0.05598778	0.03818776	0.02621778	0.01811393
23	0.04911209	0.03292049	0.02221845	0.01509494
24	0.04308078	0.02837973	0.01882920	0.01257912
25	0.03779016	0.02446528	0.01595695	0.01048260

Table II–continued

SINGLE PAYMENT PRESENT VALUE OF 1 AT COMPOUND INTEREST

n	14%	16%	18%	20%
26	0.03314926	0.02109076	0.01352284	0.00873550
27	0.02907830	0.01818169	0.01146003	0.00727958
28	0.02550728	0.01567387	0.00971189	0.00606632
29	0.02237481	0.01351196	0.00823042	0.00505526
30	0.01962702	0.01164824	0.00697493	0.00421272
31	0.01721669	0.01004159	0.00591096	0.00351060
32	0.01510236	0.00865654	0.00500929	0.00292550
33	0.01324768	0.00746253	0.00424516	0.00243792
34	0.01162077	0.00643322	0.00359759	0.00203160
35	0.01093661	0.00554588	0.00304881	0.00169300
36	0.00894181	0.00478093	0.00258373	0.00141083
37	0.00784369	0.00412149	0.00218960	0.00117569
38	0.00688043	0.00355301	0.00185560	0.00097974
39	0.00603547	0.00306294	0.00157254	0.00081645
40	0.00529427	0.00264047	0.00133266	0.00068038
41	0.00464410	0.00227626	0.00112938	0.00056698
42	0.00407377	0.00192296	0.00095710	0.00047248
43	0.00357348	0.00169163	0.00081110	0.00039374
44	0.00313463	0.00145831	0.00068737	0.00032811
45	0.00274968	0.00125716	0.00058252	0.00027343
46	0.00241200	0.00108376	0.00049366	0.00022786
47	0.00211579	0.00093427	0.00041836	0.00018988
48	0.00185595	0.00080541	0.00035454	0.00015823
49	0.00162803	0.00069432	0.00030046	0.00013186
50	0.00142810	0.00059855	0.00025462	0.00010988

Table II–continued

SINGLE PAYMENT PRESENT VALUE OF 1 AT COMPOUND INTEREST

n	22%	24%	26%	28%
1	0.81967213	0.80645161	0.79365079	0.78125000
2	0.67186240	0.65036420	0.62988158	0.61035156
3	0.55070689	0.52448726	0.49990602	0.47683716
4	0.45139909	0.42297360	0.39675081	0.37252903
5	0.36999925	0.34110774	0.31488159	0.29103830
6	0.30327808	0.27508689	0.24990603	0.22737368
7	0.24858859	0.22184426	0.19833812	0.17763568
8	0.20376114	0.17890666	0.15741120	0.13877788
9	0.16701733	0.14427957	0.12492953	0.10842022
10	0.13689945	0.11635449	0.09915042	0.08470329
11	0.11221266	0.09383427	0.07869081	0.06617445
12	0.09197759	0.07567280	0.06245302	0.05169879
13	0.07539147	0.06102645	0.04956589	0.04038968
14	0.06179629	0.04921488	0.03933801	0.03155444
15	0.05065269	0.03968942	0.03122064	0.02465190
16	0.04151860	0.03200759	0.02477829	0.01925930
17	0.03403164	0.02581258	0.01966531	0.01504633
18	0.02789479	0.02081659	0.01560739	0.01175494
19	0.02286458	0.01678758	0.01238681	0.00918355
20	0.01874146	0.01353837	0.00983081	0.00717465
21	0.01536185	0.01091804	0.00780223	0.00560519
22	0.01259168	0.00880487	0.00619224	0.00437906
23	0.01032105	0.00710070	0.00491448	0.00342114
24	0.00845988	0.00572637	0.00390038	0.00267276
25	0.00693433	0.00461804	0.00309554	0.00208810

Table II–continued

SINGLE PAYMENT PRESENT VALUE OF 1 AT COMPOUND INTEREST

n	22%	24%	26%	28%
26	0.00568387	0.00372423	0.00245678	0.00163133
27	0.00465891	0.00300341	0.00194982	0.00127447
28	0.00381878	0.00242210	0.00154748	0.00099568
29	0.00313015	0.00195331	0.00122816	0.00077788
30	0.00256570	0.00157525	0.00097473	0.00060772
31	0.00210303	0.00127036	0.00077359	0.00047478
32	0.00172379	0.00102449	0.00061396	0.00037092
33	0.00141295	0.00082620	0.00048727	0.00028978
34	0.00115815	0.00066629	0.00038672	0.00022639
35	0.00094931	0.00053733	0.00030692	0.00017687
36	0.00077812	0.00043333	0.00024359	0.00013818
37	0.00063780	0.00034946	0.00019333	0.00010795
38	0.00052279	0.00028182	0.00015343	0.00008434
39	0.00042852	0.00022728	0.00012177	0.00006589
40	0.00035124	0.00018329	0.00009664	0.00005148
41	0.00028790	0.00014781	0.00007670	0.00004022
42	0.00023599	0.00011920	0.00006087	0.00003142
43	0.00019343	0.00009613	0.00004831	0.00002455
44	0.00015855	0.00007753	0.00003834	0.00001918
45	0.00012996	0.00006252	0.00003043	0.00001498
46	0.00010652	0.00005042	0.00002415	0.00001170
47	0.00008731	0.00004066	0.00001917	0.00000914
48	0.00007157	0.00003279	0.00001521	0.00000714
49	0.00005866	0.00002644	0.00001207	0.00000558
50	0.00004808	0.00002133	0.00000958	0.00000436

Table II–continued

SINGLE PAYMENT PRESENT VALUE OF 1 AT COMPOUND INTEREST

n	30%	32%	34%	36%
1	0.76923077	0.75757576	0.74626866	0.73529412
2	0.59171598	0.57392103	0.55691691	0.54065744
3	0.45516614	0.43478866	0.41560963	0.39754223
4	0.35012780	0.32938535	0.31015644	0.29231047
5	0.26932907	0.24953435	0.23146003	0.21493417
6	0.20717621	0.18904118	0.17273137	0.15803983
7	0.15936632	0.14321301	0.12890401	0.11620576
8	0.12258947	0.10849471	0.09619702	0.08544541
9	0.94299595	0.08219296	0.07178882	0.06282751
10	0.07253815	0.06226739	0.05357375	0.04619670
11	0.05579858	0.04717227	0.03998041	0.03396816
12	0.04292198	0.03573657	0.02983613	0.02497659
13	0.03301691	0.02707316	0.02226577	0.01836514
14	0.02539762	0.02050997	0.01661624	0.01350378
15	0.01953663	0.01553785	0.01240018	0.00992925
16	0.01502818	0.01177110	0.00925387	0.00730092
17	0.01156014	0.00891750	0.00690587	0.00536832
18	0.00889241	0.00675568	0.00515363	0.00394730
19	0.00684032	0.00511794	0.00384600	0.00290242
20	0.00526178	0.00387723	0.00287015	0.00213413
21	0.00404753	0.00293729	0.00214190	0.00156922
22	0.00311348	0.00222522	0.00159843	0.00115384
23	0.00239499	0.00168578	0.00119286	0.00084841
24	0.00184230	0.00127710	0.00089019	0.00062383
25	0.00141715	0.00096750	0.00066432	0.00045870

Table II–continued

SINGLE PAYMENT PRESENT VALUE OF 1 AT COMPOUND INTEREST

n	30%	32%	34%	36%
26	0.00109012	0.00073296	0.00049576	0.00033728
27	0.00083855	0.00055527	0.00036997	0.00024800
28	0.00064504	0.00042066	0.00027610	0.00018235
29	0.00049618	0.00031868	0.00020604	0.00013408
30	0.00038168	0.00024142	0.00015376	0.00009859
31	0.00029360	0.00018290	0.00011475	0.00007249
32	0.00022585	0.00013856	0.00008563	0.00005330
33	0.00017373	0.00010497	0.00006391	0.00003919
34	0.00013364	0.00007952	0.00004769	0.00002882
35	0.00010280	0.00006024	0.00003559	0.00002119
36	0.00007908	0.00004564	0.00002656	0.00001558
37	0.00006083	0.00003458	0.00001982	0.00001146
38	0.00004679	0.00002619	0.00001479	0.00000842
39	0.00003599	0.00001984	0.00001104	0.00000619
40	0.00002769	0.00001503	0.00000824	0.00000455
41	0.00002130	0.00001139	0.00000615	0.00000335
42	0.00001638	0.00000863	0.00000459	0.00000246
43	0.00001260	0.00000654	0.00000342	0.00000181
44	0.00000969	0.00000495	0.00000256	0.00000133
45	0.00000746	0.00000375	0.00000191	0.00000097
46	0.00000574	0.00000284	0.00000142	0.00000072
47	0.00000441	0.00000215	0.00000106	0.00000053
48	0.00000339	0.00000163	0.00000079	0.00000039
49	0.00000261	0.00000124	0.00000059	0.00000029
50	0.00000201	0.00000094	0.00000044	0.00000021

Table II—continued

SINGLE PAYMENT PRESENT VALUE OF 1 AT COMPOUND INTEREST

n	38%	40%	45%	50%
1	0.72463768	0.71428571	0.68965517	0.66666667
2	0.52509977	0.51020408	0.47562426	0.44444444
3	0.38050708	0.36443149	0.32801673	0.29629630
4	0.27572977	0.26030820	0.22621843	0.19753086
5	0.19980418	0.18593443	0.15601271	0.13168724
6	0.14478564	0.13281031	0.10759497	0.08779150
7	0.10491713	0.09486451	0.07420343	0.05852766
8	0.07602690	0.06776036	0.05117478	0.03901844
9	0.05509196	0.04840026	0.03529295	0.02601229
10	0.03992171	0.03457161	0.02433997	0.01734153
11	0.02892878	0.02469401	0.01678618	0.01156102
12	0.02096288	0.01763858	0.01157668	0.00770735
13	0.01519049	0.01259898	0.00798392	0.00513823
14	0.01100760	0.00899927	0.00550615	0.00342549
15	0.00797652	0.00642805	0.00379734	0.00228366
16	0.00578009	0.00459147	0.00261886	0.00152244
17	0.00418847	0.00327962	0.00180611	0.00101496
18	0.00303512	0.00234259	0.00124559	0.00067664
19	0.00219937	0.00167328	0.00085903	0.00045109
20	0.00159374	0.00119520	0.00059243	0.00030073
21	0.00115489	0.00085371	0.00040858	0.00020049
22	0.00083687	0.00060979	0.00028178	0.00013366
23	0.00060643	0.00043556	0.00019433	0.00008910
24	0.00043944	0.00031112	0.00013402	0.00005940
25	0.00031844	0.00022223	0.00009243	0.00003960

Table II–continued

SINGLE PAYMENT PRESENT VALUE OF 1 AT COMPOUND INTEREST

n	38%	40%	45%	50%
26	0.00023075	0.00015873	0.00006374	0.00002640
27	0.00016721	0.00011338	0.00004396	0.00001760
28	0.00012117	0.00008099	0.00003032	0.00001173
29	0.00008780	0.00005785	0.00002091	0.00000782
30	0.00006362	0.00004132	0.00001442	0.00000522
31	0.00004611	0.00002951	0.00000994	0.00000348
32	0.00003341	0.00002108	0.00000686	0.00000232
33	0.00002421	0.00001506	0.00000473	0.00000155
34	0.00001754	0.00001076	0.00000326	0.00000103
35	0.00001271	0.00000768	0.00000225	0.00000069
36	0.00000921	0.00000549	0.00000155	0.00000046
37	0.00000667	0.00000392	0.00000107	0.00000031
38	0.00000484	0.00000280	0.00000074	0.00000020
39	0.00000350	0.00000200	0.00000051	0.00000014
40	0.00000254	0.00000143	0.00000035	0.00000009
41	0.00000184	0.00000102	0.00000024	0.00000006
42	0.00000133	0.00000073	0.00000017	0.00000004
43	0.00000097	0.00000052	0.00000012	0.00000003
44	0.00000070	0.00000037	0.00000008	0.00000002
45	0.00000051	0.00000027	0.00000005	0.00000001
46	0.00000037	0.00000019	0.00000004	0.00000001
47	0.00000027	0.00000014	0.00000003	0.00000001
48	0.00000019	0.00000010	0.00000002	0.00000000
49	0.00000014	0.00000007	0.00000001	0.00000000
50	0.00000010	0.00000005	0.00000001	0.00000000

Table III

AMOUNT OF 1 PER PERIOD COMPOUNDED FOR N PERIODS (UNIFORM SERIES)

n	1/8%	1/4%	1/2%	7/12%	n
1	1.00000000	1.00000000	1.00000000	1.00000000	1
2	2.00124999	2.00250000	2.00500000	2.00583333	2
3	3.00375156	3.00750625	3.01502500	3.01753403	3
4	4.00750625	4.01502502	4.03010013	4.03513631	4
5	5.01251563	5.02506258	5.05025063	5.05867460	5
6	6.01878127	6.03762523	6.07550188	6.08818354	6
7	7.02630475	7.05271930	7.10587939	7.12369794	7
8	8.03508763	8.07035110	8.14140879	8.16525285	8
9	9.04513150	9.09052697	9.18211583	9.21288349	9
10	10.05643790	10.11325329	10.22802641	10.26662531	10
11	11.06900846	11.13853642	11.27916654	11.32651396	11
12	12.08284471	12.16638277	12.33556237	12.39258529	12
13	13.09794827	13.19679872	13.39724018	13.46487537	13
14	14.11432070	14.22979072	14.46422639	14.54342048	14
15	15.13196361	15.26536520	15.53654752	15.62825710	15
16	16.15087856	16.30352861	16.61423026	16.71942193	16
17	17.17106716	17.34428743	17.69730141	17.81695189	17
18	18.19253099	18.38764815	18.78578791	18.92088411	18
19	19.21527166	19.43361727	19.87971685	20.03125593	19
20	20.23929074	20.48220131	20.97911544	21.14810493	20
21	21.26458986	21.53340682	22.08401101	22.27146887	21
22	22.29117060	22.58724033	23.19443107	23.40138577	22
23	23.31903456	23.64370843	24.31040322	24.53789386	23
24	24.34818335	24.70281770	25.43195524	25.68103157	24
25	25.37861858	25.76457475	26.55911502	26.83083759	25

Table III–continued

AMOUNT OF 1 PER PERIOD COMPOUNDED FOR N PERIODS (UNIFORM SERIES)

n	1/8%	1/4%	1/2%	7/12%
26	26.41034186	26.82898619	27.69191059	27.98735081
27	27.44335478	27.89605865	28.83037015	29.15061035
28	28.47765898	28.96579880	29.97452200	30.32065558
29	29.51325606	30.03821330	31.12439461	31.49752607
30	30.55014762	31.11330883	32.28001658	32.68126164
31	31.58833530	32.19109210	33.44141666	33.87190233
32	32.62782073	33.27156983	34.60862375	35.06948843
33	33.66860550	34.35474876	35.78166686	36.27406045
34	34.71069126	35.44063563	36.96057520	37.48565913
35	35.75407962	36.52923722	38.14537807	38.70432548
36	36.79877222	37.62056031	39.33610496	39.93010071
37	37.84477069	38.71461171	40.53278549	41.16302630
38	38.89207665	39.81139824	41.73544942	42.40314395
39	39.94069174	40.91092673	42.94412666	43.65049562
40	40.99061762	42.01320405	44.15884730	44.90512352
41	42.04185588	43.11823706	45.37964153	46.16707007
42	43.09440821	44.22603265	46.60653974	47.43637798
43	44.14827622	45.33659774	47.83957244	48.71309018
44	45.20346156	46.44993923	49.07877030	49.99724988
45	46.25996589	47.56606408	50.32416415	51.28890050
46	47.31779085	48.68497924	51.57578497	52.58808575
47	48.37693808	49.80669169	52.83366390	53.89484959
48	49.43740926	50.93120842	54.09783222	55.20923621
49	50.49920602	52.05853644	55.36832138	56.53129009
50	51.56233002	53.18868278	56.64516299	57.86105595

Table III–continued

AMOUNT OF 1 PER PERIOD COMPOUNDED FOR N PERIODS (UNIFORM SERIES)

n	1/8%	1/4%	1/2%	7/12%
51	52.62678294	54.32165449	57.92838880	59.19857877
52	53.69256642	55.45745862	59.21803075	60.54390381
53	54.75968212	56.59610227	60.51412090	61.89707659
54	55.82813173	57.73759252	61.81669150	63.25814287
55	56.89791689	58.88193650	63.12577496	64.62714870
56	57.96903929	60.02914135	64.44140384	66.00414040
57	59.04150058	61.17921420	65.76361086	67.38916455
58	60.11530246	62.33216223	67.09242891	68.78226801
59	61.19044659	63.48799264	68.42789105	70.18349791
60	62.26693465	64.64671262	69.77003051	71.59290165
61	63.34476832	65.80832940	71.11888066	73.01052691
62	64.42394928	66.97285023	72.47447507	74.43642165
63	65.50447922	68.14028235	73.83684744	75.87063411
64	66.58635982	69.31063306	75.20603168	77.31321281
65	67.66959276	70.48390964	76.58206184	78.76420655
66	68.75417975	71.66011942	77.96497215	80.22366442
67	69.84012248	72.83926971	79.35479701	81.69163580
68	70.92742263	74.02136789	80.75157099	83.16817034
69	72.01608191	75.20642131	82.15532885	84.65331800
70	73.10610202	76.39443736	83.56610549	86.14712902
71	74.19748464	77.58542345	84.98393602	87.64965394
72	75.29023150	78.77938701	86.40885570	89.16094359
73	76.38434429	79.97633548	87.84089998	90.68104909
74	77.47982472	81.17627632	89.28010448	92.21002188
75	78.57667450	82.37921701	90.72650500	93.74791367

Table III–continued

AMOUNT OF 1 PER PERIOD COMPOUNDED FOR N PERIODS
(UNIFORM SERIES)

n	1/8%	1/4%	1/2%	7/12%
76	79.67489534	83.58516505	92.18013752	95.29477650
77	80.77448896	84.79412797	93.64103821	96.85066270
78	81.87545707	86.00611329	95.10924340	98.41562490
79	82.97780139	87.22112857	96.58478962	99.98971604
80	84.08152365	88.43918139	98.06771357	101.57298939
81	85.18662555	89.66027934	99.55805214	103.16549849
82	86.29310883	90.88443004	101.05584240	104.76729723
83	87.40097522	92.11164112	102.56112161	106.37843980
84	88.51022644	93.34192022	104.07392722	107.99898070
85	89.62086422	94.57527502	105.59429685	109.62897475
86	90.73289030	95.81171321	107.12226834	111.26847710
87	91.84630642	97.05124249	108.65787968	112.91754322
88	92.96111430	98.29387060	110.20116908	114.57622889
89	94.07731569	99.53960527	111.75217492	116.24459022
90	95.19491234	100.78845429	113.31093580	117.92268367
91	96.31390598	102.04042542	114.87749048	119.61056599
92	97.43429836	103.29552649	116.45187793	121.30829429
93	98.56609123	104.55376530	118.03413732	123.01592601
94	99.67928634	105.81514972	119.62430800	124.73351891
95	100.80388545	107.07968759	121.22242954	126.46113110
96	101.92989031	108.34738681	122.82854169	128.19882103
97	103.05730267	109.61825528	124.44268440	129.94664749
98	104.18612430	110.89230091	126.06489782	131.70466960
99	105.31635695	112.16953167	127.69522231	133.47294684
100	106.44800240	113.44995550	129.33369842	135.25153903

Table III–continued

AMOUNT OF 1 PER PERIOD COMPOUNDED FOR N PERIODS
(UNIFORM SERIES)

n	1/8%	1/4%	1/2%	7/12%
101	107.58106241	114.73358038	130.98036692	137.04050634
102	108.71553874	116.02041434	132.63526875	138.83990929
103	109.85143315	117.31046537	134.29844509	140.64980876
104	110.98874745	118.60374153	135.96993732	142.47026598
105	112.12748338	119.90025089	137.64978701	144.30134253
106	113.26764274	121.20000152	139.33803594	146.14310036
107	114.40922729	122.50300152	141.03472612	147.99560178
108	115.55223882	123.80925902	142.73989975	149.85890946
109	116.69667912	125.11878217	144.45359925	151.73308643
110	117.84254997	126.43157913	146.17586725	153.61819610
111	118.98985316	127.74765807	147.90674658	155.51430225
112	120.13859048	129.06702722	149.64628032	157.42146901
113	121.28876371	130.38969479	151.39451172	159.33976091
114	122.44037467	131.71566902	153.15148428	161.26924285
115	123.59342514	133.04495820	154.91724170	163.20998010
116	124.74791692	134.37757059	156.69182791	165.16203832
117	125.90385182	135.71351452	158.47528704	167.12548354
118	127.06123163	137.05279830	160.26766348	169.10038219
119	128.22005817	138.39543030	162.06900180	171.08680109
120	129.38033324	139.74141888	163.87934681	173.08480743
121	130.54205866	141.09077242	165.69874354	175.09446881
122	131.70523623	142.44349935	167.52723726	177.11585321
123	132.86986778	143.79960810	169.36487344	179.14902902
124	134.03595511	145.15910712	171.21169781	181.19406502
125	135.20350006	146.52200489	173.06775630	183.25103040

Table III–continued

AMOUNT OF 1 PER PERIOD COMPOUNDED FOR N PERIODS
(UNIFORM SERIES)

n	1/8%	1/4%	1/2%	7/12%
126	136.37250443	147.88830990	174.93309508	185.31999474
127	137.54297006	149.25803068	176.80776056	187.40102805
128	138.71489878	150.63117575	178.69179936	189.49420071
129	139.88829240	152.00775369	180.58525836	191.59958355
130	141.06315276	153.38777308	182.48818465	193.71724778
131	142.23948170	154.77124251	184.40062557	195.84726506
132	143.41728106	156.15817062	186.32262870	197.98970744
133	144.59655266	157.54856604	188.25424184	200.14464740
134	145.77729835	158.94243746	190.19551305	202.31215785
135	146.95951997	160.33979355	192.14649062	204.49231210
136	148.14321938	161.74064304	194.10722307	206.68518392
137	149.32839839	163.14499164	196.07775919	208.89084749
138	150.51505890	164.55285713	198.05814798	211.10937744
139	151.70320272	165.96423927	200.04843872	213.34084881
140	152.89283172	167.37914987	202.04868092	215.58533709
141	154.08394776	168.79759775	204.05892432	217.84291822
142	155.27655270	170.21959174	206.07921894	220.11366858
143	156.47064838	171.64514072	208.10961504	222.39766498
144	157.66623670	173.07425357	210.15016311	224.69498469
145	158.86331950	174.50693921	212.20091393	227.00570544
146	160.06189864	175.94320655	214.26191850	229.32990538
147	161.26197602	177.38306457	216.33322809	231.66766317
148	162.46355349	178.82652223	218.41489423	234.01905787
149	163.66663293	180.27358854	220.50696870	236.38416904
150	164.87121622	181.72427251	222.60950354	238.76307669

Table III–continued

AMOUNT OF 1 PER PERIOD COMPOUNDED FOR N PERIODS (UNIFORM SERIES)

n	1/8%	1/4%	1/2%	7/12%
151	166.07730524	183.17858319	224.72255106	241.15586130
152	167.28490187	184.63652965	226.84616382	243.56260383
153	168.49400800	186.09812097	228.98039464	245.98338568
154	169.70462551	187.56336627	231.12529661	248.41828877
155	170.91675629	189.03227469	233.28092309	250.86739545
156	172.13040224	190.50485538	235.44732771	253.33078859
157	173.34556524	191.98111752	237.62456435	255.80855153
158	174.56224720	193.46107031	239.81268717	258.30076808
159	175.78045001	194.94472298	242.01175060	260.80752256
160	177.00017557	196.43208479	244.22180936	263.32889977
161	178.22142578	197.92316500	246.44291840	265.86498502
162	179.44420257	199.41797292	248.67513300	268.41586410
163	180.66850782	200.91651785	250.91850866	270.98162331
164	181.89434346	202.41880914	153.17310121	273.56234944
165	183.12171138	203.92485617	255.43896671	276.15812982
166	184.35061353	205.43466831	257.71616154	278.76905224
167	185.58105179	206.94825498	260.00474235	281.39520504
168	186.81302811	208.46562562	262.30476606	284.03667707
169	188.04654439	209.98678968	264.61628989	286.69355769
170	189.28160258	211.51175665	266.93937134	289.36593678
171	190.51820458	213.04053605	269.27406820	292.05390474
172	191.75635234	214.57313739	271.62043854	294.75755252
173	192.99604778	216.10957023	273.97854073	297.47697158
174	194.23729283	217.64984415	276.34843344	300.21225391
175	195.48008945	219.19396876	278.73017561	302.96349206

Table III–continued

AMOUNT OF 1 PER PERIOD COMPOUNDED FOR N PERIODS (UNIFORM SERIES)

n	1/8%	1/4%	1/2%	7/12%
176	196.72443956	220.74195369	281.12382648	305.73077910
177	197.97034511	222.29380857	283.52944562	308.51420864
178	199.21780804	223.84954309	285.94709284	311.31387486
179	200.46683030	225.40916695	288.37682831	314.12987246
180	201.71741384	226.97268987	290.81871245	316.96229672
181	202.96956061	228.54012159	293.27280601	319.81124345
182	204.22327256	230.11147190	295.73917004	322.67680904
183	205.47855165	231.68675058	298.21786589	325.55909042
184	206.73539984	233.26596745	300.70895522	328.45818512
185	207.99381909	234.84913237	303.21250000	331.37419120
186	209.25381136	236.43625520	305.72856250	334.30720731
187	210.51537862	238.02734584	308.25720531	337.25733269
188	211.77852285	239.62241420	310.79849134	340.22466713
189	213.04324600	241.22147024	313.35248379	343.20931102
190	214.30955001	242.82452392	315.91924621	346.21136533
191	215.57743700	244.43158523	318.49884244	349.23093163
192	216.84690879	246.04266419	321.09133666	352.26811207
193	218.11796743	247.65777085	323.69679334	355.32300939
194	219.39061489	249.27691528	326.31527731	358.39572694
195	220.66485316	250.90010756	328.94685369	361.48636868
196	221.94068422	252.52735783	331.59158796	364.59503917
197	223.21811008	254.15867623	334.24954590	367.72184356
198	224.49713272	255.79407292	336.92079363	370.86688765
199	225.77775414	257.43355810	339.60539760	374.03027783
200	227.05997633	259.07714200	342.30342450	377.21212111

Table III–continued

AMOUNT OF 1 PER PERIOD COMPOUNDED FOR N PERIODS (UNIFORM SERIES)

n	2/3%	3/4%	5/6%	11/12%
1	1.00000000	1.00000000	1.00000000	1.00000000
2	2.00666667	2.00750000	2.00833333	2.00916667
3	3.02004444	3.02255625	3.02506944	3.02758403
4	4.04017807	4.04522542	4.05027836	4.05533688
5	5.06711259	5.07556461	5.08403068	5.09251080
6	6.10089335	6.11363135	6.12639760	6.13919215
7	7.14156597	7.15948358	7.17745091	7.19546808
8	8.18917641	8.21317971	8.23726300	8.26142654
9	9.24377092	9.27477856	9.30590686	9.33715628
10	10.30539606	10.34433940	10.38345608	10.42274688
11	11.37409870	11.42192194	11.46998489	11.51828873
12	12.44992602	12.50758636	12.56556809	12.62387304
13	13.53292553	13.60139325	13.67028116	13.73959187
14	14.62314503	14.70340370	14.78420017	14.86553813
15	15.72063267	15.81367923	15.90740184	16.00180557
16	16.82543688	16.93228183	17.03996352	17.14848878
17	17.93760646	18.05927394	18.18196322	18.30568326
18	19.05719051	19.19471849	19.33347958	19.47348536
19	20.18423844	20.33867888	20.49459191	20.65199231
20	21.31880003	21.49121897	21.66538017	21.84130224
21	22.46092537	22.65240312	22.84592501	23.04151418
22	23.61066487	23.82229614	24.03630771	24.25272806
23	24.76806930	25.00096336	25.23661028	25.47504473
24	25.93318976	26.18847059	26.44691536	26.70856597
25	27.10607769	27.38488412	27.66730633	27.95339449

Table III—continued

AMOUNT OF 1 PER PERIOD COMPOUNDED FOR N PERIODS
(UNIFORM SERIES)

n	2/3%	3/4%	5/6%	11/12%
26	28.28678488	28.59027075	28.89786721	29.20963394
27	29.47536344	29.80469778	30.13868277	30.47738892
28	30.67186587	31.02823301	31.38983846	31.75676499
29	31.87634497	32.26094476	32.65142045	33.04786866
30	33.08885394	33.50290184	33.92351562	34.35080746
31	34.30944630	34.75417361	35.20621158	35.66568986
32	35.53817594	36.01482991	36.49959668	36.99262535
33	36.77509711	37.28494113	37.80375998	38.33172442
34	38.02026443	38.56457819	39.11879132	39.68309856
35	39.27373286	39.85381253	40.44478124	41.04686029
36	40.53555774	41.15271612	41.78182109	42.42312318
37	41.80579479	42.46136149	43.13000293	43.81200181
38	43.08450009	43.77982170	44.48941962	45.21361183
39	44.37173009	45.10817037	45.86016478	46.62806993
40	45.66754163	46.44648164	47.24233283	48.05549391
41	46.97199191	47.79483026	48.63601893	49.49600260
42	48.28513852	49.15329148	50.04131909	50.94971596
43	49.60703944	50.52194117	51.45833008	52.41675502
44	50.93775304	51.90085573	52.88714950	53.89724194
45	52.27733806	53.29011215	54.32787574	55.39129999
46	53.62585365	54.68978799	55.78060804	56.89905357
47	54.98335934	56.09996140	57.24544644	58.42062823
48	56.34991507	57.52071111	58.72249183	59.95615066
49	57.72558117	58.95211644	60.21184593	61.50574870
50	59.11041837	60.39425732	61.71361131	63.06955140

Table III–continued

AMOUNT OF 1 PER PERIOD COMPOUNDED FOR N PERIODS
(UNIFORM SERIES)

n	2/3%	3/4%	5/6%	11/12%
51	60.50448783	61.84721424	63.22789140	64.64768896
52	61.90785108	63.31106835	64.75479050	66.24029277
53	63.32057009	64.78590136	66.29441375	67.84749545
54	64.74270722	66.27179562	67.84686720	69.46943083
55	66.17432527	67.76883409	69.41225776	71.10623394
56	67.61548744	69.27710035	70.99069324	72.75804109
57	69.06625736	70.79667860	72.58228235	74.42498980
58	70.52669907	72.32765369	74.18713470	76.10721887
59	71.99687706	73.87011109	75.80536083	77.80486838
60	73.47685625	75.42413693	77.43707217	79.51807967
61	74.96670195	76.98981795	79.08238110	81.24699540
62	76.46647997	78.56724159	80.74140094	82.99175952
63	77.97625650	80.15649590	82.41424595	84.75251732
64	79.49609821	81.75766962	84.10103133	86.52941539
65	81.02607220	83.37085214	85.80187326	88.32260170
66	82.56624601	84.99613353	87.51688887	90.13222555
67	84.11668765	86.63360453	89.24619628	91.95843761
68	85.67746557	88.28335657	90.98991458	93.80138996
69	87.24864867	89.94548174	92.74816387	95.66123603
70	88.83030633	91.62007285	94.52106524	97.53813070
71	90.42250837	93.30722340	96.30874078	99.43223023
72	92.02532510	95.00702758	98.11131362	101.34369234
73	93.63882726	96.71958028	99.92890790	103.27267618
74	95.26308611	98.44497714	101.76164880	105.21934238
75	96.89817335	100.18331446	103.60966254	107.18385302

Table III—continued

AMOUNT OF 1 PER PERIOD COMPOUNDED FOR N PERIODS (UNIFORM SERIES)

n	2/3%	3/4%	5/6%	11/12%
76	98.54416118	101.93468932	105.47307639	109.16637167
77	100.20112225	103.69919949	107.35201869	111.16706341
78	101.86912973	105.47694349	109.24661885	113.18609482
79	103.54825726	107.26802056	111.15700734	115.22363402
80	105.23857898	109.07253072	113.08331573	117.27985067
81	106.94016950	110.89057470	115.02567670	119.35491597
82	108.65310397	112.72225401	116.98422400	121.44900269
83	110.37745799	114.56767091	118.95909254	123.56228522
84	112.11330771	116.42692845	120.95041831	125.69493950
85	113.86072977	118.30013041	122.95833846	127.84714311
86	115.61980130	120.18738139	124.98299128	130.01907525
87	117.39059997	122.08878675	127.02451621	132.21091678
88	119.17320397	124.00445265	129.08305384	134.42285018
89	120.96769200	125.93448604	131.15874596	136.65505964
90	122.77414328	127.87899469	133.25173550	138.90773102
91	124.59263757	129.83808715	135.36216663	141.18105189
92	126.42325515	131.81187280	137.49018469	143.47521153
93	128.26607685	133.80046185	139.63593623	145.79040096
94	130.12118403	135.80396531	141.79956903	148.12681297
95	131.98865859	137.82249505	143.98123210	150.48464209
96	133.86858298	139.85616377	146.18107570	152.86408464
97	135.76104020	141.90508499	148.39925133	155.26533875
98	137.66611380	143.96937313	150.63591176	157.68860435
99	139.58388790	146.04914343	152.89121103	160.13408323
100	141.51444715	148.14451201	155.16530445	162.60197899

Table III–continued

AMOUNT OF 1 PER PERIOD COMPOUNDED FOR N PERIODS (UNIFORM SERIES)

n	$\frac{2}{3}\%$	$\frac{3}{4}\%$	$\frac{5}{6}\%$	$\frac{11}{12}\%$
101	143.45787680	150.25559585	157.45834865	165.09249713
102	145.41426264	152.38251281	159.77050156	167.60584502
103	147.38369106	154.52538166	162.10192240	170.14223193
104	149.36624900	156.68432202	164.45277176	172.70186905
105	151.36202399	158.85945444	166.82321152	175.28496952
106	153.37110415	161.05090035	169.21340495	177.89174840
107	155.39357818	163.25878210	171.62351666	180.52242276
108	157.42953537	165.48322296	174.05371263	183.17721164
109	159.47906560	167.72434714	176.50416023	185.85633608
110	161.54225937	169.98227974	178.97502824	188.56001916
111	163.61920777	172.25714684	181.46648680	191.28848600
112	165.71000249	174.54907544	183.97870753	194.04196378
113	167.81473584	176.85819351	186.51186342	196.82068178
114	169.93350074	179.18462996	189.06612895	199.62487137
115	172.06639075	181.52851468	191.64168002	202.45476602
116	174.21350002	183.88997854	194.23869402	205.31060137
117	176.37492335	186.26915338	196.85734981	208.19261522
118	178.55075618	188.66617203	199.49782772	211.10104752
119	180.74109455	191.08116832	202.16030962	214.03614046
120	182.94603518	193.51427708	204.84497886	216.99813841
121	185.16567542	195.96563416	207.55202035	219.98728801
122	187.40011325	198.43537642	210.28162052	223.00383815
123	189.64944734	200.92364174	213.03396736	226.04804000
124	191.91377699	203.43056905	215.80925042	229.12014703
125	194.19320217	205.95629832	218.60766084	232.22041504

Table III–continued

AMOUNT OF 1 PER PERIOD COMPOUNDED FOR N PERIODS
(UNIFORM SERIES)

n	2/3%	3/4%	5/6%	11/12%
126	196.48782352	208.50097056	221.42939135	235.34910218
127	198.79774234	211.06472784	224.27463627	238.50646895
128	201.12306062	213.64771330	227.14359158	241.69277824
129	203.46388103	216.25007115	230.03645484	244.90829537
130	205.82030690	218.87194668	232.95342530	248.15328808
131	208.19244228	221.51348628	235.89470384	251.42802655
132	210.58039189	224.17483743	238.86049304	254.73278346
133	212.98426117	226.85614871	241.85099714	258.06783398
134	215.40415625	229.55756982	244.86642212	261.43345578
135	217.84018396	232.27925160	247.90697564	264.82992913
136	220.29245185	235.02134598	250.97286710	268.25753681
137	222.76106820	237.78400608	254.06430766	271.71656423
138	225.24614198	240.56738612	257.18151022	275.20729940
139	227.74778293	243.37164152	260.32468947	278.73003297
140	230.26610148	246.19692883	263.49406188	282.28505828
141	232.80120883	249.04340580	266.68984573	285.87267131
142	235.35321688	251.91123134	269.91226111	289.49317079
143	237.92223833	254.80056558	273.16152995	293.14685819
144	240.50838659	257.71156982	276.43787604	296.83403772
145	243.11177583	260.64440659	279.74152500	300.55501640
146	245.73252100	263.59923964	283.07270437	304.31010405
147	248.37073781	266.57623394	286.43164358	308.09961333
148	251.02654273	269.57555569	289.81857394	311.92385979
149	253.70005301	272.59737236	293.23372872	315.78316183
150	256.39138670	275.64185265	296.67734313	319.67784081

Table III–continued

AMOUNT OF 1 PER PERIOD COMPOUNDED FOR N PERIODS
(UNIFORM SERIES)

n	2/3%	3/4%	5/6%	11/12%
151	259.10066261	278.70916655	300.14965432	323.60822102
152	261.82800036	281.79948530	303.65090144	327.57462971
153	264.57352036	284.91298144	307.18132561	331.57739715
154	267.33734383	288.04982880	310.74116999	335.61685662
155	270.11959279	291.21020251	314.33067974	339.69334447
156	272.92039008	294.39427903	317.95010207	343.80720012
157	275.73985934	297.60223613	321.59968626	347.95876612
158	278.57812507	300.83425290	325.27968364	352.14838814
159	281.43531257	304.09050979	328.99034767	356.37641503
160	284.31154799	307.37118862	332.73193390	360.64319883
161	287.20695831	310.67647253	336.50470000	364.94909482
162	290.12167136	314.00654607	340.30890585	369.29446152
163	293.05581584	317.36159517	344.14481339	373.67966075
164	296.00952128	320.74180713	348.01268684	378.10505764
165	298.98291809	324.14737069	351.91279256	382.57102066
166	301.97613754	327.57847597	355.84539817	387.07792168
167	304.98931179	331.03531454	359.81077749	391.62613596
168	308.02257387	334.51807940	363.80920063	396.21604221
169	311.07605770	338.02696499	367.84094397	400.84802259
170	314.14989808	341.56216723	371.90628517	405.52246279
171	317.24423073	345.12388348	376.00550421	410.23975203
172	320.35919227	348.71231261	380.13888341	415.00028309
173	323.49492022	352.32765495	384.30670744	421.06732183
174	326.65155302	355.97011237	388.50926334	424.65265983
175	329.82923004	359.63988821	392.74684053	429.54530921

Table III–continued

AMOUNT OF 1 PER PERIOD COMPOUNDED FOR N PERIODS (UNIFORM SERIES)

n	⅔%	¾%	⅚%	11/12%
176	333.02809158	363.33718737	397.01973086	434.48280787
177	336.24827885	367.06221628	401.32822862	439.46556694
178	339.48993405	370.81518290	405.67263052	444.49400130
179	342.75320027	374.59629677	410.05323578	449.56852964
180	346.03822161	378.40576900	414.47034607	454.68957450
181	349.34514309	382.24381226	418.92426562	459.85756226
182	352.67411071	386.11064086	423.41530117	465.07292324
183	356.02527144	390.00647066	427.94376201	470.33609170
184	359.39877325	393.93151919	432.50996003	475.64750587
185	362.79470508	397.88600559	437.11420969	481.00760801
186	366.21339684	401.87015063	441.75682811	486.41684441
187	369.65481949	405.88417676	446.43813500	491.87566548
188	373.11918495	409.92830808	451.15845280	497.38452575
189	376.60664618	414.00277039	455.91810657	502.94388389
190	380.11735716	418.10779117	460.71742412	508.55420283
191	383.65147287	422.24359961	465.55673599	514.21594968
192	387.20914936	426.41042660	470.43637545	519.92959588
193	390.79054369	430.60850480	475.35667858	525.69561718
194	394.39581398	434.83806859	480.31798423	531.51449366
195	398.02511941	439.09935410	485.32063410	537.38670985
196	401.67862020	443.39259926	491.61223193	543.31275469
197	405.35647767	447.71804375	495.45134749	549.29312160
198	409.05885419	452.07592908	500.58010872	555.32830855
199	412.78591322	456.46649855	505.75160962	561.41881804
200	416.53781930	460.88999729	510.96620636	567.56515720

Table III–continued

AMOUNT OF 1 PER PERIOD COMPOUNDED FOR N PERIODS (UNIFORM SERIES)

n	1%	2%	3%	4%
1	1.00000000	1.00000000	1.00000000	1.00000000
2	2.01000000	2.02000000	2.03000000	2.04000000
3	3.03010000	3.06040000	3.09090000	3.12160000
4	4.06040100	4.12160800	4.18362700	4.24646400
5	5.10100501	5.20404016	5.30913581	5.41632256
6	6.15201506	6.30812096	6.46840988	6.63297546
7	7.21353521	7.43428338	7.66246218	7.89829448
8	8.28567056	8.58296905	8.89233605	9.21422626
9	9.36852727	9.75462843	10.15910613	10.58279531
10	10.46221254	10.94972100	11.46387931	12.00610712
11	11.56683467	12.16871542	12.80779569	13.48635141
12	12.68250301	13.41208973	14.19202956	15.02580546
13	13.80932804	14.68033152	15.61779045	16.62683768
14	14.94742132	15.97393815	17.08632416	18.29191119
15	16.09689554	17.29341692	18.59891389	20.02358764
16	17.25786449	18.63928525	20.15688130	21.82453114
17	18.43044314	20.01207096	21.76158774	23.69751239
18	19.61474757	21.41231238	23.41443537	25.64541288
19	20.81089504	22.84055863	25.11686844	27.67122940
20	22.01900399	24.29736980	26.87037449	29.77807858
21	23.23919403	25.78331719	28.67648572	31.96920172
22	24.47158598	27.29898354	30.53678030	34.24796979
23	25.71630183	28.84496321	32.45288370	36.61788858
24	26.97346485	30.42186247	34.42647022	39.08260412
25	28.24319950	32.03029972	36.45926432	41.64590829

Table III–continued

AMOUNT OF 1 PER PERIOD COMPOUNDED FOR N PERIODS (UNIFORM SERIES)

n	1%	2%	3%	4%
26	29.52563150	33.67090572	38.55304225	44.31174462
27	30.82088781	35.34432383	40.70963352	47.08421440
28	32.12909669	37.05121031	42.93092252	49.96758298
29	33.45038766	38.79223451	45.21885020	52.96628630
30	34.78489153	40.56807921	47.57541571	56.08493775
31	36.13274045	42.37944079	50.00267818	59.32833526
32	37.49406785	44.22702961	52.50275852	62.70146867
33	38.86900853	46.11157020	55.07784128	66.20952742
34	40.25769862	48.03380160	57.73017652	69.85790851
35	41.66027560	49.99447763	60.46208181	73.65222486
36	43.07687836	51.99436719	63.27594427	77.59831385
37	44.50764714	54.03425453	66.17422259	81.70224640
38	45.95272361	56.11493962	69.15944927	85.97033626
39	47.41225085	58.23723841	72.23423275	90.40914971
40	48.88637336	60.40198318	75.40125973	95.02551570
41	50.37523709	62.61002284	78.66329753	99.82653633
42	51.87898946	64.86222330	82.02319645	104.81959778
43	53.39777936	67.15946777	85.48389234	110.01238169
44	54.93175715	69.50265712	89.04840911	115.41287696
45	56.48107472	71.89271027	92.71986139	121.02939204
46	58.04588547	74.33056447	96.50145723	126.87056772
47	59.62634432	76.81717576	100.39650095	132.94539043
48	61.22260777	79.35351927	104.40839598	139.26320604
49	62.83483385	81.94058966	108.54064785	145.83373429
50	64.46318218	84.57940145	112.79686729	152.66708366

Table III–continued

AMOUNT OF 1 PER PERIOD COMPOUNDED FOR N PERIODS (UNIFORM SERIES)

n	1%	2%	3%	4%
51	66.10781401	87.27098948	117.18077331	159.77376700
52	67.76889215	90.01640927	121.69619651	167.16471768
53	69.44658107	92.81673746	126.34708240	174.85130639
54	71.14104688	95.67307221	131.13749488	182.84535865
55	72.85245735	98.58653365	136.07161972	191.15917299
56	74.58098192	101.55826432	141.15376831	199.80553991
57	76.32679174	104.58942961	146.38838136	208.79776151
58	78.09005966	107.68121820	151.78003280	218.14967197
59	79.87096025	110.83484257	157.33343379	227.87565885
60	81.66966986	114.05153942	163.05343680	237.99068520
61	83.48636655	117.33257021	168.94503991	248.51031261
62	85.32123022	120.67922161	175.01339110	259.45072511
63	87.17444252	124.09280604	181.26379284	270.82875412
64	89.04618695	127.57466216	187.70170662	282.66190428
65	90.93664882	131.12615541	194.33275782	294.96838045
66	92.84601531	134.74867852	201.16274055	307.76711567
67	94.77447546	138.44365209	208.19762277	321.07780030
68	96.72222021	142.21252513	215.44355145	334.92091231
69	98.68944242	146.05677563	222.90685800	349.31774880
70	100.67633684	149.97791114	230.59406374	364.29045876
71	102.68310021	153.97746937	238.51188565	379.86207711
72	104.70993121	158.05701875	246.66724222	396.05656019
73	106.75703052	162.21815913	255.06725949	412.89882260
74	108.82460083	166.46252231	263.71927727	430.41477550
75	110.91284684	170.79177276	272.63085559	448.63136652

Table III–continued

AMOUNT OF 1 PER PERIOD COMPOUNDED FOR N PERIODS (UNIFORM SERIES)

n	1%	2%	3%	4%
76	113.02197530	175.20760821	281.80978126	467.57662118
77	115.15219506	179.71176038	291.26407469	487.27968603
78	117.30371701	184.30599558	301.00199693	507.77087347
79	119.47675418	188.99211549	311.03205684	529.08170841
80	121.67152172	193.77195780	321.36301855	551.24497675
81	123.88823694	198.64739696	332.00390910	574.29477582
82	126.12711931	203.62034490	342.96402638	598.26656685
83	128.38839050	208.69275180	354.25294717	623.19722952
84	130.67227440	213.86660683	365.88053558	649.12511870
85	132.97899715	219.14393897	377.85695165	676.09012345
86	135.30878712	224.52681775	390.19266020	704.13372839
87	137.66187499	230.01735411	402.89844001	733.29907753
88	140.03849374	235.61770119	415.98539321	763.63104063
89	142.43887868	241.33005521	429.46495500	795.17628225
90	144.86326746	247.15665632	443.34890365	827.98333354
91	147.31190014	253.09978944	457.64937076	862.10266688
92	149.78501914	259.16178523	472.37885189	897.58677356
93	152.28286933	265.34502094	487.55021744	934.49024450
94	154.80569803	271.65192135	503.17672397	972.86985428
95	157.35375501	278.08495978	519.27202569	1012.78464845
96	159.92729256	284.64665898	535.85018645	1054.29603439
97	162.52656548	291.33959216	552.92569205	1097.46787577
98	165.15183114	298.16638400	570.51346281	1142.36659080
99	167.80334945	305.12971168	588.62886669	1189.06125443
100	170.48138294	312.23230591	607.28773270	1237.62370461

Table III–continued

AMOUNT OF 1 PER PERIOD COMPOUNDED FOR N PERIODS (UNIFORM SERIES)

n	5%	6%	7%	8%
1	1.00000000	1.00000000	1.00000000	1.00000000
2	2.05000000	2.06000000	2.07000000	2.08000000
3	3.15250000	3.18360000	3.21490000	3.24640000
4	4.31012500	4.37461600	4.43994300	4.50611200
5	5.52563125	5.63709296	5.75073901	5.86660096
6	6.80191281	6.97531854	7.15329074	7.33592904
7	8.14200845	8.39383765	8.65402109	8.92280336
8	9.54910888	9.89746791	10.25980257	10.63662763
9	11.02656432	11.49131598	11.97798875	12.48755784
10	12.57789254	13.18079494	13.81644796	14.48656247
11	14.20678716	14.97164264	15.78359932	16.64548746
12	15.91712652	16.86994120	17.88845127	18.97712646
13	17.71298285	18.88213767	20.14064286	21.49529658
14	19.59863199	21.01506593	22.55048786	24.21492030
15	21.57856359	23.27596988	25.12902201	27.15211393
16	23.65749177	25.67252808	27.88805355	30.32428304
17	25.84036636	28.21287976	30.84021730	33.75022569
18	28.13238467	30.90565255	33.99903251	37.45024374
19	30.53900391	33.75999170	37.37896479	41.44626324
20	33.06595410	36.78559120	40.99549232	45.76196430
21	35.71925181	39.99272668	44.86517678	50.42292144
22	38.50521440	43.39229028	49.00573916	55.45675516
23	41.43047512	46.99582769	53.43614090	60.89329557
24	44.50199887	50.81557735	58.17667076	66.76475922
25	47.72709882	54.86451200	63.24903772	73.10593995

Table III–continued

AMOUNT OF 1 PER PERIOD COMPOUNDED FOR N PERIODS
(UNIFORM SERIES)

n	5%	6%	7%	8%
26	51.11345376	59.15638272	68.67647036	79.95441515
27	54.66912645	63.70576568	74.48382328	87.35076836
28	58.40258277	68.52811162	80.69769091	95.33882983
29	62.32271191	73.63979832	87.34652927	103.96593622
30	66.43884750	79.05818622	94.46078632	113.28321111
31	70.76078988	84.80167739	102.07304137	123.34586800
32	75.29882937	90.88977803	110.21815426	134.21353744
33	80.06377084	97.34316471	118.93342506	145.95062044
34	85.06695938	104.18375460	128.25876481	158.62667007
35	90.32030735	111.43477987	138.23687835	172.31680368
36	95.83632272	119.12086666	148.91345984	187.10214797
37	101.62813886	127.26811866	160.33740202	203.07031981
38	107.70954580	135.90420578	172.56102017	220.31594540
39	114.09502309	145.05845813	185.64029158	238.94122103
40	120.79977424	154.76196562	199.63511199	259.05651871
41	127.83976295	165.04768356	214.60956983	280.78104021
42	135.23175110	175.95054457	230.63223972	304.24352342
43	142.99333866	187.50757724	247.77649650	329.58300530
44	151.14300559	199.75803188	266.12085125	356.94964572
45	159.70015587	212.74351379	285.74931084	386.50561738
46	168.68516366	226.50812462	306.75176260	418.42606677
47	178.11942185	241.09861210	329.22438598	452.90015211
48	188.02539294	256.56452882	353.27009300	490.13216428
49	198.42666259	272.95840053	378.99899951	530.34273742
50	209.34799572	290.33590458	406.52892947	573.77015642

Table III–continued

AMOUNT OF 1 PER PERIOD COMPOUNDED FOR N PERIODS
(UNIFORM SERIES)

n	5%	6%	7%	8%
51	220.81539550	308.75605886	435.98595454	620.67176893
52	232.85616528	328.28142239	467.50497135	671.32551044
53	245.49897354	348.97830773	501.23031935	726.03155128
54	258.77392222	370.91700620	537.31644170	785.11407538
55	272.71261833	394.17202657	575.92859262	848.92320141
56	287.34824924	418.82234816	617.24359410	917.83705752
57	302.71566171	444.95168905	661.45064569	992.26402213
58	318.85144479	472.64879040	708.75219089	1072.64514390
59	335.79401703	502.00771782	759.36484425	1159.45675541
60	353.58371788	533.12818089	813.52038335	1253.21329584
61	372.26290378	566.11587174	871.46681019	1354.47035951
62	391.87604897	601.08282405	933.46948690	1463.82798827
63	412.46985141	638.14779349	999.81235098	1581.93422733
64	434.09334398	677.43666110	1070.79921555	1709.48896552
65	456.79801118	719.08286076	1146.75516064	1847.24808276
66	480.63791174	763.22783241	1228.02802188	1996.02792938
67	505.66980733	810.02150236	1314.98998341	2156.71016373
68	531.95329770	859.62279250	1408.03928225	2330.24697683
69	559.55096258	912.20016005	1507.60203201	2517.66673497
70	588.52851071	967.93216965	1614.13417425	2720.08007377
71	618.95493625	1027.00809983	1728.12356645	2938.68647967
72	650.90268306	1089.62858582	1850.09221610	3174.78139805
73	684.44781721	1156.00630097	1980.59867123	3429.76390989
74	719.67020807	1226.36667903	2120.24057821	3705.14502268
75	756.65371848	1300.94867977	2269.65741869	4002.55662449

Table III–continued

AMOUNT OF 1 PER PERIOD COMPOUNDED FOR N PERIODS
(UNIFORM SERIES)

n	5%	6%	7%	8%
76	795.48640440	1380.00560055	2429.53343800	4323.76115445
77	836.26072462	1463.80593659	2600.60077866	4670.66204681
78	879.07376085	1552.63429278	2783.64283316	5045.31501056
79	924.02744889	1646.79235035	2979.49783148	5449.94021140
80	971.22882134	1746.59989137	3189.06267969	5886.93542831
81	1020.79026240	1852.39588485	3413.29706727	6358.89026258
82	1072.82977552	1964.53963794	3653.22786198	6868.60148358
83	1127.47126430	2083.41201622	3909.95381231	7419.08960227
84	1184.84482752	2209.41673719	4184.65057918	8013.61677045
85	1245.08706889	2342.98174142	4478.57611972	8655.70611209
86	1308.34142234	2484.56064591	4793.07644810	9349.16260105
87	1374.75849345	2634.63428466	5129.59179946	10098.09560914
88	1444.49641812	2793.71234174	5489.66322543	10906.94325787
89	1517.72123903	2962.33508225	5874.93965121	11780.49871850
90	1594.60730098	3141.07518718	6287.18542679	12723.93861598
91	1675.33766603	3330.53969841	6728.28840667	13742.85370526
92	1760.10454933	3531.37208032	7200.26859513	14843.28200168
93	1849.10977680	3744.25440514	7705.28739679	16031.74456181
94	1942.56526564	3969.90966944	8245.65751457	17315.28412676
95	2040.69352892	4209.10424961	8823.85354059	18701.50685690
96	2143.72820537	4462.65050459	9442.52328843	20198.62740545
97	2251.91461564	4731.40953486	10104.49991862	21815.51759788
98	2365.51034642	5016.29410696	10812.81491292	23561.75900572
99	2484.78586374	5318.27175337	11570.71195683	25447.69972617
100	2610.02515693	5638.36805857	12381.66179381	27484.51570427

Table III–continued

AMOUNT OF 1 PER PERIOD COMPOUNDED FOR N PERIODS (UNIFORM SERIES)

n	9%	10%	11%	12%
1	1.0000000	1.0000000	1.0000000	1.0000000
2	2.0900000	2.1000000	2.1100000	2.1200000
3	3.2781000	3.3100000	3.3421000	3.3744000
4	4.5731290	4.6410000	4.7097310	4.7793280
5	5.9847106	6.1051000	6.2278014	6.3528474
6	7.5233346	7.7156100	7.9128596	8.1151890
7	9.20043468	9.4871710	9.7832741	10.0890117
8	11.0284738	11.4358881	11.8594343	12.2996931
9	13.0210364	13.5794769	14.1639720	14.7756563
10	15.1929297	15.9374246	16.7220090	17.5487351
11	17.5602934	18.5311671	19.5614300	20.6545833
12	20.1407198	21.3842838	22.7131872	24.1331333
13	22.9533846	24.5227121	26.2116378	28.0291093
14	26.0191892	27.9749834	30.0949180	32.3926024
15	29.3609162	31.7724817	34.4053590	37.2797147
16	33.0033987	35.9497299	39.1899485	42.7532804
17	36.9737046	40.5447029	44.5008428	48.8836741
18	41.3013380	45.5991731	50.3959355	55.7497150
19	46.0184584	51.1590905	56.9394884	63.4396808
20	51.1601196	57.2749995	64.2028322	72.0524424
21	56.7645304	64.0024994	72.2651437	81.6987355
22	62.8733382	71.40274939	81.2143095	92.5025838
23	69.5319386	79.5430243	91.1478835	104.6028939
24	76.7898131	88.4973268	102.1741507	118.1552411
25	84.7008962	98.3470594	114.4133073	133.3338701

Table III—continued

AMOUNT OF 1 PER PERIOD COMPOUNDED FOR N PERIODS (UNIFORM SERIES)

n	9%	10%	11%	12%
26	93.3239769	109.1817654	127.9987711	150.3339345
27	102.7231348	121.0999419	143.0786359	169.3740066
28	112.9682169	134.2099361	159.8172859	190.6988874
29	124.1353565	148.6309297	178.3971873	214.5827539
30	136.3075385	164.4940227	199.0208779	241.3326843
31	149.5752170	181.9434250	221.9131745	271.2926065
32	164.0369865	201.1377675	247.3236237	304.8477192
33	179.8003153	222.2515442	275.5292223	342.4294455
34	196.9823437	245.4766986	306.8374368	384.5209790
35	215.7107547	271.0243685	341.5895548	431.6634965
36	236.1247226	299.1268053	380.1644058	484.4631161
37	258.3759476	330.0394859	422.9824905	543.5986900
38	282.6297829	364.0434344	470.5105644	609.8305328
39	309.0664633	401.4477779	523.2667265	684.0101967
40	337.8824450	442.5925557	581.8260664	767.0914203
41	369.2918651	487.8518112	646.8269337	860.1423908
42	403.5281330	537.6369924	718.9778964	964.3594777
43	440.8456649	592.4006916	799.0654650	1081.0826150
44	481.5217748	652.6407608	887.9626662	1211.8125288
45	525.8587345	718.9048368	986.6385595	1358.2300323
46	574.1860206	791.7953205	1096.1688010	1522.2176361
47	626.8627625	871.9748526	1217.7473691	1705.8837525
48	684.2804111	960.1723378	1352.6995797	1911.5898028
49	746.8656481	1057.1895716	1502.4965335	2141.9805791
50	815.0835564	1163.9085288	1668.7711522	2400.0182486

Table III—continued

AMOUNT OF 1 PER PERIOD COMPOUNDED FOR N PERIODS (UNIFORM SERIES)

n	14%	16%	18%	20%
1	1.000000	1.000000	1.000000	1.000000
2	2.140000	2.160000	2.180000	2.200000
3	3.439600	3.505600	3.572400	3.640000
4	4.921144	5.066496	5.215432	5.368000
5	6.610104	6.877135	7.154210	7.441600
6	8.535187	8.977477	9.441968	9.929920
7	10.730491	11.413873	12.141522	12.915904
8	13.232760	14.240093	15.326996	16.499085
9	16.085347	17.518508	19.085855	20.798902
10	19.337295	21.321469	23.521309	25.958682
11	23.044516	25.732904	28.755144	32.150419
12	27.270749	30.850169	34.931070	39.580502
13	32.088654	36.786196	42.218663	48.496603
14	37.581065	43.671987	50.818022	59.195923
15	43.842414	51.659505	60.965266	72.035108
16	50.980352	60.925026	72.939014	87.442129
17	59.117601	71.673030	87.068036	105.930555
18	68.394066	84.140715	103.740283	128.116666
19	78.969235	98.603230	123.413534	154.740000
20	91.024928	115.379747	146.627970	186.688000
21	104.768418	134.840506	174.021005	225.025600
22	120.435996	157.414987	206.344786	271.030720
23	138.297035	183.601385	244.486847	326.236863
24	158.658620	213.977607	289.494479	392.484236
25	181.870827	249.214024	342.603486	471.981083

Table III–continued

AMOUNT OF 1 PER PERIOD COMPOUNDED FOR N PERIODS
(UNIFORM SERIES)

n	14%	16%	18%	20%
26	208.332743	290.088267	405.272113	567.377300
27	238.499327	337.502390	479.221093	681.852760
28	272.889233	392.502773	566.480890	819.223312
29	312.093726	456.303216	669.447450	984.067974
30	356.786847	530.311731	790.947991	1181.881569
31	407.737006	616.161608	934.318630	1419.257883
32	465.820186	715.747465	1103.495983	1704.109459
33	532.035013	831.267059	1303.125260	2045.931351
34	607.519914	965.269789	1538.687807	2456.117621
35	693.572702	1120.712955	1816.651612	2948.341146
36	791.672881	1301.027028	2144.648902	3539.009375
37	903.507084	1510.191352	2531.685705	4247.811250
38	1030.998076	1752.821968	2988.389132	5098.373500
39	1176.337806	2034.273483	3527.299175	6119.048200
40	1342.025099	2360.757241	4163.213027	7343.857840
41	1530.908613	2739.478399	4913.591372	8813.629408
42	1746.235819	3178.794943	5799.037819	10577.355289
43	1991.708833	3688.402134	6843.864626	12693.826347
44	2271.548070	4279.546475	8076.760259	15233.591617
45	2590.564800	4965.273911	9531.577105	18281.309940
46	2954.243872	5760.717737	11248.260984	21938.571928
47	3368.838014	6683.432575	13273.947961	26327.286314
48	3841.475336	7753.781787	15664.258594	31593.743576
49	4380.281883	8995.386873	18484.825142	37913.492292
50	4994.521346	10436.649467	21813.093667	45497.190750

Table III–continued

AMOUNT OF 1 PER PERIOD COMPOUNDED FOR N PERIODS (UNIFORM SERIES)

n	22%	24%	26%	28%
1	1.000000	1.000000	1.000000	1.000000
2	2.220000	2.240000	2.260000	2.280000
3	3.708400	3.777600	3.847600	3.918400
4	5.524248	5.684224	5.847976	6.015552
5	7.739583	8.048438	8.368450	8.699907
6	10.442291	10.980063	11.544247	12.135880
7	13.739595	14.615278	15.545751	16.533927
8	17.762306	19.122945	20.587646	22.163426
9	22.670013	24.712451	26.940434	29.369186
10	28.756416	31.643440	34.944947	38.592558
11	35.962047	40.237865	45.030633	50.398474
12	44.873697	50.894953	57.738598	65.510047
13	55.745911	64.109741	73.750633	84.852860
14	69.010011	80.496079	93.925798	109.611661
15	85.192213	100.815138	119.346505	141.302926
16	104.934500	126.010772	151.376596	181.867745
17	129.020091	157.253357	191.734511	233.790714
18	158.404510	195.994162	242.585484	300.252113
19	194.253503	244.032761	306.657710	385.322705
20	237.989273	303.600624	387.388715	494.213063
21	291.346913	377.464774	489.109781	633.592720
22	356.443234	469.056320	617.278324	811.998682
23	435.860746	582.629836	778.770688	1040.358312
24	532.750110	723.460997	982.251067	1332.658640
25	650.955134	898.091636	1238.636345	1706.803059

Table III–continued

AMOUNT OF 1 PER PERIOD COMPOUNDED FOR N PERIODS
(UNIFORM SERIES)

n	22%	24%	26%	28%
26	795.165264	1114.633629	1561.681794	2185.707916
27	971.101622	1383.145700	1968.719061	2798.706132
28	1185.743978	1716.100668	2481.586016	3583.343849
29	1447.607654	2128.964828	3127.798381	4587.680126
30	1767.081337	2640.916387	3942.025960	5876.801990
31	2156.839232	3275.736320	4967.952709	7518.735119
32	2632.343863	4062.913037	6260.620413	9624.980953
33	3212.459512	5039.012166	7889.381721	12320.975619
34	3920.200605	6249.375086	9941.620968	15771.848793
35	4783.644738	7750.225106	12527.442420	20188.966455
36	5837.046581	9611.279132	15785.577449	25842.877062
37	7122.196828	11918.986123	19890.827586	33079.882639
38	8690.080131	14780.542793	25063.442758	42343.249778
39	10602.897760	18328.873063	31580.937875	54200.359716
40	12936.535267	22728.802599	39792.981723	69377.460437
41	15783.573025	28184.715222	50140.156971	88804.149359
42	19256.959091	34950.046876	63177.597783	113670.311178
43	23494.490091	43339.058126	79604.773207	145498.998308
44	28664.277911	53741.432076	100303.014240	186239.717836
45	34971.419051	66640.375774	126382.797942	238387.838830
46	42666.131242	82635.065960	159243.325408	305137.433702
47	52053.680115	102468.481790	200647.590013	390576.915135
48	63506.489741	127061.917420	252816.963416	499939.451375
49	77478.917484	157557.777600	318550.373907	639923.497760
50	94525.279331	195372.644225	401374.471119	819103.077139

Table III–continued

AMOUNT OF 1 PER PERIOD COMPOUNDED FOR N PERIODS (UNIFORM SERIES)

n	30%	32%	34%	36%
1	1.0000	1.0000	1.0000	1.0000
2	2.3000	2.3200	2.3400	2.3600
3	3.9900	4.0624	4.1356	4.2096
4	6.1870	6.3624	6.5417	6.7251
5	9.0431	9.3983	9.7659	10.1461
6	12.7560	13.4058	14.0863	14.7987
7	17.5828	18.6956	19.8756	21.1262
8	23.8576	25.6782	27.6333	29.7316
9	32.0150	34.8953	38.0287	41.4350
10	42.6195	47.0618	51.9584	57.3516
11	56.4053	63.1215	70.6243	78.9982
12	74.3270	84.3204	95.6365	108.4375
13	97.6250	112.3030	129.1529	148.4750
14	127.9125	149.2399	174.0649	202.9260
15	167.2863	197.9967	234.2470	276.9793
16	218.4722	262.3557	314.8910	377.6919
17	285.0139	347.3095	422.9539	514.6610
18	371.5180	459.4485	567.7582	700.9389
19	483.9734	607.4721	761.7961	954.2769
20	630.1655	802.8631	1021.8068	1298.8166
21	820.2151	1060.7793	1370.2211	1767.3906
22	1067.2796	1401.2287	1837.0962	2404.6512
23	1388.4635	1850.6219	2462.7089	3271.3256
24	1806.0026	2443.8209	3301.0300	4450.0029
25	2348.8033	3226.8436	4424.3801	6053.0039

Table III—continued

AMOUNT OF 1 PER PERIOD COMPOUNDED FOR N PERIODS
(UNIFORM SERIES)

n	30%	32%	34%	36%
26	3054.4443	4260.4336	5929.6694	8233.0853
27	3971.7776	5624.7723	7946.7570	11197.9960
28	5164.3109	7425.6994	10649.6543	15230.2745
29	6714.6042	9802.9233	14271.5368	20714.1734
30	8729.9855	12940.8587	19124.8593	28172.2758
31	11349.9811	17082.9335	25628.3115	38315.2951
32	14755.9755	22550.4722	34342.9374	52109.8013
33	19183.7681	29767.6233	46020.5362	70870.3298
34	24939.8985	39294.2628	61668.5185	96384.6485
35	32422.8681	51869.4269	82636.8147	131084.1219
36	42150.7285	68468.6435	110734.3317	178275.4058
37	54796.9471	90379.6094	148385.0045	242455.5519
38	71237.0312	119302.0844	198836.9061	329740.5506
39	92609.1405	157479.7515	266442.4541	448448.1488
40	120392.8827	207874.2719	357033.8885	609890.4824
41	156511.7475	274395.0390	478426.4106	829452.0560
42	203466.2718	362202.4514	641092.3902	1128055.7962
43	264507.1533	478108.2359	859064.8029	1534156.8828
44	343860.2993	631103.8714	1151147.8359	2086454.3606
45	447019.3890	833058.1102	1542539.1001	2837578.9304
46	581126.2058	1099637.7055	2067003.3942	3859108.3453
47	755465.0675	1451522.7712	2769785.5482	5248388.3497
48	982105.5877	1916011.0580	3711513.6346	7137809.1555
49	1276738.2641	2529135.5966	4973429.2704	9707421.4515
50	1659760.7433	3338459.9875	6664396.2223	13202094.1741

Table III–continued

AMOUNT OF 1 PER PERIOD COMPOUNDED FOR N PERIODS
(UNIFORM SERIES)

n	38%	40%	45%	50%
1	1.0000	1.0000	1.0000	1.0000
2	2.3800	2.4000	2.4500	2.5000
3	4.2844	4.3600	4.5525	4.7500
4	6.9124	7.1040	7.6011	8.1250
5	10.5392	10.9456	12.0216	13.1875
6	15.5441	16.3238	18.4314	20.7813
7	22.4509	23.8534	27.7255	32.1719
8	31.9822	34.3947	41.2019	49.2578
9	45.1354	49.1526	60.7428	74.8867
10	63.2869	69.8137	89.0771	113.3301
11	88.3359	98.7391	130.1618	170.9951
12	122.9040	139.2347	189.7346	257.4926
13	170.6070	195.9287	276.1151	387.2390
14	236.4376	275.3002	401.3670	581.8585
15	327.2839	386.4202	582.9821	873.7878
16	452.6518	541.9883	846.3240	1311.6817
17	625.6595	759.7837	1228.1699	1968.5225
18	864.4101	1064.6971	1781.8463	2953.7838
19	1193.8859	1491.5760	2584.6771	4431.6756
20	1648.5625	2089.2064	3748.7818	6648.5135
21	2276.0163	2925.8889	5436.7336	9973.7702
22	3141.9025	4097.2445	7884.2638	14961.6553
23	4336.8254	5737.1423	11433.1824	22443.4829
24	5985.8191	8032.9993	16579.1145	33666.2244
25	8261.4304	11247.1990	24040.7161	50500.3366

Table III–continued

AMOUNT OF 1 PER PERIOD COMPOUNDED FOR N PERIODS
(UNIFORM SERIES)

n	38%	40%	45%	50%
26	11401.7739	15747.0785	34860.0383	75751.5049
27	15735.4480	22046.9100	50548.0556	113628.2573
28	21715.9182	30866.6739	73295.6806	170443.3860
29	29968.9671	43214.3435	106279.7368	255666.0790
30	41358.1746	60501.0809	154106.6184	383500.1185
31	57075.2810	84702.5133	223455.5967	575251.1777
32	78764.8878	118584.5185	324011.6152	862877.7665
33	108696.5451	166019.3260	469817.8421	1294317.6498
34	150002.2322	232428.0563	681236.8710	1941477.4747
35	107004.0805	325400.2789	987794.4630	2912217.2121
36	185666.6311	455561.3904	1432302.9713	4368326.8182
37	394220.9509	637786.9466	2076840.3084	6552491.2273
38	544025.9122	892902.7253	3011419.4472	9828737.8408
39	750756.7589	1250064.8154	4366559.1985	14743107.7612
40	1036045.3272	1750091.7415	6331511.8378	22114662.6418
41	1429743.5516	2450129.4381	9180693.1648	33171994.9628
42	1973047.1012	3430182.2134	13312006.0889	49757993.4444
43	2722806.0000	4802256.0987	19302409.8290	74636991.1670
44	3757473.2795	6723159.5382	27988495.2520	111955487.7490
45	5185314.1257	9412424.3534	40583319.1153	167933232.6240
46	7155734.4935	13177395.0947	58845813.7171	251899849.9360
47	9874914.6011	18448354.1326	85326430.8906	377849775.9060
48	13627383.1494	25827696.7857	123723325.7910	566774664.8600
49	18805789.7462	36158776.5002	179398823.3960	850161998.2920
50	25951990.8499	50622288.1002	260128294.9260	1275242998.4400

Table IV

PRESENT VALUE OF 1 PER PERIOD RECEIVED FOR N PERIODS (UNIFORM SERIES)

n	1/8%	1/4%	1/2%	7/12%	n
1	0.99875156	0.99750623	0.99502488	0.99420050	1
2	1.99625623	1.99252492	1.98509938	1.98263513	2
3	2.99251559	2.98506227	2.97024814	2.96533732	3
4	3.98753118	3.97512446	3.95049566	3.94234034	4
5	4.98130455	4.96271766	4.92586633	4.91367722	5
6	5.97383725	5.94784804	5.89638441	5.87938083	6
7	6.96513084	6.93052174	6.86207404	6.83948384	7
8	7.95518685	7.91074487	7.82295924	7.79401874	8
9	8.94400685	8.88852357	8.77906392	8.74301780	9
10	9.93159235	9.86386391	9.73041186	9.68651314	10
11	10.91794493	10.83677198	10.67702673	10.62453667	11
12	11.90306609	11.80725384	11.61893207	11.55712014	12
13	12.88695740	12.77531555	12.55615131	12.48429509	13
14	13.86962037	13.74096314	13.48870777	13.40609288	14
15	14.85105655	14.70420264	14.41662465	14.32254470	15
16	15.83126746	15.66504004	15.33992502	15.23368156	16
17	16.81025465	16.62348133	16.25863186	16.13953427	17
18	17.78801962	17.57953250	17.17276802	17.04013350	18
19	18.76456391	18.53319950	18.08235624	17.93550969	19
20	19.73988905	19.48448828	18.98741915	18.82569315	20
21	20.71399656	20.43340477	19.88797925	19.71071398	21
22	21.68688795	21.37995488	20.78405896	20.59060213	22
23	22.65856474	22.32414452	21.67568055	21.46538738	23
24	23.62902846	23.26597957	22.56286622	22.33509930	24
25	24.59828061	24.20546591	23.44563803	23.19976732	25

Table IV—continued

PRESENT VALUE OF 1 PER PERIOD RECEIVED FOR N PERIODS (UNIFORM SERIES)

n	1/8%	1/4%	1/2%	7/12%
26	25.56632270	25.14260939	24.32401794	24.05942070
27	26.53315626	26.07741585	25.19802780	24.91408852
28	27.49878278	27.00989112	26.06768936	25.76379968
29	28.46320378	27.94004102	26.93302423	26.60858295
30	29.42642075	28.86787134	27.79405397	27.44846689
31	30.38843520	29.79338787	28.65079997	28.28347993
32	31.34924865	30.71659638	29.50328355	29.11365030
33	32.30886257	31.63750262	30.35152592	29.93900610
34	33.26727847	32.55611234	31.19554818	30.75957524
35	34.22449785	33.47243126	32.03537132	31.57538549
36	35.18052220	34.38646510	32.87101624	32.38646445
37	36.13535300	35.29821955	33.70250372	33.19283955
38	37.08899176	36.20770030	34.52985445	33.99453808
39	38.04143996	37.11491302	35.35308900	34.79158716
40	38.99269909	38.01986336	36.17222786	35.58401374
41	39.94277062	38.92255697	36.98729141	36.37184465
42	40.89165606	39.82299947	37.79829991	37.15510653
43	41.83935686	40.72119648	38.60527354	37.93382588
44	42.78587452	41.61715359	39.40823238	38.70802904
45	43.73121051	42.51087640	40.20719640	39.47774221
46	44.67536630	43.40237047	41.00218547	40.24299143
47	45.61834336	44.29164137	41.79321937	41.00380258
48	46.56014319	45.17869463	42.58031778	41.76020141
49	47.50076723	46.06353580	43.36350028	42.51221349
50	48.44021696	46.94617037	44.14278635	43.25986428

Table IV—continued

PRESENT VALUE OF 1 PER PERIOD RECEIVED FOR N PERIODS (UNIFORM SERIES)

n	1/8%	1/4%	1/2%	7/12%
51	49.37844938	47.82660386	44.91819537	44.00317907
52	50.31559934	48.70484176	45.68974664	44.74218301
53	51.25153492	49.58088953	46.45745934	45.47690108
54	52.18630205	50.45475265	47.22135258	46.20735816
55	53.11990217	51.32643656	47.98144535	46.93357895
56	54.05233675	52.19594669	48.73775657	47.65558802
57	54.98360724	53.06328847	49.49030505	48.37340980
58	55.91371510	53.92846730	50.23910950	49.08706856
59	56.84266177	54.79148858	50.98418855	49.79658846
60	57.77044871	55.65235769	51.72556075	50.50199350
61	58.69707736	56.51107999	52.46324453	51.20330754
62	59.62254918	57.36766083	53.19725824	51.90055431
63	60.54686559	58.22210557	53.92762014	52.59375739
64	61.47002806	59.07441952	54.65434839	53.28294024
65	62.39203801	59.92460800	55.37746109	53.96812617
66	63.31289689	60.77267631	56.09697621	54.64933836
67	64.23260613	61.61862974	56.81291165	55.32659986
68	65.15116717	62.46247355	57.52528522	55.99993358
69	66.068858145	63.30421302	58.23411465	56.66936230
70	66.98485038	64.14385339	58.93941756	57.33490867
71	67.89997541	64.98139989	59.64121151	57.99659520
72	68.81395796	65.81685774	60.33951394	58.65444427
73	69.72679947	66.65023216	61.03434222	59.30847815
74	70.63850134	67.48152834	61.72571366	59.95871896
75	71.54906501	68.31075146	62.41364543	60.60518869

Table IV—continued

PRESENT VALUE OF 1 PER PERIOD RECEIVED FOR N PERIODS (UNIFORM SERIES)

n	1/8%	1/4%	1/2%	7/12%
76	72.45849190	69.13790670	63.09815466	61.24790922
77	73.36678341	69.96299920	63.77925836	61.88690229
78	74.27394099	70.78603411	64.45697350	62.52218952
79	75.17996603	71.60701657	65.13131691	63.15379239
80	76.08485996	72.42595169	65.80230538	63.78173229
81	76.98862418	73.24284458	66.46995561	64.40603044
82	77.89126010	74.05770033	67.13428419	65.02670798
83	78.79276914	74.87052402	67.79530765	65.64378590
84	79.69315270	75.68132072	68.45304244	66.25728507
85	80.59241218	76.49009548	69.10750491	66.86722625
86	81.49054900	77.29685335	69.75871135	67.47363007
87	82.38756454	78.10159935	70.40667796	68.07651706
88	83.28346022	78.90433850	71.05142086	68.67590759
89	84.17823742	79.70507581	71.69295608	69.27182197
90	85.01789755	80.50381627	72.33129958	69.86428033
91	85.96444200	81.30056486	72.96646725	70.45330273
92	86.85587216	82.09532654	73.59847487	71.03890910
93	87.74618942	82.88810628	74.22733818	71.62111923
94	88.63539517	83.67890900	74.85307282	72.19995284
95	89.52349081	84.46773966	75.47569434	72.77542950
96	90.41047772	85.25460315	76.09521825	73.34756869
97	91.29635727	86.03950439	76.71165995	73.91638975
98	92.18113086	86.82244827	77.32503478	74.48191193
99	93.06479985	87.60343967	77.93535799	75.04415436
100	93.94736565	88.38248346	78.54264477	75.60313606

Table IV–continued

PRESENT VALUE OF 1 PER PERIOD RECEIVED FOR N PERIODS
(UNIFORM SERIES)

n	1/8%	1/4%	1/2%	7/12%
101	94.82882961	89.15958450	79.14691021	76.15887702
102	95.70919312	89.93474763	79.74816937	76.71139392
103	96.58845754	90.70797768	80.34643718	77.26070648
104	97.46662427	91.47927948	80.94172854	77.80683331
105	98.34369465	92.24865784	81.53405825	78.34979288
106	99.21967006	93.01611755	82.12344104	78.88960355
107	100.09455187	93.78166339	82.70989158	79.42628359
108	100.96834144	94.54530014	83.29342446	79.95985115
109	101.84104014	95.30703256	83.87405419	80.49032428
110	102.71264933	96.06686539	84.45179522	81.01772093
111	103.58317037	96.82480338	85.02666191	81.54205895
112	104.45260462	97.58085126	85.59866856	82.06335606
113	105.32095342	98.33501372	86.16782942	82.58162991
114	106.18821815	99.08729548	86.73415862	83.09689803
115	107.05440015	99.83770123	87.29767027	83.60917785
116	107.91950077	100.58623564	87.85837838	84.11848671
117	108.78352137	101.33290338	88.41629690	84.62484182
118	109.64646329	102.07770911	88.97143970	85.12826033
119	110.50832788	102.82065747	89.52382059	85.62875926
120	111.36911649	103.56175308	90.07345333	86.12635554
121	112.22883045	104.30100058	90.62035157	86.62106602
122	113.08747111	105.03840457	91.16452892	87.11290742
123	113.94503981	105.77396965	91.70599893	87.60189638
124	114.80153789	106.50770040	92.24477505	88.08804946
125	115.65696668	107.23960139	92.78087070	88.57138308

Table IV–continued

PRESENT VALUE OF 1 PER PERIOD RECEIVED FOR N PERIODS
(UNIFORM SERIES)

n	1/8%	1/4%	1/2%	7/12%
126	116.51132752	107.96967720	93.31429920	89.05191361
127	117.36462175	108.69793237	93.84507384	89.52965731
128	118.21685068	109.42437144	94.37320780	90.00463032
129	119.06801566	110.14899894	94.89871422	90.47684873
130	119.91811801	110.87181939	95.42160619	90.94632851
131	120.76715906	111.59283730	95.94189671	91.41308554
132	121.61514014	112.31205716	96.45959872	91.87713561
133	122.46206256	113.02948345	96.97472509	92.33849442
134	123.30792765	113.74512065	97.48728865	92.79717758
135	124.15273673	114.45897321	97.99730214	93.25320060
136	124.99649112	115.17104560	98.50477825	93.70657892
137	125.83919212	115.88134224	99.00972960	94.15732787
138	126.68084108	116.58986758	99.51216875	94.60546270
139	127.52143928	117.29662601	100.01210821	95.05099857
140	128.36098804	118.00162196	100.50956041	95.49395056
141	129.19948868	118.70485981	101.00453772	95.93433364
142	130.03694250	119.40634395	101.49705246	96.37216272
143	130.87335081	120.10607875	101.98711688	96.80745261
144	131.70871492	120.80406858	102.47474316	97.24021804
145	132.54303613	121.50031778	102.95994344	97.67047364
146	133.37631573	122.19483071	103.44272979	98.09823397
147	134.20855504	122.88761168	103.92311422	98.52351350
148	135.03975534	123.57866502	104.40110868	98.94632663
149	135.86991795	124.26799503	104.87672505	99.36668765
150	136.69904414	124.95560601	105.34997518	99.78461078

Table IV—continued

PRESENT VALUE OF 1 PER PERIOD RECEIVED FOR N PERIODS (UNIFORM SERIES)

n	1/8%	1/4%	1/2%	7/12%
151	137.52713522	125.64150226	105.82087082	100.20011017
152	138.35419248	126.32568804	106.28942371	100.61319987
153	139.18021721	127.00816762	106.75564548	101.02389385
154	140.00521070	127.68894525	107.21954774	101.43220601
155	140.82917423	128.36802519	107.68114203	101.83815017
156	141.65210910	129.04541166	108.14043983	102.24174005
157	142.47401657	129.72110889	108.59745257	102.64298931
158	143.29489795	130.39512109	109.05219161	103.04191152
159	144.11475451	131.06745246	109.50466827	103.43852019
160	144.93358752	131.73810719	109.95489380	103.83282872
161	145.75139827	132.40708946	110.40287940	104.22485046
162	146.56818804	133.07440346	110.84863622	104.61459866
163	147.38395809	133.74005332	111.29217534	105.00208652
164	148.19870970	134.40404321	111.73350780	105.38732715
165	149.01244415	135.06637727	112.17264458	105.77033357
166	149.82516270	135.72705962	112.60959660	106.15111874
167	150.63686661	136.38609439	113.04437473	106.52969555
168	151.44755717	137.04348567	113.47698978	106.90607680
169	152.25723562	137.69923758	113.90745251	107.28027523
170	153.06590324	138.35335419	114.33577365	107.65230349
171	153.87356129	139.00583959	114.76196383	108.02217417
172	154.68021103	139.65669785	115.18603366	108.38989979
173	155.48585371	140.30593302	115.60799369	108.75549278
174	156.29049060	140.95354914	116.02785442	109.11896552
175	157.09412294	141.59955027	116.44562629	109.48033029

Table IV–continued

PRESENT VALUE OF 1 PER PERIOD RECEIVED FOR N PERIODS (UNIFORM SERIES)

n	1/8%	1/4%	1/2%	7/12%
176	157.89675200	142.24394042	116.86131969	109.83959933
177	158.69837903	142.88672361	117.27494496	110.19678478
178	159.49900527	143.52790385	117.68651240	110.55189874
179	160.29863198	144.16748514	118.09603224	110.90495322
180	161.09726041	144.80547146	118.50351467	111.25596015
181	161.89489179	145.44186679	118.90896982	111.60493142
182	162.69152738	146.07667510	119.31240778	111.95187882
183	163.48716842	146.70990035	119.71383859	112.29681411
184	164.28181615	147.34154649	120.11327222	112.63974894
185	165.07547181	147.97161744	120.51071863	112.98069492
186	165.86813664	148.60011715	120.90618769	113.31966359
187	166.65981188	149.22704952	121.29968925	113.65666640
188	167.45049875	149.85241848	121.69123308	113.99171477
189	168.24019850	150.47622791	122.08082894	114.32482002
190	169.02891237	151.09848170	122.46848650	114.65599342
191	169.81664156	151.71918375	122.85421543	114.98524619
192	170.60338733	152.33833790	123.23802530	115.31258945
193	171.38915089	152.95594803	123.61992567	115.63803429
194	172.17393347	153.57201799	123.99992604	115.96159171
195	172.95773630	154.18655161	124.37803586	116.28327265
196	173.74056060	154.79955272	124.75426454	116.60308801
197	174.52240759	155.41102516	125.12862143	116.92104859
198	175.30327850	156.02097273	125.50111585	117.23716516
199	176.08317453	156.62939923	125.87175707	117.55144842
200	176.86209691	157.23630846	126.24055430	117.86390899

Table IV—continued

PRESENT VALUE OF 1 PER PERIOD RECEIVED FOR N PERIODS (UNIFORM SERIES)

n	$2/3\%$	$3/4\%$	$5/6\%$	$11/12\%$
1	0.99337748	0.99255583	0.99173554	0.99091660
2	1.98017631	1.97772291	1.97527491	1.97283230
3	2.96044004	2.95555624	2.95068586	2.94582887
4	3.93421196	3.92611041	3.91803557	3.90998732
5	4.90153506	4.88943961	4.87739065	4.86538793
6	5.86245205	5.84559763	6.77238066	5.81211025
7	6.81700535	6.79463785	5.82881717	6.75023312
8	7.76523710	7.73661325	7.70814611	7.67983463
9	8.70718917	8.67157642	8.63617796	8.60099220
10	9.64290315	9.59957958	9.55654013	9.51378253
11	10.57242035	10.52067452	10.46929600	10.41828162
12	11.49578180	11.43491267	11.37450842	11.31456477
13	12.41302828	12.34234508	12.27223976	12.20270663
14	13.32420028	13.24302242	13.16255183	13.08278113
15	14.22933802	14.13699495	14.04550595	13.95486157
16	15.12848148	15.02431261	14.92116292	14.81902055
17	16.02167035	15.90502492	15.78958306	15.67533002
18	16.90894405	16.77918107	16.65082618	16.52386130
19	17.79034177	17.64682984	17.50495158	17.36468502
20	18.66590242	18.50801969	18.35201810	18.19787120
21	19.53566466	19.36279870	19.19208406	19.02348921
22	20.39966688	20.21121459	20.02520734	19.84160781
23	21.25794723	21.05331473	20.85144529	20.65229510
24	22.11054361	21.88914614	21.67085484	21.45561860
25	22.95749365	22.71875547	22.48349240	22.25164518

Table IV–continued

PRESENT VALUE OF 1 PER PERIOD RECEIVED FOR N PERIODS (UNIFORM SERIES)

n	⅔%	¾%	⅚%	11/12%
26	23.79883475	23.54218905	23.28941395	23.04044114
27	24.63460406	24.35949286	24.08867499	23.82207215
28	25.46483847	25.17071251	24.88133057	24.59660328
29	26.28957464	25.97589331	25.66743528	25.36409904
30	27.10884898	26.77508021	26.44704325	26.12462333
31	27.92269766	27.56831783	27.22020818	26.87823947
32	28.73115662	28.35565045	27.98698332	27.62501021
33	29.53426154	29.13712203	28.74742147	28.36499773
34	30.33204789	29.91277621	29.50157502	29.09826365
35	31.12455088	30.68265629	30.24949588	29.82486901
36	31.91180551	31.44680525	30.99123559	30.54487433
37	32.69384653	32.20526576	31.72684521	31.25833955
38	33.47070848	32.95808016	32.45637542	31.96532408
39	34.24242564	33.70529048	33.17987645	32.66588679
40	35.00903209	34.44693844	33.89739813	33.36008600
41	35.77056168	35.18306545	34.60898988	34.04797952
42	36.52704803	35.91371260	35.31470071	34.72962463
43	37.27852453	36.63892070	36.01457921	35.40507808
44	38.02502437	37.35873022	36.70867360	36.07439611
45	38.76658050	38.07318136	37.39703167	36.73763447
46	39.50322566	38.78231401	38.07970083	37.39484836
47	40.23499238	39.48616774	38.75672810	38.04609251
48	40.96191296	40.18478189	39.42816010	38.69142115
49	41.68401949	40.87819542	40.09404307	39.33088801
50	42.40134387	41.56644707	40.75442288	39.96454633

Table IV–continued

PRESENT VALUE OF 1 PER PERIOD RECEIVED FOR N PERIODS
(UNIFORM SERIES)

n	2/3%	3/4%	5/6%	11/12%
51	43.11391776	42.24957525	41.40934500	40.59244889
52	43.82177261	42.92761812	42.05885455	41.21464795
53	44.52493968	43.60061351	42.70299625	41.83119532
54	45.22345001	44.26859902	43.34181446	42.44214235
55	45.91733445	44.93161193	43.97535318	43.04753990
56	46.60662362	45.58968926	44.60365605	43.64743838
57	47.29134797	46.24286776	45.22676633	44.24188775
58	47.97153772	46.89118388	45.84472694	44.83093749
59	48.64722290	47.53467382	46.45758044	45.41463665
60	49.31843335	48.17337352	47.06536903	45.99303384
61	49.98519869	48.80731863	47.66813457	46.56617722
62	50.64754837	49.43654455	48.26591859	47.13411450
63	51.30551162	50.06108640	48.85876223	47.69689298
64	51.95911751	50.68097906	49.44670635	48.25455952
65	52.60839487	51.29625713	50.02979142	48.80716055
66	53.25337239	51.90695497	50.60805761	49.35474208
67	53.89407853	52.51310667	51.18154473	49.89734971
68	54.53054159	53.11474607	51.75029230	50.43502861
69	55.16278966	53.71190677	52.31433947	50.96782356
70	55.79085066	54.30462210	52.87372509	51.49577892
71	56.41475231	54.89292516	53.42848770	52.01893865
72	57.03452216	55.47684880	53.97866549	52.53734631
73	57.65018758	56.05642561	54.52429635	53.05104507
74	58.26177574	56.63168795	55.06541787	53.56007769
75	58.86931365	57.20266794	55.60206731	54.06448656

Table IV—continued

PRESENT VALUE OF 1 PER PERIOD RECEIVED FOR N PERIODS
(UNIFORM SERIES)

n	⅔%	¾%	⅚%	11/12%
76	59.47282811	57.76939746	56.13428163	54.56431369
77	60.07234581	58.33190815	56.66209748	55.05960068
78	60.66789319	58.89023141	57.18555122	55.55038878
79	61.25949654	59.44439842	57.70467890	56.03671886
80	61.84718200	59.99444012	58.21951626	56.51863141
81	62.43097549	60.54038722	58.73009877	56.99616655
82	63.01090281	61.08227019	59.23646159	57.46936404
83	63.58698954	61.62011930	59.73863960	57.93826330
84	64.15926114	62.15396456	60.23666737	58.40290335
85	64.72774285	62.68383579	60.73057921	58.86332289
86	65.29245979	63.20976257	61.22040913	59.31956026
87	65.85343687	63.73177427	61.70619088	59.77165343
88	66.41069888	64.24990002	62.18795789	60.21964007
89	66.96427041	64.76416875	62.66574337	60.66355746
90	67.51417591	65.27460918	63.13958020	61.10344257
91	68.06043964	65.78124981	63.60950102	61.53933202
92	68.60308574	66.28411892	64.07553820	61.97126212
93	69.14213815	66.78324458	64.53772384	62.39926882
94	69.67762068	67.27865467	64.99608976	62.82338777
95	70.20955696	67.77037685	65.45066753	63.24365427
96	70.73797049	68.25843856	65.90148846	63.66010333
97	71.26288460	68.74286705	66.34858360	64.07276961
98	71.78432245	69.22368938	66.79198373	64.48168747
99	72.30230707	69.70093239	67.23171940	64.88689097
100	72.81686132	70.17462272	67.66782090	65.28841384

Table IV—continued

PRESENT VALUE OF 1 PER PERIOD RECEIVED FOR N PERIODS (UNIFORM SERIES)

n	2/3%	3/4%	5/6%	11/12%
101	73.32800792	70.64478682	68.10031824	65.68628952
102	73.83576944	71.11145094	68.52924123	66.08055114
103	74.34016830	71.57464113	68.95461941	66.47123152
104	74.84122677	72.03438325	69.37648206	66.85836319
105	75.33896697	72.49070298	69.79485824	67.24197839
106	75.83341088	72.94362579	70.20977676	67.62210906
107	76.32458032	73.39317696	70.62126621	67.99878684
108	76.81249699	73.83938160	71.02935492	68.37204311
109	77.29718242	74.28226461	71.43407100	68.74190895
110	77.77865801	74.72185073	71.83544231	69.10841514
111	78.25694503	75.15816450	72.23349651	69.47159222
112	78.73206458	75.59123027	72.62826100	69.83147040
113	79.20403764	76.02107223	73.01976297	70.18807968
114	79.67288505	76.44771437	73.40800294	70.54144972
115	80.13862751	76.87118052	73.79308701	70.89160996
116	80.60128559	77.29149431	74.17496232	71.23858956
117	81.06087970	77.70867922	74.55368164	71.58241740
118	81.51743015	78.12275853	74.92927105	71.92312211
119	81.97095708	78.53375536	75.30175641	72.26073207
120	82.42148052	78.94169267	75.67116338	72.59527538
121	82.86902036	79.34659322	76.03751741	72.92677990
122	83.31359636	79.74847962	76.40084371	73.25527323
123	83.75522815	80.14737432	76.76116731	73.58078272
124	84.19393523	80.54329957	77.11851304	73.90333548
125	84.62973696	80.93627749	77.47290549	74.22295836

Table IV–continued

PRESENT VALUE OF 1 PER PERIOD RECEIVED FOR N PERIODS (UNIFORM SERIES)

n	$2/3\%$	$3/4\%$	$5/6\%$	$11/12\%$
126	85.06265259	81.32633001	77.82436908	74.53967798
127	85.49270122	81.71347892	78.17292802	74.85352071
128	85.91990185	82.09774583	78.51860630	75.16451267
129	86.34427334	82.47915219	78.86142774	75.47267978
130	86.76583442	82.85771929	79.20141594	75.77804767
131	87.18460371	83.23346828	79.53859432	76.08064179
132	87.60059969	83.60642013	79.87298610	76.38048732
133	88.01384072	83.97659566	80.20461431	76.67760924
134	88.42434507	84.34401554	80.53350180	76.97203228
135	88.83213084	84.70870029	80.85967121	77.26378095
136	89.23721604	85.07067026	81.18314500	77.55287956
137	89.63961856	85.42994567	81.50394545	77.83935216
138	90.03935616	85.78654657	81.82209466	78.12322262
139	90.43644649	86.14049288	82.13761454	78.40451457
140	90.83090709	86.49180434	82.45052682	78.68325144
141	91.22275536	86.84050059	82.76085305	78.95945642
142	91.61200861	87.18660108	83.06861459	79.23315252
143	91.99868402	87.53012514	83.37383265	79.50436253
144	92.38279867	87.87109195	83.67652825	79.77310903
145	92.76436952	88.20952055	83.97672223	80.03941440
146	93.14341340	88.54542982	84.27443527	80.30330081
147	93.51994706	88.87883854	84.56968787	80.56479024
148	93.89398712	89.20976530	84.86250037	80.82390444
149	94.26555010	89.53822858	85.15289293	81.08066502
150	94.63465239	89.86424673	85.44088555	81.33509333

Table IV–continued

PRESENT VALUE OF 1 PER PERIOD RECEIVED FOR N PERIODS (UNIFORM SERIES)

n	2/3%	3/4%	5/6%	11/12%
151	95.00131029	90.18783795	85.72649807	81.58721056
152	95.36554000	90.50902029	86.00975015	81.83703772
153	95.72735759	90.82781171	86.29066131	82.08459559
154	96.08677904	91.14422998	86.56925088	82.32990480
155	96.44382021	91.45829279	86.84553806	82.57298576
156	96.79849687	91.77001765	87.11954188	82.81385873
157	97.15082468	92.07942199	87.39128121	83.05254374
158	97.500081919	92.38652307	87.66077475	83.28906069
159	97.84849586	92.69133803	87.92804107	83.52342925
160	98.19387003	92.99388390	88.19309859	83.75566896
161	98.53695695	93.29417757	88.45599655	83.98579913
162	98.87777178	93.59223580	88.71666004	84.21383894
163	99.21632956	93.88807524	88.97520004	84.43980737
164	99.55264523	94.18171239	89.23160335	84.66372324
165	99.88673364	94.47316367	89.48588762	84.88560520
166	100.21860955	94.76244533	89.73807036	85.10547171
167	100.54828760	95.04957352	89.98816896	85.32334108
168	100.87578236	95.33456429	90.23620062	85.53923146
169	101.20110828	95.61743354	90.48218243	85.75316082
170	101.52427972	95.89819706	90.72613134	85.96514697
171	101.84531095	96.17687053	90.96806414	86.17520757
172	102.16421614	96.45346951	91.20799749	86.38336010
173	102.48100939	96.72800944	91.44594793	86.64322135
174	102.79570466	97.00050565	91.68193183	86.79401014
175	103.10831586	97.27097335	91.91596545	86.99654185

Table IV–continued

PRESENT VALUE OF 1 PER PERIOD RECEIVED FOR N PERIODS
(UNIFORM SERIES)

n	2/3%	3/4%	5/6%	11/12%
176	103.41885678	97.53942764	92.14806491	87.19723387
177	103.72734115	97.80588352	92.37824619	87.39610293
178	104.03378257	98.07035585	92.60652515	87.59316558
179	104.33819457	98.33285940	92.83291750	87.78843823
180	104.64059061	98.59340884	93.05743885	87.98193714
181	104.94098402	98.85201870	93.28010464	88.17367842
182	105.23938807	99.10870342	93.50093022	88.36367804
183	105.53581593	99.36347734	93.71993080	88.55195181
184	105.83028070	99.61635468	93.93712145	88.73851542
185	106.12279536	99.86734956	94.15251714	88.92338440
186	106.41337285	100.11647599	94.36613271	89.10657414
187	106.70202598	100.36374788	94.57798285	89.28809989
188	106.98876750	100.60917904	94.78808216	89.46797677
189	107.27361007	100.85278316	94.99644512	89.64621975
190	107.55656626	101.09457386	95.20308607	89.82284369
191	107.83765039	101.33456462	95.40801925	89.99786327
192	108.11686941	101.57276886	95.61125876	90.17129309
193	108.39424296	101.80919986	95.81281860	90.34314757
194	108.66977778	102.04387083	96.01271266	90.51344103
195	108.94348786	102.27679487	96.21095471	90.68218746
196	109.21538529	102.50798498	96.45567039	90.84940146
197	109.48548208	102.73745407	96.60253725	91.01509641
198	109.75379014	102.96521496	96.79590471	91.17928629
199	110.02032134	103.19128036	96.98767409	91.34198476
200	110.28508742	103.41566289	97.17785860	91.50320538

Table IV–continued

PRESENT VALUE OF 1 PER PERIOD RECEIVED FOR N PERIODS
(UNIFORM SERIES)

n	1%	2%	3%	4%
1	0.99009901	0.98039216	0.97087379	0.96153846
2	1.97039506	1.94156094	1.91346970	1.88609467
3	2.94098521	2.88388327	2.82861135	2.77509103
4	3.90196555	3.80772870	3.71709840	3.62989522
5	4.85343124	4.71345951	4.57970719	4.45182233
6	5.79547647	5.60143089	5.41719144	5.24213686
7	6.72819453	6.47199107	6.23028296	6.00205467
8	7.65167775	7.32548144	7.01969219	6.73274487
9	8.56601758	8.16223671	7.78610892	7.43533161
10	9.47130453	8.98258501	8.53020284	8.11089578
11	10.36762825	9.78684805	9.25262411	8.76047671
12	11.25507747	10.57534122	9.95400399	9.38507376
13	12.13374007	11.34837375	10.63495533	9.98564785
14	13.00370304	12.10624877	11.29607314	10.56312293
15	13.86505252	12.84926350	11.93793509	11.11838743
16	14.71787378	13.57770931	12.56110203	11.65229561
17	15.56225127	14.29187188	13.16611847	12.16566885
18	16.39826858	14.99203125	13.75351308	12.65929697
19	17.22600850	15.67846201	14.32379911	13.13393940
20	18.04555297	16.35143334	14.87747486	13.59032634
21	18.85698313	17.01120916	15.41502414	14.02915995
22	19.66037934	17.65804820	15.93691664	14.45111533
23	20.45582113	18.29220412	16.44360839	14.85684167
24	21.24338726	18.91392560	16.93554212	15.24696314
25	22.02315570	19.52345647	17.41314769	15.62207994

Table IV—continued

PRESENT VALUE OF 1 PER PERIOD RECEIVED FOR N PERIODS (UNIFORM SERIES)

n	1%	2%	3%	4%
26	22.79520366	20.12103576	17.87684242	15.98276918
27	23.55960759	20.70689780	18.32703147	16.32958575
28	24.31644316	21.28127236	18.76410823	16.66306322
29	25.06578530	21.84438466	19.18845459	16.98371463
30	25.80770822	22.39645555	19.60044135	17.29203330
31	26.54228537	22.93770152	20.00042849	17.58849356
32	27.26958947	23.46833482	20.38876553	17.87355150
33	27.98969255	23.98856355	20.76579178	18.14764567
34	28.70266589	24.49859172	21.13183668	18.41119776
35	29.40858009	24.99861933	21.48722007	18.66461323
36	30.10750504	25.48884248	21.83225250	18.90828195
37	30.79950994	25.96945341	22.16723544	19.14257880
38	31.48466330	26.44064060	22.49246159	19.36786423
39	32.16303298	26.90258883	22.80821513	19.58448484
40	32.83468611	27.35547924	23.11477197	19.79277388
41	33.49968922	27.79948945	23.41239997	19.99305181
42	34.15810814	28.23479358	23.70135920	20.18562674
43	34.81000806	28.66156233	23.98190213	20.37079494
44	35.45545352	29.07996307	24.25427392	20.54884129
45	36.09450844	29.49015987	24.51871254	20.72003970
46	36.72723608	29.89231360	24.77544907	20.88465356
47	37.35369909	30.28658196	25.02470783	21.04293612
48	37.97395949	30.67311957	25.26670664	21.19513088
49	38.58807871	31.05207801	25.50165693	21.34147200
50	39.19611753	31.42360589	25.72976401	21.48218462

Table IV—continued

PRESENT VALUE OF 1 PER PERIOD RECEIVED FOR N PERIODS (UNIFORM SERIES)

n	1%	2%	3%	4%
51	39.79813617	31.78784892	25.95122719	21.61748521
52	40.39419423	32.14494992	26.16623999	21.74758193
53	40.98435072	32.49504894	26.37499028	21.87267493
54	41.56866408	32.83828327	26.57766047	21.99295667
55	42.14719216	33.17478752	26.77442764	22.10861218
56	42.71999224	33.50469365	26.96546373	22.21981940
57	43.28712102	33.82813103	27.15093566	22.32674943
58	43.84863468	34.14522650	27.33100549	22.42956676
59	44.40458879	34.45610441	27.50583058	22.52842957
60	44.95503841	34.76088668	27.67556367	22.62348997
61	45.50003803	35.05969282	27.84035307	22.71489421
62	46.03964161	35.35264002	28.00034279	22.80278289
63	46.57390258	35.63984316	28.15567261	22.88729124
64	47.10287385	35.92141486	28.30647826	22.96854927
65	47.62660777	36.19746555	28.45289152	23.04668199
66	48.14515621	36.46810348	28.59504031	23.12180961
67	48.65857050	36.73343478	28.73304884	23.19404770
68	49.16690149	36.99356351	28.86703771	23.26350740
69	49.67019949	37.24859168	28.99712399	23.33029558
70	50.16851435	37.49861929	29.12342135	23.39451498
71	50.66189539	37.74374441	29.24604015	23.45626440
72	51.15039148	37.98406314	29.36508752	23.51563885
73	51.63405097	38.21966975	29.48066750	23.57272966
74	52.11292175	38.45065662	29.59288106	23.62762468
75	52.58705124	38.67711433	29.70182628	23.68040834

Table IV–continued

PRESENT VALUE OF 1 PER PERIOD RECEIVED FOR N PERIODS (UNIFORM SERIES)

n	1%	2%	3%	4%
76	53.05648637	38.89913170	29.80759833	23.73116187
77	53.52127364	39.11679578	29.91028964	23.77996333
78	53.98145905	39.33019194	30.00998994	23.82688782
79	54.43708817	39.53940386	30.10678635	23.87200752
80	54.88820611	39.74451359	30.20076345	23.91539185
81	55.33485753	39.94560156	30.29200335	23.95710754
82	55.77708666	40.14274663	30.38058577	23.99721879
83	56.21493729	40.33602611	30.46658813	24.03578730
84	56.64845276	40.52551579	30.55008556	24.07287240
85	57.07767600	40.71128999	30.63115103	24.10853116
86	57.50264951	40.89342156	30.70985537	24.14281842
87	57.92341535	41.07198192	30.78626735	24.17578694
88	58.34001520	41.24704110	30.86045374	24.20748745
89	58.75249030	41.41866774	30.93247936	24.23796870
90	59.16088148	41.58692916	31.00240714	24.26727759
91	59.56522919	41.75189133	31.07029820	24.29545923
92	59.96557346	41.91361895	31.13621184	24.32255695
93	60.36195392	42.07217545	31.20020567	24.34861245
94	60.75440982	42.22762299	31.26233560	24.37366582
95	61.14298002	42.38002254	31.32265592	24.39775559
96	61.52770299	42.52943386	31.38121934	24.42091884
97	61.90861682	42.67591555	31.43807703	24.44319119
98	62.28575923	42.81952505	31.49327867	24.46460692
99	62.65916755	42.96031867	31.54687250	24.48519896
100	63.02887877	43.09835164	31.59890534	24.50499900

Table IV–continued

PRESENT VALUE OF 1 PER PERIOD RECEIVED FOR N PERIODS (UNIFORM SERIES)

n	5%	6%	7%	8%
1	0.95238095	0.94339623	0.93457944	0.92592593
2	1.85941043	1.83339267	1.80801817	1.78326475
3	2.72324803	2.67301195	2.62431604	2.57709699
4	3.54595050	3.46510561	3.38721126	3.31212684
5	4.32947667	4.21236379	4.10019744	3.99271004
6	5.07569206	4.91732433	4.76653966	4.62287966
7	5.78637340	5.58238144	5.38928940	5.20637006
8	6.46321276	6.20979381	5.97129851	5.74663894
9	7.10782168	6.80169227	6.51523225	6.24688791
10	7.72173493	7.36008705	7.02358154	6.71008140
11	8.30641422	7.88687458	7.49867434	7.13896426
12	8.86325164	8.38384394	7.94268630	7.53607802
13	9.39357299	8.85268296	8.35765074	7.90377594
14	9.89864094	9.29498393	8.74546799	8.24423698
15	10.37965804	9.71224899	9.10791401	8.55947869
16	10.83776956	10.10589527	9.44664860	8.85136916
17	11.27406625	10.47725969	9.76322299	9.12163811
18	11.68958690	10.82760348	10.05908691	9.37188714
19	12.08532086	11.15811649	10.33559524	9.60359920
20	12.46221034	11.46992122	10.59401425	9.81814741
21	12.82115271	11.76407662	10.83552733	10.01680316
22	13.16300258	12.04158172	11.06124050	10.20074366
23	13.48857388	12.30337898	11.27218738	10.37105895
24	13.79864179	12.55035753	11.46933400	10.52875828
25	14.09394457	12.78335616	11.65358318	10.67477619

Table IV—continued

PRESENT VALUE OF 1 PER PERIOD RECEIVED FOR N PERIODS (UNIFORM SERIES)

n	5%	6%	7%	8%
26	14.37518530	13.00316619	11.82577867	10.80997795
27	14.64303362	13.21053414	11.98670904	10.93516477
28	14.89812726	13.40616428	12.13711125	11.05107849
29	15.14107358	13.59072102	12.27767407	11.15840601
30	15.37245103	13.76483115	12.40904118	11.25778334
31	15.59281050	13.92908599	12.53181419	11.34979939
32	15.80267667	14.08404339	12.64655532	11.43499944
33	16.00254921	14.23022961	12.75379002	11.51388837
34	16.19290401	14.36814114	12.85400936	11.58693367
35	16.37419429	14.49824636	12.94767230	11.65456822
36	16.54685171	14.62098713	13.03520776	11.71719279
37	16.71128734	14.73678031	13.11701660	11.77517851
38	16.86789271	14.84601916	13.19347345	11.82886899
39	17.01704067	14.94907468	13.26492846	11.87858240
40	17.15908635	15.04629687	13.33170884	11.92461333
41	17.29436796	15.13801592	13.39412041	11.96723457
42	17.42320758	15.22454332	13.45244898	12.00669867
43	17.54591198	15.30617294	13.50696167	12.04323951
44	17.66277331	15.38318202	13.55790810	12.07707362
45	17.77406982	15.45583209	13.60552159	12.10840150
46	17.88006650	15.52436990	13.65002018	12.13740880
47	17.98101571	15.58902821	13.69160764	12.16426741
48	18.07715782	15.65002661	13.73047443	12.18913649
49	18.16872173	15.70757227	13.76679853	12.21216341
50	18.25592546	15.76186064	13.80074629	12.23348464

Table IV–continued

PRESENT VALUE OF 1 PER PERIOD RECEIVED FOR N PERIODS
(UNIFORM SERIES)

n	5%	6%	7%	8%
51	18.33897663	15.81307607	13.83247317	12.25322652
52	18.41807298	15.86139252	13.86212446	12.27150604
53	18.49340284	15.90697408	13.88983594	12.28843152
54	18.56514556	15.94997554	13.91573453	12.30410326
55	18.63347196	15.99054297	13.93993881	12.31861413
56	18.69854473	16.02881412	13.96255964	12.33205012
57	18.76051879	16.06491898	13.98370059	12.34449085
58	18.81954170	16.09898017	14.00345850	12.35601005
59	18.87575400	16.13111337	14.02192383	12.36667597
60	18.92928952	16.16142771	14.03918115	12.37655182
61	18.98027574	16.19002614	14.05530949	12.38569613
62	19.02883404	16.21700579	14.07038270	12.39416309
63	19.07508003	16.24245829	14.08446981	12.40200286
64	19.11912384	16.26647009	14.09763534	12.40926190
65	19.16107033	16.28912272	14.10993957	12.41598324
66	19.20101936	16.31049314	14.12143885	12.42220671
67	19.23906606	16.33065390	14.13218584	12.42796917
68	19.27530101	16.34967349	14.14222976	12.43330479
69	19.30981048	16.36761650	14.15161660	12.43824518
70	19.34267665	16.38454387	14.16038934	12.44281961
71	19.37397776	16.40051308	14.16858817	12.44705519
72	19.40378834	16.41557838	14.17625063	12.45097703
73	19.43217937	16.42979093	14.18341180	12.45460836
74	19.45921845	16.44319899	14.19010449	12.45797071
75	19.48496995	16.45584810	14.19635933	12.46108399

Table IV–continued

PRESENT VALUE OF 1 PER PERIOD RECEIVED FOR N PERIODS (UNIFORM SERIES)

n	5%	6%	7%	8%
76	19.50949519	16.46778123	14.20220498	12.46396665
77	19.53285257	16.47903889	14.20766821	12.46663579
78	19.55509768	16.48965933	14.21277403	12.46910721
79	19.57628351	16.49967862	14.21754582	12.47139557
80	19.59646048	16.50913077	14.22200544	12.47351441
81	19.61567665	16.51804790	14.22617331	12.47547631
82	19.63397776	16.52646028	14.23006851	12.47729288
83	19.65140739	16.53439649	14.23370889	12.47897489
84	19.66800704	16.54188348	14.23711111	12.48053230
85	19.68381623	16.54894668	14.24029076	12.48197436
86	19.69887260	16.55561008	14.24326239	12.48330959
87	19.71321200	16.56189630	14.24603962	12.48454592
88	19.72686857	16.56782670	14.24863516	12.48569066
89	19.73987483	16.57342141	14.25106089	12.48675061
90	19.75226174	16.57869944	14.25332794	12.48773205
91	19.76405880	16.58367872	14.25544667	12.48864079
92	19.77529410	16.58837615	14.25742680	12.48948221
93	19.78599438	16.59280769	14.25927738	12.49026131
94	19.79618512	16.59698839	14.26100690	12.49098269
95	19.80589059	16.60093244	14.26262327	12.49165064
96	19.81513390	16.60465325	14.26413390	12.49226911
97	19.82393705	16.60816344	14.26554570	12.49284177
98	19.83232100	16.61147494	14.26686514	12.49337201
99	19.84030571	16.61459900	14.26809826	12.49386297
100	19.84791020	16.61754623	14.26925071	12.49431757

Table IV–continued

PRESENT VALUE OF 1 PER PERIOD RECEIVED FOR N PERIODS (UNIFORM SERIES)

n	9%	10%	11%	12%
1	0.91743119	0.90909091	0.90090090	0.89285714
2	1.75911119	1.73553719	1.71252333	1.69005102
3	2.53129467	2.48685199	2.44371472	2.40183127
4	3.23971988	3.16986545	3.10244569	3.03734935
5	3.88965126	3.79078677	3.69589702	3.60477620
6	4.48591859	4.35526070	4.23053785	4.11140732
7	5.03295284	4.86841882	4.71219627	4.56375654
8	5.53481912	5.33492620	5.14612276	4.96763977
9	5.99524689	5.75902382	5.53704753	5.32824979
10	6.41765770	6.14456711	5.88923201	5.65022303
11	6.80519055	6.49506101	6.20651533	5.93769913
12	7.16072528	6.81369182	6.49235615	6.19437423
13	7.48690392	7.10335620	6.74987040	6.42354842
14	7.78615039	7.36668746	6.98186523	6.62816823
15	8.06068843	7.60607951	7.19086958	6.81086449
16	8.31255819	7.82370864	7.37916178	6.97398615
17	8.54363137	8.02155331	7.54879440	7.11963049
18	8.75562511	8.20141210	7.70161657	7.24967008
19	8.95011478	8.36492009	7.83929421	7.36577686
20	9.12854567	8.51356372	7.96332812	7.46944362
21	9.29224373	8.64869429	8.07507038	7.56200324
22	9.44242544	8.77154026	8.17573908	7.64464575
23	9.58020682	8.88321842	8.26643160	7.71843370
24	9.70661177	8.98474402	8.34813658	7.78431581
25	9.82257961	9.07704002	8.42174467	6.87292744

Table IV—continued

PRESENT VALUE OF 1 PER PERIOD RECEIVED FOR N PERIODS
(UNIFORM SERIES)

n	9%	10%	11%	12%
26	9.92897212	9.16094547	8.48800583	7.89565992
27	10.02657992	9.23722316	8.54780023	7.94255350
28	10.11612837	9.30656651	8.60162183	7.98442277
29	10.19828291	9.36960591	8.65010976	8.02180604
30	10.27365404	9.42691447	8.69379257	8.05518397
31	10.34280187	9.47901315	8.73314646	8.08498569
32	10.40624025	9.52637559	8.76860042	8.11159436
33	10.46444060	9.56943236	8.80054092	8.13535211
34	10.51783541	9.60857487	8.82931614	8.15654383
35	10.56682148	9.64415897	8.85523977	8.17550391
36	10.61176282	9.67650816	8.87859438	8.19241421
37	10.65299342	9.70591651	8.89963458	8.20751269
38	10.69081965	9.73265137	8.91858971	8.22099347
39	10.72552261	9.75695579	8.93566641	8.23302988
40	10.75736020	9.77905072	8.95105082	8.24377668
41	10.78656899	9.79913702	8.96491065	8.25337204
42	10.81336604	9.81739729	8.97739698	8.26193932
43	10.83795050	9.83399754	8.98864593	8.26958868
44	10.86050504	9.84908867	8.99878011	8.27641846
45	10.88119729	9.86280788	9.00791001	8.28251648
46	10.90018100	9.87527989	9.01613515	8.28796115
47	10.91759725	9.88661808	9.02354518	8.29282245
48	10.93357546	9.89692553	9.03022088	8.29716290
49	10.94823436	9.90629594	9.03623503	8.30103831
50	10.96168290	9.91481449	9.04165318	8.30449849

Table IV—continued

PRESENT VALUE OF 1 PER PERIOD RECEIVED FOR N PERIODS (UNIFORM SERIES)

n	14%	16%	18%	20%
1	0.87719298	0.86206897	0.84745763	0.83333333
2	1.64666051	1.60523187	1.56564206	1.52777778
3	2.32163203	2.24588954	2.17427293	2.10648148
4	2.91371230	2.79818064	2.69006181	2.58873457
5	3.43308097	3.27429365	3.12717102	2.99061214
6	3.88866752	3.68473591	3.49760256	3.32551012
7	4.28830484	4.03856544	3.81152759	3.60459176
8	4.63886389	4.34359090	4.07756576	3.83715980
9	4.94637184	4.60654388	4.30302183	4.03096650
10	5.21611565	4.83322748	4.49408630	4.19247209
11	5.45273302	5.02864438	4.65600534	4.32706007
12	5.66029213	5.19710722	4.79322486	4.43921673
13	5.84236151	5.34233381	4.90951259	4.53268061
14	6.00207150	5.46752915	5.00806152	4.61056717
15	6.14216799	5.57545616	5.09157756	4.67547264
16	6.26505964	5.66849669	5.16236386	4.72956054
17	6.37285933	5.74870405	5.22233378	4.77463378
18	6.46742047	5.81784831	5.27316422	4.81219482
19	6.55036883	5.87745544	5.31624087	4.84349568
20	6.62313055	5.92884090	5.35274650	4.86957973
21	6.68695662	5.97313871	5.38368347	4.89131645
22	6.74294441	6.01132647	5.40990125	4.90943037
23	6.79205650	6.04424696	5.43211970	4.92452531
24	6.83513728	6.07262669	5.45094890	4.93710442
25	6.87292744	6.09709197	5.46690565	4.94758702

Table IV–continued

PRESENT VALUE OF 1 PER PERIOD RECEIVED FOR N PERIODS (UNIFORM SERIES)

n	14%	16%	18%	20%
26	6.90607670	6.11818274	5.48042868	4.95632252
27	6.93515500	6.13636443	5.49188872	4.96360210
28	6.96066228	6.15203830	5.50160061	4.96966841
29	6.98303709	6.16555026	5.50983102	4.97472368
30	7.00266411	6.17719850	5.51680595	4.97893640
31	7.01988080	6.18724008	5.52271691	4.98244700
32	7.03498316	6.19589662	5.52772619	4.98537250
33	7.04823084	6.20335916	5.53197135	4.98781042
34	7.05985161	6.20979238	5.53556894	4.98984201
35	7.07004528	6.21533826	5.53861775	4.99153501
36	7.07898708	6.22011919	5.54120148	4.99294584
37	7.08683078	6.22424068	5.54339109	4.99412154
38	7.09371121	6.22779369	5.54524668	4.99510128
39	7.09974667	6.23085663	5.54681922	4.99591773
40	7.10504094	6.23349709	5.54815188	4.99659811
41	7.10968504	6.23577336	5.54928126	4.99716509
42	7.11375880	6.23773565	5.55023835	4.99763758
43	7.11733228	6.23942729	5.55104945	4.99803131
44	7.12046692	6.24088559	5.55173682	4.99835943
45	7.12321659	6.24214275	5.55231934	4.99863286
46	7.12562859	6.24322651	5.55281300	4.99886071
47	7.12774438	6.24416078	5.55323136	4.99905060
48	7.12960033	6.24496619	5.55358590	4.99920883
49	7.13122836	6.24566051	5.55388635	4.99934069
50	7.13265646	6.24625942	5.55414098	4.99945058

Table IV–continued

PRESENT VALUE OF 1 PER PERIOD RECEIVED FOR N PERIODS (UNIFORM SERIES)

n	22%	24%	26%	28%
1	0.81967213	0.80645161	0.79365079	0.78125000
2	1.49153453	1.45681582	1.42353238	1.39160156
3	2.04224142	1.98130308	1.92343839	1.86843872
4	2.49364051	2.40427668	2.32018920	2.24096775
5	2.86363976	2.74538442	2.63507080	2.53200606
6	3.16691784	3.02047130	2.88497682	2.75937973
7	3.41550642	3.24231557	3.08331494	2.93701541
8	3.61926756	3.42122223	3.24072614	3.07579329
9	3.78628489	3.56550180	3.36565567	3.18421351
10	3.92318433	3.68185629	3.46480609	3.26891681
11	4.03539699	3.77569056	3.54349689	3.33509125
12	4.12737459	3.851136335	3.60594992	3.38679004
13	4.20276605	3.91238980	3.65551581	3.42717972
14	4.26456234	3.961160468	3.69485381	3.45873416
15	4.31521503	4.00129410	3.72607446	3.48338606
16	4.35673363	4.03330169	3.75085274	3.50264536
17	4.39076527	4.05911427	3.77051805	3.51769169
18	4.41866006	4.07993086	3.78612544	3.52944663
19	4.44152464	4.09671844	3.79851225	3.53863018
20	4.46026610	4.11025680	3.80834306	3.54580483
21	4.47562795	4.12117484	3.81614528	3.55141002
22	4.48821963	4.12997971	3.82233753	3.55578908
23	4.49854068	4.13708041	3.82725201	3.55921022
24	4.50700056	4.14280678	3.83115636	3.56188298
25	4.51393488	4.14742483	3.83424792	3.56397108

Table IV—continued

PRESENT VALUE OF 1 PER PERIOD RECEIVED FOR N PERIODS (UNIFORM SERIES)

n	22%	24%	26%	28%
26	4.51961876	4.15114905	3.83670470	3.56560241
27	4.52427767	4.15415246	3.83865453	3.56687688
28	4.52809645	4.15657457	3.84020200	3.56787256
29	4.53122660	4.15852788	3.84143016	3.56865044
30	4.53379229	4.16010313	3.84240489	3.56925947
31	4.53589532	4.16137349	3.84317849	3.56973293
32	4.53761912	4.16239798	3.84379245	3.57010386
33	4.53903206	4.16322417	3.84427972	3.57039364
34	4.54019022	4.16389046	3.84466645	3.57062003
35	4.54113952	4.16442779	3.84497337	3.57079690
36	4.54191764	4.16486112	3.84521696	3.57093508
37	4.54255544	4.16521058	3.84541029	3.57104303
38	4.54307823	4.16549241	3.84556372	3.57112737
39	4.54350675	4.16571968	3.84568549	3.57119326
40	4.54385799	4.16590297	3.84578214	3.57124473
41	4.54414589	4.16605078	3.84588838	3.57128495
42	4.54438188	4.16616999	3.84591971	3.57131636
43	4.54457531	4.16626612	3.84596803	3.57134091
44	4.54473386	4.16634364	3.84600637	3.57136009
45	4.54486382	4.16640616	3.84603680	3.57137507
46	4.54497035	4.16645658	3.84606095	3.57138677
47	4.54505766	4.16649725	3.84608012	3.57139592
48	4.54512923	4.16653004	3.84609534	3.57140306
49	4.54518789	4.16655648	3.84610741	3.57140864
50	4.54523598	4.16657781	3.84611699	3.57141300

Table IV–continued

PRESENT VALUE OF 1 PER PERIOD RECEIVED FOR N PERIODS (UNIFORM SERIES)

n	30%	32%	34%	36%
1	0.76923077	0.75757576	0.74626866	0.73529412
2	1.36094675	1.33149679	1.30318557	1.27595156
3	1.81611288	1.76628544	1.71879520	1.67349379
4	2.16624068	2.09567079	2.02895164	1.96580426
5	2.43556975	2.34520515	2.26041167	2.18073843
6	2.64274596	2.53424632	2.43314304	2.33877825
7	2.80211228	2.67745934	2.56204704	2.45498401
8	2.92470175	2.78595404	2.65824406	2.54042942
9	3.01900135	2.86814700	2.73003288	2.60325693
10	3.09153950	2.93041440	2.78360663	2.64945363
11	3.14733808	2.97758666	2.82358704	2.68342178
12	3.19026006	3.01332323	2.85342316	2.70839837
13	3.22327697	3.04039639	2.87568893	2.72676351
14	3.24867459	3.06090635	2.89230517	2.74026728
15	3.26821122	3.07644421	2.90470535	2.75019653
16	3.28323940	3.08821531	2.91395922	2.75749745
17	3.29479954	3.09713281	2.92086509	2.76286577
18	3.30369195	3.10388849	2.92601872	2.76681307
19	3.31053227	3.10900643	2.92986472	2.76971549
20	3.31579406	3.11288366	2.93273486	2.77184963
21	3.31984158	3.11582096	2.93487676	2.77341884
22	3.32295506	3.11804618	2.93647520	2.77457268
23	3.32535005	3.11973195	2.93766806	2.77542109
24	3.32719235	3.12100906	2.93855825	2.77604492
25	3.32860950	3.12197656	2.93922258	2.77650362

Table IV–continued

PRESENT VALUE OF 1 PER PERIOD RECEIVED FOR N PERIODS (UNIFORM SERIES)

n	30%	32%	34%	36%
26	3.32969961	3.12270951	2.93971834	2.77684089
27	3.33053816	3.12326478	2.94008831	2.77708889
28	3.33118320	3.12368544	2.94036441	2.77727124
29	3.33167939	3.12400412	2.94057046	2.77740533
30	3.33206107	3.12424555	2.94072422	2.77750392
31	3.33235467	3.12442845	2.94083897	2.77757641
32	3.33258051	3.12456700	2.94092461	2.77762971
33	3.33275424	3.12467197	2.94098851	2.77766891
34	3.33288788	3.12475149	2.94103620	2.77769773
35	3.33299068	3.12481174	2.94107179	2.77771892
36	3.33306975	3.12485738	2.94109835	2.77773450
37	3.33313058	3.12489195	2.94111817	2.77774595
38	3.33317737	3.12491815	2.94113297	2.77775438
39	3.33321336	3.12493799	2.94114400	2.77776057
40	3.33324105	3.12495302	2.94115224	2.77776513
41	3.33326234	3.12496441	2.94115839	2.77776848
42	3.33327873	3.12497304	2.94116298	2.77777094
43	3.33329133	3.12497958	2.94116640	2.77777275
44	3.33330102	3.12498453	2.94116896	2.77777408
45	3.33330848	3.12498828	2.94117086	2.77777506
46	3.33331421	3.12499112	2.94117229	2.77777578
47	3.33331863	3.12499327	2.94117335	2.77777631
48	3.33332202	3.12499490	2.94117414	2.77777670
49	3.33332463	3.12499614	2.94117473	2.77777698
50	3.33332664	3.12499708	2.94117517	2.77777719

Table IV–continued

PRESENT VALUE OF 1 PER PERIOD RECEIVED FOR N PERIODS
(UNIFORM SERIES)

n	38%	40%	45%	50%
1	0.72463768	0.71428571	0.68975517	0.66666667
2	1.24973745	1.22448980	1.16527943	1.11111111
3	1.63024453	1.58892128	1.49329616	1.40740741
4	1.90597430	1.84922949	1.71951459	1.60493827
5	2.10577848	2.03516392	1.87552731	1.73662551
6	2.25056411	2.16797423	1.98312228	1.82441701
7	2.35548124	2.26283874	2.05732571	1.88294467
8	2.43150815	2.33059910	2.10850049	1.92196312
9	2.48660011	2.37899935	2.14508460	1.94797541
10	2.52652182	2.41357097	2.16813341	1.96531694
11	2.55545059	2.43826498	2.18491959	1.97687796
12	2.57641347	2.45590356	2.19649627	1.98458531
13	2.59160397	2.46850254	2.20448019	1.98972354
14	2.60261157	2.47750181	2.20998634	1.99314903
15	2.61058809	2.48392987	2.21378369	1.99543268
16	2.61636818	2.48852133	2.21640254	1.99695512
17	2.62055666	2.49180095	2.21820865	1.99797008
18	2.62359178	2.49414354	2.21945424	1.99864672
19	2.62579114	2.49581681	2.22031327	1.99909781
20	2.62738489	2.49701201	2.22090570	1.99939854
21	2.62853977	2.49786572	2.22131428	1.99959903
22	2.62937665	2.49847552	2.22159605	1.99973269
23	2.62998308	2.49881108	2.22179038	1.99982179
24	2.63042252	2.49922220	2.22192440	1.99988119
25	2.63074096	2.49944443	2.22201683	1.99992080

Table IV–continued

PRESENT VALUE OF 1 PER PERIOD RECEIVED FOR N PERIODS (UNIFORM SERIES)

n	38%	40%	45%	50%
26	2.63097171	2.49960316	2.22208057	1.99994720
27	2.63113892	2.49971655	2.22212453	1.99996480
28	2.63126009	2.49979753	2.22215485	1.99997653
29	2.63134789	2.49985538	2.22217576	1.99998436
30	2.63141151	2.49989670	2.22219018	1.99998957
31	2.63145762	2.49992622	2.22220012	1.99999305
32	2.63149103	2.49994730	2.22220698	1.99999536
33	2.63151524	2.49996235	2.22221171	1.99999691
34	2.63153278	2.49997311	2.22221497	1.00009794
35	2.63154549	2.49998079	2.22221722	1.99999863
36	2.63155471	2.49998628	2.22221877	1.99999908
37	2.63156138	2.49999020	2.22221984	1.99999939
38	2.63156622	2.49999300	2.22222058	1.99999959
39	2.63156972	2.49999500	2.22222109	1.99999973
40	2.63157226	2.49999643	2.22222144	1.99999982
41	2.63157410	2.49999745	2.22222168	1.99999988
42	2.63157544	2.49999818	2.22222185	1.99999992
43	2.63157640	2.49999870	2.22222197	1.99999995
44	2.63157710	2.49999907	2.22222205	1.99999996
45	2.63157761	2.49999934	2.22222210	1.99999998
46	2.63157798	2.49999953	2.22222214	1.99999998
47	2.63157825	2.49999966	2.22222216	1.99999999
48	2.63157844	2.49999976	2.22222218	1.99999999
49	2.63157858	2.49999983	2.22222220	2.00000000
50	2.63157868	2.49999988	2.22222220	2.00000000

Table V

CAPITAL RECOVERY FACTOR OF 1

n	1/8%	1/4%	1/2%	7/12%	n
1	1.00125000	1.00250000	1.00500000	1.00583333	1
2	0.50093770	0.50187578	0.50375312	0.50437924	2
3	0.33416701	0.33500139	0.33667221	0.33722976	3
4	0.25078174	0.25156445	0.25313279	0.25365644	4
5	0.20075062	0.20150250	0.20300997	0.20351357	5
6	0.16739659	0.16812803	0.16959546	0.17008594	6
7	0.14357232	0.14428928	0.14572843	0.14620986	7
8	0.12570415	0.12641035	0.12782886	0.12830351	8
9	0.11180671	0.11250462	0.11390736	0.11437698	9
10	0.10068879	0.10138015	0.10277057	0.10323632	10
11	0.09159233	0.09227840	0.09365903	0.09412175	11
12	0.08401197	0.08469370	0.08606643	0.08652675	12
13	0.07759784	0.07827595	0.07964224	0.08010064	13
14	0.07210003	0.07277510	0.07413609	0.07459295	14
15	0.06733528	0.06800777	0.06936436	0.06981999	15
16	0.06316614	0.06383642	0.06518937	0.06564401	16
17	0.05948750	0.06015587	0.06150579	0.06195966	17
18	0.05621761	0.05688433	0.05823173	0.05868499	18
19	0.05329194	0.05395722	0.05530253	0.05575532	19
20	0.05065885	0.05132288	0.05266645	0.05311889	20
21	0.04827654	0.04893947	0.05028163	0.05073383	21
22	0.04611081	0.04677278	0.04811380	0.04856585	22
23	0.04413342	0.04479455	0.04613465	0.04658663	23
24	0.04232083	0.04298121	0.04432061	0.04477258	24
25	0.04065325	0.04131298	0.04265186	0.04310388	25

Table V–continued

CAPITAL RECOVERY FACTOR OF 1

n	1/8%	1/4%	1/2%	7/12%
26	0.03911396	0.03977312	0.04111163	0.04156376
27	0.03768869	0.03834736	0.03968565	0.04013793
28	0.03636525	0.03702347	0.03836167	0.03881415
29	0.03513308	0.03579093	0.03712914	0.03758186
30	0.03398307	0.03464059	0.03597892	0.03643191
31	0.03290726	0.03356449	0.03490304	0.03535633
32	0.03189869	0.03255569	0.03389453	0.03434815
33	0.03095126	0.03160806	0.03294727	0.03340124
34	0.03005957	0.03071620	0.03205586	0.03251020
35	0.02921884	0.02987533	0.03121550	0.02167024
36	0.02842482	0.02908121	0.03042194	0.03087710
37	0.02767373	0.02833004	0.02967139	0.03012698
38	0.02696218	0.02761843	0.02986045	0.02941649
39	0.02628712	0.02694335	0.02828607	0.02874258
40	0.02564583	0.02630204	0.02764552	0.02810251
41	0.02503582	0.02569204	0.02703631	0.02749379
42	0.02445487	0.02511112	0.02645622	0.02691420
43	0.02390094	0.02455724	0.02590320	0.02636170
44	0.02337220	0.02402855	0.02537541	0.02583443
45	0.02286696	0.02352339	0.02487117	0.02533073
46	0.02238370	0.02304022	0.02438894	0.02484905
47	0.02192101	0.02257762	0.02392733	0.02438798
48	0.02147760	0.02213433	0.02348503	0.02394624
49	0.02105229	0.02170915	0.02306087	0.02352265
50	0.02064400	0.02130099	0.02265376	0.02311612

Table V–continued

CAPITAL RECOVERY FACTOR OF 1

n	1/8%	1/4%	1/2%	7/12%
51	0.02025173	0.02090886	0.02226269	0.02272563
52	0.01987455	0.02053184	0.02188675	0.02235027
53	0.01951161	0.02016906	0.02152507	0.02198919
54	0.01916212	0.01981974	0.02117686	0.02164157
55	0.01882534	0.01948314	0.02084139	0.02130671
56	0.01850059	0.01915858	0.02051797	0.02098390
57	0.01818724	0.01884542	0.02020598	0.02067251
58	0.01788470	0.01854308	0.01990481	0.02037196
59	0.01759242	0.01825101	0.01961392	0.02008170
60	0.01730989	0.01796869	0.01933280	0.01980120
61	0.01703662	0.01769564	0.01906096	0.01952999
62	0.01677218	0.01743142	0.01879796	0.01926762
63	0.01651613	0.01717561	0.01854337	0.01901366
64	0.01626809	0.01692780	0.01829681	0.01876773
65	0.01602769	0.01668764	0.01805789	0.01852946
66	0.01579457	0.01645476	0.01782627	0.01829848
67	0.01556842	0.01622886	0.01760163	0.01807449
68	0.01534892	0.01600961	0.01738366	0.01785716
69	0.01513579	0.01579674	0.01717206	0.01764622
70	0.01492875	0.01558996	0.01696657	0.01744138
71	0.01472755	0.01538902	0.01676693	0.01724239
72	0.01453194	0.01519368	0.01657289	0.01704901
73	0.01434169	0.01500370	0.01638422	0.01686100
74	0.01415659	0.01481887	0.01620070	0.01667814
75	0.01397642	0.01463898	0.01602214	0.01650024

Table V–continued

CAPITAL RECOVERY FACTOR OF 1

n	1/8%	1/4%	1/2%	7/12%
76	0.01380100	0.01446385	0.01584832	0.01632709
77	0.01363015	0.01429327	0.01567908	0.01615851
78	0.01346367	0.01412708	0.01551423	0.01599432
79	0.01330142	0.01396511	0.01535360	0.01583436
80	0.01314322	0.01380721	0.01519704	0.01567847
81	0.01298893	0.01365321	0.01504439	0.01552650
82	0.01283841	0.01350298	0.01489552	0.01537830
83	0.01269152	0.01335639	0.01475028	0.01523373
84	0.01254813	0.01321330	0.01460855	0.01509268
85	0.01240812	0.01307359	0.01447021	0.01495501
86	0.01227136	0.01293714	0.01433513	0.01482060
87	0.01213775	0.01280384	0.01420320	0.01468935
88	0.01200072	0.01267357	0.01407431	0.01456115
89	0.01187956	0.01254625	0.01394837	0.01443588
90	0.01175476	0.01242177	0.01382527	0.01431347
91	0.01163272	0.01230004	0.01370493	0.01419380
92	0.01151333	0.01218096	0.01358724	0.01407679
93	0.01139651	0.01206446	0.01347213	0.01396236
94	0.01128217	0.01195044	0.01335950	0.01385042
95	0.01117025	0.01183884	0.01324930	0.01374090
96	0.01106066	0.01172957	0.01314143	0.01363372
97	0.01095334	0.01162257	0.01303583	0.01352880
98	0.01084821	0.01151776	0.01293242	0.01342608
99	0.01074520	0.01141508	0.01283115	0.01332549
100	0.01064426	0.01131446	0.01273194	0.01322696

Table V–continued

CAPITAL RECOVERY FACTOR OF 1

n	1/8%	1/4%	1/2%	7/12%
101	0.01054532	0.01121584	0.01263473	0.01313045
102	0.01044832	0.01111917	0.01253947	0.01303587
103	0.01035320	0.01102439	0.01244610	0.01294319
104	0.01025992	0.01093144	0.01235457	0.01285234
105	0.01016842	0.01084027	0.01226481	0.01276328
106	0.01007865	0.01075083	0.01217679	0.01267594
107	0.00999055	0.01066307	0.01209045	0.01259029
108	0.00990409	0.01057694	0.01200575	0.01250628
109	0.00981922	0.01049241	0.01192264	0.01242385
110	0.00973590	0.01040942	0.01184107	0.01234298
111	0.00965408	0.01032793	0.01176102	0.01226361
112	0.00957372	0.01024791	0.01168242	0.01218571
113	0.00949479	0.01016932	0.01160526	0.01210923
114	0.00941724	0.01009211	0.01152948	0.01203414
115	0.00934105	0.01001625	0.01145506	0.01196041
116	0.00926617	0.00994172	0.01138195	0.01188799
117	0.00919257	0.00986846	0.01131013	0.01181686
118	0.00912022	0.00979646	0.01123956	0.01174698
119	0.00904909	0.00972567	0.01117021	0.01167832
120	0.00897915	0.00965608	0.01110205	0.01161085
121	0.00891037	0.00958764	0.01103505	0.01154454
122	0.00884271	0.00952033	0.01096918	0.01147936
123	0.00877616	0.00945412	0.01090441	0.01141528
124	0.00871068	0.00938899	0.01084072	0.01135228
125	0.00864626	0.00932491	0.01077808	0.01129033

Table V–continued

CAPITAL RECOVERY FACTOR OF 1

n	1/8%	1/4%	1/2%	7/12%
126	0.00858286	0.00926186	0.01071647	0.01122941
127	0.00852046	0.00919981	0.01065586	0.01116948
128	0.00845903	0.00913873	0.01059623	0.01111054
129	0.00839856	0.00907861	0.01053755	0.01105255
130	0.00833902	0.00901942	0.01047981	0.01099550
131	0.00828040	0.00896115	0.01042298	0.01093935
132	0.00822266	0.00890376	0.01036703	0.01088410
133	0.00816579	0.00884725	0.01031197	0.01082972
134	0.00810978	0.00879159	0.01025775	0.01077619
135	0.00805459	0.00873675	0.01020436	0.01072349
136	0.00800022	0.00868274	0.01015179	0.01067161
137	0.00794665	0.00862952	0.01010002	0.01062052
138	0.00789385	0.00857707	0.01004902	0.01057021
139	0.00784182	0.00852539	0.00999879	0.01052067
140	0.00779053	0.00847446	0.00994930	0.01047187
141	0.00773997	0.00842425	0.00990055	0.01042380
142	0.00769012	0.00837476	0.00985250	0.01037644
143	0.00764098	0.00832597	0.00980516	0.01032978
144	0.00759251	0.00827787	0.00975850	0.01028381
145	0.00754472	0.00823043	0.00971252	0.01023851
146	0.00749758	0.00818365	0.00966718	0.01019386
147	0.00745109	0.00813752	0.00962250	0.01014986
148	0.00740523	0.00809201	0.00957844	0.01010649
149	0.00735998	0.00804712	0.00953500	0.01006374
150	0.00731534	0.00800284	0.00949217	0.01002159

Table V–continued

CAPITAL RECOVERY FACTOR OF 1

n	1/8%	1/4%	1/2%	7/12%
151	0.00727129	0.00795915	0.00944993	0.00998003
152	0.00722783	0.00791605	0.00940827	0.00993905
153	0.00718493	0.00787351	0.00936719	0.00989865
154	0.00714259	0.00783153	0.00932666	0.00985880
155	0.00710080	0.00779010	0.00928668	0.00981950
156	0.00705955	0.00774921	0.00924723	0.00978074
157	0.00701882	0.00770885	0.00920832	0.00974251
158	0.00697862	0.00766900	0.00916992	0.00970479
159	0.00693891	0.00762966	0.00913203	0.00966758
160	0.00689971	0.00759082	0.00909464	0.00963087
161	0.00686100	0.00755246	0.00905773	0.00959464
162	0.00682276	0.00751459	0.00902131	0.00955890
163	0.00678500	0.00747719	0.00898536	0.00952362
164	0.00674770	0.00744025	0.00894987	0.00948881
165	0.00671085	0.00740377	0.00891483	0.00945445
166	0.00667446	0.00736773	0.00888024	0.00942053
167	0.00663848	0.00733213	0.00884608	0.00938705
168	0.00660295	0.00729695	0.00881236	0.00935401
169	0.00656783	0.00726220	0.00877906	0.00932138
170	0.00653313	0.00722787	0.00874617	0.00928917
171	0.00649884	0.00719394	0.00871369	0.00925736
172	0.00646495	0.00716042	0.00868161	0.00922595
173	0.00643145	0.00712728	0.00864992	0.00919494
174	0.00639834	0.00709454	0.00861862	0.00916431
175	0.00636561	0.00706217	0.00858770	0.00913406

Table V–continued

CAPITAL RECOVERY FACTOR OF 1

n	1/8%	1/4%	1/2%	7/12%
176	0.00633325	0.00703018	0.00855715	0.00910418
177	0.00630126	0.00699855	0.00852697	0.00907468
178	0.00626963	0.00696729	0.00849715	0.00904553
179	0.00623836	0.00693638	0.00846768	0.00901673
180	0.00620743	0.00690582	0.00843857	0.00898828
181	0.00617685	0.00687560	0.00840979	0.00896018
182	0.00614660	0.00684572	0.00838136	0.00893241
183	0.00611669	0.00681617	0.00835325	0.00890497
184	0.00608710	0.00678695	0.00832547	0.00887786
185	0.00605784	0.00675805	0.00829802	0.00885107
186	0.00602889	0.00672947	0.00827088	0.00882459
187	0.00600025	0.00670120	0.00824404	0.00879843
188	0.00597191	0.00667323	0.00821752	0.00877257
189	0.00594388	0.00664557	0.00819129	0.00874701
190	0.00591615	0.00661820	0.00816537	0.00872174
191	0.00588870	0.00659112	0.00813973	0.00869677
192	0.00586155	0.00656434	0.00811438	0.00867208
193	0.00583468	0.00653783	0.00808931	0.00864767
194	0.00580808	0.00651160	0.00806452	0.00862355
195	0.00578176	0.00648565	0.00804000	0.00859969
196	0.00575571	0.00645997	0.00801576	0.00857610
197	0.00572992	0.00643455	0.00799178	0.00855278
198	0.00570440	0.00640939	0.00796806	0.00852972
199	0.00567913	0.00638450	0.00794459	0.00850691
200	0.00565412	0.00635985	0.00792138	0.00848436

Table V–continued

CAPITAL RECOVERY FACTOR OF 1

n	2/3 %	3/4 %	5/6 %	11/12 %
1	1.00666667	1.00750000	1.00833333	1.00916667
2	0.50500554	0.50563200	0.50625864	0.50688546
3	0.33778762	0.33834579	0.33890426	0.33946303
4	0.25418051	0.25470501	0.25522994	0.25575531
5	0.20401772	0.20452242	0.20502766	0.20553346
6	0.17057709	0.17106891	0.17156139	0.17205455
7	0.14669198	0.14717488	0.14765856	0.14814303
8	0.12877907	0.12925552	0.12973288	0.13021114
9	0.11484763	0.11531929	0.11579196	0.11626566
10	0.10370321	0.10417123	0.10464038	0.10511066
11	0.09458572	0.09505094	0.09551741	0.09598512
12	0.08698843	0.08745148	0.08791589	0.08838166
13	0.08056052	0.08102188	0.08148472	0.08194903
14	0.07505141	0.07551146	0.07597311	0.07643635
15	0.07027734	0.07073639	0.07119715	0.07165961
16	0.06610049	0.06655879	0.06701891	0.06748084
17	0.06241546	0.06287321	0.06333289	0.06379451
18	0.05914030	0.05959766	0.06005708	0.06051854
19	0.05621027	0.05666740	0.05712669	0.05758815
20	0.05357362	0.05403063	0.05448992	0.05495148
21	0.05118843	0.05164543	0.05210482	0.05256659
22	0.04902041	0.04947748	0.04993706	0.05039914
23	0.04704123	0.04749846	0.04795831	0.04842077
24	0.04522729	0.04568474	0.04614493	0.04660784
25	0.04355876	0.04401650	0.04447708	0.04494050

Table V–continued

CAPITAL RECOVERY FACTOR OF 1

n	2/3%	3/4%	5/6%	11/12%
26	0.04201886	0.04247693	0.04293796	0.04340195
27	0.04059331	0.04105176	0.04151328	0.04197788
28	0.03926983	0.03972871	0.04019078	0.04065602
29	0.03803789	0.03849723	0.03895987	0.03942580
30	0.03688832	0.03734816	0.03781141	0.03827806
31	0.03581316	0.03627352	0.03673741	0.03720482
32	0.03480542	0.03526634	0.03573090	0.03619908
33	0.03385898	0.03432048	0.03478573	0.03525472
34	0.03296843	0.03343053	0.03389650	0.03436631
35	0.03212898	0.03259170	0.03305840	0.03352907
36	0.03133637	0.03179973	0.03226719	0.03273872
37	0.03058680	0.03105082	0.03151905	0.03199146
38	0.02987687	0.03034157	0.03081059	0.03128390
39	0.02920354	0.02966893	0.03013875	0.03061298
40	0.02856406	0.02903016	0.02950079	0.02997594
41	0.02795595	0.02842276	0.02889423	0.02937032
42	0.02737697	0.02784452	0.02831682	0.02879386
43	0.02682510	0.02729338	0.02776653	0.02824454
44	0.02629847	0.02676751	0.02724152	0.02772049
45	0.02579541	0.02626521	0.02674009	0.02722004
46	0.02531439	0.02578495	0.02626071	0.02674165
47	0.02485399	0.02532532	0.02580197	0.02628391
48	0.02441292	0.02488504	0.02536258	0.02584552
49	0.02399001	0.02446292	0.02494136	0.02542531
50	0.02358416	0.02405787	0.02453721	0.02502218

Table V–continued

CAPITAL RECOVERY FACTOR OF 1

n	2/3%	3/4%	5/6%	11/12%
51	0.02319437	0.02366888	0.02414914	0.02463512
52	0.02281971	0.02329503	0.02377621	0.02426322
53	0.02245932	0.02293546	0.02341756	0.02390560
54	0.02211242	0.02258938	0.02307241	0.02356149
55	0.02177827	0.02225605	0.02274001	0.02323013
56	0.02145618	0.02193478	0.02241969	0.02291085
57	0.02114552	0.02162496	0.02211080	0.02260301
58	0.02084569	0.02132597	0.02181276	0.02230602
59	0.02055616	0.02103727	0.02152501	0.02201933
60	0.02027639	0.02075836	0.02124704	0.02174242
61	0.02000592	0.02048873	0.02097837	0.02147481
62	0.01974429	0.02022795	0.02071855	0.02121606
63	0.01949108	0.01997560	0.02046716	0.02096573
64	0.01924590	0.01973127	0.02022379	0.02072343
65	0.01900837	0.01949460	0.01998809	0.02048880
66	0.01877815	0.01926524	0.01975970	0.02026148
67	0.01855491	0.01904286	0.01953829	0.02004114
68	0.01833835	0.01882716	0.01932356	0.01982749
69	0.01812816	0.01861785	0.01911522	0.01962022
70	0.01792409	0.01841464	0.01891299	0.01941907
71	0.01772586	0.01821728	0.01871661	0.01922377
72	0.01753324	0.01802554	0.01852584	0.01903408
73	0.01734600	0.01783917	0.01834045	0.01884977
74	0.01716391	0.01765796	0.01816022	0.01867062
75	0.01698678	0.01748170	0.01798494	0.01849643

Table V–continued

CAPITAL RECOVERY FACTOR OF 1

n	⅔%	¾%	⅚%	11/12%
76	0.01681440	0.01731020	0.01781443	0.01832700
77	0.01664659	0.01714328	0.01764848	0.01816214
78	0.01648318	0.01698074	0.01748693	0.01800167
79	0.01632400	0.01682244	0.01732962	0.01784544
80	0.01616889	0.01666821	0.01717637	0.01769328
81	0.01601769	0.01651790	0.01702704	0.01754504
82	0.01587027	0.01637136	0.01688149	0.01740058
83	0.01572649	0.01622847	0.01673958	0.01725975
84	0.01558621	0.01608908	0.01660118	0.01712244
85	0.01544933	0.01595308	0.01646617	0.01698851
86	0.01531570	0.01582034	0.01633442	0.01685785
87	0.01518524	0.01569076	0.01620583	0.01673034
88	0.01505781	0.01556423	0.01608028	0.01660588
89	0.01493334	0.01544064	0.01597682	0.01648436
90	0.01481170	0.01531989	0.01583793	0.01636569
91	0.01469282	0.01520190	0.01572092	0.01624977
92	0.01457660	0.01508657	0.01560658	0.01613651
93	0.01446296	0.01497382	0.01549481	0.01602583
94	0.01435181	0.01486356	0.01538554	0.01591764
95	0.01424308	0.01475571	0.01527868	0.01581186
96	0.01413668	0.01465020	0.01517416	0.01570843
97	0.01403255	0.01454696	0.01507191	0.01560725
98	0.01393062	0.01444592	0.01497186	0.01550828
99	0.01383082	0.01434701	0.01487393	0.01541143
100	0.01373308	0.01425017	0.01477807	0.01531665

Table V—continued

CAPITAL RECOVERY FACTOR OF 1

n	$2/3\%$	$3/4\%$	$5/6\%$	$11/12\%$
101	0.01363735	0.01415533	0.01468422	0.01522388
102	0.01354357	0.01406243	0.01459231	0.01513305
103	0.01345168	0.01397143	0.01450229	0.01504410
104	0.01336162	0.01388226	0.01441411	0.01495699
105	0.01327334	0.01379487	0.01432770	0.01487166
106	0.01318680	0.01370922	0.01424303	0.01478806
107	0.01310194	0.01362524	0.01416004	0.01470614
108	0.01301871	0.01354291	0.01407869	0.01462586
109	0.01293708	0.01346217	0.01399892	0.01454716
110	0.01285700	0.01338296	0.01392071	0.01447002
111	0.01277842	0.01330527	0.01384399	0.01439437
112	0.01270131	0.01322905	0.01376874	0.01432019
113	0.01262562	0.01315425	0.01369492	0.01424743
114	0.01255132	0.01308084	0.01362249	0.01417606
115	0.01247838	0.01300878	0.01355140	0.01410604
116	0.01240675	0.01293803	0.01348164	0.01403734
117	0.01233641	0.01286857	0.01341315	0.01396991
118	0.01226732	0.01280037	0.01334592	0.01390373
119	0.01219944	0.01273338	0.01327990	0.01383877
120	0.01213276	0.01266758	0.01321507	0.01377500
121	0.01206724	0.01260294	0.01315140	0.01371238
122	0.01200284	0.01253942	0.01308886	0.01365089
123	0.01193955	0.01247702	0.01302742	0.01359051
124	0.01187734	0.01241568	0.01296706	0.01353119
125	0.01181618	0.01235540	0.01290774	0.01347292

Table V–continued

CAPITAL RECOVERY FACTOR OF 1

n	2/3%	3/4%	5/6%	11/12%
126	0.01175604	0.01229614	0.01284945	0.01341567
127	0.01169690	0.01223788	0.01279215	0.01335943
128	0.01163875	0.01218060	0.01273583	0.01330415
129	0.01158154	0.01212428	0.01268047	0.01324983
130	0.01152527	0.01206888	0.01262604	0.01319643
131	0.01146992	0.01201440	0.01257251	0.01314395
132	0.01141545	0.01196080	0.01251988	0.01309235
133	0.01136185	0.01190808	0.01246811	0.01304162
134	0.01130910	0.01185621	0.01241719	0.01299173
135	0.01125719	0.01180516	0.01236710	0.01294267
136	0.01120609	0.01175493	0.01231783	0.01289443
137	0.01115578	0.01170550	0.01226934	0.01284697
138	0.01110625	0.01165684	0.01221638	0.01280029
139	0.01105749	0.01160894	0.01217469	0.01275437
140	0.01100947	0.01156179	0.01212849	0.01270919
141	0.01096218	0.01151536	0.01208301	0.01266473
142	0.01091560	0.01146965	0.01200382	0.01262098
143	0.01086972	0.01142464	0.01199417	0.01257793
144	0.01082453	0.01138031	0.01195078	0.01253555
145	0.01078000	0.01133664	0.01190806	0.01249384
146	0.01073613	0.01129364	0.01186599	0.01245279
147	0.01069291	0.01125127	0.01182457	0.01241237
148	0.01065031	0.01120953	0.01178377	0.01237258
149	0.01060833	0.01116841	0.01174358	0.01233340
150	0.01056695	0.01112790	0.01170400	0.01229482

Table V—continued

CAPITAL RECOVERY FACTOR OF 1

n	2/3%	3/4%	5/6%	11/12%
151	0.01052617	0.01108797	0.01166500	0.01225682
152	0.01048597	0.01104862	0.01162659	0.01221941
153	0.01044633	0.01100984	0.01158874	0.01218255
154	0.01040726	0.01097162	0.01155145	0.01214625
155	0.01036873	0.01093395	0.01151470	0.01211050
156	0.01033074	0.01089681	0.01147848	0.01207527
157	0.01029327	0.01086019	0.01144279	0.01204057
158	0.01025632	0.01082409	0.01140761	0.01200638
159	0.01021988	0.01078849	0.01137294	0.01197269
160	0.01018394	0.01075340	0.01133876	0.01193949
161	0.01014848	0.01071878	0.01130506	0.01190677
162	0.01011350	0.01068465	0.01127184	0.01187453
163	0.01007899	0.01065098	0.01123909	0.01184276
164	0.01004494	0.01061777	0.01120679	0.01181143
165	0.01001134	0.01058502	0.01117495	0.01178056
166	0.00997819	0.01055270	0.01114354	0.01175013
167	0.00994547	0.01052083	0.01111257	0.01172012
168	0.00991318	0.01048938	0.01108203	0.01169054
169	0.00988131	0.01045834	0.01105190	0.01166138
170	0.00984986	0.01042772	0.01102218	0.01163262
171	0.00981881	0.01039751	0.01099287	0.01160427
172	0.00978816	0.01036769	0.01096395	0.01157630
173	0.00975791	0.01033827	0.01093542	0.01154158
174	0.00972803	0.01030922	0.01090727	0.01152153
175	0.00969854	0.01028056	0.01087950	0.01149471

Table V–continued

CAPITAL RECOVERY FACTOR OF 1

n	⅔%	¾%	⅚%	11/12%
176	0.00966942	0.01025226	0.01085210	0.01146825
177	0.00964066	0.01022433	0.01082506	0.01144216
178	0.00961226	0.01019676	0.01079838	0.01141642
179	0.00958422	0.01016954	0.01077204	0.01139102
180	0.00955652	0.01014267	0.01074605	0.01136597
181	0.00952917	0.01011613	0.01072040	0.01134125
182	0.00950215	0.01008993	0.01069508	0.01131687
183	0.00947546	0.01006406	0.01067009	0.01129281
184	0.00944909	0.01003851	0.01064542	0.01126906
185	0.00942305	0.01001328	0.01062107	0.01124564
186	0.00939732	0.00998837	0.01059702	0.01122252
187	0.00937189	0.00996376	0.01057329	0.01119970
188	0.00934678	0.00993945	0.01054985	0.01117718
189	0.00932196	0.00991544	0.01052671	0.01115496
190	0.00929743	0.00989173	0.01050386	0.01113303
191	0.00927320	0.00986830	0.01048130	0.01111137
192	0.00924925	0.00984516	0.01045902	0.01109000
193	0.00922558	0.00982230	0.01043702	0.01106891
194	0.00920219	0.00979971	0.01041529	0.01104808
195	0.00917907	0.00977739	0.01039383	0.01102752
196	0.00915622	0.00975534	0.01036746	0.01100723
197	0.00913363	0.00973355	0.01035170	0.01098719
198	0.00911130	0.00971202	0.01033102	0.01096740
199	0.00908923	0.00969074	0.01031059	0.01094787
200	0.00906741	0.00966972	0.01029041	0.01092858

Table V—continued

CAPITAL RECOVERY FACTOR OF 1

n	1%	2%	3%	4%
1	1.01000000	1.02000000	1.03000000	1.04000000
2	0.50751244	0.51504950	0.52261084	0.53019608
3	0.34002211	0.34675467	0.35353036	0.36034854
4	0.25628109	0.26262375	0.26902705	0.27549005
5	0.20603980	0.21215839	0.21835457	0.22462711
6	0.17254837	0.17852581	0.18459750	0.19076190
7	0.14862828	0.15451196	0.16050635	0.16660961
8	0.13069029	0.13650980	0.14245639	0.14852783
9	0.11674037	0.12251544	0.12843386	0.13449299
10	0.10558208	0.11132653	0.11723051	0.12329094
11	0.09645408	0.10217794	0.10807745	0.11414904
12	0.08884879	0.09455960	0.10046209	0.10655217
13	0.08241482	0.08811835	0.09402954	0.10014373
14	0.07690117	0.08260197	0.08852634	0.09466897
15	0.07212378	0.07782547	0.08376658	0.08994110
16	0.06794460	0.07365013	0.07961085	0.08582000
17	0.06425806	0.06996984	0.07595253	0.08219852
18	0.06098205	0.06670210	0.07270870	0.07899333
19	0.05805175	0.06378177	0.06981388	0.07613862
20	0.05541532	0.06115672	0.06721571	0.07358175
21	0.05303075	0.05878477	0.06487178	0.07128011
22	0.05086371	0.05663140	0.06274739	0.06919881
23	0.04888584	0.05466810	0.06081390	0.06730906
24	0.04707347	0.05287110	0.05904742	0.06558683
25	0.04540675	0.05122044	0.05742787	0.06401196

Table V–continued

CAPITAL RECOVERY FACTOR OF 1

n	1%	2%	3%	4%
26	0.04386888	0.04969923	0.05593829	0.06256738
27	0.04244553	0.04829309	0.05456421	0.06123854
28	0.04112444	0.04698967	0.05329323	0.06001298
29	0.03989502	0.04577836	0.05211467	0.05887993
30	0.03874811	0.04464992	0.05101926	0.05783010
31	0.03767573	0.04359635	0.04999893	0.05685535
32	0.03667089	0.04261061	0.04904662	0.05594859
33	0.03572744	0.04168653	0.04815612	0.05510357
34	0.03483997	0.04081867	0.04732196	0.05431477
35	0.03400368	0.04000221	0.04653929	0.05357732
36	0.03321431	0.03923285	0.04580379	0.05288688
37	0.03246805	0.03850678	0.04511162	0.05223957
38	0.03176150	0.03782057	0.04445934	0.05163192
39	0.03109160	0.03717114	0.04384385	0.05106083
40	0.03045560	0.03655575	0.04326238	0.05052349
41	0.02985102	0.03597188	0.04271241	0.05001738
42	0.02927563	0.03541729	0.04219167	0.04954020
43	0.02872737	0.03488993	0.04169811	0.04908989
44	0.02820441	0.03438794	0.04122985	0.04866454
45	0.02770505	0.03390962	0.04078518	0.04826246
46	0.02722775	0.03345342	0.04036254	0.04788205
47	0.02677111	0.03301792	0.03996051	0.04752189
48	0.02633384	0.03260184	0.03957777	0.04718065
49	0.02591474	0.03220396	0.03921314	0.04685712
50	0.02551273	0.03182321	0.03886550	0.04655020

Table V–continued

CAPITAL RECOVERY FACTOR OF 1

n	1%	2%	3%	4%
51	0.02512680	0.03145856	0.03853382	0.04625885
52	0.02475603	0.03110909	0.03821718	0.04598212
53	0.02439956	0.03077392	0.03791471	0.04571915
54	0.02405658	0.03045226	0.03762558	0.04546910
55	0.02372637	0.03014337	0.03734907	0.04523124
56	0.02340823	0.02984656	0.03708447	0.04500487
57	0.02310156	0.02956120	0.03683114	0.04478932
58	0.02280573	0.02928667	0.03658848	0.04458401
59	0.02252020	0.02902243	0.03635593	0.04438836
60	0.02224445	0.02876797	0.03613296	0.04420185
61	0.02197800	0.02852278	0.03591908	0.04402398
62	0.02172041	0.02828643	0.03571385	0.04385430
63	0.02147125	0.02805848	0.03551682	0.04369237
64	0.02123013	0.02783855	0.03532760	0.04353780
65	0.02099667	0.02762624	0.03514581	0.04339019
66	0.02077052	0.02742122	0.03497110	0.04324921
67	0.02055136	0.02722316	0.03480313	0.04311451
68	0.02033888	0.02703173	0.03464159	0.04298578
69	0.02013280	0.02684665	0.03448618	0.04286272
70	0.01993282	0.02666765	0.03433663	0.04274506
71	0.01973870	0.02649446	0.03419266	0.04263253
72	0.01955019	0.02632683	0.03405404	0.04252489
73	0.01936706	0.02616454	0.03392053	0.04242190
74	0.01918910	0.02600736	0.03379191	0.04232334
75	0.01901609	0.02585508	0.03366796	0.04222900

Table V–continued

CAPITAL RECOVERY FACTOR OF 1

n	1%	2%	3%	4%
76	0.01884784	0.02570751	0.03354849	0.04213869
77	0.01868416	0.02556447	0.03343331	0.04205221
78	0.01852488	0.02542576	0.03332224	0.04196939
79	0.01836984	0.02529123	0.03321510	0.04189007
80	0.01821885	0.02516071	0.03311175	0.04181408
81	0.01807180	0.02503405	0.03301201	0.04174127
82	0.01792851	0.02491110	0.03291576	0.04167150
83	0.01778886	0.02479173	0.03282284	0.04160463
84	0.01765273	0.02467581	0.03273313	0.04154054
85	0.01751998	0.02456321	0.03264650	0.04147909
86	0.01739050	0.02445381	0.03256284	0.04142018
87	0.01726417	0.02434750	0.03248202	0.04136370
88	0.01714089	0.02424416	0.03240393	0.04130953
89	0.01702056	0.02414370	0.03232848	0.04125758
90	0.01690306	0.02404602	0.03225556	0.04120775
91	0.01678832	0.02395101	0.03218508	0.04115995
92	0.01667624	0.02385859	0.03211694	0.04111410
93	0.01656673	0.02376868	0.03205107	0.04107010
94	0.01645971	0.02368118	0.03198737	0.04102789
95	0.01635511	0.02359602	0.03192577	0.04098738
96	0.01625284	0.02351313	0.03186619	0.04094850
97	0.01615284	0.02343242	0.03180856	0.04091119
98	0.01605503	0.02335383	0.03185281	0.04087538
99	0.01595936	0.02327729	0.03179886	0.04084100
100	0.01586574	0.02320274	0.03164667	0.04080800

Table V–continued

CAPITAL RECOVERY FACTOR OF 1

n	5%	6%	7%	8%
1	1.05000000	1.06000000	1.07000000	1.08000000
2	0.53780488	0.54543689	0.55309179	0.56076923
3	0.36720856	0.37410981	0.38105166	0.38803351
4	0.28201183	0.28859149	0.29522812	0.30192080
5	0.23097480	0.23739640	0.24389069	0.25045645
6	0.19701747	0.20336263	0.20979580	0.21631539
7	0.17281982	0.17913502	0.18555322	0.19207240
8	0.15472181	0.16103594	0.16746776	0.17401476
9	0.14069008	0.14702224	0.15348647	0.16007971
10	0.12950458	0.13586796	0.14237750	0.14902949
11	0.12038889	0.12679294	0.13335690	0.14007634
12	0.11282541	0.11927703	0.12590199	0.13269502
13	0.10645577	0.11296011	0.11965085	0.12652181
14	0.10102397	0.10758941	0.11434494	0.12129685
15	0.09634229	0.10296276	0.10979462	0.11682954
16	0.09226991	0.09895214	0.10585765	0.11297687
17	0.08869914	0.09544480	0.10242519	0.10962943
18	0.08554622	0.09235654	0.09941260	0.10670210
19	0.08274501	0.08962086	0.09675301	0.10412763
20	0.08024259	0.08718456	0.09439293	0.10185221
21	0.07799611	0.08500455	0.09228900	0.09983225
22	0.07597051	0.08304557	0.09040577	0.09803207
23	0.07413682	0.08127848	0.08871393	0.09642217
24	0.07247090	0.07967900	0.08718902	0.09497796
25	0.07095246	0.07822672	0.08581052	0.09367878

Table V–continued

CAPITAL RECOVERY FACTOR OF 1

n	5%	6%	7%	8%
26	0.06956432	0.07690435	0.08456103	0.09250713
27	0.06829186	0.07569717	0.08342573	0.09144809
28	0.06712253	0.07459255	0.08239193	0.09048891
29	0.06604551	0.07357961	0.08144865	0.08961854
30	0.06505144	0.07264891	0.08058640	0.08882743
31	0.06413212	0.07179222	0.07979691	0.08810728
32	0.06328042	0.07100234	0.07907292	0.08745081
33	0.06249004	0.07027294	0.07840807	0.08685163
34	0.06175545	0.06959843	0.07779674	0.08630411
35	0.06107171	0.06897386	0.07723396	0.08580326
36	0.06043446	0.06839483	0.07671531	0.08534467
37	0.05983979	0.06785743	0.07623685	0.08492440
38	0.05928423	0.06735812	0.07579505	0.08453894
39	0.05876462	0.06689377	0.07538676	0.08418513
40	0.05827816	0.06646154	0.07500914	0.08386016
41	0.05782229	0.06605886	0.07465962	0.08356149
42	0.05739471	0.06568342	0.07433591	0.08328684
43	0.05699333	0.06533312	0.07403590	0.08303414
44	0.05661625	0.06500606	0.07375769	0.08280152
45	0.05626173	0.06470050	0.07349957	0.08258728
46	0.05592820	0.06441485	0.07325996	0.08238991
47	0.05561421	0.06414768	0.07303744	0.08220799
48	0.05531843	0.06389765	0.07283070	0.08204027
49	0.05503965	0.06366356	0.07263853	0.08188557
50	0.05477674	0.06344429	0.07245985	0.08174286

Table V–continued

CAPITAL RECOVERY FACTOR OF 1

n	5%	6%	7%	8%
51	0.05452867	0.06323880	0.07229365	0.08161116
52	0.05429450	0.06304617	0.07213901	0.08148959
53	0.05407334	0.06286551	0.07199509	0.08137735
54	0.05386438	0.06269602	0.07186110	0.08127370
55	0.05366686	0.06253696	0.07173633	0.08117796
56	0.05348010	0.06238765	0.07162011	0.08108952
57	0.05330343	0.06224744	0.07151183	0.08100780
58	0.05313626	0.06211574	0.07141093	0.08093227
59	0.05297802	0.06199200	0.07131689	0.08086247
60	0.05282818	0.06187572	0.07122923	0.08079795
61	0.05268627	0.06176642	0.07114749	0.08073830
62	0.05255183	0.06166366	0.07107127	0.08068314
63	0.05242442	0.06156704	0.07100019	0.08063214
64	0.05230365	0.06147615	0.07093388	0.08058497
65	0.05218915	0.06139066	0.07087203	0.08054135
66	0.05208057	0.06131022	0.07081431	0.08050100
67	0.05197757	0.06123454	0.07076046	0.08046367
68	0.05187896	0.06116330	0.07071021	0.08042914
69	0.05178715	0.06109625	0.07066331	0.08039719
70	0.05169915	0.06103313	0.07061953	0.08036764
71	0.05161563	0.06097370	0.07057866	0.08034029
72	0.05153633	0.06091774	0.07054051	0.08031498
73	0.05146103	0.06086505	0.07050490	0.08029157
74	0.05138953	0.06081542	0.07047164	0.08026989
75	0.05132161	0.06076867	0.07044060	0.08024984

Table V–continued

CAPITAL RECOVERY FACTOR OF 1

n	5%	6%	7%	8%
76	0.05125709	0.06072463	0.07041160	0.08023128
77	0.05119580	0.06068315	0.07038453	0.08021410
78	0.05113756	0.06064407	0.07035924	0.08019820
79	0.05108222	0.06060724	0.07033563	0.08018349
80	0.05102962	0.06057254	0.07031357	0.08016987
81	0.05097963	0.06053984	0.07029297	0.08015726
82	0.05093211	0.06050903	0.07027373	0.08014559
83	0.05088694	0.06047998	0.07025576	0.08013479
84	0.05084399	0.06045261	0.07023897	0.08012479
85	0.05080316	0.06042681	0.07022329	0.08011553
86	0.05076433	0.06040249	0.07020863	0.08010696
87	0.05072740	0.06037956	0.07019495	0.08009903
88	0.05069228	0.06035795	0.07018216	0.08009168
89	0.05065888	0.06033757	0.07017021	0.08008489
90	0.05062711	0.06031836	0.07015905	0.08007859
91	0.05059689	0.06030025	0.07014863	0.08007277
92	0.05056815	0.06028318	0.07013888	0.08006737
93	0.05054080	0.06026708	0.07012978	0.08006238
94	0.05051478	0.06025190	0.07012128	0.08005775
95	0.05049003	0.06023758	0.07011333	0.08005347
96	0.05046648	0.06022408	0.07010590	0.08004951
97	0.05044407	0.06021135	0.07009897	0.08004584
98	0.05042274	0.06019935	0.07009248	0.08004244
99	0.05040245	0.06018803	0.07008643	0.08003930
100	0.05038314	0.06017736	0.07008076	0.08003638

Table V–continued

CAPITAL RECOVERY FACTOR OF 1

n	9%	10%	11%	12%
1	1.09000000	1.10000000	1.11000000	1.12000000
2	0.56846890	0.57619048	0.58393365	0.59169811
3	0.39505476	0.40211480	0.40921307	0.41634898
4	0.30866866	0.31547080	0.32232635	0.32923444
5	0.25709246	0.26379748	0.27057031	0.27740973
6	0.22291978	0.22960738	0.23637656	0.24322572
7	0.19869052	0.20540550	0.21221527	0.21911774
8	0.18067438	0.18744402	0.19432105	0.20130284
9	0.16679880	0.17364054	0.18060166	0.18767889
10	0.15582009	0.16274539	0.16980143	0.17698416
11	0.14694666	0.15396314	0.16112101	0.16841540
12	0.13965066	0.14676332	0.15402729	0.16143681
13	0.13356656	0.14077852	0.14815099	0.15567720
14	0.12843317	0.13574622	0.14322820	0.15087125
15	0.12405888	0.13147378	0.13906524	0.14682424
16	0.12029991	0.12781662	0.13551675	0.14339002
17	0.11704625	0.12466413	0.13247148	0.14045673
18	0.11421229	0.12193022	0.12984287	0.13793731
19	0.11173041	0.11954687	0.12756250	0.13576300
20	0.10954648	0.11745962	0.12557564	0.13387878
21	0.10761663	0.11562439	0.12383793	0.13224009
22	0.10590499	0.11400506	0.12231310	0.13081051
23	0.10438188	0.11257181	0.12097118	0.12955997
24	0.10302256	0.11129978	0.11978721	0.12846344
25	0.10180625	0.11016807	0.11874024	0.12749997

Table V–continued

CAPITAL RECOVERY FACTOR OF 1

n	9%	10%	11%	12%
26	0.10071536	0.10915904	0.11781258	0.12665186
27	0.09973491	0.10825764	0.11698916	0.12590409
28	0.09885205	0.10745101	0.11625715	0.12524387
29	0.09805572	0.10672807	0.11560547	0.12466021
30	0.09733635	0.10607925	0.11502460	0.12414366
31	0.09668560	0.10549621	0.11456267	0.12368606
32	0.09609619	0.10497172	0.11404329	0.12328033
33	0.09556173	0.10449941	0.11362938	0.12292031
34	0.09507660	0.10407371	0.11325905	0.12260064
35	0.09463584	0.10368971	0.11292749	0.12231662
36	0.09423505	0.10334306	0.11263044	0.12206414
37	0.09387033	0.10302994	0.11236416	0.12183959
38	0.09353820	0.10274693	0.11212535	0.12163980
39	0.09323555	0.10249098	0.11191107	0.12146197
40	0.09295961	0.10225941	0.11171873	0.12130363
41	0.09270789	0.10204980	0.11154601	0.12116260
42	0.09247814	0.10185999	0.11139086	0.12103696
43	0.09226837	0.10168805	0.11125146	0.12092500
44	0.09207675	0.10153224	0.11112617	0.12082521
45	0.09190165	0.10139100	0.11101354	0.12073625
46	0.09174160	0.10126295	0.11091227	0.12065694
47	0.09159525	0.10114682	0.11082119	0.12058621
48	0.09146139	0.10104148	0.11073926	0.12052312
49	0.09133893	0.10094590	0.11066556	0.12046686
50	0.09122687	0.10085917	0.11059924	0.12041666

Table V–continued

CAPITAL RECOVERY FACTOR OF 1

n	14%	16%	18%	20%
1	1.14000000	1.16000000	1.18000000	1.20000000
2	0.60728972	0.62296296	0.63871560	0.65454546
3	0.43073148	0.44525787	0.45992386	0.47472527
4	0.34320478	0.35737507	0.37173867	0.38628912
5	0.29128355	0.30540938	0.31977784	0.33437970
6	0.25715750	0.27138987	0.28591013	0.30070575
7	0.23319238	0.24761268	0.26236200	0.27742393
8	0.21557002	0.23022426	0.24524436	0.26060942
9	0.20216838	0.21708249	0.23239482	0.24807946
10	0.19171354	0.20690108	0.22251464	0.23852276
11	0.18339427	0.19886075	0.21477639	0.23110379
12	0.17666933	0.19241473	0.20862781	0.22526496
13	0.17116366	0.18718411	0.20368621	0.22062000
14	0.16660914	0.18289797	0.19967806	0.21689306
15	0.16280896	0.17935752	0.19640278	0.21388212
16	0.15961540	0.17641362	0.19371008	0.21143614
17	0.15691544	0.17395225	0.19148527	0.20944015
18	0.15462115	0.17188485	0.18963946	0.20780539
19	0.15266316	0.17014166	0.18810284	0.20646245
20	0.15098600	0.16866703	0.18681998	0.20535653
21	0.14954486	0.16741617	0.18574643	0.20444394
22	0.14830317	0.16635264	0.18484626	0.20368962
23	0.14723081	0.16544658	0.18409020	0.20306526
24	0.14630284	0.16467339	0.18345430	0.20254787
25	0.14549841	0.16401262	0.18291883	0.20211873

Table V–continued

CAPITAL RECOVERY FACTOR OF 1

n	14%	16%	18%	20%
26	0.14480001	0.16344723	0.18246748	0.20176250
27	0.14419288	0.16296294	0.18208672	0.20146659
28	0.14366449	0.16254775	0.18176528	0.20122067
29	0.14320417	0.16219153	0.18149377	0.20101619
30	0.14280279	0.16188568	0.18126431	0.20084611
31	0.14245256	0.16162295	0.18107030	0.20070459
32	0.14214675	0.16139714	0.18090621	0.20058682
33	0.14187958	0.16120298	0.18076739	0.20048878
34	0.14164604	0.16103598	0.18064990	0.20040715
35	0.14144181	0.16089229	0.18055046	0.20033917
36	0.14126315	0.16076862	0.18046628	0.20028256
37	0.14110680	0.16066217	0.18039499	0.20023542
38	0.14096993	0.16057051	0.18033463	0.20019614
39	0.14085010	0.16049158	0.18028350	0.20016342
40	0.14074514	0.16042359	0.18024020	0.20013617
41	0.14065321	0.16036503	0.18020352	0.20011346
42	0.14057266	0.16031458	0.18017244	0.20009454
43	0.14050208	0.16027112	0.18014612	0.20007878
44	0.14044023	0.16023367	0.18012381	0.20006564
45	0.14038602	0.16020140	0.18010491	0.20005470
46	0.14033850	0.16017359	0.18008890	0.20004558
47	0.14029684	0.16014962	0.18007534	0.20003798
48	0.14026032	0.16012897	0.18006384	0.20003165
49	0.14022830	0.16011117	0.18005410	0.20002638
50	0.14020022	0.16009582	0.18004584	0.20002198

Table V–continued

CAPITAL RECOVERY FACTOR OF 1

n	22%	24%	26%	28%
1	1.22000000	1.24000000	1.26000000	1.28000000
2	0.67045045	0.68642857	0.70247788	0.71859649
3	0.48965807	0.50471834	0.51990228	0.53520621
4	0.40102011	0.41592551	0.43099933	0.44623578
5	0.34920593	0.36424771	0.37949645	0.39494376
6	0.31576443	0.33107416	0.34662324	0.36240028
7	0.29278235	0.30842155	0.32432626	0.34048170
8	0.27629900	0.29229320	0.30857282	0.32511938
9	0.26411114	0.28046543	0.29711893	0.31404929
10	0.25489498	0.27160213	0.28861644	0.30591173
11	0.24780709	0.26485221	0.28220711	0.29984187
12	0.24228477	0.25964831	0.27731944	0.29526483
13	0.23793854	0.25559825	0.27355921	0.29178511
14	0.23449065	0.25242297	0.27064670	0.28912312
15	0.23173816	0.24991915	0.26837896	0.28707699
16	0.22952975	0.24793583	0.26660604	0.28549850
17	0.22775073	0.24635916	0.26521555	0.28427733
18	0.22631295	0.24510219	0.26412226	0.28333053
19	0.22514791	0.24409781	0.26326096	0.28259523
20	0.22420187	0.24329380	0.26258139	0.28202342
21	0.22343233	0.24264925	0.26204453	0.28157830
22	0.22280550	0.24213194	0.26122001	0.28123153
23	0.22229431	0.24171636	0.26128408	0.28096121
24	0.22187705	0.24138224	0.26101780	0.28075038
25	0.22153620	0.24111347	0.26080734	0.28058589

Table V—continued

CAPITAL RECOVERY FACTOR OF 1

n	22%	24%	26%	28%
26	0.22125760	0.24089716	0.26064034	0.28045752
27	0.22102976	0.24072299	0.26050794	0.28035731
28	0.22084335	0.24058272	0.26040297	0.28027907
29	0.22069079	0.24046971	0.26031971	0.28021798
30	0.22056590	0.24037866	0.26025368	0.28017016
31	0.22046364	0.24030527	0.26020129	0.28013300
32	0.22037989	0.24024613	0.26015973	0.28010390
33	0.22031129	0.24019845	0.26012675	0.28008116
34	0.22025509	0.24016002	0.26010059	0.28006340
35	0.22020905	0.24012903	0.26007982	0.28004953
36	0.22017132	0.24010404	0.26006335	0.28003870
37	0.22014041	0.24008390	0.26005027	0.28003023
38	0.22011507	0.24006766	0.26003990	0.28002362
39	0.22009431	0.24005456	0.26003166	0.28001845
40	0.22007730	0.24004400	0.26002513	0.28001441
41	0.22006336	0.24003548	0.26001994	0.28001126
42	0.22005193	0.24002861	0.26001583	0.28000880
43	0.22004256	0.24002307	0.26001256	0.28000687
44	0.22003489	0.24001861	0.26000997	0.28000537
45	0.22002859	0.24001501	0.26000791	0.28000419
46	0.22002344	0.24001210	0.26000628	0.28000328
47	0.22001921	0.24000976	0.26000498	0.28000256
48	0.22001575	0.24000787	0.26000396	0.28000200
49	0.22001291	0.24000635	0.26000314	0.28000156
50	0.22001058	0.24000512	0.26000249	0.28000122

Table V–continued

CAPITAL RECOVERY FACTOR OF 1

n	30%	32%	34%	36%
1	1.30000000	1.32000000	1.34000000	1.36000000
2	0.73478261	0.75103448	0.76735043	0.78372881
3	0.55062657	0.56615991	0.58180288	0.59755226
4	0.46162922	0.47717418	0.49286537	0.50869765
5	0.41058155	0.42640193	0.44239729	0.45856027
6	0.37839430	0.39459463	0.41099105	0.42757367
7	0.35687364	0.37348840	0.39031290	0.40733463
8	0.34191521	0.35894347	0.37618818	0.39363424
9	0.33123536	0.34865716	0.36629595	0.38413419
10	0.32346344	0.34124867	0.35924616	0.37743631
11	0.31772882	0.33584245	0.35415944	0.37265852
12	0.31345407	0.33185952	0.35045626	0.36922190
13	0.31024327	0.32890448	0.34774276	0.36673514
14	0.30781784	0.32670062	0.34574498	0.36492791
15	0.30597778	0.32505059	0.34426900	0.36361038
16	0.30457724	0.32381162	0.34317570	0.36264766
17	0.30350860	0.32287928	0.34326432	0.36194303
18	0.30269166	0.32217652	0.34176131	0.36142666
19	0.30206623	0.32164617	0.34131269	0.36104791
20	0.30158688	0.32124554	0.34097866	0.36076993
21	0.30121919	0.32094270	0.34072981	0.36056581
22	0.30093696	0.32071366	0.34054434	0.36041586
23	0.30072022	0.32054036	0.34040606	0.36030569
24	0.30055371	0.32040920	0.34030294	0.36022472
25	0.30042575	0.32030990	0.34022602	0.36016521

Table V–continued

CAPITAL RECOVERY FACTOR OF 1

n	30%	32%	34%	36%
26	0.30032739	0.32023472	0.34016864	0.36012146
27	0.30025178	0.32017779	0.34012584	0.36008930
28	0.30019364	0.32013467	0.34009390	0.36006566
29	0.30014893	0.32010201	0.34007007	0.36004828
30	0.30011455	0.32007727	0.34005229	0.36003550
31	0.30008811	0.32005854	0.34003902	0.36002610
32	0.30006777	0.32004435	0.34002912	0.36001919
33	0.30005213	0.32003359	0.34002173	0.36001411
34	0.30004010	0.32002545	0.34001622	0.36001038
35	0.30003084	0.32001928	0.34001210	0.36000763
36	0.30002372	0.32001461	0.34000903	0.36000561
37	0.30001825	0.32001106	0.34000674	0.36000412
38	0.30001404	0.32000838	0.34000503	0.36000303
39	0.30001080	0.32000635	0.34000375	0.36000223
40	0.30000831	0.32000481	0.34000280	0.36000164
41	0.30000639	0.32000364	0.34000209	0.36000121
42	0.30000491	0.32000276	0.34000156	0.36000089
43	0.30000378	0.32000209	0.34000116	0.36000065
44	0.30000291	0.32000158	0.34000087	0.36000048
45	0.30000224	0.32000120	0.34000065	0.36000035
46	0.30000172	0.32000091	0.34000048	0.36000026
47	0.30000132	0.32000069	0.34000036	0.36000019
48	0.30000102	0.32000052	0.34000027	0.36000014
49	0.30000078	0.32000040	0.34000020	0.36000010
50	0.30000060	0.32000030	0.34000015	0.36000008

Table V–continued

CAPITAL RECOVERY FACTOR OF 1

n	38%	40%	45%	50%
1	1.38000000	1.40000000	1.45000000	1.50000000
2	0.80016807	0.81666667	0.85816327	0.90000000
3	0.61340491	0.62935780	0.66965953	0.71052632
4	0.52466605	0.54076577	0.58155947	0.62307692
5	0.47488376	0.49136091	0.53318339	0.57582938
6	0.44433304	0.46126010	0.50425534	0.54812030
7	0.42454170	0.44192279	0.48606791	0.53108305
8	0.41126739	0.42907422	0.47427070	0.52030135
9	0.40215554	0.42034480	0.46618208	0.51335350
10	0.39580106	0.41432384	0.46122623	0.50882378
11	0.39132042	0.41012770	0.45768275	0.50584812
12	0.38813646	0.40718211	0.45527052	0.50388360
13	0.38586143	0.40510390	0.45362168	0.50258238
14	0.38422945	0.40363240	0.45249149	0.50171863
15	0.38305545	0.40258786	0.45171532	0.50114444
16	0.38220920	0.40184506	0.45118158	0.50076238
17	0.38159831	0.40131616	0.45081422	0.50050800
18	0.38115686	0.40093923	0.45056122	0.50033855
19	0.38083760	0.40067043	0.45038690	0.50022565
20	0.38060659	0.40047865	0.45026675	0.50015041
21	0.38043936	0.40034178	0.45018393	0.50010026
22	0.38031828	0.40024407	0.45012683	0.50006684
23	0.38023058	0.40017430	0.45008746	0.50004456
24	0.38016706	0.40012449	0.45006032	0.50002970
25	0.38012104	0.40008891	0.45004160	0.50001980

Table V–continued

CAPITAL RECOVERY FACTOR OF 1

n	38%	40%	45%	50%
26	0.38008771	0.40006350	0.45002869	0.50001320
27	0.38006355	0.40004536	0.45001978	0.50000880
28	0.38004605	0.40003240	0.45001364	0.50000587
29	0.38003337	0.40002314	0.45000941	0.50000391
30	0.38002418	0.40001653	0.45000649	0.50000261
31	0.38001752	0.40001181	0.45000448	0.50000174
32	0.38001270	0.40000843	0.45000309	0.50000116
33	0.38000920	0.40000602	0.45000213	0.50000077
34	0.38000667	0.40000430	0.45000147	0.50000052
35	0.38000483	0.40000307	0.45000101	0.50000034
36	0.38000350	0.40000220	0.45000070	0.50000023
37	0.38000254	0.40000157	0.45000048	0.50000015
38	0.38000184	0.40000112	0.45000033	0.50000010
39	0.38000133	0.40000080	0.45000023	0.50000007
40	0.38000097	0.40000057	0.45000016	0.50000005
41	0.38000070	0.40000041	0.45000011	0.50000003
42	0.38000051	0.40000029	0.45000008	0.50000002
43	0.38000037	0.40000021	0.45000005	0.50000001
44	0.38000027	0.40000015	0.45000004	0.50000001
45	0.38000019	0.40000011	0.45000002	0.50000001
46	0.38000014	0.40000008	0.45000002	0.50000000
47	0.38000010	0.40000005	0.45000001	0.50000000
48	0.38000007	0.40000004	0.45000001	0.50000000
49	0.38000005	0.40000003	0.45000001	0.50000000
50	0.38000004	0.40000002	0.45000001	0.50000000

Table VI

SINKING FUND FACTOR OF 1

n	⅛%	¼%	½%	7/12%	n
1	1.00000000	1.00000000	1.00000000	1.00000000	1
2	0.49968770	0.49937578	0.49875312	0.49854591	2
3	0.33291701	0.33250139	0.33167221	0.33139643	3
4	0.24953174	0.24906445	0.24813279	0.24782310	4
5	0.19950062	0.19900250	0.29800997	0.19768024	5
6	0.16614659	0.16562803	0.16459546	0.16425260	6
7	0.14232232	0.14178928	0.14072854	0.14037653	7
8	0.12445415	0.12391035	0.12282886	0.12247018	8
9	0.11055671	0.11000462	0.10890736	0.10854365	9
10	0.09943879	0.09888015	0.09777057	0.09740299	10
11	0.09034233	0.08977840	0.08865903	0.08828842	11
12	0.08276197	0.08219370	0.08106643	0.08069341	12
13	0.07634784	0.07577595	0.07464224	0.07426730	13
14	0.07085003	0.07027510	0.06913609	0.06875962	14
15	0.06608528	0.06550777	0.06436436	0.06398666	15
16	0.06191614	0.06133642	0.06018937	0.05981068	16
17	0.05823750	0.05765587	0.05650579	0.05612632	17
18	0.05496761	0.05438433	0.05323173	0.05285165	18
19	0.05204194	0.05145722	0.05030253	0.04992198	19
20	0.04940885	0.04882288	0.04766645	0.04728556	20
21	0.04702654	0.04643947	0.04528163	0.04499005	21
22	0.04486081	0.04427278	0.04311380	0.04273251	22
23	0.04288342	0.04229455	0.04113465	0.04075329	23
24	0.04107083	0.04048121	0.03932061	0.03893925	24
25	0.03940325	0.03881298	0.03765186	0.03727055	25

Table VI–continued

SINKING FUND FACTOR OF 1

n	⅛%	¼%	½%	7/12%
26	0.03786396	0.03727312	0.03611163	0.03573043
27	0.03643869	0.03584736	0.03468565	0.03430460
28	0.03511525	0.03452347	0.03336167	0.03298082
29	0.03388308	0.03329093	0.03212914	0.03174853
30	0.03273307	0.03214059	0.03097892	0.03059857
31	0.03165726	0.03106449	0.02990304	0.02952299
32	0.03064869	0.03005569	0.02889453	0.02851482
33	0.02970126	0.02910806	0.02794727	0.02756791
34	0.02880957	0.02821620	0.02705586	0.02667687
35	0.02796884	0.02737533	0.02621550	0.02583691
36	0.02717482	0.02658121	0.02542194	0.02504376
37	0.02642373	0.02583004	0.02467139	0.02429365
38	0.02571218	0.02511843	0.02396045	0.02358316
39	0.02503712	0.02444335	0.02328607	0.02290925
40	0.02439583	0.02380204	0.02264552	0.02226917
41	0.02378582	0.02319204	0.02203631	0.02166046
42	0.02320487	0.02261112	0.02145622	0.02108087
43	0.02265094	0.02205724	0.02090320	0.02052836
44	0.02212220	0.02152855	0.02037541	0.02000110
45	0.02161696	0.02102339	0.01987117	0.01949740
46	0.02113370	0.02054022	0.01938894	0.01901571
47	0.02067101	0.02007762	0.01892733	0.01855465
48	0.02022760	0.01963433	0.01848503	0.01811291
49	0.01980229	0.01920915	0.01806087	0.01768932
50	0.01939400	0.01880099	0.01765376	0.01728278

Table VI—continued

SINKING FUND FACTOR OF 1

n	1/8%	1/4%	1/2%	7/12%
51	0.01900173	0.01840886	0.01726269	0.01689230
52	0.01862455	0.01803184	0.01688675	0.01651694
53	0.01826161	0.01766906	0.01652507	0.01615585
54	0.01791212	0.01731974	0.01617686	0.01580824
55	0.01757534	0.01698314	0.01584139	0.01547337
56	0.01725059	0.01665858	0.01551797	0.01515056
57	0.01693724	0.01634542	0.01520598	0.01483918
58	0.01663470	0.01604308	0.01490481	0.01453863
59	0.01634242	0.01575101	0.01461392	0.01424836
60	0.01605989	0.01546869	0.01433280	0.01396787
61	0.01578662	0.01519564	0.01406096	0.01366967
62	0.01552218	0.01493142	0.01379796	0.01343428
63	0.01526613	0.01467561	0.01354337	0.01318033
64	0.01501809	0.01442780	0.01329681	0.01293440
65	0.01477769	0.01418764	0.01305789	0.01269612
66	0.01454457	0.01395476	0.01282627	0.01246515
67	0.01431842	0.01372886	0.01260163	0.01224116
68	0.01409892	0.01350961	0.01238366	0.01202383
69	0.01388579	0.01329674	0.01217206	0.01181289
70	0.01367875	0.01308996	0.01196657	0.01160805
71	0.01347755	0.01288902	0.01176693	0.01140906
72	0.01328194	0.01269368	0.01157289	0.01121567
73	0.01309169	0.01250370	0.01138422	0.01102766
74	0.01296586	0.01231887	0.01120070	0.01084481
75	0.01272642	0.01213898	0.01102214	0.01066690

Table VI–continued

SINKING FUND FACTOR OF 1

n	1/8%	1/4%	1/2%	7/12%
76	0.01255100	0.01196385	0.01084832	0.01049375
77	0.01238015	0.01179327	0.01067908	0.01032517
78	0.01221367	0.01162708	0.01051423	0.01016099
79	0.01205142	0.01146511	0.01035360	0.01000103
80	0.01189322	0.01130721	0.01019704	0.00984514
81	0.01173893	0.01115321	0.01004439	0.00969316
82	0.01158841	0.01100298	0.00989552	0.00954496
83	0.01144152	0.01085639	0.00975028	0.00940040
84	0.01129813	0.01071330	0.00960855	0.00925935
85	0.01115812	0.01057359	0.00947021	0.00912168
86	0.01102136	0.01043714	0.00933513	0.00898727
87	0.01088775	0.01030384	0.00920320	0.00885602
88	0.01075719	0.01017357	0.00907431	0.00872781
89	0.01062956	0.01004625	0.00894837	0.00860255
90	0.01050476	0.00992177	0.00882527	0.00848013
91	0.01038272	0.00980004	0.00870493	0.00836047
92	0.01026333	0.00968096	0.00858724	0.00824346
93	0.01014651	0.00956446	0.00847213	0.00812903
94	0.01003217	0.00945044	0.00835950	0.00801709
95	0.00992025	0.00933884	0.00824930	0.00790757
96	0.00981066	0.00922957	0.00814143	0.00780038
97	0.00970334	0.00912257	0.00803583	0.00769547
98	0.00959821	0.00901776	0.00793242	0.00759275
99	0.00949520	0.00891508	0.00783115	0.00749216
100	0.00939426	0.00881446	0.00773194	0.00739363

Table VI–continued

SINKING FUND FACTOR OF 1

	1/8%	1/4%	1/2%	7/12%
101	0.00929532	0.00871584	0.00763473	0.00729711
102	0.00919832	0.00861917	0.00753947	0.00720254
103	0.00910320	0.00852439	0.00744610	0.00710986
104	0.00900992	0.00843144	0.00735457	0.00701901
105	0.00891842	0.00834027	0.00726481	0.00692994
106	0.00882865	0.00825083	0.00717679	0.00684261
107	0.00874055	0.00816307	0.00709045	0.00675696
108	0.00865409	0.00807694	0.00700575	0.00667294
109	0.00856922	0.00799241	0.00692264	0.00659052
110	0.00848590	0.00790942	0.00684107	0.00650965
111	0.00840408	0.00782793	0.00676102	0.00643028
112	0.00832372	0.00774791	0.00668242	0.00635237
113	0.00824479	0.00766932	0.00660526	0.00627590
114	0.00816724	0.00759211	0.00652948	0.00620081
115	0.00809105	0.00751626	0.00645506	0.00612708
116	0.00801617	0.00744172	0.00638195	0.00605466
117	0.00794257	0.00736846	0.00631013	0.00598353
118	0.00787022	0.00729646	0.00623956	0.00591365
119	0.00779909	0.00722567	0.00617021	0.00584499
120	0.00772915	0.00715607	0.00610205	0.00577751
121	0.00766037	0.00708764	0.00603505	0.00571120
122	0.00759271	0.00702033	0.00596918	0.00564602
123	0.00752616	0.00695412	0.00590441	0.00558194
124	0.00746068	0.00688899	0.00584072	0.00551894
125	0.00739626	0.00682491	0.00577808	0.00545700

Table VI–continued

SINKING FUND FACTOR OF 1

n	1/8%	1/4%	1/2%	7/12%
126	0.00733286	0.00676186	0.00571647	0.00539607
127	0.00727046	0.00669981	0.00565586	0.00533615
128	0.00720903	0.00663873	0.00559623	0.00527721
129	0.00714856	0.00657861	0.00553755	0.00522192
130	0.00708902	0.00651942	0.00547981	0.00516216
131	0.00703040	0.00646115	0.00542298	0.00510602
132	0.00697266	0.00640376	0.00536703	0.00505077
133	0.00691579	0.00634725	0.00531197	0.00499639
134	0.00685978	0.00629159	0.00525775	0.00494286
135	0.00680459	0.00623675	0.00520436	0.00489016
136	0.00675022	0.00618274	0.00515179	0.00483828
137	0.00669665	0.00612952	0.00510002	0.00478719
138	0.00664385	0.00607707	0.00504902	0.00473688
139	0.00659182	0.00602539	0.00499879	0.00468733
140	0.00654053	0.00597446	0.00494930	0.00463853
141	0.00648997	0.00592425	0.00490055	0.00459046
142	0.00644012	0.00587476	0.00485250	0.00454311
143	0.00639098	0.00582597	0.00480516	0.00449645
144	0.00634251	0.00577787	0.00475850	0.00445048
145	0.00629472	0.00573043	0.00471252	0.00440518
146	0.00624758	0.00568365	0.00466718	0.00436053
147	0.00620109	0.00563752	0.00462250	0.00431653
148	0.00615523	0.00559201	0.00457844	0.00427316
149	0.00610998	0.00554712	0.00453500	0.00423040
150	0.00606534	0.00550284	0.00449217	0.00418825

Table VI–continued

SINKING FUND FACTOR OF 1

n	1/8%	1/4%	1/2%	7/12%
151	0.00602129	0.00545915	0.00444993	0.00414670
152	0.00597783	0.00541605	0.00440827	0.00410572
153	0.00593493	0.00537351	0.00436719	0.00406532
154	0.00589259	0.00533153	0.00432666	0.00402547
155	0.00585080	0.00529010	0.00428668	0.00398617
156	0.00580955	0.00524921	0.00424723	0.00394741
157	0.00576882	0.00520885	0.00420832	0.00390917
158	0.00572862	0.00516900	0.00416992	0.00387146
159	0.00568891	0.00512966	0.00413203	0.00383425
160	0.00564971	0.00509082	0.00409464	0.00379753
161	0.00561100	0.00505247	0.00405773	0.00376131
162	0.00557276	0.00501459	0.00402131	0.00372556
163	0.00553500	0.00497719	0.00398536	0.00369029
164	0.00549770	0.00494025	0.00394987	0.00365547
165	0.00546085	0.00490377	0.00391483	0.00362111
166	0.00542445	0.00486773	0.00388024	0.00358720
167	0.00538848	0.00483213	0.00384608	0.00355372
168	0.00535295	0.00479695	0.00381236	0.00352067
169	0.00531783	0.00476220	0.00377906	0.00348804
170	0.00528313	0.00472787	0.00374617	0.00345583
171	0.00524884	0.00469394	0.00371369	0.00342403
172	0.00521495	0.00466042	0.00368161	0.00339262
173	0.00518145	0.00462728	0.00364992	0.00336160
174	0.00514834	0.00459454	0.00361862	0.00333098
175	0.00511561	0.00456217	0.00358770	0.00330073

Table VI—continued

SINKING FUND FACTOR OF 1

n	1/8%	1/4%	1/2%	7/12%
176	0.00508325	0.00453018	0.00355715	0.00327085
177	0.00505126	0.00449855	0.00352697	0.00324134
178	0.00501963	0.00446729	0.00349715	0.00321219
179	0.00498836	0.00443638	0.00346769	0.00318340
180	0.00495743	0.00440582	0.00343857	0.00315495
181	0.00492685	0.00437560	0.00340979	0.00312684
182	0.00489660	0.00434572	0.00338136	0.00309908
183	0.00486669	0.00431617	0.00335325	0.00307164
184	0.00483710	0.00428695	0.00332547	0.00304453
185	0.00480784	0.00425805	0.00329802	0.00301774
186	0.00477889	0.00422947	0.00327088	0.00299126
187	0.00475025	0.00420120	0.00324404	0.00296509
188	0.00472191	0.00417323	0.00321752	0.00293923
189	0.00469388	0.00414557	0.00319129	0.00291367
190	0.00466615	0.00411820	0.00316537	0.00288841
191	0.00463870	0.00409112	0.00313973	0.00286343
192	0.00461155	0.00406434	0.00311438	0.00283875
193	0.00458468	0.00403783	0.00308931	0.00281434
194	0.00455808	0.00401160	0.00306452	0.00279021
195	0.00453176	0.00398565	0.00304000	0.00276636
196	0.00450571	0.00395997	0.00301576	0.00274277
197	0.00447992	0.00393455	0.00299178	0.00271945
198	0.00445440	0.00390939	0.00296806	0.00269639
199	0.00442913	0.00388450	0.00294459	0.00267358
200	0.00440412	0.00385985	0.00292138	0.00265103

Table VI–continued

SINKING FUND FACTOR OF 1

n	2/3%	3/4%	5/6%	11/12%
1	1.00000000	1.00000000	1.00000000	1.00000000
2	0.49833887	0.49813200	0.49792531	0.49771879
3	0.33112096	0.33084579	0.33057092	0.33029637
4	0.24751384	0.24720501	0.24689661	0.24658864
5	0.19735105	0.19702242	0.19669433	0.19636679
6	0.16391042	0.16356891	0.16322806	0.16288788
7	0.14002531	0.13967488	0.13932523	0.13897637
8	0.12211240	0.12175552	0.12139955	0.12104447
9	0.10818096	0.10781929	0.10745863	0.10709899
10	0.09703654	0.09667123	0.09630705	0.09594400
11	0.08791905	0.08755094	0.08718407	0.08681845
12	0.08032176	0.07995148	0.07958255	0.07921499
13	0.07389385	0.07352188	0.07315139	0.07278237
14	0.06838474	0.06801146	0.06763978	0.06726968
15	0.06361067	0.06323639	0.06286382	0.06249295
16	0.05943382	0.05905879	0.05868557	0.05831418
17	0.05574880	0.05537321	0.05499956	0.05462784
18	0.05247363	0.05209766	0.05172375	0.05135188
19	0.04954361	0.04916740	0.04879336	0.04842148
20	0.04690696	0.04653063	0.04615659	0.04578482
21	0.04452176	0.04414543	0.04377148	0.04339993
22	0.04235374	0.04197748	0.04160373	0.04123247
23	0.04037456	0.03999846	0.03962497	0.03925410
24	0.03856062	0.03818474	0.03781159	0.03744117
25	0.03689210	0.03651650	0.03614374	0.03577383

Table VI–continued

SINKING FUND FACTOR OF 1

n	⅔%	¾%	⅚%	11/12%
26	0.03535220	0.03497693	0.03460463	0.03423528
27	0.03392664	0.03355176	0.03317995	0.03281121
28	0.03260317	0.03222871	0.03185744	0.03148935
29	0.03137123	0.03099723	0.03062654	0.03025914
30	0.03022166	0.02984816	0.02947808	0.02911140
31	0.02914649	0.02877352	0.02840408	0.02803815
32	0.02813875	0.02776634	0.02739756	0.02703242
33	0.02719231	0.02682048	0.02645240	0.02608805
34	0.02630176	0.02593053	0.02556316	0.02519965
35	0.02546231	0.02509170	0.02475069	0.02436240
36	0.02466970	0.02429973	0.02393385	0.02357205
37	0.02392013	0.02355082	0.02318572	0.02282480
38	0.02321020	0.02284157	0.02247725	0.02211723
39	0.02253687	0.02216893	0.02180542	0.02144631
40	0.02189739	0.02153016	0.02116746	0.02080928
41	0.02128928	0.02092276	0.02056089	0.02020365
42	0.02071031	0.02034452	0.01998349	0.01962719
43	0.02015843	0.01979338	0.01943320	0.01907787
44	0.01963180	0.01926751	0.01890818	0.01855383
45	0.01912875	0.01876521	0.01840676	0.01805338
46	0.01864772	0.01828495	0.01792738	0.01757498
47	0.01818732	0.01782532	0.01746864	0.01711724
48	0.01774626	0.01738504	0.01702925	0.01667886
49	0.01732334	0.01696292	0.01660803	0.01625864
50	0.01691749	0.01655787	0.01620388	0.01585551

Table VI–continued

SINKING FUND FACTOR OF 1

n	2/3%	3/4%	5/6%	11/12%
51	0.01652770	0.01616888	0.01581581	0.01546846
52	0.01615304	0.01579503	0.01544287	0.01509655
53	0.01579266	0.01543546	0.01508422	0.01473894
54	0.01544576	0.01508938	0.01473907	0.01439482
55	0.01511160	0.01475605	0.01440668	0.01406346
56	0.01478951	0.01443478	0.01408635	0.01374419
57	0.01447885	0.01412496	0.01377747	0.01343635
58	0.01417903	0.01382597	0.01347943	0.01313936
59	0.01388949	0.01353727	0.01319168	0.01285267
60	0.01360973	0.01325836	0.01291371	0.01257576
61	0.01333926	0.01298873	0.01264504	0.01230815
62	0.01307763	0.01272795	0.01238522	0.01204939
63	0.01282442	0.01247560	0.01213382	0.01179906
64	0.01257923	0.01223127	0.01189046	0.01155676
65	0.01234171	0.01199460	0.01165476	0.01132213
66	0.01211149	0.01176524	0.01142637	0.01109481
67	0.01188825	0.01154286	0.01120496	0.01087448
68	0.01167168	0.01132716	0.01099023	0.01066082
69	0.01146150	0.01111785	0.01078188	0.01045356
70	0.01125742	0.01091464	0.01057965	0.01025240
71	0.01105919	0.01071728	0.01038327	0.01005710
72	0.01086657	0.01052554	0.01019250	0.00986741
73	0.01067933	0.01033917	0.01007114	0.00968310
74	0.01049725	0.01015796	0.00982688	0.00950396
75	0.01032011	0.00998170	0.00965161	0.00932976

Table VI–continued

SINKING FUND FACTOR OF 1

n	⅔%	¾%	⅚%	11/12%
76	0.01014773	0.00981020	0.00948109	0.00916033
77	0.00997993	0.00964328	0.00931515	0.00899547
78	0.00981652	0.00948074	0.00915360	0.00883501
79	0.00965733	0.00932244	0.00899628	0.00867878
80	0.00950222	0.00916821	0.00884304	0.00852661
81	0.00935102	0.00901790	0.00869371	0.00837837
82	0.00920360	0.00887136	0.00854816	0.00823391
83	0.00905982	0.00872847	0.00840625	0.00809308
84	0.00891955	0.00858908	0.00826785	0.00795577
85	0.00878266	0.00845308	0.00813284	0.00782184
86	0.00864904	0.00832034	0.00800109	0.00769118
87	0.00851857	0.00819076	0.00787250	0.00756367
88	0.00839115	0.00806423	0.00774695	0.00743921
89	0.00826667	0.00794064	0.00762435	0.00731769
90	0.00814504	0.00781989	0.00750459	0.00719902
91	0.00802616	0.00770190	0.00738759	0.00708310
92	0.00790994	0.00758657	0.00727325	0.00696985
93	0.00779629	0.00747382	0.00716148	0.00685916
94	0.00768514	0.00736356	0.00705221	0.00675097
95	0.00757641	0.00725571	0.00694535	0.00664520
96	0.00747001	0.00715020	0.00684083	0.00654176
97	0.00736588	0.00704696	0.00673858	0.00644059
98	0.00726395	0.00694592	0.00663852	0.00634161
99	0.00716415	0.00684701	0.00654060	0.00624477
100	0.00706642	0.00675017	0.00644474	0.00614999

Table VI—continued

SINKING FUND FACTOR OF 1

n	⅔%	¾%	⅚%	11/12%
101	0.00697069	0.00665533	0.00635089	0.00605721
102	0.00687690	0.00656243	0.00625898	0.00596638
103	0.00678501	0.00647143	0.00616896	0.00587744
104	0.00669495	0.00638226	0.00608077	0.00579033
105	0.00660668	0.00629487	0.00599437	0.00570500
106	0.00652013	0.00620922	0.00590970	0.00562140
107	0.00643527	0.00612524	0.00582671	0.00553948
108	0.00635205	0.00604291	0.00574535	0.00545919
109	0.00627042	0.00596216	0.00566559	0.00538050
110	0.00619033	0.00588297	0.00558737	0.00530335
111	0.00611175	0.00580527	0.00551066	0.00522771
112	0.00603464	0.00572905	0.00543541	0.00515352
113	0.00595895	0.00565425	0.00536159	0.00508077
114	0.00588465	0.00558084	0.00528915	0.00500940
115	0.00581171	0.00550878	0.00521807	0.00493938
116	0.00574008	0.00543803	0.00514830	0.00487067
117	0.00566974	0.00536858	0.00507982	0.00480324
118	0.00560065	0.00530037	0.00501259	0.00473707
119	0.00553278	0.00523338	0.00494657	0.00467211
120	0.00546609	0.00516758	0.00488174	0.00460833
121	0.00540057	0.00510294	0.00481807	0.00454572
122	0.00533618	0.00503942	0.00475553	0.00448423
123	0.00527289	0.00497702	0.00469408	0.00442384
124	0.00521067	0.00491568	0.00463372	0.00436452
125	0.00514951	0.00485540	0.00457441	0.00430625

Table VI–continued

SINKING FUND FACTOR OF 1

n	$\frac{2}{3}$%	$\frac{3}{4}$%	$\frac{5}{6}$%	$\frac{11}{12}$%
126	0.00508937	0.00479614	0.00451611	0.00424901
127	0.00503024	0.00473788	0.00445882	0.00419276
128	0.00497208	0.00468060	0.00440250	0.00413748
129	0.00491488	0.00462428	0.00434714	0.00408316
130	0.00485861	0.00456888	0.00429270	0.00402977
131	0.00480325	0.00451440	0.00423918	0.00397728
132	0.00474878	0.00446080	0.00418654	0.00392568
133	0.00469518	0.00440808	0.00413478	0.00387495
134	0.00464244	0.00435621	0.00408386	0.00382507
135	0.00459052	0.00430516	0.00403377	0.00377601
136	0.00453942	0.00425493	0.00398449	0.00372776
137	0.00448911	0.00420550	0.00393601	0.00368031
138	0.00443959	0.00415684	0.00388830	0.00363362
139	0.00439082	0.00410894	0.00384136	0.00358770
140	0.00434280	0.00406179	0.00379515	0.00354252
141	0.00429551	0.00401536	0.00374967	0.00349806
142	0.00424893	0.00396965	0.00370491	0.00345431
143	0.00420305	0.00392464	0.00366084	0.00341126
144	0.00415786	0.00388031	0.00361745	0.00336889
145	0.00411333	0.00383664	0.00357473	0.00332718
146	0.00406947	0.00379364	0.00353266	0.00328612
147	0.00402624	0.00375127	0.00349123	0.00324570
148	0.00398364	0.00370954	0.00345043	0.00320591
149	0.00394166	0.00366841	0.00341025	0.00316673
150	0.00390029	0.00362790	0.00337067	0.00312815

Table VI—continued

SINKING FUND FACTOR OF 1

n	2/3%	3/4%	5/6%	11/12%
151	0.00385950	0.00358797	0.00333167	0.00309016
152	0.00381930	0.00354862	0.00329326	0.00305274
153	0.00377967	0.00350984	0.00325541	0.00301589
154	0.00374059	0.00347162	0.00321811	0.00297959
155	0.00370206	0.00343395	0.00318136	0.00294383
156	0.00366407	0.00339681	0.00314515	0.00290860
157	0.00362661	0.00336019	0.00310946	0.00287390
158	0.00358966	0.00332409	0.00307428	0.00283971
159	0.00355321	0.00328849	0.00303960	0.00280602
160	0.00351727	0.00325340	0.00300542	0.00277282
161	0.00348181	0.00321878	0.00297173	0.00274011
162	0.00344683	0.00318465	0.00293851	0.00270787
163	0.00341232	0.00315098	0.00290575	0.00267609
164	0.00337827	0.00311777	0.00287346	0.00264477
165	0.00334467	0.00308502	0.00284161	0.00261389
166	0.00331152	0.00305270	0.00281021	0.00258346
167	0.00327880	0.00302083	0.00277924	0.00255346
168	0.00324652	0.00298938	0.00278694	0.00252388
169	0.00321465	0.00295834	0.00271857	0.00249471
170	0.00318319	0.00292772	0.00268885	0.00246595
171	0.00315215	0.00289751	0.00265954	0.00243760
172	0.00312150	0.00286769	0.00263062	0.00240964
173	0.00309124	0.00283827	0.00260209	0.00237492
174	0.00306137	0.00280922	0.00257394	0.00235487
175	0.00303187	0.00278056	0.00254617	0.00232804

Table VI–continued

SINKING FUND FACTOR OF 1

n	2/3%	3/4%	5/6%	11/12%
176	0.00300275	0.00275226	0.00251877	0.00230159
177	0.00297399	0.00272433	0.00249173	0.00227549
178	0.00294560	0.00269676	0.00246504	0.00224975
179	0.00291755	0.00266954	0.00243871	0.00222436
180	0.00288985	0.00264267	0.00241272	0.00219930
181	0.00286250	0.00261613	0.00238707	0.00217459
182	0.00283548	0.00258993	0.00236175	0.00215020
183	0.00280879	0.00256406	0.00233676	0.00212614
184	0.00278242	0.00253851	0.00231209	0.00210240
185	0.00275638	0.00251328	0.00228773	0.00207897
186	0.00273065	0.00248837	0.00226369	0.00205585
187	0.00270523	0.00246376	0.00223995	0.00203303
188	0.00268011	0.00243945	0.00221652	0.00201052
189	0.00265529	0.00241544	0.00219338	0.00198829
190	0.00263077	0.00239173	0.00217053	0.00196636
191	0.00260653	0.00236830	0.00214797	0.00194471
192	0.00258258	0.00234516	0.00212569	0.00192334
193	0.00255892	0.00232230	0.00210368	0.00190224
194	0.00253552	0.00229971	0.00208195	0.00188142
195	0.00251240	0.00227739	0.00206049	0.00186086
196	0.00248955	0.00225534	0.00203412	0.00184056
197	0.00246696	0.00223355	0.00201836	0.00182052
198	0.00244464	0.00221202	0.00199768	0.00180074
199	0.00242256	0.00219074	0.00197726	0.00178120
200	0.00240074	0.00216972	0.00195708	0.00176191

Table VI–continued

SINKING FUND FACTOR OF 1

n	1%	2%	3%	4%
1	1.00000000	1.00000000	1.00000000	1.00000000
2	0.49751244	0.49504951	0.49261084	0.49019608
3	0.33002211	0.32675467	0.32353036	0.32034854
4	0.24628109	0.24262375	0.23902705	0.23549005
5	0.19603980	0.19215839	0.18835457	0.18462711
6	0.16254837	0.15852581	0.15459750	0.15076190
7	0.13862828	0.13451196	0.13050635	0.12660961
8	0.12069029	0.11650980	0.11245639	0.10852783
9	0.10674036	0.10251544	0.09843386	0.09449299
10	0.09558208	0.09132653	0.08723051	0.08329094
11	0.08645408	0.08217794	0.07807745	0.07414904
12	0.07884879	0.07455960	0.07046209	0.06655217
13	0.07241482	0.06811835	0.06402954	0.06014373
14	0.06690117	0.06260197	0.05852634	0.05466897
15	0.06212378	0.05782547	0.05376658	0.04994110
16	0.05794460	0.05365013	0.04961085	0.04582000
17	0.05425806	0.04996984	0.04595253	0.04219852
18	0.05098205	0.04670210	0.04270870	0.03899333
19	0.04805175	0.04378177	0.03981388	0.03613862
20	0.04541531	0.04115672	0.03721571	0.03358175
21	0.04303075	0.03878477	0.03487178	0.03128011
22	0.04086372	0.03663140	0.03274739	0.02919881
23	0.03888584	0.03466810	0.03081390	0.02730906
24	0.03707347	0.03287110	0.02904742	0.02558683
25	0.03540675	0.03122044	0.02742787	0.02401196

Table VI–continued

SINKING FUND FACTOR OF 1

n	1%	2%	3%	4%
26	0.03386888	0.02969923	0.02593829	0.02256738
27	0.03244553	0.02829309	0.02456421	0.02123854
28	0.03112444	0.02698967	0.02329323	0.02001298
29	0.02989502	0.02577836	0.02211467	0.01887993
30	0.02874811	0.02464992	0.02101926	0.01783010
31	0.02767573	0.02359635	0.01999893	0.01685535
32	0.02667089	0.02261061	0.01904662	0.01594859
33	0.02572744	0.02168653	0.01815612	0.01510357
34	0.02483997	0.02081867	0.01732196	0.01431477
35	0.02400368	0.02000221	0.01653929	0.01357732
36	0.02321431	0.01923285	0.01580379	0.01288688
37	0.02246805	0.01850678	0.01511162	0.01223957
38	0.02176150	0.01782057	0.01445934	0.01163192
39	0.02109160	0.01717114	0.01384385	0.01106083
40	0.02045560	0.01655575	0.01326238	0.01052349
41	0.01985102	0.01597188	0.01271241	0.01001738
42	0.01927563	0.01541729	0.01219167	0.00954020
43	0.01872737	0.01488993	0.01169811	0.00908989
44	0.01820441	0.01438794	0.01122985	0.00866454
45	0.01770505	0.01390962	0.01078518	0.00826246
46	0.01722775	0.01345342	0.01036254	0.00788205
47	0.01677111	0.01301792	0.00996051	0.00752189
48	0.01633384	0.01260184	0.00957777	0.00718065
49	0.01591474	0.01220396	0.00921314	0.00685712
50	0.01551273	0.01182321	0.00886550	0.00655020

Table VI—continued

SINKING FUND FACTOR OF 1

n	1%	2%	3%	4%
51	0.01512680	0.01145856	0.00853382	0.00625885
52	0.01475603	0.01110909	0.00821718	0.00598212
53	0.01439956	0.01077392	0.00791471	0.00571915
54	0.01405658	0.01045226	0.00762558	0.00546910
55	0.01372637	0.01014337	0.00734907	0.00523124
56	0.01340824	0.00984656	0.00708447	0.00500487
57	0.01310156	0.00956120	0.00683114	0.00478932
58	0.01280573	0.00928667	0.00658848	0.00458401
59	0.01252020	0.00902243	0.00635593	0.00438836
60	0.01224445	0.00876797	0.00613296	0.00420185
61	0.01197800	0.00852278	0.00591908	0.00402398
62	0.01172041	0.00828643	0.00571385	0.00385430
63	0.01147125	0.00805848	0.00551682	0.00369237
64	0.01123013	0.00783855	0.00532760	0.00353780
65	0.01099667	0.00762624	0.00514581	0.00339019
66	0.01077052	0.00742122	0.00497110	0.00324921
67	0.01055136	0.00722316	0.00480313	0.00311451
68	0.01033889	0.00703173	0.00464159	0.00298578
69	0.01013280	0.00684665	0.00448618	0.00286272
70	0.00993282	0.00666765	0.00433663	0.00274506
71	0.00973870	0.00649446	0.00419266	0.00263253
72	0.00955019	0.00632683	0.00405405	0.00252489
73	0.00936706	0.00616454	0.00392053	0.00242190
74	0.00918910	0.00600736	0.00379191	0.00232334
75	0.00901609	0.00585508	0.00366796	0.00222900

Table VI—continued

SINKING FUND FACTOR OF 1

n	1%	2%	3%	4%
76	0.00884784	0.00570751	0.00354849	0.00213869
77	0.00868416	0.00556447	0.00343331	0.00205221
78	0.00852488	0.00542576	0.00332224	0.00196939
79	0.00836983	0.00529123	0.00321510	0.00189007
80	0.00821885	0.00516071	0.00311175	0.00181408
81	0.00807179	0.00503405	0.00301201	0.00174127
82	0.00792851	0.00491110	0.00291576	0.00167150
83	0.00778887	0.00479173	0.00282284	0.00160463
84	0.00765273	0.00467581	0.00273313	0.00154054
85	0.00751998	0.00456321	0.00264650	0.00147909
86	0.00739050	0.00445381	0.00256284	0.00142018
87	0.00726418	0.00434750	0.00248202	0.00136370
88	0.00714089	0.00424416	0.00240393	0.00130953
89	0.00702056	0.00414370	0.00232848	0.00125758
90	0.00690306	0.00404602	0.00225556	0.00120775
91	0.00678832	0.00395101	0.00218508	0.00115995
92	0.00667624	0.00385859	0.00211694	0.00111410
93	0.00656673	0.00376868	0.00205107	0.00107010
94	0.00645971	0.00368118	0.00198737	0.00102789
95	0.00635511	0.00359602	0.00192577	0.00098738
96	0.00625284	0.00351313	0.00186619	0.00094850
97	0.00615284	0.00343242	0.00180856	0.00091119
98	0.00605503	0.00335383	0.00175281	0.00087538
99	0.00595936	0.00327729	0.00169886	0.00084100
100	0.00586574	0.00320274	0.00164667	0.00080800

Table VI–continued

SINKING FUND FACTOR OF 1

n	5%	6%	7%	8%
1	1.00000000	1.00000000	1.00000000	1.00000000
2	0.48780488	0.48543689	0.48309179	0.48076923
3	0.31720856	0.31410981	0.31105166	0.30803351
4	0.23201183	0.22859149	0.22522812	0.22192080
5	0.18097480	0.17739640	0.17389069	0.17045645
6	0.14701747	0.14336263	0.13979580	0.13631539
7	0.12281982	0.11913502	0.11555322	0.11207240
8	0.10472181	0.10103594	0.09746776	0.09401476
9	0.09069008	0.08702224	0.08348647	0.08007971
10	0.07950458	0.07586796	0.07237750	0.06902949
11	0.07038889	0.06679294	0.06335690	0.06007634
12	0.06282541	0.05927703	0.05590199	0.05269502
13	0.05645577	0.05296011	0.04965085	0.04652181
14	0.05102397	0.04758491	0.04434494	0.04129685
15	0.04634229	0.04296276	0.03979462	0.03682954
16	0.04226991	0.03895214	0.03585765	0.03297687
17	0.03869914	0.03544480	0.03242519	0.02962943
18	0.03554622	0.03235654	0.02941260	0.02670210
19	0.03274501	0.02962086	0.02675301	0.02412763
20	0.03024259	0.02718456	0.02439293	0.02185221
21	0.02799611	0.02500455	0.02228900	0.01983225
22	0.02597051	0.02304557	0.02040577	0.01803207
23	0.02413682	0.02127848	0.01871393	0.01642217
24	0.02247090	0.01967900	0.01718902	0.01497796
25	0.02095246	0.01822672	0.01581052	0.01367878

Table VI—continued

SINKING FUND FACTOR OF 1

n	5%	6%	7%	8%
26	0.01956432	0.01690435	0.01456103	0.01250713
27	0.01829186	0.01569717	0.01342573	0.01144810
28	0.01712253	0.01459255	0.01239193	0.01048891
29	0.01604551	0.01357961	0.01144865	0.00961854
30	0.01505144	0.01264891	0.01058640	0.00882743
31	0.01413212	0.01179222	0.00979691	0.00810728
32	0.01328042	0.01100234	0.00907292	0.00745081
33	0.01249004	0.01027293	0.00840807	0.00685163
34	0.01175545	0.00959843	0.00779674	0.00630411
35	0.01107171	0.00897386	0.00723396	0.00580326
36	0.01043446	0.00839483	0.00671531	0.00534467
37	0.00983979	0.00785743	0.00623685	0.00492440
38	0.00928423	0.00735812	0.00579505	0.00453894
39	0.00876462	0.00689377	0.00538676	0.00418513
40	0.00827816	0.00646154	0.00500914	0.00386016
41	0.00782229	0.00605886	0.00465962	0.00356149
42	0.00739471	0.00568342	0.00433591	0.00328684
43	0.00699333	0.00533312	0.00403590	0.00303414
44	0.00661625	0.00500606	0.00375769	0.00280152
45	0.00626173	0.00470050	0.00349957	0.00258728
46	0.00592820	0.00441485	0.00325996	0.00238991
47	0.00561421	0.00414768	0.00303744	0.00220799
48	0.00531843	0.00389766	0.00283070	0.00204027
49	0.00503965	0.00366356	0.00263853	0.00188557
50	0.00477674	0.00344429	0.00245985	0.00174286

Table VI–continued

SINKING FUND FACTOR OF 1

n	5%	6%	7%	8%
51	0.00452867	0.00323880	0.00229365	0.00161116
52	0.00424497	0.00304617	0.00213901	0.00148959
53	0.00407334	0.00286551	0.00199509	0.00137735
54	0.00386438	0.00269602	0.00186110	0.00127370
55	0.00366686	0.00253696	0.00173633	0.00117796
56	0.00348010	0.00238765	0.00162011	0.00108952
57	0.00330343	0.00224744	0.00151183	0.00100780
58	0.00313626	0.00211574	0.00141093	0.00093227
59	0.00297802	0.00199200	0.00131689	0.00086247
60	0.00282818	0.00187572	0.00122923	0.00079795
61	0.00268627	0.00176642	0.00114749	0.00073830
62	0.00255183	0.00166366	0.00107127	0.00068314
63	0.00242442	0.00156704	0.00100019	0.00063214
64	0.00230365	0.00147615	0.00093388	0.00058497
65	0.00218915	0.00139066	0.00087203	0.00054135
66	0.00208057	0.00131022	0.00081431	0.00050100
67	0.00197758	0.00123454	0.00076046	0.00046367
68	0.00187986	0.00116330	0.00071021	0.00042914
69	0.00178715	0.00109625	0.00066331	0.00039719
70	0.00169915	0.00103313	0.00061953	0.00036764
71	0.00161563	0.00097370	0.00057866	0.00034029
72	0.00153633	0.00091774	0.00054051	0.00031498
73	0.00146103	0.00086505	0.00050490	0.00029157
74	0.00138953	0.00081542	0.00047164	0.00026990
75	0.00132161	0.00076867	0.00044060	0.00024984

Table VI–continued

SINKING FUND FACTOR OF 1

n	5%	6%	7%	8%
76	0.00125709	0.00072463	0.00041160	0.00023128
77	0.00119580	0.00068315	0.00038453	0.00021410
78	0.00113756	0.00064407	0.00035924	0.00019820
79	0.00108222	0.00060724	0.00033563	0.00018349
80	0.00102962	0.00057254	0.00031357	0.00016987
81	0.00097963	0.00053984	0.00029297	0.00015726
82	0.00093211	0.00050903	0.00027373	0.00014559
83	0.00088694	0.00047998	0.00025576	0.00013479
84	0.00084399	0.00045261	0.00023897	0.00012479
85	0.00080316	0.00042681	0.00022329	0.00011553
86	0.00076433	0.00040249	0.00020863	0.00010696
87	0.00072740	0.00037956	0.00019495	0.00009903
88	0.00069228	0.00035795	0.00018216	0.00009168
89	0.00065888	0.00033757	0.00017021	0.00008489
90	0.00062711	0.00031836	0.00015905	0.00007859
91	0.00059689	0.00030025	0.00014863	0.00007277
92	0.00056815	0.00028318	0.00013888	0.00006737
93	0.00054080	0.00026708	0.00012978	0.00006238
94	0.00051478	0.00025189	0.00012128	0.00005775
95	0.00049003	0.00023758	0.00011333	0.00005347
96	0.00046648	0.00022408	0.00010590	0.00004951
97	0.00044407	0.00021135	0.00009897	0.00004584
98	0.00042274	0.00019935	0.00009248	0.00004244
99	0.00040245	0.00018803	0.00008643	0.00003930
100	0.00038314	0.00017736	0.00008076	0.00003638

Table VI–continued

SINKING FUND FACTOR OF 1

n	9%	10%	11%	12%
1	1.00000000	1.00000000	1.00000000	1.00000000
2	0.47846890	0.47619048	0.47393365	0.47169811
3	0.30505476	0.30211480	0.29921307	0.29634898
4	0.21866866	0.21547080	0.21232635	0.20923444
5	0.16709246	0.16379748	0.16057031	0.15740973
6	0.13291978	0.12960738	0.12637656	0.12322572
7	0.10869052	0.10540550	0.10221527	0.09911774
8	0.09067438	0.08744402	0.08432105	0.08130284
9	0.07679880	0.07364054	0.07060166	0.06767889
10	0.06582009	0.06274539	0.05980143	0.05698416
11	0.05694666	0.05396314	0.05112101	0.04841540
12	0.04965066	0.04676332	0.04402729	0.04143681
13	0.04356656	0.04077852	0.03815099	0.03567720
14	0.03843317	0.03574622	0.03322820	0.03087125
15	0.03405888	0.03147378	0.02906524	0.02682424
16	0.03029991	0.02781662	0.02551675	0.02339002
17	0.02704625	0.02466413	0.02247148	0.02045673
18	0.02421229	0.02193022	0.01984287	0.01793731
19	0.02173041	0.01954687	0.01756250	0.01576300
20	0.01954648	0.01745962	0.01557564	0.01387878
21	0.01761663	0.01562439	0.01383793	0.01224009
22	0.01590499	0.01400506	0.01231310	0.01081051
23	0.01438188	0.01257181	0.01097118	0.00955997
24	0.01302256	0.01129978	0.00978721	0.00846344
25	0.01180625	0.01016807	0.00874024	0.00749997

Table VI–continued

SINKING FUND FACTOR OF 1

n	9%	10%	11%	12%
26	0.01071536	0.00915904	0.00781258	0.00665186
27	0.00973491	0.00825764	0.00698916	0.00590409
28	0.00885205	0.00745101	0.00625715	0.00524387
29	0.00805572	0.00672807	0.00560547	0.00466021
30	0.00733635	0.00607925	0.00502460	0.00414366
31	0.00668560	0.00549621	0.00450627	0.00368606
32	0.00609619	0.00497172	0.00404329	0.00328033
33	0.00556173	0.00449941	0.00362938	0.00292031
34	0.00507660	0.00407371	0.00325905	0.00260064
35	0.00463584	0.00368971	0.00292749	0.00231662
36	0.00423505	0.00334306	0.00263044	0.00206414
37	0.00387033	0.00302994	0.00236416	0.00183959
38	0.00353820	0.00274693	0.00212535	0.00163980
39	0.00323555	0.00249098	0.00191107	0.00146197
40	0.00295961	0.00225941	0.00171873	0.00130363
41	0.00270789	0.00204980	0.00154601	0.00116260
42	0.00247814	0.00185999	0.00139086	0.00103696
43	0.00226837	0.00168805	0.00125146	0.00092500
44	0.00207675	0.00153224	0.00112617	0.00082521
45	0.00190165	0.00139100	0.00101354	0.00073625
46	0.00174160	0.00126295	0.00091227	0.00065694
47	0.00159525	0.00114682	0.00082119	0.00058621
48	0.00146139	0.00104148	0.00073926	0.00052312
49	0.00133893	0.00094590	0.00066556	0.00046686
50	0.00122687	0.00085917	0.00059924	0.00041666

Table VI–continued

SINKING FUND FACTOR OF 1

n	14%	16%	18%	20%
1	1.00000000	1.00000000	1.00000000	1.00000000
2	0.46728972	0.46296296	0.45871560	0.45454546
3	0.29073148	0.28525787	0.27992386	0.27472527
4	0.20320478	0.19737507	0.19173867	0.18628912
5	0.15128355	0.14540938	0.13977842	0.13437970
6	0.11715750	0.11138987	0.10591013	0.10070575
7	0.09319238	0.08761268	0.08236200	0.07742393
8	0.07557002	0.07022426	0.06524436	0.06060942
9	0.06216838	0.05708249	0.05239482	0.04807946
10	0.05171354	0.04690108	0.04251464	0.03852276
11	0.04339427	0.03886075	0.03477639	0.03110379
12	0.03666933	0.03241473	0.02862781	0.02526496
13	0.03116366	0.02718411	0.02368621	0.02062000
14	0.02660914	0.02289797	0.01967806	0.01689306
15	0.02280896	0.01935752	0.01640278	0.01388212
16	0.01961540	0.01641362	0.01371008	0.01143614
17	0.01691544	0.01395225	0.01148527	0.00944015
18	0.01462115	0.01188485	0.00963946	0.00780539
19	0.01266316	0.01014166	0.00810284	0.00646245
20	0.01098600	0.00866703	0.00681998	0.00535653
21	0.00954486	0.00741617	0.00574643	0.00444394
22	0.00830317	0.00635264	0.00484626	0.00368922
23	0.00723081	0.00544658	0.00409020	0.00306526
24	0.00630284	0.00467339	0.00345430	0.00254787
25	0.00549841	0.00401262	0.00291883	0.00211873

Table VI–continued

SINKING FUND FACTOR OF 1

n	14%	16%	18%	20%
26	0.00480001	0.00344723	0.00246748	0.00176250
27	0.00419288	0.00296294	0.00208672	0.00146659
28	0.00366449	0.00254775	0.00176528	0.00122067
29	0.00320417	0.00219153	0.00149377	0.00101619
30	0.00280279	0.00188568	0.00126431	0.00084611
31	0.00245256	0.00162295	0.00107030	0.00070459
32	0.00214675	0.00139714	0.00090621	0.00058682
33	0.00187958	0.00120298	0.00076739	0.00048878
34	0.00164604	0.00103598	0.00064990	0.00040715
35	0.00144181	0.00089229	0.00055046	0.00033917
36	0.00126315	0.00076862	0.00046628	0.00028256
37	0.00110680	0.00066217	0.00039499	0.00023542
38	0.00096993	0.00057051	0.00033463	0.00019614
39	0.00085010	0.00049158	0.00028350	0.00016342
40	0.00074514	0.00042359	0.00024020	0.00013617
41	0.00065321	0.00036503	0.00020352	0.00011346
42	0.00057266	0.00031459	0.00017244	0.00009454
43	0.00050208	0.00027112	0.00014612	0.00007878
44	0.00044023	0.00023367	0.00012381	0.00006564
45	0.00038602	0.00020140	0.00010491	0.00005470
46	0.00033850	0.00017359	0.00008890	0.00004558
47	0.00029684	0.00014962	0.00007534	0.00003798
48	0.00026032	0.00012897	0.00006384	0.00003165
49	0.00022830	0.00011117	0.00005410	0.00002638
50	0.00020022	0.00009582	0.00004584	0.00002198

Table VI–continued

SINKING FUND FACTOR OF 1

n	22%	24%	26%	28%
1	1.00000000	1.00000000	1.00000000	1.00000000
2	0.45045045	0.44642857	0.44247788	0.43859649
3	0.26965807	0.26471834	0.25990228	0.25520621
4	0.18102011	0.17592551	0.17099933	0.16623578
5	0.12920593	0.12424771	0.11949645	0.11494376
6	0.09576443	0.09107416	0.08662324	0.08240028
7	0.07278235	0.06842155	0.06432626	0.06048170
8	0.05629900	0.05229320	0.04857282	0.04511938
9	0.04411114	0.04046543	0.03711893	0.03404929
10	0.03489498	0.03160213	0.02861644	0.02591173
11	0.02780709	0.02485221	0.02220711	0.01984187
12	0.02228477	0.01964831	0.01731944	0.01526483
13	0.01793854	0.01559825	0.01355921	0.01178511
14	0.01449065	0.01242297	0.01064670	0.00912312
15	0.01173816	0.00991915	0.00837896	0.00707699
16	0.00952975	0.00793583	0.00660604	0.00549850
17	0.00775073	0.00635916	0.00521555	0.00427733
18	0.00631295	0.00510219	0.00412226	0.00333053
19	0.00514791	0.00409781	0.00326096	0.00259523
20	0.00420187	0.00329380	0.00258139	0.00202342
21	0.00343233	0.00264925	0.00204453	0.00157830
22	0.00280550	0.00213194	0.00162001	0.00123153
23	0.00229431	0.00171636	0.00128408	0.00096121
24	0.00187705	0.00138224	0.00101807	0.00075038
25	0.00153620	0.00111347	0.00080734	0.00058589

Table VI–continued

SINKING FUND FACTOR OF 1

n	22%	24%	26%	28%
26	0.00125760	0.00089716	0.00064034	0.00045752
27	0.00102976	0.00072299	0.00050794	0.00035731
28	0.00084335	0.00058272	0.00040297	0.00027907
29	0.00069079	0.00046971	0.00031971	0.00021798
30	0.00056590	0.00037866	0.00025368	0.00017016
31	0.00046364	0.00030527	0.00020129	0.00013300
32	0.00037989	0.00024613	0.00015973	0.00010390
33	0.00031129	0.00019845	0.00012675	0.00008116
34	0.00025509	0.00016002	0.00010059	0.00006340
35	0.00020905	0.00012903	0.00007982	0.00004953
36	0.00017132	0.00010404	0.00006335	0.00003870
37	0.00014041	0.00008390	0.00005027	0.00003023
38	0.00011507	0.00006766	0.00003990	0.00002362
39	0.00009431	0.00005456	0.00003166	0.00001845
40	0.00007730	0.00004400	0.00002513	0.00001441
41	0.00006336	0.00003548	0.00001994	0.00001126
42	0.00005193	0.00002861	0.00001583	0.00000880
43	0.00004256	0.00002307	0.00001256	0.00000687
44	0.00003489	0.00001861	0.00000997	0.00000537
45	0.00002859	0.00001501	0.00000791	0.00000419
46	0.00002344	0.00001210	0.00000628	0.00000328
47	0.00001921	0.00000976	0.00000498	0.00000256
48	0.00001575	0.00000787	0.00000396	0.00000200
49	0.00001291	0.00000635	0.00000314	0.00000156
50	0.00001058	0.00000512	0.00000249	0.00000122

Table VI–continued

SINKING FUND FACTOR OF 1

n	30%	32%	34%	36%
1	1.00000000	1.00000000	1.00000000	1.00000000
2	0.43478261	0.43103448	0.42735043	0.42372881
3	0.25062657	0.24615991	0.24180288	0.23755226
4	0.16162922	0.15717418	0.15286537	0.14869765
5	0.11058155	0.10640193	0.10239729	0.09856027
6	0.07839430	0.07459463	0.07099105	0.06757367
7	0.05687364	0.05348840	0.05031290	0.04733463
8	0.04191521	0.03894347	0.03618818	0.03363424
9	0.03123536	0.02865716	0.02629595	0.02413419
10	0.02346344	0.02124867	0.01924616	0.01743631
11	0.01772882	0.01584245	0.01415944	0.01265852
12	0.01345407	0.01185952	0.01045626	0.00922190
13	0.01024327	0.00890448	0.00774276	0.00673514
14	0.00781784	0.00670062	0.00574498	0.00492791
15	0.00597778	0.00505059	0.00426900	0.00361038
16	0.00457724	0.00381162	0.00317570	0.00264766
17	0.00350860	0.00287928	0.00236432	0.00194303
18	0.00269166	0.00217652	0.00176131	0.00142666
19	0.00206623	0.00164617	0.00131269	0.00104791
20	0.00158688	0.00124554	0.00097866	0.00076993
21	0.00121919	0.00094270	0.00072981	0.00056581
22	0.00093696	0.00071366	0.00054434	0.00041586
23	0.00072022	0.00054036	0.00040606	0.00030569
24	0.00055371	0.00040920	0.00030294	0.00022472
25	0.00042575	0.00030990	0.00022602	0.00016521

Table VI–continued

SINKING FUND FACTOR OF 1

n	30%	32%	34%	36%
26	0.00032739	0.00023472	0.00016864	0.00012146
27	0.00025178	0.00017779	0.00012584	0.00008930
28	0.00019364	0.00013467	0.00009390	0.00006566
29	0.00014893	0.00010201	0.00007007	0.00004828
30	0.00011455	0.00007727	0.00005229	0.00003550
31	0.00008811	0.00005854	0.00003902	0.00002610
32	0.00006777	0.00004435	0.00002912	0.00001919
33	0.00005213	0.00003359	0.00002173	0.00001411
34	0.00004010	0.00002545	0.00001622	0.00001038
35	0.00003084	0.00001928	0.00001210	0.00000763
36	0.00002372	0.00001461	0.00000903	0.00000561
37	0.00001825	0.00001106	0.00000674	0.00000412
38	0.00001404	0.00000838	0.00000503	0.00000303
39	0.00001080	0.00000635	0.00000375	0.00000223
40	0.00000831	0.00000481	0.00000280	0.00000164
41	0.00000639	0.00000364	0.00000209	0.00000121
42	0.00000491	0.00000276	0.00000156	0.00000089
43	0.00000378	0.00000209	0.00000116	0.00000065
44	0.00000291	0.00000158	0.00000087	0.00000048
45	0.00000224	0.00000120	0.00000065	0.00000035
46	0.00000172	0.00000091	0.00000048	0.00000026
47	0.00000132	0.00000069	0.00000036	0.00000019
48	0.00000102	0.00000052	0.00000027	0.00000014
49	0.00000078	0.00000040	0.00000020	0.00000010
50	0.00000060	0.00000030	0.00000015	0.00000008

Table VI–continued

SINKING FUND FACTOR OF 1

n	38%	40%	45%	50%
1	1.00000000	1.00000000	1.00000000	1.00000000
2	0.42016807	0.41666667	0.40816327	0.40000000
3	0.23340491	0.22935780	0.21965953	0.21052632
4	0.14466605	0.14076577	0.13155947	0.12307692
5	0.09488376	0.09136091	0.08318339	0.07582938
6	0.06433304	0.06126010	0.05425534	0.04812030
7	0.04454170	0.04192279	0.03606791	0.03108305
8	0.03126739	0.02907422	0.02427070	0.02030135
9	0.02215554	0.02034480	0.01618208	0.01335350
10	0.01580106	0.01432384	0.01122623	0.00882378
11	0.01132042	0.01012770	0.00768275	0.00584812
12	0.00813646	0.00718211	0.00527052	0.00388360
13	0.00586143	0.00510390	0.00362168	0.00258238
14	0.00422945	0.00363240	0.00249149	0.00171863
15	0.00305545	0.00258786	0.00171532	0.00114444
16	0.00220920	0.00184506	0.00118158	0.00076238
17	0.00159831	0.00131616	0.00081422	0.00050800
18	0.00115686	0.00093923	0.00056122	0.00033855
19	0.00083760	0.00067043	0.00038690	0.00022565
20	0.00060659	0.00047865	0.00026675	0.00015041
21	0.00043936	0.00034178	0.00018393	0.00010026
22	0.00031828	0.00024407	0.00012683	0.00006684
23	0.00023058	0.00017430	0.00008746	0.00004456
24	0.00016706	0.00012449	0.00006032	0.00002970
25	0.00012104	0.00008891	0.00004160	0.00001980

Table VI–continued

SINKING FUND FACTOR OF 1

n	38%	40%	45%	50%
26	0.00008771	0.00006350	0.00002869	0.00001320
27	0.00006355	0.00004536	0.00001978	0.00000880
28	0.00004605	0.00003240	0.00001364	0.00000587
29	0.00003337	0.00002314	0.00000941	0.00000391
30	0.00002418	0.00001653	0.00000649	0.00000261
31	0.00001752	0.00001181	0.00000448	0.00000174
32	0.00001270	0.00000843	0.00000309	0.00000116
33	0.00000920	0.00000602	0.00000213	0.00000077
34	0.00000667	0.00000430	0.00000147	0.00000052
35	0.00000483	0.00000307	0.00000101	0.00000034
36	0.00000350	0.00000220	0.00000070	0.00000023
37	0.00000254	0.00000157	0.00000048	0.00000015
38	0.00000184	0.00000112	0.00000033	0.00000010
39	0.00000133	0.00000080	0.00000023	0.00000007
40	0.00000097	0.00000057	0.00000016	0.00000005
41	0.00000070	0.00000041	0.00000011	0.00000003
42	0.00000051	0.00000029	0.00000008	0.00000002
43	0.00000037	0.00000021	0.00000005	0.00000001
44	0.00000027	0.00000015	0.00000004	0.00000001
45	0.00000019	0.00000011	0.00000002	0.00000001
46	0.00000014	0.00000008	0.00000002	0.00000000
47	0.00000010	0.00000005	0.00000001	0.00000000
48	0.00000007	0.00000004	0.00000001	0.00000000
49	0.00000005	0.00000003	0.00000001	0.00000000
50	0.00000004	0.00000002	0.00000000	0.00000000

Table VII

AMOUNT OF 1 AT CONTINUOUSLY COMPOUNDED NOMINAL INTEREST RATES

n	1/8%	1/4%	1/2%	7/12%	n
1	1.00125078	1.00250313	1.00501252	1.00585038	1
2	1.00250313	1.00501252	1.01005017	1.01173499	2
3	1.00375704	1.00752820	1.01511307	1.01765402	3
4	1.00501252	1.01005017	1.02020134	1.02360769	4
5	1.00626957	1.01257845	1.02531512	1.02959618	5
6	1.00752820	1.01511307	1.03045453	1.03561971	6
7	1.00878839	1.01765402	1.03561971	1.04167848	7
8	1.01005017	1.02020134	1.04081077	1.04777269	8
9	1.01131352	1.02275503	1.04602786	1.05390256	9
10	1.01257845	1.02531512	1.05127110	1.06006829	10
11	1.01384497	1.02788162	1.05654062	1.06627010	11
12	1.01511307	1.03045453	1.06183655	1.07250818	12
13	1.01638275	1.03303389	1.06715902	1.07878276	13
14	1.01765402	1.03561971	1.07250818	1.08509405	14
15	1.01892689	1.03821200	1.07788415	1.09144226	15
16	1.02020134	1.04081077	1.08328707	1.09782762	16
17	1.02147739	1.04341606	1.08871707	1.10425033	17
18	1.02275503	1.04602786	1.09417428	1.11071061	18
19	1.02403428	1.04864620	1.09965886	1.11720869	19
20	1.02531512	1.05127110	1.10570918	1.12374479	20
21	1.02659757	1.05390256	1.11071061	1.13031912	21
22	1.02788162	1.05654062	1.11627807	1.13693192	22
23	1.02916727	1.05918527	1.12187344	1.14358340	23
24	1.03045453	1.06183655	1.12749685	1.15027380	24
25	1.03174341	1.06449446	1.13314845	1.15700334	25

Table VII—continued

AMOUNT OF 1 AT CONTINUOUSLY COMPOUNDED NOMINAL INTEREST RATES

n	1/8%	1/4%	1/2%	7/12%
26	1.03303389	1.06715902	1.13882838	1.16377225
27	1.03432599	1.06983026	1.14453678	1.17058076
28	1.03561971	1.07250818	1.15027380	1.17742910
29	1.03695043	1.07519281	1.15603957	1.18431751
30	1.03821200	1.07788415	1.16183424	1.19124622
31	1.03951057	1.08058223	1.16765796	1.19821546
32	1.04081077	1.08328707	1.17351087	1.20522548
33	1.04211260	1.08599867	1.17939312	1.21227650
34	1.04341606	1.08871707	1.18530485	1.21936878
35	1.04472114	1.09144226	1.19124622	1.22650255
36	1.04602786	1.09417428	1.19721736	1.23367806
37	1.04733621	1.09691314	1.20321844	1.24089555
38	1.04864620	1.09865886	1.20924960	1.24815526
39	1.04995783	1.10241144	1.21531099	1.25545744
40	1.05127111	1.10517092	1.22140276	1.26280234
41	1.05258601	1.10793730	1.22752506	1.27019022
42	1.05390256	1.11071061	1.23367806	1.27762131
43	1.05522076	1.11349086	1.23986190	1.28509588
44	1.05654061	1.11627807	1.24607673	1.29261418
45	1.05786212	1.11907226	1.25232272	1.30017647
46	1.05918527	1.12187344	1.25860001	1.30778300
47	1.06051008	1.12468163	1.26490877	1.31543402
48	1.06183655	1.12749685	1.27124915	1.32312981
49	1.06316467	1.13031912	1.27762131	1.33087063
50	1.06449446	1.13314845	1.28402542	1.33865672

Table VII–continued

AMOUNT OF 1 AT CONTINUOUSLY COMPOUNDED NOMINAL INTEREST RATES

n	2/3%	3/4%	5/6%	11/12%
1	1.00668894	1.00752820	1.00836815	1.00920881
2	1.01342262	1.01511307	1.01680633	1.01850242
3	1.02020134	1.02275503	1.02531512	1.02788162
4	1.02702540	1.03045453	1.03389511	1.03734718
5	1.03389511	1.03821200	1.04254691	1.04689991
6	1.04081077	1.04602786	1.05127110	1.05654062
7	1.04777269	1.05390256	1.06006829	1.06627010
8	1.05478118	1.06183655	1.06893911	1.07608917
9	1.06183655	1.06983026	1.07788415	1.08599867
10	1.06893911	1.07788415	1.08690405	1.09599943
11	1.07608917	1.08599867	1.09599943	1.10609228
12	1.08328707	1.09417428	1.10517092	1.11627807
13	1.09053311	1.10241144	1.11441916	1.12655766
14	1.09782762	1.11071061	1.12374479	1.13693192
15	1.10517092	1.11907226	1.13314845	1.14740171
16	1.11256334	1.12749685	1.14263081	1.15796791
17	1.12000521	1.13598487	1.15219252	1.16863142
18	1.12749685	1.14453678	1.16183424	1.17939312
19	1.13503861	1.15315308	1.17155665	1.19025393
20	1.14263081	1.16183424	1.18136041	1.20121475
21	1.15027380	1.17058076	1.19124622	1.21227650
22	1.15796791	1.17939312	1.20121475	1.22344013
23	1.16571349	1.18827182	1.21126669	1.23470655
24	1.17351087	1.19721736	1.22140276	1.24607673
25	1.18136041	1.20623025	1.23162364	1.25755161

Table VII—continued

AMOUNT OF 1 AT CONTINUOUSLY COMPOUNDED NOMINAL INTEREST RATES

n	2/3%	3/4%	5/6%	11/12%
26	1.18926246	1.21531099	1.24193006	1.26913217
27	1.19721736	1.22446009	1.25232272	1.28081936
28	1.20522548	1.23367806	1.26280234	1.29261418
29	1.21328716	1.24296543	1.27336967	1.30451762
30	1.22140276	1.25232272	1.28402542	1.31653068
31	1.22957265	1.26175045	1.29477034	1.32865435
32	1.23779718	1.27124915	1.30560517	1.34088968
33	1.24607673	1.28081936	1.31653068	1.35323768
34	1.25441166	1.29294129	1.32754760	1.36569938
35	1.26280234	1.30017647	1.33865672	1.37827585
36	1.27124915	1.30996445	1.34985881	1.39096813
37	1.27975246	1.31982612	1.36115463	1.40377729
38	1.28831264	1.32976203	1.37254498	1.41670441
39	1.29693009	1.33977274	1.38403065	1.42975057
40	1.30560517	1.34985881	1.39561243	1.44291687
41	1.31433828	1.36002081	1.40729112	1.45620441
42	1.32312981	1.37025931	1.41906755	1.46961432
43	1.33198015	1.38057489	1.43094252	1.48314772
44	1.34088968	1.39096813	1.44291687	1.49680574
45	1.34985881	1.40143961	1.45499141	1.51058954
46	1.35888793	1.41198992	1.46716700	1.52450027
47	1.36797745	1.42261966	1.47944448	1.53853911
48	1.37712776	1.43332941	1.49182470	1.55270722
49	1.38633929	1.44411980	1.50430851	1.56700580
50	1.39561243	1.45499141	1.51689680	1.58143606

Table VII—continued

AMOUNT OF 1 AT CONTINUOUSLY COMPOUNDED NOMINAL INTEREST RATES

n	1%	2%	3%	4%
1	1.01005017	1.02020134	1.03045453	1.04081077
2	1.02020134	1.04081077	1.06183655	1.08328707
3	1.03045453	1.06183655	1.09417428	1.12749685
4	1.04081077	1.08328707	1.12749685	1.17351087
5	1.05127110	1.10517092	1.16183424	1.22140276
6	1.06183655	1.12749685	1.19721736	1.27124915
7	1.07250818	1.15027380	1.23367806	1.32312981
8	1.08328707	1.17351087	1.27124915	1.37712776
9	1.09417428	1.19721736	1.30996445	1.43332942
10	1.10517092	1.22140276	1.34985881	1.49182470
11	1.11627807	1.24607673	1.39096813	1.55270722
12	1.12749685	1.27124915	1.43332942	1.61607440
13	1.13882838	1.29693009	1.47698079	1.68202765
14	1.15027380	1.32312981	1.52196156	1.75067250
15	1.16183424	1.34985881	1.56831219	1.82211880
16	1.17351087	1.37712776	1.61607440	1.89648088
17	1.18530485	1.40494759	1.66529120	1.97387773
18	1.19721736	1.43332941	1.71600686	2.05443321
19	1.20924960	1.46228459	1.76826705	2.13827622
20	1.22140276	1.49182470	1.82211880	2.22554093
21	1.23367806	1.52196156	1.87761058	2.31636698
22	1.24607673	1.55270722	1.93479233	2.41089971
23	1.25860001	1.58407399	1.99371553	2.50929039
24	1.27124915	1.61607440	2.05443321	2.61169647
25	1.28402542	1.64872127	2.11700002	2.71828183

Table VII–continued

AMOUNT OF 1 AT CONTINUOUSLY COMPOUNDED NOMINAL INTEREST RATES

n	1%	2%	3%	4%
26	1.29693009	1.68202765	2.18147227	2.82921701
27	1.30996445	1.71600686	2.24790799	2.94467955
28	1.32312981	1.75067250	2.31636698	3.06485420
29	1.33642749	1.78603843	2.38691085	3.18993328
30	1.34985881	1.82211880	2.45960311	3.32011692
31	1.36342511	1.85892804	2.53450918	3.45561347
32	1.37712776	1.89648088	2.61169647	3.59663973
33	1.39096813	1.93479233	2.69123445	3.74342138
34	1.40494759	1.97387773	2.77319476	3.89619330
35	1.41906755	2.01375271	2.85766512	4.05519997
36	1.43332941	2.05443321	2.94467955	4.22069582
37	1.44773461	2.09593551	3.03435839	4.39294568
38	1.46228459	2.13827622	3.12676837	4.57222520
39	1.47698079	2.18147227	3.22199264	4.75882125
40	1.49182470	2.22554093	3.32011692	4.95303242
41	1.50681779	2.27049984	3.42122954	5.15516951
42	1.52196156	2.31636698	3.52542149	5.36555597
43	1.53725752	2.36316069	3.63278656	5.58452846
44	1.55270722	2.41089971	3.74342138	5.81243739
45	1.56831219	2.45960311	3.85742553	6.04964746
46	1.58407399	2.50929039	3.97490163	6.29653826
47	1.59999419	2.55998142	4.09595540	6.55350486
48	1.61607440	2.61169647	4.22069582	6.82095847
49	1.63231622	2.66445624	4.34923514	7.09932706
50	1.64872127	2.71828183	4.48168907	7.38905610

Table VII–continued

AMOUNT OF 1 AT CONTINUOUSLY COMPOUNDED NOMINAL INTEREST RATES

n	5%	6%	7%	8%
1	1.05127110	1.06183655	1.07250818	1.08328707
2	1.10517092	1.12749685	1.15027380	1.17351087
3	1.16183424	1.19721736	1.23367806	1.27124915
4	1.22140276	1.27124915	1.32312981	1.37712776
5	1.28402542	1.34985881	1.41906755	1.49182470
6	1.34985881	1.43332942	1.52196156	1.61607440
7	1.41906755	1.52196156	1.63231622	1.75067250
8	1.49182470	1.61607440	1.75067250	1.89648088
9	1.56831219	1.71600686	1.87761058	2.05443321
10	1.64872127	1.82211880	2.01375271	2.22554093
11	1.73325302	1.93479233	2.15976625	2.41089971
12	1.82211880	2.05443321	2.31636698	2.61169647
13	1.91554083	2.18147227	2.48432253	2.82921701
14	2.01375721	2.31636698	2.66445624	3.06485420
15	2.11700002	2.45960311	2.85765112	3.32011692
16	2.22554093	2.61169647	3.06485420	3.59663973
17	2.33964685	2.77319476	3.28708121	3.89619330
18	2.45960311	2.94467955	3.52542149	4.22069582
19	2.58570966	3.12676837	3.78104339	4.57225195
20	2.71828183	3.32011692	4.05519997	4.95303242
21	2.85765112	3.52542149	4.34923514	5.36555597
22	3.00416602	3.74342138	4.66459027	5.81243739
23	3.15819291	3.97490163	5.00281123	6.29653826
24	3.32011692	4.22069582	5.36555597	6.82095847
25	3.49034296	4.48168907	5.75460268	7.38905610

Table VII–continued

AMOUNT OF 1 AT CONTINUOUSLY COMPOUNDED NOMINAL INTEREST RATES

n	5%	6%	7%	8%
26	3.66929667	4.75882125	6.17185845	8.00446891
27	3.85742553	5.05309032	6.61936868	8.67113766
28	4.05519997	5.36555597	7.09932706	9.39331286
29	4.26311451	5.69734342	7.61408636	10.17567430
30	4.48168907	6.04964746	8.16616991	11.02317638
31	4.71147018	6.42373677	8.75828404	11.94126442
32	4.95303242	6.82095847	9.39331286	12.93581731
33	5.20697983	7.24274298	10.07442465	14.01320361
34	5.47394739	7.69060920	10.80490286	15.18032224
35	5.75460268	8.16616991	11.58834672	16.44464677
36	6.04964746	8.67113766	12.42859666	17.81427318
37	6.35981952	9.20733086	13.32977160	19.29797175
38	6.68589444	9.77668041	14.29628910	20.90524323
39	7.02868758	10.38123656	15.33288702	22.64637964
40	7.38905610	11.02311764	16.44464671	24.53253019
41	7.76790110	11.70481154	17.63701820	26.57577269
42	8.16616991	12.42859666	18.91584631	28.78919087
43	8.58485840	13.19713816	20.28739992	31.18695816
44	9.02501350	14.01320360	21.75840239	33.78442846
45	9.48773583	14.87973172	23.33606458	36.59823444
46	9.97418245	15.79984294	25.02812018	39.64639406
47	10.48556972	16.77685067	26.84286365	42.94842597
48	11.02317638	17.81427318	28.78919087	46.52547443
49	11.58834672	18.91584631	30.87664274	50.40044477
50	12.18249396	20.08553692	33.11545195	54.59815002

Table VII–continued

AMOUNT OF 1 AT CONTINUOUSLY COMPOUNDED NOMINAL INTEREST RATES

n	9%	10%	11%	12%
1	1.09417428	1.10517092	1.11627807	1.12749685
2	1.19721736	1.22140276	1.24607673	1.27124915
3	1.30996445	1.34985881	1.39096813	1.43332942
4	1.43332942	1.49182470	1.55270722	1.61607440
5	1.56831219	1.64872127	1.73325302	1.82211880
6	1.71600686	1.82211880	1.93479233	2.05443321
7	1.87761058	2.01375271	2.15976625	2.31636698
8	2.05443321	2.22554093	2.41089971	2.61169647
9	2.24790799	2.45960311	2.69123447	2.94467955
10	2.45960311	2.71828183	3.00416602	3.32011692
11	2.69123447	3.00416602	3.35348465	3.74342138
12	2.94467955	3.32011692	3.74342138	4.22069582
13	3.22199264	3.66929667	4.17869919	4.75882125
14	3.52542149	4.05519997	4.66459027	5.36555597
15	3.85742553	4.48168907	5.20697983	6.04964746
16	4.22069582	4.95303242	5.81243739	6.82095847
17	4.61817682	5.47394739	6.48829640	7.69060920
18	5.05309032	6.04964746	7.24274298	8.67113766
19	5.52896148	6.68589444	8.08491516	9.77668041
20	6.04964747	7.38905610	9.02501350	11.02317638
21	6.61936868	8.16616991	10.07442465	12.42859666
22	7.24274298	9.02501350	11.24585931	14.01320361
23	7.92482312	9.97418245	12.55350613	15.79984295
24	8.67113766	11.02317638	14.01320361	17.81427318
25	9.48773584	12.18249396	15.64263188	20.08553692

Table VII–continued

AMOUNT OF 1 AT CONTINUOUSLY COMPOUNDED NOMINAL INTEREST RATES

n	9%	10%	11%	12%
26	10.38123656	13.46373803	17.46152693	22.64637964
27	11.35888208	14.87973172	19.49191959	25.53372174
28	12.42859666	16.44464677	21.75840239	28.78919087
29	13.59905085	18.17414537	24.28842744	32.45972207
30	14.87973172	20.08553692	27.11263891	36.59823443
31	16.28101980	22.19795128	30.26524425	41.26439410
32	17.81427318	24.53253019	33.78442846	46.52547443
33	19.49191959	27.11263892	37.71281661	52.45732594
34	21.32755716	29.96410004	42.09799015	59.14546983
35	23.33606458	33.11545195	46.99306322	66.68633102
36	25.53372174	36.59823444	54.45732593	75.18862827
37	27.93834170	40.44730435	58.55696257	84.77494165
38	30.56941502	44.70118448	65.36585319	95.58347980
39	33.44826778	49.40244491	72.96646848	107.77007254
40	36.59823444	54.59815002	81.45086864	121.51041748
41	40.04484695	60.34028758	90.92181848	137.00261314
42	43.81604173	66.68633103	101.49403210	154.47001497
43	47.94238607	73.69979368	113.29556231	174.16445555
44	52.45732594	81.45086865	126.46935169	196.36987528
45	57.39745703	90.01713128	141.17496387	221.40641613
46	62.80282144	99.48431562	157.59051627	249.63503710
47	68.71723216	109.94717242	175.91483742	281.46271837
48	75.18862828	121.51041749	196.36987528	317.34832880
49	82.26946349	134.28977965	219.20338547	357.80924157
50	90.01713128	148.41315906	244.69193217	403.42879333

Table VII–continued

AMOUNT OF 1 AT CONTINUOUSLY COMPOUNDED NOMINAL INTEREST RATES

n	13%	14%	15%	16%
1	1.1388284	1.1502738	1.1618342	1.1735108
2	1.2969301	1.3231298	1.3498588	1.3771278
3	1.4769808	1.5219616	1.5683122	1.6160744
4	1.6820277	1.7506725	1.8221188	1.8964809
5	1.9155408	2.0137527	2.1170002	2.2255409
6	2.1814723	2.3163670	2.4596031	2.6116965
7	2.4843225	2.6644562	2.8576511	3.0648542
8	2.8292170	3.0648542	3.3201169	3.5966397
9	3.2219926	3.5254215	3.8574255	4.2206958
10	3.6692967	4.0552000	4.4816891	4.9530324
11	4.1786992	4.6645903	5.2069798	5.8124374
12	4.7588213	5.3655560	6.0496475	6.8209585
13	5.4194807	6.1718584	7.0286876	8.0044689
14	6.1718585	7.0993271	8.1661699	9.3933313
15	7.0286876	8.1661699	9.4877358	11.0231764
16	8.0044689	9.3933129	11.0231764	12.9358173
17	9.1157164	10.8049029	12.8071038	15.1803222
18	10.3812366	12.4285967	14.8797317	17.8142732
19	11.8224469	14.2962891	17.2877818	20.9052432
20	13.4637380	16.4446468	20.0855369	24.5325302
21	15.3328870	18.9158463	23.3360646	28.7891909
22	17.4615269	21.7584024	27.1126389	33.7844285
23	19.8856825	25.0281202	31.5003923	39.6463941
24	22.6463796	28.7891909	36.5982344	46.5254744
25	25.7903399	33.1154520	42.5210820	54.5981500

Table VII–continued

AMOUNT OF 1 AT CONTINUOUSLY COMPOUNDED NOMINAL INTEREST RATES

n	13%	14%	15%	16%
26	29.3707711	38.0918367	49.4024491	64.0715226
27	33.4482678	43.8160417	57.3974570	75.1886283
28	38.0918367	50.4004448	66.6863310	88.2346727
29	43.3800648	57.9743111	77.4784629	103.5443476
30	49.4024491	66.6863310	90.0171313	121.5104175
31	56.2609112	76.7075393	104.5849856	142.5937959
32	64.0715226	88.2346727	121.5104175	167.3353696
33	72.9664685	101.4940321	141.1749639	196.3698753
34	83.0962853	116.7459259	164.0219073	230.4421834
35	94.6324083	134.2897797	190.5662684	270.4264074
36	107.7700726	154.4700150	221.4064161	317.3483289
37	122.7316175	177.6828110	257.2375558	372.4117139
38	139.7702495	204.3838819	298.8674009	437.0291947
39	159.1743273	235.0974243	347.2343804	512.8585109
40	181.2722418	270.4264074	403.4287934	601.8450378
41	206.4379741	311.0644109	468.7173867	706.2716946
42	235.0974243	357.8092416	544.5719100	828.8175114
43	267.7356197	411.5785956	632.7022926	972.6263597
44	304.9049229	473.4280747	735.0951890	1141.3876066
45	347.2343804	544.5719100	854.0587623	1339.4307643
46	395.4403681	626.4067996	992.2747153	1571.8365628
47	450.3387151	720.5393290	1152.8587424	1844.5672939
48	512.8585108	828.8175112	1339.4307640	2164.6197717
49	584.0578288	953.3670672	1556.1965273	2540.2048336
50	665.1416329	1096.6331581	1808.0424138	2980.9579868

Table VII–continued

AMOUNT OF 1 AT CONTINUOUSLY COMPOUNDED NOMINAL INTEREST RATES

n	17%	18%	19%	20%
1	1.1853049	1.1972174	1.2092496	1.2214028
2	1.4049476	1.4333294	1.4622846	1.4918247
3	1.6652912	1.7160069	1.7682671	1.8221188
4	1.9738777	2.0544332	2.1382762	2.2255409
5	2.3396469	2.4596031	2.5857097	2.7182818
6	2.7731947	2.9446796	3.1267684	3.3201169
7	3.2870812	3.5254215	3.7810434	4.0552000
8	3.8961933	4.2206958	4.5722252	4.0496475
9	4.6181768	5.0530903	5.5289615	7.3890561
10	5.4739474	6.0496475	6.6858944	9.0250135
11	6.4882964	7.2427430	8.0849152	11.0231764
12	7.6906092	8.6711377	9.7766804	13.4637380
13	9.1157164	10.3812366	11.8224469	16.4446468
14	10.8049029	12.4285967	14.2962891	20.0855369
15	12.8071038	14.8797317	17.2877818	24.5325302
16	15.1803222	17.8142732	20.9052432	29.9641001
17	17.9933096	21.3275572	25.2796570	36.5982344
18	21.3275572	25.5337218	30.5694150	44.7011845
19	25.2796570	30.5694150	36.9660528	54.5981500
20	29.9641001	36.5982344	44.7011845	66.6863310
21	35.5165932	43.8160417	54.0548894	81.4508687
22	42.0979902	52.4573260	65.3658532	99.4843156
23	49.8989520	62.8028215	79.0436317	121.5104175
24	59.14546985	75.1886283	95.5834798	148.4131591
25	70.1054124	90.0171313	115.5842845	

Table VII–continued

AMOUNT OF 1 AT CONTINUOUSLY COMPOUNDED NOMINAL INTEREST RATES

n	17%	18%	19%	20%
26	83.0962854	107.7700726	139.7702495	181.2722419
27	98.4944302	129.0242021	169.0171180	221.4064162
28	116.7459259	154.4700150	204.3838820	270.4264074
29	138.3795123	184.9341841	247.1511270	330.2995599
30	164.0219073	221.4064162	298.8674009	403.4287935
31	194.4159624	265.0716058	361.4052843	492.7490411
32	230.4421835	317.3483289	437.0291946	601.8450379
33	273.1442380	379.9349295	528.4773778	735.0951892
34	323.7591904	454.8646945	639.0610564	897.8472916
35	383.7533391	544.5719101	772.7843254	1096.6331584
36	454.8646945	651.9709462	934.4891345	1339.4307644
37	539.1533291	780.5509371	1130.0306099	1635.9844300
38	639.0610566	934.4891347	1366.4890604	1998.1958951
39	757.4821706	1118.7866177	1652.4263465	2440.6019776
40	897.8472916	1339.4307643	1998.1958946	2980.9579870
41	1064.2227505	1603.5897677	2416.3175816	3640.9503073
42	1261.4283891	1919.8455133	2921.9310633	4447.0667477
43	1495.1771892	2298.4723830	3533.3439627	5431.6595914
44	1772.2407759	2751.7710456	4272.6947653	6634.2440062
45	2100.6455894	3294.4680751	5166.7544258	8103.0839276
46	2489.9054080	3944.1943817	6247.8957106	9897.1290588
47	2951.2969595	4722.0579973	7555.2653741	12088.3807301
48	3498.1866037	5653.3298241	9136.2016138	14764.7815654
49	4146.4175522	6768.2646249	11047.9481255	18033.7449277
50	4914.7688403	8103.0839271	13359.7268256	22026.4657946

Table VII–continued

AMOUNT OF 1 AT CONTINUOUSLY COMPOUNDED NOMINAL INTEREST RATES

n	21%	22%	23%	24%
1	1.233678	1.246077	1.258600	1.271249
2	1.521962	1.552707	1.584073	1.616074
3	1.877611	1.934792	1.993715	2.054433
4	2.316367	2.410900	2.509290	2.611696
5	2.857651	3.004166	3.158193	3.320116
6	3.525421	3.743421	3.974902	4.220695
7	4.349235	4.664590	5.002811	5.365556
8	5.365556	5.812437	6.296538	6.820958
9	6.619369	7.242743	7.924823	8.671137
10	8.166170	9.025013	9.974182	11.023176
11	10.074424	11.245859	12.553506	14.013204
12	12.428597	14.013204	15.779843	17.814273
13	15.332887	17.461153	19.885682	22.646380
14	18.915846	21.758402	25.028120	28.789191
15	23.336065	27.112639	31.500392	36.598234
16	28.789191	33.784428	39.646394	46.525474
17	35.516593	42.097990	49.898952	59.145470
18	43.816042	52.457326	62.802821	75.188628
19	54.054889	65.365853	79.043632	95.583480
20	66.686331	81.450869	99.484316	121.510418
21	82.269463	101.494032	125.210961	154.470015
22	101.494032	126.469352	157.590516	196.369875
23	125.210961	157.590516	198.343425	249.635037
24	154.470015	196.369875	249.635037	317.348329
25	190.566268	244.691932	314.190660	403.428794

Table VII—continued

AMOUNT OF 1 AT CONTINUOUSLY COMPOUNDED NOMINAL INTEREST RATES

n	21%	22%	23%	24%
26	235.097424	304.904923	395.440368	512.858511
27	290.034534	379.934930	497.701125	651.970946
28	357.809242	473.428075	626.406800	828.817512
29	441.421411	589.927708	788.395604	1053.633557
30	541.571910	735.095189	992.274715	1339.430764
31	671.826418	915.985010	1248.876967	1702.750221
32	828.817511	1141.387606	1571.836563	2164.619772
33	1022.493979	1422.256537	1978.313513	2751.771046
34	1261.428389	1722.240776	2489.905407	3498.186604
35	1556.196528	2208.347991	3133.794970	4447.066748
36	1919.845513	2751.771045	3944.194381	5653.329824
37	2368.471288	3428.917867	4964.163087	7186.790736
38	2921.931063	4272.694765	6247.895711	9136.201616
39	3604.722246	5324.105524	7863.601603	11614.388542
40	4447.066747	6634.244005	9897.129056	14764.781565
41	5486.248677	8266.777079	12456.526728	18769.716019
42	8768.264624	10301.038555	15677.784663	23860.985541
43	8349.859570	12835.884445	19732.059933	30333.275595
44	10301.038556	15994.496923	24834.770827	38561.127945
45	12708.165261	19930.370433	31257.042809	49020.801135
46	15677.784664	24834.770828	39340.114390	62317.651791
47	19341.338969	30946.030038	49513.468361	79221.261889
48	23860.985536	38561.127935	62317.651770	100709.961863
49	29436.774345	48050.124224	78432.997137	128027.453448
50	36315.502664	59874.141697	98715.770974	162754.791414

Table VII–continued

AMOUNT OF 1 AT CONTINUOUSLY COMPOUNDED NOMINAL INTEREST RATES

n	25%	26%	27%	28%
1	1.28402	1.29693	1.30996	1.32313
2	1.64872	1.68203	1.71601	1.75067
3	2.11700	2.18147	2.24791	2.31637
4	2.71828	2.82922	2.94468	3.06485
5	3.49034	3.66930	3.85743	4.05520
6	4.48169	4.75882	5.05309	5.36556
7	5.74460	6.17186	6.61937	7.09933
8	7.38906	8.00447	8.67114	9.39333
9	9.48774	10.38123	11.35888	12.42860
10	12.18249	13.46374	14.87973	16.44465
11	15.64623	17.46153	19.49192	21.75840
12	20.08554	22.64638	25.53372	28.78919
13	25.79033	29.37077	33.44827	38.09184
14	33.11545	38.09184	43.81604	50.40044
15	42.52108	49.40245	57.39746	66.68633
16	54.59815	64.07152	75.18863	88.23467
17	70.10541	83.09629	98.49443	116.74593
18	90.01713	107.77007	129.02420	154.47002
19	115.58428	139.77025	169.01712	204.38388
20	148.41316	181.27224	221.40642	270.42641
21	190.56627	235.09742	290.03453	357.80924
22	244.69193	304.90492	379.93493	473.42807
23	314.19066	395.44037	497.70125	626.40680
24	403.42879	512.85851	651.97095	828.81751
25	518.01282	665.14163	854.05876	1096.63316

Table VII—continued

AMOUNT OF 1 AT CONTINUOUSLY COMPOUNDED NOMINAL INTEREST RATES

n	25%	26%	27%	28%
26	665.14163	862.64220	1118.78662	1450.98803
27	854.05876	1118.78662	1465.57070	1919.84551
28	1096.63316	1450.98803	1919.84551	2540.20483
29	1408.10485	1881.83003	2514.92937	3361.02075
30	1808.04241	2440.60198	3294.46808	4447.06075
31	2321.57241	3165.29013	4315.63606	5884.04659
32	2980.95799	4105.16001	5653.32982	7785.35746
33	3827.62582	5324.10553	7405.66110	10301.03856
34	4914.76884	6904.99264	9701.15277	13629.61121
35	6310.68811	8955.29270	12708.16526	18033.74492
36	8103.08393	11614.38854	16647.24473	23860.09554
37	10404.56571	15063.04994	21807.29880	31571.18132
38	13359.72683	19535.72266	28566.78619	41772.77121
39	17154.22881	25336.46648	37421.47438	55270.79893
40	22026.46579	32859.62567	49020.80113	73130.44182
41	28282.54191	42616.63717	64215.50683	96761.06776
42	36315.50267	55270.79893	84120.03113	128027.45342
43	46630.02844	71682.36205	110194.25038	169396.94042
44	59874.14170	92967.01202	144350.55068	224134.14199
45	76879.91974	120571.71496	189094.08982	296558.56523
46	98715.77098	156373.08473	247706.53550	392385.47875
47	126753.55897	202804.95834	324486.75572	519176.92487
48	162754.79137	263023.85219	425066.11473	686938.46716
49	208981.28881	341123.54741	556821.49951	908908.76514
50	268337.28644	442413.39191	729416.36976	1202604.28384

Table VII–continued

AMOUNT OF 1 AT CONTINUOUSLY COMPOUNDED NOMINAL INTEREST RATES

n	29%	30%	31%	32%
1	1.33643	1.34986	1.36343	1.37713
2	1.78604	1.82212	1.85893	1.89648
3	2.38691	2.45960	2.53451	2.61170
4	3.18993	3.32012	3.45561	3.59664
5	4.26311	4.48169	4.71147	4.95303
6	5.69734	6.04965	6.42374	6.82096
7	7.61409	8.16617	8.75828	9.39333
8	10.17567	11.02318	11.94126	12.93582
9	13.59905	14.87973	16.28102	17.81427
10	18.17415	20.08554	22.19795	24.53253
11	24.28843	27.11264	30.26524	33.78443
12	32.45972	36.59823	41.26439	46.52547
13	43.38006	49.40245	56.26091	64.07153
14	57.97431	66.68633	76.70754	88.23467
15	77.47846	90.01713	104.58450	121.51042
16	103.54435	121.51042	142.59380	167.33537
17	138.37951	164.02191	194.41596	230.44218
18	184.93418	221.40642	265.07161	317.34833
19	247.15113	298.86740	361.40553	437.02919
20	330.29956	403.42879	492.74904	601.84504
21	441.42141	544.57191	671.82642	828.81751
22	589.92771	735.09519	915.98501	1141.38761
23	788.39560	992.27472	1248.87697	1571.83656
24	1053.63356	1339.43076	1702.75022	2164.61977
25	1408.10485	1808.04241	2321.57242	2980.95799

Table VII–continued

AMOUNT OF 1 AT CONTINUOUSLY COMPOUNDED NOMINAL INTEREST RATES

n	29%	30%	31%	32%
26	1881.83003	2440.60198	3165.29013	4105.16001
27	2514.92937	3294.46808	4315.63606	5653.32982
28	3361.02075	4447.06675	5884.04659	7785.35746
29	4491.76051	6002.91222	8022.45690	10721.43192
30	6002.91222	8103.08393	10938.01921	14764.78156
31	8022.45689	10938.01921	14913.17009	20332.99063
32	10721.43192	14764.78156	20332.99063	28001.12592
33	14328.41632	19930.37044	27722.51007	38561.12794
34	19148.88943	26903.18607	37797.56645	53103.59991
35	25591.10220	36315.50267	51534.15135	73130.44182
36	34200.65243	49020.80113	70262.95619	100709.96185
37	45706.69202	66171.16016	95798.27906	138690.48461
38	61083.67960	89321.72335	130613.77956	190994.51700
39	81633.90849	120571.71496	178082.10731	263023.85220
40	109097.79926	162754.79139	242801.61748	362217.44955
41	145801.29781	219695.98863	331041.82303	498819.70650
42	194852.86218	296558.56524	451350.73535	686938.46721
43	260406.72114	400312.19125	615382.92785	946002.03559
44	348014.70020	540364.93714	839028.53864	1302765.66831
45	465096.41158	729416.36970	1143952.58104	1794074.77224
46	621567.62902	984609.11102	1559693.67837	2470670.18015
47	830680.06508	1329083.28053	2126525.53145	3402428.50157
48	1110143.67272	1794074.77221	2899358.31542	4685578.75569
49	1483626.51987	2421747.63271	3953057.94211	6452640.59637
50	1982759.26312	3269017.37175	5389698.47590	8886110.51855

Table VII—continued

AMOUNT OF 1 AT CONTINUOUSLY COMPOUNDED NOMINAL INTEREST RATES

n	35%	40%	45%	50%
1	1.4191	1.4918	1.5683	1.6487
2	2.0138	2.2255	2.4596	2.7183
3	2.8577	3.3201	3.8574	4.4817
4	4.0552	4.9530	6.0496	7.3891
5	5.7546	7.3891	9.4877	12.1825
6	8.1662	11.0232	14.8797	20.0855
7	11.5883	16.4446	23.3361	33.1155
8	16.4446	24.5325	36.5982	54.5982
9	23.3361	36.5982	57.3975	90.0171
10	33.1155	54.5982	90.0171	148.4132
11	46.9930	81.4509	141.1750	244.6919
12	66.6863	121.5104	221.4064	403.4288
13	94.6324	181.2722	347.2344	665.1416
14	134.2898	270.4264	544.5719	1096.6332
15	190.5663	403.4288	854.0588	1808.0424
16	270.4264	601.8450	1339.4308	2980.9580
17	383.7533	897.8473	2100.6456	4914.7688
18	544.5719	1339.4308	3294.4681	8103.0839
19	772.7843	1998.1959	5166.7544	13359.7268
20	1096.6332	2980.9580	8103.0839	22026.4658
21	1556.1965	4447.0667	12708.1653	36315.5027
22	2208.3480	6634.2440	19930.3704	59874.1417
23	3133.7950	9897.1291	31257.0428	98715.7710
24	4447.0667	14764.7816	49020.8011	162754.7914
25	6310.6881	22026.4658	76879.9198	268337.2865

Table VII–continued

AMOUNT OF 1 AT CONTINUOUSLY COMPOUNDED NOMINAL INTEREST RATES

n	35%	40%	45%	50%
26	8955.2927	32859.6257	120571.7150	442413.3919
27	12708.1653	49020.8011	189094.0898	729416.3697
28	18033.7449	73130.4418	296558.5652	1202604.2840
29	25591.1022	109097.7993	465096.4116	1982759.2632
30	36315.5027	162754.7914	729416.3697	3269017.3719
31	51534.1514	242801.6175	1143952.5809	5389698.4753
32	71130.4418	362217.4496	1794074.7722	8886110.5188
33	103777.0368	540364.9372	2813669.3270	14650719.4260
34	147266.6252	806129.7591	4412711.8914	24154952.7485
35	208981.2889	1202604.2841	6920509.8303	39824784.3892
36	296558.5653	1794074.7726	10853519.8966	65659969.1231
37	420836.6362	2676445.0551	17021707.5092	108254987.7250
38	597195.6137	3992786.8351	26695351.3042	178482300.9220
39	847460.9156	5956538.0130	41866644.7466	294267565.9700
40	1202604.2841	8886110.5202	65659969.1209	485165195.2940
41	1706576.7133	13256519.1399	102975329.6700	799902177.2750
42	2421747.6331	19776402.6577	161497464.3260	1318815734.1400
43	3436623.4769	29502925.9152	253278441.2260	2174359553.0100
44	4876800.8528	44013193.5330	397219665.6970	3584912845.1600
45	6920509.8312	65659969.1347	622964442.0240	5910522061.4200
46	9820670.9212	97953163.6015	977002725.5430	9744803444.0000
47	13936195.4096	146128948.6720	1532245280.0000	16066464716.0000
48	19776402.6565	217998774.6700	2403038943.3300	26489122122.1000
49	28064051.2377	325215956.1090	3768715257.0300	43673179085.0000
50	39824784.3935	485165195.3900	5910522061.1900	72004899316.0000

Table VIII

PRESENT VALUE OF 1 AT CONTINUOUSLY COMPOUNDED NOMINAL INTEREST RATES

n	1/8%	1/4%	1/2%	7/12%
1	0.9987507809	0.9975031224	0.9950124792	0.9941836475
2	0.9975031224	0.9950124792	0.9900498338	0.9884011250
3	0.9962570225	0.9925280548	0.9851119396	0.9826522357
4	0.9950124792	0.9900498338	0.9801986734	0.9769367839
5	0.9937694907	0.9875778005	0.9753099121	0.9712545752
6	0.9925280549	0.9851119396	0.9704455336	0.9656054163
7	0.9912881699	0.9826522357	0.9656054163	0.9599891148
8	0.9900498338	0.9801986734	0.9607894392	0.9544054798
9	0.9988130447	0.9777512372	0.9559974819	0.9488543211
10	0.9875778006	0.9753099121	0.9512294246	0.9433354499
11	0.9863440995	0.9728748626	0.9464851481	0.9378486784
12	0.9851119397	0.9704455336	0.9417645337	0.9323938199
13	0.9838813190	0.9680224499	0.9370674635	0.9269706888
14	0.9826522357	0.9656054163	0.9323938200	0.9215791006
15	0.9814246878	0.9631944178	0.9277434865	0.9162188717
16	0.9801986734	0.9607894392	0.9231163465	0.9108898198
17	0.9789741905	0.9583904656	0.9185122846	0.9055917635
18	0.9777512373	0.9559974819	0.9139311854	0.9003245226
19	0.9765298118	0.9536104732	0.9093729346	0.8950879179
20	0.9753099121	0.9512294246	0.9048374128	0.8898817711
21	0.9740915364	0.9488543212	0.9003245228	0.8847059050
22	0.9728746827	0.9464851481	0.8958341355	0.8795601436
23	0.9716593491	0.9441218905	0.8913661441	0.8744443118
24	0.9704455337	0.9417645337	0.8869204369	0.8693582355
25	0.9692332346	0.9394130630	0.8824969028	0.8643017415

Table VIII—continued

PRESENT VALUE OF 1 AT CONTINUOUSLY COMPOUNDED NOMINAL INTEREST RATES

n	1/8%	1/4%	1/2%	7/12%
26	0.9680224500	0.9370674635	0.8780954311	0.8592746580
27	0.9668131779	0.9437277208	0.8737159119	0.8542768137
28	0.9656054164	0.9323938201	0.8693582356	0.8493080386
29	0.9643991637	0.9300657468	0.8650222933	0.8443681637
30	0.9631944179	0.9277434865	0.8607079767	0.8394570208
31	0.9619911770	0.9254270246	0.8564151777	0.8345744429
32	0.9607894393	0.9231163466	0.8521437892	0.8297202638
33	0.9595892028	0.9208114380	0.8478937044	0.8248943183
34	0.9583904657	0.9185122846	0.8436648169	0.8200964422
35	0.9571932261	0.9162188718	0.8394570210	0.8153264722
36	0.9559974820	0.9139311855	0.8352702117	0.8105842461
37	0.9548032317	0.9116492112	0.8311042841	0.8058696024
38	0.9536104733	0.9093729347	0.8269591342	0.8011823807
39	0.9524192049	0.9071023418	0.8228346584	0.7965224216
40	0.9512294247	0.9048374183	0.8187307534	0.7918895664
41	0.9500411308	0.9025781500	0.8146473167	0.7872836576
42	0.9488543213	0.9003245228	0.8105842463	0.7827045383
43	0.9476689944	0.8980765227	0.8065414405	0.7781520529
44	0.9464851482	0.8958341355	0.8025187983	0.7736260462
45	0.9453027809	0.8935973473	0.7985162191	0.7691263645
46	0.9441218906	0.8913661441	0.7945336029	0.7646528544
47	0.9429424756	0.8891405120	0.7905708500	0.7602053639
48	0.9417645338	0.8869204370	0.7866278614	0.7557837416
49	0.9405880636	0.8847059052	0.7827045386	0.7513878369
50	0.9394130631	0.8842969028	0.7788007834	0.7470175004

Table VIII—continued

PRESENT VALUE OF 1 AT CONTINUOUSLY COMPOUNDED NOMINAL INTEREST RATES

n	2/3%	3/4%	5/6%	11/12%
1	0.9933555063	0.9925280548	0.9917012926	0.9908752191
2	0.9867551618	0.9851119396	0.9834714538	0.9818336999
3	0.9801986733	0.9777512372	0.9753099121	0.9728746826
4	0.9736857494	0.9704455336	0.9672161005	0.9639974143
5	0.9672161005	0.9631944178	0.9591894571	0.9552011492
6	0.9607894392	0.9559974819	0.9512294246	0.9464851480
7	0.9544054798	0.9488543211	0.9433354499	0.9378486784
8	0.9480639385	0.9417645336	0.9355069851	0.9292910148
9	0.9417645336	0.9347277207	0.9277434864	0.9108114379
10	0.9355069851	0.9277434864	0.9200444147	0.9124092353
11	0.9292910148	0.9208114379	0.9124092354	0.9040837010
12	0.9231163464	0.9139311853	0.9048374181	0.8958341354
13	0.9169827056	0.9071023416	0.8973284372	0.8876598452
14	0.9108898198	0.9003245226	0.8898817711	0.8795601436
15	0.9048374181	0.8935973472	0.8824969027	0.8715343501
16	0.8988252315	0.8869204368	0.8751733192	0.8635817901
17	0.8928529929	0.8802934159	0.8679105119	0.8557017955
18	0.8869204368	0.8737159118	0.8607079765	0.8478937042
19	0.8810272995	0.8671875544	0.8535652129	0.8401568599
20	0.8751733191	0.8607079765	0.8464817250	0.8324906127
21	0.8693582355	0.8542768137	0.8394570209	0.8248943183
22	0.8635817901	0.8478937042	0.8324906127	0.8173673384
23	0.8578437263	0.8415582889	0.8255820168	0.8099090406
24	0.8521437890	0.8352702115	0.8187307532	0.8025187981
25	0.8464817250	0.8290291183	0.8119363463	0.7951959899

Table VIII–continued

PRESENT VALUE OF 1 AT CONTINUOUSLY COMPOUNDED NOMINAL INTEREST RATES

n	$\frac{2}{3}$%	$\frac{3}{4}$%	$\frac{5}{6}$%	$\frac{11}{12}$%
26	0.8408572825	0.8228346582	0.8051983242	0.7879400008
27	0.8352702115	0.8166864827	0.7985162189	0.7807502209
28	0.8297202638	0.8105842461	0.7918895665	0.7736260463
29	0.8242071927	0.8045276050	0.7853179067	0.7665668781
30	0.8187307532	0.7985162189	0.7788007832	0.7595721234
31	0.8132907018	0.7925497495	0.7723377435	0.7526411942
32	0.8078867968	0.7866278612	0.7659283385	0.7457735082
33	0.8025187981	0.7807502209	0.7595721234	0.7389684884
34	0.7971864669	0.7734303258	0.7532686566	0.7322255629
35	0.7918895664	0.7691263645	0.7470175005	0.7255441651
36	0.7866278612	0.7633794945	0.7408182209	0.7189237336
37	0.7814011173	0.7576755647	0.7346703873	0.7123637121
38	0.7762091024	0.7520142545	0.7285735727	0.7058635493
39	0.7710515859	0.7463952452	0.7225273539	0.6994226991
40	0.7659283385	0.7408182208	0.7165313108	0.6930406203
41	0.7608391324	0.7352828677	0.7105850271	0.6867167765
42	0.7557837416	0.7297888744	0.7046880899	0.6804506364
43	0.7507619412	0.7243359319	0.6988400897	0.6742416734
44	0.7457735082	0.7189237336	0.6930406203	0.6680893659
45	0.7408182208	0.7135519749	0.6872892790	0.6619931969
46	0.7358958588	0.7082203536	0.6815856664	0.6559526540
47	0.7310062034	0.7029285700	0.6759293864	0.6499672298
48	0.7261490372	0.6976763262	0.6703200463	0.6440364213
49	0.7213241445	0.6924633270	0.6647572564	0.6381597301
50	0.7165313107	0.6872892789	0.6592406304	0.6323366624

Table VIII–continued

PRESENT VALUE OF 1 AT CONTINUOUSLY COMPOUNDED NOMINAL INTEREST RATES

n	1%	2%	3%	4%
1	0.9900498338	0.9801986733	0.9704455336	0.9607894392
2	0.9801986733	0.9607894392	0.9417645336	0.9231163464
3	0.9704455336	0.9417645336	0.9139311853	0.8869204367
4	0.9607894392	0.9231163464	0.8869204367	0.8521437890
5	0.9512294245	0.9048374181	0.8607079764	0.8187307531
6	0.9417645336	0.8869204368	0.8352702114	0.7866278611
7	0.9323938199	0.8693582354	0.8105842460	0.7557837415
8	0.9231163464	0.8521437890	0.7866278611	0.7261490371
9	0.9139311853	0.8352702115	0.7633794944	0.6976763261
10	0.9048374181	0.8187307531	0.7408182207	0.6703200460
11	0.8958341353	0.8025187980	0.7189237335	0.6440364211
12	0.8869204368	0.7866278611	0.6976763261	0.6187833918
13	0.8780954310	0.7710515859	0.6770568745	0.5945205480
14	0.8693582354	0.7557837415	0.6570468198	0.5712090639
15	0.8607079765	0.7408182208	0.6376281517	0.5488116361
16	0.8521437890	0.7261490372	0.6187833918	0.5272924241
17	0.8436648167	0.7117703228	0.6004955789	0.5066169924
18	0.8352702115	0.6976763262	0.5827482524	0.4867522560
19	0.8269591340	0.6838614093	0.5655254387	0.4676664270
20	0.8187307531	0.6703200461	0.5488116361	0.4493289641
21	0.8105842460	0.6570468199	0.5325918010	0.4317105234
22	0.8025187980	0.6440364212	0.5168513345	0.4147829117
23	0.7945336026	0.6312836456	0.5015760691	0.3985190411
24	0.7866278611	0.6187833919	0.4867522560	0.3828928860
25	0.7788007832	0.6065306598	0.4723665528	0.3678794412

Table VIII—continued

PRESENT VALUE OF 1 AT CONTINUOUSLY COMPOUNDED NOMINAL INTEREST RATES

n	1%	2%	3%	4%
26	0.7710515859	0.5945205481	0.4584060113	0.3534546820
27	0.7633794944	0.5827482525	0.4448580663	0.3395955257
28	0.7557837415	0.5712090640	0.4317105235	0.3262797946
29	0.7482635677	0.5598983667	0.4189515493	0.3134861809
30	0.7408182208	0.5488116362	0.4065696598	0.3011942119
31	0.7334469563	0.5379444377	0.3945537104	0.2893842180
32	0.7261490372	0.5272924242	0.3828928860	0.2780373005
33	0.7189237335	0.5168513346	0.3715766911	0.2671353020
34	0.7117703229	0.5066169925	0.3605949402	0.2566607770
35	0.7046880898	0.4965853039	0.3499377492	0.2465969640
36	0.6976763262	0.4867522561	0.3395955257	0.2369277587
37	0.6907343307	0.4771139156	0.3295589611	0.2276376884
38	0.6838614093	0.4676664271	0.3198190219	0.2187118870
39	0.6770568746	0.4584060114	0.3103669413	0.2101360712
40	0.6703200461	0.4493289642	0.3011942120	0.2018965180
41	0.6636502502	0.4404316546	0.2922925777	0.1939800423
42	0.6570468199	0.4317105235	0.2836540265	0.1863739761
43	0.6505090948	0.4231620824	0.2752707831	0.1790661479
44	0.6440364212	0.4147829118	0.2671353020	0.1720448638
45	0.6376281517	0.4065696599	0.2592402607	0.1652988882
46	0.6312836456	0.3985190412	0.2515785531	0.1588174261
47	0.6250022684	0.3906278355	0.2441432832	0.1525901058
48	0.6187833919	0.3828928861	0.2369277587	0.1466069621
49	0.6126263943	0.3753110990	0.2299254852	0.1408584209
50	0.6065306598	0.3678794413	0.2231301602	0.1353352833

Table VIII—continued

PRESENT VALUE OF 1 AT CONTINUOUSLY COMPOUNDED NOMINAL INTEREST RATES

n	5%	6%	7%	8%
1	0.9512294245	0.9417645336	0.9323938199	0.9231163464
2	0.9048374180	0.8869204367	0.8693582354	0.8521437890
3	0.8607079764	0.8352702114	0.8105842460	0.7866278611
4	0.8187307531	0.7866278611	0.7557837415	0.7261490371
5	0.7788007831	0.7408182207	0.7046880897	0.6703200461
6	0.7408182207	0.6976763261	0.6570468198	0.6187833918
7	0.7046880898	0.6570468198	0.6126263942	0.5712090639
8	0.6703200461	0.6187833918	0.5712090639	0.5272924241
9	0.6376281517	0.5827482524	0.5325918010	0.4867522560
10	0.6065306597	0.5488116361	0.4965853038	0.4493289641
11	0.5769498104	0.5168513345	0.4630130683	0.4147829117
12	0.5488116361	0.4867522560	0.4317105234	0.3828928860
13	0.5220457768	0.4584060113	0.4025242241	0.3534546820
14	0.4965853038	0.4317105235	0.3753110989	0.3262797946
15	0.4723665528	0.4065696598	0.3499377491	0.3011942119
16	0.4493289642	0.3828928860	0.3262797946	0.2780373005
17	0.4274149320	0.3605949402	0.3042212641	0.2566607770
18	0.4065696598	0.3395955257	0.2836540265	0.2369277587
19	0.3867410235	0.3198190218	0.2644772613	0.2187118870
20	0.3678794412	0.3011942119	0.2465969640	0.2018965180
21	0.3499377492	0.2836540265	0.2299254852	0.1863739761
22	0.3328710837	0.2671353020	0.2143811014	0.1720448638
23	0.3166367694	0.2515785531	0.1998876141	0.1588174261
24	0.3011942120	0.2369277587	0.1863739761	0.1466069621
25	0.2865047969	0.2231301602	0.1737739435	0.1353352833

Table VIII—continued

PRESENT VALUE OF 1 AT CONTINUOUSLY COMPOUNDED NOMINAL INTEREST RATES

n	5%	6%	7%	8%
26	0.2725317931	0.2101360712	0.1620257509	0.1249302122
27	0.2592402607	0.1978986991	0.1510718089	0.1153251211
28	0.2465969640	0.1863739761	0.1408584209	0.1064585044
29	0.2345702881	0.1755204006	0.1313355212	0.0982735856
30	0.2231301602	0.1652988882	0.1224564283	0.0907179533
31	0.2122479739	0.1556726304	0.1141776169	0.0837432256
32	0.2018965180	0.1466069622	0.1064585044	0.0773047405
33	0.1920499087	0.1380692373	0.0992612516	0.0713612696
34	0.1826835241	0.1300287109	0.0925505775	0.0658747544
35	0.1737739435	0.1224564283	0.0862935865	0.0608100626
36	0.1652988883	0.1153251211	0.0804596068	0.0561347628
37	0.1572371663	0.1086091088	0.0750200401	0.0518189172
38	0.1495686193	0.1022842067	0.0699482218	0.0478348895
39	0.1422740716	0.0963276382	0.0652192897	0.0441571684
40	0.1353352833	0.0907179533	0.0608100626	0.0407622040
41	0.1287349036	0.0854349510	0.0566989266	0.0376282568
42	0.1224564283	0.0804596068	0.0528657287	0.0347352590
43	0.1164841578	0.0757740040	0.0492916788	0.0320646853
44	0.1108031584	0.0713612696	0.0459592567	0.0295994352
45	0.1053992246	0.0672055128	0.0428521269	0.0273237225
46	0.1002588437	0.0632917684	0.0399550583	0.0252229748
47	0.0953691622	0.0596059427	0.0372538494	0.0232837404
48	0.0907179533	0.0561347628	0.0347352590	0.0214936013
49	0.0862935865	0.0528657288	0.0323869408	0.0198410947
50	0.0820849986	0.0497870684	0.0301973834	0.0183156389

Table VIII—continued

PRESENT VALUE OF 1 AT CONTINUOUSLY COMPOUNDED NOMINAL INTEREST RATES

n	9%	10%	11%	12%
1	0.9139311853	0.9048374180	0.8958341353	0.8869204367
2	0.8352702114	0.8187307531	0.8025187980	0.7866278671
3	0.7633794944	0.7408182207	0.7189237334	0.6976763261
4	0.6976763261	0.6703200461	0.6440364211	0.6187833918
5	0.6376281516	0.6065306597	0.5769498104	0.5488116361
6	0.5827482524	0.5488116361	0.5168513345	0.4867522560
7	0.5325918010	0.4965853038	0.4630130683	0.4317105235
8	0.4867522560	0.4493289641	0.4147829117	0.3828928860
9	0.4448580662	0.4065696598	0.3715766910	0.3395955257
10	0.4065696598	0.3678794412	0.3328710837	0.3011942119
11	0.3715766910	0.3328710837	0.2981972795	0.2671353020
12	0.3395955257	0.3011942119	0.2671353020	0.2369277587
13	0.3103669413	0.2725317931	0.2393089223	0.2101360712
14	0.2836540265	0.2465969640	0.2143811015	0.1863739761
15	0.2592402607	0.2231301602	0.1920499086	0.1652988882
16	0.2369277587	0.2018965180	0.1720448638	0.1466069621
17	0.2165356673	0.1826835241	0.1541236618	0.1300287109
18	0.1978986991	0.1652988882	0.1380692373	0.1153251211
19	0.1808657926	0.1495686192	0.1236871358	0.1022842067
20	0.1652988882	0.1353352833	0.1108031584	0.0907179533
21	0.1510718089	0.1224564283	0.0992612516	0.0804596068
22	0.1380692373	0.1108031584	0.0889216175	0.0713612696
23	0.1261857817	0.1002588437	0.0796590203	0.0632917684
24		0.0907179533	0.0713612696	0.0561347628
25	0.1053992246	0.0820849986	0.0639278612	0.0497870684

Table VIII–continued

PRESENT VALUE OF 1 AT CONTINUOUSLY COMPOUNDED NOMINAL INTEREST RATES

n	9%	10%	11%	12%
26	0.0963276382	0.0742735782	0.0572687603	0.0441571684
27	0.0880368326	0.0672055127	0.0513033103	0.0391638951
28	0.0804596068	0.0608100626	0.0459592567	0.0347352590
29	0.0735345438	0.0550232201	0.0411718709	0.0308074110
30	0.0672055127	0.0497870684	0.0368831674	0.0273237225
31	0.0614212139	0.0550492024	0.0330412004	0.0242339679
32	0.0561347628	0.0407622040	0.0295994352	0.0214936014
33	0.0513033103	0.0368831674	0.0265161844	0.0190631143
34	0.0468876952	0.0333732700	0.0237541031	0.0169074657
35	0.0428521269	0.0301973834	0.0212797364	0.0149955768
36	0.0391638951	0.0273237225	0.0190631143	0.0132998835
37	0.0357931051	0.0247235265	0.0170773885	0.0117959385
38	0.0327124349	0.0223707719	0.0152985076	0.0104620589
39	0.0298969144	0.0202419114	0.0137049253	0.0092790139
40	0.0273237225	0.0183156389	0.0122773399	0.0082297471
41	0.0249720020	0.0165726754	0.0109984602	0.0072991308
42	0.0228226914	0.0149955768	0.0098527961	0.0064737483
43	0.0208583694	0.0135685590	0.0088264710	0.0057416997
44	0.0190631143	0.0122773399	0.0079070541	0.0050924308
45	0.0174223746	0.0111089965	0.0070834089	0.0045165809
46	0.0159228515	0.0100518357	0.0063455595	0.0040058479
47	0.0145523906	0.0090952771	0.0056845688	0.0035528684
48	0.0132998835	0.0082297471	0.0050924308	0.0031511116
49	0.0121551783	0.0074465831	0.0045619733	0.0027947853
50	0.0111089965	0.0067379470	0.0040867714	0.0024787522

Table VIII—continued

PRESENT VALUE OF 1 AT CONTINUOUSLY COMPOUNDED NOMINAL INTEREST RATES

n	13%	14%	15%	16%
1	0.8780954309	0.8693582354	0.8607079764	0.8521437890
2	0.7710515858	0.7557837415	0.7408182207	0.7261490371
3	0.6770568745	0.6570468198	0.6376281516	0.6187833918
4	0.5945205480	0.5712090639	0.5488116361	0.5272924240
5	0.5220457768	0.4965853038	0.4723665528	0.4493289641
6	0.4584060113	0.4317105234	0.4065696598	0.3828928860
7	0.4025242240	0.3753110989	0.3499377491	0.3262797946
8	0.3534546820	0.3262797946	0.3011942119	0.2780373005
9	0.3103669413	0.2836540265	0.2592402607	0.2369277587
10	0.2725317930	0.2465969640	0.2231301602	0.2018965180
11	0.2393089223	0.2143811014	0.1920499086	0.1720448638
12	0.2101360712	0.1863739761	0.1652988882	0.1466069621
13	0.1845195240	0.1620257509	0.1422740716	0.1249302122
14	0.1620257509	0.1408584209	0.1224564283	0.1064585044
15	0.1422740716	0.1224564283	0.1053992246	0.0907179533
16	0.1249302122	0.1064585044	0.0907179533	0.0773047404
17	0.1097006485	0.0925505775	0.0780816660	0.0658747544
18	0.0963276382	0.0804596068	0.0672055127	0.0561347628
19	0.0845848590	0.0699482218	0.0578443209	0.0478348895
20	0.0742735782	0.0608100626	0.0497870684	0.0407622040
21	0.0652192897	0.0528657287	0.0428521269	0.0347352589
22	0.0572687603	0.0459592567	0.0368831674	0.0295994352
23	0.0502874367	0.0399550583	0.0317456364	0.0252229748
24	0.0441571684	0.0347352589	0.0273237225	0.0214936013
25	0.0387742078	0.0301973834	0.0235177459	0.0183156389

Table VIII–continued

PRESENT VALUE OF 1 AT CONTINUOUSLY COMPOUNDED NOMINAL INTEREST RATES

n	13%	14%	15%	16%
26	0.0340474547	0.0262523440	0.0202419114	0.0156075579
27	0.0298969144	0.0228226914	0.0174223746	0.0132998835
28	0.0262523440	0.0198410947	0.0149955768	0.0113334132
29	0.0230520633	0.0172490191	0.0129068126	0.0096576976
30	0.0202419114	0.0149955768	0.0111089965	0.0082297470
31	0.0177743300	0.0130365282	0.0095616019	0.0070129278
32	0.0156075579	0.0113334132	0.0082297471	0.0059760229
33	0.0137049253	0.0098527961	0.0070834089	0.0050924308
34	0.0120342323	0.0085656094	0.0060967466	0.0043394833
35	0.0105672044	0.0074465831	0.0052475184	0.0036978637
36	0.0092790139	0.0064737483	0.0045165809	0.0031511116
37	0.0081478597	0.0056280064	0.0038874572	0.0026852002
38	0.0071545984	0.0048927537	0.0033459655	0.0022881767
39	0.0062824201	0.0042535557	0.0028798992	0.0019498555
40	0.0055165644	0.0036978637	0.0024787522	0.0016615573
41	0.0048440700	0.0032147683	0.0021334818	0.0014158857
42	0.0042535557	0.0027947853	0.0018363048	0.0012065382
43	0.0037350279	0.0024296696	0.0015805222	0.0010281440
44	0.0032797109	0.0021122533	0.0013603680	0.0008761266
45	0.0028798992	0.0018363048	0.0011708796	0.0007465858
46	0.0025288263	0.0015964067	0.0010077854	0.0006361985
47	0.0022205508	0.0013878493	0.0008674090	0.0005421326
48	0.0019498555	0.0012065382	0.0007465858	0.0004619749
49	0.0017121592	0.0010489139	0.0006425924	0.0003936690
50	0.0015034392	0.0009118820	0.0005530844	0.0003354626

Table VIII–continued

PRESENT VALUE OF 1 AT CONTINUOUSLY COMPOUNDED NOMINAL INTEREST RATES

n	17%	18%	19%	20%
1	0.8436648166	0.8352702114	0.8269591339	0.8187307531
2	0.7117703228	0.6976763261	0.6838614092	0.6703200460
3	0.6004955788	0.5827482524	0.5655254387	0.5488116361
4	0.5066169924	0.4867522560	0.4676666427	0.4493289641
5	0.4274149319	0.4065696597	0.3867410235	0.3678794412
6	0.3605949402	0.3395955256	0.3198190218	0.3011942119
7	0.3042212641	0.2836540265	0.2644772613	0.2465969639
8	0.2566607770	0.2369277587	0.2187118870	0.2018965180
9	0.2165356673	0.1978986991	0.1808657926	0.1652988882
10	0.1826835241	0.1652988882	0.1495686192	0.1353352832
11	0.1541236618	0.1380692373	0.1236871358	0.1108031584
12	0.1300287109	0.1153251210	0.1022842067	0.0907179533
13	0.1097006485	0.0963276382	0.0845848590	0.0742735782
14	0.0925505775	0.0804596068	0.0699482218	0.0608100626
15	0.0780816660	0.0672055127	0.0578443209	0.0497870684
16	0.0658747544	0.0561347628	0.0478348895	0.0407622040
17	0.0555762126	0.0468876952	0.0395574988	0.0333732700
18	0.0468876952	0.0391638951	0.0327124349	0.0273237224
19	0.0395574989	0.0327124349	0.0270518469	0.0223707719
20	0.0333732700	0.0273237224	0.0223707719	0.0183156389
21	0.0281558537	0.0228226914	0.0184997141	0.0149955768
22	0.0237541031	0.0190631143	0.0152985076	0.0122773399
23	0.0200405011	0.0159228515	0.0126512406	0.0100518357
24	0.0169074657	0.0132998835	0.0104620589	0.0082297470
25	0.0142642339	0.0111089965	0.0086516952	0.0067379470

Table VIII–continued

PRESENT VALUE OF 1 AT CONTINUOUSLY COMPOUNDED NOMINAL INTEREST RATES

n	17%	18%	19%	20%
26	0.0120342323	0.0092790139	0.0071545984	0.0055165644
27	0.0101528584	0.0077504839	0.0059165605	0.0045165809
28	0.0085656094	0.0064737483	0.0048927537	0.0036978637
29	0.0072265033	0.0054073291	0.0040461074	0.0030275547
30	0.0060967466	0.0045165809	0.0033459655	0.0024787522
31	0.0051436106	0.0037725655	0.0027669767	0.0020294306
32	0.0043394833	0.0031511116	0.0022881767	0.0016615573
33	0.0036610694	0.0026320297	0.0018922286	0.0013603680
34	0.0030887154	0.0021984560	0.0015647957	0.0011137751
35	0.0026058405	0.0018363048	0.0012940221	0.0009118820
36	0.0021984560	0.0015338107	0.0010701034	0.0007465858
37	0.0018547599	0.0012811464	0.0008849318	0.0006112528
38	0.0015647557	0.0010701034	0.0007318024	0.0005004514
39	0.0013201631	0.0008938255	0.0006051707	0.0004097350
40	0.0011137751	0.0007465858	0.0005004514	0.0003354626
41	0.0009396529	0.0006236009	0.0004138529	0.0002746536
42	0.0007927521	0.0005208752	0.0003422394	0.0002248673
43	0.0006688171	0.0004350716	0.0002830180	0.0001841058
44	0.0005642574	0.0003634023	0.0002340443	0.0001507331
45	0.0004760441	0.0003035391	0.0001935451	0.0001234098
46	0.0004016217	0.0002535372	0.0001600539	0.0001010394
47	0.0003388341	0.0002117721	0.0001323580	0.0000827241
48	0.0002858624	0.0001768869	0.0001094547	0.0000677287
49	0.0002411720	0.0001477484	0.0000905145	0.0000554516
50	0.0002034684	0.0001234098	0.0000748518	0.0000453998

Table VIII–continued

PRESENT VALUE OF 1 AT CONTINUOUSLY COMPOUNDED NOMINAL INTEREST RATES

n	21%	22%	23%	24%
1	0.8105842460	0.8025187980	0.7945336025	0.7866278611
2	0.6570468198	0.6440364211	0.6312836455	0.6187833918
3	0.5325918010	0.5168513345	0.5015760691	0.4867522560
4	0.4317105234	0.4147829117	0.3985190411	0.3828928860
5	0.3499377491	0.3328710837	0.3166367694	0.3011942119
6	0.2836540265	0.2671353020	0.2515785531	0.2369277587
7	0.2299254852	0.2143811014	0.1998876141	0.1863739760
8	0.1863739760	0.1720448638	0.1588174261	0.1466069621
9	0.1510718088	0.1380692373	0.1261857817	0.1153225121
10	0.1224564283	0.1108031584	0.1002588437	0.0907179533
11	0.0992612516	0.0889216175	0.0796590203	0.0713612696
12	0.0804596068	0.0713612696	0.0632917684	0.0561347628
13	0.0652192897	0.0572687603	0.0502874367	0.0441571684
14	0.0528657287	0.0459592567	0.0399550583	0.0347352589
15	0.0428521269	0.0368831674	0.0317456364	0.0273237224
16	0.0347352589	0.0295994352	0.0252229748	0.0214936013
17	0.0281558537	0.0237541031	0.0200405011	0.0169074657
18	0.0228226914	0.0190631143	0.0159228515	0.0132998835
19	0.0184997141	0.0152985076	0.0126512406	0.0104620589
20	0.0149955768	0.0122773399	0.0100518357	0.0082297470
21	0.0121551783	0.0098527961	0.0079865213	0.0064737483
22	0.0098527961	0.0079070541	0.0063455595	0.0050924308
23	0.0079865213	0.0063455595	0.0050417603	0.0040058479
24	0.0064737483	0.0050924308	0.0040058479	0.0031511116
25	0.0052475184	0.0040867714	0.0031827808	0.0024787552

Table VIII—continued

PRESENT VALUE OF 1 AT CONTINUOUSLY COMPOUNDED NOMINAL INTEREST RATES

n	21%	22%	23%	24%
26	0.0042535557	0.0032797109	0.0025288263	0.0019498555
27	0.0034478653	0.0026320297	0.0020092375	0.0015338107
28	0.0027947853	0.0021122533	0.0015964067	0.0012065382
29	0.0022654089	0.0016951230	0.0012683988	0.0009490966
30	0.0018363048	0.0013603680	0.0010077854	0.0007465858
31	0.0014884797	0.0010917209	0.0008007194	0.0005872852
32	0.0012065382	0.0008761266	0.0006361985	0.0004619749
33	0.0009780009	0.0007031080	0.0005054811	0.0003634023
34	0.0007927521	0.0005642574	0.0004016217	0.0002858624
35	0.0006425924	0.0004528272	0.0003191019	0.0002248673
36	0.0005208752	0.0003634023	0.0002535372	0.0001768869
37	0.0004222133	0.0002916372	0.0002014438	0.0001391442
38	0.0003422394	0.0002340443	0.0001600539	0.0001094547
39	0.0002774139	0.0001878250	0.0001271682	0.0000861001
40	0.0002248673	0.0001507331	0.0001010394	0.0000677287
41	0.0001822739	0.0001209661	0.0000802729	0.0000532773
42	0.0001477484	0.0000970776	0.0000637845	0.0000419094
43	0.0001197625	0.0000779066	0.0000506789	0.0000329671
44	0.0000970776	0.0000625215	0.0000402661	0.0000259329
45	0.0000786896	0.0000501747	0.0000319928	0.0000203995
46	0.0000637845	0.0000402661	0.0000254193	0.0000160468
47	0.0000517027	0.0000323143	0.0000201965	0.0000126229
48	0.0000419094	0.0000259329	0.0000160468	0.0000099295
49	0.0000339711	0.0000208116	0.0000127497	0.0000078108
50	0.0000275364	0.0000167017	0.0000101301	0.0000061442

Table VIII–continued

PRESENT VALUE OF 1 AT CONTINUOUSLY COMPOUNDED NOMINAL INTEREST RATES

n	25%	26%	27%	28%
1	0.7788007831	0.7710515858	0.7633794943	0.7557837415
2	0.6065306597	0.5945205480	0.5827482524	0.5712090639
3	0.4723665528	0.4584060113	0.4448580662	0.4317105234
4	0.3678794412	0.3534546820	0.3395955256	0.3262797946
5	0.2865047969	0.2725317930	0.2592402606	0.2465969639
6	0.2231301602	0.2101360712	0.1978986991	0.1863739760
7	0.1737739435	0.1620257509	0.1510718088	0.1408584209
8	0.1353352832	0.1249302122	0.1153251210	0.1064585044
9	0.1053992246	0.0963276382	0.0880368326	0.0804596068
10	0.0820849986	0.0742735782	0.0672055127	0.0608100626
11	0.0639278612	0.0572687603	0.0513033103	0.0459592567
12	0.0497870684	0.0441571684	0.0391638951	0.0347352589
13	0.0387742078	0.0340474547	0.0298969144	0.0262523440
14	0.0301973834	0.0262523440	0.0228226914	0.0198410947
15	0.0235177459	0.0202419114	0.0174223746	0.0149955768
16	0.0183156389	0.0150755790	0.0132998835	0.0113334132
17	0.0142642339	0.0120342323	0.0101528584	0.0085656094
18	0.0111089965	0.0092790139	0.0077504839	0.0064737483
19	0.0086516952	0.0071545984	0.0059165605	0.0048927537
20	0.0067379470	0.0055165644	0.0045165809	0.0036978637
21	0.0052475184	0.0042535557	0.0034478653	0.0027947853
22	0.0040867714	0.0032797109	0.0026320297	0.0021122533
23	0.0031827808	0.0025288263	0.0020092375	0.0015964067
24	0.0024787522	0.0019498555	0.0015338107	0.0012065382
25	0.0019304541	0.0015034392	0.0011708796	0.0009118820

Table VIII–continued

PRESENT VALUE OF 1 AT CONTINUOUSLY COMPOUNDED NOMINAL INTEREST RATES

n	25%	26%	27%	28%
26	0.0015034392	0.0011592292	0.0008938255	0.0006891856
27	0.0011708796	0.0008938255	0.0006823281	0.0005208762
28	0.0009118820	0.0006891856	0.0005208752	0.0003936690
29	0.0007101744	0.0005313976	0.0003976255	0.0002975287
30	0.0005530844	0.0004097350	0.0003035391	0.0002248673
31	0.0004307425	0.0003159268	0.0002317156	0.0001699511
32	0.0003354626	0.0002435959	0.0001768869	0.0001284463
33	0.0002612586	0.0001878250	0.0001350318	0.0000970776
34	0.0002034684	0.0001448227	0.0001030805	0.0000733697
35	0.0001584613	0.0001116658	0.0000786896	0.0000554516
36	0.0001234098	0.0000861001	0.0000600700	0.0000419094
37	0.0000961117	0.0000663876	0.0000458562	0.0000316745
38	0.0000748518	0.0000511883	0.0000350057	0.0000239390
39	0.0000582947	0.0000394688	0.0000267226	0.0000180927
40	0.0000453999	0.0000304325	0.0000203995	0.0000136742
41	0.0000353575	0.0000234650	0.0000155726	0.0000103347
42	0.0000275364	0.0000180927	0.0000118878	0.0000078108
43	0.0000214454	0.0000139504	0.0000090749	0.0000059033
44	0.0000167017	0.0000107565	0.0000069276	0.0000044616
45	0.0000130073	0.0000082938	0.0000052884	0.0000033720
46	0.0000101301	0.0000063950	0.0000040370	0.0000025485
47	0.0000078893	0.0000049308	0.0000030818	0.0000019261
48	0.0000061442	0.0000038019	0.0000023526	0.0000014557
49	0.0000047851	0.0000029315	0.0000017959	0.0000011002
50	0.0000130073	0.0000022603	0.0000013710	0.0000008315

Table VIII–continued

PRESENT VALUE OF 1 AT CONTINUOUSLY COMPOUNDED NOMINAL INTEREST RATES

n	29%	30%	31%	32%
1	0.7482635676	0.7408182207	0.7334469562	0.7261490371
2	0.5598983666	0.5488116361	0.5379444376	0.5272924241
3	0.4189515493	0.4065696597	0.3945537104	0.3828928860
4	0.3134861809	0.3011942119	0.2893842179	0.2780373005
5	0.2345702881	0.2231301602	0.2122479738	0.2018965180
6	0.1755204006	0.1652988882	0.1556726304	0.1466069621
7	0.1313355212	0.1224564283	0.1141776169	0.1064585044
8	0.0982735856	0.0907179533	0.0837432256	0.0773047404
9	0.0735345438	0.0672055127	0.0614212139	0.0561347628
10	0.0550232201	0.0497870684	0.0450492024	0.0407622041
11	0.0411718709	0.0368831674	0.0330412004	0.0295994352
12	0.0308074110	0.0273237224	0.0242339678	0.0214936013
13	0.0230520633	0.0202419114	0.0177743300	0.0156075579
14	0.0172490191	0.0149955768	0.0130365282	0.0113334132
15	0.0129068126	0.0111089965	0.0095616019	0.0082297470
16	0.0096576976	0.0082297470	0.0070129278	0.0059760229
17	0.0072265033	0.0060967466	0.0051436106	0.0043394833
18	0.0054073291	0.0045165809	0.0037725655	0.0031511116
19	0.0040461074	0.0033459655	0.0027669767	0.0022881767
20	0.0030275547	0.0024787522	0.0020294306	0.0016615573
21	0.0022654089	0.0018363048	0.0014884797	0.0012065382
22	0.0016951230	0.0013603680	0.0010917209	0.0008761266
23	0.0012683988	0.0010077854	0.0008007194	0.0006361985
24	0.0009490966	0.0007465858	0.0005872852	0.0004619749
25	0.0007101744	0.0005530844	0.0004307425	0.0003354626

Table VIII–continued

PRESENT VALUE OF 1 AT CONTINUOUSLY COMPOUNDED NOMINAL INTEREST RATES

n	29%	30%	31%	32%
26	0.0005313976	0.0004097350	0.0003159268	0.0002435959
27	0.0003976255	0.0003035391	0.0002317156	0.0001768869
28	0.0002975287	0.0002248673	0.0001699511	0.0001284463
29	0.0002262990	0.0001665858	0.0001246501	0.0000932711
30	0.0001665858	0.0001234098	0.0000914242	0.0000677287
31	0.0001246501	0.0000914242	0.0000670548	0.0000491812
32	0.0000932711	0.0000677287	0.0000491812	0.0000357128
33	0.0000697914	0.0000501747	0.0000360718	0.0000259329
34	0.0000522223	0.0000371703	0.0000264567	0.0000188311
35	0.0000390761	0.0000275364	0.0000194046	0.0000136742
36	0.0000292392	0.0000203995	0.0000142323	0.0000099295
37	0.0000218786	0.0000151123	0.0000104386	0.0000072103
38	0.0000163710	0.0000111955	0.0000076562	0.0000052358
39	0.0000122498	0.0000082938	0.0000056154	0.0000038019
40	0.0000091661	0.0000061442	0.0000041186	0.0000027608
41	0.0000068586	0.0000045517	0.0000030208	0.0000020047
42	0.0000051321	0.0000003372	0.0000022156	0.0000014557
43	0.0000038401	0.0000024981	0.0000016250	0.0000010571
44	0.0000028734	0.0000018506	0.0000011919	0.0000007676
45	0.0000021501	0.0000013710	0.0000008742	0.0000005574
46	0.0000016088	0.0000010156	0.0000006412	0.0000004047
47	0.0000012038	0.0000007524	0.0000004703	0.0000002939
48	0.0000009008	0.0000005574	0.0000003449	0.0000002134
49	0.0000000674	0.0000004129	0.0000002530	0.0000001550
50	0.0000005043	0.0000003059	0.0000001855	0.0000001125

Table VIII–continued

PRESENT VALUE OF 1 AT CONTINUOUSLY COMPOUNDED NOMINAL INTEREST RATES

n	35%	40%	45%	50%
1	0.7046880897	0.6703200460	0.6376281516	0.6065306597
2	0.4965853038	0.4493289641	0.4065696597	0.3678794412
3	0.3499377491	0.3011942119	0.2592402607	0.2231301602
4	0.2465969639	0.2018965180	0.1652988882	0.1353352832
5	0.1737739435	0.1353352832	0.1053992246	0.0820849986
6	0.1224564283	0.0907179533	0.0672055127	0.0497870684
7	0.0862935865	0.0608100626	0.0428521269	0.0301973834
8	0.0608100626	0.0407622040	0.0273237224	0.0183156389
9	0.0428521269	0.0273237224	0.0174223746	0.0111089965
10	0.0301973834	0.0183156389	0.0111089965	0.0067379470
11	0.0212797364	0.0122773399	0.0070834089	0.0040867714
12	0.0149955769	0.0082297470	0.0045165809	0.0024787522
13	0.0105672044	0.0055165644	0.0028798992	0.0015034392
14	0.0074465831	0.0036978637	0.0018363048	0.0009118820
15	0.0052475184	0.0024787522	0.0011708796	0.0005530844
16	0.0036978637	0.0016615573	0.0007465858	0.0003354626
17	0.0026058405	0.0011137751	0.0004760441	0.0002034684
18	0.0018363048	0.0007465858	0.0003035391	0.0001234098
19	0.0012940221	0.0005004514	0.0001935451	0.0000748518
20	0.0009118820	0.0003354626	0.0001234098	0.0000453999
21	0.0006425924	0.0002248673	0.0000786896	0.0000275364
22	0.0004528272	0.0001507331	0.0000501747	0.0000167017
23	0.0000319102	0.0001010394	0.0000319928	0.0000101301
24	0.0002248673	0.0000677287	0.0000203995	0.0000061442
25	0.0001584613	0.0000453999	0.0000130073	0.0000037267

Table VIII–continued

PRESENT VALUE OF 1 AT CONTINUOUSLY COMPOUNDED NOMINAL INTEREST RATES

n	35%	40%	45%	50%
26	0.0001116658	0.0000304325	0.0000082938	0.0000022603
27	0.0000786898	0.0000203995	0.0000052884	0.0000013710
28	0.0000554516	0.0000136742	0.0000033720	0.0000008315
29	0.0000390761	0.0000091661	0.0000021501	0.0000005043
30	0.0000275364	0.0000061442	0.0000013710	0.0000003059
31	0.0000194046	0.0000041186	0.0000008742	0.0000001855
32	0.0000136742	0.0000027608	0.0000005574	0.0000001125
33	0.0000096360	0.0000018506	0.0000003554	0.0000000683
34	0.0000067904	0.0000012405	0.0000002266	0.0000000414
35	0.0000047851	0.0000008315	0.0000001445	0.0000000251
36	0.0000033720	0.0000005574	0.0000000921	0.0000000152
37	0.0000023762	0.0000003736	0.0000000587	0.0000000092
38	0.0000016745	0.0000002505	0.0000000375	0.0000000056
39	0.0000011800	0.0000001679	0.0000000239	0.0000000034
40	0.0000008315	0.0000001125	0.0000000152	0.0000000021
41	0.0000005858	0.0000000754	0.0000000097	0.0000000013
42	0.0000004129	0.0000000506	0.0000000062	0.0000000008
43	0.0000002910	0.0000000339	0.0000000039	0.0000000005
44	0.0000002051	0.0000000227	0.0000000025	0.0000000003
45	0.0000001445	0.0000000152	0.0000000016	0.0000000002
46	0.0000001018	0.0000000102	0.0000000010	0.0000000001
47	0.0000000718	0.0000000068	0.0000000007	0.0000000001
48	0.0000000506	0.0000000046	0.0000000004	0.0000000000
49	0.0000000356	0.0000000031	0.0000000003	0.0000000000
50	0.0000000251	0.0000000021	0.0000000002	0.0000000000

Table IX

AMOUNT OF 1 PER PERIOD FOR n PERIODS (UNIFORM SERIES) AT CONTINUOUSLY COMPOUNDED NOMINAL INTEREST RATES

n	1/8%	1/4%	1/2%	7/12%	n
1	1.00000000	1.00000000	1.00000000	1.00000000	1
2	2.00125078	2.00250312	2.00501252	2.00585038	2
3	3.00375390	3.00751565	3.01506269	3.01758537	3
4	4.00751094	4.01504384	4.03017575	4.03523939	4
5	5.01252347	5.02509401	5.05037709	5.05884708	5
6	6.01879304	6.03767246	6.07569221	6.08844325	6
7	7.02632123	7.05278552	7.10614675	7.12406296	7
8	8.03510962	8.07043955	8.14176646	8.16574144	8
9	9.04515980	9.09064089	9.18257723	9.21351413	9
10	10.05647331	10.11339592	10.22860509	10.26741670	10
11	11.06905177	11.13871104	11.27987618	11.32748499	11
12	12.08289673	12.16659266	12.33641680	12.39375508	12
13	13.09800980	13.19704719	13.39825335	13.46626327	13
14	14.11439255	14.23008108	14.46541237	14.54504603	14
15	15.13204657	15.26570079	15.53792055	15.63014008	15
16	16.15097345	16.30391279	16.61580470	16.72158234	16
17	17.17117480	17.34472356	17.69909177	17.81940996	17
18	18.19265218	18.38813962	18.78780883	18.92366029	18
19	19.21540722	19.43416748	19.88198312	20.03437090	19
20	20.23944150	20.48281368	20.09164197	21.15157959	20
21	21.26475661	21.53408477	22.08681289	22.27532437	21
22	22.29135418	22.58798734	23.19752350	23.40564349	22
23	23.31923580	23.64452795	24.31380157	24.54257541	23
24	24.34840306	24.70371322	25.43567501	25.68615881	24
25	25.37885760	25.76554977	26.56317186	26.83643261	25

Table IX–continued

AMOUNT OF 1 PER PERIOD FOR n PERIODS (UNIFORM SERIES) AT CONTINUOUSLY COMPOUNDED NOMINAL INTEREST RATES

n	1/8%	1/4%	1/2%	7/12%
26	26.41060101	26.83004423	27.69632031	27.99343595
27	27.44366349	27.89720325	28.83514870	29.15720819
28	28.47796090	28.96703351	29.97968548	30.32778895
29	29.51358060	30.03954169	31.12995928	31.50521805
30	30.55049565	31.11473450	32.28599885	32.68953556
31	31.58870764	32.19261865	33.44783309	33.88078178
32	32.62821822	33.27320088	34.61549105	35.07899724
33	33.66902899	34.35648795	35.78900192	36.28422271
34	34.71114159	35.44248662	36.96839504	37.49649922
35	35.75455765	36.53120369	38.15369989	38.71586800
36	36.79927879	37.62264595	39.34494611	39.94237055
37	37.84530665	38.71682024	40.54216347	41.17604861
38	38.89264286	39.81373338	41.74538191	42.41694416
39	39.94128906	40.91339223	42.95463151	43.66509942
40	40.99124689	42.01580367	44.95463151	44.92055658
41	42.04251799	43.12097459	45.39134525	46.18335920
42	43.09510399	44.22891189	46.61887032	47.45354942
43	44.14900655	45.33962250	47.85254838	48.73117073
44	45.20422732	46.45311337	49.09241027	50.01626661
45	46.26076794	47.56939144	50.33848700	51.30888080
46	47.31863005	48.68846369	51.59080972	52.60905726
47	48.37781532	49.81033713	52.84949073	53.91684026
48	49.43832540	50.93501876	54.11431850	55.23227428
49	50.50016195	52.06251561	55.38556765	56.55540409
50	51.56332662	53.19283473	56.66318896	57.88627472

Table IX—continued

AMOUNT OF 1 PER PERIOD FOR n PERIODS (UNIFORM SERIES) AT CONTINUOUSLY COMPOUNDED NOMINAL INTEREST RATES

n	2/3%	3/4%	5/6%	11/12%
1	1.00000000	1.00000000	1.00000000	1.00000000
2	2.00668894	2.00752820	2.00836815	2.00920881
3	3.02011156	3.02264126	3.02517448	3.02771123
4	4.04031290	4.04539629	4.05048960	4.05559285
5	5.06733830	5.07585083	5.08438472	5.09294003
6	6.10123341	6.11406283	6.12693162	6.13983994
7	7.14204419	7.16009068	7.17820272	7.19638055
8	8.18981688	8.21399325	8.23827101	8.26265065
9	9.24459806	9.27582979	9.30721012	9.33873982
10	10.30643461	10.34566005	10.38509427	10.42473850
11	11.37537371	11.42354420	11.47199832	11.52073792
12	12.45146289	12.50954288	12.56799774	12.62683020
13	13.53474995	13.60371716	13.67316866	13.74310827
14	14.62528306	14.70612860	14.78758782	14.86966593
15	15.72311068	15.81683921	15.91133260	16.00659785
16	16.82828160	16.93591147	17.04448106	17.15399956
17	17.94084494	18.06340832	18.18711187	18.31196747
18	19.06085014	19.19939319	19.33930439	19.48059888
19	20.18834698	20.34392997	20.50113863	20.65999200
20	21.32338560	21.49708305	21.67269528	21.85024592
21	22.46601641	22.65891730	22.85405569	23.05146067
22	23.61629021	23.82949805	24.04530191	24.26373717
23	24.77425812	25.00889117	25.24651666	25.48717730
24	25.93997161	26.19716299	26.45778335	26.72188385
25	27.11348248	27.39438036	27.67918611	27.96796058

Table IX–continued

AMOUNT OF 1 PER PERIOD FOR n PERIODS (UNIFORM SERIES)
AT CONTINUOUSLY COMPOUNDED NOMINAL INTEREST RATES

n	$\frac{2}{3}\%$	$\frac{3}{4}\%$	$\frac{5}{6}\%$	$\frac{11}{12}\%$
26	28.29484289	28.60061061	28.91080975	29.22551220
27	29.48410535	29.81592159	30.15273980	30.49464436
28	30.68132271	31.04038168	31.40506252	31.77546372
29	31.88654819	32.27405974	32.66786486	33.06807791
30	33.09983534	33.51702517	33.94123453	34.37259553
31	34.32123810	34.76934788	35.22525995	35.68912620
32	35.55081075	36.03109833	36.52003028	37.01778056
33	36.78860793	37.30234748	37.82563545	38.35867024
34	38.03468466	38.58316684	39.14216613	39.71190791
35	39.28909632	39.87362846	40.46971373	41.07760730
36	40.55189866	41.17380493	41.80837046	42.45588315
37	41.82314781	42.48376938	43.15822926	43.84685127
38	43.10290027	43.80355955	44.51938389	45.25062856
39	44.39121291	45.13335753	45.89192887	46.66733297
40	45.68814300	46.47313026	47.27595952	48.09708353
41	46.99374817	47.82298907	48.67157195	49.54000040
42	48.30808646	49.18300988	50.07886307	50.99620481
43	49.63121627	50.55326919	51.49793061	52.46581913
44	50.96319642	51.93384408	52.92887314	53.94896685
45	52.30408609	53.32481221	54.37179000	55.44577260
46	53.66394490	54.72625182	55.82678142	56.95636214
47	55.01283283	56.13824174	57.29394842	58.48086241
48	56.38081028	57.56086139	58.77339290	60.01940152
49	57.75793804	58.99419081	60.26521760	61.57210873
50	59.14427733	60.43831060	61.76952611	63.13911454

Table IX—continued

AMOUNT OF 1 PER PERIOD FOR n PERIODS (UNIFORM SERIES) AT CONTINUOUSLY COMPOUNDED NOMINAL INTEREST RATES

n	1%	2%	3%	4%
1	1.00000000	1.00000000	1.00000000	1.00000000
2	2.01005017	2.02020134	2.03045453	2.04081077
3	3.03025151	3.06101211	3.09229108	3.12409784
4	4.06070604	4.12284866	4.18646536	4.25159469
5	5.10151682	5.20613573	5.31396222	5.42510556
6	6.15278791	6.31130665	6.47579646	6.64650832
7	7.21462446	7.43880350	7.67301382	7.91775747
8	8.28713264	8.58907730	8.90669188	9.24088729
9	9.37041971	9.76258817	10.17794103	10.61801505
10	10.46459399	10.95980553	11.48790548	12.05134446
11	11.56976491	12.18120829	12.83776429	13.54316916
12	12.68604298	13.42728502	14.22873242	15.09587638
13	13.81353983	14.69853417	15.66206183	16.71195078
14	14.95236821	15.99546426	17.13904263	18.39397843
15	16.10264201	17.31859407	18.66100418	20.14465093
16	17.26447625	18.66845288	20.22931637	21.96676973
17	18.43798713	20.04558064	21.84539077	23.86325061
18	19.62329198	21.45052823	23.51068196	25.83712834
19	20.82050934	22.88385764	25.22668883	27.89156155
20	22.02975894	24.34614223	26.99495588	30.02983778
21	23.25116170	25.83796693	28.81707468	32.25537870
22	24.48483976	27.35992849	30.69468526	34.57174568
23	25.73091649	28.91263571	32.62947759	36.98264539
24	26.98951650	30.49670969	34.62319312	39.49193578
25	28.26076565	32.11278409	36.67762634	42.10363225

Table IX–continued

AMOUNT OF 1 PER PERIOD FOR n PERIODS (UNIFORM SERIES)
AT CONTINUOUSLY COMPOUNDED NOMINAL INTEREST RATES

n	1%	2%	3%	4%
26	29.54479106	33.76150536	38.79462635	44.82191408
27	30.84172115	35.44353301	40.97609862	47.65113109
28	32.15168560	37.15953987	43.22400660	50.59581064
29	33.47481541	38.91021237	45.54037358	53.66066485
30	34.81124290	40.69625080	47.92728443	56.85059812
31	36.16110171	42.51836960	50.38688754	60.17071504
32	37.52452682	44.37729765	52.92139672	63.62632851
33	38.90165459	46.27377852	55.53309319	67.22296823
34	40.29262271	48.20857086	58.22432767	70.96638961
35	41.69757030	50.18244859	60.99752243	74.86258291
36	43.11663785	52.19620130	63.85517355	78.91778288
37	44.54996727	54.25063451	66.79985310	83.13847870
38	45.99770188	56.34657002	69.83421149	87.53142438
39	47.45998647	58.48484624	72.96097986	92.10364957
40	48.93696726	60.66631851	76.18297250	96.86247082
41	50.42879196	62.89185944	79.50308942	101.81550324
42	51.93560975	65.16235927	82.92431895	106.97067275
43	53.45757130	67.47872625	86.44974044	112.33622872
44	54.99482883	69.84188694	90.08252700	117.92075719
45	56.54753604	72.25278665	93.82594837	123.73319458
46	58.11584823	74.71238976	97.68337390	129.78284205
47	59.69992221	77.22168015	101.65827553	136.07938031
48	61.29991641	79.78166156	105.75423093	142.63288517
49	62.91599081	82.39335804	109.97492675	149.45384364
50	64.54830703	85.05781428	114.32416189	156.55317070

Table IX–continued

AMOUNT OF 1 PER PERIOD FOR n PERIODS (UNIFORM SERIES) AT CONTINUOUSLY COMPOUNDED NOMINAL INTEREST RATES

n	6%	8%	10%	12%
1	1.00000000	1.00000000	1.00000000	1.00000000
2	2.06183655	2.08328707	2.10517092	2.12749685
3	3.18933340	3.25679794	3.32657368	3.39874600
4	4.38655076	4.52804709	4.67643248	4.83207542
5	5.65779991	5.90517485	6.16825718	6.44814982
6	7.00765872	7.39699955	7.81697845	8.27026862
7	8.44098813	9.01307395	9.63909725	10.32470183
8	9.96294969	10.76374645	11.65284996	12.64106881
9	11.57902409	12.66022733	13.87839089	15.25276528
10	13.29503095	14.71466054	16.33799400	18.19744483
11	15.11714975	16.94020147	19.05627583	21.51756175
12	17.05194209	19.35110118	22.06044185	25.26098313
13	19.10637530	21.96279765	25.38055588	29.48167895
14	21.28784756	24.79201467	29.04985544	34.24050019
15	23.60421454	27.85686887	33.10505541	39.60605616
16	26.06381765	31.17698579	37.58674448	45.65570363
17	28.67551412	34.77362552	42.53977690	52.47666209
18	31.44870889	38.66981882	48.01372429	60.16727129
19	34.39338844	42.89051463	54.06337176	68.83840895
20	37.52015680	47.46273983	60.74926620	78.61508936
21	40.84027373	52.41577225	68.13832230	89.63826574
22	44.36569521	57.78132822	76.30449221	102.06686240
23	48.10911659	63.59376562	85.32950571	116.08006600
24	52.08401822	69.89030388	95.30368816	131.87990895
25	56.30471403	76.71126235	106.32686454	149.69418212

Table IX—continued

AMOUNT OF 1 PER PERIOD FOR n PERIODS (UNIFORM SERIES) AT CONTINUOUSLY COMPOUNDED NOMINAL INTEREST RATES

n	6%	8%	10%	12%
26	60.78640310	84.10031844	118.50935850	169.77971904
27	65.54522435	92.10478736	131.97309653	192.42609868
28	70.59831466	100.77592501	146.85282825	217.95982042
29	75.96387063	110.16925630	163.29747502	246.74901130
30	81.66121406	120.34493061	181.47162039	279.20873337
31	87.71086152	131.36810698	201.55715731	315.80696780
32	94.13459829	143.30937140	223.75510859	357.07136190
33	100.95555676	156.24518871	248.28763878	403.59683633
34	108.19829974	170.25839232	275.40027770	456.05416226
35	115.88890894	185.43871456	305.36437774	515.19963210
36	124.05507885	201.88336133	338.47982969	581.88596312
37	132.72621651	219.69763451	375.07806413	657.07459139
38	141.93354737	238.99560626	415.52536848	741.84953304
39	151.71022778	259.90084949	460.22655279	837.43301284
40	162.09146434	282.54722913	509.62900206	945.20308538
41	173.11464072	307.07975932	564.22715208	1066.71350286
42	184.81945226	333.65553202	624.56743967	1203.71611599
43	197.24804892	362.44472289	691.25377069	1358.18613097
44	210.44518707	393.63168105	764.95356438	1532.35058652
45	224.45839068	427.41610951	846.40443303	1728.72046180
46	239.33812240	464.01434395	936.42156430	1950.12687792
47	255.13796534	503.66073801	1035.90587991	2199.76191503
48	271.91481601	546.60916398	1145.85305234	2481.22463340
49	289.72908919	593.13463841	1267.36346983	2798.57296220
50	308.64493550	643.53508318	1401.65324948	3156.38220377

Table IX–continued

AMOUNT OF 1 PER PERIOD FOR n PERIODS (UNIFORM SERIES)
AT CONTINUOUSLY COMPOUNDED NOMINAL INTEREST RATES

n	14%	16%	18%	20%
1	1.000000	1.000000	1.000000	1.000000
2	2.150274	2.173511	2.197217	2.221403
3	3.473404	3.550639	3.630547	3.713227
4	4.995365	5.166713	5.346554	5.535346
5	6.746038	7.063194	7.400987	7.760887
6	8.759790	9.288735	9.860590	10.479169
7	11.076157	11.900431	12.805270	13.799286
8	13.740614	14.965286	16.330691	17.854486
9	16.805468	18.561925	20.551387	22.807518
10	20.330889	22.782621	25.604477	28.857166
11	24.386089	27.735653	31.654125	36.246222
12	29.050680	33.548091	38.896868	45.271235
13	34.416235	40.369049	47.568005	56.294412
14	40.588094	48.373518	57.949242	69.758150
15	47.687421	57.766850	70.377838	86.202797
16	55.853591	68.790026	85.257570	106.288334
17	65.246922	81.725843	103.071843	130.820864
18	76.051825	96.906165	124.399401	160.784964
19	88.480422	114.720439	149.933122	197.383198
20	102.776711	135.625682	180.502537	242.084383
21	119.221358	160.158212	217.100772	296.682533
22	138.137204	188.947403	260.916814	363.368864
23	159.895606	222.731831	313.374139	444.819732
24	184.923727	262.378226	376.176961	544.304048
25	213.712917	308.903700	451.365589	665.814466

Table IX–continued

AMOUNT OF 1 PER PERIOD FOR n PERIODS (UNIFORM SERIES)
AT CONTINUOUSLY COMPOUNDED NOMINAL INTEREST RATES

n	14%	16%	18%	20%
26	246.828369	363.501850	541.382721	814.227625
27	284.920206	427.573373	649.152793	995.499867
28	328.736248	502.762001	778.176995	1216.906283
29	379.136693	590.996674	932.647010	1487.332690
30	437.111004	694.541021	1117.581194	1817.632250
31	503.797335	816.051439	1338.987610	2221.061044
32	580.504874	958.645235	1604.059216	2713.810085
33	668.739547	1125.980604	1921.407545	3315.655123
34	770.233579	1322.350479	2301.342475	4050.750312
35	886.979505	1552.792663	2756.207169	4948.597603
36	1021.269284	1823.219070	3300.779079	6045.230762
37	1175.739299	2140.567399	3952.750025	7384.661526
38	1353.422110	2512.979113	4733.300963	9020.645956
39	1557.805992	2950.008308	5667.790097	11018.841851
40	1792.903416	3462.866819	6786.576715	13459.443829
41	2063.329824	4064.711857	8126.007479	16440.401816
42	2374.394235	4770.983551	9729.597247	20081.352123
43	2732.203476	5599.801063	11649.442760	24528.418871
44	3143.782072	6572.427422	13947.915143	29960.078462
45	3617.210147	7713.815029	16699.686189	36594.322469
46	4161.782057	9053.245793	19994.154264	44697.406396
47	4788.188856	10625.082356	23938.348646	54594.535455
48	5508.728185	12469.649650	28660.406643	66682.916185
49	6337.545697	14634.269422	34313.736467	81447.697750
50	7290.912764	17174.474255	41082.001092	99481.442678

Table IX—continued

AMOUNT OF 1 PER PERIOD FOR n PERIODS (UNIFORM SERIES)
AT CONTINUOUSLY COMPOUNDED NOMINAL INTEREST RATES

n	22%	24%	26%	28%
1	1.00000	1.00000	1.00000	1.00000
2	2.24608	2.27125	2.29693	2.32313
3	3.79878	3.88732	3.97896	4.07380
4	5.73358	5.94176	6.16043	6.39017
5	8.14448	8.55345	8.98965	9.45502
6	11.14864	11.87357	12.65894	13.51022
7	14.89206	16.09427	17.41776	18.87578
8	19.55665	21.45982	23.58962	25.97511
9	25.36909	28.28078	31.59409	35.36844
10	32.61183	36.95192	41.97533	47.79703
11	41.63685	47.97510	55.43907	65.30643
12	52.88271	61.98830	72.90059	86.00008
13	66.89591	79.80257	95.54697	114.78927
14	84.35744	102.44895	124.91774	152.88111
15	106.11584	131.23814	163.00958	203.28156
16	133.22848	167.83638	212.41203	269.96789
17	167.01291	214.36185	276.48355	358.20256
18	209.11090	273.50732	359.57984	474.94849
19	261.56822	348.69595	467.34991	629.41850
20	326.93408	444.27943	607.12016	833.80238
21	408.38495	565.78985	788.39240	1104.22879
22	509.87898	720.25986	1023.48983	1462.03803
23	636.34833	916.62974	1328.39475	1935.46611
24	793.93885	1166.26477	1723.83512	2561.87291
25	990.30872	1483.61310	2236.69363	3390.69042

Table IX–continued

AMOUNT OF 1 PER PERIOD FOR n PERIODS (UNIFORM SERIES) AT CONTINUOUSLY COMPOUNDED NOMINAL INTEREST RATES

n	22%	24%	26%	28%
26	1235.00065	1887.04190	2901.83526	4487.32358
27	1539.90558	2399.90041	3764.47746	5938.31160
28	1919.84051	3051.87135	4883.26408	7858.15711
29	2393.26858	3880.68887	6334.25210	10398.36195
30	2983.19629	4934.32242	8216.08213	13759.38269
31	3718.29148	6273.75319	10656.68410	18206.44944
32	4634.27649	7976.50341	13821.97424	24090.49603
33	5775.66409	10141.12318	17927.13424	31875.85349
34	7197.92063	12892.89422	23251.23977	42176.89205
35	8970.16141	16391.08083	30156.23241	55806.50326
36	11178.50940	20838.14758	39111.52511	73840.24818
37	13930.28044	26491.47740	50725.91365	97701.23372
38	17359.19831	33678.26814	65788.96359	129272.41503
39	21631.89307	42814.46975	85324.68624	171045.18625
40	26955.99860	54428.85829	110661.15272	226315.98518
41	33590.24260	69193.63986	143520.77839	299446.42700
42	41857.01968	87963.35588	186137.41556	396207.49475
43	52158.05824	111824.34142	241408.21449	524234.94818
44	64993.94268	142157.59902	313090.57654	693631.88859
45	80988.43961	180718.72696	406057.58857	917766.03059
46	100918.81004	229739.52810	526629.30352	1214324.59581
47	125753.58087	292057.17989	683002.38826	1606710.07457
48	156699.61090	371278.44177	885807.34659	2125886.99942
49	195260.73884	471988.40364	1148831.19878	2812825.46660
50	243310.86306	600015.85709	1489954.74620	3721734.23172

Table IX–continued

AMOUNT OF 1 PER PERIOD FOR n PERIODS (UNIFORM SERIES)
AT CONTINUOUSLY COMPOUNDED NOMINAL INTEREST RATES

n	30%	32%	34%	36%
1	1.0000	1.0000	1.0000	1.0000
2	2.3499	2.3771	2.4049	2.4333
3	4.1720	4.2736	4.3788	4.4878
4	6.6316	6.8853	7.1520	7.4324
5	9.9517	10.4819	11.0482	11.6531
6	14.4334	15.4350	16.5222	17.7028
7	20.4830	22.2559	24.2128	26.3739
8	28.6492	31.6493	35.0177	38.8025
9	39.6724	44.5851	50.1980	56.6168
10	54.5521	62.3994	71.5256	82.1505
11	74.6376	86.9319	101.4897	118.7487
12	101.7503	120.7163	143.5876	171.2060
13	138.3485	167.2418	202.7331	246.3947
14	187.7510	231.3133	285.8294	354.1648
15	254.4373	319.5480	402.5753	508.6348
16	344.4544	441.0584	566.5972	730.0412
17	465.9649	608.3938	797.0394	1047.3895
18	629.9868	838.8360	1120.7986	1502.2542
19	851.3932	1156.1843	1575.6633	2154.2252
20	1150.2606	1593.2135	2214.7244	3088.7143
21	1553.6894	2195.0585	3112.5716	4428.1451
22	2098.2613	3023.8760	4374.0000	6347.9906
23	2833.3565	4165.2636	6146.2408	9099.7616
24	3825.6312	5737.1002	8636.1462	13043.9560
25	5165.0619	7901.7200	12134.3328	18697.2858

Table IX—continued

AMOUNT OF 1 PER PERIOD FOR n PERIODS (UNIFORM SERIES)
AT CONTINUOUSLY COMPOUNDED NOMINAL INTEREST RATES

n	30%	32%	34%	36%
26	6973.1044	10882.6780	17049.1017	26800.3698
27	9413.7063	14987.8380	23954.0943	38414.7583
28	12708.1744	20641.1678	33655.2471	55062.0030
29	17155.2422	28426.5253	47284.8583	78922.9886
30	23158.1534	39147.9572	66433.7477	113123.6410
31	31261.2373	53912.7387	93336.9338	162144.4422
32	42199.2565	74245.7294	131134.5002	232407.3983
33	56964.0381	102246.8553	184238.1002	333117.3602
34	76894.4085	140807.9832	258845.8749	477467.9109
35	103797.5946	193911.5831	363665.8883	684369.8012
36	140113.0972	267042.0249	510932.5135	980928.3665
37	189133.8984	367751.9868	717834.4038	1405994.4813
38	255305.0585	506442.4714	1008520.7160	2015254.2467
39	344626.7819	697436.9884	1416919.7500	2888524.1896
40	465198.4968	960460.8406	1990698.9888	4140207.6857
41	627953.2882	1322678.2902	2796828.7478	5934282.4583
42	847649.2769	1821497.9966	3929398.8104	8505782.6017
43	1144207.8421	2508436.4639	5520600.3911	12191589.3969
44	1544520.0334	3454438.4994	7756155.2180	17474564.6928
45	2084884.9705	4757204.1677	10896992.5855	25046808.5807
46	2814301.3402	6551278.9400	15309704.4772	35900328.4796
47	3798910.4512	9021949.1201	21509333.4176	51456997.8025
48	5127993.7317	12424377.6217	30219487.1595	73754829.5352
49	6922068.5040	17109956.3773	42456796.6729	105714967.6380
50	9343816.1367	23562596.9738	59649575.1887	151524373.6760

Table IX–continued

AMOUNT OF 1 PER PERIOD FOR n PERIODS (UNIFORM SERIES)
AT CONTINUOUSLY COMPOUNDED NOMINAL INTEREST RATES

n	38%	40%	45%	50%
1	1.000	1.000	1.000	1.000
2	2.462	2.492	2.568	2.649
3	4.601	4.717	5.028	5.367
4	7.727	8.037	8.885	9.849
5	12.300	12.991	14.935	17.238
6	20.161	20.380	24.423	29.420
7	28.762	31.403	39.302	49.506
8	43.058	47.847	62.639	82.621
9	63.964	72.380	99.237	137.219
10	94.533	108.978	156.634	227.237
11	139.234	163.576	246.651	375.650
12	204.600	245.027	387.826	620.342
13	300.184	366.538	609.233	1023.770
14	439.954	547.810	956.467	1688.912
15	644.338	818.236	1501.039	2785.545
16	943.205	1221.665	2355.098	4593.588
17	1380.234	1823.510	3694.529	7574.546
18	2019.295	2721.357	5795.174	12489.314
19	2953.785	4060.788	9089.642	20592.398
20	4320.274	6058.984	14256.397	33952.125
21	6318.469	9039.942	22359.481	55978.591
22	9240.401	13487.009	35067.646	92294.094
23	13513.095	20121.253	54998.016	152168.235
24	19760.991	30018.382	86255.059	250884.006
25	28897.193	44783.163	135275.860	413638.798

Table IX–continued

AMOUNT OF 1 PER PERIOD FOR n PERIODS (UNIFORM SERIES) AT CONTINUOUSLY COMPOUNDED NOMINAL INTEREST RATES

n	38%	40%	45%	50%
26	42256.919	66809.629	212155.780	681976.084
27	61792.642	99669.255	332727.495	1124389.476
28	90359.428	148690.056	521821.585	1853805.846
29	132132.200	221820.498	818380.150	3056410.130
30	193215.879	330918.297	1283476.562	5039169.393
31	282537.603	493673.089	2012892.931	8308186.765
32	413151.382	736474.706	3156845.512	13697885.240
33	604145.899	1098692.156	4950920.284	22583995.759
34	883434.238	1639057.093	7764589.611	37234715.185
35	1291833.272	1445186.852	12177301.503	61389667.934
36	1889028.886	3647791.136	19097811.333	101214452.322
37	2762298.829	5441865.909	29951331.230	166874421.444
38	4039268.008	8118310.964	46973038.739	275129409.171
39	5906560.361	12111097.799	73668390.044	453611710.090
40	8637073.193	18067635.812	115535034.789	747879276.067
41	12629860.028	26953746.332	181195003.909	1233044471.350
42	18468450.685	40210265.472	284170333.581	2032946649.000
43	27006131.827	59986668.129	445667797.906	3351762382.999
44	39490651.391	89489594.045	698946239.137	5526121935.999
45	57746571.956	133502787.578	1096165905.000	9111034781.000
46	84441923.263	199162756.712	1719130346.999	15021556842.300
47	123478124.090	297115920.313	2696133072.390	24766360286.000
48	180560159.000	443244869.000	4228378352.121	40832825001.900
49	264030339.000	661243643.659	6631417295.490	67321947124.000
50	386087496.793	986459599.768	10400132551.400	110995126209.000

Table X

PRESENT VALUE OF 1 PER PERIOD FOR n PERIODS (UNIFORM SERIES) AT CONTINUOUSLY COMPOUNDED NOMINAL INTEREST RATES

n	1/8%	1/4%	1/2%	7/12%	n
1	0.99875078	0.99750312	0.99501248	0.99418365	1
2	1.99625390	1.99251560	1.98506231	1.98258477	2
3	2.99251092	2.98504365	2.97017425	2.96523701	3
4	3.98752340	3.97509349	3.95037292	3.94217379	4
5	4.98129289	4.96267129	4.92568284	4.91342837	5
6	5.97382095	5.94778323	5.89612837	5.87903378	6
7	6.96510911	6.93043546	6.86173379	6.83902290	7
8	7.95515895	7.91063414	7.82252323	7.79342838	8
9	8.94397200	8.88838538	8.77852071	8.74228270	9
10	9.93154980	9.86369529	9.72975013	9.68561815	10
11	10.91789390	10.83656997	10.67623528	10.62346683	11
12	11.90300583	11.80701550	11.61799981	11.55586065	12
13	12.88688716	12.77503795	12.55506728	12.48283134	13
14	13.86953939	13.74064337	13.48746110	13.40441044	14
15	14.85096408	14.70383779	14.41520458	14.32062931	15
16	15.83116275	15.66462723	15.33832093	15.23151913	16
17	16.81013695	16.62301769	16.25683322	16.13711089	17
18	17.78788818	17.57901517	17.17076440	17.03743541	18
19	18.76441800	18.53262565	18.08013733	17.93252333	19
20	19.73972791	19.48385507	18.98497475	18.82240510	20
21	20.71381944	20.43270939	19.88529928	19.70711101	21
22	21.68669413	21.37919454	20.78111334	20.58667115	22
23	22.65835347	22.32331643	21.67249956	21.46111546	23
24	23.62879900	23.26508096	22.55941999	22.33047370	24
25	24.59803224	24.20449403	23.44191690	23.19477544	25

Table X–continued

PRESENT VALUE OF 1 PER PERIOD FOR n PERIODS (UNIFORM SERIES) AT CONTINUOUSLY COMPOUNDED NOMINAL INTEREST RATES

n	1/8%	1/4%	1/2%	7/12%
26	25.56605469	25.14156149	24.32001233	24.05405010
27	26.53286787	26.07628921	25.19372824	24.90832691
28	27.49847329	27.00868303	26.06308647	25.75763495
29	28.46287245	27.93874878	26.92810877	26.60200311
30	29.42606687	28.86649227	27.78881675	27.44146014
31	30.38805805	29.79191929	28.64523192	28.27603458
32	31.34884749	30.71503564	29.49737571	29.10575484
33	32.30843669	31.63584708	30.34526942	29.93064916
34	33.26682716	32.55435936	31.18893423	30.75074560
35	34.22402038	33.47057823	32.02839125	31.56607207
36	35.18001786	34.38450942	32.86366147	32.37665632
37	36.13482110	35.29615863	33.69476575	33.18252592
38	37.08843157	36.20553156	34.52172488	33.98370830
39	38.04085077	37.11263390	35.34455954	34.78023073
40	38.99208020	38.01747132	36.16329030	35.57212029
41	39.94212133	38.92004947	36.97793761	36.35940395
42	40.89097565	39.82037400	37.78852186	37.14210849
43	41.83864464	40.71845052	38.59506330	37.92026054
44	42.78512980	41.61428465	39.39758210	38.69388659
45	43.73043258	42.50788200	40.19609832	39.46301295
46	44.67455447	43.39924815	40.99063192	40.22766581
47	45.61749694	44.28838866	41.78120277	40.98787117
48	46.55926147	45.17530909	42.56783063	41.74365491
49	47.49984954	46.06001500	43.35053517	42.49504275
50	48.43926261	46.94251190	44.12933595	43.24206025

Table X—continued

PRESENT VALUE OF 1 PER PERIOD FOR n PERIODS (UNIFORM SERIES) AT CONTINUOUSLY COMPOUNDED NOMINAL INTEREST RATES

n	2/3%	3/4%	5/6%	11/12%
1	0.99335551	0.99252805	0.99170129	0.99087522
2	1.98011067	1.97763999	1.97517275	1.97270892
3	2.96030934	2.95539123	2.95048266	2.94558360
4	3.93399509	3.92583677	3.91769876	3.90958102
5	4.90121119	4.88903118	4.87688822	4.86478217
6	5.86200063	5.84502867	5.82811764	5.81126731
7	6.81640611	6.79388299	6.77145309	6.74911599
8	7.76447005	7.73564751	7.70696008	7.67840701
9	8.70623458	8.67037524	8.63470356	8.59921844
10	9.64174157	9.59811873	9.55474798	9.51162768
11	10.57103258	10.51893016	10.46715721	10.41571138
12	11.49414893	11.43286135	11.37199463	11.31154552
13	12.41113163	12.33996369	12.26932307	12.19920536
14	13.32202145	13.24028821	13.15920484	13.07877655
15	14.22685887	14.13388556	14.04170174	13.95029985
16	15.12568410	15.02080600	14.19687506	14.81388164
17	16.01853710	15.90109941	15.78478557	15.66958344
18	16.90545753	16.77481532	16.64549355	16.51747714
19	17.78648483	17.64200288	17.49905876	17.35763400
20	18.66165815	18.50271086	18.34554049	18.19012462
21	19.53101639	19.35698767	19.18499751	19.01501894
22	20.39459818	20.20488137	20.01748812	19.83238627
23	21.25244190	21.04643966	20.84307014	20.64229531
24	22.10458569	21.88170987	21.66180089	21.44481411
25	22.95106742	22.71073899	22.47373724	22.24001010

Table X—continued

PRESENT VALUE OF 1 PER PERIOD FOR n PERIODS (UNIFORM SERIES) AT CONTINUOUSLY COMPOUNDED NOMINAL INTEREST RATES

n	2/3%	3/4%	5/6%	11/12%
26	23.79192470	23.53357365	23.27893556	23.02795010
27	24.62719491	24.35026013	24.07745178	23.80870032
28	25.45691518	25.16084438	24.86934135	24.58232637
29	26.28112237	25.96537198	25.65465925	25.34889325
30	27.09985312	26.76388820	26.43346004	26.10846537
31	27.91314382	27.55643795	27.20579778	26.86110657
32	28.72103062	28.34306581	27.97172612	27.60688007
33	29.52354942	29.12381604	28.73129824	28.34584856
34	30.32073588	29.89873253	29.48456690	29.07807413
35	31.11262545	30.66785890	30.23158440	29.80361829
36	31.89925331	31.43123839	30.97240262	30.52254202
37	32.68065443	32.18891396	31.70707301	31.23490574
38	33.45686353	32.94092821	32.43564658	31.94076929
39	34.22791512	33.68732346	33.15817393	32.64019198
40	34.99384346	34.42814168	33.87470524	33.33323261
41	35.75468259	35.16342455	34.58529027	34.01994938
42	36.51046633	35.89321342	35.28999784	34.70040002
43	37.26122827	36.61754935	35.98881845	35.37464169
44	38.00700178	37.33647308	36.68185907	36.04273106
45	38.74782000	38.05002506	37.36914835	36.70472425
46	39.48371586	38.75824541	38.05073402	37.36067991
47	40.21472206	39.46117398	38.72666340	38.01064414
48	40.94087110	40.15885031	39.39698345	38.65468056
49	41.66219525	40.85131364	40.06174071	39.29284029
50	42.37872656	41.53860292	40.72098134	39.92517695

Table X–continued

PRESENT VALUE OF 1 PER PERIOD FOR n PERIODS (UNIFORM SERIES) AT CONTINUOUSLY COMPOUNDED NOMINAL INTEREST RATES

n	1%	2%	3%	4%
1	0.99004983	0.98019867	0.97044553	0.96078944
2	1.97024851	1.94098811	1.91221007	1.88390579
3	2.94069404	2.88275265	2.82614125	2.77082622
4	3.90148348	3.80586899	3.71306169	3.62297001
5	4.85271290	4.71070641	4.57376967	4.44170076
6	5.79447744	5.59762685	5.40903988	5.22832863
7	6.72687126	6.46698508	6.21962412	5.98411237
8	7.64998760	7.31912887	7.00625198	6.71026140
9	8.56391879	8.15439908	7.76963148	7.40793773
10	9.46875621	8.97312984	8.51044970	8.07825778
11	10.36459034	9.77564863	9.22937343	8.72229420
12	11.25151078	10.56227650	9.92704976	9.34107759
13	12.12960621	11.33332808	10.60410663	9.93559814
14	12.99896445	12.08911182	11.26115345	10.50680720
15	13.85967242	12.82993004	11.89878160	11.05561884
16	14.71181621	13.55607908	12.51756500	11.58291126
17	15.55548103	14.26784940	13.11806058	12.08952825
18	16.39075124	14.96552573	13.70080883	12.57628051
19	17.21771037	15.64938714	14.26633427	13.04394694
20	18.03644113	16.31970719	14.81514590	13.49327590
21	18.84702537	16.97675401	15.34773770	13.92498642
22	19.64954417	17.62079043	15.86458904	14.33976934
23	20.44407777	18.25207407	16.36616511	14.73828838
24	21.23070563	18.87085746	16.85291736	15.12118126
25	22.00950642	19.47738812	17.32528392	15.48906070

Table X–continued

PRESENT VALUE OF 1 PER PERIOD FOR n PERIODS (UNIFORM SERIES) AT CONTINUOUSLY COMPOUNDED NOMINAL INTEREST RATES

n	1%	2%	3%	4%
26	22.78055800	20.07190867	17.78368993	15.84251539
27	23.54393750	20.65465692	18.22854799	16.18211091
28	24.29972124	21.22586599	18.66025852	16.50839071
29	25.04798481	21.78576436	19.07921007	16.82187689
30	25.78880303	22.33457599	19.48577973	17.12307110
31	26.52224998	22.87252043	19.88033344	17.41245532
32	27.24839902	23.39981285	20.26322632	17.69049262
33	27.96732275	23.91666419	20.63480301	17.95762792
34	28.67909308	24.42328118	20.99539795	18.21428870
35	29.38378117	24.91986648	21.34533570	18.46088566
36	30.08145749	25.40661874	21.68493123	18.69781342
37	30.77219182	25.88373266	22.01449019	18.92545111
38	31.45605323	26.35139908	22.33430921	19.14416299
39	32.13311011	26.80980509	22.64467615	19.35429907
40	32.80343016	27.25913406	22.94587037	19.55619558
41	33.46708041	27.69956571	23.23816294	19.75017563
42	34.12412723	28.13127624	23.52181697	19.93654960
43	34.77463632	28.55443832	23.79708775	20.11561575
44	35.41867274	28.96922123	24.06422305	20.28766061
45	36.05630089	29.37579089	24.32346332	20.45295950
46	36.68758454	29.77430993	24.57504187	20.61177693
47	37.31258681	30.16493777	24.81918515	20.76436703
48	37.93137020	30.54783065	25.05611291	20.91097400
49	38.54399659	30.92314175	25.28603840	21.05183242
50	39.15052725	31.29102119	25.50916856	21.18716770

Table X–continued

PRESENT VALUE OF 1 PER PERIOD FOR n PERIODS (UNIFORM SERIES) AT CONTINUOUSLY COMPOUNDED NOMINAL INTEREST RATES

n	6%	8%	10%	12%
1	0.94176453	0.92311635	0.90483742	0.88692044
2	1.82868497	1.77526014	1.72356817	1.67354830
3	2.66395518	2.56188800	2.46438639	2.37122462
4	3.45058304	3.28803703	3.13470644	2.99000802
5	4.19140126	3.95835708	3.74123710	3.53881965
6	4.88907759	4.57714047	4.29004873	4.02557191
7	5.54612441	5.14834954	4.78663404	4.45728243
8	6.16490780	5.67564196	5.23596300	4.84017532
9	6.74765605	6.16239422	5.64253266	5.17977084
10	7.29646769	6.61172318	6.01041210	5.48096506
11	7.81331902	7.02650609	6.34328319	5.74810036
12	8.30007128	7.40939898	6.64447740	5.98502812
13	8.75847729	7.76285366	6.91700919	6.19516419
14	9.19011878	8.08913345	7.16360616	6.38153816
15	9.59675748	8.39032767	7.38673632	6.54683705
16	9.97965036	8.66836497	7.58863283	6.69344401
17	10.34024530	8.92502574	7.77131636	6.82347272
18	10.67984083	9.16195350	7.93661525	6.93879785
19	10.99965985	9.38066539	8.08618387	7.04108205
20	11.30085406	9.58256191	8.22151915	7.13180001
21	11.58450809	9.76893588	8.34397558	7.21225961
22	11.85164339	9.94098075	8.45477874	7.28362088
23	12.10322194	10.09979817	8.55503758	7.34691265
24	12.34014970	10.24640514	8.64575553	7.40304741
25	12.56327986	10.38174042	8.72784053	7.45283448

Table X–continued

PRESENT VALUE OF 1 PER PERIOD FOR n PERIODS (UNIFORM SERIES) AT CONTINUOUSLY COMPOUNDED NOMINAL INTEREST RATES

n	6%	8%	10%	12%
26	12.77341593	10.50667063	8.80211411	7.49699165
27	12.97131463	10.62199575	8.86931962	7.53615555
28	13.15768861	10.72845426	8.93012968	7.57089080
29	13.33320901	10.82672784	8.98515290	7.60169822
30	13.49850790	10.91744579	9.03493997	7.62902194
31	13.65418053	11.00118902	9.07998918	7.65325591
32	13.80078749	11.07849376	9.12075138	7.67474951
33	13.93885673	11.14985503	9.15763455	7.69381262
34	14.06888544	11.21572978	9.19100782	7.71072009
35	14.19134187	11.27653985	9.22120520	7.72571566
36	14.30666699	11.33267461	9.24852892	7.73901555
37	14.41527610	11.38449353	9.27325245	7.75081149
38	14.51756030	11.43232842	9.29562322	7.76127354
39	14.61388794	11.47648559	9.31586513	7.77055256
40	14.70460589	11.51724779	9.33418077	7.77878231
41	14.79004084	11.55487605	9.35075345	7.78608144
42	14.87050045	11.58961131	9.36574902	7.79255518
43	14.94627446	11.62167599	9.37931758	7.79829688
44	15.01763572	11.65127543	9.39159492	7.80338932
45	15.08484124	11.67859915	9.40270392	7.80790590
46	15.14813301	11.70382212	9.41275575	7.81191174
47	15.20773895	11.72710586	9.42185103	7.81546461
48	15.26387371	11.74859946	9.43008078	7.81861572
49	15.31673944	11.76844056	9.43752736	7.82141051
50	15.36652651	11.78675620	9.44426531	7.82388926

Table X—continued

PRESENT VALUE OF 1 PER PERIOD FOR n PERIODS (UNIFORM SERIES) AT CONTINUOUSLY COMPOUNDED NOMINAL INTEREST RATES

n	14%	16%	18%	20%
1	0.86935824	0.85214379	0.83527021	0.81873075
2	1.62514198	1.57829283	1.53294654	1.48905080
3	2.28218880	2.19707622	2.11569479	2.03786244
4	2.85339786	2.72436864	2.60244705	2.48719140
5	3.34998316	3.17369761	3.00901671	2.85507084
6	3.78169369	3.55659049	3.34861223	3.15626505
7	4.15700479	3.88287029	3.63226626	3.40286202
8	4.48328458	4.16090759	3.86919402	3.60475853
9	4.76693861	4.39783535	4.06709272	3.77005742
10	5.01353557	4.59973186	4.23239160	3.90539271
11	5.22791667	4.77177673	4.37046084	4.01619586
12	5.41429065	4.91838369	4.48578596	4.10691382
13	5.57631640	5.04331390	4.58211360	4.18118740
14	5.71717482	5.14977241	4.66257321	4.24199746
15	5.83963125	5.24049036	4.72797872	4.29178453
16	5.94608975	5.31779510	4.78591348	4.33254673
17	6.03864033	5.38366985	4.83280118	4.36592000
18	6.11909994	5.43980462	4.87196507	4.41561450
19	6.18904816	5.48763951	4.90467751	4.43393013
20	6.24985822	5.52840171	4.93200123	4.44892571
21	6.30272395	5.56313697	4.95482392	4.46120305
22	6.34868321	5.59273641	4.97388704	4.47125489
23	6.38863827	5.61795938	4.98980989	4.47948463
24	6.42337353	5.63945298	5.00310977	4.48622258
25	6.45357091	5.65776862	5.01421877	

Table X—continued

PRESENT VALUE OF 1 PER PERIOD FOR n PERIODS (UNIFORM SERIES) AT CONTINUOUSLY COMPOUNDED NOMINAL INTEREST RATES

n	14%	16%	18%	20%
26	6.47982353	5.67337618	5.02349778	4.49173915
27	6.50264594	5.68667606	5.03124827	4.49625573
28	6.52248704	5.69800948	5.03772201	4.49995359
29	6.53973606	5.70766717	5.04312934	4.50298114
30	6.55473164	5.71589692	5.04764592	4.50545990
31	6.56776816	5.72290985	5.05141849	4.50748933
32	6.57910158	5.72888587	5.05456960	4.50915088
33	6.58895437	5.73397830	5.05720163	4.51051125
34	6.59751998	5.73831778	5.05940009	4.51162503
35	6.60496657	5.74201565	5.06123639	4.51253691
36	6.61144031	5.74516676	5.06277020	4.51328350
37	6.61706832	5.74785196	5.06405135	4.51389475
38	6.62196107	5.75014014	5.06512145	4.51439520
39	6.62621463	5.75208999	5.06601528	4.51480493
40	6.62991249	5.75375155	5.06676186	4.51514040
41	6.63312726	5.75516744	5.06738546	4.51541505
42	6.63592205	5.75637397	5.06790634	4.51563992
43	6.63835172	5.75740212	5.06834141	4.51582402
44	6.64046397	5.75827824	5.06870481	4.51597476
45	6.64230027	5.75902483	5.06900835	4.51609817
46	6.64389668	5.75966103	5.06926189	4.51619921
47	6.64528453	5.76020316	5.06947366	4.51628193
48	6.64649107	5.76066514	5.06965055	4.51634966
49	6.64753998	5.76105880	5.06979830	4.51640511
50	6.64845186	5.76139427	5.06992171	4.51645051

Table X–continued

PRESENT VALUE OF 1 PER PERIOD FOR n PERIODS (UNIFORM SERIES) AT CONTINUOUSLY COMPOUNDED NOMINAL INTEREST RATES

n	22%	24%	26%	28%
1	0.80251880	0.78662786	0.77105159	0.75578374
2	1.44655522	1.40541125	1.36557213	1.32699281
3	1.96340655	1.89216351	1.82397815	1.75870333
4	2.37818947	2.27505640	2.17743283	2.08498312
5	2.71106055	2.57625061	2.44996462	2.33158009
6	2.97819585	2.81317837	2.66010069	2.51795406
7	3.19257695	2.99955234	2.82212644	2.65881248
8	3.36462182	3.14615930	2.94705665	2.76527099
9	3.50269105	3.26148443	3.04338429	2.84573060
10	3.61349421	3.35220238	3.11765787	2.90654066
11	3.70241583	3.42356365	3.17492663	2.95471392
12	3.77377710	3.47969841	3.21908380	2.98723517
13	3.83104586	3.52385558	3.25313125	3.02348752
14	3.87700512	3.55859084	3.27938360	3.03332861
15	3.91388828	3.58591456	3.29962551	3.04832419
16	3.94348772	3.60740816	3.31523307	3.05965760
17	3.96724182	3.62431563	3.32726730	3.06822321
18	3.98630494	3.63761551	3.33654631	3.07469696
19	4.00160344	3.64807757	3.34370091	3.07958971
20	4.01388078	3.65630732	3.34921748	3.08328758
21	4.02373358	3.66278107	3.35347103	3.08608236
22	4.03164063	3.66787350	3.35675074	3.08819462
23	4.03798619	3.67187934	3.35927957	3.08979102
24	4.04307862	3.67503046	3.36122943	3.09099756
25	4.04716540	3.67750921	3.36273286	3.09190944

Table X–continued

PRESENT VALUE OF 1 PER PERIOD FOR n PERIODS (UNIFORM SERIES) AT CONTINUOUSLY COMPOUNDED NOMINAL INTEREST RATES

n	22%	24%	26%	28%
26	4.05044511	3.67945906	3.36389209	3.09259863
27	4.05307714	3.68099287	3.36478592	3.09311950
28	4.05518939	3.68219941	3.36547511	3.09351317
29	4.05688451	3.68314851	3.36600650	3.09381070
30	4.05824488	3.68389509	3.36641624	3.09403557
31	4.05933660	3.68448238	3.36673216	3.09420552
32	4.06021273	3.68494435	3.36697576	3.09433397
33	4.06091584	3.68530776	3.36716359	3.09443104
34	4.06148009	3.68559362	3.36730841	3.09450441
35	4.06193292	3.68581849	3.36742007	3.09455987
36	4.06229632	3.68599537	3.36750617	3.09460177
37	4.06258796	3.68613452	3.36757256	3.09463345
38	4.06282200	3.68624397	3.36762375	3.09465739
39	4.06300983	3.68633007	3.36766322	3.09467548
40	4.06316056	3.68639780	3.36769365	3.09468916
41	4.06328153	3.68645108	3.36771712	3.09469949
42	4.06337861	3.68649299	3.36773521	3.09470730
43	4.06345651	3.68652596	3.36774916	3.09471320
44	4.06351903	3.68655189	3.36775992	3.09471767
45	4.06356921	3.68657229	3.36776821	3.09472104
46	4.06360948	3.68658833	3.36777460	3.09472359
47	4.06364179	3.68660096	3.36777954	3.09472551
48	4.06366772	3.68661089	3.36778334	3.09472697
49	4.06368853	3.68661870	3.36778627	3.09472807
50	4.06370524	3.68662484	3.36778853	3.09472890

Table X–continued

PRESENT VALUE OF 1 PER PERIOD FOR n PERIODS (UNIFORM SERIES) AT CONTINUOUSLY COMPOUNDED NOMINAL INTEREST RATES

n	30%	32%	34%	36%
1	0.74081822	0.72614904	0.71170323	0.69767633
2	1.28962986	1.25344164	1.21838732	1.18442858
3	1.69619952	1.63633435	1.57898226	1.52402411
4	1.99739373	1.91437165	1.83564303	1.76095187
5	2.22052389	2.11626817	2.01832656	1.92625076
6	2.38582278	2.26287513	2.14835527	2.04157588
7	2.50827921	2.36933363	2.24090585	2.12203548
8	2.59899716	2.44663837	2.30678060	2.17817025
9	2.66620267	2.50277314	2.35366829	2.21733414
10	2.71598974	2.54353534	2.38704156	2.24465786
11	2.75287291	2.57313478	2.41079567	2.26372098
12	2.78019663	2.59462838	2.42770313	2.27702086
13	2.80043854	2.61023593	2.43973737	2.28629987
14	2.81543412	2.62156935	2.44830298	2.29277362
15	2.82654311	2.62979909	2.45439972	2.29729020
16	2.83477286	2.63577512	2.45873921	2.30044132
17	2.84086961	2.64011460	2.46182792	2.30263977
18	2.84538619	2.64326571	2.46402638	2.30417358
19	2.84873215	2.64555389	2.46559117	2.30524369
20	2.85121091	2.64721545	2.46670495	2.30599027
21	2.85304721	2.64842198	2.46749770	2.30651115
22	2.85440758	2.64929811	2.46806196	2.30687455
23	2.85541537	2.64993431	2.46846358	2.30712809
24	2.85616195	2.65039628	2.46874944	2.30730497
25	2.85671504	2.65073175	2.46895291	2.30742838

Table X—continued

PRESENT VALUE OF 1 PER PERIOD FOR n PERIODS (UNIFORM SERIES) AT CONTINUOUSLY COMPOUNDED NOMINAL INTEREST RATES

n	30%	32%	34%	36%
26	2.85712477	2.65097534	2.46909773	2.30751448
27	2.85742831	2.65115223	2.46920081	2.30757455
28	2.85765318	2.65128068	2.46927418	2.30761646
29	2.85781976	2.65137395	2.46932640	2.30764770
30	2.85794317	2.65144168	2.46936357	2.30766610
31	2.85803460	2.65149086	2.46939003	2.30768033
32	2.85810233	2.65152657	2.46940886	2.30769026
33	2.85815250	2.65155250	2.46942227	2.30769719
34	2.85818967	2.65157133	2.46943181	2.30770202
35	2.85821721	2.65158501	2.46943860	2.30770540
36	2.85823761	2.65159494	2.46944343	2.30770775
37	2.85825272	2.65160215	2.46944687	2.30770939
38	2.85826391	2.65160738	2.46944932	2.30771053
39	2.85827221	2.65161119	2.46945106	2.30771133
40	2.85827835	2.65161395	2.46945230	2.30771189
41	2.85828290	2.65161595	2.46945318	2.30771228
42	2.85828628	2.65161741	2.46945381	2.30771255
43	2.85828877	2.65161846	2.46945426	2.30771274
44	2.85829062	2.65161923	2.46945458	2.30771287
45	2.85829200	2.65161979	2.46945481	2.30771296
46	2.85829301	2.65162019	2.46945497	2.30771303
47	2.85829376	2.65162049	2.46945508	2.30771307
48	2.85829432	2.65162070	2.46945516	2.30771311
49	2.85829473	2.65162086	2.46945522	2.30771313
50	2.85829504	2.65162097	2.46945526	2.30771314

Table X–continued

PRESENT VALUE OF 1 PER PERIOD FOR n PERIODS (UNIFORM SERIES) AT CONTINUOUSLY COMPOUNDED NOMINAL INTEREST RATES

n	38%	40%	45%	50%
1	0.68386141	0.67032004	0.63762815	0.60653066
2	1.15152784	1.11964901	1.04419781	0.97441010
3	1.47134686	1.42084322	1.30343807	1.19754026
4	1.69005875	1.62273974	1.46873696	1.33287554
5	1.83962736	1.75807502	1.57413619	1.41496054
6	1.95356566	1.84879298	1.64134170	1.46474761
7	2.01185979	1.90960304	1.68419382	1.49494500
8	2.05969468	1.95036524	1.71151755	1.51326063
9	2.09240712	1.97768897	1.72893992	1.52436963
10	2.11477789	1.99600461	1.74004892	1.53110758
11	2.13007640	2.00828194	1.74713233	1.53519435
12	2.14053846	2.01651169	1.75164891	1.53767310
13	2.14769305	2.02202826	1.75452881	1.53917654
14	2.15258581	2.02572612	1.75636511	1.54008842
15	2.15593177	2.02820487	1.75753599	1.54064151
16	2.15821995	2.02986643	1.75828258	1.54097697
17	2.15978475	2.03098020	1.75875862	1.54118044
18	2.16085485	2.03172679	1.75906216	1.54130385
19	2.16158665	2.03222724	1.75925571	1.54137870
20	2.16208710	2.03256270	1.75937912	1.54142410
21	2.16242934	2.03278757	1.75945781	1.54145164
22	2.16266339	2.03293830	1.75950798	1.54146834
23	2.16282344	2.03303934	1.75953997	1.54147847
24	2.16293290	2.03310707	1.75956037	1.54148461
25	2.16300775	2.03331524	1.75957338	1.54148834

Table X–continued

PRESENT VALUE OF 1 PER PERIOD FOR n PERIODS (UNIFORM SERIES) AT CONTINUOUSLY COMPOUNDED NOMINAL INTEREST RATES

n	38%	40%	45%	50%
26	2.16305894	2.03318291	1.75958167	1.54149060
27	2.16309394	2.03320331	1.75958696	1.54149197
28	2.16311788	2.03321698	1.75959033	1.54149280
29	2.16314251	2.03322615	1.75959248	1.54149331
30	2.16314545	2.03323229	1.75959386	1.54149361
31	2.16315310	2.03323641	1.75959473	1.54149380
32	2.16315834	2.03323917	1.75959529	1.54149391
33	2.16316192	2.03322410	1.75959564	1.54149398
34	2.16316437	2.03324226	1.75959587	1.54149402
35	2.16316604	2.03324309	1.75959601	1.54149404
36	2.16316719	2.03324365	1.75959611	1.54149406
37	2.16316797	2.03324402	1.75959616	1.54149407
38	2.16316851	2.03324427	1.75959620	1.54149407
39	2.16316887	2.03324444	1.75959623	1.54149408
40	2.16316912	2.03324455	1.75959624	1.54149408
41	2.16316929	2.03324463	1.75959625	1.54149408
42	2.16316941	2.03324468	1.75959626	1.54149408
43	2.16316949	2.03324471	1.75959626	1.54149408
44	2.16316955	2.03324474	1.75959626	1.54149408
45	2.16316958	2.03324475	1.75959626	1.54149408
46	2.16316961	2.03324476	1.75959626	1.54149408
47	2.16316963	2.03324477	1.75959627	1.54149408
48	2.16316964	2.03324477	1.75959627	1.54149408
49	2.16316965	2.03324478	1.75959627	1.54149408
50	2.16316965	2.03324478	1.75959627	1.54149408

Table XI

CAPITAL RECOVERY FACTOR OF 1 AT CONTINUOUSLY COMPOUNDED NOMINAL INTEREST RATES

n	1/8%	1/4%	1/2%	7/12%	n
1	1.00125078	1.00250313	1.00501252	1.00585038	1
2	0.50093828	0.50187813	0.50376252	0.50439205	2
3	0.33416754	0.33500348	0.33668058	0.33724117	3
4	0.25078222	0.25156641	0.25314066	0.25366715	4
5	0.20075109	0.20150438	0.20301754	0.20352388	5
6	0.16739705	0.16812987	0.16960282	0.17009598	6
7	0.14357277	0.14429108	0.14573576	0.14621972	7
8	0.12570459	0.12641212	0.12783599	0.12831323	8
9	0.11180715	0.11250637	0.11391441	0.11438660	9
10	0.10068922	0.10138188	0.10277756	0.10324586	10
11	0.09159276	0.09228012	0.09366598	0.09413123	11
12	0.08401240	0.08469541	0.08607334	0.08653618	12
13	0.07759826	0.07827765	0.07964912	0.08011003	13
14	0.07210045	0.07277680	0.07414294	0.07460231	14
15	0.06733570	0.06800946	0.06937120	0.06982933	15
16	0.06316655	0.06383810	0.06519618	0.06565333	16
17	0.05948792	0.06015755	0.06151260	0.06196896	17
18	0.05621803	0.05688601	0.05823853	0.05869428	18
19	0.05329236	0.05395889	0.05530931	0.05576460	19
20	0.05065926	0.05132455	0.05267323	0.05312817	20
21	0.04827695	0.04894114	0.05028841	0.05074310	21
22	0.04611122	0.04677445	0.04812057	0.04857512	22
23	0.04413383	0.04479621	0.04614142	0.04659590	23
24	0.04232124	0.04298287	0.04432738	0.04478185	24
25	0.04065366	0.04131464	0.04265863	0.04311316	25

Table XI—continued

CAPITAL RECOVERY FACTOR OF 1 AT CONTINUOUSLY COMPOUNDED NOMINAL INTEREST RATES

n	1/8%	1/4%	1/2%	7/12%
26	0.03911437	0.03977478	0.04111840	0.04157304
27	0.03768910	0.03834901	0.03969242	0.04014722
28	0.03636566	0.03702513	0.03836844	0.03882344
29	0.03513349	0.03579258	0.03713592	0.03759115
30	0.03398347	0.03464224	0.03598570	0.03644121
31	0.03290766	0.03356615	0.03490982	0.03536564
32	0.03189910	0.03255734	0.03390132	0.03435747
33	0.03095167	0.03160971	0.03295407	0.03341057
34	0.03005998	0.03071785	0.03206265	0.03251954
35	0.02921924	0.02987699	0.03122230	0.03167958
36	0.02842523	0.02908286	0.03042875	0.03088645
37	0.02767414	0.02833170	0.02967820	0.03013634
38	0.02696259	0.02762009	0.02896727	0.02942586
39	0.02628753	0.02694500	0.02829290	0.02875197
40	0.02564624	0.02630370	0.02765235	0.02811190
41	0.02503623	0.02569370	0.02704315	0.02750320
42	0.02445527	0.02511277	0.02646306	0.02692362
43	0.02390135	0.02455889	0.02591005	0.02637113
44	0.02337261	0.02403021	0.02538227	0.02584388
45	0.02286737	0.02352505	0.02487804	0.02534018
46	0.02238411	0.02304187	0.02439582	0.02485851
47	0.02192141	0.02257928	0.02393421	0.02439746
48	0.02147800	0.02213599	0.02349192	0.02395574
49	0.02105270	0.02171080	0.02306777	0.02353216
50	0.02064441	0.02130265	0.02266066	0.02312563

Table XI–continued

CAPITAL RECOVERY FACTOR OF 1 AT CONTINUOUSLY COMPOUNDED NOMINAL INTEREST RATES

n	2/3%	3/4%	5/6%	11/12%
1	1.00668894	1.00752820	1.00836815	1.00920881
2	0.50502228	0.50565320	0.50628483	0.50691716
3	0.33780254	0.33836468	0.33892760	0.33949130
4	0.25419452	0.25472277	0.25525189	0.25578188
5	0.20403120	0.20453950	0.20504878	0.20555905
6	0.17059022	0.17108556	0.17158199	0.17207950
7	0.14670487	0.14719123	0.14767879	0.14816755
8	0.12879179	0.12927166	0.12975285	0.13023535
9	0.11486021	0.11533526	0.11581173	0.11628964
10	0.10371570	0.10418708	0.10466001	0.10513448
11	0.09459814	0.09506670	0.09553692	0.09600880
12	0.08700079	0.08746717	0.08793532	0.08840525
13	0.08057283	0.08103752	0.08150409	0.08197255
14	0.07506368	0.07552706	0.07599243	0.07645982
15	0.07028958	0.07075195	0.07121644	0.07168305
16	0.06611271	0.06657432	0.06703817	0.06750425
17	0.06242767	0.06288873	0.06335214	0.06381791
18	0.05915250	0.05961317	0.06007632	0.06054193
19	0.05622246	0.05668291	0.05714593	0.05761154
20	0.05358581	0.05404613	0.05450916	0.05497488
21	0.05120061	0.05166093	0.05212406	0.05259001
22	0.04903259	0.04949299	0.04995632	0.05042258
23	0.04705342	0.04751397	0.04797758	0.04844423
24	0.04523948	0.04570027	0.04616421	0.04663132
25	0.04357096	0.04403203	0.04449638	0.04496401

Table XI—continued

CAPITAL RECOVERY FACTOR OF 1 AT CONTINUOUSLY COMPOUNDED NOMINAL INTEREST RATES

n	2/3%	3/4%	5/6%	11/12%
26	0.04203107	0.04249248	0.04295729	0.04342549
27	0.04060552	0.04106732	0.04153263	0.04200145
28	0.03928206	0.03974429	0.04021015	0.04067963
29	0.03805013	0.03851283	0.03897927	0.03944945
30	0.03690057	0.03736378	0.03783084	0.03830175
31	0.03582542	0.03628916	0.03675687	0.03722855
32	0.03481769	0.03528200	0.03575039	0.03622285
33	0.03387127	0.03433616	0.03480525	0.03527853
34	0.03298073	0.03344623	0.03391605	0.03439017
35	0.03214129	0.03260743	0.03307799	0.03355297
36	0.03134870	0.03181548	0.03228681	0.03276267
37	0.03059914	0.03106660	0.03153870	0.03201546
38	0.02988923	0.03035737	0.03083028	0.03130795
39	0.02921592	0.02968476	0.03015848	0.03063707
40	0.02857646	0.02904601	0.02952055	0.03000009
41	0.02796836	0.02843864	0.02891403	0.02939452
42	0.02738941	0.02786042	0.02833666	0.02881811
43	0.02683755	0.02730931	0.02778641	0.02826884
44	0.02631094	0.02678346	0.02726143	0.02774485
45	0.02580790	0.02628119	0.02676004	0.02724445
46	0.02532690	0.02580096	0.02628070	0.02676611
47	0.02486652	0.02534136	0.02582200	0.02630842
48	0.02442547	0.02490111	0.02538265	0.02587009
49	0.02400258	0.02447902	0.02496147	0.02544993
50	0.02359674	0.02407399	0.02455737	0.02504685

Table XI–continued

CAPITAL RECOVERY FACTOR OF 1 AT CONTINUOUSLY COMPOUNDED NOMINAL INTEREST RATES

n	1%	2%	3%	4%
1	1.01005017	1.02020134	1.03045453	1.04081077
2	0.50755019	0.51520151	0.52295510	0.53081211
3	0.34005578	0.34689067	0.35383936	0.36090318
4	0.25631276	0.26275208	0.26931952	0.27601664
5	0.20607030	0.21228239	0.21863803	0.22513898
6	0.17257812	0.17864714	0.18487569	0.19126571
7	0.14865752	0.15463156	0.16078142	0.16710916
8	0.13071917	0.13662828	0.14272967	0.14902549
9	0.11676897	0.12263319	0.12870623	0.13499034
10	0.10561049	0.11144383	0.11750260	0.12378907
11	0.09648235	0.10229500	0.10834972	0.11464874
12	0.08887695	0.09467656	0.10073486	0.10705403
13	0.08244291	0.08823534	0.09430309	0.10064819
14	0.07692920	0.08271906	0.08880085	0.09517639
15	0.07215178	0.07794275	0.08404222	0.09045174
16	0.06797257	0.07376764	0.07988744	0.08633408
17	0.06428602	0.07008765	0.07623078	0.08271621
18	0.06101002	0.06682024	0.07298839	0.07951477
19	0.05807973	0.06390027	0.07009509	0.07666391
20	0.05544331	0.06127561	0.06749849	0.07411099
21	0.05305877	0.05890408	0.06515618	0.07181336
22	0.05089177	0.05675114	0.06303346	0.06973613
23	0.04891392	0.05478829	0.06110167	0.06785048
24	0.04710159	0.05299176	0.05933691	0.06613240
25	0.04543491	0.05134159	0.05771911	0.06456169

Table XI—continued

CAPITAL RECOVERY FACTOR OF 1 AT CONTINUOUSLY COMPOUNDED NOMINAL INTEREST RATES

n	1%	2%	3%	4%
26	0.04389708	0.04982087	0.05623130	0.06312129
27	0.04247378	0.04841523	0.05485900	0.06179663
28	0.04115724	0.04711233	0.05358983	0.06057526
29	0.03992337	0.04590153	0.05241307	0.05944640
30	0.03877652	0.04473628	0.05131948	0.05840074
31	0.03770419	0.04372059	0.05030097	0.05743015
32	0.03669940	0.04273538	0.04935048	0.05652754
33	0.03575601	0.04181185	0.04846181	0.05568664
34	0.03486861	0.04094454	0.04762949	0.05490195
35	0.03403238	0.04012863	0.04684864	0.05416858
36	0.03324307	0.03935982	0.04611497	0.05348219
37	0.03249687	0.03863430	0.04542463	0.05283890
38	0.03179038	0.03794865	0.04477416	0.05223525
39	0.03112055	0.03729979	0.04416049	0.05166811
40	0.03048462	0.03668495	0.04358083	0.05113469
41	0.02988011	0.03610165	0.04303266	0.05063246
42	0.02930478	0.03554762	0.04251372	0.05015913
43	0.02875659	0.03502083	0.04202195	0.04971262
44	0.02823369	0.03451940	0.04155547	0.04929105
45	0.02773440	0.03404164	0.04111257	0.04889268
46	0.02725718	0.03358600	0.04069169	0.04851595
47	0.02680061	0.03315107	0.04029141	0.04815943
48	0.02636340	0.03273555	0.03991042	0.04782178
49	0.02594438	0.03233824	0.03954752	0.04750180
50	0.02554244	0.03195805	0.03920159	0.04719838

Table XI–continued

CAPITAL RECOVERY FACTOR OF 1 AT CONTINUOUSLY COMPOUNDED NOMINAL INTEREST RATES

n	6%	8%	10%	12%
1	1.06183655	1.08328707	1.10517092	1.12749685
2	0.54684105	0.56329773	0.58019173	0.59753280
3	0.37538169	0.39033713	0.40578052	0.42172302
4	0.28980610	0.30413283	0.31900914	0.33444726
5	0.23858369	0.25263006	0.26729127	0.28258010
6	0.20453756	0.21847702	0.23309759	0.24841191
7	0.18030609	0.19423701	0.20891507	0.22435195
8	0.16220843	0.17619152	0.19098683	0.20660409
9	0.14819961	0.16227459	0.17722538	0.19305873
10	0.13705262	0.15124650	0.16637794	0.18244962
11	0.12798658	0.14231824	0.15764707	0.17397052
12	0.12048089	0.13496371	0.15050093	0.16708359
13	0.11417510	0.12881861	0.14457115	0.16146222
14	0.10881170	0.12362264	0.13959450	0.15670203
15	0.10420186	0.11918486	0.13537778	0.15274552
16	0.10020391	0.11536201	0.13177604	0.14939992
17	0.09670950	0.11204449	0.12867833	0.14655294
18	0.09363435	0.10914703	0.12599830	0.14411718
19	0.09091190	0.10660225	0.12366773	0.14202363
20	0.08848889	0.10435623	0.12163202	0.14021706
21	0.08632218	0.10236529	0.11984695	0.13865280
22	0.08437648	0.10059370	0.11827631	0.13729435
23	0.08262263	0.09901188	0.11689019	0.13611160
24	0.08103629	0.09759520	0.11566369	0.13507951
25	0.07959705	0.09632296	0.11457588	0.13417714

Table XI–continued

CAPITAL RECOVERY FACTOR OF 1 AT CONTINUOUSLY COMPOUNDED NOMINAL INTEREST RATES

n	6%	8%	10%	12%
26	0.07828759	0.09517763	0.11360907	0.13338684
27	0.07709319	0.09414427	0.11274822	0.13269365
28	0.07600119	0.09321007	0.11198046	0.13208485
29	0.07500070	0.09236401	0.11129471	0.13154955
30	0.07408226	0.09159652	0.11068142	0.13107840
31	0.07323764	0.09089927	0.11013229	0.13066334
32	0.07245963	0.09026498	0.10964009	0.13029741
33	0.07174190	0.08968726	0.10919850	0.12997457
34	0.07107884	0.08916049	0.10880200	0.12968957
35	0.07046550	0.08867968	0.10844569	0.12943785
36	0.06989748	0.08824042	0.10812530	0.12921540
37	0.06937085	0.08783878	0.10783703	0.12901875
38	0.06888210	0.08747125	0.10757751	0.12884483
39	0.06841806	0.08713469	0.10734376	0.12869098
40	0.06800590	0.08682630	0.10713313	0.12855483
41	0.06761307	0.08654355	0.10694325	0.12843431
42	0.06724723	0.08628417	0.10677203	0.12832761
43	0.06690631	0.08604611	0.10661756	0.12823313
44	0.06658838	0.08582751	0.10647819	0.12814944
45	0.06639172	0.08562671	0.10635239	0.12807531
46	0.06601474	0.08544217	0.10623881	0.12800964
47	0.06575599	0.08527253	0.10613626	0.12795145
48	0.06551417	0.08511653	0.10604363	0.12789988
49	0.06528805	0.08497303	0.10595996	0.12785418
50	0.06507652	0.08484098	0.10588436	0.12781367

Table XI—continued

CAPITAL RECOVERY FACTOR OF 1 AT CONTINUOUSLY COMPOUNDED NOMINAL INTEREST RATES

n	14%	16%	18%	20%
1	1.15027380	1.17351087	1.19721736	1.22140276
2	0.61533085	0.63359599	0.65233847	0.67156876
3	0.43817584	0.45515035	0.47265797	0.49071026
4	0.35045936	0.36705752	0.38425374	0.40205993
5	0.29850896	0.31508988	0.33233448	0.35025401
6	0.26443178	0.28116816	0.29863117	0.31683017
7	0.24055781	0.25754143	0.27531021	0.29387028
8	0.22305075	0.24033218	0.25845176	0.27741109
9	0.20977824	0.22738459	0.24587588	0.26524795
10	0.19946004	0.21740398	0.23627303	0.25605620
11	0.19128078	0.20956555	0.22880883	0.24899184
12	0.18469640	0.20331883	0.22292637	0.24349184
13	0.17932985	0.19828232	0.21823990	0.23916651
14	0.17491157	0.19418334	0.21447384	0.23573800
15	0.17124369	0.19082184	0.21142638	0.23300331
16	0.16817775	0.18804786	0.20894653	0.23081113
17	0.16560019	0.18574690	0.20691933	0.22904680
18	0.16342273	0.18383013	0.20525599	0.22762224
19	0.16157573	0.18222771	0.20388700	0.22646905
20	0.16000363	0.18088411	0.20275745	0.22553355
21	0.15866156	0.17975470	0.20182352	0.22477336
22	0.15751298	0.17880335	0.20105000	0.22415478
23	0.15652788	0.17800058	0.20040844	0.22365086
24	0.15568143	0.17732216	0.19987569	0.22323997
25	0.15495297	0.17674813	0.19943286	0.22290468

Table XI–continued

CAPITAL RECOVERY FACTOR OF 1 AT CONTINUOUSLY COMPOUNDED NOMINAL INTEREST RATES

n	14%	16%	18%	20%
26	0.15432520	0.17626189	0.19906449	0.22263092
27	0.15378355	0.17584966	0.19875783	0.22240728
28	0.15331575	0.17549988	0.19850242	0.22222451
29	0.15291137	0.17520293	0.19828958	0.22207510
30	0.15256155	0.17495067	0.19811215	0.22195292
31	0.15225872	0.17473628	0.19796420	0.22185299
32	0.15199644	0.17455401	0.19784078	0.22177124
33	0.15176915	0.17439899	0.19773781	0.22170436
34	0.15157211	0.17426710	0.19765189	0.22164963
35	0.15140122	0.17415487	0.19758018	0.22160484
36	0.15125297	0.17405935	0.19752032	0.22156818
37	0.15112433	0.17397804	0.19747035	0.22153817
38	0.15101267	0.17390881	0.19742863	0.22151362
39	0.15091573	0.17384985	0.19739380	0.22149351
40	0.15083155	0.17379965	0.19736471	0.22147706
41	0.15075845	0.17375689	0.19734042	0.22146358
42	0.15069496	0.17372047	0.19732014	0.22145256
43	0.15063980	0.17368945	0.19730320	0.22144353
44	0.15059189	0.17366302	0.19728906	0.22143614
45	0.15055026	0.17364051	0.19727724	0.22143008
46	0.15051408	0.17362133	0.19726738	0.22142513
47	0.15048265	0.17360499	0.19725914	0.22142108
48	0.15045533	0.17359107	0.19725225	0.22141775
49	0.15043159	0.17357920	0.19724651	0.22141504
50	0.15041096	0.17356910	0.19724170	0.22141281

Table XI–continued

CAPITAL RECOVERY FACTOR OF 1 AT CONTINUOUSLY COMPOUNDED NOMINAL INTEREST RATES

n	22%	24%	26%	28%
1	1.24607673	1.27124915	1.29693009	1.32312981
2	0.69129750	0.71153550	0.73229379	0.75358359
3	0.50931887	0.52849556	0.54825218	0.56860073
4	0.42048794	0.43954954	0.45925642	0.47962019
5	0.36885934	0.38816100	0.40816916	0.42889370
6	0.33577375	0.35546982	0.37592562	0.39714783
7	0.31322659	0.33338308	0.35434273	0.37610776
8	0.29721022	0.31784786	0.33932161	0.36162821
9	0.28549478	0.30660885	0.32858157	0.35140361
10	0.27674045	0.29831135	0.32075360	0.34405161
11	0.27009392	0.29209330	0.31496791	0.33844224
12	0.26498650	0.28738123	0.31064740	0.33475771
13	0.26102533	0.28378007	0.30739614	0.33184143
14	0.25793105	0.28101011	0.30493535	0.32967084
15	0.25550039	0.27886889	0.30306470	0.32804910
16	0.25358263	0.27720733	0.30163792	0.32683396
17	0.25206429	0.27591416	0.30054694	0.32592153
18	0.25085888	0.27490536	0.29971111	0.32523530
19	0.24989982	0.27411698	0.29906981	0.32471858
20	0.24913545	0.27349999	0.29857721	0.32432914
21	0.24852540	0.27301659	0.29819849	0.32403542
22	0.24803798	0.27263754	0.29790714	0.32381379
23	0.24764820	0.27234010	0.29768288	0.32364648
24	0.24733627	0.27210659	0.29751019	0.32352015
25	0.24708652	0.27192318	0.29737718	0.32342474

Table XI–continued

CAPITAL RECOVERY FACTOR OF 1 AT CONTINUOUSLY COMPOUNDED NOMINAL INTEREST RATES

n	22%	24%	26%	28%
26	0.24688645	0.27177908	0.29727470	0.32335266
27	0.24672612	0.27166583	0.29719573	0.32329821
28	0.24659761	0.27157682	0.29713487	0.32325707
29	0.24649457	0.27150684	0.29708796	0.32322598
30	0.24641194	0.27145181	0.29705180	0.32320249
31	0.24634567	0.27140854	0.29702392	0.32318474
32	0.24629251	0.27137452	0.29700243	0.32317132
33	0.24624987	0.27134776	0.29698587	0.32316118
34	0.24621566	0.27132671	0.29697310	0.32315352
35	0.24618821	0.27131016	0.29696325	0.32314773
36	0.24616619	0.27129714	0.29695565	0.32314336
37	0.24614852	0.27128690	0.29694980	0.32314005
38	0.24613434	0.27128843	0.29694529	0.32313755
39	0.24612296	0.27127251	0.29694181	0.32313566
40	0.24611383	0.27126752	0.29693912	0.32313423
41	0.24610650	0.27126360	0.29693705	0.32313315
42	0.24610062	0.27126052	0.29693546	0.32313234
43	0.24609590	0.27125809	0.29693423	0.32313172
44	0.24609212	0.27125618	0.29693328	0.32313125
45	0.24608908	0.27125468	0.29693255	0.32313090
46	0.24608664	0.27125350	0.29693199	0.32313064
47	0.24608468	0.27125257	0.29693155	0.32313043
48	0.24608311	0.27125184	0.29693122	0.32313029
49	0.24608185	0.27125127	0.29693096	0.32313017
50	0.24608084	0.27125082	0.29693076	0.32313008

Table XI—continued

CAPITAL RECOVERY FACTOR OF 1 AT CONTINUOUSLY COMPOUNDED NOMINAL INTEREST RATES

n	30%	32%	34%	36%
1	1.34985881	1.37712776	1.40494759	1.43332942
2	0.77541629	0.79780351	0.82075707	0.84428898
3	0.58955329	0.61112205	0.63331934	0.65615760
4	0.50065242	0.52236461	0.54477682	0.56787469
5	0.45034418	0.47252991	0.49545996	0.51914321
6	0.41914262	0.44191568	0.46547236	0.48981770
7	0.39867970	0.42205960	0.44624811	0.47124566
8	0.38476379	0.40872407	0.43350460	0.45910094
9	0.37506526	0.39955679	0.42486870	0.45099202
10	0.36818990	0.39315357	0.41892861	0.44550219
11	0.36325687	0.38863102	0.41480081	0.44175056
12	0.35968679	0.38541165	0.41191198	0.43917033
13	0.35708693	0.38310713	0.40988018	0.43738794
14	0.35518501	0.38145091	0.40844618	0.43615296
15	0.35378905	0.38025718	0.40743160	0.43529546
16	0.35276195	0.37939504	0.40671251	0.43469920
17	0.35200489	0.37877144	0.40620223	0.43428417
18	0.35144614	0.37831989	0.40583981	0.43399508
19	0.35103335	0.37799268	0.40558224	0.43379362
20	0.35072818	0.37775543	0.40539811	0.43365317
21	0.35050244	0.37758333	0.40526887	0.43355524
22	0.35033539	0.37745847	0.40517621	0.43348694
23	0.35021175	0.37736785	0.40511029	0.43343931
24	0.35012020	0.37730207	0.40506338	0.43340608
25	0.35005242	0.37725432	0.40503000	0.43338290

Table XI—continued

CAPITAL RECOVERY FACTOR OF 1 AT CONTINUOUSLY COMPOUNDED NOMINAL INTEREST RATES

n	30%	32%	34%	36%
26	0.35000222	0.37721965	0.40500624	0.43336673
27	0.34996504	0.37719449	0.40498934	0.43335545
28	0.34993750	0.37717621	0.40497730	0.43334758
29	0.34991710	0.37716294	0.40496874	0.43334209
30	0.34990199	0.37715331	0.40496264	0.43333825
31	0.34989080	0.37714631	0.40495830	0.43333558
32	0.34988250	0.37714123	0.40495522	0.43333372
33	0.34987636	0.37713754	0.40495302	0.43333242
34	0.34987181	0.37713487	0.40495145	0.43333151
35	0.34986844	0.37713292	0.40495034	0.43333088
36	0.34986594	0.37713151	0.40494955	0.43333043
37	0.34986409	0.37713048	0.40494898	0.43333013
38	0.34986272	0.37712974	0.40494858	0.43332991
39	0.34986171	0.37712920	0.40494830	0.43332976
40	0.34986096	0.37712881	0.40494809	0.43332966
41	0.34986040	0.37712852	0.40494795	0.43332958
42	0.34985999	0.37712831	0.40494785	0.43332953
43	0.34985968	0.37712816	0.40494778	0.43332950
44	0.34985946	0.37712805	0.40494772	0.43332947
45	0.34985929	0.37712797	0.40494768	0.43332946
46	0.34985916	0.37712792	0.40494766	0.43332944
47	0.34985907	0.37712788	0.40494764	0.43332943
48	0.34985900	0.37712784	0.40494762	0.43332943
49	0.34985895	0.37712782	0.40494761	0.43332942
50	0.34985891	0.37712781	0.40494760	0.43332942

Table XI–continued

CAPITAL RECOVERY FACTOR OF 1 AT CONTINUOUSLY COMPOUNDED NOMINAL INTEREST RATES

n	38%	40%	45%	50%
1	1.46228459	1.49182470	1.56831219	1.64872127
2	0.86841149	0.89313704	0.95767295	1.02636194
3	0.67964939	0.70380742	0.76720177	0.83504499
4	0.59169541	0.61624176	0.68085711	0.75025759
5	0.54358835	0.56880394	0.63526905	0.70673349
6	0.51188451	0.54089344	0.60925766	0.68271147
7	0.49705253	0.52366905	0.59375589	0.66892033
8	0.48550885	0.51272448	0.58427680	0.66082470
9	0.47791847	0.50564068	0.57838910	0.65600887
10	0.47286290	0.50100085	0.57469649	0.65312197
11	0.46946673	0.49793805	0.57236649	0.65138333
12	0.46717217	0.49590588	0.57089066	0.65033329
13	0.46561588	0.49455293	0.56995359	0.64969805
14	0.46455756	0.49365015	0.56935770	0.64931337
15	0.46383657	0.49304684	0.56897839	0.64908027
16	0.46334480	0.49264325	0.56873680	0.64893897
17	0.46300910	0.49237309	0.56858286	0.64885329
18	0.46277981	0.49219216	0.56848474	0.64880134
19	0.46262314	0.49207096	0.56842220	0.64876983
20	0.46251606	0.49198974	0.56838233	0.64875072
21	0.46244286	0.49193532	0.56835691	0.64873913
22	0.46239281	0.49189884	0.56834070	0.64873211
23	0.46235859	0.49187440	0.56833037	0.64872784
24	0.46233519	0.49185801	0.56832378	0.64872526
25	0.46231919	0.49184703	0.56831958	0.64872369

Table XI–continued

CAPITAL RECOVERY FACTOR OF 1 AT CONTINUOUSLY COMPOUNDED NOMINAL INTEREST RATES

n	38%	40%	45%	50%
26	0.46230825	0.49183967	0.56831690	0.64872274
27	0.46230077	0.49183473	0.56831519	0.64872216
28	0.46229566	0.49183142	0.56831410	0.64872181
29	0.46239216	0.49182921	0.56831341	0.64872160
30	0.46228977	0.49182772	0.56831296	0.64872147
31	0.46228813	0.49182672	0.56831268	0.64872139
32	0.46228701	0.49182606	0.56831250	0.64872134
33	0.46228624	0.49182561	0.56831239	0.64872132
34	0.46228572	0.49182531	0.56831231	0.64872130
35	0.46228536	0.49182511	0.56831227	0.64872129
36	0.46228512	0.49182497	0.56831224	0.64872128
37	0.46228495	0.49182488	0.56831222	0.64872128
38	0.46228484	0.49182482	0.56831221	0.64872127
39	0.46228476	0.49182478	0.56831220	0.64872127
40	0.46228471	0.49182475	0.56831219	0.64872127
41	0.46228467	0.49182473	0.56831219	0.64872127
42	0.46228464	0.49182472	0.56831219	0.64872127
43	0.46228463	0.49182471	0.56831219	0.64872127
44	0.46228461	0.49182471	0.56831219	0.64872127
45	0.46228461	0.49182471	0.56831219	0.64872127
46	0.46228460	0.49182470	0.56831219	0.64872127
47	0.46228460	0.49182470	0.56831219	0.64872127
48	0.46228460	0.49182470	0.56831219	0.64872127
49	0.46228459	0.49182470	0.56831219	0.64872127
50	0.46228459	0.49182470	0.56831219	0.64872127

Table XII

SINKING FUND FACTOR OF 1 AT CONTINUOUSLY COMPOUNDED NOMINAL INTEREST RATES

n	1/8%	1/4%	1/2%	7/12%	n
1	1.00000000	1.00000000	1.00000000	1.00000000	1
2	0.49968750	0.49937500	0.49875000	0.49854167	2
3	0.33291675	0.33250035	0.33166806	0.33139079	3
4	0.24953145	0.24906328	0.24812814	0.24781677	4
5	0.19950031	0.19900125	0.19800502	0.19767350	5
6	0.16614627	0.16562674	0.16459030	0.16424560	6
7	0.14232199	0.14178795	0.14072324	0.14036934	7
8	0.12445381	0.12390899	0.12282347	0.12246285	8
9	0.11055637	0.11000325	0.10890189	0.10853622	9
10	0.09943844	0.09887876	0.09776504	0.09739548	10
11	0.09034198	0.08977699	0.08865346	0.08828085	11
12	0.08276161	0.08219228	0.08106082	0.08068580	12
13	0.07634748	0.07577453	0.07463659	0.07425965	13
14	0.07084967	0.07027367	0.06913042	0.06875193	14
15	0.06608491	0.06550633	0.06435868	0.06397895	15
16	0.06191577	0.06133497	0.06018366	0.05980295	16
17	0.05823713	0.05765442	0.05650007	0.05611858	17
18	0.05496725	0.05438288	0.05326005	0.05284390	18
19	0.05204157	0.05145577	0.05029679	0.04991422	19
20	0.04940848	0.04882142	0.04766071	0.04727779	20
21	0.04702617	0.04643801	0.04527589	0.04489272	21
22	0.04486044	0.04427132	0.04310805	0.04272474	22
23	0.04288305	0.04229308	0.04112890	0.04074552	23
24	0.04107046	0.04047974	0.03931486	0.03893147	24
25	0.03940288	0.03881151	0.03764611	0.03726278	25

Table XII–continued

SINKING FUND FACTOR OF 1 AT CONTINUOUSLY COMPOUNDED NOMINAL INTEREST RATES

n	1/8%	1/4%	1/2%	7/12%
26	0.03786358	0.03727165	0.03610588	0.03572266
27	0.03643832	0.03584589	0.03467990	0.03429684
28	0.03511487	0.03452200	0.03335592	0.03297306
29	0.03388271	0.03328946	0.03212340	0.03174077
30	0.03273269	0.03213911	0.03097318	0.03059083
31	0.03165688	0.03106302	0.02989730	0.02951526
32	0.03064832	0.03005422	0.02888880	0.02850709
33	0.02970089	0.02910658	0.02794154	0.02756019
34	0.02880919	0.02821472	0.02705013	0.02666916
35	0.02796846	0.02737386	0.02620978	0.02582920
36	0.02717444	0.02657974	0.02541622	0.02503607
37	0.02642336	0.02582857	0.02466568	0.02428596
38	0.02571180	0.02511696	0.02395475	0.02357548
39	0.02503675	0.02441875	0.02328038	0.02290159
40	0.02439545	0.02380059	0.02263983	0.02226152
41	0.02378545	0.02319057	0.02203063	0.02165282
42	0.02320449	0.02260965	0.02145054	0.02107324
43	0.02265057	0.02205576	0.02089753	0.02052075
44	0.02212182	0.02152708	0.02036975	0.01999350
45	0.02161659	0.02102192	0.01986552	0.01948980
46	0.02113333	0.02053875	0.01938330	0.01900813
47	0.02067063	0.02007615	0.01892169	0.01854708
48	0.02022722	0.01963286	0.01847940	0.01810536
49	0.01980192	0.01920768	0.01805525	0.01768178
50	0.01939363	0.01879952	0.01764814	0.01727525

Table XII–continued

SINKING FUND FACTOR OF 1 AT CONTINUOUSLY COMPOUNDED NOMINAL INTEREST RATES

n	2/3%	3/4%	5/6%	11/12%
1	1.00000000	1.00000000	1.00000000	1.00000000
2	0.49833334	0.49812501	0.49791668	0.49770835
3	0.33111360	0.33083648	0.33055945	0.33028249
4	0.24750558	0.24719457	0.24688373	0.24657308
5	0.19734226	0.19701131	0.19668063	0.19635204
6	0.16390129	0.16355736	0.16321383	0.16287070
7	0.14001594	0.13966304	0.13931064	0.13895874
8	0.12210285	0.12174347	0.12138469	0.12102654
9	0.10817128	0.10780707	0.10744358	0.10708083
10	0.09702676	0.09665889	0.09629186	0.09592567
11	0.08790920	0.08753851	0.08716877	0.08680000
12	0.08031185	0.07993897	0.07956717	0.07919644
13	0.07388389	0.07350932	0.07313594	0.07276374
14	0.06837475	0.06799886	0.06762428	0.06725101
15	0.06360065	0.06322376	0.06284829	0.06247424
16	0.05942377	0.05904613	0.05867002	0.05829544
17	0.05573873	0.05536054	0.05498399	0.05460910
18	0.05246356	0.05208498	0.05170817	0.05133312
19	0.04953353	0.04915471	0.04877778	0.04840273
20	0.04689687	0.04651794	0.04614101	0.04576608
21	0.04451167	0.04413274	0.04375591	0.04338120
22	0.04234365	0.04196480	0.04158817	0.04121377
23	0.04036448	0.03998578	0.03960942	0.03923542
24	0.03855054	0.03817207	0.03779606	0.03742251
25	0.03688202	0.03650384	0.03612823	0.03575520

Table XII–continued

SINKING FUND FACTOR OF 1 AT CONTINUOUSLY COMPOUNDED NOMINAL INTEREST RATES

n	2/3%	3/4%	5/6%	11/12%
26	0.03534213	0.03496429	0.03458914	0.03421668
27	0.03391658	0.03359128	0.03316448	0.03279264
28	0.03259312	0.03221610	0.03184200	0.03147082
29	0.03136119	0.03098464	0.03061112	0.03024064
30	0.03021163	0.02983558	0.02946269	0.02909294
31	0.02913648	0.02876097	0.02838872	0.02801974
32	0.02812875	0.02775380	0.02738223	0.02701405
33	0.02718233	0.02680796	0.02643710	0.02606973
34	0.02629179	0.02591804	0.02554790	0.02518136
35	0.02545235	0.02507923	0.02470984	0.02434416
36	0.02465976	0.02428729	0.02391866	0.02355386
37	0.02391020	0.02353840	0.02317055	0.02280665
38	0.02320030	0.02282918	0.02246213	0.02209914
39	0.02256981	0.02215656	0.02179032	0.02142827
40	0.02188752	0.02151781	0.02115240	0.02079128
41	0.02127943	0.02091045	0.02054585	0.02018571
42	0.02070047	0.02033222	0.01996850	0.01960930
43	0.02014861	0.01978111	0.01941826	0.01906003
44	0.01962200	0.01925527	0.01889328	0.01853604
45	0.01911897	0.01875300	0.01839189	0.01803564
46	0.01863796	0.01827277	0.01791255	0.01755730
47	0.01817758	0.01781317	0.01745385	0.01709961
48	0.01773653	0.01737292	0.01701450	0.01666128
49	0.01731364	0.01695082	0.01659332	0.01624112
50	0.01690781	0.01654580	0.01618921	0.01583804

Table XII—continued

SINKING FUND FACTOR OF 1 AT CONTINUOUSLY COMPOUNDED NOMINAL INTEREST RATES

n	1%	2%	3%	4%
1	1.00000000	1.00000000	1.00000000	1.00000000
2	0.49750002	0.49500017	0.49250056	0.49000133
3	0.33000561	0.32668933	0.32338482	0.32009241
4	0.24626259	0.24255074	0.23886499	0.23520586
5	0.19602013	0.19208105	0.18818350	0.18432821
6	0.16252795	0.15844580	0.15442116	0.15045494
7	0.13860735	0.13443022	0.13032689	0.12629839
8	0.12066900	0.11642694	0.11227513	0.10821472
9	0.10671881	0.10243185	0.09825170	0.09417956
10	0.09556032	0.09124249	0.08704807	0.08297829
11	0.08643218	0.08209366	0.07789518	0.07383796
12	0.07882679	0.07447522	0.07028033	0.06624326
13	0.07239274	0.06803400	0.06384855	0.05983742
14	0.06687904	0.06251772	0.05834632	0.05436562
15	0.06210161	0.05774141	0.05358768	0.04964097
16	0.05792241	0.05356630	0.04943321	0.04552331
17	0.05423586	0.04988631	0.04577625	0.04190544
18	0.05095985	0.04661890	0.04253386	0.03870399
19	0.04802956	0.04369893	0.03964056	0.03585314
20	0.04539314	0.04107427	0.03704396	0.03330021
21	0.04300860	0.03870274	0.03470165	0.03100258
22	0.04084160	0.03654980	0.03257893	0.02892535
23	0.03886375	0.03458695	0.03064713	0.02703971
24	0.03705142	0.03279042	0.02888237	0.02532163
25	0.03538475	0.03114025	0.02726458	0.02375092

Table XII–continued

SINKING FUND FACTOR OF 1 AT CONTINUOUSLY COMPOUNDED NOMINAL INTEREST RATES

n	1%	2%	3%	4%
26	0.03384691	0.02961953	0.02577677	0.02231052
27	0.03242361	0.02821389	0.02440447	0.02098586
28	0.03110257	0.02691099	0.02313529	0.01976448
29	0.02987320	0.02570019	0.02195854	0.01863562
30	0.02872635	0.02457229	0.02086494	0.01758996
31	0.02765402	0.02351925	0.01984643	0.01661938
32	0.02664924	0.02253404	0.01889595	0.01571676
33	0.02570585	0.02161051	0.01800728	0.01487587
34	0.02481844	0.02074320	0.01717495	0.01409118
35	0.02398221	0.01992729	0.01639411	0.01335781
36	0.02319290	0.01915848	0.01566044	0.01267142
37	0.02244671	0.01843296	0.01497009	0.01202812
38	0.02174022	0.01774731	0.01431963	0.01142447
39	0.02107038	0.01709845	0.01370596	0.01085733
40	0.02043445	0.01648361	0.01312629	0.01032392
41	0.01982994	0.01590031	0.01257813	0.00982169
42	0.01925461	0.01534628	0.01205919	0.00934836
43	0.01870642	0.01481949	0.01156741	0.00890185
44	0.01818353	0.01431806	0.01110093	0.00848027
45	0.01768424	0.01384030	0.01065803	0.00808191
46	0.01720701	0.01338466	0.01023716	0.00770518
47	0.01675044	0.01294973	0.00983688	0.00734865
48	0.01631324	0.01253421	0.00945589	0.00701101
49	0.01589421	0.01213690	0.00909298	0.00669103
50	0.01549227	0.01175671	0.00874706	0.00638761

Table XII–continued

SINKING FUND FACTOR OF 1 AT CONTINUOUSLY COMPOUNDED NOMINAL INTEREST RATES

n	6%	8%	10%	12%
1	1.00000000	1.00000000	1.00000000	1.00000000
2	0.48500450	0.48001066	0.47502081	0.47003595
3	0.31354514	0.30705006	0.30060961	0.29422616
4	0.22796955	0.22084576	0.21383822	0.20695041
5	0.17674715	0.16934300	0.16212035	0.15508325
6	0.14270101	0.13518995	0.12792667	0.12091506
7	0.11846954	0.11094994	0.10374416	0.09685510
8	0.10037188	0.09290446	0.08581592	0.07910723
9	0.08636306	0.07898752	0.07205446	0.06556188
10	0.07521607	0.06795943	0.06120702	0.05495277
11	0.06615004	0.05903118	0.05247615	0.04647367
12	0.05864435	0.05167665	0.04530008	0.03958674
13	0.05233855	0.04553154	0.03940024	0.03391937
14	0.04697516	0.04033557	0.03442358	0.02920518
15	0.04236532	0.03589779	0.03020687	0.02524866
16	0.03836736	0.03207494	0.02660512	0.02190307
17	0.03487296	0.02875743	0.02350741	0.01905609
18	0.03179781	0.02585996	0.02082738	0.01662033
19	0.02907536	0.02331518	0.01849681	0.01452677
20	0.02665234	0.02106916	0.01646110	0.01272020
21	0.02448563	0.01907823	0.01467603	0.01115595
22	0.02253994	0.01730663	0.01310539	0.00977499
23	0.02078608	0.01572481	0.01171928	0.00861474
24	0.01919975	0.01430814	0.01049277	0.00758266
25	0.01776050	0.01303590	0.00940496	0.00668029

Table XII–continued

SINKING FUND FACTOR OF 1 AT CONTINUOUSLY COMPOUNDED NOMINAL INTEREST RATES

n	6%	8%	10%	12%
26	0.01645105	0.01189056	0.00843815	0.00588999
27	0.01525664	0.01085720	0.00757730	0.00519680
28	0.01416464	0.00992300	0.00680954	0.00458800
29	0.01316415	0.00907694	0.00612379	0.00405270
30	0.01224572	0.00830945	0.00551050	0.00358155
31	0.01140110	0.00761220	0.00491372	0.00316649
32	0.01062309	0.00697791	0.00446917	0.00280056
33	0.00990535	0.00640020	0.00402759	0.00247772
34	0.00924229	0.00587343	0.00363108	0.00219272
35	0.00862895	0.00539262	0.00327478	0.00194100
36	0.00806094	0.00495336	0.00295439	0.00171855
37	0.00753431	0.00455171	0.00266611	0.00152190
38	0.00704555	0.00418418	0.00240659	0.00134798
39	0.00659151	0.00384762	0.00217284	0.00119413
40	0.00616936	0.00353923	0.00196221	0.00105797
41	0.00577652	0.00325648	0.00177236	0.00093746
42	0.00541069	0.00299710	0.00160111	0.00083076
43	0.00506976	0.00275904	0.00144665	0.00073628
44	0.00475183	0.00254045	0.00130727	0.00065259
45	0.00445517	0.00233964	0.00118147	0.00057846
46	0.00417819	0.00215511	0.00106790	0.00051279
47	0.00391945	0.00198546	0.00096534	0.00045459
48	0.00367762	0.00182946	0.00087271	0.00040303
49	0.00345150	0.00168596	0.00078904	0.00035733
50	0.00323997	0.00155392	0.00071344	0.00031682

Table XII–continued

SINKING FUND FACTOR OF 1 AT CONTINUOUSLY COMPOUNDED NOMINAL INTEREST RATES

n	14%	16%	18%	20%
1	1.00000000	1.00000000	1.00000000	1.00000000
2	0.46505705	0.46008512	0.45512111	0.45016600
3	0.28790204	0.28163947	0.27544060	0.26930750
4	0.20018557	0.19354665	0.18703637	0.18065717
5	0.14823516	0.14157901	0.13511711	0.12885125
6	0.11415798	0.10765729	0.10141381	0.09542741
7	0.09028402	0.18403057	0.07809285	0.07246752
8	0.07277695	0.06682131	0.06123440	0.05600833
9	0.05950444	0.05387372	0.04865852	0.04384519
10	0.04918624	0.04389311	0.03905567	0.03465344
11	0.04100699	0.03605468	0.03159146	0.02758908
12	0.03442260	0.02980796	0.02570901	0.02208908
13	0.02905605	0.02477145	0.02102253	0.01776375
14	0.02463777	0.02067247	0.01725648	0.01433524
15	0.02096989	0.01731097	0.01420902	0.01160055
16	0.01790395	0.01453699	0.01172916	0.00940837
17	0.01532639	0.01223603	0.00970197	0.00764404
18	0.01314893	0.01031926	0.00803862	0.00621949
19	0.01130194	0.00871684	0.00666964	0.00506629
20	0.00972983	0.00737323	0.00554009	0.00413079
21	0.00838776	0.00624383	0.00460616	0.00337061
22	0.00723918	0.00529248	0.00383264	0.00275202
23	0.00625408	0.00448970	0.00319107	0.00224810
24	0.00540763	0.00381129	0.00265832	0.00183721
25	0.00467917	0.00323725	0.00221550	0.00150192

Table XII–continued

SINKING FUND FACTOR OF 1 AT CONTINUOUSLY COMPOUNDED NOMINAL INTEREST RATES

n	14%	16%	18%	20%
26	0.00405140	0.00275101	0.00184712	0.00122816
27	0.00350975	0.00233878	0.00154047	0.00100452
28	0.00304195	0.00198901	0.00128505	0.00082176
29	0.00263757	0.00169206	0.00107222	0.00067234
30	0.00228775	0.00143980	0.00089479	0.00055017
31	0.00198493	0.00122541	0.00074683	0.00045024
32	0.00172264	0.00104314	0.00062342	0.00036849
33	0.00149535	0.00088811	0.00052045	0.00030160
34	0.00129831	0.00075623	0.00043453	0.00024687
35	0.00112742	0.00064400	0.00036282	0.00020208
36	0.00097917	0.00054848	0.00030296	0.00016542
37	0.00085053	0.00046717	0.00025299	0.00013542
38	0.00073887	0.00039793	0.00021127	0.00011086
39	0.00064193	0.00033898	0.00017644	0.00009075
40	0.00055775	0.00028878	0.00014735	0.00007430
41	0.00048465	0.00024602	0.00012306	0.00006083
42	0.00042116	0.00020960	0.00010278	0.00004980
43	0.00036601	0.00017858	0.00008584	0.00004077
44	0.00031809	0.00015215	0.00007170	0.00003338
45	0.00027646	0.00012964	0.00005988	0.00002733
46	0.00024028	0.00011046	0.00005001	0.00002237
47	0.00020885	0.00009412	0.00004177	0.00001832
48	0.00018153	0.00008020	0.00003489	0.00001500
49	0.00015779	0.00006833	0.00002914	0.00001228
50	0.00013716	0.00005823	0.00002434	0.00001005

Table XII–continued

SINKING FUND FACTOR OF 1 AT CONTINUOUSLY COMPOUNDED NOMINAL INTEREST RATES

n	22%	24%	26%	28%
1	1.00000000	1.00000000	1.00000000	1.00000000
2	0.44522076	0.44028635	0.43536371	0.43045378
3	0.26324214	0.25724640	0.25132210	0.24547092
4	0.17444112	0.16830039	0.16232633	0.15649038
5	0.12278261	0.11691185	0.11123907	0.10576388
6	0.08969702	0.08422067	0.07899553	0.07401802
7	0.06714986	0.06213393	0.05741265	0.05297794
8	0.05113349	0.04659871	0.04239152	0.03849840
9	0.03941805	0.03535970	0.03165149	0.02827380
10	0.03066372	0.02706219	0.02382352	0.02092180
11	0.02401719	0.02084415	0.01803782	0.01531243
12	0.01890977	0.01613208	0.01371731	0.01162790
13	0.01494860	0.01253092	0.01046606	0.00871162
14	0.01185432	0.00976096	0.00800527	0.00654103
15	0.00942366	0.00761974	0.00613461	0.00491929
16	0.00750590	0.00595818	0.00470783	0.00370414
17	0.00598756	0.00466501	0.00361685	0.00279172
18	0.00478216	0.00365621	0.00278102	0.00210549
19	0.00382309	0.00286783	0.00213972	0.00158877
20	0.00305872	0.00225084	0.00164712	0.00119932
21	0.00244867	0.00176744	0.00126840	0.00090561
22	0.00196125	0.00138839	0.00097705	0.00068398
23	0.00157147	0.00109095	0.00075279	0.00051667
24	0.00125954	0.00085744	0.00058010	0.00039034
25	0.00100979	0.00067403	0.00044709	0.00029493

Table XII—continued

SINKING FUND FACTOR OF 1 AT CONTINUOUSLY COMPOUNDED NOMINAL INTEREST RATES

n	22%	24%	26%	28%
26	0.00080972	0.00052993	0.00034461	0.00022285
27	0.00064939	0.00041668	0.00026564	0.00016840
28	0.00052088	0.00032767	0.00020478	0.00012726
29	0.00041784	0.00025769	0.00015787	0.00009617
30	0.00033521	0.00020266	0.00012171	0.00007268
31	0.00026894	0.00015939	0.00009384	0.00005493
32	0.00021578	0.00012537	0.00007235	0.00004151
33	0.00017314	0.00009861	0.00005578	0.00003137
34	0.00013893	0.00007756	0.00004301	0.00002371
35	0.00011148	0.00006101	0.00003316	0.00001792
36	0.00008946	0.00004799	0.00002557	0.00001354
37	0.00007179	0.00003775	0.00001971	0.00001024
38	0.00005761	0.00002969	0.00001520	0.00000774
39	0.00004623	0.00002336	0.00001172	0.00000585
40	0.00003710	0.00001837	0.00000904	0.00000442
41	0.00002977	0.00001445	0.00000697	0.00000334
42	0.00002389	0.00001137	0.00000537	0.00000252
43	0.00001917	0.00000894	0.00000414	0.00000191
44	0.00001539	0.00000703	0.00000319	0.00000144
45	0.00001235	0.00000553	0.00000246	0.00000109
46	0.00000991	0.00000435	0.00000190	0.00000082
47	0.00000795	0.00000342	0.00000146	0.00000062
48	0.00006382	0.00000269	0.00000113	0.00000047
49	0.00000512	0.00000212	0.00000087	0.00000036
50	0.00000411	0.00000167	0.00000067	0.00000027

Table XII–continued

SINKING FUND FACTOR OF 1 AT CONTINUOUSLY COMPOUNDED NOMINAL INTEREST RATES

n	30%	32%	34%	36%
1	1.00000000	1.00000000	1.00000000	1.00000000
2	0.42555748	0.42067575	0.41580948	0.41095957
3	0.23969448	0.23399429	0.22837175	0.22282818
4	0.15079361	0.14523685	0.13982064	0.13454528
5	0.10048537	0.09540214	0.09051237	0.08581380
6	0.06928381	0.06478792	0.06052477	0.05648829
7	0.04888209	0.04493183	0.04130052	0.03791624
8	0.03490498	0.03159631	0.02855701	0.02577152
9	0.02520645	0.02242903	0.01992111	0.01766260
10	0.01833110	0.01600258	0.01398102	0.01217278
11	0.01339806	0.01150326	0.00985322	0.00842114
12	0.00982788	0.00828388	0.00696439	0.00584091
13	0.00722812	0.00597937	0.00493259	0.00405853
14	0.00532620	0.00432314	0.00349859	0.00282354
15	0.00393024	0.00312942	0.00248401	0.00196605
16	0.00290314	0.00226727	0.00176492	0.00136979
17	0.00214608	0.00164367	0.00125464	0.00095475
18	0.00158733	0.00119213	0.00089222	0.00066567
19	0.00117455	0.00086491	0.00063465	0.00046420
20	0.00086937	0.00062766	0.00045152	0.00032376
21	0.00064363	0.00045557	0.00032128	0.00022583
22	0.00047659	0.00033070	0.00022862	0.00015753
23	0.00035294	0.00024008	0.00016270	0.00010989
24	0.00026139	0.00017430	0.00011579	0.00007666
25	0.00019361	0.00012655	0.00008241	0.00005348

Table XII–continued

SINKING FUND FACTOR OF 1 AT CONTINUOUSLY COMPOUNDED NOMINAL INTEREST RATES

n	30%	32%	34%	36%
26	0.00014341	0.00009189	0.00005865	0.00003731
27	0.00010623	0.00006672	0.00004175	0.00002603
28	0.00007869	0.00004845	0.00002971	0.00001816
29	0.00005829	0.00003518	0.00002115	0.00001267
30	0.00004318	0.00002554	0.00001505	0.00000884
31	0.00003199	0.00001855	0.00001071	0.00000617
32	0.00002370	0.00001347	0.00000763	0.00000430
33	0.00001755	0.00000978	0.00000543	0.00000300
34	0.00001300	0.00000710	0.00000386	0.00000209
35	0.00000963	0.00000516	0.00000275	0.00000146
36	0.00000714	0.00000374	0.00000196	0.00000102
37	0.00000529	0.00000272	0.00000139	0.00000071
38	0.00000392	0.00000197	0.00000099	0.00000050
39	0.00000290	0.00000143	0.00000071	0.00000035
40	0.00000215	0.00000104	0.00000050	0.00000024
41	0.00000159	0.00000076	0.00000036	0.00000017
42	0.00000118	0.00000055	0.00000025	0.00000012
43	0.00000087	0.00000040	0.00000018	0.00000008
44	0.00000065	0.00000029	0.00000013	0.00000006
45	0.00000048	0.00000021	0.00000009	0.00000004
46	0.00000036	0.00000015	0.00000007	0.00000003
47	0.00000026	0.00000011	0.00000005	0.00000002
48	0.00000020	0.00000008	0.00000003	0.00000001
49	0.00000014	0.00000006	0.00000002	0.00000001
50	0.00000011	0.00000004	0.00000002	0.00000001

Table XII–continued

SINKING FUND FACTOR OF 1 AT CONTINUOUSLY COMPOUNDED NOMINAL INTEREST RATES

n	38%	40%	45%	50%
1	1.00000000	1.00000000	1.00000000	1.00000000
2	0.40612690	0.40131234	0.38936077	0.37754067
3	0.21736480	0.21198272	0.19888959	0.18632372
4	0.12941082	0.12441707	0.11254492	0.10153632
5	0.08130376	0.07697924	0.06695687	0.05801222
6	0.04959992	0.04906875	0.04094547	0.03399020
7	0.03476794	0.03184435	0.02544370	0.02019966
8	0.02322426	0.02089978	0.01596462	0.01210343
9	0.01563388	0.01381599	0.01007691	0.00728760
10	0.01057831	0.00917615	0.00638430	0.00440070
11	0.00718214	0.00611335	0.00405431	0.00266205
12	0.00488758	0.00408118	0.00257847	0.00161202
13	0.00333129	0.00272823	0.00164141	0.00097678
14	0.00227297	0.00182545	0.00104551	0.00059210
15	0.00155198	0.00122214	0.00066621	0.00035900
16	0.00106021	0.00081856	0.00042461	0.00021769
17	0.00072451	0.00054839	0.00027067	0.00013202
18	0.00049522	0.00036746	0.00017256	0.00008007
19	0.00033855	0.00024626	0.00011002	0.00004856
20	0.00023147	0.00016504	0.00007014	0.00002945
21	0.00015827	0.00011062	0.00004472	0.00001786
22	0.00010822	0.00007415	0.00002852	0.00001083
23	0.00007400	0.00004970	0.00001818	0.00000657
24	0.00005060	0.00003331	0.00001159	0.00000399
25	0.00003461	0.00002233	0.00000739	0.00000242

Table XII–continued

SINKING FUND FACTOR OF 1 AT CONTINUOUSLY COMPOUNDED NOMINAL INTEREST RATES

n	38%	40%	45%	50%
26	0.00002366	0.00001497	0.00000471	0.00000147
27	0.00001618	0.00001003	0.00000301	0.00000089
28	0.00001107	0.00000673	0.00000192	0.00000054
29	0.00000757	0.00000451	0.00000122	0.00000033
30	0.00000518	0.00000302	0.00000078	0.00000020
31	0.00000354	0.00000203	0.00000050	0.00000012
32	0.00000242	0.00000136	0.00000032	0.00000007
33	0.00000166	0.00000091	0.00000020	0.00000004
34	0.00000113	0.00000061	0.00000013	0.00000003
35	0.00000077	0.00000041	0.00000008	0.00000002
36	0.00000053	0.00000027	0.00000005	0.00000001
37	0.00000036	0.00000018	0.00000003	0.00000000
38	0.00000025	0.00000012	0.00000002	0.00000000
39	0.00000017	0.00000008	0.00000001	0.00000000
40	0.00000012	0.00000006	0.00000001	0.00000000
41	0.00000008	0.00000004	0.00000001	0.00000000
42	0.00000005	0.00000002	0.00000000	0.00000000
43	0.00000004	0.00000002	0.00000000	0.00000000
44	0.00000003	0.00000001	0.00000000	0.00000000
45	0.00000002	0.00000001	0.00000000	0.00000000
46	0.00000001	0.00000001	0.00000000	0.00000000
47	0.00000001	0.00000000	0.00000000	0.00000000
48	0.00000001	0.00000000	0.00000000	0.00000000
49	0.00000000	0.00000000	0.00000000	0.00000000
50	0.00000000	0.00000000	0.00000000	0.00000000

Table XIII

FACTORS TO CONVERT A GRADIENT SERIES TO AN EQUIVALENT UNIFORM SERIES

n	½%	1%	2%	3%	n
1	0.00000000	0.00000000	0.00000000	0.00000000	1
2	0.49875292	0.49751239	0.49504949	0.49261083	2
3	0.99667486	0.99336652	0.98679910	0.98029700	3
4	1.49376557	1.48756241	1.47524946	1.46306064	4
5	1.99002496	1.98010019	1.96040147	1.94090477	5
6	2.48545320	2.47097997	2.44225630	2.41383324	6
7	2.98005024	2.96020195	2.92081536	2.88185079	7
8	3.47381609	3.44776636	3.39608035	3.34496298	8
9	3.96675083	3.93367343	3.86805318	3.80317623	9
10	4.45885450	4.41792345	4.33673607	4.25649780	10
11	4.95012710	4.90051671	4.80213145	4.70493579	11
12	5.44056869	5.38145359	5.26424203	5.14849914	12
13	5.93017933	5.86073443	5.72307076	5.58719762	13
14	6.41895905	6.33835966	6.17862087	6.02104180	14
15	6.90690795	6.81432972	6.63089581	6.45004310	15
16	7.39402602	7.28864509	7.07989931	6.87421373	16
17	7.88031339	7.76130626	7.52563532	7.29356669	17
18	8.36577008	8.23231379	7.96810806	7.70811580	18
19	8.85039620	8.70166824	8.40732201	8.11787564	19
20	9.33419180	9.16937022	8.84328187	8.52286160	20
21	9.81715698	9.63542036	9.27599261	8.92308981	21
22	10.29929181	10.09981935	9.70545942	9.31857715	22
23	10.78059637	10.56256787	10.13168775	9.70934128	23
24	11.26107078	11.02366666	10.55468330	10.09540057	24
25	11.74071513	11.48311650	10.97445198	10.47677413	25

Table XIII–continued

FACTORS TO CONVERT A GRADIENT SERIES TO AN EQUIVALENT UNIFORM SERIES

n	½%	1%	2%	3%
26	12.21952950	11.94091817	11.39099997	10.85348178
27	12.69751402	12.39707251	11.80433366	11.22554404
28	13.17466878	12.85158039	12.21445971	11.59298213
29	13.65099391	13.30444269	12.62138497	11.95581793
30	14.12648952	13.75566035	13.02511656	12.31407401
31	14.60115573	14.20523432	13.42566180	12.66777359
32	15.07499267	14.65316560	13.82302826	13.01694051
33	15.54800046	15.09945520	14.21722373	13.36159925
34	16.02017924	15.54410419	14.60825620	13.70177491
35	16.49152916	15.98711364	14.99613392	14.03749317
36	16.96205035	16.42848467	15.38086532	14.36878031
37	17.43174296	16.86821844	15.76245909	14.69566318
38	17.90060714	17.30631612	16.14092410	15.01816917
39	18.36864303	17.74277892	16.51626943	15.33632623
40	18.83585081	18.17760809	16.88850441	15.65016281
41	19.30223063	18.61080490	17.25763852	15.95970790
42	19.76778267	19.04237065	17.62368150	16.26499095
43	20.23250708	19.47230668	17.98664326	16.56604193
44	20.69640405	19.90061436	18.34653392	16.86289123
45	21.15947376	20.32729508	18.70336378	17.15556972
46	21.62171639	20.75235027	19.05714337	17.44410868
47	22.08313212	21.17578139	19.40788337	17.72853982
48	22.54372114	21.59758993	19.75559469	18.00889525
49	23.00348366	22.01777740	20.10028839	18.28520744
50	23.46241987	22.43634536	20.44197574	18.55750926
75	34.66793965	32.37933915	28.04343886	24.16342483
100	45.36126127	41.34256875	33.98628231	27.84444701

Table XIII—continued

FACTORS TO CONVERT A GRADIENT SERIES TO AN EQUIVALENT UNIFORM SERIES

n	4%	6%	8%	10%
1	0.00000000	0.00000000	0.00000000	0.00000000
2	0.49019608	0.48543689	0.48076923	0.47619048
3	0.97385956	0.96117603	0.94873223	0.93655589
4	1.45099546	1.42723384	1.40395978	1.38116785
5	1.92161081	1.88363330	1.84647159	1.81012596
6	2.38571462	2.33040382	2.27634603	2.22355718
7	2.84331789	2.76758123	2.69366488	2.62161502
8	3.29443359	3.19520765	3.09852394	3.00447859
9	3.73907664	3.61333142	3.49103272	3.37235148
10	4.17726392	4.02200696	3.87131391	3.72546051
11	4.60901420	4.42129468	4.23950296	4.06405438
12	5.03434819	4.81126079	4.59574746	4.38840219
13	5.45328846	5.19197718	4.94020666	4.69879191
14	5.86585943	5.56352123	5.27305076	4.99552875
15	6.27208736	5.92597568	5.59446032	5.27893347
16	6.67200031	6.27942838	5.90462560	5.54934069
17	7.06562811	6.62397213	6.20374581	5.80709715
18	7.45300234	6.95970450	6.49202842	6.05256000
19	7.83415626	7.28672755	6.76968847	6.28609504
20	8.20912484	7.60514767	7.03694779	6.50807505
21	8.57794465	7.91507534	7.29403429	6.71887814
22	8.94065390	8.21662487	7.54118120	6.91888615
23	9.29729233	8.50991420	7.77862637	7.10848309
24	9.64790120	8.79506467	8.00661152	7.28805368
25	9.99252326	9.07220075	8.22538155	7.45798195

Table XIII–continued

FACTORS TO CONVERT A GRADIENT SERIES TO AN EQUIVALENT UNIFORM SERIES

n	4%	6%	8%	10%
26	10.33120270	9.34144979	8.43518383	7.61864997
27	10.66398508	9.60294182	8.63626753	7.77043659
28	10.99091735	9.85680929	8.82888299	7.91371632
29	11.31204771	10.10318680	9.01328105	8.04885833
30	11.62742565	10.34221092	9.18971248	8.17622552
31	11.93710187	10.57401989	9.35842739	8.29617366
32	12.24112821	10.79875341	9.51967471	8.40905065
33	12.53955764	11.01655244	9.67370163	8.51519592
34	12.83244420	11.22755892	9.82075319	8.61493982
35	13.11984293	11.43191560	9.96107176	8.70860321
36	13.40180984	11.62976577	10.09489667	8.79649703
37	13.67840187	11.82125312	10.22246382	8.87892202
38	13.94967682	12.00652146	10.34400535	8.95616851
39	14.21569329	12.18571458	10.45974927	9.02851623
40	14.47651068	12.35889761	10.56991925	9.09623423
41	14.73218908	12.52644901	10.67473431	9.15958086
42	14.98278927	12.68827602	10.77440862	9.21880375
43	15.22837263	12.84459890	10.86915135	9.27413994
44	15.46900113	12.99555854	10.95916642	9.32581594
45	15.70473725	13.14129479	11.04465246	9.37404789
46	16.13269515	13.28194628	11.12580263	9.41904178
47	16.16178458	13.41765031	11.20280459	9.46099363
48	16.38322293	13.54854272	11.27584039	9.50008974
49	16.60002309	13.67475777	11.34508648	9.53650697
50	16.81224944	13.79642802	11.41071365	9.57041298
75	20.82062214	15.70582938	12.26577471	9.94098649
100	22.97999991	16.37107286	12.45451985	9.99274290

Table XIII—continued

FACTORS TO CONVERT A GRADIENT SERIES TO AN EQUIVALENT UNIFORM SERIES

n	12%	14%	16%	18%
1	0.00000000	0.00000000	0.00000000	0.00000000
2	0.47169811	0.46728972	0.46296296	0.45871560
3	0.92460882	0.91289685	0.90141488	0.89015788
4	1.35885212	1.33700619	1.31562326	1.29469620
5	1.77459450	1.73987334	1.70595682	1.67283773
6	2.17204741	2.12182162	2.07287987	2.02521791
7	2.55146541	2.48323828	2.41694538	2.35258891
8	2.91314391	2.82457007	2.73878700	2.65580627
9	3.25741668	3.14631818	3.03911012	2.93581436
10	3.58465299	3.44903280	3.31868231	3.19363104
11	3.89525461	3.73330725	3.57832334	3.43033195
12	4.18965257	3.99977198	3.81889500	3.64703496
13	4.46830386	4.24908839	4.04129106	3.84488503
14	4.73168795	4.48194267	4.24642734	4.02503991
15	4.98030338	4.69903968	4.43523234	4.18865701
16	5.21466426	4.90109714	4.60863838	4.33688143
17	5.43529694	5.08883992	4.76757350	4.47083551
18	5.64273662	5.26299480	4.91295408	4.59160985
19	5.83752422	5.42428552	5.04567840	4.70025588
20	6.02020333	5.57342834	5.16662095	4.79777987
21	6.19131732	5.71112797	5.27662780	4.88513840
22	6.35140671	5.83807400	5.37651265	4.96323517
23	6.50100672	5.95493787	5.46705384	5.03291894
24	6.64064498	6.06237018	5.54899207	5.09498258
25	6.77083962	6.16099858	5.62302886	5.15016304

Table XIII–continued

FACTORS TO CONVERT A GRADIENT SERIES TO AN EQUIVALENT UNIFORM SERIES

n	12%	14%	16%	18%
26	6.89209741	6.25142605	5.68982567	5.19914208
27	7.00491226	6.33422952	5.75000354	5.24254763
28	7.10976388	6.40995904	5.80414328	5.28095573
29	7.20711670	6.47913711	5.85278606	5.31489274
30	7.29741895	6.54225845	5.89643437	5.34483795
31	7.38110195	6.59979000	5.93555327	5.37122634
32	7.45857965	6.65217118	5.97057184	5.39445141
33	7.53024819	6.69981434	6.00188479	5.41486813
34	7.59648580	6.74310540	6.02985429	5.43279583
35	7.65765270	6.78240466	6.05481175	5.44852103
36	7.63834753	6.81804766	6.07705970	5.46230020
37	7.76612569	6.85034619	6.09687371	5.47436240
38	7.81406339	6.87958937	6.11450421	5.48491177
39	7.85819422	6.90604470	6.13017835	5.49412990
40	7.89879147	6.92995927	6.14410178	5.50217798
41	7.93611228	6.95156085	6.15646030	5.50919888
42	7.97039813	6.97105904	6.16742154	5.51531900
43	8.00187547	6.98864642	6.17713647	5.52065000
44	8.03075628	7.00449964	6.18574085	5.52529040
45	8.05723872	7.01878051	6.19335660	5.52932695
46	8.08150776	7.03163700	6.20009302	5.53283599
47	8.10373582	7.04320430	6.20604803	5.53588461
48	8.12408342	7.05360572	6.21130920	5.53853166
49	8.14269980	7.06295361	6.21595477	5.54082876
50	8.15972354	7.07135022	6.22005457	5.54282110
75	8.31806478	7.13880933	6.24890171	5.55525083
100	8.33213603	7.14265320	6.24996417	5.55554907

Table XIII–continued

FACTORS TO CONVERT A GRADIENT SERIES TO AN EQUIVALENT UNIFORM SERIES

n	20%	22%	25%	30%
1	0.00000000	0.00000000	0.00000000	0.00000000
2	0.45454545	0.45045045	0.44444444	0.43478261
3	0.87912088	0.86829900	0.85245902	0.82706767
4	1.27421759	1.25417975	1.22493225	1.17827703
5	1.64050742	1.60895603	1.56306521	1.49030753
6	1.97882762	1.93369741	1.86833203	1.76544740
7	2.29016258	2.22965248	2.14243372	2.00628181
8	2.57562310	2.49821826	2.38724780	2.21559453
9	2.83642423	2.74090810	2.60477675	2.39627252
10	3.07386216	2.95931900	2.79709750	2.55121868
11	3.28929132	3.15509987	2.96631427	2.68327675
12	3.48410211	3.32992166	3.11451630	2.79517053
13	3.65969993	3.48545017	3.24374170	2.88945812
14	3.81748613	3.62332220	3.35594777	2.96850073
15	3.95884101	3.74512532	3.45298815	3.03444456
16	4.08510920	3.85238151	3.53659639	3.08921380
17	4.19758752	3.94653443	3.60837543	3.13451260
18	4.29751528	4.02894033	3.66979233	3.17183377
19	4.38606695	4.10086212	3.72217730	3.20247216
20	4.46434693	4.16346636	3.76672624	3.22754101
21	4.53338642	4.21782264	3.80450607	3.24798987
22	4.59414195	4.26490497	3.83646195	3.26462282
23	4.64749539	4.30559478	3.86342577	3.27811642
24	4.69425524	4.34068517	3.88612545	3.28903661
25	4.73515888	4.37088589	3.90519451	3.29785427

Table XIII—continued

FACTORS TO CONVERT A GRADIENT SERIES TO AN EQUIVALENT UNIFORM SERIES

n	20%	22%	25%	30%
26	4.77087557	4.39682907	3.92118161	3.30495938
27	4.80201004	4.41907511	3.93455978	3.31067346
28	4.82910643	4.43811879	3.94573516	3.31526058
29	4.85265246	4.45439522	3.95505513	3.31893685
30	4.87308373	4.46828569	3.96281577	3.32187856
31	4.89078799	4.48012326	3.96926865	3.32422906
32	4.90610932	4.49019788	3.97462689	3.32610462
33	4.91935213	4.49876135	3.99143049	3.32759932
34	4.93078507	4.50603170	3.98275121	3.32878908
35	4.94064459	4.51219729	3.98579655	3.32973505
36	4.94913831	4.51742044	3.98831354	3.33048641
37	4.95644816	4.52184079	3.99039176	3.33108260
38	4.96273321	4.52557817	3.99210607	3.33155523
39	4.96813230	4.52873527	3.99351894	3.33192958
40	4.97276636	4.53139992	3.99468238	3.33222585
41	4.97674057	4.53364710	3.99563967	3.33246013
42	4.98014627	4.53554077	3.99642673	3.33264526
43	4.98306263	4.53713538	3.99707337	3.33279145
44	4.98555823	4.53847722	3.99760428	3.33290680
45	4.98769235	4.53960561	3.99803989	3.33299778
46	4.98951618	4.54055392	3.99839708	3.33306948
47	4.99107390	4.54135039	3.99868980	3.33312596
48	4.99240356	4.54201896	3.99892954	3.33317042
49	4.99353792	4.54257986	3.99912580	3.33320540
50	4.99450516	4.54305019	3.99928637	3.33323292
75	4.99991361	4.54542954	3.99999596	3.33333312
100	4.99999879	4.54545431	3.99999998	3.33333333

Table XIII–continued

FACTORS TO CONVERT A GRADIENT SERIES TO AN EQUIVALENT UNIFORM SERIES

n	35%	40%	45%	50%
1	0.00000000	0.00000000	0.00000000	0.00000000
2	0.42553191	0.41666667	0.40816327	0.40000000
3	0.80287597	0.77981651	0.75782537	0.73684211
4	1.13412359	1.09234234	1.05280468	1.01538462
5	1.42202460	1.35798860	1.29796237	1.24170616
6	1.66983404	1.58109857	1.49881768	1.42255639
7	1.88114555	1.76635123	1.66116590	1.56483730
8	2.05972679	1.91851551	1.79074314	1.67517843
9	2.20936935	2.04224207	1.89296521	1.75963695
10	2.33376229	2.14190391	1.97275042	1.82352434
11	2.43639382	2.22148833	2.03442175	1.87134136
12	2.52048218	2.28453660	2.08167501	1.90679347
13	2.58893388	2.33412333	2.11759598	1.93285801
14	2.64432532	2.37286604	2.14470934	1.95187834
15	2.68890309	2.40295539	2.16504494	1.96566672
16	2.72459809	2.42619767	2.18021047	1.97560384
17	2.75304878	2.44406303	2.19146281	1.98272816
18	2.77562985	2.45773446	2.19977360	1.98781224
19	2.79348314	2.46815449	2.20588663	1.99142537
20	2.80754873	2.47606747	2.21036652	1.99398362
21	2.81859443	2.48205674	2.21363864	1.99578896
22	2.82724297	2.48657634	2.21602140	1.99705915
23	2.83399622	2.48997759	2.21775180	1.99795041
24	2.83925640	2.49253081	2.21900532	1.99857424
25	2.84334424	2.49444306	2.21991133	1.99900991

Table XIII—continued

FACTORS TO CONVERT A GRADIENT SERIES TO AN EQUIVALENT UNIFORM SERIES

n	35%	40%	45%	50%
26	2.84651434	2.49587225	2.22056480	1.99931355
27	2.84896794	2.49693835	2.22103523	1.99952477
28	2.85086358	2.49773218	2.22137330	1.99967145
29	2.85232570	2.49832232	2.22161586	1.99977314
30	2.85345171	2.49876035	2.22178962	1.99984355
31	2.85431762	2.49908503	2.22191393	1.99989222
32	2.85498263	2.49932538	2.22200275	1.99992583
33	2.85549272	2.49950307	2.22206613	1.99994901
34	2.85588351	2.49963430	2.22211131	1.99996498
35	2.85618258	2.49973110	2.22214348	1.99997596
36	2.85641220	2.49980244	2.22216637	1.99998352
37	2.85658585	2.49985497	2.22218263	1.99998871
38	2.85671911	2.49989361	2.22219418	1.99999227
39	2.85682071	2.49992200	2.22220237	1.99999471
40	2.85689811	2.49994286	2.22220818	1.99999638
41	2.85695703	2.49995817	2.22221230	1.99999753
42	2.85700185	2.49996939	2.22221521	1.99999831
43	2.85703592	2.49997762	2.22221727	1.99999885
44	2.85706180	2.49998364	2.22221873	1.99999921
45	2.85708145	2.49998805	2.22221976	1.99999946
46	2.85709636	2.49991273	2.22222049	1.99999964
47	2.85710767	2.49993631	2.22222100	1.99999975
48	2.85711624	2.49999535	2.22222136	1.99999983
49	2.85712273	2.49999661	2.22222162	1.99999989
50	2.85712764	2.49999753	2.22222180	1.99999992
75	2.85714285	2.49999999	2.22222222	2.00000000
100	2.85714286	2.50000000	2.22222222	2.00000000

Table XIV

NOMINAL RATES OF INTEREST FROM EFFECTIVE RATES (%)

Effective Rate	Nominal Rate when Converted n Times per Year					
	2	3	4	6	12	e^j
0.25	0.249844	0.249792	0.249766	0.249740	0.249714	0.249688
0.50	0.499376	0.499169	0.499065	0.498961	0.498875	0.498754
0.75	0.748599	0.748132	0.747899	0.747666	0.747433	0.747202
1.00	0.997512	0.996685	0.996271	0.995858	0.995445	0.995033
1.25	1.246118	1.244827	1.244183	1.243539	1.242895	1.242252
1.50	1.494417	1.492561	1.491635	1.490709	1.489785	1.488861
1.75	1.742410	1.739889	1.738631	1.737373	1.736118	1.734864
2.00	1.990099	1.986813	1.985172	1.983534	1.981896	1.980263
2.25	2.237484	2.233333	2.231261	2.229192	2.227125	2.234192
2.50	2.484567	2.479451	2.476898	2.474349	2.471803	2.469261
2.75	2.731349	2.725170	2.722087	2.719009	2.715936	2.726449
3.00	2.977831	2.970490	2.966829	2.963173	2.959523	2.955880
3.25	3.224014	3.215414	3.211125	3.206844	3.202571	3.217194
3.50	3.469899	3.459942	3.454978	3.450024	3.445076	3.440143
3.75	3.715488	3.704078	3.698390	3.692714	3.687049	3.681397
4.00	3.960780	3.947821	3.941362	3.934917	3.928486	3.922071
4.25	4.205779	4.191174	4.183897	4.176636	4.169392	4.162168
4.50	4.450483	4.434138	4.425996	4.417873	4.409769	4.401689
4.75	4.694895	4.676715	4.667661	4.658629	4.649620	4.640637
5.00	4.979015	4.918907	4.908893	4.898907	4.888947	4.879016
5.25	5.182845	5.160714	5.149696	5.138709	5.127752	5.116829
5.50	5.426386	5.402139	5.390069	5.378036	5.366037	5.354077
5.75	5.669638	5.643182	5.630016	5.616891	5.603805	5.590763
6.00	5.912603	5.883847	5.869538	5.855276	5.841058	5.826891
6.25	6.155281	6.124133	6.108637	6.093193	6.077802	6.062462

Table XIV–continued

NOMINAL RATES OF INTEREST FROM EFFECTIVE RATES (%)

Effective Rate	Nominal Rate when Converted n Times per Year					
	2	3	4	6	12	e^j
6.50	6.397674	6.364042	6.347313	6.330644	6.314033	6.297480
6.75	6.639783	6.603576	6.585571	6.567630	6.549756	6.531947
7.00	6.881608	6.842736	6.823410	6.804156	6.784974	6.765865
7.25	7.123152	7.081524	7.060832	7.040220	7.019688	6.999237
7.50	7.364414	7.319942	7.297840	7.275827	7.253903	7.232066
7.75	7.605395	7.557990	7.534435	7.510977	7.487618	7.464354
8.00	7.846097	7.779567	7.770619	7.745673	7.720836	7.696104
8.25	8.086520	8.032984	8.006393	7.979917	7.953560	7.927318
8.50	8.326666	8.269932	8.241758	8.213711	8.185792	8.157999
8.75	8.566536	8.506517	8.476718	8.447057	8.417533	8.388148
9.00	8.806130	8.742740	8.711272	8.679955	8.648787	8.617770
9.25	9.045450	9.822578	8.945424	8.912408	8.879555	8.846865
9.50	9.284495	9.214104	9.179173	9.144420	9.109840	9.075436
9.75	9.523268	9.449247	9.412524	9.375989	9.339643	9.303487
10.00	9.761770	9.684034	9.645475	9.607120	9.568967	9.531018
10.50	10.237960	10.152543	10.110190	10.068071	10.026187	9.984533
11.00	10.713075	10.619641	10.573331	10.527288	10.481513	10.436002
11.50	11.187120	11.085338	11.034909	10.984784	10.934961	10.885440
12.00	11.660105	11.549645	11.494938	11.440573	11.386550	11.332869
12.50	12.132034	12.012574	11.953428	11.894670	11.836295	11.778304
13.00	12.602916	12.474131	12.410394	12.347088	12.284213	12.221763
13.50	13.072757	12.934329	12.865845	12.797842	12.730316	12.663265
14.00	13.541565	13.393178	13.319793	13.246943	13.174620	13.102826
14.50	14.009346	13.850687	13.772252	13.694405	13.617144	13.540464
15.00	14.476106	14.306865	14.223231	14.140243	14.057899	13.976194

Table XIV–continued

NOMINAL RATES OF INTEREST FROM EFFECTIVE RATES (%)

Effective Rate	Nominal Rate when Converted n Times per Year					
	2	3	4	6	12	e^j
15.50	14.941852	14.761724	14.672740	14.584469	14.496901	14.410034
16.00	15.406592	15.215272	15.120794	15.027094	14.934165	14.842001
16.50	15.870331	15.667518	15.567401	15.468132	15.369703	15.272109
17.00	16.333076	16.118472	16.012574	15.907596	15.803533	15.700375
17.50	16.794834	16.568144	16.456320	16.345498	16.235665	16.126815
18.00	17.255610	17.016541	16.898654	16.781848	16.666115	16.551444
18.50	17.715411	17.463674	17.339584	17.216662	17.094897	16.974277
19.00	18.174242	17.909551	17.779120	17.649949	17.522023	17.395331
19.50	18.632111	18.354180	18.217274	18.081722	17.947507	17.814619
20.00	19.089023	18.797570	18.654056	18.511991	18.371364	18.232156
21.00	20.000000	19.680670	19.523539	19.368068	19.214241	19.062036
22.00	20.907220	20.558919	20.387650	20.218270	20.050756	19.885086
23.00	21.810730	21.432381	21.246465	21.062683	20.881010	20.701417
24.00	22.710574	22.301121	22.100059	21.901395	21.705097	21.511138
25.00	23.606798	23.165203	22.948505	22.734489	22.523116	22.314355
26.00	24.499443	24.024689	23.791876	23.562047	23.335160	23.111172
27.00	25.388553	24.879639	24.630242	24.384150	24.141316	23.901690
28.00	26.274170	25.730113	25.463672	25.200876	24.941673	24.686008
29.00	27.156334	26.576170	26.292232	26.012303	25.736321	25.464222
30.00	28.035085	27.417865	27.115988	26.818503	26.525340	26.236427
32.00	29.782506	29.088392	28.749349	28.415524	28.086828	27.763174
34.00	31.516738	30.742131	30.364253	29.992504	29.626777	29.266961

Table XIV–continued

NOMINAL RATES OF INTEREST FROM EFFECTIVE RATES (%)

Effective Rate i_e	Nominal Rate when Converted n Times per Year					
	2	3	4	6	12	e^j
36.00	33.238076	32.379495	31.961179	31.549993	31.145802	30.748470
38.00	34.946802	34.000884	33.540588	33.088509	32.644483	32.208350
40.00	36.643191	35.606682	35.102922	34.608555	34.123386	33.647224
42.00	38.327505	37.197259	36.648606	36.110612	35.583048	35.065687
44.00	40.000000	38.772970	38.178046	37.595141	37.023983	36.464311
46.00	41.660919	40.334158	39.691637	39.062586	38.446691	37.843644
48.00	43.310501	41.881153	41.189756	40.513374	39.851644	39.204209
50.00	44.948974	43.414273	42.672768	41.947916	41.239299	40.546511
55.00	48.997992	47.188358	46.316472	45.465745	44.635605	43.825493
60.00	52.982212	50.882128	49.87306	48.890247	47.932928	47.000363
65.00	56.904652	54.499725	53.347241	52.226701	51.137115	50.077529
70.00	60.768096	58.044957	56.743338	55.479938	54.153503	53.062825
75.00	64.575131	61.521339	60.065326	58.654390	57.286975	55.961579
80.00	68.328157	64.932120	63.316873	61.754141	60.242016	58.778667
85.00	72.029410	68.280308	66.501370	64.782949	63.122748	61.518564
90.00	75.680975	71.568698	69.621954	67.744290	65.932974	64.185389
95.00	79.284801	74.799893	72.681542	70.641388	68.676212	66.782937
99.00	82.134720	77.345301	75.087124	72.914825	70.824763	68.813464
125.00	100.000000	93.111209	89.897948	86.828545	83.895831	81.093022

Table XV

EFFECTIVE INTEREST RATES FROM NOMINAL RATES (%)

Nominal Rate	Effective Rate when Converted n Times per Year					
	2	4	6	12	52	e^j
$\frac{1}{4}$	0.2501563	0.2502345	0.2502606	0.2502867	0.2503067	0.2503128
1	1.0025000	1.0037563	1.0041759	1.0045961	1.0049196	1.0050167
2	2.0100000	2.0150501	2.0167409	2.0184356	2.0197417	2.0201340
3	3.0225000	3.0339191	3.0377509	3.0415957	3.0445620	3.0454534
4	4.0400000	4.0604010	4.0672622	4.0741543	4.0794770	4.0810774
5	5.0625000	5.0945337	5.1053313	5.1161898	5.1245842	5.1271096
6	6.0900000	6.1363551	6.1520151	6.1677812	6.1799819	6.1836547
7	7.1225000	7.1859031	7.2073705	7.2290081	7.2457696	7.2508181
8	8.1600000	8.2432160	8.2714551	8.2999507	8.3220474	8.3287068
9	9.2025000	9.3083319	9.3443264	9.3806898	9.4089166	9.4174284
10	10.2500000	10.3812891	10.4260424	10.4713067	10.5064793	10.5170918
11	11.3025000	11.4621259	11.5166614	11.5718836	11.6148386	11.6278070
12	12.3600000	12.5508810	12.6162419	12.6825030	12.7340987	12.7496852
13	13.4225000	13.6475928	13.7248427	13.8032482	13.8643647	13.8828383
14	14.4900000	14.7523001	14.8425229	14.9342029	15.0057425	15.0273799
15	15.5625000	15.8650415	15.9693418	16.0754518	16.1583394	16.1834243
16	16.6400000	16.9858560	17.1053592	17.2270798	17.3222633	17.3510871
17	17.7225000	18.1147825	18.2506351	18.3891728	18.4976234	18.5304851
18	18.8100000	19.2518601	19.4052297	19.5618171	19.6845300	19.7217363
19	19.9025000	20.3971278	20.5692035	20.7450998	20.8830940	20.9249598
20	21.0000000	21.5506250	21.7426174	21.9391085	22.0934278	22.1402758
21	22.1025000	22.7123909	22.9255326	23.1439315	23.3156447	23.3678060
22	23.2100000	23.8824651	24.1180106	24.3596578	24.5498590	24.6076731
23	24.3225000	25.0608869	25.3201130	25.5863770	25.7961861	25.8600010
24	25.4400000	26.2476960	26.5319018	26.8241795	27.0547426	27.1249150
25	26.5625000	27.4429321	27.7534396	28.0731561	28.3256461	28.4025417

Table XV–continued

EFFECTIVE INTEREST RATES FROM NOMINAL RATES (%)

Nominal Rate	Effective Rate when Converted n Times per Year					
	2	4	6	12	52	e^j
26	27.6900000	28.6466351	28.9847888	29.3333985	29.6090154	29.6930087
27	28.8225000	29.8588447	30.2260125	30.6049990	30.9049702	30.9964451
28	29.9600000	31.0796010	31.4771738	31.8880506	32.2136315	32.3129812
29	31.1025000	32.3089441	32.7383640	33.1826469	33.5351215	33.6427488
30	32.2500000	33.5469141	34.0095641	34.4888824	34.8695635	34.9858808
31	33.4025000	34.7935513	35.2909210	35.8068521	36.2170819	36.3425114
32	34.5600000	36.0488960	36.5824716	37.1366516	37.5778022	37.7127764
33	35.7225000	37.3129888	37.8842807	38.4783775	38.9518513	39.0968128
34	36.8900000	38.5858701	39.1964133	39.8321270	40.3393571	40.4947591
35	38.0625000	39.8675806	40.5189350	41.1979978	41.7404489	41.9067549
36	39.2400000	41.1581610	41.8519112	42.5760887	43.1552569	43.3329415
37	40.4225000	42.4576522	43.1954082	43.9664988	44.5839128	44.7734615
38	41.6100000	43.7660951	44.5494921	45.3693283	46.0265496	46.2284589
39	42.8025000	45.0835306	45.9142297	46.7846778	47.4833013	47.6980794
40	44.0000000	46.4100000	47.2896878	48.2126490	48.9543032	49.1824698
41	45.2025000	47.7455444	48.6759338	49.6533439	50.4396919	50.6817785
42	46.4100000	49.0902051	50.0730352	51.1068657	51.9396055	52.1961556
43	47.6225000	50.4440234	51.4810599	52.5733181	53.4541832	53.7257524
44	48.8400000	51.8070410	52.9000762	54.0528055	54.9835655	55.2707219
45	50.0625000	53.1792993	54.3301526	55.5454331	56.5278941	56.8312185
46	51.2900000	54.5608401	55.7713579	57.0513071	58.0873124	58.4073985
47	52.5225000	55.9517050	57.2237613	58.5705342	59.6619647	59.9994193
48	53.7600000	57.3519360	58.6874323	60.1032219	61.2519971	61.6074402
49	55.0025000	58.7615750	60.1624407	61.6494785	62.8575567	63.2316220
50	56.2500000	60.1806641	61.6488568	63.2094133	64.4787921	64.8721271

Table XV–continued

EFFECTIVE INTEREST RATES FROM NOMINAL RATES (%)

Nominal Rate	Effective Rate when Converted n Times per Year					
	2	4	6	12	52	e^j
55	62.5625000	67.4193384	69.2545286	71.2181330	72.8254076	73.3253018
60	69.0000000	74.9006250	77.1561000	79.5856326	81.5870306	82.2118800
65	75.5625000	82.6298853	85.3627097	88.3264646	90.7838718	91.5540829
70	82.2500000	90.6125391	93.8837066	97.4557108	100.4371053	101.3752707
75	89.0625000	98.8540649	102.7286530	106.9889992	110.5689140	111.7000017
80	96.0000000	107.3600000	111.9073273	116.9425213	121.2025365	122.5540928
85	103.0625000	116.1359399	121.4297280	127.3330504	132.3623159	133.9646852
90	110.2500000	125.1875391	131.3060766	138.1779599	144.0737516	145.9603111
95	117.5625000	134.5205103	141.5468205	149.4952423	156.3635529	158.5709659
99	123.5025000	142.1933516	150.0089477	158.9016751	166.6305727	169.1234472

Table XVI

CONTINUOUSLY COMPOUNDED RATES EQUIVALENT TO NOMINAL RATES (%)

Continuous Compounding	Equivalent Rates Compounded		
	Annually	Semi-Annually	Quarterly
0.1249803	0.1250585	0.1250192	0.1250000 (1/8)
0.1249609	0.1250390	0.1250000	0.1249803
0.1249219	0.1250000	0.1249608	0.1249414
0.1250000 (1/8)	0.1250781	0.1250390	0.1250194
0.2499218	0.2502344	0.2500779	0.2500000 (1/4)
0.2498438	0.2501563	0.2500000	0.2499216
0.2496880	0.2500000	0.2498437	0.2497657
0.2500000 (1/4)	0.2503128	0.2501562	0.2500780
0.2915601	0.2919856	0.2917725	0.2916667 (7/24)
0.2914540	0.2918792	0.2916667	0.2915599
0.2912421	0.2916667	0.2914541	0.2913479
0.2916667 (7/24)	0.2920923	0.2918791	0.2917726
0.3331943	0.3337501	0.3334718	0.3333333 (1/3)
0.3330556	0.3336109	0.3333333	0.3331940
0.3327789	0.3333333	0.3330558	0.3329170
0.3333333 (1/3)	0.3338895	0.3336109	0.3334719
0.4164496	0.4173180	0.4168833	0.4166667 (5/12)
0.4162331	0.4171006	0.4166667	0.4164497
0.4158010	0.4166667	0.4162334	0.4160171
0.4166667 (5/12)	0.4175358	0.4171007	0.4168835
0.4996876	0.5009382	0.5003120	0.5000000 (1/2)
0.4993760	0.5006250	0.5000000	0.4996875
0.4987541	0.5000000	0.4993762	0.4990650
0.5000000 (1/2)	0.5012521	0.5006234	0.5003104

Table XVI–continued

CONTINUOUSLY COMPOUNDED RATES EQUIVALENT TO NOMINAL RATES (%)

Continuous Compounding	Equivalent Rates Compounded		
	Annually	Semi-Annually	Quarterly
0.5829083	0.5846105	0.5837584	0.5833333 (7/12)
0.5824842	0.5841839	0.5833333	0.5829081
0.5816386	0.5833333	0.5824851	0.5820614
0.5833333 (7/12)	0.5850379	0.5841846	0.5837584
0.6245121	0.6264663	0.6254882	0.6250000 (5/8)
0.6240255	0.6259765	0.6250000	0.6245122
0.6230550	0.6250000	0.6240266	0.6235402
0.6250000 (5/8)	0.6269572	0.6297758	0.6254883
0.6661116	0.6683350	0.6672220	0.6666667 (2/3)
0.6655580	0.6677771	0.6666667	0.6661116
0.6644543	0.6666667	0.6655592	0.6650061
0.6666667 (2/3)	0.6688936	0.6677787	0.6672219
0.7492977	0.7521119	0.7507029	0.7500000 (3/4)
0.7485973	0.7514063	0.7500000	0.7492978
0.7472015	0.7500000	0.7485988	0.7478992
0.7500000 (3/4)	0.7528196	0.7514078	0.7507030
0.8740444	0.8778752	0.8759569	0.8750000 (7/8)
0.8730915	0.8769140	0.8750000	0.8740447
0.8711941	0.8750000	0.8730940	0.8721430
0.8750000 (7/8)	0.8788393	0.8769166	0.8759572
0.9987518	1.0037560	1.0012497	1.0000000 (1)
0.9975083	1.0025000	1.0000000	0.9987525
0.9950331	1.0000000	0.9975122	0.9962711
1.0000000 (1)	1.0050166	1.0025041	1.0012510
1.2480507	1.2558714	1.2519528	1.2500000 (1 1/4)
1.2461099	1.2539063	1.2500000	1.2480528
1.2422520	1.2500000	1.2461180	1.2441830
1.2500000 (1 1/4)	1.2578450	1.2539142	1.2519550

Table XVI–continued

CONTINUOUSLY COMPOUNDED RATES EQUIVALENT TO NOMINAL RATES (%)

Continuous Compounding	Equivalent Rates Compounded Annually	Semi-Annually	Quarterly
1.4971942	1.5084584	1.5028120	1.5000000 (1 1/2)
1.4944029	1.5056250	1.5000000	1.4971974
1.4888612	1.5000000	1.4944166	1.4916351
1.5000000 (1 1/2)	1.5113065	1.5056390	1.5028155
1.7461829	1.7615178	1.7538278	1.7500000 (1 3/4)
1.7423881	1.7576563	1.7500000	1.7461880
1.7348639	1.7500000	1.7424099	1.7386312
1.7500000 (1 3/4)	1.7654021	1.7576785	1.7538332
1.9950164	2.0150499	2.0049998	2.0000000 (2)
1.9900661	2.0100000	2.0000000	1.9950244
1.9802627	2.0000000	1.9900985	1.9851722
2.0000000 (2)	2.0201339	2.0100331	2.0050082
2.2436958	2.2690559	2.2563282	2.2500000 (2 1/4)
2.2374379	2.2626563	2.2500000	2.2437071
2.2250610	2.2500000	2.2374841	2.2312608
2.2500000 (2 1/4)	2.2755034	2.2627039	2.2563398
2.4922202	2.5235356	2.5078127	2.5000000 (2 1/2)
2.4845041	2.5156250	2.5000000	2.4922360
2.4692613	2.5000000	2.4845671	2.4768982
2.5000000 (2 1/2)	2.5315121	2.5156901	2.5078288
2.7405900	2.7784896	2.7594529	2.7500000 (2 3/4)
2.7312653	2.7689063	2.7500000	2.7406113
2.7128668	2.7500000	2.7313492	2.7220867
2.7500000 (2 3/4)	2.7881614	2.7689931	2.7594744
2.9888059	3.0339191	3.0112497	3.0000000 (3)
2.9777225	3.0225000	3.0000000	2.9888333
2.9558802	3.0000000	2.9778312	2.9668286
3.0000000 (3)	3.0454533	3.0226128	3.0112781

Table XVI–continued

CONTINUOUSLY COMPOUNDED RATES EQUIVALENT TO NOMINAL RATES (%)

Continuous Compounding	Equivalent Rates Compounded		
	Annually	Semi-Annually	Quarterly
3.2368680	3.2898244	3.2632032	3.2500000 (3 1/4)
3.2238764	3.2764063	3.2500000	3.2369028
3.1983047	3.2500000	3.2240144	3.2111248
3.2500000 (3 1/4)	3.3033893	3.2765498	3.2632390
3.4847762	3.5462060	3.5153121	3.5000000 (3 1/2)
3.4697277	3.5306250	3.5000000	3.4848199
3.4401428	3.5000000	3.4698994	3.4549783
3.5000000 (3 1/2)	3.5619708	3.5308043	3.5153571
3.7325310	3.8030648	3.7675780	3.7500000 (3 3/4)
3.7152771	3.7851563	3.7500000	3.7325845
3.6813973	3.7500000	3.7154877	3.6983905
3.7500000 (3 3/4)	3.8211996	3.7853769	3.7676329
3.9801323	4.0604010	4.0200000	4.0000000 (4)
3.9605254	4.0400000	4.0000000	3.9801970
3.9220713	4.0000000	3.9607803	3.9413623
4.0000000 (4)	4.0810773	4.0402675	4.0200664
4.2275804	4.3182152	4.2725778	4.2500000 (4 1/4)
4.2054735	4.2951563	4.2500000	4.2276582
4.1621676	4.2500000	4.2057786	4.1838971
4.2500000 (4 1/4)	4.3416055	4.2954774	4.2726576
4.4748756	4.5765084	4.5253121	4.5000000 (4 1/2)
4.4501218	4.5506250	4.5000000	4.4749680
4.4016886	4.5000000	4.4504830	4.4259961
4.5000000 (4 1/2)	4.6027860	4.5510068	4.5254077
4.7220181	4.8352811	4.7782028	4.7500000 (4 3/4)
4.6944713	4.8064063	4.7500000	4.7221262
4.6406373	4.7500000	4.6948949	4.6676606
4.7500000 (4 3/4)	4.8646201	4.8068553	4.7783148

Table XVI–continued

CONTINUOUSLY COMPOUNDED RATES EQUIVALENT TO NOMINAL RATES (%)

Continuous Compounding	Equivalent Rates Compounded		
	Annually	Semi-Annually	Quarterly
4.9690079	5.0945336	5.0312497	5.0000000 (5)
4.9385225	5.0625000	5.0000000	4.9691340
4.8790164	5.0000000	4.9390149	4.9088934
5.0000000 (5)	5.1271095	5.0630240	5.0313800
5.2158453	5.3542666	5.2844528	5.2500000 (5 1/4)
5.1822764	5.3189063	5.2500000	5.2159918
5.1168288	5.2500000	5.1828452	5.1496956
5.2500000 (5 1/4)	5.3902561	5.3195130	5.2846040
5.4625302	5.6144805	5.5378120	5.5000000 (5 1/2)
5.4257335	5.5756250	5.5000000	5.4626984
5.3540767	5.5000000	5.4263857	5.3900694
5.5000000 (5 1/2)	5.6540614	5.5763228	5.5379862
5.7090633	5.8751764	5.7913274	5.5750000 (5 3/4)
5.6688946	5.8326563	5.5750000	5.7092554
5.4251415	5.5750000	5.4993916	5.4620985
5.5750000 (5 3/4)	5.7333318	5.6534283	5.6140314
5.9554448	6.1363548	6.0450000	6.0000000 (6)
5.9117604	6.0900000	6.0000000	5.9556624
5.8268908	6.0000000	5.9126028	5.8695380
6.0000000 (6)	6.1836545	6.0909064	6.0452256
6.2016746	6.3980162	6.2988278	6.2500000 (6 1/4)
6.1543318	6.3476563	6.2500000	6.2019201
6.0624622	6.2500000	6.1552810	6.1086368
6.2500000 (6 1/4)	6.4494457	6.3486811	6.2990826
6.4477527	6.6601608	6.5528121	6.5000000 (6 1/2)
6.3966092	6.6056250	6.5000000	6.4480285
6.2974800	6.5000000	6.3976741	6.3473134
6.5000000 (6 1/2)	6.7159024	6.6067785	6.5530996

Table XVI—continued

CONTINUOUSLY COMPOUNDED RATES EQUIVALENT TO NOMINAL RATES (%)

Continuous Compounding	Equivalent Rates Compounded		
	Annually	Semi-Annually	Quarterly
6.6936797	6.9227898	6.8069531	6.7500000 (6 3/4)
6.6385935	6.8639063	6.7500000	6.6939878
6.5319467	6.7500000	6.6397830	6.5855708
6.7500000 (6 3/4)	6.9830259	6.8651984	6.8072747
6.9394553	7.1859032	7.0612498	7.0000000 (7)
6.8802853	7.1225000	7.0000000	6.9397986
6.7658648	7.0000000	6.8816082	6.8234096
7.0000000 (7)	7.2508180	7.1239414	7.0616083
7.1850801	7.4495018	7.3157028	7.2500000 (7 1/4)
7.1216855	7.3814063	7.2500000	7.1854610
6.9992371	7.2500000	7.1231515	7.0608322
7.2500000 (7 1/4)	7.5192805	7.3830085	7.3161014
7.4305543	7.7135866	7.5703124	7.5000000 (7 1/2)
7.3627946	7.6406250	7.5000000	7.4309753
7.2320662	7.5000000	7.3644135	7.2978405
7.5000000 (7 1/2)	7.7884150	7.6423992	7.5707538
7.6758777	7.9781577	7.8250780	7.7500000 (7 3/4)
7.6036134	7.9001563	7.7500000	7.6763422
7.4643543	7.7500000	7.6053947	7.5344349
7.7500000 (7 3/4)	8.0582232	7.9021146	7.8255650
7.9210508	8.2432159	8.0800000	8.0000000 (8)
7.8441426	8.1600000	8.0000000	7.9215606
7.6961041	8.0000000	7.8460968	7.7706186
8.0000000 (8)	8.3287065	8.1621543	8.0805351
8.1660737	8.5087617	8.3350777	8.2500000 (8 1/4)
8.0843830	8.4201563	8.2500000	8.1666326
7.9273181	8.2500000	8.0865203	8.0063926
8.2500000 (8 1/4)	8.5998671	8.4225199	8.3356656

Table XVI—continued

CONTINUOUSLY COMPOUNDED RATES EQUIVALENT TO NOMINAL RATES (%)

Continuous Compounding	Equivalent Rates Compounded Annually	Semi-Annually	Quarterly
8.4109473	8.7747966	8.5903128	8.5000000 (8 1/2)
8.3243350	8.6806250	8.5000000	8.4115571
8.1579987	8.5000000	8.3266663	8.2417577
8.5000000 (8 1/2)	8.8717065	8.6832108	8.5909548
8.6556704	9.0413198	8.8457033	8.7500000 (8 3/4)
8.5639940	8.9414063	8.7500000	8.6563344
8.3881484	8.7500000	8.5665361	8.4767176
8.7500000 (8 3/4)	9.1442264	8.9442282	8.8464042
8.9002440	9.3083324	9.1012504	9.0000000 (9)
8.8033771	9.2025000	9.0000000	8.9009658
8.6177696	9.0000000	8.8061300	8.7112719
9.0000000 (9)	9.4174283	9.2055718	9.1020133
9.1446677	9.5758346	9.3569529	9.2500000 (9 1/4)
9.0424685	9.4639063	9.2500000	9.1454504
8.8468648	9.2500000	9.0454495	8.9454235
9.2500000 (9 1/4)	9.6913140	9.4672422	9.3577819
9.3889427	9.8438281	9.6128125	9.5000000 (9 1/2)
9.2812746	9.7256250	9.5000000	9.3897897
9.0754364	9.5000000	9.2844952	9.1791729
9.5000000 (9 1/2)	9.9658854	9.7292402	9.6137106
9.6330682	10.1123125	9.8688281	9.7500000 (9 3/4)
9.5197958	9.9876563	9.7500000	9.6339829
9.3034866	9.7500000	9.5232684	9.4125239
9.7500000 (9 3/4)	10.2411442	9.9915657	9.8697995
9.8770450	10.3812891	10.1250000	10.0000000 (10)
9.7580328	10.2500000	10.0000000	9.8780306
9.5310180	10.0000000	9.7617696	9.6454756
10.0000000 (10)	10.5170918	10.2542193	10.1260482

Table XVI—continued

CONTINUOUSLY COMPOUNDED RATES EQUIVALENT TO NOMINAL RATES (%)

Continuous Compounding	Equivalent Rates Compounded		
	Annually	Semi-Annually	Quarterly
10.3645527	10.9207201	10.6378125	10.5000000 (10 1/2)
10.2336573	10.7756250	10.5000000	10.3656906
9.9845335	10.5000000	10.2379604	10.1101905
10.5000000 (10 1/2)	11.0710610	10.7805124	10.6390263
10.8514670	11.4621259	11.1512500	11.0000000 (11)
10.7081534	11.3025000	11.0000000	10.8527717
10.4360015	11.0000000	10.7130750	10.5733309
11.0000000 (11)	11.6278070	11.3081229	11.1526460
11.3377892	12.0055113	11.6653125	11.5000000 (11 1/2)
11.1815264	11.8306250	11.5000000	11.3392760
10.8854405	11.5000000	11.1871208	11.0349093
11.5000000 (11 1/2)	12.1873438	11.8370541	11.6669082
11.8235209	12.5508810	12.1800000	12.0000000 (12)
11.6537816	12.3600000	12.0000000	11.8252056
11.3328685	12.0000000	11.6601049	11.4949379
12.0000000 (12)	12.7496852	12.3673093	12.1818136
12.3086635	13.0982399	12.6953125	12.5000000 (12 1/2)
12.1249244	12.8906250	12.5000000	12.3105627
11.7783036	12.5000000	12.1320343	11.9534288
12.5000000 (12 1/2)	13.3148453	12.8988918	12.6973630
12.7932183	13.6475928	13.2112500	13.0000000 (13)
12.5949598	13.4225000	13.0000000	12.7953488
12.2217633	13.0000000	12.6029163	12.4103939
13.0000000 (13)	13.8828383	13.4318049	13.2135573
13.2771869	14.1989446	13.7278125	13.5000000 (13 1/2)
13.0638932	13.9556250	13.5000000	13.2795664
12.6632651	13.5000000	13.0727575	12.8658451
13.5000000 (13 1/2)	14.4536784	13.9660519	13.7303972

Table XVI—continued

CONTINUOUSLY COMPOUNDED RATES EQUIVALENT TO NOMINAL RATES (%)

Continuous Compounding	Equivalent Rates Compounded		
	Annually	Semi-Annually	Quarterly
13.7605707	14.7523001	14.2450000	14.0000000 (14)
13.5317297	14.4900000	14.0000000	13.7632173
13.1028262	14.0000000	13.5415650	13.3197939
14.0000000 (14)	15.0273799	14.5016363	14.2478835
14.2433710	15.3076641	14.7628125	14.5000000 (14 1/2)
13.9984744	15.0256250	14.5000000	14.2463035
13.5404637	14.5000000	14.0093456	13.7722519
14.5000000 (14 1/2)	15.6039570	15.0385612	14.7660171
14.7255893	15.8650415	15.2812500	15.0000000 (15)
14.4641323	15.5625000	15.0000000	14.7288271
13.9761942	15.0000000	14.4761059	14.2232305
15.0000000 (15)	16.1834243	15.5768302	15.2847988
15.6882853	16.9858560	16.3200000	16.0000000 (16)
15.3922082	16.6400000	16.0000000	15.6921938
14.8420005	16.0000000	15.4065923	15.1207943
16.0000000 (16)	17.3510871	16.6574135	16.3243097
16.6486699	18.1147825	17.3612500	17.0000000 (17)
16.3159974	17.7225000	17.0000000	16.6533331
15.7003749	17.0000000	16.3330765	16.0125734
17.0000000 (17)	18.5304851	17.7434133	17.3664226
17.6067542	19.2518601	18.4050000	18.0000000 (18)
17.2355393	18.8100000	18.0000000	17.6122604
16.5514439	18.0000000	17.2556098	16.8986542
18.0000000 (18)	19.7217363	18.8348567	18.4111440
18.5625491	20.3971278	19.4512500	19.0000000 (19)
18.1508727	19.9025000	19.0000000	18.5689907
17.3953307	19.0000000	18.1742423	17.7791209
19.0000000 (19)	20.9249598	19.9317710	19.4584804
19.5160657	21.5506250	20.5000000	20.0000000 (20)
19.0620360	21.0000000	20.0000000	19.5235393
18.2321557	20.0000000	19.0890230	18.6540558
20.0000000 (20)	22.1402758	21.0341836	20.5084386

Table XVI–continued

CONTINUOUSLY COMPOUNDED RATES EQUIVALENT TO NOMINAL RATES (%)

Continuous Compounding		Equivalent Rates Compounded			
		Annually	Semi-Annually	Quarterly	
21.4163068		23.8824651	22.6050000	22.0000000	(22)
20.8720031		23.2100000	22.0000000	21.4261501	
19.8850859		22.0000000	20.9072203	20.3876500	
22.0000000	(22)	24.6076731	23.2556141	22.6162459	
23.3075633		26.2476960	24.7200000	24.0000000	(24)
22.6657371		25.4400000	24.0000000	23.3202098	
21.5111380		24.0000000	22.7105745	22.1000588	
24.0000000	(24)	27.1249150	25.4993703	24.7346186	
25.1899197		28.6466351	26.8450000	26.0000000	(26)
24.4435266		27.6900000	26.0000000	25.2058325	
23.1111721		26.0000000	24.4994432	23.7918765	
26.0000000	(26)	29.6930087	27.7656767	26.8636098	
27.0634594		31.0796010	28.9800000	28.0000000	(28)
26.2056525		29.9600000	28.0000000	27.0831301	
24.6860078		28.0000000	26.2741700	25.4636718	
28.0000000	(28)	32.3129812	30.0547598	29.0032725	
28.9282646		33.5469141	31.1250000	30.0000000	(30)
27.9523885		32.2500000	30.0000000	28.9522118	
26.2364265		30.0000000	28.0350850	27.1159890	
30.0000000	(30)	34.9858808	32.3668485	31.1536604	
33.5525936		39.8675806	36.5312500	35.0000000	(35)
32.2536295		38.0625000	35.0000000	33.5896678	
30.0104593		35.0000000	32.3790008	31.1649344	
35.0000000	(35)	41.9067549	38.2492433	36.5769058	
38.1240719		46.4100000	42.0000000	40.0000000	(40)
36.4643114		44.0000000	40.0000000	38.1780460	
33.6472237		40.0000000	36.6431913	35.1029224	
40.0000000	(40)	49.1824698	44.2805516	42.0683672	

Table XVI–continued

CONTINUOUSLY COMPOUNDED RATES EQUIVALENT TO NOMINAL RATES (%)

Continuous Compounding		Equivalent Rates Compounded			
		Annually	Semi-Annually	Quarterly	
42.6438940		53.1792993	47.5312500	45.0000000	(45)
40.5881688		50.0625000	45.0000000	42.7188724	
37.1563556		45.0000000	40.8318916	38.9367987	
45.0000000	(45)	56.8312185	50.4645432	47.6289028	
47.1132143		60.1806641	53.1250000	50.0000000	(50)
44.6287103		56.2500000	50.0000000	47.2135955	
40.5465108		50.0000000	44.9489743	42.6727679	
50.0000000	(50)	64.8721271	56.8050833	53.2593812	

Table XVII

MONTHLY PAYMENTS NECESSARY TO AMORTIZE A LOAN OF $1

years	6%	7%	8%	9%	10%
1	0.08606643	0.08652675	0.08698843	0.08745148	0.08791589
1½	0.05823173	0.05868499	0.05914030	0.05959766	0.06005708
2	0.04432061	0.04477258	0.04522729	0.04568474	0.04614493
2½	0.03597892	0.03643191	0.03688832	0.03734816	0.03781141
3	0.03042194	0.03087710	0.03133637	0.03179973	0.03226719
3½	0.02645622	0.02691420	0.02737697	0.02784452	0.02831682
4	0.02348503	0.02394624	0.02441292	0.02488504	0.02536258
4½	0.02117686	0.02164157	0.02211242	0.02258938	0.02307241
5	0.01933280	0.01980120	0.02027639	0.02075836	0.02124704
6	0.01657289	0.01704901	0.01753324	0.01802554	0.01852584
7	0.01460855	0.01509268	0.01558621	0.01608908	0.01660118
8	0.01314143	0.01363372	0.01413668	0.01465020	0.01517416
9	0.01200575	0.01250628	0.01301871	0.01354291	0.01407869
10	0.01110205	0.01161085	0.01213276	0.01266758	0.01321507
11	0.01036703	0.01088410	0.01141545	0.01196080	0.01251988
12	0.00975850	0.01028381	0.01082453	0.01138031	0.01195078
13	0.00924723	0.00978074	0.01033074	0.01089681	0.01147848
14	0.00881236	0.00935401	0.00991318	0.01048938	0.01108203
15	0.00843857	0.00898828	0.00955652	0.01014267	0.01074605
16	0.00811438	0.00867208	0.00924925	0.00984516	0.01045902
17	0.00783101	0.00839661	0.00898257	0.00958804	0.01021210
18	0.00758162	0.00815502	0.00874963	0.00936445	0.00999844
19	0.00736083	0.00794192	0.00854501	0.00916897	0.00981259
20	0.00716431	0.00775299	0.00836440	0.00899726	0.00965022
25	0.00644300	0.00706779	0.00771816	0.00839196	0.00908701
30	0.00599551	0.00665303	0.00733765	0.00804623	0.00877572
35	0.00570190	0.00638856	0.00710261	0.00783993	0.00859672
40	0.00550214	0.00621431	0.00695312	0.00771262	0.00849146

Table XVIII

IMPLICIT PRICE DEFLATORS, GROSS NATIONAL PRODUCT, 1947–77 (1972 = 100)

	Quarters			
	I	II	III	IV
1947	48.470	49.000	49.860	51.420
1948	52.290	52.900	53.790	53.530
1949	52.980	52.490	52.430	52.440
1950	52.280	52.720	54.300	55.160
1951	56.890	57.180	57.200	57.800
1952	57.690	57.640	58.000	58.650
1953	58.730	58.880	59.080	58.810
1954	59.540	59.740	59.610	59.900
1955	60.440	60.760	61.180	61.500
1956	62.030	62.540	63.250	63.770
1957	64.510	64.770	65.370	65.440
1958	65.690	65.830	66.210	66.410
1959	66.980	67.450	67.700	67.950
1960	68.420	68.550	68.810	68.940
1961	68.850	69.180	69.480	69.590
1962	70.170	70.410	70.600	71.030
1963	71.320	71.370	71.580	72.070
1964	72.280	72.530	72.930	73.080
1965	73.680	74.060	74.560	74.920
1966	75.680	76.570	77.020	77.730
1967	78.190	78.480	79.240	80.150
1968	81.180	82.120	82.880	84.040
1969	84.950	86.050	87.400	88.480
1970	89.810	90.910	91.740	92.990
1971	94.400	95.730	96.530	97.380
1972	98.760	99.450	100.290	101.440
1973	102.890	104.650	106.570	109.050
1974	111.560	114.640	118.030	121.600
1975	124.210	125.960	128.200	130.170
1976	131.470	133.060	134.560	136.350
1977	138.130	140.520	142.290	

Table XIX

IMPLICIT PRICE DEFLATORS FOR GROSS NATIONAL PRODUCT COMPOUNDED ANNUAL RATES OF CHANGE

(1972 = 100)

Terminal Quarter	Initial Quarter																										
	4-72	1-73	2-73	3-73	4-73	1-74	2-74	3-74	4-74	1-75	2-75	3-75	4-75	1-76	2-76	3-76	4-76	1-77	2-77	3-77	4-77	1-78	2-78	3-78	4-78	1-79	1972=100
1-73	5.8																										102.89
2-73	6.4	7.0																									104.65
3-73	6.8	7.3	7.5																								106.57
4-73	7.5	8.1	8.6	9.6																							109.05
1-74	7.7	8.2	8.5	9.0	8.4																						111.28
2-74	8.3	8.8	9.3	9.8	9.9	11.5																					114.34
3-74	8.8	9.3	9.7	10.3	10.5	11.5	11.6																				117.52
4-74	9.2	9.7	10.2	10.7	11.0	11.9	12.1	12.6																			121.06
1-75	9.4	9.9	10.3	10.8	11.0	11.6	11.6	11.6	10.6																		124.16
2-75	9.0	9.4	9.7	10.0	10.1	10.4	10.2	9.7	8.2	5.9																	125.95
3-75	8.9	9.2	9.4	9.7	9.7	9.9	9.6	9.1	7.9	6.6	7.3																128.19
4-75	8.7	8.9	9.1	9.3	9.3	9.4	9.0	8.5	7.5	6.5	6.8	6.2															130.14
1-76	8.3	8.5	8.7	8.8	8.7	8.7	8.3	7.7	6.8	5.8	5.8	5.1	3.9														131.30
2-76	8.1	8.2	8.3	8.4	8.3	8.3	7.8	7.3	6.4	5.6	5.5	4.9	4.3	4.7													132.79
3-76	7.8	8.0	8.0	8.1	7.9	7.9	7.4	6.9	6.2	5.4	5.3	4.8	4.4	4.6	4.5												134.35
4-76	7.7	7.8	7.9	7.9	7.7	7.7	7.3	6.8	6.1	5.5	5.4	5.0	4.7	5.0	5.1	5.7											136.34
1-77	7.5	7.6	7.7	7.7	7.5	7.5	7.2	6.7	6.1	5.5	5.5	5.2	5.0	5.2	5.4	5.9	6.0										138.34
2-77	7.5	7.6	7.6	7.7	7.5	7.4	7.2	6.8	6.2	5.8	5.8	5.5	5.4	5.7	6.0	6.5	6.8	7.7									140.93
3-77	7.4	7.5	7.5	7.5	7.4	7.3	7.0	6.7	6.1	5.7	5.7	5.5	5.4	5.6	5.8	6.1	6.2	6.2	4.8								142.59
4-77	7.4	7.4	7.4	7.3	7.2	7.1	6.9	6.6	6.1	5.7	5.7	5.5	5.4	5.6	5.8	6.0	6.2	6.3	5.6	6.4							144.82
1-78	7.3	7.4	7.4	7.2	7.1	7.1	6.9	6.6	6.2	5.8	5.8	5.7	5.6	5.8	6.0	6.2	6.2	6.3	5.8	6.4	6.3						147.05
2-78	7.3	7.4	7.5	7.6	7.4	7.4	7.1	6.9	6.5	6.2	6.2	6.1	6.1	6.4	6.6	6.9	7.0	7.2	7.0	7.8	8.5	10.7					150.82
3-78					7.5	7.4	7.2	6.9	6.5	6.2	6.3	6.2	6.2	6.4	6.6	6.9	7.0	7.2	7.0	7.6	8.0	8.9	7.2				153.45
4-78					7.5	7.5	7.2	7.0	6.9	6.4	6.4	6.4	6.4	6.6	6.8	7.1	7.2	7.4	7.3	7.8	8.2	8.8	7.9	8.7			156.68
1-79					7.4	7.3	7.3	7.1	6.8	6.6	6.6	6.6	6.6	6.9	7.1	7.3	7.4	7.6	7.6	8.1	8.4	9.0	8.4	9.0	9.3		160.22
2-79					7.5	7.3	7.2	7.3	7.0	6.8	6.8	6.8	6.8	7.1	7.3	7.5	7.7	7.9	7.9	8.3	8.7	9.1	8.8	9.3	9.6	9.9	164.03

Table XX

IMPLICIT PRICE DEFLATORS FOR GROSS NATIONAL PRODUCT COMPOUNDED ANNUAL RATES OF CHANGE

(1958 = 100)

Terminal Quarter	Initial Quarter																			
	3-70	4-70	1-71	2-71	3-71	4-71	1-72	2-72	3-72	4-72	1-73	2-73	3-73	4-73	1-74	2-74	3-74	4-74	1-75	1958=100
4-70	6.4																			137.88
1-71	5.5	4.7																		139.47
2-71	5.3	4.8	4.8																	141.13
3-71	4.8	4.0	3.7	2.6																142.03
4-71	4.1	3.5	3.1	2.2	1.9															142.70
1-72	4.3	3.9	3.7	3.3	3.7	5.5														144.62
2-72	4.0	3.6	3.3	3.0	3.1	3.7	1.9													145.31
3-72	3.9	3.5	3.3	3.0	3.1	3.6	2.6	3.3												146.50
4-72	3.9	3.6	3.4	3.2	3.3	3.7	3.1	3.7	4.0											147.96
1-73	4.1	3.8	3.7	3.5	3.7	4.0	3.7	4.3	4.8	5.5										149.95
2-73	4.3	4.1	4.1	4.0	4.2	4.6	4.4	5.0	5.6	6.4	7.3									152.61
3-73	4.7	4.5	4.5	4.5	4.7	5.1	5.0	5.7	6.3	7.0	7.8	8.3								155.67
4-73	5.0	4.8	4.9	4.9	5.1	5.5	5.5	6.2	6.7	7.4	8.1	8.5	8.6							158.93
1-74	5.5	5.4	5.5	5.5	5.8	6.3	6.4	7.0	7.6	8.4	9.1	9.7	10.5	12.3						163.61
2-74	5.7	5.7	5.8	5.8	6.1	6.6	6.7	7.3	7.9	8.5	9.2	9.6	10.1	10.8	9.4					167.31
3-74	6.1	6.1	6.2	6.3	6.6	7.0	7.2	7.8	8.4	9.0	9.6	10.1	10.5	11.2	10.6	11.9				172.07
4-74	6.6	6.6	6.7	6.9	7.2	7.6	7.8	8.4	9.0	9.7	10.3	10.8	11.3	12.0	11.9	13.1	14.4			177.97
1-75	6.7	6.7	6.8	7.0	7.3	7.7	7.9	8.4	9.0	9.5	10.1	10.5	10.8	11.3	11.0	11.6	11.4	8.5		181.62
2-75	6.6	6.6	6.7	6.8	7.1	7.5	7.7	8.2	8.6	9.1	9.5	9.8	10.0	10.2	9.8	9.9	9.2	6.7	5.0	183.85

3.2%

7.4%

12.0%

6.7%

Table XXI

AGE-REDUCING FACTORS FOR DEPRECIABLE ASSETS (DOUBLE DECLINING BALANCE)

Unad-justed Life in Years*	Annual Growth Rate of Depreciable Assets (or Surrogate)					
	0%	5%	10%	15%	20%	30%
3	0.764706	0.779434	0.793105	0.805796	0.817576	0.838674
4	0.765306	0.783763	0.800807	0.816513	0.830958	0.856400
5	0.764997	0.787301	0.807768	0.826454	0.843444	0.872744
6	0.764619	0.790793	0.814637	0.836176	0.855495	0.888002
7	0.764285	0.794327	0.821473	0.845701	0.867098	0.902108
8	0.764006	0.797901	0.828260	0.854994	0.878200	0.915005
9	0.763774	0.801503	0.834974	0.864019	0.888754	0.926670
10	0.763581	0.805120	0.841596	0.872745	0.898728	0.937116
11	0.763417	0.808741	0.848107	0.881150	0.908101	0.946384
12	0.763278	0.812359	0.854496	0.889216	0.916864	0.954534
13	0.763158	0.815967	0.860750	0.896930	0.925017	0.961645
14	0.763054	0.819560	0.866861	0.904286	0.932565	0.967801
15	0.762962	0.823134	0.872822	0.911279	0.939523	0.973094
20	0.762634	0.840616	0.900195	0.940831	0.966249	0.989670
25	0.762432	0.857275	0.923311	0.962058	0.982189	0.996331
30	0.762297	0.872956	0.942215	0.976483	0.991014	0.998766

*Accumulated Depreciation/Depreciation Charges for Year.

Table XXII

AGE-REDUCING FACTORS FOR DEPRECIABLE ASSETS (SUM OF THE YEARS' DIGITS)

Unadjusted Life in Years*	Annual Growth Rate of Depreciable Assets (or Surrogate)					
	0%	5%	10%	15%	20%	30%
3	0.857143	0.865991	0.874202	0.881823	0.888898	0.901575
4	0.833333	0.846666	0.858928	0.870188	0.880513	0.898633
5	0.818182	0.835965	0.852168	0.866872	0.880169	0.902953
6	0.807692	0.829889	0.849913	0.867850	0.883822	0.910458
7	0.800000	0.826571	0.850291	0.871241	0.889576	0.919252
8	0.794118	0.825025	0.852309	0.876041	0.896423	0.928347
9	0.789474	0.824677	0.855390	0.881666	0.903779	0.937203
10	0.785714	0.825173	0.859175	0.887756	0.911283	0.945519
11	0.782609	0.826282	0.863428	0.894070	0.918707	0.953141
12	0.780000	0.827845	0.867988	0.900449	0.925903	0.959998
13	0.777778	0.829752	0.872742	0.906780	0.932775	0.966081
14	0.775862	0.831921	0.877607	0.912985	0.939262	0.971411
15	0.774194	0.834294	0.882520	0.919008	0.945330	0.976036
20	0.768293	0.847901	0.906506	0.945383	0.969205	0.990728
25	0.764706	0.862605	0.927800	0.964872	0.983715	0.996701
30	0.762295	0.877202	0.945545	0.978234	0.991789	0.998891

*Accumulated Depreciation/Depreciation Charges for Year.

Table XXIII

EXPONENTIAL FUNCTIONS

x	e^x	e^{-x}
0.000000	1.000000	1.000000
0.001250	1.001251	0.998751
0.002500	1.002503	0.997503
0.003333	1.003339	0.996673
0.003750	1.003757	0.996257
0.004167	1.004176	0.995842
0.005000	1.005013	0.995012
0.005833	1.005850	0.994184
0.006250	1.006270	0.993769
0.006667	1.006689	0.993355
0.007500	1.007528	0.992528
0.008333	1.008365	0.991705
0.008750	1.008789	0.991288
0.009167	1.009209	0.990874
0.010000	1.010050	0.990050
0.012500	1.012578	0.987578
0.015000	1.015113	0.985112
0.017500	1.017654	0.982652
0.020000	1.020201	0.980199
0.030000	1.030454	0.970446
0.040000	1.040811	0.960789
0.050000	1.051271	0.951229
0.060000	1.061837	0.941765
0.070000	1.072508	0.932934
0.080000	1.083287	0.923117

Table XXIII–continued

EXPONENTIAL FUNCTIONS

x	e^x	e^{-x}
0.080000	1.083287	0.923117
0.090000	1.094174	0.913931
0.100000	1.105171	0.904837
0.110000	1.116278	0.895834
0.120000	1.127497	0.886920
0.130000	1.138828	0.878095
0.140000	1.150274	0.869358
0.150000	1.161834	0.860708
0.160000	1.173511	0.852144
0.170000	1.185305	0.843665
0.180000	1.197217	0.835270
0.190000	1.209250	0.826959
0.200000	1.221403	0.818731
0.300000	1.349859	0.740818
0.400000	1.491825	0.670320
0.500000	1.648721	0.606531
0.600000	1.822119	0.548812
0.700000	2.013753	0.496585
0.800000	2.225541	0.449329
0.900000	2.459603	0.406570
1.000000	2.718282	0.367879
1.100000	3.004166	0.332871
1.200000	3.320117	0.301194
1.300000	3.669297	0.272532
1.400000	4.055200	0.246597
1.500000	4.481689	0.223130

Table XXIII–continued

EXPONENTIAL FUNCTIONS

x	e^x	e^{-x}
1.600000	4.953032	0.201897
1.700000	5.473947	0.182684
1.800000	6.049647	0.165299
1.900000	6.685894	0.149569
2.000000	7.389056	0.135335
2.100000	8.166170	0.122456
2.200000	9.025013	0.110803
2.300000	9.974182	0.100259
3.300000	27.112639	0.036883
3.400000	29.964100	0.033373
3.500000	33.115452	0.030197
3.600000	36.598234	0.027324
3.700000	40.447304	0.024724
3.800000	44.701184	0.022371
3.900000	49.402449	0.020242
4.000000	54.598150	0.018316
4.100000	60.340288	0.016573
4.200000	66.686331	0.014996
4.300000	73.699794	0.013569
4.400000	81.450869	0.012277
4.500000	90.017131	0.011109
4.600000	99.484316	0.010052
4.700000	109.947173	0.009095
4.800000	121.510418	0.008230
4.900000	134.289780	0.007447

Table XXIII–continued

EXPONENTIAL FUNCTIONS

x	e^x	e^{-x}
5.000000	148.413159	0.006738
5.500000	244.691932	0.004087
6.000000	403.428794	0.002479
6.500000	665.141633	0.001503
7.000000	1096.633158	0.000912
7.500000	1808.042414	0.000553
8.000000	2980.957987	0.000335
8.500000	4914.768840	0.000203
9.000000	8103.083928	0.000123
9.500000	13359.726830	0.000074
10.000000	22026.465795	0.000045

Table XXIV

SIX PLACE MANTISSAS

N.	0	1	2	3	4	5	6	7	8	9	D.
100	000000	000434	000868	001301	001734	002166	002598	003029	003461	003891	432
1	4321	4751	5181	5609	6038	6466	6894	7321	7748	8174	428
2	8600	9026	9451	9876	010300	010724	011147	011570	011993	012415	424
3	012837	013259	013680	014100	4521	4940	5360	5779	6197	6616	420
4	7033	7451	7868	8284	8700	9116	9532	9947	020361	020775	416
105	021189	021603	022016	022428	022841	023252	023664	024075	4486	4896	412
6	5306	5715	6125	6533	6942	7350	7757	8164	8571	8978	408
7	9384	9789	030195	030600	031004	031408	031812	032216	032619	033021	404
8	033424	033826	4227	4628	5029	5430	5830	6230	6629	7028	400
9	7426	7825	8223	8620	9017	9414	9811	040207	040602	040998	397
110	041393	041787	042182	042576	042969	043362	043755	044148	044540	044932	393
1	5323	5714	6105	6495	6885	7275	7664	8053	8442	8830	390
2	9218	9606	9993	050380	050766	051153	051538	051924	052309	052694	386
3	053078	053463	053846	4230	4613	4996	5378	5760	6142	6524	383
4	6905	7286	7666	8046	8426	8805	9185	9563	9942	060320	379
115	060698	061075	061452	061829	062206	062582	062958	063333	063709	4083	376
6	4458	4832	5206	5580	5953	6326	6699	7071	7443	7815	373
7	8186	8557	8928	9298	9668	070038	070407	070776	071145	071514	370
8	071882	072250	072617	072985	073352	3718	4085	4451	4816	5182	366
9	5547	5912	6276	6640	7004	7368	7731	8094	8457	8819	363
120	079181	079543	079904	080266	080626	080987	081347	081707	082067	082426	360
1	082785	083144	083503	3861	4219	4576	4934	5291	5647	6004	357
2	6360	6716	7071	7426	7781	8136	8490	8845	9198	9552	355
3	9905	090258	090611	090963	091315	091667	092018	092370	092721	093071	352
4	093422	3772	4122	4471	4820	5169	5518	5866	6215	6562	349
125	6910	7257	7604	7951	8298	8644	8990	9335	9681	100026	346
6	100371	100715	101059	101403	101747	102091	102434	102777	103119	3462	343
7	3804	4146	4487	4828	5169	5510	5851	6191	6531	6871	341
8	7210	7549	7888	8227	8565	8903	9241	9579	9916	110253	338
9	110590	110926	111263	111599	111934	112270	112605	112940	113275	3609	335
130	113943	114277	114611	114944	115278	115611	115943	116276	116608	116940	333
1	7271	7603	7934	8265	8595	8926	9256	9586	9915	120245	330
2	120574	120903	121231	121560	121888	122216	122544	122871	123198	3525	328
3	3852	4178	4504	4830	5156	5481	5806	6131	6456	6781	325
4	7105	7429	7753	8076	8399	8722	9045	9368	9690	130012	323
135	130334	130655	130977	131298	131619	131939	132260	132580	132900	3219	321
6	3539	3858	4177	4496	4814	5133	5451	5769	6086	6403	318
7	6721	7037	7354	7671	7987	8303	8618	8934	9249	9564	316
8	9879	140194	140508	140822	141136	141450	141763	142076	142389	142702	314
9	143015	3327	3639	3951	4263	4574	4885	5196	5507	5818	311
140	146128	146438	146748	147058	147367	147676	147985	148294	148603	148911	309
1	9219	9527	9835	150142	150449	150756	151063	151370	151676	151982	307
2	152288	152594	152900	3205	3510	3815	4120	4424	4728	5032	305
3	5336	5640	5943	6246	6549	6852	7154	7457	7759	8061	303
4	8362	8664	8965	9266	9567	9868	160168	160469	160769	161068	301
145	161368	161667	161967	162266	162564	162863	3161	3460	3758	4055	299
6	4353	4650	4947	5244	5541	5838	6134	6430	6726	7022	297
7	7317	7613	7908	8203	8497	8792	9086	9380	9674	9968	295
8	170262	170555	170848	171141	171434	171726	172019	172311	172603	172895	293
9	3186	3478	3769	4060	4351	4641	4932	5222	5512	5802	291
150	176091	176381	176670	176959	177248	177536	177825	178113	178401	178689	289
1	8977	9264	9552	9839	180126	180413	180699	180986	181272	181558	287
2	181844	182129	182415	182700	2985	3270	3555	3839	4123	4407	285
3	4691	4975	5259	5542	5825	6108	6391	6674	6956	7239	283
4	7521	7803	8084	8366	8647	8928	9209	9490	9771	190051	281
155	190332	190612	190892	191171	191451	191730	192010	192289	192567	2846	279
6	3125	3403	3681	3959	4237	4514	4792	5069	5346	5623	278
7	5900	6176	6453	6729	7005	7281	7556	7832	8107	8382	276
8	8657	8932	9206	9481	9755	200029	200303	200577	200850	201124	274
9	201397	201670	201943	202216	202488	2761	3033	3305	3577	3848	272
N.	0	1	2	3	4	5	6	7	8	9	D.

Table XXIV–continued

SIX PLACE MANTISSAS

N.	0	1	2	3	4	5	6	7	8	9	D.
160	204120	204391	204663	204934	205204	205475	205746	206016	206286	206556	271
1	6826	7096	7365	7634	7904	8173	8441	8710	8979	9247	269
2	9515	9783	210051	210319	210586	210853	211121	211388	211654	211921	267
3	212188	212454	2720	2986	3252	3518	3783	4049	4314	4579	266
4	4844	5109	5373	5638	5902	6166	6430	6694	6957	7221	264
165	7484	7747	8010	8273	8536	8798	9060	9323	9585	9846	262
6	220108	220370	220631	220892	221153	221414	221675	221936	222196	222456	261
7	2716	2976	3236	3496	3755	4015	4274	4533	4792	5051	259
8	5309	5568	5826	6084	6342	6600	6858	7115	7372	7630	258
9	7887	8144	8400	8657	8913	9170	9426	9682	9938	230193	256
170	230449	230704	230960	231215	231470	231724	231979	232234	232488	232742	255
1	2996	3250	3504	3757	4011	4264	4517	4770	5023	5276	253
2	5528	5781	6033	6285	6537	6789	7041	7292	7544	7795	252
3	8046	8297	8548	8799	9049	9299	9550	9800	240050	240300	250
4	240549	240799	241048	241297	241546	241795	242044	242293	2541	2790	249
175	3038	3286	3534	3782	4030	4277	4525	4772	5019	5266	248
6	5513	5759	6006	6252	6499	6745	6991	7237	7482	7728	246
7	7973	8219	8464	8709	8954	9198	9443	9687	9932	250176	245
8	250420	250664	250908	251151	251395	251638	251881	252125	252368	2610	243
9	2853	3096	3338	3580	3822	4064	4306	4548	4790	5031	242
180	255273	255514	255755	255996	256237	256477	256718	256958	257198	257439	241
1	7679	7918	8158	8398	8637	8877	9116	9355	9594	9833	239
2	260071	260310	260548	260787	261025	261263	261501	261739	261976	262214	238
3	2451	2688	2925	3162	3399	3636	3873	4109	4346	4582	237
4	4818	5054	5290	5525	5761	5996	6232	6467	6702	6937	235
185	7172	7406	7641	7875	8110	8344	8578	8812	9046	9279	234
6	9513	9746	9980	270213	270446	270679	270912	271144	271377	271609	233
7	271842	272074	272306	2538	2770	3001	3233	3464	3696	3927	232
8	4158	4389	4620	4850	5081	5311	5542	5772	6002	6232	230
9	6462	6692	6921	7151	7380	7609	7838	8067	8296	8525	229
190	278754	278982	279211	279439	279667	279895	280123	280351	280578	280806	228
1	281033	281261	281488	281715	281942	282169	2396	2622	2849	3075	227
2	3301	3527	3753	3979	4205	4431	4656	4882	5107	5332	226
3	5557	5782	6007	6232	6456	6681	6905	7130	7354	7578	225
4	7802	8026	8249	8473	8696	8920	9143	9366	9589	9812	223
195	290035	290257	290480	290702	290925	291147	291369	291591	291813	292034	222
6	2256	2478	2699	2920	3141	3363	3584	3804	4025	4246	221
7	4466	4687	4907	5127	5347	5567	5787	6007	6226	6446	220
8	6665	6884	7104	7323	7542	7761	7979	8198	8416	8635	219
9	8853	9071	3289	9507	9725	9943	300161	300378	300595	300813	218
200	301030	301247	301464	301681	301898	302114	302331	302547	302764	302980	217
1	3196	3412	3628	3844	4059	4275	4491	4706	4921	5136	216
2	5351	5566	5781	5996	6211	6425	6639	6854	7068	7282	215
3	7496	7710	7924	8137	8351	8564	8778	8991	9204	9417	213
4	9630	9843	310056	310268	310481	310693	310906	311118	311330	311542	212
205	311754	311966	2177	2389	2600	2812	3023	3234	3445	3656	211
6	3867	4078	4289	4499	4710	4920	5130	5340	5551	5760	210
7	5970	6180	6390	6599	6809	7018	7227	7436	7646	7854	209
8	8063	8272	8481	8689	8898	9106	9314	9522	9730	9938	208
9	320146	320354	320562	320769	320977	321184	321391	321598	321805	322012	207
210	322219	322426	322633	322839	323046	323252	323458	323665	323871	324077	206
1	4282	4488	4694	4899	5105	5310	5516	5721	5926	6131	205
2	6336	6541	6745	6950	7155	7359	7563	7767	7972	8176	204
3	8380	8583	8787	8991	9194	9398	9601	9805	330008	330211	203
4	330414	330617	330819	331022	331225	331427	331630	331832	2034	2236	202
215	2438	2640	2842	3044	3246	3447	3649	3850	4051	4253	202
6	4454	4655	4856	5057	5257	5458	5658	5859	6059	6260	201
7	6460	6660	6860	7060	7260	7459	7659	7858	8058	8257	200
8	8456	8656	8855	9054	9253	9451	9650	9849	340047	340246	199
9	340444	340642	340841	341039	341237	341435	341632	341830	2028	2225	198
N.	0	1	2	3	4	5	6	7	8	9	D.

Table XXIV–continued

SIX PLACE MANTISSAS

N.	0	1	2	3	4	5	6	7	8	9	D.
220	342423	342620	342817	343014	343212	343409	343606	343802	343999	344196	197
1	4392	4589	4785	4981	5178	5374	5570	5766	5962	6157	196
2	6353	6549	6744	6939	7135	7330	7525	7720	7915	8110	195
3	8305	8500	8694	8889	9083	9278	9472	9666	9860	350054	194
4	350248	350442	350636	350829	351023	351216	351410	351603	351796	1989	193
225	2183	2375	2568	2761	2954	3147	3339	3532	3724	3916	193
6	4108	4301	4493	4685	4876	5068	5260	5452	5643	5834	192
7	6026	6217	6408	6599	6790	6981	7172	7363	7554	7744	191
8	7935	8125	8316	8506	8696	8886	9076	9266	9456	9646	190
9	9835	360025	360215	360404	360593	360783	360972	361161	361350	361539	189
230	361728	361917	362105	362294	362482	362671	362859	363048	363236	363424	188
1	3612	3800	3988	4176	4363	4551	4739	4926	5113	5301	188
2	5488	5675	5862	6049	6236	6423	6610	6796	6983	7169	187
3	7356	7542	7729	7915	8101	8287	8473	8659	8845	9030	186
4	9216	9401	9587	9772	9958	370143	370328	370513	370698	370883	185
235	371068	371253	371437	371622	371806	1991	2175	2360	2544	2728	184
6	2912	3096	3280	3464	3647	3831	4015	4198	4382	4565	184
7	4748	4932	5115	5298	5481	5664	5846	6029	6212	6394	183
8	6577	6759	6942	7124	7306	7488	7670	7852	8034	8216	182
9	8398	8580	8761	8943	9124	9306	9487	9668	9849	380030	181
240	380211	380392	380573	380754	380934	381115	381296	381476	381656	381837	181
1	2017	2197	2377	2557	2737	2917	3097	3277	3456	3636	180
2	3815	3995	4174	4353	4533	4712	4891	5070	5249	5428	179
3	5606	5785	5964	6142	6321	6499	6677	6856	7034	7212	178
4	7390	7568	7746	7923	8101	8279	8456	8634	8811	8989	178
245	9166	9343	9520	9698	9875	390051	390228	390405	390582	390759	177
6	390935	391112	391288	391464	391641	1817	1993	2169	2345	2521	176
7	2697	2873	3048	3224	3400	3575	3751	3926	4101	4277	176
8	4452	4627	4802	4977	5152	5326	5501	5676	5850	6025	175
9	6199	6374	6548	6722	6896	7071	7245	7419	7592	7766	174
250	397940	398114	398287	398461	398634	398808	398981	399154	399328	399501	173
1	9674	9847	400020	400192	400365	400538	400711	400883	401056	401228	173
2	401401	401573	1745	1917	2089	2261	2433	2605	2777	2949	172
3	3121	3292	3464	3635	3807	3978	4149	4320	4492	4663	171
4	4834	5005	5176	5346	5517	5688	5858	6029	6199	6370	171
255	6540	6710	6881	7051	7221	7391	7561	7731	7901	8070	170
6	8240	8410	8579	8749	8918	9087	9257	9426	9595	9764	169
7	9933	410102	410271	410440	410609	410777	410964	411114	411283	411451	169
8	411620	1788	1956	2124	2293	2461	2629	2796	2964	3132	168
9	3300	3467	3635	3803	3970	4137	4305	4472	4639	4806	167
260	414973	415140	415307	415474	415641	415808	415974	416141	416308	416474	167
1	6641	6807	6973	7139	7306	7472	7638	7804	7970	8135	166
2	8301	8467	8633	8798	8964	9129	9295	9460	9625	9791	165
3	9956	420121	420286	420451	420616	420781	420945	421110	421275	421439	165
4	421604	1768	1933	2097	2261	2426	2590	2754	2918	3082	164
265	3246	3410	3574	3737	3901	4065	4228	4392	4555	4718	164
6	4882	5045	5208	5371	5534	5697	5860	6023	6186	6349	163
7	6511	6674	6836	6999	7161	7324	7486	7648	7811	7973	162
8	8135	8297	8459	8621	8783	8944	9106	9268	9429	9591	162
9	9752	9914	430075	430236	430398	430559	430720	430881	431042	431203	161
270	431364	431525	431685	431846	432007	432167	432328	432488	432649	432809	161
1	2969	3130	3290	3450	3610	3770	3930	4090	4249	4409	160
2	4569	4729	4868	5048	5207	5367	5526	5685	5844	6004	159
3	6163	6322	6481	6640	6799	6957	7116	7275	7433	7592	159
4	7751	7909	8067	8226	8384	8542	8701	8859	9017	9175	158
275	9333	9491	9648	9806	9964	440122	440279	440437	440594	440752	158
6	440909	441066	441224	441381	441538	1695	1852	2009	2166	2323	157
7	2480	2637	2793	2950	3106	3263	3419	3576	3732	3889	157
8	4045	4201	4357	4513	4669	4825	4981	5137	5293	5449	156
9	5604	5760	5915	6071	6226	6382	6537	6692	6848	7003	155
N.	0	1	2	3	4	5	6	7	8	9	D.

Table XXIV—continued

SIX PLACE MANTISSAS

N.	0	1	2	3	4	5	6	7	8	9	D.
280	447158	447313	447468	447623	447778	447933	448088	448242	448397	448552	155
1	8706	8861	9015	9170	9324	9478	9633	9787	9941	450095	154
2	450249	450403	450557	450711	450865	451018	451172	451326	451479	1633	154
3	1786	1940	2093	2247	2400	2553	2706	2859	3012	3165	153
4	3318	3471	3624	3777	3930	4082	4235	4387	4540	4692	153
285	4845	4997	5150	5302	5454	5606	5758	5910	6062	6214	152
6	6366	6518	6670	6821	6973	7125	7276	7428	7579	7731	152
7	7882	8033	8184	8336	8487	8638	8789	8940	9091	9242	151
8	9392	9543	9694	9845	9995	460146	460296	460447	460597	460748	151
9	460898	461048	461198	461348	461499	1649	1799	1948	2098	2248	150
290	462398	462548	462697	462847	462997	463146	463296	463445	463594	463744	150
1	3893	4042	4191	4340	4490	4639	4788	4936	5085	5234	149
2	5383	5532	5680	5829	5977	6126	6274	6423	6571	6719	149
3	6868	7016	7164	7312	7460	7608	7756	7904	8052	8200	148
4	8347	8495	8643	8790	8938	9085	9233	9380	9527	9675	148
295	9822	9969	470116	470263	470410	470557	470704	470851	470998	471145	147
6	471292	471438	1585	1732	1878	2025	2171	2318	2464	2610	146
7	2756	2903	3049	3195	3341	3487	3633	3779	3925	4071	146
8	4216	4362	4508	4653	4799	4944	5090	5235	5381	5526	146
9	5671	5816	5962	6107	6252	6397	6542	6687	6832	6976	145
300	477121	477266	477411	477555	477700	477844	477989	478133	478278	478422	145
1	8566	8711	8855	8999	9143	9287	9431	9575	9719	9863	144
2	480007	480151	480294	480438	480582	480725	480869	481012	481156	481299	144
3	1443	1586	1729	1872	2016	2159	2302	2445	2588	2731	143
4	2874	3016	3159	3302	3445	3587	3730	3872	4015	4157	143
305	4300	4442	4585	4727	4869	5011	5153	5295	5437	5579	142
6	5721	5863	6005	6147	6289	6430	6572	6714	6855	6997	142
7	7138	7280	7421	7563	7704	7845	7986	8127	8269	8410	141
8	8551	8692	8833	8974	9114	9255	9396	9537	9677	9818	141
9	9958	490099	490239	490380	490520	490661	490801	490941	491081	491222	140
310	491362	491502	491642	491782	491922	492062	492201	492341	492481	492621	140
1	2760	2900	3040	3179	3319	3458	3597	3737	3876	4015	139
2	4155	4294	4433	4572	4711	4850	4989	5128	5267	5406	139
3	5544	5683	5822	5960	6099	6238	6376	6515	6653	6791	139
4	6930	7068	7206	7344	7483	7621	7759	7897	8035	8173	138
315	8311	8448	8586	8724	8862	8999	9137	9275	9412	9550	138
6	9687	9824	9962	500099	500236	500374	500511	500648	500785	500922	137
7	501059	501196	501333	1470	1607	1744	1880	2017	2154	2291	137
8	2427	2564	2700	2837	2973	3109	3246	3382	3518	3655	136
9	3791	3927	4063	4199	4335	4471	4607	4743	4878	5014	136
320	505150	505286	505421	505557	505693	505828	505964	506099	506234	506370	136
1	6505	6640	6776	6911	7046	7181	7316	7451	7586	7721	135
2	7856	7991	8126	8260	8395	8530	8664	8799	8934	9068	135
3	9203	9337	9471	9606	9740	9874	510009	510143	510277	510411	134
4	510545	510679	510813	510947	511081	511215	1349	1482	1616	1750	134
325	1883	2017	2151	2284	2418	2551	2684	2818	2951	3084	133
6	3218	3351	3484	3617	3750	3883	4016	4149	4282	4415	133
7	4548	4681	4813	4946	5079	5211	5344	5476	5609	5741	133
8	5874	6006	6139	6271	6403	6535	6668	6800	6932	7064	132
9	7196	7328	7460	7592	7724	7855	7987	8119	8251	8382	132
330	518514	518646	518777	518909	519040	519171	519303	519434	519566	519697	131
1	9828	9959	520090	520221	520353	520484	520615	520745	520876	521007	131
2	521138	521269	1400	1530	1661	1792	1922	2053	2183	2314	131
3	2444	2575	2705	2835	2966	3096	3226	3356	3486	3616	130
4	3746	3876	4006	4136	4266	4396	4526	4656	4785	4915	130
335	5045	5174	5304	5434	5563	5693	5822	5951	6081	6210	129
6	6339	6469	6598	6727	6856	6985	7114	7243	7372	7501	129
7	7630	7759	7888	8016	8145	8274	8402	8531	8660	8788	129
8	8917	9045	9174	9302	9430	9559	9687	9815	9943	530072	128
9	530200	530328	530456	530584	530712	530840	530968	531096	531223	1351	128
N.	0	1	2	3	4	5	6	7	8	9	D.

Table XXIV–continued

SIX PLACE MANTISSAS

N.	0	1	2	3	4	5	6	7	8	9	D.
340	531479	531607	531734	531862	531990	532117	532245	532372	532500	532627	128
1	2754	2882	3009	3136	3264	3391	3518	3645	3772	3899	127
2	4026	4153	4280	4407	4534	4661	4787	4914	5041	5167	127
3	5294	5421	5547	5674	5800	5927	6053	6180	6306	6432	126
4	6558	6685	6811	6937	7063	7189	7315	7441	7567	7693	126
345	7819	7945	8071	8197	8322	8448	8574	8699	8825	8951	126
6	9076	9202	9327	9452	9578	9703	9829	9954	540079	540204	125
7	540329	540455	540580	540705	540830	540955	541080	541205	1330	1454	125
8	1579	1704	1829	1953	2078	2203	2327	2452	2576	2701	125
9	2825	2950	3074	3199	3323	3447	3571	3696	3820	3944	124
350	544068	544192	544316	544440	544564	544688	544812	544936	545060	545183	124
1	5307	5431	5555	5678	5802	5925	6049	6172	6296	6419	124
2	6543	6666	6789	6913	7036	7159	7282	7405	7529	7652	123
3	7775	7898	8021	8144	8267	8389	8512	8635	8758	8881	123
4	9003	9126	9249	9371	9494	9616	9739	9861	9984	550106	123
355	550228	550351	550473	550595	550717	550840	550962	551084	551206	1328	122
6	1450	1572	1694	1816	1938	2060	2181	2303	2425	2547	122
7	2668	2790	2911	3033	3155	3276	3398	3519	3640	3762	121
8	3883	4004	4126	4247	4368	4489	4610	4731	4852	4973	121
9	5094	5215	5336	5457	5578	5699	5820	5940	6061	6182	121
360	556303	556423	556544	556664	556785	556905	557026	557146	557267	557387	120
1	7507	7627	7748	7868	7988	8108	8228	8349	8469	8589	120
2	8709	8829	8948	9068	9188	9308	9428	9548	9667	9787	120
3	9907	560026	560146	560265	560385	560504	560624	560743	560863	560982	119
4	561101	1221	1340	1459	1578	1698	1817	1936	2055	2174	119
365	2293	2412	2531	2650	2769	2887	3006	3125	3244	3362	119
6	3481	3600	3718	3837	3955	4074	4192	4311	4429	4548	119
7	4666	4784	4903	5021	5139	5257	5376	5494	5612	5730	118
8	5848	5966	6084	6202	6320	6437	6555	6673	6791	6909	118
9	7026	7144	7262	7379	7497	7614	7732	7849	7967	8084	118
370	568202	568319	568436	568554	568671	568788	568905	569023	569140	569257	117
1	9374	9491	9608	9725	9842	9959	570076	570193	570309	570426	117
2	570543	570660	570776	570893	571010	571126	1243	1359	1476	1592	117
3	1709	1825	1942	2058	2174	2291	2407	2523	2639	2755	116
4	2872	2988	3104	3220	3336	3452	3568	3684	3800	3915	116
375	4031	4147	4263	4379	4494	4610	4726	4841	4957	5072	116
6	5188	5303	5419	5534	5650	5765	5880	5996	6111	6226	115
7	6341	6457	6572	6687	6802	6917	7032	7147	7262	7377	115
8	7492	7607	7722	7836	7951	8066	8181	8295	8410	8525	115
9	8639	8754	8868	8983	9097	9212	9326	9441	9555	9669	114
380	579784	579898	580012	580126	580241	580355	580469	580583	580697	580811	114
1	580925	581039	1153	1267	1381	1495	1608	1722	1836	1950	114
2	2063	2177	2291	2404	2518	2631	2745	2858	2972	3085	114
3	3199	3312	3426	3539	3652	3765	3879	3992	4105	4218	113
4	4331	4444	4557	4670	4783	4896	5009	5122	5235	5348	113
385	5461	5574	5686	5799	5912	6024	6137	6250	6362	6475	113
6	6587	6700	6812	6925	7037	7149	7262	7374	7486	7599	112
7	7711	7823	7935	8047	8160	8272	8384	8496	8608	8720	112
8	8832	8944	9056	9167	9279	9391	9503	9615	9726	9838	112
9	9950	590061	590173	590284	590396	590507	590619	590730	590842	590953	112
390	591065	591176	591287	591399	591510	591621	591732	591843	591955	592066	111
1	2177	2288	2399	2510	2621	2732	2843	2954	3064	3175	111
2	3286	3397	3508	3618	3729	3840	3950	4061	4171	4282	111
3	4393	4503	4614	4724	4834	4945	5055	5165	5276	5380	110
4	5496	5606	5717	5827	5937	6047	6157	6267	6377	6487	110
395	6597	6707	6817	6927	7037	7146	7256	7366	7476	7586	110
6	7695	7805	7914	8024	8134	8243	8353	8462	8572	8681	110
7	8791	8900	9009	9119	9228	9337	9446	9556	9665	9774	109
8	9883	9992	600101	600210	600319	600428	600537	600646	600755	600864	109
9	600973	601082	1191	1299	1408	1517	1625	1734	1843	1951	109
N.	0	1	2	3	4	5	6	7	8	9	D.

Table XXIV–continued

SIX PLACE MANTISSAS

N.	0	1	2	3	4	5	6	7	8	9	D.
400	602060	602169	602277	602386	602494	602603	602711	602819	602928	603036	108
1	3144	3253	3361	3469	3577	3686	3794	3902	4010	4118	108
2	4226	4334	4442	4550	4658	4766	4874	4982	5089	5197	108
3	5305	5413	5521	5628	5736	5844	5951	6059	6166	6274	108
4	6381	6489	6596	6704	6811	6919	7026	7133	7241	7348	107
405	7455	7562	7669	7777	7884	7991	8098	8205	8312	8419	107
6	8526	8633	8740	8847	8954	9061	9167	9274	9381	9488	107
7	9594	9701	9808	9914	610021	610128	610234	610341	610447	610554	107
8	610660	610767	610873	610979	1086	1192	1298	1405	1511	1617	106
9	1723	1829	1936	2042	2148	2254	2360	2466	2572	2678	106
410	612784	612890	612996	613102	613207	613313	613419	613525	613630	613736	106
1	3842	3947	4053	4159	4264	4370	4475	4581	4686	4792	106
2	4897	5003	5108	5213	5319	5424	5529	5634	5740	5845	105
3	5950	6055	6160	6265	6370	6476	6581	6686	6790	6895	105
4	7000	7105	7210	7315	7420	7525	7629	7734	7839	7943	105
415	8048	8153	8257	8362	8466	8571	8676	8780	8884	8989	105
6	9093	9198	9302	9406	9511	9615	9719	9824	9928	620032	104
7	620136	620240	620344	620448	620552	620656	620760	620864	620968	1072	104
8	1176	1280	1384	1488	1592	1695	1799	1903	2007	2110	104
9	2214	2318	2421	2525	2628	2732	2835	2939	3042	3146	104
420	623249	623353	623456	623559	623663	623766	623869	623973	624076	624179	103
1	4282	4385	4488	4591	4695	4798	4901	5004	5107	5210	103
2	5312	5415	5518	5621	5724	5827	5929	6032	6135	6238	103
3	6340	6443	6546	6648	6751	6853	6956	7058	7161	7263	103
4	7366	7468	7571	7673	7775	7878	7980	8082	8185	8287	102
425	8389	8491	8593	8695	8797	8900	9002	9104	9206	9308	102
6	9410	9512	9613	9715	9817	9919	630021	630123	630224	630326	102
7	630428	630530	630631	630733	630835	630936	1038	1139	1241	1342	102
8	1444	1545	1647	1748	1849	1951	2052	2153	2255	2356	101
9	2457	2559	2660	2761	2862	2963	3064	3165	3266	3367	101
430	633468	633569	633670	633771	633872	633973	634074	634175	634276	634376	101
1	4477	4578	4679	4779	4880	4981	5081	5182	5283	5383	101
2	5484	5584	5685	5785	5886	5986	6087	6187	6287	6388	100
3	6488	6588	6688	6789	6889	6989	7089	7189	7290	7390	100
4	7490	7590	7690	7790	7890	7990	8090	8190	8290	8389	100
435	8489	8589	8689	8789	8888	8988	9088	9188	9287	9387	100
6	9486	9586	9686	9785	9889	9984	640084	640183	640283	640382	99
7	640481	640581	640680	640779	640879	640978	1077	1177	1276	1375	99
8	1474	1573	1672	1771	1871	1970	2069	2168	2267	2366	99
9	2465	2563	2662	2761	2860	2959	3058	3156	3255	3354	99
440	643453	643551	643650	643749	643847	643946	644044	644143	644242	644340	98
1	4439	4537	4636	4734	4832	4931	5029	5127	5226	5324	98
2	5422	5521	5619	5717	5815	5913	6011	6110	6208	6306	98
3	6404	6502	6600	6698	6796	6894	6992	7089	7187	7285	98
4	7383	7481	7579	7676	7774	7872	7969	8067	8165	8262	98
445	8360	8458	8555	8653	8750	8848	8945	9043	9140	9237	97
6	9335	9432	9530	9627	9724	9821	9919	650016	650113	650210	97
7	650308	650405	650502	650599	650696	650793	650890	0987	1084	1181	97
8	1278	1375	1472	1569	1666	1762	1859	1956	2053	2150	97
9	2246	2343	2440	2536	2633	2730	2826	2923	3019	3116	97
450	653213	653309	653405	653502	653598	653695	653791	653888	653984	654080	96
1	4177	4273	4369	4465	4562	4658	4754	4850	4946	5042	96
2	5138	5235	5331	5427	5523	5619	5715	5810	5906	6002	96
3	6098	6194	6290	6386	6482	6577	6673	6769	6864	6960	96
4	7056	7152	7247	7343	7438	7534	7629	7725	7820	7916	96
455	8011	8107	8202	8298	8393	8488	8584	8679	8774	8870	95
6	8965	9060	9155	9250	9346	9441	9536	9631	9726	9821	95
7	9916	660011	660106	660201	660296	660391	660486	660581	660676	660771	95
8	660865	0960	1055	1150	1245	1339	1434	1529	1623	1718	95
9	1813	1907	2002	2096	2191	2286	2380	2475	2569	2663	95
N.	0	1	2	3	4	5	6	7	8	9	D.

Table XXIV—continued

SIX PLACE MANTISSAS

N.	0	1	2	3	4	5	6	7	8	9	D.
460	662758	662852	662947	663041	663135	663230	663324	663418	663512	663607	94
1	3701	3795	3889	3983	4078	4172	4266	4360	4454	4548	94
2	4642	4736	4830	4924	5018	5112	5206	5299	5393	5487	94
3	5581	5675	5769	5862	5956	6050	6143	6237	6331	6424	94
4	6518	6612	6705	6799	6892	6986	7079	7173	7266	7360	94
465	7453	7546	7640	7733	7826	7920	8013	8106	8199	8293	93
6	8386	8479	8572	8665	8759	8852	8945	9038	9131	9224	93
7	9317	9410	9503	9596	9689	9782	9875	9967	670060	670153	93
8	670246	670339	670431	670524	670617	670710	670802	670895	0988	1080	93
9	1173	1265	1358	1451	1543	1636	1728	1821	1913	2005	93
470	672098	672190	672283	672375	672467	672560	672652	672744	672836	672929	92
1	3021	3113	3205	3297	3390	3482	3574	3666	3758	3850	92
2	3942	4034	4126	4218	4310	4402	4494	4586	4677	4769	92
3	4861	4953	5045	5137	5228	5320	5412	5503	5595	5687	92
4	5778	5870	5962	6053	6145	6236	6328	6419	6511	6602	92
475	6694	6785	6876	6968	7059	7151	7242	7333	7424	7516	91
6	7607	7698	7789	7881	7972	8063	8154	8245	8336	8427	91
7	8518	8609	8700	8791	8882	8973	9064	9155	9246	9337	91
8	9428	9519	9610	9700	9791	9882	9973	680063	680154	680245	91
9	680336	680426	680517	680607	680698	680789	680879	0970	1060	1151	91
480	681241	681332	681422	681513	681603	681693	681784	681874	681964	682055	90
1	2145	2235	2326	2416	2506	2596	2686	2777	2867	2957	90
2	3047	3137	3227	3317	3407	3497	3587	3677	3767	3857	90
3	3947	4037	4127	4217	4307	4396	4486	4576	4666	4756	90
4	4845	4935	5025	5114	5204	5294	5383	5473	5563	5652	90
485	5742	5831	5921	6010	6100	6189	6279	6368	6458	6547	89
6	6636	6726	6815	6904	6994	7083	7172	7261	7351	7440	89
7	7529	7618	7707	7796	7886	7975	8064	8153	8242	8331	89
8	8420	8509	8598	8687	8776	8865	8953	9042	9131	9220	89
9	9309	9398	9486	9575	9664	9753	9841	9930	690019	690107	89
490	690196	690285	690373	690462	690550	690639	690728	690816	690905	690993	89
1	1081	1170	1258	1347	1435	1524	1612	1700	1789	1877	88
2	1965	2053	2142	2230	2318	2406	2494	2583	2671	2759	88
3	2847	2935	3023	3111	3199	3287	3375	3463	3551	3639	88
4	3727	3815	3903	3991	4078	4166	4254	4342	4430	4517	88
495	4605	4693	4781	4868	4956	5044	5131	5219	5307	5394	88
6	5482	5569	5657	5744	5832	5919	6007	6094	6182	6269	87
7	6356	6444	6531	6618	6706	6793	6880	6968	7055	7142	87
8	7229	7317	7404	7491	7578	7665	7752	7839	7926	8014	87
9	8101	8188	8275	8362	8449	8535	8622	8709	8796	8883	87
500	698970	699057	699144	699231	699317	699404	699491	699578	699664	699751	87
1	9838	9924	700011	700098	700184	700271	700358	700444	700531	700617	87
2	700704	700790	0877	0963	1050	1136	1222	1309	1395	1482	86
3	1568	1654	1741	1827	1913	1999	2086	2172	2258	2344	86
4	2431	2517	2603	2689	2775	2861	2947	3033	3119	3205	86
505	3291	3377	3463	3549	3635	3721	3807	3893	3979	4065	86
6	4151	4236	4322	4408	4494	4579	4665	4751	4837	4922	86
7	5008	5094	5179	5265	5350	5436	5522	5607	5693	5778	86
8	5864	5949	6035	6120	6206	6291	6376	6462	6547	6632	85
9	6718	6803	6888	6974	7059	7144	7229	7315	7400	7485	85
510	707570	707655	707740	707826	707911	707996	708081	708166	708251	708336	85
1	8421	8506	8591	8676	8761	8846	8931	9015	9100	9185	85
2	9270	9355	9440	9524	9609	9694	9779	9863	9948	710033	85
3	710117	710202	710287	710371	710456	710540	710625	710710	710794	0879	85
4	0963	1048	1132	1217	1301	1385	1470	1554	1639	1723	84
515	1807	1892	1976	2060	2144	2229	2313	2397	2481	2566	84
6	2650	2734	2818	2902	2986	3070	3154	3238	3323	3407	84
7	3491	3575	3659	3742	3826	3910	3994	4078	4162	4246	84
8	4330	4414	4497	4581	4665	4749	4833	4916	5000	5084	84
9	5167	5251	5335	5418	5502	5586	5669	5753	5836	5920	84
N.	0	1	2	3	4	5	6	7	8	9	D.

Table XXIV—continued

SIX PLACE MANTISSAS

N.	0	1	2	3	4	5	6	7	8	9	D.
520	716003	716087	716170	716254	716337	716421	716504	716588	716671	716754	83
1	6838	6921	7004	7088	7171	7254	7338	7421	7504	7587	83
2	7671	7754	7837	7920	8003	8086	8169	8253	8336	8419	83
3	8502	8585	8668	8751	8834	8917	9000	9083	9165	9248	83
4	9331	9414	9497	9580	9663	9745	9828	9911	9994	720077	83
525	720159	720242	720325	720407	720490	720573	720655	720738	720821	0903	83
6	0986	1068	1151	1233	1316	1398	1481	1563	1646	1728	82
7	1811	1893	1975	2058	2140	2222	2305	2387	2469	2552	82
8	2634	2716	2798	2881	2963	3045	3127	3209	3291	3374	82
9	3456	3538	3620	3702	3784	3866	3948	4030	4112	4194	82
530	724276	724358	724440	724522	724604	724685	724767	724849	724931	725013	82
1	5095	5176	5258	5340	5422	5503	5585	5667	5748	5830	82
2	5912	5993	6075	6156	6238	6320	6401	6483	6564	6646	82
3	6727	6809	6890	6972	7053	7134	7216	7297	7379	7460	81
4	7541	7623	7704	7785	7866	7948	8029	8110	8191	8273	81
535	8354	8435	8516	8597	8678	8759	8841	8922	9003	9084	81
6	9165	9246	9327	9408	9489	9570	9651	9732	9813	9893	81
7	9974	730055	730136	730217	730298	730378	730459	730540	730621	730702	81
8	730782	0863	0944	1024	1105	1186	1266	1347	1428	1508	81
9	1589	1669	1750	1830	1911	1991	2072	2152	2233	2313	81
540	732394	732474	732555	732635	732715	732796	732876	732956	733037	733117	80
1	3197	3278	3358	3438	3518	3598	3679	3759	3839	3919	80
2	3999	4079	4160	4240	4320	4400	4480	4560	4640	4720	80
3	4800	4880	4960	5040	5120	5200	5279	5359	5439	5519	80
4	5599	5679	5759	5838	5918	5998	6078	6157	6237	6317	80
545	6397	6476	6556	6635	6715	6795	6874	6954	7034	7113	80
6	7193	7272	7352	7431	7511	7590	7670	7749	7829	7908	79
7	7987	8067	8146	8225	8305	8384	8463	8543	8622	8701	79
8	8781	8860	8939	9018	9097	9177	9256	9335	9414	9493	79
9	9572	9651	9731	9810	9889	9968	740047	740126	740205	740284	79
550	740363	740442	740521	740600	740678	740757	740836	740915	740994	741073	79
1	1152	1230	1309	1388	1467	1546	1624	1703	1782	1860	79
2	1939	2018	2096	2175	2254	2332	2411	2489	2568	2647	79
3	2725	2804	2882	2961	3039	3118	3196	3275	3353	3431	78
4	3510	3588	3667	3745	3823	3902	3980	4058	4136	4215	78
555	4293	4371	4449	4528	4606	4684	4762	4840	4919	4997	78
6	5075	5153	5231	5309	5387	5465	5543	5621	5699	5777	78
7	5855	5933	6011	6089	6167	6245	6323	6401	6479	6556	78
8	6634	6712	6790	6868	6945	7023	7101	7179	7256	7334	78
9	7412	7489	7567	7645	7722	7800	7878	7955	8033	8110	78
560	748188	748266	748343	748421	748498	748576	748653	748731	748808	748885	77
1	8963	9040	9118	9195	9272	9350	9427	9504	9582	9659	77
2	9736	9814	9891	9968	750045	750123	750200	750277	750354	750431	77
3	750508	750586	750663	750740	0817	0894	0971	1048	1125	1202	77
4	1279	1356	1433	1510	1587	1664	1741	1818	1895	1972	77
565	2048	2125	2202	2279	2356	2433	2509	2586	2663	2740	77
6	2816	2893	2970	3047	3123	3200	3277	3353	3430	3506	77
7	3583	3660	3736	3813	3889	3966	4042	4119	4195	4272	77
8	4348	4425	4501	4578	4654	4730	4807	4883	4960	5036	76
9	5112	5189	5265	5341	5417	5494	5570	5646	5722	5799	76
570	755875	755951	756027	756103	756180	756256	756332	756408	756484	756560	76
1	6636	6712	6788	6864	6940	7016	7092	7168	7244	7320	76
2	7396	7472	7548	7624	7700	7775	7851	7927	8003	8079	76
3	8155	8230	8306	8382	8458	8533	8609	8685	8761	8836	76
4	8912	8988	9063	9139	9214	9290	9366	9441	9517	9592	76
575	9668	9743	9819	9894	9970	760045	760121	760196	760272	760347	75
6	760422	760498	760573	760649	760724	0799	0875	0950	1025	1101	75
7	1176	1251	1326	1402	1477	1552	1627	1702	1778	1853	75
8	1928	2003	2078	2153	2228	2303	2378	2453	2529	2604	75
9	2679	2754	2829	2904	2978	3053	3128	3203	3278	3353	75
N.	0	1	2	3	4	5	6	7	8	9	D.

Table XXIV–continued

SIX PLACE MANTISSAS

N.	0	1	2	3	4	5	6	7	8	9	D.
580	763428	763503	763578	763653	763727	763802	763877	763952	764027	764101	75
1	4176	4251	4326	4400	4475	4550	4624	4699	4774	4848	75
2	4923	4998	5072	5147	5221	5296	5370	5445	5520	5594	75
3	5669	5743	5818	5892	5966	6041	6115	6190	6264	6338	74
4	6413	6487	6562	6636	6710	6785	6859	6933	7007	7082	74
585	7156	7230	7304	7379	7453	7527	7601	7675	7749	7823	74
6	7898	7972	8046	8120	8194	8268	8342	8416	8490	8564	74
7	8638	8712	8786	8860	8934	9008	9082	9156	9230	9303	74
8	9377	9451	9525	9599	9673	9746	9820	9894	9968	770042	74
9	770115	770189	770263	770336	770410	770484	770557	770631	770705	0778	74
590	770852	770926	770999	771073	771146	771220	771293	771367	771440	771514	74
1	1587	1661	1734	1808	1881	1955	2028	2102	2175	2248	73
2	2322	2395	2468	2542	2615	2688	2762	2835	2908	2981	73
3	3055	3128	3201	3274	3348	3421	3494	3567	3640	3713	73
4	3786	3860	3933	4006	4079	4152	4225	4298	4371	4444	73
595	4517	4590	4663	4736	4809	4882	4955	5028	5100	5173	73
6	5246	5319	5392	5465	5538	5610	5683	5756	5829	5902	73
7	5974	6047	6120	6193	6265	6338	6411	6483	6556	6629	73
8	6701	6774	6846	6919	6992	7064	7137	7209	7282	7354	73
9	7427	7499	7572	7644	7717	7789	7862	7934	8006	8079	72
600	778151	778224	778296	778368	778441	778513	778585	778658	778730	778802	72
1	8874	8947	9019	9091	9163	9236	9308	9380	9452	9524	72
2	9596	9669	9741	9813	9885	3957	780029	780101	780173	780245	72
3	780317	780389	780461	780533	780605	780677	0749	0821	0893	0965	72
4	1037	1109	1181	1253	1324	1396	1468	1540	1612	1684	72
605	1755	1827	1899	1971	2042	2114	2186	2258	2329	2401	72
6	2473	2544	2616	2688	2759	2831	2902	2974	3046	3117	72
7	3189	3260	3332	3403	3475	3546	3618	3689	3761	3832	71
8	3904	3975	4046	4118	4189	4261	4332	4403	4475	4546	71
9	4617	4689	4760	4831	4902	4974	5045	5116	5187	5259	71
610	785330	785401	785472	785543	785615	785686	785757	785828	785899	785970	71
1	6041	6112	6183	6254	6325	6396	6467	6538	6609	6680	71
2	6751	6822	6893	6964	7035	7106	7177	7248	7319	7390	71
3	7460	7531	7602	7673	7744	7815	7885	7956	8027	8098	71
4	8168	8239	8310	8381	8451	8522	8593	8663	8734	8804	71
615	8875	8946	9016	9087	9157	9228	9299	9369	9440	9510	71
6	9581	9651	9722	9792	9863	9933	790004	790074	790144	790215	70
7	790285	790356	790426	790496	790567	790637	0707	0778	0848	0918	70
8	0988	1059	1129	1199	1269	1340	1410	1480	1550	1620	70
9	1691	1761	1831	1901	1971	2041	2111	2181	2252	2322	70
620	792392	792462	792532	792602	792672	792742	792812	792882	792952	793022	70
1	3092	3162	3231	3301	3371	3441	3511	3581	3651	3721	70
2	3790	3860	3930	4000	4070	4139	4209	4279	4349	4418	70
3	4488	4558	4627	4697	4767	4836	4906	4976	5045	5115	70
4	5185	5254	5324	5393	5463	5532	5602	5672	5741	5811	70
625	5880	5949	6019	6088	6158	6227	6297	6366	6436	6505	69
6	6574	6644	6713	6782	6852	6921	6990	7060	7129	7198	69
7	7268	7337	7406	7475	7545	7614	7683	7752	7821	7890	69
8	7960	8029	8098	8167	8236	8305	8374	8443	8513	8582	69
9	8651	8720	8789	8858	8927	8996	9065	9134	9203	9272	69
630	799341	799409	799478	799547	799616	799685	799754	799823	799892	799961	69
1	800029	800098	800167	800236	800305	800373	800442	800511	800580	800648	69
2	0717	0786	0854	0923	0992	1061	1129	1198	1266	1335	69
3	1404	1472	1541	1609	1678	1747	1815	1884	1952	2021	69
4	2089	2158	2226	2295	2363	2432	2500	2568	2637	2705	68
635	2774	2842	2910	2979	3047	3116	3184	3252	3321	3389	68
6	3457	3525	3594	3662	3730	3798	3867	3935	4003	4071	68
7	4139	4208	4276	4344	4412	4480	4548	4616	4685	4753	68
8	4821	4889	4957	5025	5093	5161	5229	5297	5365	5433	68
9	5501	5569	5637	5705	5773	5841	5908	5976	6044	6112	68
N.	0	1	2	3	4	5	6	7	8	9	D.

Table XXIV—continued

SIX PLACE MANTISSAS

N	0	1	2	3	4	5	6	7	8	9	D.
640	806180	806248	806316	806384	806451	806519	806587	806655	806723	806790	68
1	6858	6926	6994	7061	7129	7197	7264	7332	7400	7467	68
2	7535	7603	7670	7738	7806	7873	7941	8008	8076	8143	68
3	8211	8279	8346	8414	8481	8549	8616	8684	8751	8818	67
4	8886	8953	9021	9088	9156	9223	9290	9358	9425	9492	67
645	9560	9627	9694	9762	9829	9896	9964	810031	810098	810165	67
6	810233	810300	810367	810434	810501	810569	810636	0703	0770	0837	67
7	0904	0971	1039	1106	1173	1240	1307	1374	1441	1508	67
8	1575	1642	1709	1776	1843	1910	1977	2044	2111	2178	67
9	2245	2312	2379	2445	2512	2579	2646	2713	2780	2847	67
650	812913	812980	813047	813114	813181	813247	813314	813381	813448	813514	67
1	3581	3648	3714	3781	3848	3914	3981	4048	4114	4181	67
2	4248	4314	4381	4447	4514	4581	4647	4714	4780	4847	67
3	4913	4980	5046	5113	5179	5246	5312	5378	5445	5511	66
4	5578	5644	5711	5777	5843	5910	5976	6042	6109	6175	66
655	6241	6308	6374	6440	6506	6573	6639	6705	6771	6838	66
6	6904	6970	7036	7102	7169	7235	7301	7367	7433	7499	66
7	7565	7631	7698	7764	7830	7896	7962	8028	8094	8160	66
8	8226	8292	8358	8424	8490	8556	8622	8688	8754	8820	66
9	8885	8951	9017	9083	9149	9215	9281	9346	9412	9478	66
660	819544	819610	819676	819741	819807	819873	819939	820004	820070	820136	66
1	820201	820267	820333	820399	820464	820530	820595	0661	0727	0792	66
2	0858	0924	0989	1055	1120	1186	1251	1317	1382	1448	66
3	1514	1579	1645	1710	1775	1841	1906	1972	2037	2103	65
4	2168	2233	2299	2364	2430	2495	2560	2626	2691	2756	65
665	2822	2887	2952	3018	3083	3148	3213	3279	3344	3409	65
6	3474	3539	3605	3670	3735	3800	3865	3930	3996	4061	65
7	4126	4191	4256	4321	4386	4451	4516	4581	4646	4711	65
8	4776	4841	4906	4971	5036	5101	5166	5231	5296	5361	65
9	5426	5491	5556	5621	5686	5751	5815	5880	5945	6010	65
670	826075	826140	826204	826269	826334	826399	826464	826528	826593	826658	65
1	6723	6787	6852	6917	6981	7046	7111	7175	7240	7305	65
2	7369	7434	7499	7563	7628	7692	7757	7821	7886	7951	65
3	8015	8080	8144	8209	8273	8338	8402	8467	8531	8595	64
4	8660	8724	8789	8853	8918	8982	9046	9111	9175	9239	64
675	9304	9368	9432	9497	9561	9625	9690	9754	9818	9882	64
6	9947	830011	830075	830139	830204	830268	830332	830396	830460	830525	64
7	830589	0653	0717	0781	0845	0909	0973	1037	1102	1166	64
8	1230	1294	1358	1422	1486	1550	1614	1678	1742	1806	64
9	1870	1934	1998	2062	2126	2189	2253	2317	2381	2445	64
680	832509	832573	832637	832700	832764	832828	832892	832956	833020	833083	64
1	3147	3211	3275	3338	3402	3466	3530	3593	3657	3721	64
2	3784	3848	3912	3975	4039	4103	4166	4230	4294	4357	64
3	4421	4484	4548	4611	4675	4739	4802	4866	4929	4993	64
4	5056	5120	5183	5247	5310	5373	5437	5500	5564	5627	63
685	5691	5754	5817	5881	5944	6007	6071	6134	6197	6261	63
6	6324	6387	6451	6514	6577	6641	6704	6767	6830	6894	63
7	6957	7020	7083	7146	7210	7273	7336	7399	7462	7525	63
8	7588	7652	7715	7778	7841	7904	7967	8030	8093	8156	63
9	8219	8282	8345	8408	8471	8534	8597	8660	8723	8786	63
690	838849	838912	838975	839038	839101	839164	839227	839289	839352	839415	63
1	9478	9541	9604	9667	9729	9792	9855	9918	9981	840043	63
2	840106	840169	840232	840294	840357	840420	840482	840545	840608	0671	63
3	0733	0796	0859	0921	0984	1046	1109	1172	1234	1297	63
4	1359	1422	1485	1547	1610	1672	1735	1797	1860	1922	63
695	1985	2047	2110	2172	2235	2297	2360	2422	2484	2547	62
6	2609	2672	2734	2796	2859	2921	2983	3046	3108	3170	62
7	3233	3295	3357	3420	3482	3544	3606	3669	3731	3793	62
8	3855	3918	3980	4042	4104	4166	4229	4291	4353	4415	62
9	4477	4539	4601	4664	4726	4788	4850	4912	4974	5036	62
N.	0	1	2	3	4	5	6	7	8	9	D.

Table XXIV–continued

SIX PLACE MANTISSAS

N.	0	1	2	3	4	5	6	7	8	9	D.
700	845098	845160	845222	845284	845346	845408	845470	845532	845594	845656	62
1	5718	5780	5842	5904	5966	6028	6090	6151	6213	6275	62
2	6337	6399	6461	6523	6585	6646	6708	6770	6832	6894	62
3	6955	7017	7079	7141	7202	7264	7326	7388	7449	7511	62
4	7573	7634	7696	7758	7819	7881	7943	8004	8066	8128	62
705	8189	8251	8312	8374	8435	8497	8559	8620	8682	8743	62
6	8805	8866	8928	8989	9051	9112	9174	9235	9297	9358	61
7	9419	9481	9542	9604	9665	9726	9788	9849	9911	9972	61
8	850033	850095	850156	850217	850279	850340	850401	850462	850524	850585	61
9	0646	0707	0769	0830	0891	0952	1014	1075	1136	1197	61
710	851258	851320	851381	851442	851503	851564	851625	851686	851747	851809	61
1	1870	1931	1992	2053	2114	2175	2236	2297	2358	2419	61
2	2480	2541	2602	2663	2724	2785	2846	2907	2968	3029	61
3	3090	3150	3211	3272	3333	3394	3455	3516	3577	3637	61
4	3698	3759	3820	3881	3941	4002	4063	4124	4185	4245	61
715	4306	4367	4428	4488	4549	4610	4670	4731	4792	4852	61
6	4913	4974	5034	5095	5156	5216	5277	5337	5398	5459	61
7	5519	5580	5640	5701	5761	5822	5882	5943	6003	6064	61
8	6124	6185	6245	6306	6366	6427	6487	6548	6608	6668	60
9	6729	6789	6850	6910	6970	7031	7091	7152	7212	7272	60
720	857332	857393	857453	857513	857574	857634	857694	857755	857815	857875	60
1	7935	7995	8056	8116	8176	8236	8297	8357	8417	8477	60
2	8537	8597	8657	8718	8778	8838	8898	8958	9018	9078	60
3	9138	9198	9258	9318	9379	9439	9499	9559	9619	9679	60
4	9739	9799	9859	9918	9978	860038	860098	860158	860218	860278	60
725	860338	860398	860458	860518	860578	0637	0697	0757	0817	0877	60
6	0937	0996	1056	1116	1176	1236	1295	1355	1415	1475	60
7	1534	1594	1654	1714	1773	1833	1893	1952	2012	2072	60
8	2131	2191	2251	2310	2370	2430	2489	2549	2608	2668	60
9	2728	2787	2847	2906	2966	3025	3085	3144	3204	3263	60
730	863323	863382	863442	863501	863561	863620	863680	863739	863799	863858	59
1	3917	3977	4036	4096	4155	4214	4274	4333	4392	4452	59
2	4511	4570	4630	4689	4748	4808	4867	4926	4985	5045	59
3	5104	5163	5222	5282	5341	5400	5459	5519	5578	5637	59
4	5696	5755	5814	5874	5933	5992	6051	6110	6169	6228	59
735	6287	6346	6405	6465	6524	6583	6642	6701	6760	6819	59
6	6878	6937	6996	7055	7114	7173	7232	7291	7350	7409	59
7	7467	7526	7585	7644	7703	7762	7821	7880	7939	7998	59
8	8056	8115	8174	8233	8292	8350	8409	8468	8527	8586	59
9	8644	8703	8762	8821	8879	8938	8997	9056	9114	9173	59
740	869232	869290	869349	869408	869466	869525	869584	869642	869701	869760	59
1	9818	9877	9935	9994	870053	870111	870170	870228	870287	870345	59
2	870404	870462	870521	870579	0638	0696	0755	0813	0872	0930	58
3	0989	1047	1106	1164	1223	1281	1339	1398	1456	1515	58
4	1573	1631	1690	1748	1806	1865	1923	1981	2040	2098	58
745	2156	2215	2273	2331	2389	2448	2506	2564	2622	2681	58
6	2739	2797	2855	2913	2972	3030	3088	3146	3204	3262	58
7	3321	3379	3437	3495	3553	3611	3669	3727	3785	3844	58
8	3902	3960	4018	4076	4134	4192	4250	4308	4366	4424	58
9	4482	4540	4598	4656	4714	4772	4830	4888	4945	5003	58
750	875061	875119	875177	875235	875293	875351	875409	875466	875524	875582	58
1	5640	5698	5756	5813	5871	5929	5987	6045	6102	6160	58
2	6218	6276	6333	6391	6449	6507	6564	6622	6680	6737	58
3	6795	6853	6910	6968	7026	7083	7141	7199	7256	7314	58
4	7371	7429	7487	7544	7602	7659	7717	7774	7832	7889	58
755	7947	8004	8062	8119	8177	8234	8292	8349	8407	8464	57
6	8522	8579	8637	8694	8752	8809	8866	8924	8981	9039	57
7	9096	9153	9211	9268	9325	9383	9440	9497	9555	9612	57
8	9669	9726	9784	9841	9898	9956	880013	880070	880127	880185	57
9	880242	880299	880356	880413	880471	880528	0585	0642	0699	0756	57
N.	0	1	2	3	4	5	6	7	8	9	D

Table XXIV—continued

SIX PLACE MANTISSAS

N.	0	1	2	3	4	5	6	7	8	9	D.
760	880814	880871	880928	880985	881042	881099	881156	881213	881271	881328	57
1	1385	1442	1499	1556	1613	1670	1727	1784	1841	1898	57
2	1955	2012	2069	2126	2183	2240	2297	2354	2411	2468	57
3	2525	2581	2638	2695	2752	2809	2866	2923	2980	3037	57
4	3093	3150	3207	3264	3321	3377	3434	3491	3548	3605	57
765	3661	3718	3775	3832	3888	3945	4002	4059	4115	4172	57
6	4229	4285	4342	4399	4455	4512	4569	4625	4682	4739	57
7	4795	4852	4909	4965	5022	5078	5135	5192	5248	5305	57
8	5361	5418	5474	5531	5587	5644	5700	5757	5813	5870	57
9	5926	5983	6039	6096	6152	6209	6265	6321	6378	6434	56
770	886491	886547	886604	886660	886716	886773	886829	886885	886942	886998	56
1	7054	7111	7167	7223	7280	7336	7392	7449	7505	7561	56
2	7617	7674	7730	7786	7842	7898	7955	8011	8067	8123	56
3	8179	8236	8292	8348	8404	8460	8516	8573	8629	8685	56
4	8741	8797	8853	8909	8965	9021	9077	9134	9190	9246	56
775	9302	9358	9414	9470	9526	9582	9638	9694	9750	9806	56
6	9862	9918	9974	890030	890086	890141	890197	890253	890309	890365	56
7	890421	890477	890533	0589	0645	0700	0756	0812	0868	0924	56
8	0980	1035	1091	1147	1203	1259	1314	1370	1426	1482	56
9	1537	1593	1649	1705	1760	1816	1872	1928	1983	2039	56
780	892095	892150	892206	892262	892317	892373	892429	892484	892540	892595	56
1	2651	2707	2762	2818	2873	2929	2985	3040	3096	3151	56
2	3207	3262	3318	3373	3429	3484	3540	3595	3651	3706	56
3	3762	3817	3873	3928	3984	4039	4094	4150	4205	4261	55
4	4316	4371	4427	4482	4538	4593	4648	4704	4759	4814	55
785	4870	4925	4980	5036	5091	5146	5201	5257	5312	5367	55
6	5423	5478	5533	5588	5644	5699	5754	5809	5864	5920	55
7	5975	6030	6085	6140	6195	6251	6306	6361	6416	6471	55
8	6526	6581	6636	6692	6747	6802	6857	6912	6967	7022	55
9	7077	7132	7187	7242	7297	7352	7407	7462	7517	7572	55
790	897627	897682	897737	897792	897847	897902	897957	898012	898067	898122	55
1	8176	8231	8286	8341	8396	8451	8506	8561	8615	8670	55
2	8725	8780	8835	8890	8944	8999	9054	9109	9164	9218	55
3	9273	9328	9383	9437	9492	9547	9602	9656	9711	9766	55
4	9821	9875	9930	9985	900039	900094	900149	900203	900258	900312	55
795	900367	900422	900476	900531	0586	0640	0695	0749	0804	0859	55
6	0913	0968	1022	1077	1131	1186	1240	1295	1349	1404	55
7	1458	1513	1567	1622	1676	1731	1785	1840	1894	1948	54
8	2003	2057	2112	2166	2221	2275	2329	2384	2438	2492	54
9	2547	2601	2655	2710	2764	2818	2873	2927	2981	3036	54
800	903090	903144	903199	903253	903307	903361	903416	903470	903524	903578	54
1	3633	3687	3741	3795	3849	3904	3958	4012	4066	4120	54
2	4174	4229	4283	4337	4391	4445	4499	4553	4607	4661	54
3	4716	4770	4824	4878	4932	4986	5040	5094	5148	5202	54
4	5256	5310	5364	5418	5472	5526	5580	5634	5688	5742	54
805	5796	5850	5904	5958	6012	6066	6119	6173	6227	6281	54
6	6335	6389	6443	6497	6551	6604	6658	6712	6766	6820	54
7	6874	6927	6981	7035	7089	7143	7196	7250	7304	7358	54
8	7411	7465	7519	7573	7626	7680	7734	7787	7841	7895	54
9	7949	8002	8056	8110	8163	8217	8270	8324	8378	8431	54
810	908485	908539	908592	908646	908699	908753	908807	908860	908914	908967	54
1	9021	9074	9128	9181	9235	9289	9342	9396	9449	9503	54
2	9556	9610	9663	9716	9770	9823	9877	9930	9984	910037	53
3	910091	910144	910197	910251	910304	910358	910411	910464	910518	0571	53
4	0624	0678	0731	0784	0838	0891	0944	0998	1051	1104	53
815	1158	1211	1264	1317	1371	1424	1477	1530	1584	1637	53
6	1690	1743	1797	1850	1903	1956	2009	2063	2116	2169	53
7	2222	2275	2328	2381	2435	2488	2541	2594	2647	2700	53
8	2753	2806	2859	2913	2966	3019	3072	3125	3178	3231	53
9	3284	3337	3390	3443	3496	3549	3602	3655	3708	3761	53
N.	0	1	2	3	4	5	6	7	8	9	D.

Table XXIV–continued

SIX PLACE MANTISSAS

N.	0	1	2	3	4	5	6	7	8	9	D.
820	913814	913867	913920	913973	914026	914079	914132	914184	914237	914290	53
1	4343	4396	4449	4502	4555	4608	4660	4713	4766	4819	53
2	4872	4925	4977	5030	5083	5136	5189	5241	5294	5347	53
3	5400	5453	5505	5558	5611	5664	5716	5769	5822	5875	53
4	5927	5980	6033	6085	6138	6191	6243	6296	6349	6401	53
825	6454	6507	6559	6612	6664	6717	6770	6822	6875	6927	53
6	6980	7033	7085	7138	7190	7243	7295	7348	7400	7453	53
7	7506	7558	7611	7663	7716	7768	7820	7873	7925	7978	52
8	8030	8083	8135	8188	8240	8293	8345	8397	8450	8502	52
9	8555	8607	8659	8712	8764	8816	8869	8921	8973	9026	52
830	919078	919130	919183	919235	919287	919340	919392	919444	919496	919549	52
1	9601	9653	9706	9758	9810	9862	9914	9967	920019	920071	52
2	920123	920176	920228	920280	920332	920384	920436	920489	0541	0593	52
3	0645	0697	0749	0801	0853	0906	0958	1010	1062	1114	52
4	1166	1218	1270	1322	1374	1426	1478	1530	1582	1634	52
835	1686	1738	1790	1842	1894	1946	1998	2050	2102	2154	52
6	2206	2258	2310	2362	2414	2466	2518	2570	2622	2674	52
7	2725	2777	2829	2881	2933	2985	3037	3089	3140	3192	52
8	3244	3296	3348	3399	3451	3503	3555	3607	3658	3710	52
9	3762	3814	3865	3917	3969	4021	4072	4124	4176	4228	52
840	924279	924331	924383	924434	924486	924538	924589	924641	924693	924744	52
1	4796	4848	4899	4951	5003	5054	5106	5157	5209	5261	52
2	5312	5364	5415	5467	5518	5570	5621	5673	5725	5776	52
3	5828	5879	5931	5982	6034	6085	6137	6188	6240	6291	51
4	6342	6394	6445	6497	6548	6600	6651	6702	6754	6805	51
845	6857	6908	6959	7011	7062	7114	7165	7216	7268	7319	51
6	7370	7422	7473	7524	7576	7627	7678	7730	7781	7832	51
7	7883	7935	7986	8037	8088	8140	8191	8242	8293	8345	51
8	8396	8447	8498	8549	8601	8652	8703	8754	8805	8857	51
9	8908	8959	9010	9061	9112	9163	9215	9266	9317	9368	51
850	929419	929470	929521	929572	929623	929674	929725	929776	929827	929879	51
1	9930	9981	930032	930083	930134	930185	930236	930287	930338	930389	51
2	930440	930491	0542	0592	0643	0694	0745	0796	0847	0898	51
3	0949	1000	1051	1102	1153	1204	1254	1305	1356	1407	51
4	1458	1509	1560	1610	1661	1712	1763	1814	1865	1915	51
855	1966	2017	2068	2118	2169	2220	2271	2322	2372	2423	51
6	2474	2524	2575	2626	2677	2727	2778	2829	2879	2930	51
7	2981	3031	3082	3133	3183	3234	3285	3335	3386	3437	51
8	3487	3538	3589	3639	3690	3740	3791	3841	3892	3943	51
9	3993	4044	4094	4145	4195	4246	4296	4347	4397	4448	51
860	934498	934549	934599	934650	934700	934751	934801	934852	934902	934953	50
1	5003	5054	5104	5154	5205	5255	5306	5356	5406	5457	50
2	5507	5558	5608	5658	5709	5759	5809	5860	5910	5960	50
3	6011	6061	6111	6162	6212	6262	6313	6363	6413	6463	50
4	6514	6564	6614	6665	6715	6765	6815	6865	6916	6966	50
865	7016	7066	7117	7167	7217	7267	7317	7367	7418	7468	50
6	7518	7568	7618	7668	7718	7769	7819	7869	7919	7969	50
7	8019	8069	8119	8169	8219	8269	8320	8370	8420	8470	50
8	8520	8570	8620	8670	8720	8770	8820	8870	8920	8970	50
9	9020	9070	9120	9170	9220	9270	9320	9369	9419	9469	50
870	939519	939569	939619	939669	939719	939769	939819	939869	939918	939968	50
1	940018	940068	940118	940168	940218	940267	940317	940367	940417	940467	50
2	0516	0566	0616	0666	0716	0765	0815	0865	0915	0964	50
3	1014	1064	1114	1163	1213	1263	1313	1362	1412	1462	50
4	1511	1561	1611	1660	1710	1760	1809	1859	1909	1958	50
875	2008	2058	2107	2157	2207	2256	2306	2355	2405	2455	50
6	2504	2554	2603	2653	2702	2752	2801	2851	2901	2950	50
7	3000	3049	3099	3148	3198	3247	3297	3346	3396	3445	49
8	3495	3544	3593	3643	3692	3742	3791	3841	3890	3939	49
9	3989	4038	4088	4137	4186	4236	4285	4335	4384	4433	49
N.	0	1	2	3	4	5	6	7	8	9	D.

Table XXIV—continued

SIX PLACE MANTISSAS

N.	0	1	2	3	4	5	6	7	8	9	D.
880	944483	944532	944581	944631	944680	944729	944779	944828	944877	944927	49
1	4976	5025	5074	5124	5173	5222	5272	5321	5370	5419	49
2	5469	5518	5567	5616	5665	5715	5764	5813	5862	5912	49
3	5961	6010	6059	6108	6157	6207	6256	6305	6354	6403	49
4	6452	6501	6551	6600	6649	6698	6747	6796	6845	6894	49
885	6943	6992	7041	7090	7140	7189	7238	7287	7336	7385	49
6	7434	7483	7532	7581	7630	7679	7728	7777	7826	7875	49
7	7924	7973	8022	8070	8119	8168	8217	8266	8315	8364	49
8	8413	8462	8511	8560	8609	8657	8706	8755	8804	8853	49
9	8902	8951	8999	9048	9097	9146	9195	9244	9292	9341	49
890	949390	949439	949488	949536	949585	949634	949683	949731	949780	949829	49
1	9878	9926	9975	950024	950073	950121	950170	950219	950267	950316	49
2	950365	950414	950462	0511	0560	0608	0657	0706	0754	0803	49
3	0851	0900	0949	0997	1046	1095	1143	1192	1240	1289	49
4	1338	1386	1435	1483	1532	1580	1629	1677	1726	1775	49
895	1823	1872	1920	1969	2017	2066	2114	2163	2211	2260	48
6	2308	2356	2405	2453	2502	2550	2599	2647	2696	2744	48
7	2792	2841	2889	2938	2986	3034	3083	3131	3180	3228	48
8	3276	3325	3373	3421	3470	3518	3566	3615	3663	3711	48
9	3760	3808	3856	3905	3953	4001	4049	4098	4146	4194	48
900	954243	954291	954339	954387	954435	954484	954532	954580	954628	954677	48
1	4725	4773	4821	4869	4918	4966	5014	5062	5110	5158	48
2	5207	5255	5303	5351	5399	5447	5495	5543	5592	5640	48
3	5688	5736	5784	5832	5880	5928	5976	6024	6072	6120	48
4	6168	6216	6265	6313	6361	6409	6457	6505	6553	6601	48
905	6649	6697	6745	6793	6840	6888	6936	6984	7032	7080	48
6	7128	7176	7224	7272	7320	7368	7416	7464	7512	7559	48
7	7607	7655	7703	7751	7799	7847	7894	7942	7990	8038	48
8	8086	8134	8181	8229	8277	8325	8373	8421	8468	8516	48
9	8564	8612	8659	8707	8755	8803	8850	8898	8946	8994	48
910	959041	959089	959137	959185	959232	959280	959328	959375	959423	959471	48
1	9518	9566	9614	9661	9709	9757	9804	9852	9900	9947	48
2	9995	960042	960090	960138	960185	960233	960280	960328	960376	960423	48
3	960471	0518	0566	0613	0661	0709	0756	0804	0851	0899	48
4	0946	0994	1041	1089	1136	1184	1231	1279	1326	1374	48
915	1421	1469	1516	1563	1611	1658	1706	1753	1801	1848	47
6	1895	1943	1990	2038	2085	2132	2180	2227	2275	2322	47
7	2369	2417	2464	2511	2559	2606	2653	2701	2748	2795	47
8	2843	2890	2937	2985	3032	3079	3126	3174	3221	3268	47
9	3316	3363	3410	3457	3504	3552	3599	3646	3693	3741	47
920	963788	963835	963882	963929	963977	964024	964071	964118	964165	964212	47
1	4260	4307	4354	4401	4448	4495	4542	4590	4637	4684	47
2	4731	4778	4825	4872	4919	4966	5013	5061	5108	5155	47
3	5202	5249	5296	5343	5390	5437	5484	5531	5578	5625	47
4	5672	5719	5766	5813	5860	5907	5954	6001	6048	6095	47
925	6142	6189	6236	6283	6329	6376	6423	6470	6517	6564	47
6	6611	6658	6705	6752	6799	6845	6892	6939	6986	7033	47
7	7080	7127	7173	7220	7267	7314	7361	7408	7454	7501	47
8	7548	7595	7642	7688	7735	7782	7829	7875	7922	7969	47
9	8016	8062	8109	8156	8203	8249	8296	8343	8390	8436	47
930	968483	968530	968576	968623	968670	968716	968763	968810	968856	968903	47
1	8950	8996	9043	9090	9136	9183	9229	9276	9323	9369	47
2	9416	9463	9509	9556	9602	9649	9695	9742	9789	9835	47
3	9882	9928	9975	970021	970068	970114	970161	970207	970254	970300	47
4	970347	970393	970440	0486	0533	0579	0626	0672	0719	0765	46
935	0812	0858	0904	0951	0997	1044	1090	1137	1183	1229	46
6	1276	1322	1369	1415	1461	1508	1554	1601	1647	1693	46
7	1740	1786	1832	1879	1925	1971	2018	2064	2110	2157	46
8	2203	2249	2295	2342	2388	2434	2481	2527	2573	2619	46
9	2666	2712	2758	2804	2851	2897	2943	2989	3035	3082	46
N.	0	1	2	3	4	5	6	7	8	9	D.

Table XXIV–continued

SIX PLACE MANTISSAS

N.	0	1	2	3	4	5	6	7	8	9	D.
940	973128	973174	973220	973266	973313	973359	973405	973451	973497	973543	46
1	3590	3636	3682	3728	3774	3820	3866	3913	3959	4005	46
2	4051	4097	4143	4189	4235	4281	4327	4374	4420	4466	46
3	4512	4558	4604	4650	4696	4742	4788	4834	4880	4926	46
4	4972	5018	5064	5110	5156	5202	5248	5294	5340	5386	46
945	5432	5478	5524	5570	5616	5662	5707	5753	5799	5845	46
6	5891	5937	5983	6029	6075	6121	6167	6212	6258	6304	46
7	6350	6396	6442	6488	6533	6579	6625	6671	6717	6763	46
8	6808	6854	6900	6946	6992	7037	7083	7129	7175	7220	46
9	7266	7312	7358	7403	7449	7495	7541	7586	7632	7678	46
950	977724	977769	977815	977861	977906	977952	977998	978043	978089	978135	46
1	8181	8226	8272	8317	8363	8409	8454	8500	8546	8591	46
2	8637	8683	8728	8774	8819	8865	8911	8956	9002	9047	46
3	9093	9138	9184	9230	9275	9321	9366	9412	9457	9503	46
4	9548	9594	9639	9685	9730	9776	9821	9867	9912	9958	46
955	980003	980049	980094	980140	980185	980231	980276	980322	980367	980412	45
6	0458	0503	0549	0594	0640	0685	0730	0776	0821	0867	45
7	0912	0957	1003	1048	1093	1139	1184	1229	1275	1320	45
8	1366	1411	1456	1501	1547	1592	1637	1683	1728	1773	45
9	1819	1864	1909	1954	2000	2045	2090	2135	2181	2226	45
960	982271	982316	982362	982407	982452	982497	982543	982588	982633	982678	45
1	2723	2769	2814	2859	2904	2949	2994	3040	3085	3130	45
2	3175	3220	3265	3310	3356	3401	3446	3491	3536	3581	45
3	3626	3671	3716	3762	3807	3852	3897	3942	3987	4032	45
4	4077	4122	4167	4212	4257	4302	4347	4392	4437	4482	45
965	4527	4572	4617	4662	4707	4752	4797	4842	4887	4932	45
6	4977	5022	5067	5112	5157	5202	5247	5292	5337	5382	45
7	5426	5471	5516	5561	5606	5651	5696	5741	5786	5830	45
8	5875	5920	5965	6010	6055	6100	6144	6189	6234	6279	45
9	6324	6369	6413	6458	6503	6548	6593	6637	6682	6727	45
970	986772	986817	986861	986906	986951	986996	987040	987085	987130	987175	45
1	7219	7264	7309	7353	7398	7443	7488	7532	7577	7622	45
2	7666	7711	7756	7800	7845	7890	7934	7979	8024	8068	45
3	8113	8157	8202	8247	8291	8336	8381	8425	8470	8514	45
4	8559	8604	8648	8693	8737	8782	8826	8871	8916	8960	45
975	9005	9049	9094	9138	9183	9227	9272	9316	9361	9405	45
6	9450	9494	9539	9583	9628	9672	9717	9761	9806	9850	44
7	9895	9939	9983	990028	990072	990117	990161	990206	990250	990294	44
8	990339	990383	990428	0472	0516	0561	0605	0650	0694	0738	44
9	0783	0827	0871	0916	0960	1004	1049	1093	1137	1182	44
980	991226	991270	991315	991359	991403	991448	991492	991536	991580	991625	44
1	1669	1713	1758	1802	1846	1890	1935	1979	2023	2067	44
2	2111	2156	2200	2244	2288	2333	2377	2421	2465	2509	44
3	2554	2598	2642	2686	2730	2774	2819	2863	2907	2951	44
4	2995	3039	3083	3127	3172	3216	3260	3304	3348	3392	44
985	3436	3480	3524	3568	3613	3657	3701	3745	3789	3833	44
6	3877	3921	3965	4009	4053	4097	4141	4185	4229	4273	44
7	4317	4361	4405	4449	4493	4537	4581	4625	4669	4713	44
8	4757	4801	4845	4889	4933	4977	5021	5065	5108	5152	44
9	5196	5240	5284	5328	5372	5416	5460	5504	5547	5591	44
990	995635	995679	995723	995767	995811	995854	995898	995942	995986	996030	44
1	6074	6117	6161	6205	6249	6293	6337	6380	6424	6468	44
2	6512	6555	6599	6643	6687	6731	6774	6818	6862	6906	44
3	6949	6993	7037	7080	7124	7168	7212	7255	7299	7343	44
4	7386	7430	7474	7517	7561	7605	7648	7692	7736	7779	44
995	7823	7867	7910	7954	7998	8041	8085	8129	8172	8216	44
6	8259	8303	8347	8390	8434	8477	8521	8564	8608	8652	44
7	8695	8739	8782	8826	8869	8913	8956	9000	9043	9087	44
8	9131	9174	9218	9261	9305	9348	9392	9435	9479	9522	44
9	9565	9609	9652	9696	9739	9783	9826	9870	9913	9957	43
N.	0	1	2	3	4	5	6	7	8	9	D.

Table XXV

SEVEN PLACE MANTISSAS

10000–10509

N.		0	1	2	3	4	5	6	7	8	9	D.
1000	000	0000	0434	0869	1303	1737	2171	2605	3039	3473	3907	434
1001		4341	4775	5208	5642	6076	6510	6943	7377	7810	8244	434
1002		8677	9111	9544	9977	*0411	*0844	*1277	*1710	*2143	*2576	433
1003	001	3009	3442	3875	4308	4741	5174	5607	6039	6472	6905	433
1004		7337	7770	8202	8635	9067	9499	9932	*0364	*0796	*1228	432
1005	002	1661	2093	2525	2957	3389	3821	4253	4685	5116	5548	432
1006		5980	6411	6843	7275	7706	8138	8569	9001	9432	9863	431
1007	003	0295	0726	1157	1588	2019	2451	2882	3313	3744	4174	431
1008		4605	5036	5467	5898	6328	6759	7190	7620	8051	8481	431
1009		8912	9342	9772	*0203	*0633	*1063	*1493	*1924	*2354	*2784	430
1010	004	3214	3644	4074	4504	4933	5363	5793	6223	6652	7082	430
1011		7512	7941	8371	8800	9229	9659	*0088	*0517	*0947	*1376	429
1012	005	1805	2234	2663	3092	3521	3950	4379	4808	5237	5666	429
1013		6094	6523	6952	7380	7809	8238	8666	9094	9523	9951	429
1014	006	0380	0808	1236	1664	2092	2521	2949	3377	3805	4233	428
1015		4660	5088	5516	5944	6372	6799	7227	7655	8082	8510	428
1016		8937	9365	9792	*0219	*0647	*1074	*1501	*1928	*2355	*2782	427
1017	007	3210	3637	4064	4490	4917	5344	5771	6198	6624	7051	427
1018		7478	7904	8331	8757	9184	9610	*0037	*0463	*0889	*1316	426
1019	008	1742	2168	2594	3020	3446	3872	4298	4724	5150	5576	426
1020		6002	6427	6853	7279	7704	8130	8556	8981	9407	9832	426
1021	009	0257	0683	1108	1533	1959	2384	2809	3234	3659	4084	425
1022		4509	4934	5359	5784	6208	6633	7058	7483	7907	8332	425
1023		8756	9181	9605	*0030	*0454	*0878	*1303	*1727	*2151	*2575	424
1024	010	3000	3424	3848	4272	4696	5120	5544	5967	6391	6815	424
1025		7239	7662	8086	8510	8933	9357	9780	*0204	*0627	*1050	424
1026	011	1474	1897	2320	2743	3166	3590	4013	4436	4859	5282	423
1027		5704	6127	6550	6973	7396	7818	8241	8664	9086	9509	423
1028		9931	*0354	*0776	*1198	*1621	*2043	*2465	*2887	*3310	*3732	422
1029	012	4154	4576	4998	5420	5842	6264	6685	7107	7529	7951	422
1030		8372	8794	9215	9637	*0059	*0480	*0901	*1323	*1744	*2165	422
1031	013	2587	3008	3429	3850	4271	4692	5113	5534	5955	6376	421
1032		6797	7218	7639	8059	8480	8901	9321	9742	*0162	*0583	421
1033	014	1003	1424	1844	2264	2685	3105	3525	3945	4365	4785	420
1034		5205	5625	6045	6465	6885	7305	7725	8144	8564	8984	420
1035		9403	9823	*0243	*0662	*1082	*1501	*1920	*2340	*2759	*3178	420
1036	015	3598	4017	4436	4855	5274	5693	6112	6531	6950	7369	419
1037		7788	8206	8625	9044	9462	9881	*0300	*0718	*1137	*1555	419
1038	016	1974	2392	2810	3229	3647	4065	4483	4901	5319	5737	418
1039		6155	6573	6991	7409	7827	8245	8663	9080	9498	9916	418
1040	017	0333	0751	1168	1586	2003	2421	2838	3256	3673	4090	417
1041		4507	4924	5342	5759	6176	6593	7010	7427	7844	8260	417
1042		8677	9094	9511	9927	*0344	*0761	*1177	*1594	*2010	*2427	417
1043	018	2843	3259	3676	4092	4508	4925	5341	5757	6173	6589	416
1044		7005	7421	7837	8253	8669	9084	9500	9916	*0332	*0747	416
1045	019	1163	1578	1994	2410	2825	3240	3656	4071	4486	4902	415
1046		5317	5732	6147	6562	6977	7392	7807	8222	8637	9052	415
1047		9467	9882	*0296	*0711	*1126	*1540	*1955	*2369	*2784	*3198	415
1048	020	3613	4027	4442	4856	5270	5684	6099	6513	6927	7341	414
1049		7755	8169	8583	8997	9411	9824	*0238	*0652	*1066	*1479	414
1050	021	1893	2307	2720	3134	3547	3961	4374	4787	5201	5614	413
N.		0	1	2	3	4	5	6	7	8	9	D.

Table XXV–continued

SEVEN PLACE MANTISSAS

10500–11009

N.		0	1	2	3	4	5	6	7	8	9	D.
1050	021	1893	2307	2720	3134	3547	3961	4374	4787	5201	5614	413
1051		6027	6440	6854	7267	7680	8093	8506	8919	9332	9745	413
1052	022	0157	0570	0983	1396	1808	2221	2634	3046	3459	3871	413
1053		4284	4696	5109	5521	5933	6345	6758	7170	7582	7994	412
1054		8406	8818	9230	9642	*0054	*0466	*0878	*1289	*1701	*2113	412
1055	023	2525	2936	3348	3759	4171	4582	4994	5405	5817	6228	411
1056		6639	7050	7462	7873	8284	8695	9106	9517	9928	*0339	411
1057	024	0750	1161	1572	1982	2393	2804	3214	3625	4036	4446	411
1058		4857	5267	5678	6088	6498	6909	7319	7729	8139	8549	410
1059		8960	9370	9780	*0190	*0600	*1010	*1419	*1829	*2239	*2649	410
1060	025	3059	3468	3878	4288	4697	5107	5516	5926	6335	6744	410
1061		7154	7563	7972	8382	8791	9200	9609	*0018	*0427	*0836	409
1062	026	1245	1654	2063	2472	2881	3289	3698	4107	4515	4924	409
1063		5333	5741	6150	6558	6967	7375	7783	8192	8600	9008	408
1064		9416	9824	*0233	*0641	*1049	*1457	*1865	*2273	*2680	*3088	408
1065	027	3496	3904	4312	4719	5127	5535	5942	6350	6757	7165	408
1066		7572	7979	8387	8794	9201	9609	*0016	*0423	*0830	*1237	407
1067	028	1644	2051	2458	2865	3272	3679	4086	4492	4899	5306	407
1068		5713	6119	6526	6932	7339	7745	8152	8558	8964	9371	406
1069		9777	*0183	*0590	*0996	*1402	*1808	*2214	*2620	*3026	*3432	406
1070	029	3838	4244	4649	5055	5461	5867	6272	6678	7084	7489	406
1071		7895	8300	8706	9111	9516	9922	*0327	*0732	*1138	*1543	405
1072	030	1948	2353	2758	3163	3568	3973	4378	4783	5188	5592	405
1073		5997	6402	6807	7211	7616	8020	8425	8830	9234	9638	405
1074	031	0043	0447	0851	1256	1660	2064	2468	2872	3277	3681	404
1075		4085	4489	4893	5296	5700	6104	6508	6912	7315	7719	404
1076		8123	8526	8930	9333	9737	*0140	*0544	*0947	*1350	*1754	403
1077	032	2157	2560	2963	3367	3770	4173	4576	4979	5382	5785	403
1078		6188	6590	6993	7396	7799	8201	8604	9007	9409	9812	403
1079	033	0214	0617	1019	1422	1824	2226	2629	3031	3433	3835	402
1080		4238	4640	5042	5444	5846	6248	6650	7052	7453	7855	402
1081		8257	8659	9060	9462	9864	*0265	*0667	*1068	*1470	*1871	402
1082	034	2273	2674	3075	3477	3878	4279	4680	5081	5482	5884	401
1083		6285	6686	7087	7487	7888	8289	8690	9091	9491	9892	401
1084	035	0293	0693	1094	1495	1895	2296	2696	3096	3497	3897	400
1085		4297	4698	5098	5498	5898	6298	6698	7098	7498	7898	400
1086		8298	8698	9098	9498	9898	*0297	*0697	*1097	*1496	*1896	400
1087	036	2295	2695	3094	3494	3893	4293	4692	5091	5491	5890	399
1088		6289	6688	7087	7486	7885	8284	8683	9082	9481	9880	399
1089	037	0279	0678	1076	1475	1874	2272	2671	3070	3468	3867	399
1090		4265	4663	5062	5460	5858	6257	6655	7053	7451	7849	398
1091		8248	8646	9044	9442	9839	*0237	*0635	*1033	*1431	*1829	398
1092	038	2226	2624	3022	3419	3817	4214	4612	5009	5407	5804	398
1093		6202	6599	6996	7393	7791	8188	8585	8982	9379	9776	397
1094	039	0173	0570	0967	1364	1761	2158	2554	2951	3348	3745	397
1095		4141	4538	4934	5331	5727	6124	6520	6917	7313	7709	397
1096		8106	8502	8898	9294	9690	*0086	*0482	*0878	*1274	*1670	396
1097	040	2066	2462	2858	3254	3650	4045	4441	4837	5232	5628	396
1098		6023	6419	6814	7210	7605	8001	8396	8791	9187	9582	395
1099		9977	*0372	*0767	*1162	*1557	*1952	*2347	*2742	*3137	*3532	395
1100	041	3927	4322	4716	5111	5506	5900	6295	6690	7084	7479	395
N.		0	1	2	3	4	5	6	7	8	9	D.

Table XXVI

TABLE OF ROOTS

x	$\sqrt{x}$	$\sqrt[3]{x}$	$\sqrt[4]{x}$
0.125	0.353553391	0.500000000	0.594603558
0.250	0.500000000	0.629960525	0.707106781
0.375	0.612372436	0.721124785	0.782542290
0.500	0.707106781	0.793700526	0.840896415
0.625	0.790569415	0.854987973	0.889139705
0.750	0.866025404	0.908560296	0.930604859
0.875	0.935414346	0.956465591	0.967168210
1.000	1.000000000	1.000000000	1.000000000
1.250	1.118033989	1.077217345	1.057371263
1.500	1.224744871	1.144714243	1.106681920
1.750	1.322875656	1.205071132	1.150163317
2.000	1.414213562	1.259921050	1.189207115
2.250	1.500000000	1.310370697	1.224744871
2.500	1.581138830	1.357208808	1.257433430
2.750	1.658312395	1.401019665	1.287754788
3.000	1.732050808	1.442249570	1.316074013
3.500	1.870828693	1.518294486	1.367782400
4.000	2.000000000	1.587401052	1.414213562
4.500	2.121320344	1.650963624	1.456475315
5.000	2.236067977	1.709975947	1.495348781
5.500	2.345207880	1.765174168	1.531407157
6.000	2.449489743	1.817120593	1.565084580
6.500	2.549509757	1.866255578	1.596718434
7.000	2.645751311	1.912931183	1.626576562
7.500	2.738612788	1.957433821	1.654875460
8.000	2.828427125	2.000000000	1.681792831
8.500	2.915475947	2.040827551	1.707476485
9.000	3.000000000	2.080083823	1.732050808
9.500	3.082207001	2.117911792	1.755621543
10.000	3.162277660	2.154434690	1.778279410
11.000	3.316624790	2.223980091	1.821160287
12.000	3.464101615	2.289428485	1.861209718

Table XXVI–continued

TABLE OF ROOTS

$\sqrt[5]{x}$	$\sqrt[6]{x}$	$\sqrt[7]{x}$
0.659753955	0.707106781	0.742997145
0.757858283	0.793700526	0.820335356
0.821875915	0.849190665	0.869255253
0.870550563	0.890898718	0.905723664
0.910282102	0.924655597	0.935061127
0.944087511	0.953184293	0.959735610
0.973647181	0.977990589	0.981104881
1.000000000	1.000000000	1.000000000
1.045639553	1.037890816	1.032391185
1.084471771	1.069913194	1.059634023
1.118426915	1.097757319	1.083227610
1.148698355	1.122462048	1.104089514
1.176079023	1.144714243	1.122824262
1.201124434	1.164993051	1.139852281
1.224239925	1.183646765	1.155478352
1.245730940	1.200936955	1.169930813
1.284735157	1.232190929	1.195980246
1.319507911	1.259921050	1.219013654
1.350960039	1.284898293	1.239698493
1.379729661	1.307660486	1.258498951
1.406282388	1.328598573	1.275751532
1.430969081	1.348006155	1.291708342
1.454061151	1.366109651	1.306563373
1.475773162	1.383087554	1.320469248
1.496277870	1.399083207	1.333548306
1.515716567	1.414213562	1.345900193
1.534206383	1.428575357	1.357607199
1.551845574	1.442249570	1.368738107
1.568717427	1.455304708	1.379351021
1.584893192	1.467799268	1.389495494
1.615394266	1.491301475	1.408543888
1.643751830	1.513085749	1.426161635

Table XXVI–continued

TABLE OF ROOTS

x	$\sqrt{x}$	$\sqrt[3]{x}$	$\sqrt[4]{x}$
13.000	3.605551275	2.351334688	1.898828922
14.000	3.741657387	2.410142264	1.934336420
15.000	3.872983346	2.466212074	1.967989671
16.000	4.000000000	2.519842100	2.000000000
17.000	4.123105626	2.571281591	2.030543185
18.000	4.242640687	2.620741394	2.059767144
19.000	4.358898944	2.668401649	2.087797630
20.000	4.472135955	2.714417617	2.114742527
21.000	4.582575695	2.758924176	2.140695143
22.000	4.690415760	2.802039331	2.165367710
23.000	4.795831523	2.843866980	2.189938703
24.000	4.898979486	2.884499141	2.213363839
25.000	5.000000000	2.924017738	2.236067977
28.000	5.291502622	3.036588972	2.300326634
31.000	5.567764363	3.141380652	2.359611062
34.000	5.830951895	3.239611801	2.414736403
37.000	6.082762530	3.332221852	2.466325715
40.000	6.324555320	3.419951893	2.514866859
43.000	6.557438524	3.503398060	2.560749602
46.000	6.782329983	3.583047871	2.604290687
49.000	7.000000000	3.659305710	2.645711311
50.000	7.071067812	3.684031499	2.659147948
55.000	7.416198487	3.802952461	2.723269815
60.000	7.745966692	3.914867641	2.783157684
65.000	8.062257748	4.020725759	2.839411514
70.000	8.366600265	4.121285300	2.892507609
75.000	8.660254038	4.217163327	2.942830956
80.000	8.944271910	4.308869380	2.990697562
85.000	9.219544457	4.396829672	3.036370277
90.000	9.486832981	4.481404747	3.080070288
95.000	9.746794345	4.562902635	3.121985641
99.000	9.949874371	4.626065009	3.154342146

Table XXVI–continued

TABLE OF ROOTS

$\sqrt[5]{x}$	$\sqrt[6]{x}$	$\sqrt[7]{x}$
1.670277652	1.533406237	1.442562919
1.695218203	1.552463289	1.457916250
1.718771928	1.570417802	1.472356700
1.741101127	1.587401052	1.485994289
1.762340348	1.603521622	1.498919872
1.782602458	1.618870407	1.511209391
1.801983127	1.633524303	1.522926998
1.820564203	1.647548972	1.534127405
1.838416287	1.661000956	1.544857660
1.855600736	1.673929309	1.555158537
1.872171231	1.686376880	1.565065608
1.888175023	1.698381330	1.574610106
1.903653939	1.709975947	1.583819609
1.947294361	1.742581123	1.609670043
1.987340755	1.772394045	1.633246253
2.024397458	1.799892164	1.654941713
2.058924136	1.825437441	1.675054021
2.091279105	1.849311194	1.693813980
2.121747461	1.871736643	1.711404370
2.150560013	1.892894046	1.727972526
2.177906424	1.912931183	1.743639034
2.186724148	1.919383104	1.748678622
2.228807384	1.950116012	1.772651006
2.267933155	1.978602446	1.794822921
2.304531620	2.005174745	1.815463920
2.338942837	2.030094899	1.834786070
2.371440610	2.053573307	1.852959362
2.402248868	2.075781631	1.870122254
2.431553251	2.096861863	1.886389086
2.459509486	2.116932863	1.901855432
2.486249570	2.136095184	1.916602029
2.506842442	2.150828912	1.927927695

Table XXVII

TABLE OF POWERS

x	x^2	x^3	x^4	x^5
0.125	0.01562500	0.0019531	0.0002441	0.000030518
0.250	0.06250000	0.0156250	0.0039063	0.000976563
0.375	0.14062500	0.0527344	0.0197754	0.007415772
0.500	0.25000000	0.1250000	0.0625000	0.031250000
0.625	0.39062500	0.2441406	0.1525879	0.095367432
0.750	0.56250000	0.4218750	0.3164063	0.237304688
0.875	0.76562500	0.6699219	0.5861816	0.512908936
1.000	1.00000000	1.0000000	1.0000000	1.000000000
1.250	1.56250000	1.9531250	2.4414063	3.051757812
1.500	2.25000000	3.3750000	5.0625000	7.593750000
1.750	3.06250000	5.3593750	9.3789063	16.41308594
2.000	4.00000000	8.0000000	16.000000	32.00000000
2.250	5.06250000	11.390625	25.628906	57.66503906
2.500	6.25000000	15.625000	39.062500	97.65625000
2.750	7.56250000	20.796875	57.191406	157.2763672
3.000	9.00000000	27.000000	81.000000	243.0000000
3.500	12.2500000	42.875000	150.06250	525.2187500
4.000	16.0000000	64.000000	256.00000	1024.000000
4.500	20.2500000	91.125000	410.06250	1845.281250
5.000	25.0000000	125.00000	625.00000	3125.000000
5.500	30.2500000	166.37500	915.06250	5032.843750
6.000	36.0000000	216.00000	1296.0000	7776.000000
6.500	42.2500000	274.62500	1785.0625	11602.90625
7.000	49.0000000	343.00000	2401.0000	16807.00000
7.500	56.2500000	421.87500	3164.0625	23730.46875

Table XXVII–continued

TABLE OF POWERS

x	x^2	x^3	x^4	x^5
8.000	64.000000	512.00000	4096.0000	32768.00000
8.500	72.250000	614.12500	5220.0625	44370.53125
9.000	81.000000	729.00000	6561.0000	59049.00000
9.500	90.250000	857.37500	8145.0625	77378.09375
10	100.00000	1000.0000	10000.000	100000.0000
11	121.00000	1331.0000	14641.000	161051.0000
12	144.00000	1728.0000	20736.000	248832.0000
13	169.00000	2197.0000	28561.000	371293.0000
14	196.00000	2744.0000	38416.000	537824.0000
15	225.00000	3375.0000	50625.000	759375.0000
16	256.00000	4096.0000	65536.000	1048576.000
17	289.00000	4913.0000	83521.000	1419857.000
18	324.00000	5832.0000	104976.00	1889568.000
19	361.00000	6859.0000	130321.00	2476099.000
20	400.00000	8000.0000	160000.00	3200000.000
21	441.00000	9261.0000	194481.00	4084101.000
22	484.00000	10648.000	234256.00	5153632.000
23	529.00000	12167.000	279841.00	8436343.000
24	576.00000	13824.000	331776.00	7962624.000
25	625.00000	15625.000	390625.00	9765625.000
28	784.00000	21952.000	614656.00	17210368.00
31	961.00000	29791.000	923521.00	28629151.00
34	1156.0000	39304.000	1336336.0	45435424.00
37	1369.0000	50653.000	1874161.0	69343957.00
40	1600.0000	64000.000	2560000.0	102400000.0

Table XXVII–continued

TABLE OF POWERS

x	x^2	x^3	x^4	x^5
43	1849.0000	79507.000	3418801.0	147008443.0
46	2116.0000	97336.000	4477456.0	205962976.0
49	2401.0000	117649.00	5764801.0	282475249.0
50	2500.0000	125000.00	6250000.0	312500000.0
55	3025.0000	166375.00	9150625.0	503284375.0
60	3600.0000	216000.00	12960000	777600000.0
65	4225.0000	274625.00	17850625	1160290625
70	4900.0000	343000.00	24010000	1680700000
75	5625.0000	421875.00	31640625	2373046875
80	6400.0000	512000.00	40960000	3276800000
85	7225.0000	614125.00	52200625	4437053125
90	8100.0000	729000.00	65610000	5904900000
95	9025.0000	857375.00	81450625	7737809375
99	9801.0000	970299.00	96059601	9509900499

INDEX OF CASES AND EXAMPLES

GENERAL INDEX

G